NEWNES
PICTORIAL KNOWLEDGE

VOLUME NINE

United Kingdom
GEORGE NEWNES LTD.
LONDON: 15-17, LONG ACRE, LONDON, W.C.2

Australia
GEORGE NEWNES (AUSTRALIA) PTY., LTD.

ADELAIDE :   S.A.A.C.C. HOUSE, 32, HINDMARSH SQUARE
BRISBANE :   ROUBIN BUILDING, 117, QUEEN STREET
MELBOURNE : PRUDENTIAL BUILDING, 150, QUEEN STREET
PERTH :   N.M.L.A. BUILDING, 81, ST. GEORGE'S TERRACE
SYDNEY :   NEWNES HOUSE, 20-22, MARGARET STREET

NEWNES
PICTORIAL
KNOWLEDGE

General Editor
PETER FINCH, M.A.

Associate Editors:
WALTER SHEPHERD
CEDRIC DOVER

VOLUME 9

GEORGE NEWNES LIMITED
15–17 LONG ACRE
LONDON, W.C.2

Acknowledgments

FOR permission to include the following copyright poems in this Work the Publishers are indebted to the courtesy of the late Mr. W. B. Yeats, for "The Lake Isle of Innisfree," from *Poems*, by W. B. Yeats, published by Messrs. Macmillan & Co. Ltd.; the late Mr. Rudyard Kipling, for "Big Steamers," from *A School History of England*, by C. R. L. Fletcher and Rudyard Kipling, published by The Oxford University Press; the late Mr. Lloyd Osbourne, for "The Gardener," from *A Child's Garden of Verses*, by Robert Louis Stevenson, published by Messrs. Longmans, Green & Co.; Mr. John Masefield, for "Cargoes"; the Proprietors of *Punch*, for "The Cat and the Broom," by A. A. Kenny, and "Crab-Apple," by Ethel Talbot; Mr. Walter De La Mare, for "Someone" and "Old Shellover"; Mr. Alfred Noyes, for "The Elfin Artist," published by Messrs. William Blackwood & Sons; Mrs. Robert Bridges and The Oxford University Press, for "A Child's Poem," by Robert Bridges; Messrs. Macmillan & Co. Ltd., for "Who has seen the Wind?" from *Poetical Works of Christina Rossetti*; Sir Henry Newbolt, for "Drake's Drum," from *Poems Old and New*, published by John Murray; Messrs. Frederick Warne & Co. Ltd., for "The Owl and the Pussy Cat," by Edward Lear; Messrs. George G. Harrap & Co. Ltd., for "Goblins' Lanterns," from *The Littlest One His Book*, by Marion St. John Webb; Miss Rose Fyleman, for "A Fairy Went A-Marketing."

PRINTED IN GREAT BRITAIN
BY THE WHITEFRIARS PRESS LTD., LONDON AND TONBRIDGE AND
BOUND BY HAZELL, WATSON & VINEY LTD., AYLESBURY AND LONDON
N.P.K. 1037760. W.P. 1220

CONTENTS OF VOLUME NINE

PAGE

THE STORY OF THE EARLY CIVILISATIONS IN THE WORLD'S HISTORY
HOW LEARNING AND UNDERSTANDING SPREAD FROM THE
MEDITERRANEAN

GREAT NATIONS OF THE PAST I
IN AMERICA BEFORE COLUMBUS 25
AUSTRALIA'S OLDEST INHABITANTS 35

HOW BRITAIN AND OTHER COUNTRIES OF THE WORLD ARE GOVERNED
CONCERNING PARLIAMENTS AND PEOPLE ; LOCAL GOVERNMENT
AND COURTS OF LAW

CITIZENS OF BRITAIN 43
OUR PARLIAMENT—AND OTHERS 47
ELECTING YOUR M.P. 59
HOW LAWS ARE MADE 67
IN THE COURTS OF JUSTICE 76
HOW THE POLICE WORK 83

A CHILDREN'S TREASURY OF VERSE
LITTLE MASTERPIECES OF TO-DAY AND YESTERDAY

THE LAKE ISLE OF INNISFREE. W. B. Yeats 93
BIG STEAMERS. Rudyard Kipling 94
I KNOW A BANK. William Shakespeare 94
THE GARDENER. Robert Louis Stevenson 95
THE FAIRIES. William Allingham 96
A MARCH DAY. William Wordsworth 96
CARGOES. John Masefield 97
SEVEN YEARS OLD. Jean Ingelow 98
THE VOWELS. Jonathan Swift 98
THE CAT AND THE BROOM. A. A. Kenny 99
SOMEONE. Walter De La Mare 99
THE NAUGHTY BOY. John Keats 100
WHO IS IT ? Enid Blyton 101
THE FAIRIES' SONG. William Shakespeare 102
SIGNS OF RAIN. Edward Jenner 103
ENGLAND. William Shakespeare 104
TO THE LADY-BIRD. Anon 104

PAGE

A CHILDREN'S TREASURY OF VERSE (Contd.)

THE THRUSH'S NEST. John Clare 104
SPRING. Thomas Nash 105
CRAB-APPLE. Ethel Talbot 106
THE DOVE. John Keats 106
THE BEGGAR MAID. Tennyson 107
RABBIT-SONG. Enid Blyton 108
WINTER. William Shakespeare 109
THE ELFIN ARTIST. Alfred Noyes 110
HOME-THOUGHTS FROM ABROAD. Robert Browning . . . 111
FIRST SPRING MORNING—A CHILD'S POEM. Robert Bridges . . 112
THE OWL. Tennyson 112
WHO HAS SEEN THE WIND? Christina Rossetti 113
THE WIND IN A FROLIC. William Howitt 114
THE LUCKY DUCKS. Enid Blyton 115
THERE WAS AN OLD WOMAN. Anon 116
DRAKE'S DRUM. Henry Newbolt 117
EARL HALDAN'S DAUGHTER. Charles Kingsley 118
WATER JEWELS. Mrs. M. I. Butts 118
THE OWL AND THE PUSSY-CAT. Edward Lear 119
MR. NOBODY. Anon 120
MORNING. Robert Browning 120
GOBLINS' LANTERNS. Marion St. John Webb 121
A FAIRY WENT A-MARKETING. Rose Fyleman 122
FOUR DUCKS. William Allingham 122
THE FIRST WILD ROSE. Enid Blyton 123
OLD SHELLOVER. Walter De La Mare 123
THE ELF AND THE DORMOUSE. Oliver Herford 124
THE MOUNTAIN AND THE SQUIRREL. Ralph Waldo Emerson . . 124

YOUR OWN SPECIAL CORNER : READING, WRITING AND ARITHMETIC— A HELPING HAND FOR TINY FOLK

THE LETTERS OF THE ALPHABET 125
WHEN WE BEGIN TO READ 130
MAKING LETTERS BIG AND SMALL 139
GAMES TO PLAY WITH FIGURES 143

FIRST STEPS IN DRAWING, " HOW-TO-MAKE " AND GEOGRAPHY—A HELPING HAND FOR TINY FOLK

EASY DRAWING 153
PRETTY WORK FOR LITTLE FINGERS 159
JUNE AND ROBIN LEARN GEOGRAPHY 173

PAGE

**FAMILIAR THINGS AND HOW THEY ARE MADE
INDUSTRIES THAT SERVE OUR EVERYDAY NEEDS**

THE POTTER'S ANCIENT CRAFT 189
MAKING A DAILY NEWSPAPER 199
OUR CLOCKS AND WATCHES 213
A CAKE OF SOAP 219
THE STORY OF LEATHER 225
THE WONDER OF GLASS 233
GOOD THINGS FOR THE LARDER 242
HOW SCENT IS MADE 253
TOYS AND GAMES 261
MONEY AND ITS HISTORY 270
WHAT IS A FILM ? 285

**THE SECRET OF MAN'S SUPREMACY—
ABOUT THE MENTAL EQUIPMENT OF THE HUMAN BEING**

HOW THE BRAIN AND THE MIND WORK 315

**QUESTIONS AND ANSWERS
ON THINGS THAT INTEREST YOU AND ME**

AIRCRAFT 331
ASTRONOMY 333
CALENDAR, THE 338
CHEMISTRY 339
EDUCATION 343
ELECTRICITY 344
GEOGRAPHY 347
GEOLOGY 353
GOVERNMENT, INSTITUTIONS AND CUSTOMS 354
HISTORY AND INTERNATIONAL AFFAIRS 359
HUMAN BODY 367
LANGUAGE 371
LEGAL 373
LITERATURE AND ART 374
MECHANISMS 377
METALS 384
METEOROLOGY AND GENERAL SCIENCE 385
MONEY 388
NAMES AND PHRASES 391
NATURAL HISTORY—
    MAMMALS 397
    BIRDS 401
    FISH 401
    REPTILES 402
    INSECTS 404
    PLANTS 405
    TREES 408

PAGE

QUESTIONS AND ANSWERS
ON THINGS THAT INTEREST YOU AND ME (Contd.)

NAVAL AND MILITARY 409
PHOTOGRAPHY 410
PHYSICS (GENERAL) 412
     HEAT 414
     LIGHT 418
     SOUND 420
PRINTING 421
RAILWAYS 422
ROADS 428
SHIPS 428
SPORT 431
STEAM 434
MISCELLANEOUS 434
ABBREVIATIONS IN GENERAL USE 446

Colour Plates

AN ABORIGINAL CEREMONIAL DANCE . . . . . . *Facing* 224
A WINE GLASS IN THE MAKING . . . . ,, 225
SOWING THE SEED ON A NEW TEA ESTATE . . . . . ,, 240
LUNCH-TIME WITH A GOLDFINCH FAMILY . . . . . ,, 241
A MISTLE THRUSH AND ITS YOUNG . . . . . . ,, 336
CONSULTING THE WITCH-DOCTOR . . . . ,, 337
TWO MEMBERS OF THE ANTELOPE FAMILY . . . . . ,, 352
A REMARKABLE EXAMPLE OF ANIMAL CAMOUFLAGE . . . ,, 353

Special Colour Supplements

EARLY CIVILISATIONS: *Plates 1 and 2*—EGYPT . . . *Between* 24–25
EARLY CIVILISATIONS: *Plates 3 and 4*—BABYLON AND ASSYRIA ,, 24–25
FUN WITH COLOURS . . . . ,, 160–161
GEOGRAPHICAL TERMS: *Plates 1, 2, 3 and 4* . . . . ,, 184–185
BRITISH UNIFORMS: *Plates 1, 2 and 3*—THE DEFENCE FORCES ,, 408–409
BRITISH UNIFORMS: *Plate 4*—COMMONWEALTH FORCES . . ,, 408–409

Special Transart Supplement

THE DOG ROSE . . . . *Between* 400–401

Photo=tone Supplements

TREASURES OF THE PAST . . . . *Between* 8–9
AUSTRALIAN ABORIGINES . . . . ,, 40–41
THROUGH THE MICROSCOPE . . . . ,, 328–329
RED MEN OF AMERICA . . . . ,, 360–361

The Story of
the early
Civilisations in
the World's History

How Learning
and Understanding
Spread from
the Mediterranean

John Tarlton.

EXPLORING A ROMAN FORTRESS

Our knowledge of ancient civilisation for which there is little or no written history depends on the archæologist and his scientific " digging up the past." Gaps in our knowledge of more recent times may also be filled by his painstaking work on historic sites. This picture shows the excavation of a famous site in Monmouthshire, the great Roman fortress of Isca Silurum (A.D. 74–78) at Caerleon.

GREAT NATIONS OF THE PAST

A COMMON definition of the word "archæology" is the "science of antiquities." This seems rather a dull way to sum up a subject that covers such a wide field and is so full of excitement and interest. To carry out " digs " on supposed sites of ancient cities; to unearth pottery and other relics often thousands of years old; to reconstruct details in the lives of ancient peoples—all these are branches of archæological work.

To-day, more than ever before, knowledge of archæology is made available not only to the expert but to anybody that it intrigues. Excavations, or " digs " as

they are familiarly called, take place each year in many countries. Fast-moving news systems—television, radio, and newspapers—give us information about these digs in record time, and photographs in magazines and books can almost take us, in imagination, to the spot. It would be impossible to mention all the excavations that have taken place and that are even now going on. It is only practical to consider some of the most important of those that have been carried out recently and to give an account of theories put forward to support discoveries that have been made in the past.

In conjunction with the geologist, the

Specially drawn for this work.

HOW MAN FIRST LEARNED TO MAKE FIRE

The first and most important step forward made by our early ancestors was the discovery of how to make fire at will. At first it was probably by the slow and tedious method of friction, rubbing one piece of wood against another until sufficient heat was generated to produce a flame. Later came the use of flint with dry tinder to catch the spark and spring into flame.

archæologist has worked in different countries, including Great Britain, so that we can form some sort of picture to-day of how the ancient Britons lived long before the Romans came.

So, with the aid of the archæologist, the geologist, the zoologist, and the scholar of languages known as the philologist, all aided by the historian who can connect one phase with another and give great help in fitting the jigsaw pieces together, we have to-day a fairly good picture of how men lived during those thousands of years before history began to be written for all to read. We can to some extent trace the progress of man from those far-off days when there was little difference between him and the other animals that roamed the earth. There was a difference, however: in man there was something more vital than instinct, and because of his power to reason man

advanced slowly from his savage animal state till there came a time when he ceased to roam and seek shelter in caves but built huts for himself and cultivated the land with tools he had made.

Fire-making and Stone-cutting

He learned to do these things very slowly. We know that he existed long ages before he had learned to make fire and to fashion weapons and tools from stone. Yet our earliest records show that he possessed this knowledge at least 50,000 years ago. This earliest period of history is usually known as the Stone Age and his progress through this long period is divided into the Early, Middle and Late Stone Ages. In the Late Stone Age men made their axes sharp on some kind of grindstone and had begun to build huts with the wood they cut down in the forests.

In certain parts of Europe they even built these huts on piles driven into the water. This gave them protection from the animals, and by now they had begun to use boats, usually made by hacking out the centre of a great log they had cut down in the forests; another piece of wood, shaped with their axes, was used as a paddle. The Stone Age man was a hunter and a fisherman, and, with his fire, he cooked the food he had caught in a large pot or jar of clay. The art of making pottery came in during this Late Stone Age and marks another advance towards civilisation.

The Stone Age faded as he discovered the use of metals. Copper was the first, then copper mixed with some other metal to form bronze, a period sometimes referred to as the Bronze Age. Later came the discovery of iron, but the Iron Age which probably began about 2000 B.C. comes into that period which can best be termed the Historic Age. Roughly, the long, long period known as the Stone Age came to an end about 4000 B.C. But about this time, and even before it, changes had begun to take place in some parts of the world much more rapidly, even before the use of metals was understood.

While the Stone Age lingered on in

W. F. Mansell.

A SPORTSMAN IN ANCIENT EGYPT

A great deal of information about the everyday life of the early Egyptians has been gained from the paintings in the tombs which have been discovered in comparatively recent times. Here is a mural painting from Thebes, dating from the 1600–1450 B.C. period. It shows the man, accompanied by his wife and daughter, standing in a red canoe among the reeds, engaged in the sport of knocking down birds with the sticks he carries.

some parts of Europe, in the Near East a much higher civilisation had begun to develop. It was in Egypt where real civilisation, as we know it, had its first beginnings well before 4000 B.C.

On the Banks of the Nile

In the main this progress was due to the fertility of the Nile Valley. At different times in various parts of the world prehistoric man found some place where he could settle and grow his own food, having discovered by virtue of his powers of observation and reason the elementary facts about seeds and their growth in the soil.

In the country we know to this day as Egypt there were ideal conditions of climate and soil. The wandering tribes who first came here probably settled in small villages, especially in the delta of the Nile. Presently a leader emerged and he put an end to village quarrels by a process of conquest and was able to unite all this part of the Nile Valley into one kingdom of Lower Egypt.

Egypt's Early Kings

Farther along the Nile a similar process took place and a kingdom of Upper Egypt came into existence. They had barely discovered the use of metals but they knew a good deal about irrigation and the cultivation of their fertile lands. Somewhere about 4300 B.C. the King of Lower Egypt (at the delta end of the Nile) conquered Upper Egypt and the two kingdoms became one. What was probably the first real government was formed and the king of Egypt now ruled several million people.

Agriculture prospered and the first agricultural tools were made. The plough was evolved and oxen employed to draw it. There was corn for all and it even became the coin of the realm with which to pay men for carrying out other tasks.

One step leads to another. The king could collect wealth from his subjects and pay others to carry out different tasks: the king's taxes were used to pay men to see that the farmers looked after their lands and paid their due share to the king. To keep a record of what had been paid some method of accounts was necessary. From that it was an obvious step to find some way of putting down a record of events that mattered.

Our Earliest Calendar

Thus some form of writing came into existence and a calendar was devised by the learned men employed by the king. The first calendar was invented and brought into use in the year 4236 B.C. With certain alterations so far as names are concerned this is the same twelve-months calendar we use to-day. Each year was given the name of some important event. Long centuries later the Palermo Stone was discovered and is still preserved. This is a black granite slab which was erected in Lower Egypt and it gives the names of some 700 years from what we now date 3400 B.C. to 2700 B.C.

Later, the Egyptians altered this system by naming the year of the King's reign: the tenth year of the reign of King Tehutmes, and so on. They had invented a system of writing by pictorial methods at an early date. Pictures became sound signs, and this gradually developed into combining pictures which led eventually to the formation of an alphabet. It was a somewhat complicated affair, or so it seems to us to-day, but their hieroglyphic writing can now be deciphered by trained experts. From the hieroglyphic style a more free and running hand known as Hieratic was developed, and this was used for writing on papyrus by the ordinary man in the course of his business.

They had learned to make a tough, pale-yellow paper by splitting a kind of river reed, known as papyrus, and on this they wrote with a pointed reed, dipped in a mixture of soot and gum.

Years later, when Egyptian civilisation had ceased to progress and the country itself was occupied by the Romans, all knowledge of hieroglyphics died out.

Before 4000 B.C. the Egyptians were a highly civilised nation and they progressed steadily towards a still higher standard for many centuries. They were an attractive people, dignified but without foolish pride, determined and even strong-minded, yet in the main a kindly people.

These ancient Egyptians were the first among the human race to have a standard of conduct and to cultivate what we sometimes call to-day "a way of life." In the tomb of one great noble are the words he wrote regarding his own endeavours during his life: there were none whom he had oppressed, no shepherd had been expelled and none was wretched on his great estate, nor did anyone go hungry in his time.

When Women Wove Fine Linen

The period of the Great Pyramids began about 3000 B.C. We have pictures of the life and conditions under which the people lived. These pictures show us not only the great nobles in their palaces and gardens or with their families at meals; they show us the potter working at his wheel, the labourer planting and cultivating the fields; cows being milked, while donkeys are used to bear the loads of grain from the fields at harvest time.

There were coppersmiths who made the tools used to build the pyramids and palaces; glass-makers who fashioned coloured bottles and vases, while women wove fine linen cloth on their hand looms. The earliest known tapestry used in the palace of the Pharaoh was made when the Pyramids were being built. Luxurious furniture was made by skilled craftsmen and the building

of seagoing ships as well as river-craft made transport a fairly simple matter.

There were free men and slaves; mostly the slaves were men who had been taken in battle, but even they seem to have been well treated by their owners. Then there were landowners, lords, officials, and the skilled workers, all ruled by the great Pharaoh or King. The word 'Pharaoh' meant the royal estates at first, but over a long period the term was also used to denote the reigning king.

W. F. Mansell.

DESCRIBED IN CUNEIFORM

Somewhere about 4000 B.C. the Sumerians settled in the Plain of Shinar (Babylon) and gradually built up one of the earliest civilisations. Our picture shows a statue of one of their rulers, Gudea, probably about 2450 B.C., and the type of writing they developed, known as Cuneiform, meaning wedge-shaped, is plainly seen on the inscription.

Our present-day science of Egyptology is entirely devoted to the study of the records and remains of early civilisations in Egypt. The traveller in Egypt has always been astounded by the vast number of ruins of tombs and temples that are strung along the banks of the River Nile. An important discovery, to which we owe much of our subsequent knowledge of ancient Egypt, occurred in 1799 when Napoleon Bonaparte's soldiers unearthed, by fortunate chance, a slab of black basalt with an inscription honouring one of the Ptolemys, a king of Egypt in 195 B.C. Written in three languages—Greek, hieroglyphics and " Demotic " writing, a more advanced style of hieroglyphs—the Rosetta Stone has proved invaluable as a key in helping to decipher the writing on monuments and on the tough pale-yellow paper, papyrus.

Over the past hundred years or so there has been great archæological activity in Egypt. Much is now known about the lives of the ancient Egyptians from the earliest beginnings of their civilisation to its zenith in about 1353 B.C., and then, on to the wane of power some thirty years before the Birth of Christ.

Gods of the Sun and River

It may seem strange to us that the Egyptians should have taken so much trouble and spent so much time and energy in building themselves such large, costly and ornate burial places—like the Great Pyramids. The truth is that they were an extremely religious people. Their priests taught that the soul lived on after death and still had need of the body. Therefore, they reasoned, the body must be well guarded and preserved and, when buried, must be near things indispensable to it in life. Thus, the Pharaoh was buried in a palatial tomb, often a pyramid, with his luxurious belongings around him and the poor man took with him his smaller needs, eating utensils and other necessities.

The Egyptians had

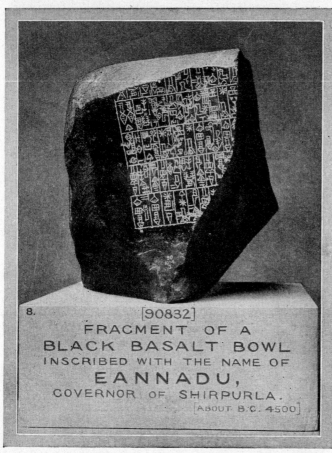

8.   [90832]
FRAGMENT OF A
BLACK BASALT BOWL
INSCRIBED WITH THE NAME OF
EANNADU,
GOVERNOR OF SHIRPURLA.
[ABOUT B.C. 4500]

British Museum.

BABYLONIA'S EARLIEST RECORD

Civilisation existed in Babylonia almost as early as it did in Egypt. Not much is known of its history before about 3500 B.C. but its people, the Sumerians, had founded city-states long before then. Probably the above fragment, with its cuneiform inscription, now in the British Museum, is the earliest record in existence. Shirpurla is an older name for Lagash, an ancient city in S. Babylonia (Iraq).

IN ANCIENT UR OF THE CHALDEES

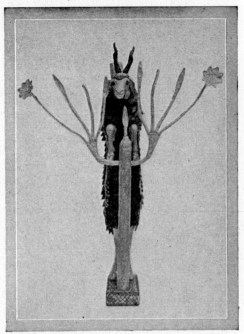

Excavations in recent years have told us much concerning the Sumerian races in the valley of the Euphrates. Here is a rein ring of metal found in the Chaldean tombs.

Like the Egyptians, the great ones of Babylon had their treasures buried with them at death. Here is an ornament, a goat of lapis lazuli, shell and gold from the Royal graves at Ur.

British Museum.

Ur of the Chaldees was a city in ancient Babylonia and is mentioned in Genesis as the home of Abraham. Excavations in recent years have added to our knowledge of this civilisation of some 5,000 years ago. Our picture shows a mosaic illustrating the first stages in the preparations for a feast.

British Museum.

HIS FAME LIVES ON

It is only within the last century that the key to the ancient writing of the Babylon civilisation has been evolved. Here is a memorial tablet to a famous man discovered in the land of the Euphrates.

A KING'S STATUE

Larsa, an ancient Sumerian city, referred to in Genesis xiv. as Ellasar, lasted as a kingdom from about 2325 to 2100 B.C., when it was conquered by Hammurapi, King of Babylon. Here is a statue of one of its kings, Arad-Sin.

many gods, chief among which was Re (pronounced Ray) the Sun-god to whom all their temples were erected. Almost equal to Re was Osiris, the god of the Nile and all the fertile soil.

Most of the history of ancient Egypt has been learned within comparatively recent times. One of the most wonderful discoveries was made in 1922 when the tomb of Tutankhamen was unearthed in the Valley of the Kings. For centuries it had been hidden and so escaped the fate of many other tombs after the conquest of Egypt when robbers took all the valuables they could.

This Egyptian king, whose name and portrait figured prominently in the newspapers of the world more than 3,000 years after his death, was one of the last Pharaohs of the eighteenth dynasty and was only just eighteen years old when he died (about 1340 B.C.). He

was son-in-law of Akhnaton, the heretic king, who had roused the anger of the priests by changes in their religion. Akhnaton's royal residence at Tell-el-Amarna and tombs in the same neighbourhood were excavated in the nineteenth century, when letters were found written on clay tablets by the Mesopotamian kings and Syrian governors to the rulers of Egypt. Tutankhamen succeeded to the throne in 1346 B.C. after the death of Smenkh-kara, another son-in-law of Akhnaton.

Egypt's Greatness Wanes

It was after the death of Tutankhamen that Egypt's power began to wane. She had extended her dominion over neighbouring lands and had brought foreigners into the country, and perhaps this fact, combined with the religious troubles caused by Akhnaton, had a weakening effect on Egyptian character. Once or

TREASURES OF THE PAST

E.N.A.

Egypt is one of the most important countries in the history of mankind since it was in the Nile valley that the earliest civilisation developed and spread slowly to other Mediterranean lands. Our knowledge of those far-off days is largely due to the work of the archaeologists who have dug the treasures and records of the past from the sands of the desert. One of the most remarkable discoveries was the tomb of King Tutankhamen in 1922, and this photograph shows the massive gold mask which covered the head of the king.

This carved wooden figure, varnished with black resin, was taken from Tutankhamen's tomb. It represents the sacred goose of Amun. These geese were kept by the ancient kings.

This vase is made of pure silver, and is in the form of a pomegranate, a fruit which, owing to the number of its seeds, was taken to typify plenty. It is now in the Cairo Museum.

Another of the remarkable treasures taken from the king's tomb was this royal couch. The cows supporting the seat represent the goddess Hathor, held in reverence by the ancient Egyptians.

This is a panel from Tutankhamen's throne. It shows the queen, holding a small vase in one hand, standing before the king, while the sun sheds its beneficent rays on husband and wife

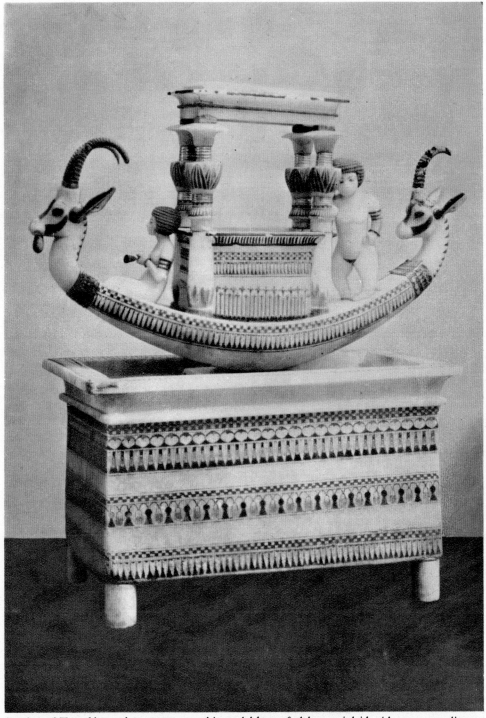

Another of Tutankhamen's treasures was this model boat of alabaster, inlaid with paste, standing on a pedestal. The cabin is in the form of a shrine, guarded by a dwarf, while at the other end of the boat a girl is seated, holding a lotus flower. The horns of the ibexes are natural ones. The boat was probably intended to represent the vessel in which the king would make his journey into the next world.

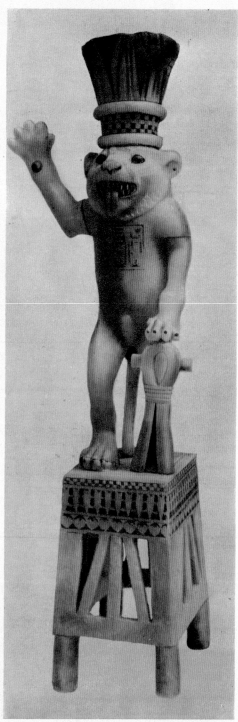

This is a photograph of the actual casket which contained the mummy of Tutankhamen. It was made of solid gold, the value of which to-day would be considerably over £50,000.

Known as a "Lion Gardant" vase, this alabaster figure in the form of a lion was a receptacle for costly oils. The crown forms a sealed vase and the topmost part represents the lotus flower.

twice there was some effort at national revival, but in the years 664–342 B.C. Egypt was under Ethiopian influence, and then finally submitted to the armies under Alexander the Great. Ptolemy succeeded Alexander and under him and his successors Egypt for a time enjoyed peace and prosperity.

Other civilisations had arisen by now, and the Romans became overlords of Egypt in 30 B.C. She was drained of wealth, taxed in corn to feed Rome, and became little better than a slave-state of the mighty Roman Empire. Egyptian institutions and civilisation still continued to influence the world for centuries but her own long years of greatness and supremacy had passed.

Long before then, however, another civilisation had risen to considerable greatness farther East. Mesopotamia is a land which has been divided many times and borne different names. It is men-

tioned in Genesis and other books of the Bible, while the Hebrew name for it means the Syria of the Two Rivers. Both Babylon and Assyria have formed part of Mesopotamia, and it is under these names they first appear as civilised nations.

In the Land of Mesopotamia

The valleys of the Tigris and Euphrates in Lower Mesopotamia, now known as Iraq, have been very good hunting grounds for the archæologist. Some very recent excavations found prehistoric settlements believed to have been in existence as long ago as 5,000 B.C. It is difficult to believe that relics as old as this could still be attainable, but such familiar things as cream bowls and vases have been found, often in fragments, but, nevertheless, reparable and perfectly authentic.

One of the most exciting digs ever

Copyright.

THE TEMPLE OF KING SOLOMON

Among those earlier nations that developed a high civilisation was the Hebrew race. Led by Moses and later by Joshua, they settled in Palestine about 1200 B.C. King David became King about 1000 B.C. and was succeeded by his son Solomon about 969 B.C. Renowned for his wisdom and his great buildings, chief of which was the famous Temple, Solomon ruled until 937 B.C. Our picture shows a reconstruction of this Temple as it was in those days.

Specially drawn for this work.

WHEN BABYLON FLOURISHED

From about 2200 B.C. the country of the Sumerians between the Tigris and the Euphrates became known as Babylon, and the city of that name flourished as a great trading centre. Schools were built and boys and girls taught to read and write.

began in A.D. 1855 at Ur, on the banks of the River Euphrates, on behalf of the British Museum. More research went on at this site after the First World War in a joint expedition from Britain and the United States, led by the famous British archæologist, Sir Leonard Woolley. Facts established at these two, widely separated, digs have taught us a great deal about ancient Ur, which was founded about 3500 B.C. Houses and streets, statues and documents have been found and the main temple or *ziggurrat* is estimated to have been 70 feet high.

The British School of Archæology in Iraq has been responsible for a great many Mesopotamian digs. It was established in 1932 and one of its main aims since has been to trace the development of Man in Mesopotamia from Neolithic times until the end of the Assyrian Empire in about 612 B.C. (The Neolithic period in all places is that in which Man first begins to lead a settled life.) Work at Nimrud (or Kalah), an Assyrian city situated about 22 miles south of modern Mosul and ancient Nineveh on the east bank of the Tigris, has been particularly fruitful. Nimrud was the military capital of ancient Assyria, founded in 883 B.C. by King Assur-nasir-pal II. It is mentioned in the Old Testament as Calah and was one of the most important cities in Assyria: Nineveh being the administrative capital; Assur, the traditional and religious capital; and Khorsbad. The first dig at Nimrud was in 1845 by A. H. Layard, who concentrated on the temple and a chain of palaces. In 1949 the British School of Archæology took over and seven seasons of work have now been completed.

Some time before 3500 B.C. a race of people called the Sumerians came from Arabia and overran the plain of Shinar, later known as Sumer. Here, between the two great rivers, they settled, and, so far as can be traced, the lines along which they developed were not unlike the Egyptians' earlier progress on the Nile. They learned the art of irrigation by controlling the flood of the rivers with dykes and leading the water across their fields in trenches. They baked clay to form bricks and with them built great towers as temples to their gods.

They had little stone and no material

such as the reed-pith for papyrus was discovered. All their records were made on clay tablets and in comparatively recent times considerable numbers of these tablets have been recovered. The early writing of the Sumerians, like the Egyptians, was formed by pictures. Later the pictures became signs for words or syllables, and from these more simple signs, triangular or wedge-shaped, were developed. This ancient form of script has been called Cuneiform, a name first used in A.D. 1700.

In different forms this method continued in use right down to the Christian era, but it was not until about 1802 that the key to some of the earlier Cuneiform writing was worked out and the early history of the Sumerians and their successors revealed. These ancient Sumerians had

a curiously modern time-saving method of putting their signature at the end of their letters. They had little rollers or cylinders on which were engraved the picture and sign, and sometimes the owner's full name. When the letter was written on the soft clay with a reed the writer used his cylinder or seal over the clay at the end of the letter and this was his signature. To-day we still use seals in a somewhat similar way and for much the same purpose. " Signed, sealed and delivered," is a phrase in very common use in legal documents to-day.

How Babylon Became a City

The Sumerians, too, were the first to introduce drill and discipline into their army and to group men into what we should call a phalanx instead of loose, irregular bodies, fighting where and how they chose. As the Sumerians had

W. F. Mansell.

ASSYRIA'S WARRIOR KING AND HUNTSMAN

About 1400 B.C. Assyria became independent and later conquered Babylon. The Assyrians were a military race, but literature and art were also encouraged by King Ashurbanipal, seen in the sculptured panel above. During his reign (668–626 B.C.) Assyria was at the zenith of her power, but in 607 B.C. she was defeated by the Medes and as a nation disappeared from history.

Specially drawn for this work.

WISE MEN OF THE EAST

For a time the people known as the Chaldeans were lords of Babylon, but their greatest work lay in their astronomical observations. They made the first long series of records and even after losing their independence were encouraged to continue their scientific work.

Semites appeared and about 2200 B.C. they seized Babylon, a small village on the Euphrates. A hundred years later Babylon became the first city of the land and under their king, Hammurapi, made further conquests, including a part known as Assyria. From now on the name of this country became known as Babylon. Hammurapi made a code of laws which laid down among other things that justice must be done to the widow, the orphan and the poor. Women were given an important place and became scribes or engaged in business. Schools were built and boys and girls were taught the three or four hundred signs of their language so that they could read and write.

Babylon flourished. They produced grain and dates, had flocks and herds, and made leather as well as woollen clothing. Their donkey caravans travelled far on peaceful trading expeditions. Many of the letters written by Hammurapi have been found in comparatively recent times and give a picture of a busy, commercial country. Art and architecture, however, seem to have been neglected to some extent and there was no advance in this sphere on the old Sumerian standards.

formed themselves into separate city-states there was a good deal of fighting. The earliest city to gain leadership in Sumer was Ur and here Abraham was born. " In Ur of the Chaldees " it says in Genesis, and Chaldea is the Biblical name for this region of the Euphrates-Tigris plain.

About 2750 B.C. a great king, Sargon, became ruler of the country north of Sumer. He defeated the Sumerian city-kings and, as a result, his people, the Akkadians, learned a great deal of the arts of civilisation. The rulers of the new and larger country became known as kings of Sumer and Akkad.

They prospered and lasted for over oo years, but then a new tribe of

When the Assyrians Gained Power

Away to the north-west of Babylon and standing on the Tigris was a small city-kingdom known as Assur. The people of Assur had learned much from the Sumerians and they also had trading expeditions from the Phœnicians, Egyptians, and other races such as the Hittites. Assur grew and its people became known as the Assyrians. They were a race of fighters since they often had to defend their borders against enemies on the other side and they were the first to bring horses into their armies and to use chariots. They developed powerful weapons for destroying the walls of a city and used archers to shoot at the defenders of the city walls. They even had something very similar to what we now call a "tank" which was protected in front by metal armour-plate. This carried a heavy battering-ram to pierce the walls of an opposing city.

Gradually Assyria grew stronger until it had gained lordship over a great empire in Western Asia. Under the king known as Sargon II (722–705 B.C.) Assyria reached the height of her power as a military empire. Nineveh, north of Assur, became the chief city and great palaces and temples were built along the Tigris. The arts of peace flourished, too, and one great collection of 22,000 clay tablets was discovered in the library rooms at Nineveh. This was probably the earliest library known in Asia.

One large flat tablet, part of an Assyrian book consisting of many such tablets, tells the story of the Flood and how the hero built a great ship and survived the destructive waters. But in 606 B.C. Nineveh was destroyed by the Chaldeans from the South and the Medes from the North. A new Chaldean empire arose with Babylon as its

capital. Greatest among all the rulers of this new kingdom of Babylon was Nebuchadnezzar, who ruled from 604–561 B.C. His story is told in the Bible. He conquered the little kingdom of Judah, destroyed Jerusalem, and took away many Hebrews as captives to Babylon. It was he who possibly built the famous palace with its hanging gardens of Babylon, though tradition also associates the gardens with the fabulous Queen Semiramis.

W. F. Mansell.

TRIBUTE TO A MIGHTY KING

The Assyrians became the dominant race in Babylon about 1300 B.C. to 607 B.C. and five of their kings bore the name Shalmaneser. On a black obelisk Shalmaneser III (860–825 B.C.) told of his exploits and power. Our picture shows the bearers of Jehu, King of Israel, bringing tribute to the powerful ruler. The other two panels also show tribute-bearers bringing apes, ivory tusks and staves to Shalmaneser.

Specially drawn for this work.

TRADING WITH PHŒNICIAN SAILORS

The fame of the Phœnicians has remained in history owing to their supremacy as sailors over all other early nations. They sailed not as conquerors but for trade and commerce and established colonies. Alone among early nations they had sailed beyond the Mediterranean and traded with the Tin Islands (Scilly and Cornwall).

The Chaldean Astronomers

Other nations from the North had begun to progress from their semi-barbaric state. These belonged to a white race, usually classified as Indo-Europeans, and most prominent of these in the earliest days were the Medes and Persians. Among the Persians a great king arose, Cyrus (600–529 B.C.), whose youthful story is told in Volume II. Cyrus conquered Babylon and the Persians learned a great deal of the arts of civilisation which influenced them strongly as a nation. The Chaldeans were renowned as astronomers and even under Persian rule their work continued.

It is worth mentioning that about 500 B.C. one Chaldean astronomer made tables showing the time taken by the sun and the moon in their revolutions and giving the dates of eclipses and other events. He calculated the length of the year to within less than 27 minutes of the final conclusions arrived at by astronomers many centuries later. This was 2,000 years before the telescope was invented. A century later another Chaldean astronomer compiled tables of even greater accuracy.

Darius succeeded Cyrus and it was he who erected a great triumphal monument on the cliffs at Behistun. This was inscribed in three languages, Persian, Babylonian and Elamite, proclaiming the great events that had taken place in the expansion of the Persian empire. Through the efforts of an Englishman, Sir Henry Rawlinson, who worked on his task for some years, the translation of the Babylonian from the Persian cuneiform was completed by 1847 and the completely forgotten lost language of Babylon became understood. After two or three thousand years the clay tablets which had been unearthed in Mesopotamia could be read again and great gaps in world history could be filled in.

Persians and Hebrews

By this period, the beginning of the fifth century B.C., there were several peoples or nations in this Eastern part of the world who had in varying degrees made considerable progress from their semi-savage wandering tribe condition towards a state of settled civilisation in which arts and crafts could advance. Egypt no longer held pride of place and for a time the Persians were dominant, though near at hand the Greeks had begun to make their place in history.

There was, too, a small country known as Palestine which was at times the battlefield between the nations of the Nile and the Euphrates. From about 2500 B.C. Egypt held Palestine. The history of the Hebrew inhabitants of this country is told in Genesis, beginning with the journey of Abraham from Ur to the valley of the Euphrates and down into Palestine.

One group of Hebrew tribes became slaves in Egypt and suffered great hardships. Eventually they were led out of Egypt by their great leader and law-giver, Moses, and later, under Joshua, entered Canaan, as that part of Palestine which included the coastal region and the valley of the Jordan was then called. Most of the industries which began in Palestine had been learned by the tribes in Egypt.

Among these Hebrews who had come to Canaan with Joshua there were some who still thought regretfully of the days when they had wandered as shepherds in the open lands instead of living in towns. One such man, whose name is unknown, was inspired to write a history of the Hebrews. This history survived and is the earliest history ever written, though it was not published in the sense that we understand the word until centuries later.

Others also had written and there came a time when the Persian kings, beginning with Cyrus, permitted the Hebrew exiles in Babylon to return to Palestine and Jerusalem was rebuilt. Here some of the Hebrew leaders

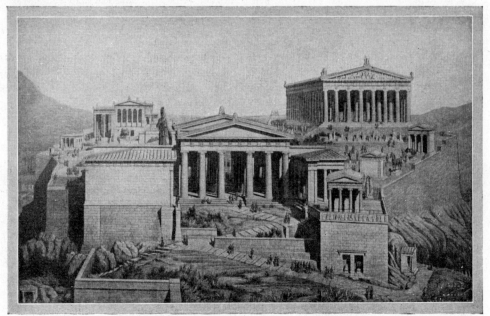

W. F. Mansell.

HOW THE ATHENIANS SAW THE ACROPOLIS

The ancient citadel of Athens, the Acropolis, is said to have been built by Cecrops, legendary first king of Athens, and in its long history it has been fortress, sanctuary and museum. For more than 2,000 years its buildings have served as models to architects. Though the original buildings were destroyed during the Persian war they were rebuilt in the age of Pericles (499 to 429 B.C.). Our picture gives a restored view showing the scene in its great days.

THREE GODS OF GREEK MYTHOLOGY

The ancient Greeks had a wonderful religion of mythology and the stories of their gods have come down to us through the ages. Three of their deities are seen above, carved in stone by a Greek sculptor. On the left is Poseidon, the god of the sea whose symbol of power is a trident; then Dionysus, or Bacchus, god of wine and fertility, and Demeter, known to the Romans as Ceres, the goddess of Agriculture.

arranged the addresses of their prophets as a book of hymns and we know it to-day as the Book of Psalms. They had, too, the Law given to them by Moses, but it was not until the Christian era that these different works, including that of the early historian, were put together to become the Sacred Book of the Hebrews, the Old Testament as we know it to-day.

Voyages of the Phœnicians

One other nation should be mentioned as playing a part in the progress of mankind in those far-off days. The Phœnicians lived in a small territory north of Palestine, measuring about 200 miles long by 15 miles in depth. Not a great deal is known about their early history; they were not a military people and although they founded colonies and settlements they made no conquests. Yet by 1200 B.C. they had become skilled navigators and their ships ventured out over the seas as far as the Atlantic coast of Spain. One of their rulers, Hiram, king of Tyre, was the ally of David and Solomon during the brief period of Hebrew prosperity in Palestine.

It is believed that the Phœnicians came with their ships to Cornwall to obtain tin, and there is some little evidence that they may have adventured as far south as Sumatra about 450 B.C., but there are no real records of these more distant voyages. Their settlement at Carthage became an important commercial state and even a rival eventually to the growing power of Rome.

They learned from the Egyptians how to manufacture goods and for purposes of trade made metal goods and glassware. They spread their acquired knowledge to other countries. At first they used clay tablets as the Babylonians did but quickly adopted papyrus when they realised its advantages as used in Egypt. In languages, too, they were adepts and it was from the Phœnicians that the Greeks learned their alphabet, which was a Phœnician improvement on other systems they had seen, and it is of course the basis of our alphabet to-day. To Greece, too, they brought as traders the pale-yellow paper obtained from the Egyptians, as well as the ink and pens with which to write.

Asia's Knowledge Comes to Greece

The Phœnicians made no fresh contribution to knowledge but improved the inventions and devices of others and as merchants spread them far and wide. When at last Alexander the Great besieged and conquered their great city of Tyre in 332 B.C. the days of the Phœnicians came to an end, though some of their city-states outside the mother-country, such as Carthage, carried on, but Phœnicia itself had passed from history.

Persia was really the last of the great early civilisations of the Orient and much of what they had learned and discovered passed to the Greeks in Europe.

In recent years there have been a number of Italian excavations in the Minoan Palace at Phaistos in Crete, which was really the first part of Europe to step from the Late Stone Age into the age of a higher civilisation. By 1955 A.D. it had been established that four palaces were built, at different times, on the same spot. Rich pottery, including a wine pourer, fruit stands and a jar still containing grape seeds were among the remarkable finds.

It was probably a little later than 2000 B.C. when the tribesmen of the

W. F. Mansell.

THE TEMPLE OF THESEUS THE HERO

In Greek legend Theseus was the great hero of Athens and Attica. He slew the bull of Marathon, killed the Minotaur, led an expedition against the Amazons and married their queen. When after many adventures he was himself slain his bones were brought to Athens in 469 B.C., where a marble temple was built to receive them. To-day the temple remains the best preserved of all ancient Greek buildings.

Specially drawn for this work.

WHEN ROME DEFEATED THE GREEKS OF CORINTH

One of the greatest cities of ancient Greece was Corinth, famed for its painting and its work in clay and bronze. The third order of Greek architecture, the Corinthian, took its name from the city. As a result of its defiance of Rome when the new Empire was expanding, the Roman legions attacked Corinth and utterly destroyed it in the year 146 B.C.

Balkan mountains came down into the Greek peninsula. In the days of their wandering their leaders became shepherd-kings ruling over a group of villages. As they began to settle down these villages grew into one city. Even after 1000 B.C., long after the Egyptians had seen their greatest era, the Greeks remained a rough and barbarous people. It was the traders from the East, the Phœnicians, bringing woollen garments, metal trays, handsome ivory combs, and porcelain dishes, who roused the desire for knowledge in these early Greeks.

Even in their semi-savage state the Greeks had natural mental ability. Early in their history their poets and bards sang songs of battle and brave adventure as well as of the great gods dwelling among the clouds above the summit of Mount Olympus: Zeus, the sky-god with lightning in his hand; Apollo, the sun-god, musician, and protector of the shepherds; Athena, the warrior goddess who protected them all, especially in their peaceful tasks since she bore the olive branch of peace. These were the greatest, but there were many others. Many of the stories and songs were ascribed to Homer and we can read his *Iliad* and *Odyssey* to-day. Of the work Homer and other Greek poets did you can read in Volume VII.

The Greeks became good sailors and built their own ships on Phœnician lines. They founded colonies and their city-states developed in power. The Greeks were not so much a united nation as a group of states and they called all men not of Greek blood barbarians and themselves Hellenes, or the descendants of Helen.

Architecture made great advances around 600 B.C. At first they copied Egyptian models, but in this, as well as in sculpture and other arts, they gradually developed their own. In science, they learned all that the Egyptians, the Phœnicians, and the astronomers of Babylon had discovered and then went much further ahead. History began to be recorded by such men as Herodotus, generally known as "the Father of History," who travelled widely in the known world of his time and collected material for his great work.

Herodotus was born about 484 B.C. and died in 424 B.C. His history records the story of Croesus (595–546 B.C.) whose name we still use to describe someone possessed of great wealth, and of the manner in which he was defeated in battle by Cyrus, King of Persia and founder of a great Empire.

There had been records of events before Herodotus began, but it was he who tried to give a history of the world so far as it was then known. At the time he wrote, the "civilised world" was almost entirely gathered in those countries which lie around the Eastern end of the Mediterranean.

Hecateus (550–476 B.C.) was a great traveller and wrote a Journey Round the World, giving a geographical account of Europe, Asia and Northern Africa (Libya), with a map. It was a quaint map of the world, according to our modern knowledge, but it was a beginning.

Where Democracy Began

Their great city was Athens, a centre of industry and commerce, and also the home of art and literature. Their Government was the first real attempt at democracy ever known. In another city-state, Sparta, which took an almost opposite point of view from that

W. F. Mansell.

AMONG THE RUINS OF ANCIENT ROME

From the Greeks whom they conquered the Romans learned much about architecture, but they also learned something nearer home. It was from the Etruscans, who had been masters of Italy before the Romans, that the secret of the arch was learned, and this enabled the Romans to build larger temples and palaces than the Greeks. Above, we see the House of the Vestals connected with the Temple dedicated to Vesta, the goddess of the hearth and the fire.

of the citizens of Athens, strict discipline and military valour were the
virtues considered most desirable.

Yet there was war between Athens
and Sparta (459–446 B.C.) and victory
went to Sparta. Athens recovered
something of her power and men such
as Plato and Aristotle in the fourth
century B.C. brought new learning to
the world. Alexander, son of the king
of Macedonia, was a pupil of Aristotle,
a fact which had a very great effect on
world history in due course.

Macedonia was a kingdom to the
north of Greece, but her people were
undoubtedly of the Hellenic race and
spoke Greek. Under Alexander,
Macedonia became a great Empire,
which included Greece, as well as
Persia, Babylon, Egypt, and other
lands reaching down even to the
Punjab in India. Alexander the Great
spread Greek ideas and culture through
all the countries he conquered. He
died suddenly in Babylon in the month
of June, 323 B.C., at the age of 33, but
few men have left so great a mark on
the course of world affairs. A military
genius of great personal courage, he
was also a wise and practical states-
man, a conqueror who respected the
customs and laws of the country he had
conquered while eager to give them the
culture and knowledge of Greece.

After his death his empire was
divided among his generals. Ptolemy,
for instance, ruled Egypt and under him
and his successors the ancient civilisation revived and prospered till the
Romans came. Antipater, a regent of
Macedonia, was nominally the ruler of
Greece, but the city-states carried on
along their own lines, forming leagues
and unfortunately quarrelling among
themselves.

The Rise of the Romans

Meantime, a new power had begun
to arise in the West. We have read in
an earlier volume the story of Romulus
and Remus, and between 500–275 B.C.
the Romans gained control of the
entire Italian peninsula south of the
River Po. They conquered some of
the Italian cities founded by the Greeks,
but the Romans did not destroy. They
were too anxious to learn and admired
the Greek sculptors so much that they
employed them for their own great
works.

We are chiefly concerned here with
the growth of civilisations, but wars
and conquests played their part even
while the scientists and artists worked.
Rome became a great military nation,
but in general she did not seek to
oppress or make slaves of the people
she had conquered. There were exceptions, however, such as Egypt. Then
there was Carthage, the little trading
colony of the Phœnicians which had
grown into a great and splendid seaport
city, spreading not only far inland on
the north coast of Africa, but also
spreading her power and influence in
various parts of Europe.

Carthage became a rival to Rome.
In 216 B.C. at Cannæ in Southern Italy,
their great general, Hannibal, annihi-
lated a Roman army of 70,000 men.
Rome had her revenge in 202 B.C. when
at Zama, five days' march from Carthage, Hannibal was defeated and
Rome became mistress of the Mediterranean. Carthage recovered to some
extent but Rome never ceased to fear
her. "Carthage must be destroyed!"
said Cato, the Roman senator, in every
speech, and in 146 B.C. his words were
fulfilled. At the end of the third Punic
War the Romans captured Carthage
and utterly destroyed it. The territory
became a Roman province.

In that same year another great city,
Corinth, in Greece, was taken and
destroyed by the Romans. With that
defeat Greece, too, ceased to be an
independent country and became part
of the Roman Empire. But Greek
civilisation lived on. The Romans had
destroyed a strong city but made no
attempt to destroy Grecian culture
and art. It has been said, indeed, that
in their defeat the Greeks conquered

the Romans. It was Greek art and literature that became the standard of Rome.

Here we need not go into all the details of the rise of the mighty Roman Empire. It became a great military nation, with a well-trained, disciplined army which could be supported by other armies belonging to countries under Roman control. To conquer a seafaring nation such as Carthage they built a powerful navy. Their central government in Rome, the Senate, showed great ability in carrying on their wars. Rome itself became a city of wealth and enormous power.

Rome Learns from Greece

In the Roman home were to be found statues, paintings and ornaments brought from Greece and other civilised lands of the East. Greeks who were brought to Rome as prisoners of war became teachers to the Romans. It was these Greeks who founded schools to which the Romans sent their children, or in other cases an educated Greek slave was engaged as tutor to a family. Presently there were Roman poets and writers, modelling their style on the Greek books brought into their country, but writing stories of Rome in Latin. A library stocked with papyrus rolls, which were the books of those days, became an important feature in well-ordered Roman houses.

The city had its troubles; there was civil strife and revolution. Rome ceased to be a republic and became an empire. Under the Roman eagle the legions went North, South, East and West. Egypt, parts of Asia Minor, the lands of the Danube, and a great part of Europe, including France (Gaul) and Spain, were all part of this Roman Empire by the time Julius Cæsar

STATUE OF A LADY

Another example of Roman sculpture, which gives some idea of the high standard it attained, is seen in this statue of a lady or priestess which dates from the third century B.C.

British Museum.

A PRIEST OF ROME

The rise of the Romans marked the decline of Greece, but Greek sculptors taught Romans their art. Here is the head of a priest, the work of a sculptor who lived before Julius Cæsar.

figured in history. Gaul had not been completely conquered when Cæsar became governor and made the country we know as France one of the finest provinces of the Roman Empire. The French became proud to belong to that empire and to this day France owes much to the influence of the Romans.

The Romans come to Britain

It is now we come to the British Isles. Julius Cæsar gazed across the waters now known as the English Channel and wondered about the unknown land on the opposite side. In 55 B.C., and again in 54 B.C., he crossed the Channel, the second time with a larger force. The ill-armed Britons with their war-chariots were no match for the Roman legions, but for various reasons Cæsar was unable to remain and conquer the country. The real Roman invasion did not come till nearly a century later, A.D. 43, and then, under Aulus Plautus, it was completely successful.

With the coming of the Romans the civilisation of Britain began. Julius Cæsar in his writings described the Britons as he saw them in those far-off years of 55 and 54 B.C. Fair-haired warriors bedaubed with blue war-paint they were; they had wicker coracles for crossing rivers, by the side of which they built their settlements of primitive huts.

Not very much is known of Great Britain before this visit of Julius Cæsar. The Mesolithic (or Middle Stone Age) period set in after the last Ice Age in about 10,000 B.C. In the later part of this period, when Britain was still joined to the Continent, Man was in an exceedingly primitive state. In A.D. 1949 a Mesolithic site was unearthed at Star Carr in Yorkshire, known to have existed earlier than 5,000 B.C. From discoveries found on this site—implements and rough dwelling places—something has been learned of the hunter-fishers who lived at this time. Another early sign of habitation is Stonehenge, on the Salis-

bury Plain in Wiltshire, which may have been erected about 1800 B.C. It is a collection of huge stones, some of which may have come from Wales, and the burial pits surrounding the area may have been used in the early Bronze Age, nearly 4,000 years ago. Stonehenge must have been a prehistoric sanctuary, possibly connected with sun-worship.

Barrows and Dolmens

Evidence of Neolithic man is clearly visible in several parts of the country in the huge burial mounds, or barrows, that remind one of the care taken by the ancient Egyptians in disposing of their dead. Also common are *dolmens*, which consist of two or more upright slabs of stone with other stones placed horizontally on top—as at Stonehenge. A well-known example is Kit's Coty House, high on the south bank of the North Downs, near Aylesford, in Kent.

Naturally enough the Romans brought their own way of life and this was gradually adopted by the less civilized Britons. Religion, too, spread from the Mediterranean. One of the most popular cults was the worship of the god, Mithras. This was a cult of Persian origin and Mithras was esteemed the God of Light. Three temples to him have been excavated on Hadrian's Wall in the North of England and in A.D. 1949, at Carrawburgh, in Northumberland, altars and other relics of the Mithras worship were discovered. Even more recently a temple was unearthed right in the heart of London at Walbrook, believed to have been built towards the end of the second century A.D. A marble head of the god was found and also a head of the goddess Minerva, or Athena as she was called by the Greeks. Both are remarkable examples of marble sculpture.

The Romans built beautiful villas all over the countryside. A great number of these were destroyed by later invaders but, fortunately for posterity some did survive and the remains of these still exist to-day. As early as 1823 traces of a Roman villa were found at Lullingstone,

A ROMAN VILLA IN SOMERSET

Illustrated London News.

It was the Romans who brought civilisation to Britain when they began their occupation of the country in A.D. 43. They remained as rulers for over 360 years and many records of their great work as builders still remain. The photograph above shows excavators uncovering the fine mosaic floor of a large room in what was once a Roman villa at Low Ham, near Langport, Somerset, first discovered in 1946.

in Kent. Excavations from 1949–54 revealed fine tessellated pavements and mosaic floors, once part of the stately residence of a well-to-do Roman. Pictures of the gods, Jupiter and Europa, and, strangely, a chapel of Christian worship, were other outstanding finds and it is thought that the villa was built at the time of the Emperor Trajan (A.D. 98–117).

Roman London

In London, parts of the Roman Wall and a fort at Cripplegate have been found. The Wall must have been a most effective fortification; it is 11 feet wide at ground level with an extended ditch 16 feet wide and a substantial bank on the inside constructed from earth taken from the ditch. It probably surrounded London, but to-day much of it has been built on and the only visible parts are from Aldermanbury Postern, past the Cripplegate fort to St. Giles Church—somewhere around this area it gets lost again beneath modern London offices.

It was not until A.D. 407 that the Romans, for reasons of their own, bade good-bye to Britain, never to return. Orderly government ceased to exist and the country broke up into separate kingdoms. But the Romans had left much behind them, and though the story of our British civilisation made little progress through the six centuries that followed the departure of the Romans, a good deal of our heritage from them remained.

Donald McLeish.

THE STATELY PONT DU GARD BUILT BY THE ROMANS

It was Julius Cæsar who conquered the tribes of Gaul, the country we now know as France, and the influence of the Romans has remained strong ever since. In France, too, the Romans built some of their finest structures and the photograph above shows the stately three-tiered Pont du Gard, part of an aqueduct which carried water for 26 miles to Nîmes. The bridge has stood firm since 19 B.C. but a modern road now crosses the main tier.

EARLY CIVILISATIONS—Plate 1—Egypt

Specially painted for this work.

It was in the fertile valley of the Nile that man first emerged from his primitive state and gradually attained a stage of high civilisation. Long before 4000 B.C. the Egyptians were a well-governed nation of several millions. In the Plate above are seen some examples of their work; (1) Reproduction of a bas-relief at Tel-el-Amarna. (2) Mummy of a cat. (3) Riverside scene. (4) A very early Egyptian with bow and arrow. (5) Internal plan of Great Pyramid. (6) Obelisk. (7) Colossus of Thebes. (8) Great Pyramid of Gizeh.

EARLY CIVILISATIONS—Plate 2—Egypt

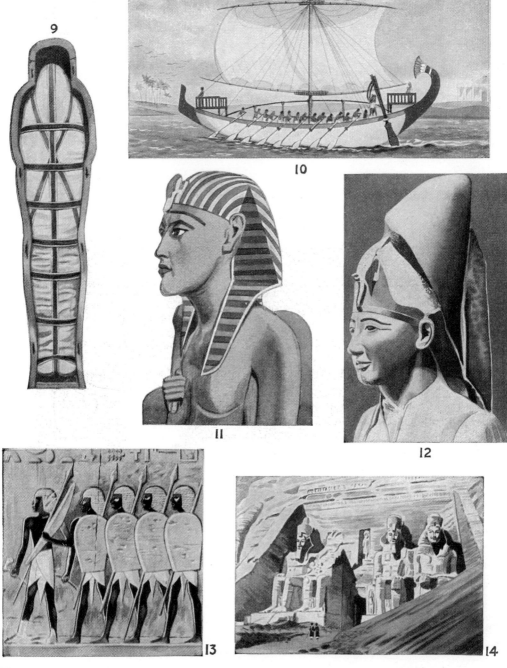

The ancient Egyptians believed that there was another life after death, but it was necessary to preserve the body. Embalming became a fine art, and (9) shows the mummy of a king in its coffin. From drawings in their tombs we know what their ships (10) were like. Here, too, are preserved portraits of their kings (11), one of whom, Thotmes III, is seen in this picture (12). In a temple at Deir-el-Bahri is this drawing of their warriors, armed with spears and shields (13), while in (14) we have a view of the Rock Temple at Abu Simbel.

EARLY CIVILISATIONS—Plate 3—Babylon and Assyria

Between the rivers Tigris and Euphrates lies the plain of Shinar. The earliest inhabitants were known as Sumerians, but the land became known as Babylon, of which Assyria formed a part. Its history can be traced back beyond 3500 B.C. Above are seen (1) Sumerians marching to battle 2500 B.C.; (2) Babylonian map of the world; (3) Assyrian battering-ram; (4) Ornament showing a goat caught in a thicket at Ur; (5) Assyrian god—winged bull with human face; (6) Raft of inflated skins, and a skin-covered basket-boat; (7) In the Hanging Gardens at Babylon.

EARLY CIVILISATIONS—Plate 4—Babylon and Assyria

For a time Assyria became dominant in Babylon. Their capital was Nineveh and they reached their height as a military empire about 722 B.C. Nineveh was destroyed in 606 B.C. and Babylon again became the capital. In (8) is seen a plough and seed drill used in Babylon; (9) Portrait of an Assyrian; (10) Assyrians torturing their captives; (11) Temple of the Moongod at Ur; (12) Sargon I, King of Assyria, was found like Moses floating in a wicker basket; (13) Sennacherib, the Assyrian king mentioned in 2 Kings xix. 36; (14) Clay model of Assyrian demon; (15) Caged lion being released for the hunt.

IN AMERICA BEFORE COLUMBUS

RUINS OF A PRE-COLOMBIAN FORTRESS IN PERU

All the original inhabitants of North and South America came of the same stock. In the North they remained largely a primitive people, but on the Mexican plateau and farther South in Peru higher stages of civilisation were attained. Our photograph shows the remains of a fortress on what is now the Peru-Bolivia border which was probably built by the Andes people who preceded the Incas.

MODERN world history really begins with the discovery of America in 1492. Even to-day we still speak of the Western hemisphere across the ocean as the New World, and it was the joining of the two halves of the whole world that gave a new impetus to Western civilisation.

It also extended that civilisation which had slowly spread over the Old World. The New World was well populated when the streams of explorers and adventurers from Europe followed the course Columbus had set across the uncharted seas. There were certain forms of comparatively high civilisations in the New World when the Europeans arrived there, but they faded out before the more advanced and virile civilisations from the Eastern hemisphere.

Although it was another explorer, Amerigo Vespucci, who gave his name to America, the credit for the discovery rightly goes to Columbus; and the period in its history before its existence was known to the Old World is generally referred to as the pre-Colombian era. Compared with the Old World not a great deal is known of life in America in the pre-Colombian period. We can trace the growth of civilisation in the Old World over a period of more than 6,000 years through Egypt, Babylon (or Mesopotamia as it became known later), Greece and Rome till it spread all over Europe and Eastern Asia as well as the northern parts of Africa.

Primitive Races of the North

While all this progress had been made in the Old World, what was happening in that vast land mass we know to-day as North and South America? Columbus believed, of course, that he had reached the coasts of India and the people found in the newly discovered continent were called Indians. They remain Indians, American Indians to this day.

Not many people realise that these early Indians, and indeed all the other tribes in America at that time, originated in Asia. For when the ice sheets of the

By permission of Dr. Gann.

DESCENDANTS OF THE MAYAS

Most of the ceremonial centres of the Mayas were in the lowland regions of Guatemala. The tribes of the mountains were not so fond of ceremony. Some of the customs of the ancient Mayas are still practised by their descendants to-day. Our picture shows members of one branch of the Maya people, the Kekchi Indians, dressed to give a performance of their " Devil Dance."

Great Ice Age receded northwards, the Asiatic nomads hunted their game farther and farther north and finally crossed the ice-choked Bering Straits from Siberia to Alaska. They wandered south across America, some settling near rivers and forests, others for ever on the move, hunting bison on the plains. Always they adapted their primitive ways to the climatic and geographical conditions of their region. These were so varied that the language, looks and occupations of the people soon differed considerably from tribe to tribe.

Indians and Eskimos

We know that by A.D. 300 the south-west of North America was populated by a nomadic people whose speciality was the making of coiled baskets. These people were superseded around A.D. 800 by the first of the pueblo Indians, who hunted and learned to cultivate maize, to make glazed pottery and eventually even to weave cotton cloth. Although a purely primitive people, they were usually peaceful. In the thirteenth century another large tribe existed in the south-east; to-day we know this tribe as the Mound Builders, because they built huge burial mounds for their dead.

In the extreme north, living in snow " igloos " in the freezing winters, the Eskimos fished and hunted.

Strangely, there was a vast difference between these primitive peoples in the North and those that lived in Middle and South America. Although by A.D. 1100 the pueblo Indians had learned to build stone terraced houses and to make decorative pottery, they were far behind

IN THE LAND OF THE MAYAS

By permission of Dr. Gann.

Although there are few descendants of the Mayas, and those that now exist are mostly peasants, one thousand years ago the Mayas lived very much more cultured lives. They built temples and houses which were often decorated with beautiful carvings. It was because of their love of art and architecture that they had very little time for wars, and for this reason it was not difficult for the warlike Aztecs to overcome them. The picture above shows a reconstruction of a Maya citadel.

the civilisations that had grown up on the Mexican Plateau, in Central America and on the Andean Highlands in the South.

The Mayas

One of the first and certainly the most outstanding of these civilisations was that of the Mayas in the densely forested areas of Guatemala, south-east Mexico and western Honduras, and on the limestone plateau of Yucatan. Not only did the people of the Maya build cities and huge temples, but they had a system of picture writing and their buildings were often carved with inscriptions in hieroglyphics.

The first city that we know of was Uaxactun in the southern forested area, built about A.D. 300 and followed by the cities of Tikal, Copan and Palenque in the same area. These probably formed the peaceful group that is to-day known as the Old Empire. Indeed, the Mayas seem to have been at peace generally until affected, much later in the twelfth century, by the invasion of a fiercer people from North Mexico.

Before this time there appears to have been some sort of government among the Maya. Probably each city or settlement had its own leader, who was to some extent responsible for the progress of his region. Roads were built, and architecture and religion encouraged. The people grew cotton and maize, made excellent carvings in wood, freestone and jade, and were often clever at making pottery. Skilled builders erected impressive temples and houses for the priests and rulers, which were often surrounded by the thatched dwellings of the people.

Religion played a very big part in their lives and the priests were often leaders of the people. The chief gods were those of the weather and crops. The ruins of their temples still stand to-day, and the remarkably accurate calender that they formed has helped us to reconstruct Maya history.

When the Warrior Aztecs came

As time passed, the peaceful Old Empire of the Mayas declined and gave place to a New Empire, which had a different chief city, Chichen Itza in Yucatan, and which was constantly disturbed by the influence and activities of a

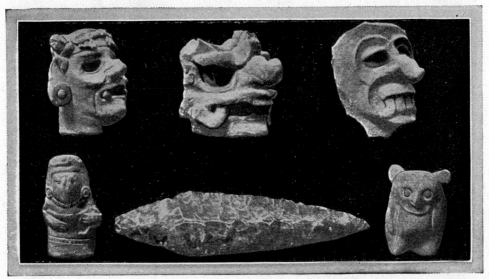

By permission of Dr. Gann.

FROM OLD TIME RUINED CITIES

Yucatan, Honduras, Guatemala and a portion of the country running up into Mexico are the home of the mysterious Maya Empire, and here we see some carvings which have been found in the ruins of their ancient cities. The third head is that of Tlaloc, the Mexican god of rain.

Dorien Leigh.

THE SILVER MINES OF VANISHED INCAS

It was because of the stories of untold wealth in gold and silver to be found in the land of the Incas that certain Spanish adventurers, led by Don Francisco Pizarro, made their way to Peru. The stories were based on truth and our picture shows the ruins of an Inca silver mine. The ore was milled in the round stone towers. In the background a herd of llamas is seen passing along the ancient highway.

war-like tribe, the Aztecs of North Mexico.

The Aztecs were skilled metal workers and specialised in making war weapons—spears and wooden swords. This was unfortunate for the Mayas, who knew very little about such crafts, and it is obvious that from the twelfth century to the latter half of the fifteenth, when civil war, hurricane and pestilence struck them, the Mayas were losing their position as most important people of Central America. Although the Aztecs soon took over this position they never reached such a high standard of culture as the early Mayas.

The Aztec merchants were quick to realize the value of trade and often travelled far selling their goods, using the cacao bean and axe-shaped copper plates as a form of currency. There was a system of education and a calendar similar to that of the Mayas was used. In spite of all this, the Aztecs were first and foremost a violent tribe. Their religion was cruel, human sacrifice by corrupt priests to hosts of weird gods being the main feature. Most of the wars were fought to obtain prisoners for sacrifice. The priests encouraged the ordinary people to be superstitious and most lived in constant fear of the end of the world. Records of events in the lives of the war chiefs were kept by the priests; it was one of the few useful things that they did.

Cortés and Montezuma

These were the people who dominated Central America when a small Spanish force of no more than about 400 men landed on the coast of Vera Cruz in 1519. Led by a hardy general, Hernando Cortés, they founded a settlement at Vera Cruz and from there marched across Mexico until they arrived at Tenochtitlan, the capital Aztec city built in 1325 on the site that is now Mexico City, and then the residence of the main war chief, Montezuma II.

Montezuma was in a difficult position. He was far from being all-powerful and was therefore not in the position to attack the oncoming invaders without first consulting cautious advisers. While he was still only thinking about a plan of action, Cortés entered the city and Montezuma was obliged to receive him without fight or question. He was immediately seized by the Spaniard as a hostage.

From the first the Aztecs stood no chance against the invaders. They were in the middle of harvesting and could not give full attention to any war; they were under no one clear and authoritative command; many of them betrayed their cause to the Spaniards; and finally, the unflinching generalship of Cortés and the superior military technique and weapons of the Spaniards, who had cannons, soon broke their resistance.

Death of Montezuma

The events that followed soon favoured Spain. Montezuma was killed by his own people while trying to pacify them and Cortés, after only a few defeats obtained complete control of the Aztec lands. By 1521 Cortés was in full control and Mexico became the centre of a Spanish dominion, New Spain. The rule of the Aztecs was over, but their spirit was not yet dead, for, in the nineteenth century many of their descendants were among those who threw off Spanish rule and made Mexico a republic.

Many interesting relics of these early civilisations have been unearthed. The British archæologist, Alfred P. Maudslay, did a great deal in the 1880's and

90's, and some of the pictures that illustrate this chapter were taken by Dr. Thomas Gann, also British, an amateur archæologist in British Honduras in the early part of the present century. To-day, the Carnegie Institute of Washington, with Eric Thompson of Great Britain, is carrying on valuable excavations in these areas.

Among the Incas of Peru

The Incas of Peru in South America were the third high civilisation of pre-Colombian America, and they are probably the one of which you have heard most.

Before the supremacy of the Incas South America was a land of many scattered tribes. They were situated according to climate, many on the Andean plateau, the hot coastal plains and the fertile valleys within the mountain belt. Few lived in the hot, damp tropical forests of the east. Most lived by fishing, hunting, potato and maize cultivation and metal work.

By the fifteenth century the Incas had become head of all the tribes including the Great Chimu, with their huge empire and capital city of Chan Chan on the coast of Peru. Soon the Inca kingdom extended across Peru, much of Ecuador, Chile, Bolivia and N.W. Argentina. Village life came under a central Inca government, which had complete control over everyone. Inca culture and the Quechea language were taught. Government was so centralised, in fact, that when the Spaniards finally overcame the Inca King, Atualpha, the whole Inca rule was punctured immediately.

Nevertheless, the system was effective, for much improvement was made in road building, land cultivation and social laws. Many great cities were built. The Inca pottery and weaving were superb and have never been equalled to this day. Wool for weaving was obtained from llamas, kept on the Andes, which were also used as beasts of burden and eaten for meat.

PERU, THE LAND OF THE INCAS

One of the cities of Peru in the days when the Incas were extending their power was Chan Chan, capital of the Great Chimu kingdom, on the coast near Trujillo. The people of Chimu, like the Incas, were sun worshippers, and here are the remains of the temples of the Sun and Moon at Chan Chan, photographed from the air. The Great Chimu were conquered by the Incas shortly before the Spanish conquest.

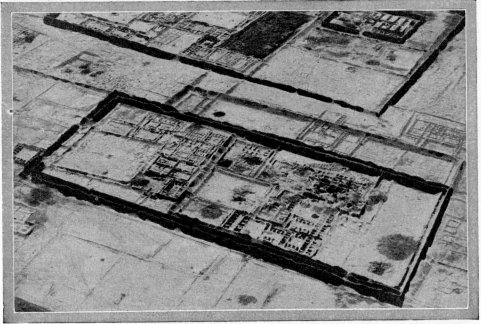

New York Times.

The ruins of Chan Chan occupy an area of eleven square miles and the city contained palaces, burial grounds, reservoirs and sunken gardens. The Incas had become rulers of this city and of a great empire extending from Quito to Chile and from the Pacific coast to beyond the Andes by the time the Spaniards, under Pizarro, descended upon them in 1532.

This was the state of the different parts of America at the end of the fifteenth century just before this New World was discovered. Following Columbus, the Spaniards and the Portuguese came. These two nations signed a treaty, dividing the whole of the newly-discovered world into two halves: Central and South America, except Brazil, were to become Spanish-controlled, while Portugal took Brazil and any other parts she desired.

Stories of the wealth and splendour of both the Aztecs and the Incas reached the ears of the explorers and adventurers. What happened in Mexico, the land of the Aztecs, we have seen. It was a similar story over again in Peru.

Daring and Treachery

In Mexico the Spanish conquerors heard stories of the even greater wealth of the Incas farther south in Peru.

IN THE SERVANTS' HALL

Both photographs on this page were taken at Machu Picchu in Peru and show ruins of bygone Inca buildings. This is part of the " residence of the servants."

Francisco Pizarro, in the service of Charles V of Spain, sailed from Panama at the end of 1531. He had with him a force of less than 200 men, but by an extraordinary mixture of daring and treachery he became eventually the real master of the country of the Incas. The king, Atualpha, agreed to give the Spaniards a vast store of treasure if they would restore him to his rightful place.

Pizarro played his cards skilfully and when it suited him he turned on Atualpha and had him executed. A puppet emperor was set up and Pizarro, with another adventurer, Almagro, held the country. Almagro was eventually slain by Pizarro's brothers, but in 1541 Pizarro himself was assassinated.

Nevertheless, the Inca rule had gone and Peru had become a Spanish possession. For four centuries the Inca civilisation had been dominant; for another three centuries the land belonged to Spain. Not until 1824 did Spanish rule come to an end and Peru became a

Dorien Leigh.
WITH THE SUN WORSHIPPERS

The Incas were worshippers of the sun and had many temples, with priests who had considerable powers. Here are the ruins of the house in which the " virgins of the sun " lived.

republic. It still remains Spanish in its culture and language, while Brazil, which broke away from Portugal a year or two earlier, still uses the Portuguese language and has cultural links with its first conquerors from the Old World.

Pioneers from England and France

In North America there was no real form of civilisation to be changed. The native Indians may at times have resisted the encroachment of the white adventurers from Europe, but there were no great kingdoms to be overthrown. Mostly the story is of slow and steady development of lands along the coasts or the great waterways. Emigrants from Europe, chiefly English and French at first, founded their colonies, and gradually two great countries, the United States and Canada, with a purely European civilisation, have grown to greatness, retaining the languages they had learned in their Motherland.

The original Red Indians are still there, but the new civilisation made little impact on them, beyond restricting their freedom to some extent, until recent times. They live to-day in great reservations, retaining much of their old traditions but benefiting more and more from education and new industries (canning, farming and lumbering).

Dorien Leigh.

IN THE CITY OF CHAN CHAN

When Pizarro, the Spanish explorer and daring adventurer, completed his conquest of Peru he founded Lima, which still remains the capital of the country. Some of the great cities which had been built under the rule of the Incas fell into ruins. Here we have a photograph of the walls of what was once an imposing building in the city of Chan Chan.

Other civilisations existed while European culture was developing. We know now that the Chinese language is the oldest living tongue and has survived with little change through more than 5,000 years. The civilisation that existed in China long before Greece or Rome existed did not spread beyond the bounds of that vast country and has exercised little influence on world progress.

Indian civilisation, too, existed before 4,000 B.C., and their teachers and philosophers made great contributions to knowledge. From the first to the fifteenth century almost the whole of South-east Asia was under Indian influence, and their philosophy will play its part in future world developments.

European Influence

Farther south, civilisation came with the European adventurers seeking new worlds beyond the seas. The Maoris of New Zealand had a primitive civilisation of their own which has been developed and largely influenced by the Europeans. It was indeed a European civilisation which spread through the Old World and was later taken to the New Worlds of America and then to Australia and the islands in the Southern Seas—a development of that civilisation which first began on the Nile and in the valley of the Tigris and Euphrates, passing eventually to the Ancient Greeks.

People still speak of 'the glory that was Greece'; and certainly, we owe much to the Greeks of ancient time and their high civilisation. To all that Greece gave to the world other races have added their portion, and with the dawn of Christianity the world of Roman civilisation took on a higher conception of life on this earth.

Camera Press.

THE LAST INCA STRONGHOLD

Here is another picture of the ruins of Machu Picchu. The Incas built this city, probably in the latter half of the fifteenth century, on a high ridge guarded by deep precipices. They called the city Vitcos, and it is certain that the conquering Spaniards knew little or nothing about it. Its beautiful temples and staircases were discovered, hidden in mountain vegetation, in comparatively recent times.

A Stone Age
Race that
has survived

The Aborigines
and their
Primitive Ways

Australian News & Information Bureau.

DANCING A CORROBOREE

Nowadays there are only about fifty thousand full-blood Aborigines in Australia and the number is still growing less. Even those trained as stockmen and working on the modern cattle stations often cling to their old customs. Here, for example, Aboriginal stockmen are dancing a corroboree to celebrate the home-coming of one of their number who had been in hospital.

AUSTRALIA'S OLDEST INHABITANTS

THE first people to inhabit Australia were not the white settlers who landed there in 1788. Their new country was already the homeland of some three hundred thousand primitive natives—the Aborigines, or blackfellows as they are now called. The word "aborigine" means the native, or original inhabitant of a country.

The Aborigines did not take kindly to the white man and his ways, or to other outside influences. For his part, the white man had little understanding of the Aborigines. As settlement went on, and an increasing area of the great continent was opened up to European influences, so the Aborigines retreated and their numbers diminished. To-day there are only about fifty thousand full-blood Aborigines in Australia and the number is still decreasing.

Meet the Aborigine

Let us meet a typical Aborigine and see what he looks like. He is about five and a half feet tall, and has a chocolate-brown skin. His hair is curly, his head narrow. He has thick skullbones; a low, sloping forehead, with prominent eyebrow ridges; and a nose that is

3—2

pushed in at the top and splayed out at the nostrils. His mouth is wide and stands out from the rest of his face. He holds himself very erect. He is what ethnologists (scientists who study the different races of mankind) call the Australoid type.

Although, since the coming of the white man, many Aborigines have taken to wearing the *naga* or loincloth, it is more natural for them to wear no clothes at all. Their possessions are few— implements and weapons made of wood or stone, some of them very cleverly (the boomerang, for example) and simple ornaments and sacred objects. If they live on the coast, they may also have bark or dug-out canoes. Only in a few regions do they build huts; but they often erect rough shelters, called *mia-mias*, made of bark and bushes.

No one knows for certain how long these people have lived in Australia or where they came from. It is thought that many thousands of years ago similar people lived in southern India and in time moved on, through Ceylon, the Malay Peninsula and the East Indies— and so, eventually, to Australia. There is nothing to show that they had large canoes, but they may well have crossed the sea on simple rafts, in the best Kon-Tiki fashion.

Tribes and Traditions

While we may safely speak of the Aborigines in these general terms, we must not forget that they are not all of a kind. They are divided into tribes, and each tribe has its own language, territory, and probably rites and customs. Within each tribe are a number of local groups or clans, each named after an animal or bird. These clans also have their own allotted parts of the tribal territory.

This territory has special meaning for the Aborigine. He believes that his spirit dwelt in this territory before his life on earth and will continue to live in

Australian National Publicity Assoc.

ABORIGINAL FISHERMEN AND THEIR CATCH

Some of the most primitive Aborigines are to be found on remote parts of the north Australian coast. In this picture we see three fishermen from the Northern Territory aboard their dug-out canoe. The fish that they are hauling out of the water is a huge groper. Gropers often reach a weight of several hundredweight.

it after his death. In this territory he will hunt the game and gather the wild fruits and tubers that are food for himself and his family.

Within the whole tribal territory, certain things and places will be regarded as sacred. There may be "dreaming rocks," for example, which are associated in myth and legend with the Great Beings of the "Eternal Dreamtime" who made all things, and still, in spirit form, frequent these places— or so the Aborigine believes. Stones or cairns often mark these sacred sites. If they are destroyed, or if the proper ceremonies are not observed, disaster will surely follow.

The Aborigines have many myths and legends. In some tribes they tell of Darana, the Ancestral Spirit who made the first humans ; in others, of the Goanna Men or the Rainbow Snake. These and many other legendary figures are the Ancestral Beings who once roamed the tribal territory and exist there to-day as spirits, or as actual landmarks.

Special rites, songs and dances commemorate these Beings. But not all Aboriginal songs and dances are religious; many are quite light-hearted affairs carried out for the sheer joy of it all.

A Corroboree

You like songs and dances? Good! Then let's take a look at a typical corroboree—this is the Aboriginal name for a dance festival for the menfolk of the tribe or clan.

The Aborigines prepare for a corro-

Camera Press.

CARVED BY THE ABORIGINES OF OLD

In some parts of Australia remarkable rock carvings and cave paintings made long ago by the Aborigines may be seen. The carvings seen in this picture had been so worn away by time and weather that they had to be chalked before they could be photographed. The life-size figures probably represent men in ceremonial dress.

boree with great care and enthusiasm, using coloured clays and feathers to decorate their bodies in patterns suited to whatever dance they are to perform, and sometimes wearing strange conical head-dresses made of pandanus palm, or grass and bark. Music for the occasion is provided by a didjeridoo, a large wooden flute made from the hollowed-out limb of a tree; and corroboree sticks, pieces of wood which are tapped together to provide the rhythm. Some tribes also favour the "Bullroarer," a flat piece of polished wood which is whirled vigorously at the end of a cord and makes a deep humming sound.

How the Aborigines prance and stamp!

Camera Press.

HUNTING CROCODILES IN THE NORTHERN TERRITORY

Crocodile hunting is a profitable business and the white hunters who get their livelihood in this way usually employ Aboriginals to help them. This picture shows the Aboriginal assistants of a white hunter hauling a " croc " out of the Finniss River. By the time the season is over, they may have caught no fewer than five hundred of these creatures.

to convince the victim that the cause of his illness really has been removed.

Family Life

Although there have been cases of Aborigines attacking white people, they are by nature kindly and straightforward. They take great care of their children and old folk and have a high regard for family ties and life.

An Aboriginal baby is cared for by everyone in the family. As soon as a baby boy can walk, he is given toy spears to play with and, like small boys the world over, thoroughly enjoys trying to do all the things that grown-ups do. A little girl has small baskets and dishes as playthings, and amuses herself by trying to prepare food in the way that mother prepares it.

The boys are also taught simple songs and dances about the Ancestral Beings, perhaps, or the birds and animals of the bush. They may even learn some of the songs and dances of the grown-ups, although most of these will remain a secret from them until they are much older. Meanwhile, they have all the fun of make-believe, fighting mock battles with their toy spears, hunting small lizards and birds, learning bushcraft, and sometimes joining up with their sisters to play mothers and fathers.

At last the great moment comes when, with secret rites and ceremonies, the boy is admitted to manhood. He is now a full member of his tribe, and in due course

Some corroborees continue all through the night, the dance-ground lit by the moon and bordered by small fires lit to keep the mosquitoes and sand-flies at bay.

The Aborigines are firm believers in magic. " Bone-pointing," for example, may cause illness or death, although the victim may be saved if the invisible spear thrown by the sorcerer is magically withdrawn by another medicine-man. The latter, by a simple piece of conjuring, often produces an actual piece of bone he will marry and raise his own family. If he is a born leader or shows some special skill, our Aborigine may become a headman or perhaps a medicine-man. When he is about fifty years old, he may take his place as an elder of the tribe and take a share in maintaining tribal law and custom. As he grows older, he and his wife will be cared for by their children. His age will not be held against him, for the old are wise and therefore worthy of respect.

Hunting and Fishing

People who do not understand the Aborigines often think that they are extremely lazy. The truth is that the Aborigine, in his natural state, does not see any point in being energetic until food is needed. Then he will take up his boomerang, and his spears and spearthrower, and go off into the bush with his dog to hunt his next meal.

They are wonderful trackers and hunters, and can follow trails through the bush that would not be visible to European eyes. They know their way across the dry lands far better than any white man and can often live in desert regions where he would starve or die of thirst.

Animals of all kinds, from kangaroos to snakes, certain kinds of ants and caterpillars, crocodile and turtle eggs, wild fruits and honey—all these are food to the Aborigine. In the deserts and barren regions they can often find water where others would fail—in native soaks or wells, in hollows in the trees, even in some kinds of frogs which carry their own water supply stored in their bodies. Along the coasts and rivers, they spear and net fish, and harpoon turtles.

The nets of the fishermen are made from grass by the womenfolk, and the hooks are of bone. For boat-building the Aborigines often use strips of bark, which are heated, bent to the required shape and fixed together. Fish are also

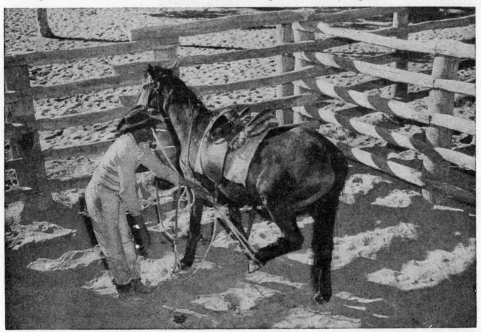

Australian News & Information Bureau.

ABORIGINES OFTEN MAKE GOOD STOCKMEN

The future holds little for Aborigines who are unable to accept the ways of the white man and find a useful place in his communities. But training can often make good stockmen, mechanics and carpenters of the " blackfellows." Here, for example, is a skilled Aboriginal stockman at the Beswick Cattle Station, near Katherine in the Northern Territory. He has just put a saddle on a colt he is breaking in.

caught in stone weirs built across the river, and sometimes with the help of special leaves. These leaves, dropped into the water, give out juices that stupefy the fish and make them an easy catch for the Aborigines.

Aboriginal Food

The Aborigines' ideas of good cooking are very different from ours. Turtle, kangaroo, possum and any other food that needs cooking is put on the fire just as it is. In some tribes, however, flat stones are put on the fire first and covered with wet honeysuckle leaves. The meat, cut in strips and placed on the leaves, is then covered with stones

and more leaves. More strips of meat, and more stones and leaves, are added and finally, the strange sandwich is covered with paper-bark and earth and left to cook for an hour.

Aborigines like honey as much as you and I do. But theirs comes straight from the hive of the wild honey bee, high up in a tree, perhaps. To reach the hive, the Aborigine slings a rope around the tree and secures it so that it forms a loose circle. Standing within the circle, he leans against the rope and climbs up the tree, using footholds that he cuts as he goes up and shifting the rope higher at each step.

If you see Aborigines raking out a hole in the ground, you may well find that they are digging for honey ants. Their "flour" is made from grass seed. Their drink is water, to which honeysuckle leaves or green-tree ants may be added.

When Aborigines travel, their food is carried in dilly bags or baskets made of grasses, or of pandanus fibre, by the womenfolk, and a lighted fire-stick is often borne by one of the travellers. Fire is important—it provides warmth at night, a means of cooking food, and is generally the centre of things in social life.

For lighting a fire all an Aborigine needs is a hard stick, with a point on it, and a piece of softer wood with a hole in it. The point of the hard stick is inserted in the hole and the stick is rotated between the hands until the friction causes a spark.

Camera Press.

A FAMOUS ABORIGINAL ARTIST

This is Albert Namatjira, one of several Aboriginal artists of the Hermansburg school of central Australia who have become famous for their colourful paintings. In this picture he is seen outlining the design of " The Flying Ants," a family totem.

AUSTRALIAN ABORIGINES

Australian News & Information Bureau

When the First Fleet reached Australia the continent was the home of primitive tribes of natives. The Aborigines, or blackfellows as they are often called, then numbered about 300,000. To-day there are only about 50,000 full-blood Aborigines. This Aboriginal stockman is seen decorating a didjeridoo, or large flute, in readiness for a corroboree. A corroboree is a sort of dance festival in which only the men take part. They usually decorate their bodies elaborately for the occasion.

SOME TYPICAL BLACKFELLOWS

This cheerful young girl has a bow in her hair and wears a frock. But many Aborigines, especially in Arnhem Land and other Reserves, wear little or no clothing and live their old tribal life as hunters and nomads.

This happy Aboriginal lad may become a stockman when he grows up. But he may prefer to live with his tribe and follow its old-established rites and customs. Missions now care for many of the Aborigines.

Ready for the corroboree. His body streaked with white clay, this Aborigine plays his didjeridoo, a flute made from the hollowed-out limb of a tree. Its wailing notes can be heard miles away.

Photos: Camera Press

No one is better at bushcraft than the Aborigine. He can read trails through the bush invisible to our eyes. This old man is employed as a police blacktracker in Western Australia.

Aborigines dressed for a male dance festival, or corroboree, stand facing a sacred emblem. Their bodies are decorated with coloured clays and small feathers. The shape and patterns of their conical headdresses, like the designs on their bodies, have definite meanings according to the dance or rite in which they are to take part. Dancing and singing are enjoyed by the Aborigines and form an important part of their day-to-day life.

Photos: Australian News & Information Bureau

These dancers are taking part in a Warrangan Corroboree, which is associated with flying-fox mythology. The dancers are decorated with birds' down. The wooden cross-piece in the headdress of the central figure represents the horns of a buffalo. Rhythm for the dancers is given by the Aborigines in the foreground clapping boomerangs together. The Aborigines have a rich store of myths and legends.

USING A BOOMERANG

Photos: E.N.A.

This young Aborigine is receiving his first lesson in throwing a boomerang, a weapon he will use when he reaches manhood. Skilfully shaped, the boomerang has a back-curving flight.

This hunter poses proudly with the pelican he has slain with his boomerang. Aborigines live mainly on what they can take with their throwing spears and boomerangs and on wild fruits and tubers.

Camera Press

These Aborigines dance to the sounds of the didjeridoo and corroboree sticks. The latter, played by the man in the foreground (left), beat out the rhythm. The boots and trousers of this musician contrast sharply with the bare feet and loincloths of the painted dancers. Another instrument sometimes used is the "Bullroarer," a flat piece of wood that makes a humming sound when it is whirled at the end of a rope.

E.N.A.

THIS IS WHERE WE ARE

The dark little Aboriginal girl watches intently as her fair Australian school friend turns the globe.
Nowadays it is more and more difficult for the Aborigines to live their old tribal life. Their future
as a race depends on their ability to learn the white man's ways, as this little girl is learning them at
a school at La Perouse, New South Wales.

Material that will burn easily is close at hand and, lit by the spark, is soon fanned into a flame. Usually a camp fire is not allowed to go out once it has been lit.

Although Aborigines have few possessions of their own, and although the things they make are primitive by our standards, they take great pride in their craftsmanship and artistry, often carefully decorating even the most ordinary objects. In some parts of the country, their paintings can be seen on the walls of rocks and caves. Some of the finest work of this kind can be seen in the Kimberleys in Western Australia, or at Oenpelli, in Arnhem Land.

The cave paintings at Oenpelli are particularly beautiful, if rather mystifying. There, in the " galleries," can be seen the strange figures of men and beasts, of spirits and Ancestral Beings.

Works of this kind are usually connected with Aboriginal rites and ceremonies ; some have been in existence for so long that even the Aborigines cannot explain their meaning.

In the Great Victoria Desert, long wooden boards play an important part in sacred ceremonies. Painted with ochres and carefully greased, they are kept in special shelters when they are not in use. The designs carved upon them tell of the travels of the Ancestral Beings.

Not all tribes attempt to preserve their sacred emblems. Some are quite content to throw them away when the particular ceremony for which they have been so painstakingly made is over. When the time for the ceremony approaches again, they will lovingly make a new set, working happily with ochres and brushes and carving tools.

Evidence of Aboriginal skill in carving

and decorating such things can be found in many different forms, from the strange dancing masks of the Cape York Peninsula to the carved and coloured grave posts of Bathurst and Melville Islands. Parakeet feathers, stringy-bark, grasses and other materials are used by these primitive artists and craftsmen, who make their emblems and designs for the sheer pleasure that it gives them.

Several Aboriginal artists have taken to using the white man's materials and techniques and have become renowned for their paintings. Albert Namatjira, Edwin Pareoultja and others of the Hermansburg school of central Australia are probably the best known. But they are the exceptions. The true home of the Aboriginal artist and craftsman is the tribe, where the tools and methods of old are still lovingly employed.

The Aborigine To-day

The cave art of the Aborigines is often compared with that of the Stone Age man in prehistoric Europe. Indeed, it is sometimes said that the Aborigines are a Stone Age people who have lingered on, without change, into modern times. Certainly the gulf between them and the white people who have made Australia into one of the great nations of the world is wide. It has been difficult, often impossible, for the Aborigines to re-adjust themselves to the pace and outlook of the present world, despite the help they have received—and are still receiving from missionaries and administrators.

Men skilled in Aboriginal problems now watch over their interests in the various States and the Northern Territory, and strive to find them a place in the general life of the nation. In New South Wales, for example, there is an Aborigines Welfare Board, which includes a trained anthropologist. (An anthropologist is a scientist who studies the development of mankind and its races.) In the Northern Territory, the Director of Native Affairs is also an experienced anthropologist.

It would be wrong to imagine that all Aborigines live the life of old. Many have been trained to become skilled stockmen, mechanics and carpenters. For primitive though these people may be, they are not lacking in intelligence.

An Intelligent People

Some are employed by the police to help in tracking down criminals and others who have offended against the law—work in which they excel. Many tales are told of their skill in following a trail through the bush. On one occasion, a little girl was lost in the bush in New South Wales. After her father and his friends had searched for a whole day in vain, the police went to work with their Aboriginal tracker. For some time, he studied the hard, dry ground around the homestead, then at last made off confidently, reading signs that no one else had noticed. Before long, he had led the searchers to where the little girl, exhausted by her wanderings, lay fast asleep.

What will happen to the Aborigines eventually? Their numbers are growing less and before long even the Reserves set aside for them may have to yield to the march of progress. In Arnhem Land, for example, valuable bauxite deposits are to be worked and other mineral wealth is said to be there awaiting development.

But increasing contact with the white man need not lead to the extinction of the Aborigine now that his problems are understood by governments and scientists. Two leading Australian anthropologists, R. M. and C. H. Berndt, who have long studied the Aborigine, sum up the matter thus : " The Aborigines cannot continue to live in their old way, and indeed few of them are able to do so now. Life is changing for them just as it is, in a different sense, for us; and the white man is the new power in the land. It seems certain that they must, in the coming generation, become more fully absorbed into the main stream of Australian life."

How Britain
And Other Countries
of the World
are Governed

Concerning
Parliaments and People,
Local Government
and Courts of Law

Specially drawn for this work by Dennis Adams.

ALL MEMBERS OF ONE NATION

When we speak of the British Nation it means all the fifty millions or more people who, mainly by birth and a few by adoption, are citizens of the United Kingdom. In the pages which follow is set forth the story of how we are governed, how we make our laws, what rights and privileges belong to us, and how the laws are enforced while justice is given to all.

CITIZENS OF BRITAIN

WHEN St. Paul described himself as a " citizen of no mean city " he used a word which had a proud and honourable meaning even in those days. It still remains the same good word which many people are proud to use to-day. The dictionary gives the meaning of the word citizen as " a burgess, freeman of a city; townsman; a member, native or naturalised, of a State," all having the same idea of being a member of a city, town or village with all the rights and privileges of the country to which one belongs.

" I am an American citizen," says the traveller from the United States, and is proud of it since the possession of his passport gives him the protection of that great country. " I am a British citizen " is a statement which might be made quietly and unboast-ingly, but the one who said it would certainly not speak in tones of apology. If he were proud of nothing else his British citizenship would be one important fact to his credit and advantage.

After the war there were in Europe many unfortunate people who were described as " stateless persons." They were no longer citizens of any country nor could they claim the protection of any State, and one of the problems for the United Nations' statesmen to solve was how these unfortunate people could regain the rights of citizenship in one country or another.

Your Rights and Privileges

Most of you who read this will be British citizens by right of birth. From the moment you were born you were a member of this great nation,

43

and the State, or the nation, assumed at once certain duties towards you. You became entitled to certain rights. Many of these rights are so taken for granted that we don't really think about them. When your parents had decided on your Christian name it was by law duly entered in the Register of Births and a certificate was given to prove, whenever necessary, that you were born on such and such a day in a certain parish in Great Britain. It might be said that with that certificate a good many rights and privileges were conferred upon you.

There are people whose duty it is to see that every child is fed and clothed and protected from dangerous diseases; to ensure that in due course he shall be properly educated and fitted to play his part as a citizen. Here again, these privileges are usually taken for granted, and, in the vast majority of cases, our parents take charge of everything for us so that there is no need for anyone to worry one little bit about Acts of Parliament, the machinery of government, or the various officials and committees whose duty it is to ensure that every youngster in Britain enjoys the rights and privileges that are his heritage.

Progress and Improvements

Now and again, however, a case occurs in which a child is neglected, and very quickly someone steps in to ensure that these rights of the child are restored. In effect the State says: This child is a British citizen and has the right to be properly cared for, educated and protected until old enough to take his place as a wage-earner, capable of looking after himself. That is our duty and the child's right.

Go back two hundred years, or even a

Specially drawn for this work.
IN THE GOOD OLD DAYS
Not by any means the least among the many advantages we enjoy to-day compared with the so-called good old days of the past are the paved and well-kept streets of our towns. Small wonder that disease flourished in the dirt and squalor of city streets such as our artist shows above.

Topical Press

MODERN LIGHTING IN NIGHT'S DARKNESS

Not until 1813 were the first public gas-lamps installed in London, and until 1886 the best street lighting available was that of the flat batswing gas-burner. Only in comparatively recent times have the highways outside the towns been illuminated. Our picture taken near Croydon, Surrey, gives a good example of how modern highways are lighted to-day.

good deal less, and you would find that for most young people life was very different from what it is to-day, not merely in the material things but in the attitude of the State towards children. A hundred years ago children were sent down the mines to work long hours; only a comparatively small number of children went to school and it was no concern of the State or anybody except the parents whether the child learnt to read or not. Even the children whose parents could afford to send them to school had a very much harder time than any child could have to-day.

It may be said that the grown-ups also had a harder time, and that is true. To-day we have well-kept roads and streets with clean pavements and lamps to light us at night; there are public libraries and parks; pure water is obtained by turning a tap at home instead of going out to the nearest well. These, and many other improvements in our modern world, have all come about through our system of government.

In a Civilised State

Police are on guard night and day for the protection of peaceful citizens. There is a Medical Officer of Health in each district to see that certain rules are strictly kept to avoid disease. We are an organised civilised society— and we are governed by ourselves. That is the important fact to bear in mind. These improvements, rights and privileges have not just happened in the way that the sunshine and the rain come to us. The attitude of the State towards children, the schools, the parks, the well-kept roads, and all the thousand and one advantages we have to-day compared with one or two hundred years ago have all been worked for and an organisation built up.

They have come about by the efforts of good citizens through many years. Men and women who thought of the community instead of thinking always and solely of themselves have brought these things about by influencing and building up our system of government. As citizens in Britain to-day we have many rights. What we sometimes overlook as we grow older is that we have certain duties to carry out in return for those rights.

We can avoid some of these duties and take no interest in the privileges of citizenship beyond enjoying them and taking it for granted that somebody else will guard our rights. That is not good citizenship. Our first duty is to understand how we are governed and how our voice, although it may not be very powerful, can affect the government of the country, the county, and the town or village in which we live.

For the Country's Good

How does Parliament work? What does it mean when someone says that a Bill is before Parliament? How does this Bill become an Act of Parliament and the law of the country? Who decides which person shall be Prime Minister? How does a person become a Member of Parliament, or a member of the County Council, or the local Urban Council?

How does the British Parliament compare with the systems of government in other countries? Why are we known as a Democracy? What is the Civil Service and what connection has it with Parliament? When an Act of Parliament has become the law of the country what happens if someone disobeys? What are the Courts of Justice? Are there different kinds of law courts? Who appoints the different judges and by what rules do they make their decisions?

Here we are only dealing with the main facts which we should know if we are to become good citizens. Apart from understanding our system of government and taking an interest in what is being done in our country, county and town, there are many ways in which we can contribute in some way or other to the betterment of the country in which we were born.

There are societies and associations, some national and some local, whose object is the preservation of public rights, such as country paths or open spaces, or of certain woodlands and even mountains or parts of the seashore. Then there are societies for the promotion of city, town and countryside improvements, ratepayers' associations to safeguard the interests of those who live in the district, and other similar bodies.

All these have as their object the general good of the community in which they live. That is the essence of good citizenship. We do not live just for ourselves but as part of a community in a highly complex society. It is because of the good citizens of the past that we enjoy so many rights to-day.

The Voice of Every Citizen

Never in our history has there been a time when the question of Parliament and the government of the country was the concern of every citizen to such an extent as it is to-day. More and more is Parliament, with the County and local councils carrying out its decrees, controlling our everyday life.

That is why one of the first essentials of the good citizen is to have some knowledge of the system under which we are governed, and how the laws, passed by the government elected by the citizens of the country, as well as those laws which have come down to us through long centuries, are enforced when necessary in the Courts of Justice.

OUR PARLIAMENT—AND OTHERS

THE MOTHER OF PARLIAMENTS

Our system of Parliamentary government has been developed through some eight centuries and has been taken as a model by the self-governing Dominions and many other countries. The building of the Houses of Parliament, seen above, was begun in 1840 on the site of the old Palace of Westminster. Considerable damage was done to the building during the Second World War, and the rebuilt House of Commons was opened in October, 1950.

FOR many years, journalists and cartoonists have depicted Prime Ministers or other heads of governments as ship captains standing at the helm of the " Ship of State," particularly in times of political or international storm. That is not a bad comparison in starting to describe how we are governed.

In many ways a nation is like a great ship, a self-contained community relying on its own qualities and abilities in the face of the world's storms. Governments, in their various forms all over the world, may well be compared to the machinery of a ship, with parliamentary government driving the " Ship of State " along, and local government like marine auxiliary machinery providing the every-day services of our lives, such as local transport, education, cleaning services and the like.

Serving the People

To-day, the more advanced nations have governments of democracy, in which the State exists to serve its people, and practically every adult citizen has a voice in freely choosing his or her parliamentary representative and local councillor. By contrast, there are certain nations, usually those which have been cut off for generations from the main stream of world thought, which live under that more primitive form of government called dictatorship, where a single man or group of men wields absolute power and all citizens are treated as mere servants of the State.

The British system of national and local government, evolved out of more than 800 years of practically bloodless struggle and peaceful development, is generally recognised as the prime example of democratic government. That is why the Parliament in London is constantly described as " Mother of Parliaments." So many governing assemblies throughout the world are modelled on it.

Chief among these are the parliaments of the British Commonwealth whose now independent nations have closely modelled their parliaments, in both form and spirit, on the " Mother " Parliament.

The " Mother of Parliaments " at Westminster traces her descent from the Witenagemot, or Council of Wise Men, which advised the kings of the Anglo-Saxon era before the Norman Conquest of England in 1066; but real parliamentary history did not begin until the Thirteenth Century.

Down the centuries the power of government has steadily shifted from the peers to the commoners. So to-day we have the House of Commons dominant, while the House of Lords serves rather as a council of elders and experts to add its wisdom to parliamentary legislation which passes through its hands.

Nowadays the House of Lords has no final power to block any legislation sent to it by the Commons. The character of the Lords itself is changing, moreover. The Life Peerages Act of 1958 provides for the creation of " life peers " whose rank and membership of the House of Lords do not depend upon heritage and cannot be passed on, as son succeeds father in the ordinary peerage. Suitable men and women can be " promoted " to the Lords under this act, but life peerages so granted expire on the death of the holders. In this way their past services to the country can be recognised and advantage still taken of their experience and knowledge, which will show itself in debates in the Lords.

So the line of legislation runs from The Commons, through The Lords, to The Crown. The Acts of Parliament under which we are governed and taxed, must finally receive the approval of the Sovereign—or The Crown, as the term is used in this case. Theoretically, the Sovereign has the right to veto (refuse to approve) such Acts; but in practice, this right has long fallen into abeyance.

The Two-Party System

Another characteristic feature of the British parliamentary machine is the two-party system, which has also been largely adopted by the Parliaments of the British Commonwealth. It is in striking contrast to such other democratic parliaments as the French National Assembly, where eight or nine parties and additional splinter groups are ranged around the debating chamber.

Although there are actually three political parties represented in the British House of Commons—the Conservative, Labour and Liberal Parties—it is still known as a two-party system, because two major parties hold the large majority of the seats between them.

This century began with the political battle of the Liberals against the Conservatives, but gradually the Labour Party came into parliamentary existence and over the past twenty years or so has ousted the Liberals as the main opponents of the Conservatives.

To use another simile, the British system under which we are governed is like a great pyramid. At the top is the Prime Minister, who, with the assistance of his Ministers, shapes the course for the nation in many fields, including health, education, defence, insurance, trade and finance. Laws to fulfil these policies are then drafted by experts and presented to the House of Commons. There they must duly be passed by the predominant vote of the party in power, perhaps with the acquiescence of the opposing party or in face of their fierce criticism and objection, which can be expressed in terms of votes cast at what is called the " division " of the House.

Even though the Prime Minister has a sufficient number of party supporters in the House to assure him of a comfortable majority vote for all his legislation, he must also be constantly alert to public opinion as well as the national good. For he must put his government to the test of a general election at least every five years, permitting the people as a whole to express their approval or disapproval of the government through their votes.

Two prime functions of the House of Commons are to serve as watchdog of public expenditure, and to be the protector of the citizen. In the second category, the House of Commons is the zealous guardian of one of our most cherished rights, the right of free speech.

This right is most flamboyantly displayed at what is called " Speakers' Corner," just inside the railings at the Marble Arch end of London's widespread Hyde Park. Here, practically every afternoon and evening of the year, are to be heard the speakers standing on boxes and portable platforms to preach their pet theme, even denouncing in the fiercest terms the unwritten British Constitution, the political parties, the government of the day or any other pet hate they may have.

In guarding the interests of the individual, any Member of Parliament may bring before the House any case in which he or she considers that an injustice has been done to a citizen by officialdom, and demand a satisfactory explanation and redress of a grievance from the Government Minister responsible for the sphere of administration in which the injustice has occurred.

This watchdog function is not confined to the United Kingdom, but extends to all Colonial Territories, though definitely not to those lands which have achieved their final independence and become members of the Commonwealth.

For instance, although the East African Colony of Kenya has a substantial measure of internal self-government, members of the " Mother of Parliaments " may, and do, bring before the House some offence they believe has been committed against the rights of some humble African tribal folk or individual. The Secretary of State for the Colonies must then call for a report on the matter from the Governor of

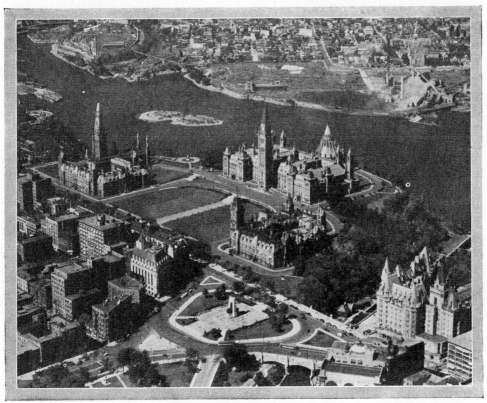

Royal Canadian Air Force.

IN THE CAPITAL OF CANADA

Canada is a self-governing Dominion of the British Commonwealth. A Governor-General, appointed by the Sovereign, acts as the representative of the British Sovereign. Parliament consists of a Senate and a House of Commons, but each of the provinces also has its own parliament and administration. The Speaker's Chair is indeed a replica of the one used at Westminster. Our photograph shows the Parliament Building at Ottawa.

E.N.A.

THE MEETING PLACE OF DENMARK'S PARLIAMENT

This aerial view shows the old Christiansborg Palace at Copenhagen, the Danish capital, which houses Parliament, the Courts of Justice and the Foreign Office. Like New Zealand, Denmark has a Sovereign as Head of State. Parliament comprises a single chamber, the *Folketing* (Diet) of some 179 members, who are elected for a period of four years. Every Dane, male and female, above the age of twenty-three has the right to vote at election time. The Cabinet is known as the *Statsraadet* (State Council).

Kenya, and at least explain the true position in the House of Commons.

The House of Commons constantly gives evidence of its sense of ultimate responsibility for the well-being of the people of all Colonial Territories until the day those people have been trained to the point where they can assume their independence—a basic tenet of British colonial policy. It is the House of Commons, too, which must pass the final Act to grant such independence to a colony or group of colonies.

The people of the United Kingdom as a whole contribute to the welfare of colonial peoples through taxation, the main channel of this aid being called the Colonial Development and Welfare Fund.

Yet the House of Commons—or Parliament as a whole—is far from being the only body which regulates our lives.

From this upper tier of government, authority to organise many aspects of our daily life passes down through county, borough, urban and rural district councils, the so-called local authorities. These are really miniature local parliaments, and operate in similar form, though they are largely subject in their various spheres of responsibility to the policy of the central authority, the Government of the day.

Moving to Independence

British colonies which have already moved—or are moving—into the final stage of complete independence all show the influence of both Westminster and the British local government systems.

First of these is the Gold Coast, or Ghana, to use the new name of this country. When the Gold Coast Commission, under a distinguished African judge of the Colony, Mr. Justice Coussey, was planning the shape of an independent constitution, it did not confine its studies to the British system. Among other systems seriously studied, with the idea of application to the Gold Coast, were the United States' and French forms of government. The Commission, however, finally decided that the "Mother of Parliaments" and the local government system in the United Kingdom should become the model for this newly independent West African territory.

Next of the new independents is the Federation of the British West Indies, a grouping of British island colonies in the Caribbean area—Barbados, Jamaica with the Turks and Caicos Islands and the Cayman Islands, Trinidad and Tobago, Leeward Islands and Windward Islands. Jamaica and Trinidad are the major units in this Federation with long traditions of British rule and an advanced degree of self-government.

Malaya displays another form of federal association within the British framework, being, in the main, a grouping of Malayan States, each with its individual princely ruler. Its federal legislature is at Kuala Lumpur.

Yet another form, but still on the purely British pattern, is shown by Malta. This is known as a diarchy, meaning government by two independent authorities.

Malta holds a unique position in the British family of nations. This key island in the Central Mediterranean has

E.N.A.

THE HALL OF THE KNIGHTS

The seat of government of the Netherlands (or Holland) is the city known as The Hague, which has through many years been an important meeting-place for statesmen of all nations. Our photograph shows the Hall of the Knights in the Binnenhof where both houses of the Netherlands Parliament meet.

a remarkable history. In ancient times it was held by the Phoenicians, Greeks, Carthaginians and Romans, in turn, and finally conquered by the Arabs. From 1090 to 1530 it was joined to Sicily under Neapolitan kings, but then was handed over to the Knights of St. John, whose rule was ended by Napoleon in 1798.

But the Maltese defied and fought Napoleon for their liberty, and then, of their own free will and choice, were annexed to the British Crown under the Treaty of Paris in 1814.

Malta has a most advanced form of self-government with a Legislative Assembly of forty members, elected by all adult citizens under a proportional representation voting system. The Prime Minister and his Ministers, who number a maximum of seven, form the Executive Council. Under the diarchy system, legislative and administrative powers concerning defence and external relations are reserved to the Governor appointed by the Crown, advised by the Nominated Council composed of the Lieutenant Governor, the Legal Secretary and one officer each from the three fighting services.

A Picturesque Kingdom

Probably the most picturesque member of this worldwide family of nations is Tonga—with the very suitable alternative name of the Friendly Islands.

This independent Polynesian kingdom became a protectorate of Great Britain in 1900. Her Majesty Queen Salote Tupou has ruled over this realm of 150 islands and islets since the death of her father in 1918, being a Queen in her own right who lives in the shade of the great tree which is the British Crown.

The government consists of a Privy Council, Cabinet, Legislative Assembly and Judiciary. The Assembly, which meets annually, is composed of seven nobles elected by their peers, seven elected representatives of the people, and

High Commissioner for New Zealand.

CORONATION DAY IN WELLINGTON, THE CAPITAL OF NEW ZEALAND

This was the scene outside Parliament House, Wellington, during the official Coronation ceremony on June 2nd, 1953—the day on which Queen Elizabeth II was crowned in Westminster Abbey in distant London. Like the United Kingdom, New Zealand is a constitutional monarchy, the Queen's representative in the Dominion being the Governor-General.

AN IMPRESSIVE CEREMONY AT CANBERRA, THE AUSTRALIAN FEDERAL CAPITAL

Australia is a federation of States, each of which has its own government. The Federal capital is Canberra and it is here that the members of the Federal House of Representatives and the Senate meet. Our picture shows the outside of the Federal Parliament House at Canberra, with guards of honour drawn up for the opening of the Commonwealth Parliament by the Governor-General.

seven Ministers of the Crown. The system is not closely modelled on the British system, but is democratic and well suited to a happy people.

Federal Systems

One major difference between the United Kingdom machinery and that in such independent, but loyal members of the British Commonwealth as Australia and Canada, is the federal system, under which these vast territories are divided into States or Provinces. These States and Provinces are also jealous of their rights, to be preserved from encroachment by the central or federal Government.

In the case of Australia, this was due to the fact that the six States—New South Wales, Victoria, Queensland, South Australia, Western Australia and Tasmania—began life as separate colonies. When they came together to form the Commonwealth of Australia on January 1st, 1901, they ceded some of their authority to the new Federal Government, but carefully guarded their individual rights in such fields as railways and education.

The result is that Australia has seven parliaments, one in each State, and a central parliament in Canberra, to serve a population of about ten million citizens.

Across the Atlantic

The same federal system applies to that other great democracy on the opposite side of the Atlantic from Great Britain. The United States also grew out of a handful of colonies which combined to throw off the control of a king and parliament in London in 1776. By the Declaration of Independence drawn up in Philadelphia, thirteen States formed the first American Union, which has developed into the fifty States of to-day.

In an effort to avoid what they regarded

as certain tyrannical aspects of the British form of government of those days, the original Americans drafted a constitution with counter-balances which would avert any danger of tyranny or dictatorship, a truly democratic constitution. Even in writing this, they departed from the British example, since Great Britain has never had, to this day, a written constitution.

The United States Constitution

Under the United States Constitution, the Government of the nation is entrusted to three separate authorities:—(1) the Executive power which is vested in the President; (2) the Legislative which lies in the two Houses of Congress; and (3) the Judicial authority of the Supreme Court of the United States. The President is elected every fourth year, on the Tuesday after the first Monday in November, with a Vice-President who will step into the supreme office should the President die.

Under the President, the administrative business of the nation is conducted by ten heads of departments who form the " Cabinet," but this term is used in a very different sense from its usual meaning in Britain. The members of the President's Cabinet are not Ministers responsible to a parliament. They are chosen by the President, but must be confirmed in their posts by the Senate, and generally they are experts who do not sit in Congress. Each presides over a separate department of State, such as Army, Navy, State Department (Foreign Affairs) and Labour.

While the President holds the power to shape the policy of the nation, the whole power to pass legislation putting main aspects of this policy into operation is vested in a Congress consisting of a Senate and a House of Representatives.

The Senate consists of two members from each one of the fifty States, chosen by popular vote for a term of six years. The House of Representatives is chosen under a rather more complicated electoral system, members being selected every second year by the vote of citizens, who are qualified under the varying rules of individual States to vote for members of the State legislature.

As the Constitution forbids disqualification from voting rights on the grounds of race, colour or sex, the electorate theoretically consists of all citizens over twenty-one years of age.

Varying State regulations for registration on the lists of voters, however, do exclude quite a few citizens.

The National Government, consisting of the executive President and legislative Congress, has authority over general taxation, treaties and other dealings with foreign powers, the Army, Navy and Air Force, foreign and inter-state commerce, postal services, coinage, weights and measures and the trial and punishment of crime against the United States.

The third arm of government is protective. The Supreme Court of the United States, consisting of the Chief Justice and eight Associates appointed by the President, with the advice and consent of the Senate, are the " nine wise men " who make the final decision on questions arising out of the Constitution, including the rights and protection of the individual citizen.

The Supreme Court stands at the peak of a complex interlocking of State and Federal Courts with the judges of many courts selected and appointed on various systems, according to State.

The major difference between the American and United Kingdom judiciaries is that there can be strong political influence within the American system, while the British judiciary is completely independent of the Executive as represented by the Government, chosen from men of the highest integrity and experience in the legal profession without political considerations and free of all outside influences.

Many complexities are added to the American political scene by the fact that each one of the fifty States has its own republican form of constitution,

Camera Press.

IN THE SOVIET UNION

The governmental system in the Soviet Union is very different from that of the Western democracies. There is only one party, the Communist Party, and the making of laws by decree and executive authority is vested in the Council of Ministers, which is closely related to the leadership of the Party. Our picture was taken during the opening of the Twenty-first Congress of the Communist Party of the Soviet Union and shows Mr. Khrushchev making his long opening speech.

deriving authority from the people of the State, and not from the United States Congress. Each State has a legislature of two Houses, a Governor and other executive officials along a similar pattern to the President and his Cabinet, and its own judicial system.

Republicans and Democrats

Like the United Kingdom, the United States has the two-party system in Congress, perhaps even more deeply entrenched. There are the Republicans, very roughly approximating to the Conservative Party in Britain, and the Democrats, forming an approximation to the British Liberal Party—with the late President Franklin Delano Roosevelt as their classic exponent of policy.

One of the weaknesses of the American system in British eyes is that the Chief Executive, the President, and his Cabinet members have no direct place in Congressional machinery.

So, from time to time, you have a President belonging to one party and propounding policy from its point of view, and a Congress controlled by the other party, which is liable to reject much of the President's policy. This tends to paralyse progressive government.

Yet, even in Congress itself there are no truly binding party lines, and members of one party often line up with the other party against their own President's policy, if they consider that the "folks back home" would like it that way.

Responsible to Parliament

This would be a practical impossibility in Britain, where the Prime Minister, as Chief Executive, and his colleagues are in Parliament and directly responsible to it. If a British Prime Minister's followers switched from one side of the House to the other on casual issues, as they do in the U.S. Congress, the Prime Minister would soon be overthrown and a general election would probably be necessary.

On the other side of the international political fence is that vast nation, or collection of nations, called the Union of Socialist Soviet Republics, which extends from the Pacific Ocean to the Baltic, and from Archangel or Murmansk in the Arctic north, to Odessa on the Black Sea and the Persian border in the south.

This vast land mass, unified as the U.S.S.R., incorporates fifteen nominally autonomous republics covering many different races and languages. In practice they are strictly subordinated to the present leaders of "All-the-Russias," who sit in the Kremlin in Moscow.

The Russian Revolution

It is ironical that the Tsar Nicholas II was submitting to the first waves of real liberalism just at the time he was overthrown and killed in the 1917 Revolution. This was really a double revolution. The first began on March 12th, 1917, when moderates, first under Prince George Lvoff and later under Alexander Kerensky, formed governments.

The second revolution, which gave birth to the Russia of to-day, came on November 7th, 1917, when the Revolutionary Committee of the Petrograd (now Leningrad) Soviet seized power and handed it over next day to the All-Russian Congress of Soviet. Russians know this as the October Revolution, although for us it happened in November, because the Russians used an Eastern calendar which lagged behind the Gregorian Calendar of the West.

Vladimir Ilyich Ulianov, better known to the world as V. I. Lenin (his revolutionary pseudonym) soon became the leader of this movement, and worked to apply the Communist principles of the famous political philosopher of the late nineteenth century, Karl Marx.

Russia, ravaged and nearly ruined by the first few years of World War I, now had to fight a civil war against Tsarist loyalists, who were later actively supported by Britain and several European nations. The last traces of Tsarism,

however, were wiped off the Russian map when one of the then little-known Soviet leaders, Josef Vissarionovich Djugashvili, of Georgia, who chose the pseudonym Stalin (Man of Steel), entered Sebastopol on November 15th, 1920.

For two more years Lenin shaped the destiny of the new Communist or Marxist nation, but then was stricken by a paralysing illness which finally killed him in January, 1924.

Stalin, who had achieved the key position of power as First Secretary of the Communist Party, now set about achieving his dictatorship, first by ousting his most serious rival, Trotsky, and driving him into exile. After ruthlessly disposing of his other opponents, Stalin became virtual dictator of the Soviet Union by his fiftieth birthday on December 21st, 1929, and retained this power until his death in 1953.

He was succeeded by a triumvirate of his closest colleagues, which has since changed several times and shown signs of becoming a slightly more liberal "collective leadership."

The Soviet System

Theoretically, the Soviet Union is a "socialist" state of workers and peasants, with the Soviets or councils of "workers by hand and brain" as its political units in which all central and political authority is vested.

Again, theoretically, the highest organ of the state power of the U.S.S.R. is the Supreme Soviet, consisting of two chambers supposedly with all legislative rights. These are (1) the Council of the Union elected on the basis of one deputy for every 300,000 of the population and numbering around 700 members; and (2) the Council of Nationalities elected by republics or regions, and numbering over 600.

As the millions of Russian citizens are offered no choice of candidates at the polls, there is little true democracy about a Russian election, and the two Chambers of Parliament so elected are called together only at rare intervals.

Legislation by decree and executive authority is vested in the supreme executive organ, the Council of Ministers which was formerly known as the Council of People's Commissars, but this closely interlocks with the supreme hierarchy of the Communist Party.

Each of the individual republics making up the Union has its own provincial organisation modelled on the Federal one.

Although the leaders of the Soviet Union insist that they are the heads of a real democracy, this word has a meaning in their vocabulary entirely different from the way it is understood in the Western world.

European Parliaments

Modern Switzerland, consisting of twenty-two Cantons which are fiercely proud of their provincially autonomous status, was born at the Congress of Vienna in 1815, when Austria, Great Britain, Portugal, Prussia and Russia guaranteed the perpetual neutrality and inviolability of the little mountain nation.

In 1848, a new constitution, prepared without foreign influence, was brought into force, and this was superseded by the present constitution in 1874.

Under this constitution, the individual has even more influence on his form of government, since 50,000 citizens can act together to have any matter of principle put to a referendum by direct popular vote. Cantons also hold their own referendums to decide such questions as female suffrage.

The Federal Government, consisting of Parliament and an Executive Federal Council, has full authority in matters of peace, war and treaties. It controls the Army, in which all male Swiss do service, the railways, posts and telegraphs, the monetary system and weights and measures of the Republic.

Supreme legislative authority is vested in a Parliament of two Chambers, a *Standerat* (Council of States) and a *Nationalrat* (National Council).

Away in the North of Europe are three States also setting examples of democracy as Constitutional Monarchies,

Camera Press.

EVERYONE APPROVES

Delegates at the Twenty-first Congress of the Communist Party of the Soviet Union unanimously accept Mr. Khrushchev's report. The hall in which they are sitting is in the Kremlin, Moscow. China and the countries of Eastern Europe have largely adopted the Soviet system. Their interpretation of the word " democracy " is entirely different from ours.

on similar lines to our own. These States are Sweden, Norway and Denmark.

We can take the Swedish Parliament, or Diet as it is called, as typical. This consists of two chambers elected by universal suffrage. Executive power is in the hands of the King, who must act on the advice of the Council of State headed by the Prime Minister. All the members of the Council of State are responsible for the acts of the Government. It is a form of government in many ways similar to that of Britain.

In reading about the parliaments of the world in the newspapers, it is sometimes confusing to see these legislative chambers given their correct name in their own language. For instance, in the Federal Republic of Western Germany the Lower and Upper Houses are the *Bundestag* and the *Bundesrat*, in Poland the parliament is still called the *Sejm*, as it was before the Communists came to power. Norway has its *Storting*, Iceland its *Althing*, and Israel its *Knesset*. In Japan the parliament is known as the Diet.

The Chinese System

And while we are in the Far East, we could conclude with a look at the form of government in the most populous single country of the world—the People's Republic of China, which has a Chinese adaptation of the system of Soviet Russian Communism.

Here again we have a theoretical democracy, with real control in the hands of a small group of leading Communists. The most notable of these is Mao Tse-tung, the Chairman of the Central Committee of the Chinese Communist Party since 1936, and Chairman of the People's Republic of China from its establishment in 1949 until he relinquished the latter office in 1958. He remains, however, the virtual leader of the Chinese people.

Mao Tse-tung and his associates lived a precarious existence for years before the war as controllers of a small Com-munised section of North-West China, and were constantly engaged in a form of guerilla warfare with the Nationalist forces of Marshal Chiang Kai-shek.

After the Japanese had been beaten in the Pacific war, the Communists began to work for control of the whole of China, and in 1949 they swept away Chiang's Government, which fled to the large island of Formosa and set itself up there with the claim to be the legitimate government of all China.

But the Communist Government in Peking is firmly in the saddle of China proper, though it is still being shaped and reshaped towards a form of government which will suit the Chinese people. It does enjoy the distinction of being the first Government to exercise real control over this vast land, and has even forcefully extended its authority to the remote mountain country of Tibet.

A "People's Republic"

Again, in what are called the " General Principles " of the Constitution of this State, we have the declaration of theoretical democracy.

It is solemnly declared that the People's Republic of China is a people's democratic state led by the working class and based on an alliance of the workers and the peasants, with all power belonging to the people, as represented by the National People's Congress and the local congresses. The National People's Congress is stated to be the highest organ of state authority and sole law-making body.

In practice, the real power is wielded by Mao Tse-tung, with Liu Shao-Chi as Chairman of the Central People's Government Council and Marshal Chu Teh as Vice-Chairman, and a State Council headed by the able Chou En-lia as Premier.

These men are reshaping a land of more than 600 million people who have been known down the centuries for their individualism. It is one of the most interesting experiments in government going on in the world to-day.

ELECTING YOUR M.P.

Central Press.

WHEN CITIZENS GO TO THE POLL

Our system of voting for Members of Parliament and of local government councils is by secret ballot, and the place where electors record their votes is the polling booth. Here we have the scene in the polling booth on Election Day. The policeman, who is usually on or about the premises, has just looked in, but his role is mainly that of guide to electors.

OUR present Parliament evolved gradually over eight centuries from a meeting of the barons, church leaders and the knights of the shire. In 1215 the powerful barons forced King John to grant certain rights and compelled him to sign a document, the Great Charter, otherwise Magna Charter, at Runnymede. The charter was not intended to benefit the common people so much as the barons themselves, but it laid down broad principles such as the right of every man to justice, which apply to-day. It also asserted that the king could not levy taxes without the consent of Parliament.

Parliament versus King

The next landmark was another quarrel between king and subjects on this question of taxation without Parliament's consent when Charles I levied a tax (Ship Money). This resulted in the Civil War which began in 1642 between King and Parliament. The King lost the fight and was beheaded. The Civil War led to the nearest approach to a dictatorship without any Parliament at all that England has ever had. Oliver Cromwell became Lord Protector, but later dismissed Parliament. This lasted only a few years and the Monarchy was restored in 1660 and Parliament was recalled.

About thirty years later Parliament was again in opposition to the King, James II, who had succeeded Charles II. The Bill of Rights declared William and Mary to be King and Queen, asserted the Protestant Faith of the country (James was a Catholic) and ordered that in future the king must act on Parliament's wishes as made known to him through his Ministers.

At that time, however, Parliament represented only a very small class of people, but in 1832 the Reform Bill brought a change. The " rotten " boroughs were abolished and the number of voters was increased to about 100,000. Since then, the right to vote has been extended several times and in 1918 the Representation of the People Act gave the vote to women for the first time. Further extensions since then have given every man and woman of twenty-one years or over the right to vote.

The Representation of the People Act, 1948, abolished Plural Voting which was a privilege enjoyed by certain electors who had two votes. A business man residing in a different constituency from the one in which his business was situated could vote in each. Graduates of the various Universities also elected twelve Members of Parliament besides having a vote in their own constituencies.

Candidates for the Commons

Any person over twenty-one may become a candidate for Parliament provided he is not a member of the House of Lords, a clergyman of the Church of England, a criminal or a lunatic, an undischarged bankrupt or an alien. He (or she) must be nominated by voters in the constituency and deposit £150. If he fails to secure one-eighth of the votes cast he forfeits the £150. This rule is aimed to prevent frivolous candidatures.

Normally, a Parliament lasts for five years, though it need not remain so long if the Government feels that it cannot go on without making sure that the country generally favours its policy. Then Parliament is dissolved and a General Election takes place.

On Nomination Day

The register of voters is brought up to date every year so that within the year after your twenty-first birthday your name should be on the register with your electoral number. A day is fixed for the election, each party has chosen its candidates and on a stated date, about three weeks before polling day, accompanied by their leading supporters, who are electors in the district, or constituency as it is always called, the candidates go to the Town Hall or Council offices to hand in the nomination papers to the Returning Officer who is usually the Town Clerk or other important local official. If there is only one candidate he is returned unopposed and there is no election. There may be two or three or even more candidates. Usually a candidate belongs to a particular party, Conservative, Labour, Liberal, or other party. There are sometimes Independent candidates, but if they are to stand a chance of winning the seat they need strong local support.

Following nomination the work of electioneering begins. Each candidate puts his case to the electors by public meetings and a printed address, setting forth his policy and principles. His supporters canvass from door to door and at factories and business houses.

There are smaller parties such as Co-operative (allied to Labour), Independent Labour (I.L.P.), Communist, Scottish Nationalist and Welsh Nationalist and there have been such parties as Commonwealth. Broadly speaking, Britain prefers the two-party system as it makes for clear decisions.

When Election Day Comes

On Election Day the voters go to the polling stations (usually a school or hall vacated for the day) where a poll clerk asks the name and address and voting number. The notice which has been delivered earlier will have told the voter at which station he must vote and what his number on the register is. The clerk checks these items and hands the elector a ballot or voting paper which bears the names of the candidates in alphabetical order. The voter then goes to one of the polling booths where he places a " X " in the blank space opposite the name of the candidate for whom he wishes to vote.

No other mark must be made on the paper or it will be spoiled. The voter folds the paper and drops it through a slot in a steel box. Thus he has recorded his vote, a right for which men have struggled for centuries.

If the new voter is a girl of twenty-one or twenty-two she, too, may reflect on the thought that for this privilege many women fought fiercely, went to prison, and some even died in the early years of this present century to gain the right for her. One of the most famous of these women, who were known as Suffragettes because they were fighting for the Suffrage (the vote), was Mrs. Pankhurst. Under her leadership, the militant or fighting section of the Suffragette movement carried on a campaign against members of the Government as well as against certain M.P.'s. Women were arrested and went on hunger-strike in prison and took other drastic measures to call attention to their cause.

When the war of 1914–18 came the Suffragettes ceased their campaign and threw all their energies into the war effort. This, and the changed attitude towards votes for women throughout the country when peace came in 1918, induced the Government to introduce the Representation of the People Bill which gave the vote to women for the first time in our history. In the general election in December 1918, women as well as men, were able to vote for a Parliamentary candidate. There were even 16 women candidates. Only one was elected, Countess Markievicz, for a Dublin division, but she refused to take her seat. In November 1919, Lady

COUNTING THE VOTES *Centra Press.*

After the excitement of Election Day, when the polling stations have closed down and the last voting paper has been dropped in the box, the big task of counting the votes begins. Our picture shows a scene in Caxton Hall, Westminster, shortly after the counting of the votes had begun after an election in Parliament's own division.

Astor was elected for Plymouth and became the first woman to sit in the House of Commons as an M.P.

While the elector is casting his vote, millions of others throughout the country are doing the same thing on Election Day. When the polling station has been closed, the steel boxes are sealed and taken to a central point, usually the town hall, where the counting may begin at once in the case of a big town, but it may be postponed until the following day in the case of a scattered constituency.

The counting is scrupulously watched

and the candidates have their representatives present. If there is any doubt as to the number of votes given for any candidate he, or his agent, can ask for the votes to be counted all over again and if the Returning Officer, who is the official responsible for organizing the counting of the votes, agrees, there is another count. There have been times when, to dispel all doubts, there have been several recounts in a constituency. It takes a lot of time, but justice must be fully done ; the person who is returned to Parliament must be the one the majority of voters want as their representative in the House of Commons.

Declaration of the Poll

After the votes have been counted the Returning Officer reads out the figures and declares that the candidate with the largest number of votes has been duly elected a Member of Parliament. Votes of thanks are passed to the officials and then the Returning Officer followed by the new M.P., and after him, the defeated candidate, go into the open to announce the result to the waiting crowd.

There are speeches by the successful and the unsuccessful candidates. The supporters of the winning candidate are, naturally, very jubilant, whereas the supporters of the losing candidate may be very disappointed, and there are, sometimes, hectic scenes at the declaration of the poll because of the high feelings which have been roused in the members of the various parties.

Results from all parts of the country are quickly telephoned by reporters to the Press Association which, in turn, sends them to the newspapers and the B.B.C. The results are broadcast by the B.B.C. for most of the night and, at intervals, it gives what is called " the state of the parties," showing how many seats have been won. Listening to these announcements can be a very exciting experience, because the state of the parties seems to change from hour to hour in the course of the night as the results come in, and there is doubt as to which party is eventually to form the Government.

In some general elections the final result is fairly clear from the early stages of the announcements when it is found that what were believed to be " safe " seats have fallen to the opposing party. Where there is a considerable change in this way from one party to the other and a new Government is elected with a very big majority, people refer to it as a " Landslide election," but that has not happened very often in our history.

What it Costs

The newly-elected M.P. is given a certificate by the Returning Officer to show that he has been declared elected. Later his agent prepares a full statement of all the money spent on the election. There are certain rules which must be observed: no bribery or corrupt practice of any kind is permitted, and each candidate's expenses for the election must not exceed £450 plus 6½d. per head in boroughs, or £450 plus 2d. for each voter in straggling areas. Roughly, this means a limit of between £1,000 and £1,500 which any candidate can spend on posters, circulars, postages, hire of halls, office expenses and all other expenditure on the election.

If the candidate (or his agent) has spent more than the permitted amount, he may be unseated on a petition by his opponent. This means a by-election in that constituency.

Strictly speaking, an M.P. cannot resign, but under certain conditions he may be compelled to retire quite honourably. He cannot, for instance, hold an office of profit under the Crown and remain an M.P. Therefore, when a member wishes to resign for health or other personal reasons he applies for the post of Steward of the Chiltern Hundreds. There are no duties attached to this position, but it carries a nominal salary of 20s. a year. Having accepted this post, the M.P. automatically retires —and soon gives up his position as a

Steward of the Chiltern Hundreds, leaving it vacant for the next applicant.

The Stewardship of the manor of Northstead in Yorkshire has been granted in the same way since 1841, but is not often used. Indeed, the whole question is under review and it may be that an M.P. will be able to resign in a simple, straightforward way without applying for any stewardship, though this has been the custom for over two centuries.

Other Voting Systems

The system of voting in the university elections was a form of what is known as the Alternative Vote. A good many people have argued, written, and urged for years past that our present system of voting is unfair and does not result in a House of Commons which is truly representative of the country. Those who take this point of view desire to have Proportional Representation, or, failing that, the Alternative Vote.

Under our present system the majority of constituencies return one member of Parliament. There are a few which return two members but they make no difference to the argument. Supposing, as frequently happens, three or even four candidates stand for election. When the votes are counted the result may be something like this:

Green	. . .	25,000
Brown	. . .	20,000
White	. . .	15,000

Mr. Green is elected. Actually, 35,000 people have voted against him and 25,000 people have voted for him. He does not really represent the majority of the people. In a great number of constituencies throughout the country Mr. Green's party may be as lucky as he has been with the result

Sport & General.

WHEN THE QUEEN DRIVES TO PARLIAMENT

When a new Government takes office and at the beginning of each new Session, as the Parliamentary year is called, the Sovereign drives in state to Westminster. From the Throne in the House of Lords the Queen reads what is known as "the Queen's Speech," which outlines the Government plans for the months ahead. Our photograph shows the State procession as it drove through Parliament Square when Queen Elizabeth II opened the first new session of her reign. The Queen and the Duke of Edinburgh rode in the Irish State Coach, drawn by four Windsor greys, seen above.

that the Green party becomes the winning side and can claim that the country has returned them to power. Yet in actual fact it may be that more people have voted against them than have voted for them.

By Proportional Representation

Where there are three or more parties that is bound to happen at times. The "P.R." or Proportional Representation system would do away with single-member constituencies and would have a small number of much larger constituencies. These would return, say, six members each. The voter would put "1," "2," "3" and so on against the six selected names on a list of possibly fifteen or twenty candidates.

The counting of the votes would be much more complicated than it is at present and would involve transferring votes from a candidate, who had more than sufficient to elect him, to a member of his party who had not sufficient. The system is too complicated to be described briefly, and that is the chief argument against "P.R."

The Alternative Vote would have the same constituencies as at present, but where there were more than two candidates the voter would put "1," "2," "3" against the candidates' names instead of the single "X" he puts now. Then, supposing the man who received most votes had not a clear majority over his other opponents combined, the "second preferences" would be counted and allocated. This might result in the man who stood second on the first count coming out on top and being elected.

Those are the two systems, in brief and not in full detail, one of which it is urged should replace our present very simple if sometimes a little unfair method of electing M.P.s. Our present system really demands two parties only and gives little chance for minorities to have any representation at all. No one would claim that our present system is

absolutely fair, but it is simple and straightforward, and, generally speaking, ensures stability of government.

Forming a Government

When the results of practically all the elections are known, the country knows that, let us say, the Green party have more members of the new House of Commons than any of the other parties, and usually more than all the other parties combined. They have a working majority. Soon after the results are known, the Queen will send for the leader of the successful party and ask him to form a Government. The leader himself becomes the Prime Minister, and his task now is to appoint the Ministers to serve under him.

The chief Ministers are the Lord President of the Council and Leader of the House of Commons, the Chancellor of the Exchequer, the Foreign Secretary, the Lord High Chancellor, the Lord Privy Seal, Chancellor of the Duchy of Lancaster, the Secretaries of State for the Home Department, for Commonwealth Relations, the Colonies, and for Scotland; the Ministers of Defence, Labour and National Service, Health, Education, Agriculture and Fisheries, Housing and Local Government; President of the Board of Trade.

Other Ministers

These Ministers form the Cabinet, but changes may be made as the Prime Minister decides. Other Ministers of Cabinet rank, though not necessarily members at present, are: The First Lord of the Admiralty, the Secretaries of State for War and for Air, the Ministers of Supply, Transport and Civil Aviation, Food, Works, Pensions and National Insurance, and Power; the Postmaster General and the Paymaster General, as well as two Ministers of State (Foreign Office and Colonial Office). Also members of the Government, though they are not of Cabinet rank, are the Attorney-General and the Solicitor-General, the Lord Advocate,

Copyright.

A PRESENTATION TO A DISTINGUISHED PARLIAMENTARIAN

Some Members of Parliament serve well and faithfully in a humble capacity; others attain the highest offices that a political career can bring. Of the latter kind is Sir Winston Churchill, one of the greatest figures of our times, whose leadership and achievements have commanded the admiration of both friend and foe alike. Our picture shows the scene in Westminster Hall on November 30th, 1954 (his eightieth birthday), when his own portrait, by Mr. Graham Sutherland, was presented to him by both Houses of Parliament.

and the Parliamentary Under-Secretaries to the various Ministries.

Probably before all these posts are filled, but with his Cabinet Ministers all appointed, the Prime Minister will submit the list to the Queen. The Prime Minister will himself be "sworn in" and later his Ministers will see the Queen and "kiss hands" on their appointment to their high offices. The country has a Government and the new House of Commons can be summoned to meet it and, indeed, to say what they think about it, criticise it, and tell the Ministers what they ought to do. The Government will sit on one side of the House with all the members of their Party behind them, while the Opposition sit on the opposite side.

The leader of the party which has failed to win the election becomes officially the Leader of Her Majesty's Opposition. There is an official opening of Parliament by the Queen, who drives to the House of Lords and from the Throne makes what is known as "The Queen's Speech." This Speech is later read in the House of Commons, though most members will probably have been present in the House of Lords when it was actually delivered.

An Important Occasion

The M.P.s crowd into that part of the House of Lords which is technically "outside the Chamber." The benches of the House of Lords are for this occasion filled with the peers and peeresses, all impressively arrayed for this important State occasion.

In actual fact, the Queen's Speech is the work of the new Prime Minister

and sets forth the Government programme. It is rather typical of the way
in which changes and alterations in
our way of Government have been
grafted on to the old traditions. Thus
there will be a debate on the Queen's
Speech (which is really the Government
programme) but this debate takes place
on a motion to the effect " That a humble
Address of Thanks be presented to Her
Majesty for Her Majesty's Most Gracious
Speech."

Putting down an Amendment

Those members who do not agree
with the Government's programme
simply put down an addition to the
effect that while thanking Her Majesty
for the Speech " humbly regret " that
no mention was made of something
that the member—or members—think
should have been included. All sorts
of amendments of this kind may be
put down, and these are debated, if
the Speaker finds there is time. In
this matter the Speaker has practically
the powers of an autocrat, and it can
be understood that only a man of
supreme tact and ability can fill such
a position.

This debate lets the Government know
the general feeling in the House and if
there is any subject on which a large
number of members feel strongly the
Government will make a note of it.

How the Government Learns

One may be tempted to say, " Yes,
but all this talk doesn't get anywhere,
and it is all rather farcical to make
this pretence of thanking the Queen for
a Speech someone else wrote when
probably half the speeches are com-
plaining or criticising the Speech or
regretting that something was said or
something else has been left out. What
good is it anyway ? "

It serves a good many purposes,
apart from giving the Government an
opportunity of finding their feet, as it
were. It brings forward subjects which
the ordinary people in the country

have talked about but which have been
overlooked by the Government; it
enables the Ministers to get everything
in right perspective. Somebody makes
a strong speech about the supply of
milk for children. It has been talked
about before, but the members of the
Government are not aware that anyone
is really excited about it. Other
members, both on the Government
side as well as the Opposition, take up
the subject and the Government realise
that if this particular amendment is
voted upon it will be very strongly
supported.

If that amendment were actually
carried it would be a serious matter.
The Government promise that if the
amendment is withdrawn they will
bring in a Bill as early as possible
dealing with this subject. The Minister
responsible for bringing in such a Bill
is given instructions to get busy, and in
due course the Bill comes before the
House. The Government sensed the
feeling of the House and acted wisely.

Questions in the House

Once the debate on the Queen's
Speech is over and the motion of thanks
duly passed the House of Commons
settles down to the hard, practical
work of running and governing the
country. The broad outline of what
that work will be has been sketched
out; the new Ministers have taken
charge of their departments and learned
something of the practical details of
their everyday work. Each Minister is
responsible to Parliament for what his
department does, and Parliament is, of
course, responsible to the country.

The Minister, or his Under-Secre-
tary, answers all questions asked by
members concerning the work of his
department. These replies are usually
prepared by officials of the department,
but the Minister is responsible for them.
In this way a continual check is kept on
all departments and the responsibility
of Government officials to the public is
maintained.

HOW LAWS ARE MADE

THE QUEEN WILLS IT

At one time the King proclaimed the laws which governed the nation. To-day a Bill is prepared, debated, and when necessary amended, in Parliament, and finally goes to the Queen for the Royal Assent. When this has been given the clerk of Parliament announces in the old Norman French " La reyne le veult "—the Queen wills it—and the Bill becomes an Act and part of the law of the country.

ONE of the main tasks, though not by any means the only one, carried out by the House of Commons is to make new laws for the better government of the country. Many of these new laws are, of course, extensions, improvements, or enlargements of old laws.

As an example, there have been many Acts of Parliament passed during the last century or so dealing with factories, and since 1870 there have been a number of new Education Acts. There have also been quite a few Acts dealing with the question of who shall vote at an election (Representation of the People Acts) and a series on Unemployment and Pensions Insurance or Health Insurance.

When the Government has decided to make new laws governing, for instance, the supply of milk to school children, the first thing to be done is to draft out a Bill which states just what can be done and how it must be done, and what steps will be taken against anyone who fails to do all he is called upon to do by this new law. Actually, such a matter as this would probably be dealt with as a clause in a much bigger Bill covering many other points concerning children's welfare, but for the sake of simplicity this single example is taken.

Different Government departments would have to be consulted. The Ministry of Agriculture and the Milk Marketing Board may have to make certain arrangements to see that the milk is regularly supplied. Someone must also make sure that the children get the milk when it has been delivered to the school—so the Ministry of Education comes in. Then, as it is first and foremost a question concerning the health of the future citizens of the country, the Ministry of Health will have an interest in the new Bill.

Drafting the Bill

One way and another everybody's ideas are boiled down to different clauses, and the parliamentary lawyers are given the statements showing just what it is proposed to do. They proceed to draft out the Bill in its correct form, so that there can be no loopholes which will allow someone who ought to do something to say that he doesn't intend to do it. The legal men have to make certain that when this Bill eventually becomes an Act and is the law of the land, it cannot be ignored by anyone who has to carry out its terms.

5-2

Someone else meantime calculates how much all this will cost, and this is set forth in what is known as the financial resolution which is passed before the House of Commons settles down to discuss the main Bill itself.

All this preparation takes some time, probably several weeks, before the Bill is printed and copies are available to all M.P.s. On that same day there will be an item on the Order Paper of the House "That the School Children's Milk Bill be read for the first time." At some stage during that day the Speaker will read this out and ask those in favour to say "Aye," and those who are not in favour of the Bill to say "No." Usually at this stage nobody says anything at all, and the Speaker merely announces: "The Ayes have it."

In the Committee Stage

That is all that happens on the First Reading. The Bill is now public and can be read by anybody. Some time later, when the members, the Press and the public have all had time to learn all they wish to know about the Bill, it comes up for Second Reading. On this occasion members say what they think about it generally, and then, after this debate on the Second Reading, the Bill passes to the Committee stage. If it is an important Bill the Committee will be the full House, but the Speaker no longer sits in the Chair, which is taken instead by the Chairman of Committees.

Fox Photos.

LONDON COUNTY COUNCIL IN SESSION

For the purposes of local government London is an administrative county covering an area of 117 square miles. Its Council consists of a chairman, 20 aldermen and 124 councillors, and full meetings are usually held fortnightly. Much of its work is carried on through the different committees, such as Finance, General Purposes, Education, Housing and Public Health, Town Planning. Almost everything that affects the life and welfare of the Londoner is watched over by the County Council.

Specially drawn for this work.

THE CITIZENS ACCLAIM THEIR NEW MAYOR

In this picture our artist has depicted a scene in the Middle Ages when the Mayor of the City appeared before the citizens after being chosen by the leading merchants as chief ruler of their city. So long ago as 1100 the chief official of London was given the title of Mayor and it was soon in general use in other cities and large towns which had become boroughs.

Bills which are not quite so important are dealt with by a smaller Committee, made up of members in proportion to the numbers of their party. This Committee is usually referred to as "the Committee upstairs." In committee any member may propose an amendment and, if agreed to by a majority, all sorts of alterations may be made in the Bill. Every detail can be argued about and perhaps voted upon. Sometimes even the Minister in charge of the Bill may himself propose an amendment because something has been suggested since the Bill was first prepared.

The Royal Assent

This Committee stage may take quite a long time as there are many other matters coming before the House. Finally the Committee passes the last clause and the amended Bill is reported to the House in what is called the Report Stage. Some time later the Bill in its new and amended form comes before the House for its Third Reading. There is not likely to be much trouble at this stage ; everything that can be said has been said and all the alterations the Government are prepared to make have been made.

Now the Bill is sent to the House of Lords and, after it has been passed by them, it is taken to the Queen to receive the Royal Assent. After that it is no longer a Bill but has become an Act of Parliament and the law of the country which must be obeyed.

The House of Lords might have altered the Bill and sent it back to the House of Commons for them to pass the alteration. Very occasionally this does happen, but for various reasons it is a somewhat rare occurrence in these days, although up to 1911 it often happened. Traditionally the House of Lords was superior to the House of Commons, but in practice it has little real authority. During the Parliament of 1906–10 the House of Lords opposed the Government of the day, which took up the challenge, and, being returned to power again after a General Election, finally succeeded by the Parliament Act of 1911 in establishing certain rules which curtailed the power of the House of Lords considerably. Other restrictions were imposed by an Act passed in 1948.

One of the rules governing the House of Lords is that it has no power over Money Bills. If the Speaker of the House of Commons certifies that a Bill is a Money Bill then the House of Lords can do nothing about it. Any other Bill may be rejected by the House of Lords, but the House of Commons could then wait for one year and pass it again, and after that it would go to the Queen for the Royal Assent without the Lords having any powers to prevent it becoming law.

The House of Lords also has certain judicial authority, although, generally speaking, an appeal to the House of Lords is dealt with by a special committee known as the Lords of Appeal, who are peers with legal qualifications for such a task.

Although the House of Lords in a political sense has little power it does exercise a considerable influence. Its debates are often more outspoken than those made in the House of Commons, and sometimes may represent more accurately just what the country as a whole is thinking than either House of Commons or even the Press. So far as the actual business of making laws is concerned, the House of Lords has little power compared with the House of Commons.

Our Civil Service

Once a Bill has become an Act it must be administered. This practical side is carried out by the Civil Service in the first place, as from them come the necessary instructions. Thus in the case of our Milk Bill the officers of the Ministry of Education will make all arrangements with the Education Committees of the county and local councils, while other Ministries concerned see to their part in the programme. The Ministry of Health will want to know that the milk is pure and supplied in the right kind of bottle; the Minister of Agriculture and the head of the Milk Marketing Board will decide about the form of contract with the milk suppliers. One way and another a good many people will have work to do before all the school children in the country have their middle-of-the-morning milk.

The practical government of the country, that is the carrying into effect of whatever the Government orders, is the work of the Civil Service. They are impartial and are not concerned with policy but simply to see that the laws are carried out and that the machinery of government runs smoothly. There are some 600,000 Civil Servants employed in the many Government departments at the present time.

There has been and always will be a good deal of criticism of our Civil Service, though it is generally admitted that it is both the most efficient and the most honest in the world. Very great care is taken to make sure that it shall be so. Its faults are due to the fact that it is at one and the same time the servant and the master of the public. It is carrying out the duties which the people of the country, through the Parliament they elected, asked to be done.

How the Money Is Obtained

If the country as a whole desires that education in the higher grade schools shall be free they elect as their Members of Parliament more men who are pledged to bring this about than those who are opposed to it. It will naturally cost money, and either through income tax or local rates, or

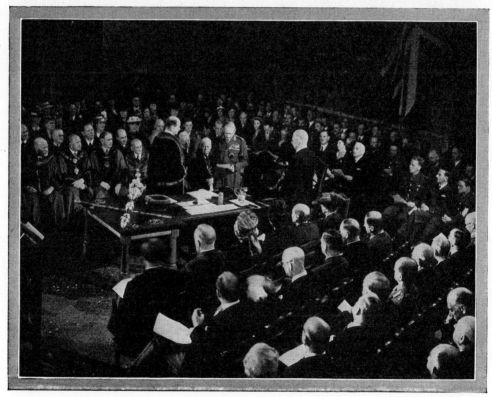

P.N.A.

THE FREEDOM OF THE CITY

It has always been regarded as a great honour to be made a Freeman of a great city, and although in modern days it carries no particular privileges, it is the custom to confer the Freedom of the City upon notable personages as a mark of high distinction. Our picture shows the scene in the Guildhall when the Freedom of the City of London was conferred upon Field Marshal Lord Montgomery.

Fox Photos.

AT KEW GARDENS IN BLOSSOM TIME

Parks and open spaces are among the many privileges conferred upon the citizens of this country, mainly through the different branches of government, both national and local. Here we have a scene in one of the most famous of our public gardens, the Royal Botanic Gardens at Kew where many valuable and remarkable plants are to be seen. Our picture shows a beautiful Magnolia tree when in full bloom.

probably both, the Government will obtain the money required. The Tax Inspector, who is a Civil Servant, is merely carrying out the commands of Parliament when, in due course, he asks for more income tax from the people in his district.

Apart from making laws, Parliament has many other tasks. It must raise the money to pay for our Defence Forces; there are big sums required for pensions of all kinds, for medical and other health services, as well as the cost of running such Ministries as the Foreign Office, Home Office, and others. Certain departments, such as the Post Office, are more than self-supporting and bring in profit to the Government.

Normally once a year the Chancellor of the Exchequer tells the House of Commons how much he thinks it will cost to run the country during the coming year and how he is proposing to collect this money. The day when this statement is made to the House is known as Budget Day and the country learns just what taxes will have to be paid during the coming year and how they must be paid.

The debate and committee work dealing with these important matters of finance take a considerable amount of time. The House becomes a Committee of Supply or a Committee of Ways and Means, and discusses all matters dealing with the provision of money for the Forces and the Civil Service.

When M.P.s Ask Questions

At times there are full debates on Foreign Affairs or any other subject of immediate national importance. On every day except Friday a full hour is allotted at the beginning of the day's proceedings to "Question Time." A member must give his question to one of the clerks at the table just below the Speaker at least one full day before he can expect an answer. Every day there are any number up to as many as a hundred questions to be answered by different Ministers. Those questions which are not replied to verbally will receive written answers.

The Minister who replies is responsible for the information he gives, but the Civil Service have the task of preparing the answer for him. If the member asks a supplementary question, as he may, the Minister will have to answer that from his notes. Usually Ministers are very wary, and if the supplementary question seems a dangerous one they give a tactful but non-committal reply as far as possible. Or they may inform the member that they must have notice in writing of that particular question.

If the member is not at all satisfied with the answer he receives and feels that it deserves more attention he can give notice to raise the matter on the Adjournment. This means that he can arrange with the officials of the House, usually the Speaker's secretary, that one night in the near future when the House has finished its work for the day but before it is finally closed, he will raise the matter again. This time the Minister, having had time to look into the question more carefully and to discuss it with the head Civil

A. W. Kerr.

A CALL AT THE EMPLOYMENT EXCHANGE

As an example of the way in which the Government of a country can organise a service for the general benefit of the community the Employment Exchanges may be quoted as a case in point. Originally begun and managed by local authorities in 1905, they became national in 1910, proved their value during 1914 to 1920 and again in 1939 were of great importance in organising the nation's labour resources. Our photograph shows a scene in a Croydon Exchange.

Servants in his department, will do his best to give a full explanation.

Not all Members of Parliament are present when the House is sitting. There is no rule which compels a member to be there, but when there is important business on hand and a vote, known as a "division," is to be taken, he will probably be warned in a specially underlined notice from an official of his party, known as a Whip. As the Chief Whip and his assistants have considerable power, it will be bad policy on the part of a member to ignore their urgent requests.

The notice which the Whips send out is also known as a "Whip," and this notice may be underlined once, twice or three times. A "three-line Whip" is almost in the nature of a command to the member that he must be present. Each party has its Whips, and they keep members regularly informed of the programme before the House during the week ahead.

Passing on the Work

Parliament makes the laws, keeps careful watch on all matters affecting the country, and raises the money necessary to run the country as a whole. The Law Courts, Civil Service and Local Government services see that these laws are carried into effect. Parliament has conferred certain definite powers and duties on the "local authorities," i.e., County Councils, municipal borough councils, urban and rural district councils and parish councils.

The widest powers have been given to the most important authorities, which are the county and the borough councils. But in the main their schemes for inspiring local services and so on need to be approved by a Government department. The County Councils exercise considerable control over the councils of the smaller boroughs, and over the urban and the other local councils.

The larger boroughs, governing cities such as Manchester, Birmingham, Liverpool, and many others, are known as "County Boroughs" and are quite independent of the County Councils. It is natural, too, that London has a special system of its own and is administered by the London County Council, the City of London Corporation, and twenty-eight Metropolitan Boroughs, one of which is now known as the City of Westminster.

The members of these councils are elected by the votes of the citizens in much the same way as Members of Parliament are elected.

Broadly speaking, every adult now has a vote in the district in which he lives. They must be persons "resident there on the qualifying date, who, on that date and the date of the poll, are of full age and not subject to any legal incapacity to vote, and either British subjects or citizens of the republic of Ireland."

This applies to both the parliamentary and local government elections. An additional privilege of voting at local government elections may be possessed by persons having a non-resident qualification. For instance, a person living in London and owning a shop in, say, a Surrey town (with a rateable value of £10 or over) would be entitled to vote at elections held for the ward in which his business was situated, providing he has been registered as having a non-resident's qualification in that ward.

The local Registration Officer is responsible for the preparation of the lists of voters, both for parliamentary and local elections. These lists have to be shown publicly so that anyone may inspect the list to find out if his name has been correctly entered. If it is not on he can claim to have it inserted; any person on the list can object to the name of someone else, if he has good reason to believe that it ought not to be there.

Our Local Government

Similarly a candidate for the local or County Council must have certain modest qualifications, either through having resided in the district for a year before the election or by virtue of the fact that he is qualified as an elector.

All this local government is carried on under laws which Parliament has passed. The local councils carry out the laws relating to the welfare of the people in their own area. Public Health, Education and all branches of local government are dealt with in detail by the committees of the local councils: the Education Committee; the Cleansing Committee to see that rubbish is collected and the roads kept clean; the Highways Committee to attend to road repairs, new roads, drains to keep the streets in good order; a Public Assistance Committee to see that any person in want is cared for properly; probably

Fox Photos.

THE SPEAKER'S CHAIR

The Speaker of the House of Commons has very considerable powers and the Chair which he occupies when the House is sitting plays its part in the making of Britain's laws. The new chair in the rebuilt House of Commons is of black bean, and was the gift of Australia; the chairs at the table were South Africa's gift and many other fittings and furniture were given by other members of the British Commonwealth.

there is a Town Planning Committee and a Parks and Recreation Committee, as well as one to look after the affairs of the local library, while a Housing Committee will deal with the building, letting, and maintenance of houses.

The history of local government is one of steady growth and increasing responsibility. Councillors receive no payment for their services, though the Mayor of a big borough may receive an allowance for the heavy expenses he has to meet, and councillors may also receive payment for legitimate out-of-pocket expenses when on the business of the council. On this question of expenses, and indeed of most of the payments made by the local council, the Minister of Health exercises a control by the District Auditors who are appointed and paid by him.

IN THE COURTS OF JUSTICE

THE MAJESTY OF THE LAW
Originally the Law Courts formed part of the Parliament meeting at Westminster Hall and a judge of the High Court is still addressed as " My Lord " (though he is usually a knight and referred to as " Mr. Justice —") simply because he is historically a Lord of the high court of Parliament and administers the law as directed by Parliament (Statutory Law) or as established by precedents over long years (Common Law).

PARLIAMENT makes our laws; the Civil Service sees that all arrangements are made for the laws to be put into force. County, borough, urban and rural district councils receive full information of what part they must take in putting a new law into operation.

Quite often, of course, the law may not affect the work of the local councils at all. There are many laws which have existed for centuries before the present system of local government came into being. Some of them indeed may be solely concerned with the order that certain acts shall not be committed. " Thou shalt not steal " is not only one of the Ten Commandments but the law of this land, and indeed of all civilised countries.

The Law of the Land

When a person breaks the law he is liable to a penalty. To enforce the laws and to see that those who break them are punished is the duty of the police and those officers of the law such as judges and magistrates. Then there are many cases in which two

people quarrel concerning their rights. One asserts that the other has put up a fence and in so doing has taken land belonging to the one who complains. To settle the matter the case must be brought into a court of law, where a judge will listen to both sides and decide on the evidence brought before him which of the two is right.

Like so many of our firmly-established systems the laws of this country did not begin as a written set of rules. In many cases they just grew until they were regarded as the law of the land. It is easy to understand how quite early in history it came about that if one member of the tribe or community took another person's weapon or other personal property, the chief or elders decided that the property should be restored to its rightful owner and the thief punished, not merely because he had done wrong but also as a warning to others.

Later the King of the country established courts to deal with wrong-doers and to settle disputes between two persons regarding their rights. The one kind of court came to be known in due time as the criminal court and the other as a civil court. At first the judges appointed by the King found out what were the customs and unwritten rules in the district. In this way there grew up what we now know as Common Law.

Common Law and Statute Law

No Act of Parliament was passed to establish these laws, but from time to time cases came before the judges who considered every aspect of the case as well as the customs of the people. They delivered careful judgment, stating their reasons for coming to their decision. That judgment in turn was quoted and became regarded as the accepted law in future cases.

In this way our Common Law represents the ancient rules and customs of long years ago, modified and developed in accordance with modern conditions by our judges. In the course of time a certain amount of this old-time Common Law has been embodied in Acts of Parliament, but much of it still remains unwritten except for the decisions of judges in earlier cases.

The other kind of law we have in this country is known as Statute Law, which means that it is written and laid down by the authority of Parliament. This kind of law must be administered by the judges exactly as it is written. Such laws as the Factory Acts, Bankruptcy Laws and those relating to companies, as well as all the recent Health and Unemployment Acts, are Statutes and must be carried out precisely as Parliament has laid down.

According to the Act

Sometimes there are cases in which the judge himself feels that in the

P. A. Reuter.

THE JUDGES ATTEND WESTMINSTER ABBEY

It is a long-standing custom that just before the opening of the Law Courts after they have been closed for the summer vacation the Judges attend divine service at Westminster Abbey or other church, and here we see the procession of judges, led by the Lord Chancellor, leaving the service, at which they dedicate themselves to administer true justice to all men.

particular case before him it is not quite fair on the one accused of breaking the law, and he may say, as happens on occasion: " It certainly seems rather unfair, but it is clearly laid down in the Act that this shall be done, and the defendant failed to do so. Therefore ——" and he delivers judgment in accordance with the Act of Parliament and not according to his own ideas.

Whenever any law, civil or criminal, is broken, or when two people have a dispute which they cannot settle between themselves, the case will be tried before a properly appointed judge or magistrates in a Court of Law. It may be a comparatively small affair: a minor theft, a dispute between neighbours, or a motorist exceeding the speed limit in a built-up area. In such a case the offender will be tried before magistrates known as Justices of the Peace, sitting in a Police Court. J.P.s are not paid for their services and are not usually lawyers, but they have the help of the Clerk of the Court, who is a lawyer and is paid. There is no jury and the magistrates usually deal with the cases there and then. They are also called upon to hear a certain amount of evidence in cases they will not be called upon to judge.

Every Man's Right

In these cases, what they are called upon to do is to decide if the police have been justified in arresting a certain person for a particular crime. They must satisfy themselves that there is at least good reason for thinking the man had some connection with the crime. They can then commit him for trial before a higher court, either the Quarter Sessions or the Assizes.

There is a reason for this. In Magna Carta and in the Habeas Corpus Act of 1679 safeguards are given against wrongful arrest and imprisonment. A man cannot be arrested and held in prison simply because the police think he is just the sort of man who might have carried out a recent burglary and

if they can keep him under lock and key for two or three weeks they will have a better chance of proving that he did it.

They cannot do that. They must have some real evidence about his movements or that he has had possession of some of the stolen property since it disappeared from its rightful place, and they must bring the accused person before the magistrates as soon as possible, probably on the day following his arrest, and give him a chance of saying anything he may wish about his conduct.

This question of wrongful arrest and detention is a very important one. A person cannot be kept in ignorance of the crime of which he is accused. He must be told why he has been arrested, and the magistrates must be told the crime of which he is accused and the reasons why the police have acted. They may remand the case for a week to give the police time to gather further evidence and also to give the man time to arrange with a lawyer about his defence.

If the magistrates are satisfied that there is a good case against the accused man they will commit him for trial at the Quarter Sessions, or in more serious cases to the Assizes. In certain cases the accused person, or his lawyer, may ask that he should be allowed out on bail. That is, one or two other responsible persons will agree to stand surety for him: they will see that he is at the Court again at the time and on the day stated by the magistrates, otherwise they will be called upon to pay a considerable sum of money.

Magistrates deal with about 92 per cent. of all the cases that are heard in Great Britain.

J.P.s, Stipendiaries, Recorders and Judges

In London and certain other large cities a paid magistrate known as a Stipendiary takes the place of the J.P.s in some police courts. A Stipendiary must be a barrister of at

Barratt.

A JUDGE ON CIRCUIT

From the time of Henry II it has been a custom for English judges to make regular journeys to different parts of the country to give fair trial to wrong-doers and settle disputes of importance. England and Wales is divided into seven circuits and three times each year the judges visit the towns at which Assizes are held. In this picture the Judge on the South-eastern Circuit is seen as he leaves the Assize Court at Lewes, Sussex.

least five years' standing. Most cities and boroughs have also their own Court of Quarter Sessions. In the case of counties a number of magistrates are on the bench at Quarter Sessions under the chairmanship of one who has had considerable experience. In the city courts there is only one judge, known as the Recorder, and he is an experienced barrister who receives a salary.

There is, too, a County Court for the trial of civil cases and this is presided over by a judge. Here, cases in which not more than £200 is involved are dealt with, bankrupts are examined, and a good deal of other judicial work is carried through.

At the Assize Courts a Judge of the Queen's Bench tries the cases. England and Wales is divided into circuits and the Assizes are held in the larger cities and towns usually three times a year. In London there is a special court known as the Central Criminal Court which deals with cases of serious crime in the same way as the Assize Courts.

Trial by Jury

In both the Court of Quarter Sessions and at the Assizes there is a jury of twelve men (or men and women nowadays). They are chosen from ordinary citizens, sworn to return a true verdict in accordance with the evidence they hear. The system of trial by jury has existed in England since very early days.

When the jury has heard all the evidence the Judge will sum up, going carefully over all that has been brought forward and explaining any points of law which may have cropped up. The task of the jury is to decide whether the accused person is " Guilty " or " Not Guilty." They have nothing to do with the sentence. The Judge alone decides that.

If the verdict is " Guilty " the Judge first of all asks the police whether the prisoner in the dock has ever been convicted of any crimes before. Until then anything relating to a man's wrong-doing in the past has been most carefully avoided. Until after the verdict no mention must be made of a person's previous convictions. This means that an accused man is tried solely on the evidence dealing with the particular crime for which he has been arrested.

The Judge, however, will take into consideration a man's previous record. If it is the first time he has been guilty of such a crime or of any crime at all, it can naturally be expected that his sentence will be much more lenient than the one imposed on a man who has repeatedly committed the same crime, or has a criminal record.

Scotland's Third Verdict

It should be mentioned here that in Scotland there are certain differences in the way in which the law courts are conducted and in the names given to different officials of the court. Another curious difference is that in England a jury must return a verdict of "Guilty" or "Not Guilty," unless, of course, they cannot agree, in which case a fresh jury has to be sworn in and the trial begun all over again. In Scotland the jury can bring in a verdict of " Not Proven " which means that they are not satisfied on the evidence that the prisoner is guilty, but find it equally difficult to assert that he is innocent.

There is one special kind of Court which is very different from all the others. If a person under seventeen years

Fox Photos.

PUMP COURT IN THE TEMPLE

The four English legal societies which govern that branch of the profession to which barristers belong are known as Inns of Court and have their habitation in the particular districts from which they take their names: Lincoln's Inn, Inner Temple, Middle Temple and Gray's Inn. Our photograph shows a corner in the Middle Temple known as Pump Court.

of age is accused of a crime he appears before a Children's Court. Names are not made public, and the parents or guardians must appear with the accused youngster. The magistrates in this case have to consider how best they can help the young wrong-doer and prevent him or her from committing further wrongs. Frequently where parents are considered to be reasonably sensible sort of people the young person will be put on probation. Such a "sentence" means that the Court does not propose to punish the offender for this particular offence, but if he offends again it will be taken into consideration when the Court hears the subsequent charge and he is likely to be punished for both.

The making of a probation order also carries the condition that the young offender must lead what is called

A. W. Kerr.

THE ROYAL COURTS OF JUSTICE

Generally known as the Law Courts, the Royal Courts of Justice on the North side of the Strand, London, are the headquarters of the administration of justice in England. The present building was opened by Queen Victoria in 1882 and the business of the supreme court was then transferred here.

" an honest and industrious life " and report regularly to the probation officer at whatever time and place he fixes. The probationer must not change his job or school without telling the probation officer and, generally, he is under the supervision of the probation officer during the whole of the time the magistrates have said the probation shall last— possibly one or two and, in some cases, even three years.

If the child comes from a bad home, or if there have been previous occasions on which he has done wrong, the magistrates may send him away to a special school or home where he can be properly looked after and trained to earn his living without stealing or doing anything wrong.

Duties of the Lawyers

There are very many rules and regulations about the way in which the laws of the country must be administered. Only a few can be mentioned here, but their importance is obvious in most cases. An accused person has the right to legal aid, that is to have a solicitor to advise him and help him prepare his case; if it is merely a case in the police court the solicitor can defend him and act as his advocate. A solicitor may also appear in certain special cases at Quarter Sessions, but here it is generally the rule that a barrister must appear as the advocate to plead the cause of the accused. In all higher Courts a barrister only can conduct a case before the judge.

Solicitors and Barristers

Both solicitors and barristers are lawyers, but their tasks are somewhat different. In the main the barrister is the advocate who " pleads " before the judge and jury, and his branch of the profession is usually regarded as the higher one. The solicitor is more concerned with advising clients, and he " briefs " the barrister, that is, gives him all the facts about the case so that the barrister can present it properly before the judge. A barrister, too, is usually specially learned in one particular branch of the law and his views may be sought by the solicitor on some knotty point.

In this case the solicitor will say that he has " Counsel's Opinion " and some barristers are largely occupied in this kind of work, particularly when they have specialised in some highly technical or complicated side of the law, as, for instance, Patent Law. The solicitor is more concerned with the preparation of legal deeds such as partnership agreements, transfer of property, leases of land, wills, and many matters in which some kind of legal and binding arrangement is desirable.

On Becoming a " Silk "

Barristers themselves are divided into two classes: the ordinary barrister and the higher ranking Q.C. or Queen's Counsel. To become a Q.C. a man must have attained some eminence as a barrister before being nominated by the Lord Chancellor. The expression " to take silk " sometimes used when a man becomes a Q.C., comes from the fact that he wears a silk gown instead of the usual stuff gown of the ordinary, or junior, barrister. The first to hold this rank was Francis Bacon, created Queen's Counsel by Elizabeth I.

In most cases, whether in the criminal or civil courts, there is a right of appeal to a higher court. At times there may be an appeal from the Court of Appeal to the House of Lords, which is the highest tribunal in the land. In criminal cases the appeal is heard by the judges of the Court of Criminal Appeal.

Appointing Judges

Who appoints our judges ? County Court judges must be barristers of at least seven years' standing and are appointed by the Lord Chancellor. They are styled " Judge —— " and addressed as " Your Honour." Judges of the High Court must be barristers of ten years' standing and are appointed by the Crown. Once they are appointed they cannot be dismissed except on an address from both Houses of Parliament showing that they have been guilty of some grave fault. They cannot sit in Parliament themselves once they become judges. Officially they are referred to as " Mr. Justice —— " and addressed as " My Lord."

The Lord Chancellor

Chief among the judges is the Lord Chief Justice; he ranks next to the Lord High Chancellor (usually known as the Lord Chancellor) who is the head of all the judicial services in the country. The Lord Chancellor is a Cabinet Minister, Privy Councillor, Keeper of the Great Seal, and issues the royal commissions opening and proroguing Parliament : he appoints all Justices of the Peace, certain judges of the High Court, and all County Court judges. He is also the President or Speaker of the House of Lords, where he sits on the historic, though possibly not too comfortable, seat known as the Woolsack, a large square cushion of wool covered with red cloth.

HOW THE POLICE WORK

Central Press.

ON POINT DUTY IN A LONDON STREET

Here is a typical British policeman controlling the traffic near the Royal Courts of Justice in the Strand, London. The whole world knows his blue uniform which shows him to belong to one of the finest Police Forces that there is. It is because of our police that we are able to go about our work and play in safety and in peace.

THE whole world knows the blue uniform of the officers and constables of Britain's Police Forces. Indeed, the fame of our police is so widespread that it is now almost taken for granted that a foreigner, if asked for his impressions after his first visit to Britain, will voice the opinion that " your policemen are wonderful "—and most foreigners will say as much in all sincerity.

If you live in Britain, whether in town or country, the policeman—and the police woman—are part of the scene of your daily life. In the country, you will see the constable cycling along his " beat " and notice, perhaps, on the outskirts of the village the neat brick house which is both his home and his office.

In the towns, you will see policemen controlling the traffic at busy crossroads, patrolling the streets, or driving along in smart radio-equipped cars. While you are at school, a policeman may come along to talk to your class about road safety and the Highway Code, and to give friendly advice on such matters as the brakes on your bicycle ; and when school is over for the day, you will probably find a policeman waiting at the crossing over the main road to shepherd you and your classmates safely to the other side.

In Old London

Have you ever paused to consider what life would be like without a Police Force ? The men and women of our Police Forces exist to safeguard our lives and our property. It is precisely because we have efficient Police Forces that we are able to go about our work and play in safety and in peace. Without police to make sure that the laws our representatives in

6–2

Parliament make are obeyed, without police to prevent and detect crime, daily life would be as uncertain and risky as it was in times gone by when Britain had no men to maintain her laws other than the parish constables, who were usually as ineffective as they were old and who were quite often hand in glove with the very criminals they were supposed to bring to justice.

Picture Post Library.

THE LAST OF THE " CHARLIES "

Before Peel founded his " New Police," the maintenance of law and order lay in the hands of the parish constables, and the night watch-men or " Charlies." Here, standing outside his box, armed with his truncheon, lantern, cutlass and rattle, is the last representative of those ineffective guardians of the peace. He died in 1880 at the age of ninety-five.

In those times, even London was likely to be as dangerous a place for the peaceful citizens as the heaths and remo-ter stretches of main road which were the hunting grounds of ruthless high-waymen. The night watchmen who, since the reign of Charles II, had supplemented the work of the parish constables in London were useless in the suppression of crime and were jeeringly called " Charlies." This is how Henry Fielding has described them : " They were chosen out of those poor, old, decrepit people who are from their want of bodily strength, rendered incapable of getting a living by work. These men, armed only with a pole, which some of them are scarce able to lift, are to secure the persons and houses of His Majesty's subjects from the attacks of young, bold, stout, and desperate and well-armed villains. . . . If the poor old fellows should run away from such enemies, no one—I think—can wonder: unless he should wonder that they are able even to make their escape."

The Bow Street Runners

Henry Fielding was not only a skilful playwright and novelist whose literary work paved the way for such masters as Thackeray and Dickens. He was also a magistrate and the founder of the Bow Street Police, the early ancestor of our present Police Forces.

In theory, the constables of his time were volunteers who served for a while and then retired. But in 1749, the year in which Fielding was chosen chairman of the Westminster quarter sessions, he persuaded the more efficient of his men to stay in service, paying them a small salary for the work they did. This was the beginning of the Bow Street Police Force whose officers were soon to be famous as the Bow Street Runners. Before many years had pas-sed, the Bow Street Police Force had its well-armed foot and horse patrols ; its officers wore uniform, their red waistcoats leading to their nickname of " Robin Redbreasts." Moreover, they were charged not only to keep law and order in their district, but to befriend the poor and unfortunate. This was a new and peculiarly British attitude to police work and the commencement of the great tradition of public service which lies behind our Police Forces to this day.

But even at the height of their activity, the Bow Street Runners could not fulfil all the duties of a national or even a London police force. They were comparatively few in number and constituted a small island of law and order in the lawless sea of Britain's capital. In London as a whole, crime and disorder went seemingly unchecked. There were riots and street battles between rival mobs which could only be put down by calling in the Army. In the more disreputable parts of the great city, gangs of thieves and cut-throats would gather by night at the street corners to waylay the luckless traveller ; and so desperate was the situation that people who had been robbed were often prepared to settle with the thieves, virtually paying blackmail for the return of the whole or some part of what had been stolen from them. On all sides, the peaceful law-abiding public were in need of protection, although many leading statesmen and citizens disliked the idea of having a police force because they felt such a force would be too powerful a weapon in the hands of an unscrupulous government.

The " New Police "

The great William Pitt had unsuccessfully tried to bring a police force into being in 1785, but it was not until the time of Sir Robert Peel that Parliament passed a Bill " for Improving the Police in and near the Metropolis " (1829).

When Peel took office as Home Secretary in 1822, he had at once announced his intention of giving London " as perfect a system of police as was consistent with the character of a free country,"

Picture Post Library.

A NINETEENTH CENTURY " PEELER "

" Peelers," or " Bobbies," were what Londoners called the members of Peel's " New Police " which came into being as a result of his Act of 1829. At first the police were universally unpopular and were attacked in the newspapers and in public speeches. But within about five years their true worth was recognised, so much so that people suggested they should take on other duties such as fire-fighting.

but seven years elapsed before he had sufficiently overcome opposition to bring the " New Police " into being.

Londoners soon came to know the men of the " New Police " as " Peelers " or " Bobbies," and it was not long before their work in putting down crime towns. Writing of the change which the establishment of these forces brought about, Charles Reith, the well-known police historian, says: "Wherever the police appeared crime was at once brought under control and ceased, automatically, to be either a local or a national problem."

From such beginnings have our present police Forces grown. To-day there are 130 Police Forces in England and Wales and 47 in Scotland. Some are small, others large. The largest of all is the Metropolitan Police Force which has a strength of about 20,000. Nowadays local authorities are required by law to maintain an efficient Police Force, but the officers and men of such Forces are the servants of the Crown whose conditions of work are laid down in regulations made by the Home Secretary (in the case of England and Wales) and by the Secretary of State for Scotland (in the case of Scottish Police Forces). The Metropolitan Police Force is commanded by Commissioners directly responsible to the Home Secretary, but your local police will probably have a Chief Constable at their head.

Picture Post Library.

THE FRIEND OF HOMELESS CHILDREN

This illustration, taken from an old nineteenth century picture, shows how even in those early days the police befriended the poor, the homeless and the unfortunate. The policemen of to-day are no less our friends and protectors ; and as they are always ready to help us, so we must be willing to assist them in every possible way.

and violence won them widespread gratitude. Controlled by two Commissioners, the Force had its first headquarters in a private house in Whitehall Place where once the Palace of Scotland had stood and which soon came to be called Scotland Yard. So much was this name linked with the police that it was retained when the headquarters was moved to a new and more imposing building on the Thames Embankment in 1890.

The "New Police" became the model for the police forces of provincial

If you wish to become a Policeman—

The first requirements of a policeman or police woman are height and physical fitness. Policemen must not be less than 5 ft. 8 in. tall, and police women not less than 5 ft. 4 in. tall. Once a recruit is accepted, he or she has to undergo an arduous but interesting training at one of the District Training Schools in Great Britain. The training of police women differs very little from that of policemen, for both have to be fitted to deal with any and every emergency.

In the case of the Metropolitan Police Force, every recruit has twelve or thirteen weeks' training at the school at Hendon or at Peel House, Westminster. If the recruit passes his examinations, he next goes to a police station where he works under the guidance of an experienced officer. Nor until two years have elapsed can he call himself a fully-fledged Police Constable, and even then he finds that there is still plenty for him to learn.

During those two years he will have taken further examinations, and may receive training for one of the specialist branches of police work. There is so much for the Police recruit to learn, not only at the training school but by experience, that senior Police Officers are often heard to say that it takes ten years to make a policeman !

Training of recruits for the provincial Police Forces follows the same pattern. Policemen and police women need to have had a good education, and in addition they must be proficient in a variety of other subjects such as criminal law, local regulations and by-laws, police procedure, and how to give evidence in court.

Later in his training, the recruit may

Barratts Photo Press.

MOUNTED POLICE AND THEIR HORSES IN TRAINING

Members of the Metropolitan Mounted Police play an important part especially on ceremonial occasions such as Royal processions and parades. Not only the men but the horses, too, undergo special training for these duties. In this picture, taken at the Mounted Training Establishment at Imber Court, the police are taking their horses through the special lane of flags and banners, while others provide the noise to accustom the horses to cheering crowds, fluttering flags, and other distractions.

Fox Photos.

THE COUNTRY POLICEMAN AT WORK

The country policeman has no busy crossroads to control, but he has other duties connected with the work and people of the farms and villages in his area. When the sheep are dipped, for example, he will call at the farm to make sure that this is being done properly and in accordance with the law. Often, too, he is called upon to give advice about new regulations.

For all there is opportunity, for the senior officers of Britain's Police Forces are men who have worked their way up through the ranks. About one policeman in seven holds a rank higher than a constable. Those who show great promise in their work will probably be sent for special training to the new police college at Ryton-on-Dunsmore, Warwickshire. The College was formally opened in October, 1948, an event which was described by the Home Secretary as "a landmark in police history" and is a police University where officers from all parts of Britain go to add still further to their knowledge and experience.

At your Local Police Station

Your local Central Police Station is equipped to deal with everything from returning a lost child to its anxious parents to solving a serious crime and arresting those who have

find chances of using interests that have until now been only hobbies. If he is a good mechanic, driver, or motor cyclist, he may be employed on motor patrol duties. If he is a good horseman, a job may be found for him in the mounted branch. Radio enthusiasts will find places for themselves in the police wireless branch, while good watermen will be employed in the river police and photographic experts in certain specialised kinds of detective work.

committed it. The Central Police Station is the nerve-centre of Police activity in your town or district. Like Scotland Yard, it has its Information Room where reports are received from—and instructions issued to—patrolling police cars by radio telephone. The Information Room has radio-telephone links, too, with County and other adjoining police centres and with such local services as the Fire Brigade.

FOR SAFETY ON OUR ROADS

These motor cycle police and the police car are familiar sights to all of us who live in Britain's towns and cities. The car is equipped with two-way radio telephone communication with the Information Room at headquarters and a loudspeaker which enables careless drivers to be cautioned.

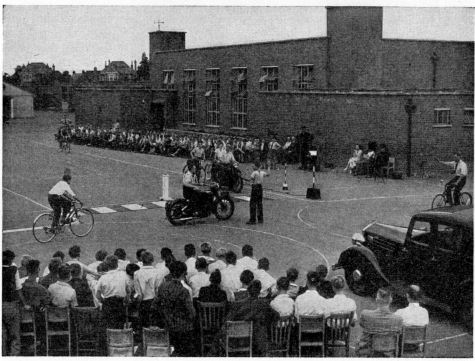

Photos : Central Press.

Here we see a demonstration of " safety-first " rules for cyclists when approaching cross-roads, given by the police to the pupils at a Middlesex Secondary School. Some of the pupils themselves took part in the different scenes both as cyclists and traffic controllers.

The Central Police Station has its own Criminal Investigation Department composed of skilled plain-clothes detectives, finger-print experts, and photographers whose work, if need be, can be supplemented by that of highly-specialised detectives from Scotland Yard. For Scotland Yard, in addition to being the headquarters of the Metropolitan Police Force, is also the centre for able detectives experienced in dealing with particular types of crimes and has in its many departments every scientific device that can assist in the solution of crime and the capture of the criminal. While each provincial Police Force is trained and equipped to fend for itself in its own area, Chief Constables can at any time call for assistance from Scotland Yard, and this they will certainly do in cases where something more than local knowledge is needed.

But most of us are naturally law-abiding and are unlikely to encounter members of a Criminal Investigation Department outside a detective novel or film where their work is likely to be romantically but inaccurately depicted. For us, the Police are the good-natured men we see controlling the crowds at a cup final, the men who see us safely across the road, the men who are ready to tell us the way to this or that street. We see our policemen and police women as friends who are always ready to be helpful and courteous, and we scarcely pause to think of the duties they undertake or the risks they sometimes run on our behalf.

A Policeman's Life

A song from one of the famous Gilbert and Sullivan operas complains that a policeman's lot "is not a happy one"—an opinion that seems to have little real foundation beyond the fact that a policeman is never really "off duty." He works a six day week, eight hours on and sixteen hours off, and has eighteen days or more annual leave. But even when he

Keystone.

THE FINGER-PRINT DEPARTMENT AT SCOTLAND YARD

Scotland Yard is not only the headquarters of the Metropolitan Police Force ; it has expert detectives and every scientific device which can assist in police work—and these are available to Police Forces throughout the country. The finger-print department is one of the most important, for here detectives can check the prints of a suspect and compare them with prints from articles touched by the criminal.

TALKING BEACONS FOR ROAD CROSSINGS

Among the various devices used by the Police during a Pedestrian Crossing Week were the talking beacons seen above. Operated by remote control these beacons give warning and good advice from a loud speaker fitted in the base.

is officially off duty and has changed from uniform into civilian clothes, he is still a police officer and if duty calls he has to answer. This is true even of his annual leave. Should some grave emergency arise requiring every officer to be on duty, then he will have to cut short his holiday and obey the order which recalls him to his station.

But after all, our Police are, like ourselves, only human, and require rest and relaxation as much as any of us do. You will find that all Police Forces have recreation clubs which provide every kind of game, sport and amusement for their members.

Our policemen, too, have the satisfaction of knowing that theirs is indeed a worth-while job which can only be performed efficiently by men of the highest character and intelligence. Our policemen and women are the servants of the public of which you and I are members ; and as they are always

ready to help us when we need them—whether it be to catch the burglar who has broken into our home or to tell us the best way to the railway station—so we must be ready to assist them in their work in every possible way.

If you travel abroad, you will notice that most Continental police are armed. The French *gendarme*, for example, has his pistol, just as the Spanish *civile* has his carbine. The British constable does not carry firearms nor does he inspire fear or distrust. The power of our police does not rest on armed force, but on the support and approval of the ordinary men and women whose lives and interest they protect. Our Police work in co-operation with the public in seeing that our laws are obeyed. Compare Britain's record with that of other nations and you will find the measure of police efficiency in the comparative absence of crime and disorder in the United Kingdom.

Fox Photos.

LEARNING THE " SAFETY FIRST " RULE

These beacons can move their heads round, and their lips move as they give their Safety First advice. Among the many tasks of the Police the safeguarding of school children at road crossings has a special place.

ONE MADCAP WINDY DAY

Specially drawn for this work.

It is Nature in her many moods that more than any other subject inspires the poet to take his pen and tell us of what he has seen. Though he may write of many things there is nearly always some touch of Nature's wonders in the background. In the drawing above the artist depicts a scene such as the one which inspired William Howitt when he wrote his gay, galloping, carefree poem "The Wind in a Frolic" which appears in "A Children's Treasury of Verse" in the following pages.

A Children's
Treasury
of Verse

Little Masterpieces
of To=Day
and Yesterday

THE JOY OF LIFE

Here set out in the following pages is an anthology or collection of poems which has been specially prepared for *you*. The poems selected are from the published works of some of our greatest poets whilst, in addition, there are verses written by the most popular children's poets of to-day.

A CHILDREN'S TREASURY OF VERSE

The Lake Isle of Innisfree

I WILL arise and go now, and go to Innisfree,
  And a small cabin build there, of clay and wattles made ;
Nine bean rows will I have there, a hive for the honey-bee,
And live alone in the bee-loud glade.

And I shall have some peace there, for peace comes dropping slow,
Dropping from the veils of the morning to where the cricket sings ;
There midnight's all a-glimmer, and noon a purple glow,
And evening full of the linnet's wings.

I will arise and go now, for always night and day
I hear lake water lapping with low sounds by the shore;
While I stand on the roadway, or on the pavements gray,
I hear it in the deep heart's core.

W. B. Yeats.

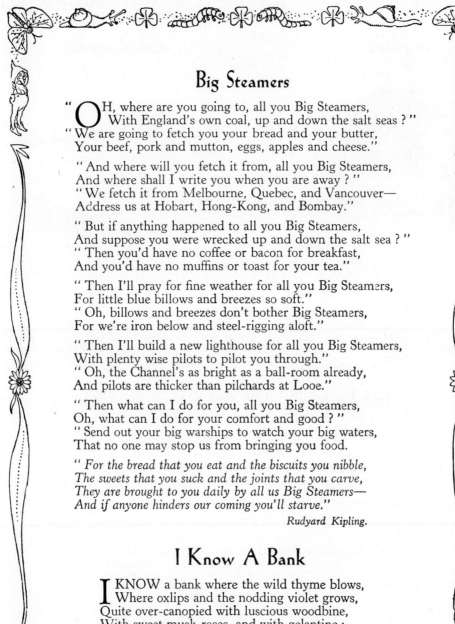

Big Steamers

"OH, where are you going to, all you Big Steamers,
  With England's own coal, up and down the salt seas?"
"We are going to fetch you your bread and your butter,
  Your beef, pork and mutton, eggs, apples and cheese."

"And where will you fetch it from, all you Big Steamers,
  And where shall I write you when you are away?"
"We fetch it from Melbourne, Quebec, and Vancouver—
  Address us at Hobart, Hong-Kong, and Bombay."

"But if anything happened to all you Big Steamers,
  And suppose you were wrecked up and down the salt sea?"
"Then you'd have no coffee or bacon for breakfast,
  And you'd have no muffins or toast for your tea."

"Then I'll pray for fine weather for all you Big Steamers,
  For little blue billows and breezes so soft."
"Oh, billows and breezes don't bother Big Steamers,
  For we're iron below and steel-rigging aloft."

"Then I'll build a new lighthouse for all you Big Steamers,
  With plenty wise pilots to pilot you through."
"Oh, the Channel's as bright as a ball-room already,
  And pilots are thicker than pilchards at Looe."

"Then what can I do for you, all you Big Steamers,
  Oh, what can I do for your comfort and good?"
"Send out your big warships to watch your big waters,
  That no one may stop us from bringing you food.

"For the bread that you eat and the biscuits you nibble,
  The sweets that you suck and the joints that you carve,
They are brought to you daily by all us Big Steamers—
  And if anyone hinders our coming you'll starve."

                              Rudyard Kipling.

I Know A Bank

I KNOW a bank where the wild thyme blows,
  Where oxlips and the nodding violet grows,
Quite over-canopied with luscious woodbine,
With sweet musk-roses, and with gelantine:
There sleeps Titania, some time of the night,
Lull'd in these flowers with dances and delight;
And there the snake throws her enamell'd skin,
Weed wide enough to **wrap** a fairy in.

                              William Shakespeare.

The Gardener

THE gardener does not love to talk,
He makes me keep the gravel walk;
And when he puts his tools away,
He locks the door and takes the key.

Away behind the currant row
Where no one else but Cook may go;
Far in the plots, I see him dig,
Old and serious, brown and big.

He digs the flowers, green, red and blue,
Nor wishes to be spoken to.
He digs the flowers and cuts the hay,
And never seems to want to play.

Silly gardener! Summer goes,
And winter comes with pinching toes,
When in the garden bare and brown
You must lay your barrow down.

Well now, while the summer stays,
Profit by these garden days!
O how much wiser you would be
To play at Indian wars with me!

Robert Louis Stevenson.

The Fairies

UP the airy mountain,
　　Down the rushy glen,
We daren't go a-hunting
For fear of little men ;
Wee folk, good folk,
Trooping all together :
Green jacket, red cap,
And white owl's feather !

Down along the rocky shore
Some make their home,
They live on crispy pancakes
Of yellow tide-foam ;
Some in the reeds
Of the black mountain-lake,
With frogs for their watch-dogs,
All night awake.

High on the hill-top
The old King sits ;
He is now so old and grey
He's nigh lost his wits ;
With a bridge of white mist
Columbkill he crosses,
On his stately journeys
From Slieveleague to Rosses ;
Or going up with music
On cold starry nights,
To sup with the Queen
Of the gay Northern Lights.

They stole little Bridget
For seven years long ;
When she came down again
Her friends were all gone.
They took her lightly back,
Between the night and morrow,
They thought that she was fast
　　asleep,
But she was dead with sorrow.
They have kept her ever since
Deep within the lake,
On a bed of flag leaves,
Watching till she wake.

By the craggy hill-side,
Through the mosses bare,
They have planted thorn-trees
For pleasure here and there.
Is any man so daring
As dig one up in spite,
He shall find their thornies set
In his bed at night.

Up the airy mountain,
Down the rushy glen,
We daren't go a-hunting
For fear of little men ;
Wee folk, good folk,
Trooping all together ;
Green jacket, red cap,
And white owl's feather !

William Allingham.

A March Day

THE cock is crowing,
　　The stream is flowing,
The small birds twitter,
The lake doth glitter,
The green field sleeps in the
　　sun ;
The oldest and youngest
Are at work with the strongest ;
The cattle are grazing,
Their heads never raising,
There are forty feeding like one !

Like an army defeated,
The snow hath retreated,
And now doth fare ill
On the top of the bare hill ;
The ploughboy is
　　whooping-anon-anon ;
There's joy in the mountains ;
There's life in the fountains ;
Small clouds are sailing ;
Blue sky prevailing ;
The rain is over and gone !

William Wordsworth.

Cargoes

QUINQUIREME of Nineveh from distant Ophir
Rowing home to haven in sunny Palestine,
With a cargo of ivory,
And apes and peacocks,
Sandalwood, cedarwood, and sweet white wine.

Stately Spanish galleon coming from the Isthmus,
Dipping through the Tropics by the palm-green shores
With a cargo of diamonds,
Emeralds, amethysts,
Topazes, and cinnamon and gold moidores.

Dirty British coaster with a salt-caked smoke-stack,
Butting through the Channel in the mad March days,
With a cargo of Tyne coal,
Road-rail, pig-lead,
Firewood, ironware and cheap tin trays.

John Masefield.

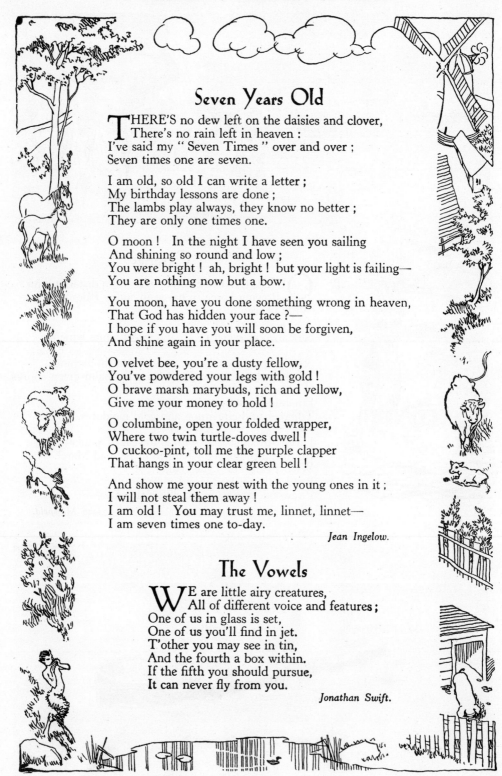

Seven Years Old

THERE'S no dew left on the daisies and clover,
  There's no rain left in heaven :
I've said my " Seven Times " over and over ;
Seven times one are seven.

I am old, so old I can write a letter ;
My birthday lessons are done ;
The lambs play always, they know no better ;
They are only one times one.

O moon !   In the night I have seen you sailing
And shining so round and low ;
You were bright ! ah, bright ! but your light is failing—
You are nothing now but a bow.

You moon, have you done something wrong in heaven,
That God has hidden your face ?—
I hope if you have you will soon be forgiven,
And shine again in your place.

O velvet bee, you're a dusty fellow,
You've powdered your legs with gold !
O brave marsh marybuds, rich and yellow,
Give me your money to hold !

O columbine, open your folded wrapper,
Where two twin turtle-doves dwell !
O cuckoo-pint, toll me the purple clapper
That hangs in your clear green bell !

And show me your nest with the young ones in it ;
I will not steal them away !
I am old !   You may trust me, linnet, linnet—
I am seven times one to-day.

Jean Ingelow.

The Vowels

WE are little airy creatures,
  All of different voice and features ;
One of us in glass is set,
One of us you'll find in jet.
T'other you may see in tin,
And the fourth a box within.
If the fifth you should pursue,
It can never fly from you.

Jonathan Swift.

The Cat and the Broom

THE broom looks tattered and tired to-day,
The raggedest stick of a broom ;
It couldn't reach up for a cobweb grey
Or sweep out the smallest room.

And Trusty Tompkins, our little black cat,
With fur like the finest silk,
Is curled up tight in a ball on the mat
Too sleepy to drink his milk.

But the bad old broom looks rakish and sly,
As if it had been on the spree ;
And Puss from a narrow satin eye
Looks wickedly out at me.

Ho ho ! I know what the rascal pair
In the midnight hours were at ;
It wasn't mousing or sweeping the stair
That made them look like that.

I know by the old broom's battered plight
And Tompkins' look of sin
They were both of them out with a witch last night,
And they've only just got in.

A. A. Kenny.

Someone

SOMEONE came knocking
At my wee, small door ;
Someone came knocking,
I'm sure—sure—sure ;
I listened, I opened,
I looked to left and right,
But nought there was a-stirring
In the still dark night ;

Only the busy beetle
Tap-tapping in the wall,
Only from the forest
The screech-owl's call,
Only the cricket whistling
While the dewdrops fall,
So I know not who came knocking,
At all, at all, at all.

Walter De La Mare.

The Naughty Boy

1

THERE was a naughty Boy,
A naughty Boy was he,
He would not stop at home,
He could not quiet be—
He took
In his Knapsack
A Book
Full of vowels
And a shirt
With some towels—
A slight cap
For night-cap—
A hair brush,
Comb ditto,
New stockings,
For old ones
Would split O !
This knapsack
Tight at's back
He rivetted close
And followed his Nose,
To the North,
To the North,
And followed his nose
To the North.

2

There was a naughty Boy,
And a naughty Boy was he,
He ran away to Scotland
The people for to see—
Then he found
That the ground
Was as hard,
That a yard,
Was as long,
That a song
Was as merry,
That a cherry
Was as red—
That lead
Was as weighty,
That fourscore
Was as eighty,
That a door
Was as wooden
As in England—
So he stood in his shoes
And he wonder'd,
He wonder'd,
He stood in his shoes
And he wonder'd.

John Keats.

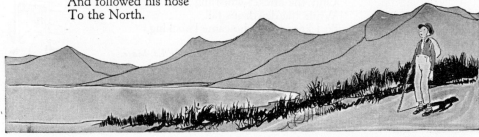

Who Is It?

WHO goes slipping by the old oak tree,
Who goes tripping with a one-two-three,
Who's been waking up the primrose pale,
Who's been shaking ev'ry wee lamb's tail?

Who's been marching where the daffodils grow,
Who's been starching all their frills just so,
Who's that playing with the bunny over there,
Playing and straying with the wind in his hair?

P'raps 'tis a tricksy elf, little and shy,
Or a wee pixie man, just so high.
There he goes creeping, look, on tip-tip-toe,
Who is it peeping there?   I don't know.

Enid Blyton.

The Fairies' Song

YOU spotted snakes with double tongue,
Thorny hedge-hogs, be not seen;
Newts, and blind-worms, do no wrong;
Come not near our fairy queen.

Philomel, with melody,
Sing in our sweet lullaby;
Lulla, lulla, lullaby; lulla, lulla, lullaby;
Never harm, nor spell, nor charm,
Come our lovely lady nigh;
So, good night, with lullaby.

Weaving spiders come not here;
Hence, you long-legged spinners, hence!
Beetles black, approach not near;
Worm, nor snail, do no offence.
Hence, away! now all is well.
One aloof stand sentinel.

William Shakespeare.

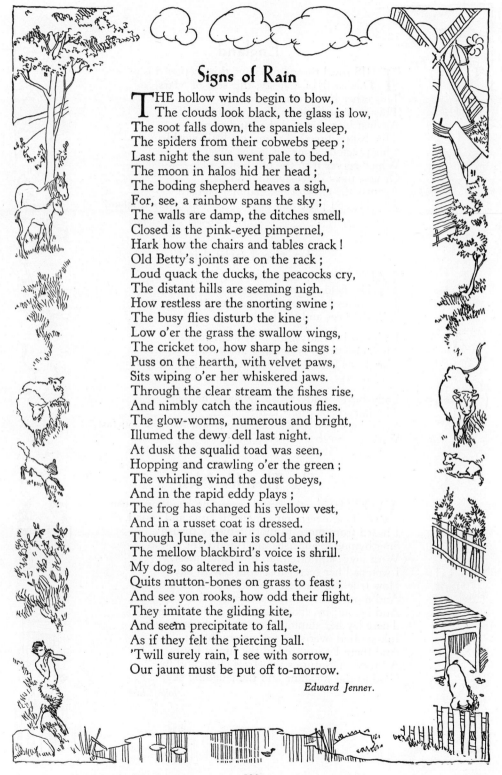

Signs of Rain

THE hollow winds begin to blow,
The clouds look black, the glass is low,
The soot falls down, the spaniels sleep,
The spiders from their cobwebs peep ;
Last night the sun went pale to bed,
The moon in halos hid her head ;
The boding shepherd heaves a sigh,
For, see, a rainbow spans the sky ;
The walls are damp, the ditches smell,
Closed is the pink-eyed pimpernel,
Hark how the chairs and tables crack !
Old Betty's joints are on the rack ;
Loud quack the ducks, the peacocks cry,
The distant hills are seeming nigh.
How restless are the snorting swine ;
The busy flies disturb the kine ;
Low o'er the grass the swallow wings,
The cricket too, how sharp he sings ;
Puss on the hearth, with velvet paws,
Sits wiping o'er her whiskered jaws.
Through the clear stream the fishes rise,
And nimbly catch the incautious flies.
The glow-worms, numerous and bright,
Illumed the dewy dell last night.
At dusk the squalid toad was seen,
Hopping and crawling o'er the green ;
The whirling wind the dust obeys,
And in the rapid eddy plays ;
The frog has changed his yellow vest,
And in a russet coat is dressed.
Though June, the air is cold and still,
The mellow blackbird's voice is shrill.
My dog, so altered in his taste,
Quits mutton-bones on grass to feast ;
And see yon rooks, how odd their flight,
They imitate the gliding kite,
And seem precipitate to fall,
As if they felt the piercing ball.
'Twill surely rain, I see with sorrow,
Our jaunt must be put off to-morrow.

Edward Jenner.

England

THIS royal throne of kings, this scepter'd isle,
   This earth of majesty, this seat of Mars,
This other Eden, demi-paradise,
This fortress built by Nature for herself
Against infection and the hand of war,
This happy breed of men, this little world,
This precious stone set in the silver sea,
Which serves it in the office of a wall
Or as a moat defensive to a house,
Against the envy of less happier lands,
This blessed plot, this earth, this realm, this England.

William Shakespeare.

To the Lady-bird

LADY-BIRD ! Lady-bird ! fly away home ;
   The field-mouse is gone to her nest,
The daisies have shut up their sweet sleepy eyes,
And the bees and the birds are at rest.

Lady-bird ! Lady-bird ! fly away home ;
The glow-worm is lighting her lamp,
The dew's falling fast, and your fine speckled wings
Will be wet with the close-clinging damp.

Lady-bird ! Lady-bird ! fly away home ;
The fairy-bells tinkle afar ;
Make haste, or they'll catch you, and harness you fast,
With a cobweb to Oberon's car.

Anon.

The Thrush's Nest

WITHIN a thick and spreading hawthorn bush
   That overhung a molehill large and round,
I heard from morn to morn a merry thrush
Sing hymns to sunrise, and I drank the sound
With joy ; and often, an intruding guest,
I watched her secret toil from day to day—
How true she warped the moss, to form a nest,
And modelled it within with wood and clay ;
And by and by, like heath bells gilt with dew,
There lay her shining eggs, as bright as flowers,
Ink-spotted over shells of greeny blue ;
And there I witnessed in the sunny hours,
A brood of Nature's minstrels chirp and fly,
Glad as the sunshine and the laughing sky.

John Clare.

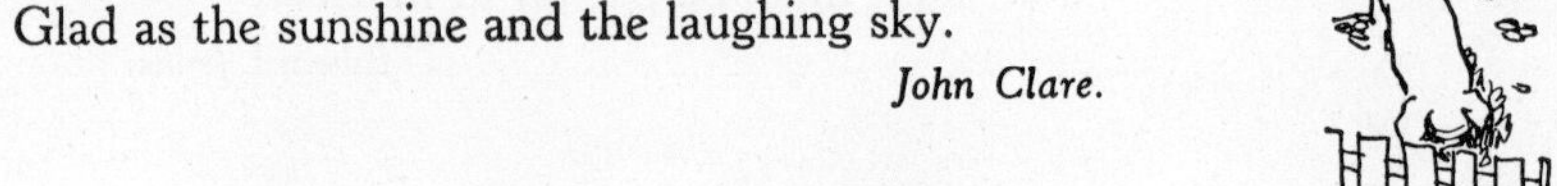

Spring

SPRING, the sweet Spring, is the year's
  pleasant king ;
Then blooms each thing, then maids dance
  in a ring,
Cold doth not sting, the pretty birds do sing,
Cuckoo, jug-jug, pu-we, to-witta-woo !

The palm and may make country houses gay,
Lambs frisk and play, the shepherds pipe all day,
And we hear aye birds tune this merry lay :
Cuckoo, jug-jug, pu-we, to-witta-woo !

The fields breathe sweet, the daisies kiss our feet,
Young lovers meet, old wives a-sunning sit,
In every street these tunes our ears do greet :
Cuckoo, jug-jug, pu-we, to-witta-woo !
Spring, the sweet Spring !

Thomas Nash.

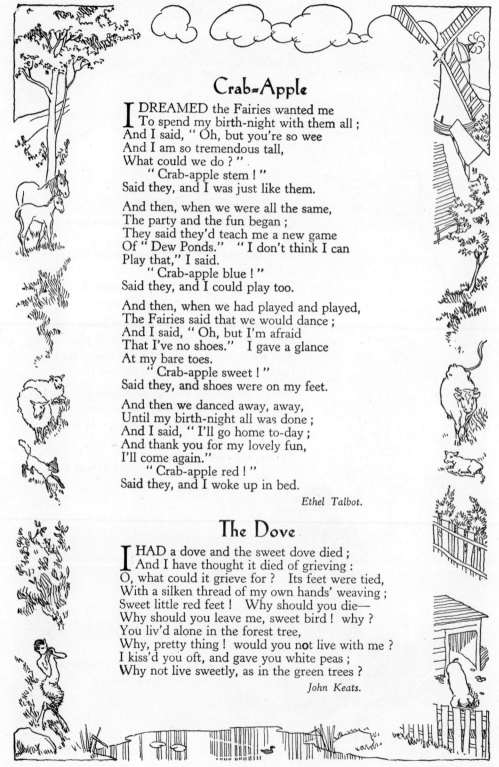

Crab-Apple

I DREAMED the Fairies wanted me
To spend my birth-night with them all ;
And I said, " Oh, but you're so wee
And I am so tremendous tall,
What could we do ? "
   " Crab-apple stem ! "
Said they, and I was just like them.

And then, when we were all the same,
The party and the fun began ;
They said they'd teach me a new game
Of " Dew Ponds." " I don't think I can
Play that," I said.
   " Crab-apple blue ! "
Said they, and I could play too.

And then, when we had played and played,
The Fairies said that we would dance ;
And I said, " Oh, but I'm afraid
That I've no shoes." I gave a glance
At my bare toes.
   " Crab-apple sweet ! "
Said they, and shoes were on my feet.

And then we danced away, away,
Until my birth-night all was done ;
And I said, " I'll go home to-day ;
And thank you for my lovely fun,
I'll come again."
   " Crab-apple red ! "
Said they, and I woke up in bed.

Ethel Talbot.

The Dove

I HAD a dove and the sweet dove died ;
And I have thought it died of grieving :
O, what could it grieve for ? Its feet were tied,
With a silken thread of my own hands' weaving ;
Sweet little red feet ! Why should you die—
Why should you leave me, sweet bird ! why ?
You liv'd alone in the forest tree,
Why, pretty thing ! would you not live with me ?
I kiss'd you oft, and gave you white peas ;
Why not live sweetly, as in the green trees ?

John Keats.

The Beggar Maid

HER arms across her breast she laid,
  She was more fair than words
    can say :
Bare-footed came the beggar maid
Before the king Cophetua.
In robe and crown the king stept down,
To meet and greet her on her way ;
" It is no wonder," said the lords,
" She is more beautiful than day."

As shines the moon in clouded skies,
She in her poor attire was seen :
One praised her ankles, one her eyes,
One her dark hair and lovesome mien.
So sweet a face, such angel grace,
In all that land had never been :
Cophetua sware a royal oath :
" This beggar maid shall be my queen ! "

Tennyson.

Rabbit=Song

NOBODY knows, nobody knows,
  Where the very first violet grows,
Nobody sees, nobody sees,
The wind that awakens the shiv'ring trees,
Nobody hears with prick'd up ears,
The splash of a weeping fairy's tears,
No one but me, just only me,
A bunny that peeps by an old oak tree.

Nobody spies, nobody spies,
The things I see with my two brown eyes,
Nobody creeps, nobody peeps,
In a shadowy dell where a pixie sleeps,
Nobody knows, nobody goes,
Where I am a-dancing on soft tippytoes,
No one but me, just only me,
A bunny that peeps by an old oak tree.

Enid Blyton.

Winter

WHEN icicles hang by the wall,
  And Dick the shepherd blows his nail,
And Tom bears logs into the hall,
And milk comes frozen home in pail,
When blood is nipp'd, and ways be foul,
Then nightly sings the staring owl,
Tu-who ;
Tu-whit, tu-who, a merry note,
While greasy Joan doth keel the pot.

When all around the wind doth blow,
And coughing drowns the parson's saw,
And birds sit brooding in the snow,
And Marion's nose looks red and raw,
When roasted crabs hiss in the bowl,
Then nightly sings the staring owl,
Tu-who ;
Tu-whit, tu-who, a merry note,
While greasy Joan doth keel the pot.

William Shakespeare.

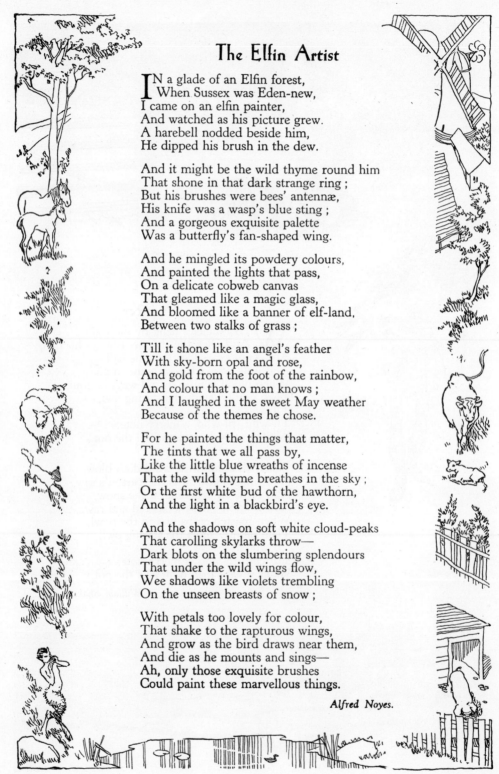

The Elfin Artist

IN a glade of an Elfin forest,
When Sussex was Eden-new,
I came on an elfin painter,
And watched as his picture grew.
A harebell nodded beside him,
He dipped his brush in the dew.

And it might be the wild thyme round him
That shone in that dark strange ring ;
But his brushes were bees' antennæ,
His knife was a wasp's blue sting ;
And a gorgeous exquisite palette
Was a butterfly's fan-shaped wing.

And he mingled its powdery colours,
And painted the lights that pass,
On a delicate cobweb canvas
That gleamed like a magic glass,
And bloomed like a banner of elf-land,
Between two stalks of grass ;

Till it shone like an angel's feather
With sky-born opal and rose,
And gold from the foot of the rainbow,
And colour that no man knows ;
And I laughed in the sweet May weather
Because of the themes he chose.

For he painted the things that matter,
The tints that we all pass by,
Like the little blue wreaths of incense
That the wild thyme breathes in the sky ;
Or the first white bud of the hawthorn,
And the light in a blackbird's eye.

And the shadows on soft white cloud-peaks
That carolling skylarks throw—
Dark blots on the slumbering splendours
That under the wild wings flow,
Wee shadows like violets trembling
On the unseen breasts of snow ;

With petals too lovely for colour,
That shake to the rapturous wings,
And grow as the bird draws near them,
And die as he mounts and sings—
Ah, only those exquisite brushes
Could paint these marvellous things.

Alfred Noyes.

Home=Thoughts From Abroad

OH, to be in England
    Now that April's there,
And whoever wakes in England
Sees, some morning, unaware,
That the lowest boughs and the brushwood sheaf
Round the elm-tree bole are in tiny leaf,
While the chaffinch sings on the orchard bough
In England—now !

And after April, when May follows,
And the whitethroat builds, and all the swallows !
Hark, where my blossomed pear-tree in the hedge
Leans to the field and scatters on the clover
Blossoms and dewdrops—at the bent spray's edge—
That's the wise thrush ; he sings each song twice over,
Lest you should think he never could recapture
The first fine careless rapture !
And though the fields look rough with hoary dew,
All will be gay when noontide wakes anew
The buttercups, the little children's dower
—Far brighter than this gaudy melon-flower !

                                        Robert Browning.

First Spring Morning—
A Child's Poem

LOOK! Look! The spring is come:
O feel the gentle air,
That wanders thro' the boughs to burst
The thick buds everywhere!
The birds are glad to see
The high unclouded sun:
Winter is fled away, they sing,
The gay time is begun.

Adown the meadows green
Let us go dance and play,
And look for violets in the lane,
And ramble far away
To gather primroses,
That in the woodland grow,
And hunt for oxlips, or if yet
The blades of bluebells show:

There the old woodman gruff
Hath half the coppice cut,
And weaves the hurdles all day long
Beside his willow hut.
We'll steal on him, and then
Startle him, all with glee
Singing our song of winter fled
And summer soon to be.

Robert Bridges.

The Owl

WHEN cats run home and light is come,
And dew is cold upon the ground,
And the far-off stream is dumb
And the whirring sail goes round,
And the whirring sail goes round:
Alone and warming his five wits
The white owl in the belfry sits.

When merry milkmaids click the latch,
And rarely smells the new-mown hay,
And the cock hath sung beneath the thatch
Twice or thrice his roundelay,
Twice or thrice his roundelay;
Alone and warming his five wits
The white owl in the belfry sits.

Tennyson.

Who Has Seen the Wind?

WHO has seen the wind?
  Neither I nor you;
But when the leaves hang trembling,
The wind is passing through.

Who has seen the wind?
Neither you nor I;
But when the trees bow down their heads,
The wind is passing by.

O wind, why do you never rest,
Wandering, whistling to and fro,
Bringing rain out of the west,
From the dim north bringing snow?

Christina Rossetti.

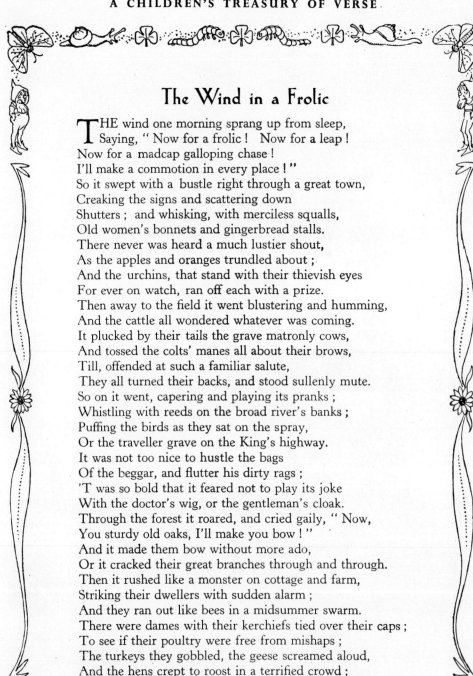

The Wind in a Frolic

THE wind one morning sprang up from sleep,
Saying, " Now for a frolic !   Now for a leap !
Now for a madcap galloping chase !
I'll make a commotion in every place ! "
So it swept with a bustle right through a great town,
Creaking the signs and scattering down
Shutters ; and whisking, with merciless squalls,
Old women's bonnets and gingerbread stalls.
There never was heard a much lustier shout,
As the apples and oranges trundled about ;
And the urchins, that stand with their thievish eyes
For ever on watch, ran off each with a prize.
Then away to the field it went blustering and humming,
And the cattle all wondered whatever was coming.
It plucked by their tails the grave matronly cows,
And tossed the colts' manes all about their brows,
Till, offended at such a familiar salute,
They all turned their backs, and stood sullenly mute.
So on it went, capering and playing its pranks ;
Whistling with reeds on the broad river's banks ;
Puffing the birds as they sat on the spray,
Or the traveller grave on the King's highway.
It was not too nice to hustle the bags
Of the beggar, and flutter his dirty rags ;
'T was so bold that it feared not to play its joke
With the doctor's wig, or the gentleman's cloak.
Through the forest it roared, and cried gaily, " Now,
You sturdy old oaks, I'll make you bow ! "
And it made them bow without more ado,
Or it cracked their great branches through and through.
Then it rushed like a monster on cottage and farm,
Striking their dwellers with sudden alarm ;
And they ran out like bees in a midsummer swarm.
There were dames with their kerchiefs tied over their caps ;
To see if their poultry were free from mishaps ;
The turkeys they gobbled, the geese screamed aloud,
And the hens crept to roost in a terrified crowd ;
There was rearing of ladders, and logs laying on
Where the thatch from the roof threatened soon to be gone.

But the wind had passed on, and had met in a lane
With a schoolboy, who panted and struggled in vain ;
For it tossed him and twirled him, then passed, and he stood
With his hat in a pool and his shoe in the mud.

*   *   *   ●   ●

But away went the wind in its holiday glee,
And now it was far on the billowy sea,
And the lordly ships felt its staggering blow,
And the little boats darted to and fro.
But lo ! it was night, and it sank to rest,
On the sea-bird's rock in the gleaming West,
Laughing to think, in its fearful fun,
How little of mischief it had done.

William Howitt.

The Lucky Ducks

THE ducks go out on rainy days,
  And never wear goloshes,
And no one calls to them and says,
" Put on your mackintoshes."

They never wrap their necks about
With scarves when it is chilly,
And never take umbrellas out,
They wouldn't be so silly.

But when it rains I have to do
Exactly what I'm told,
And even put on gaiters too,
In case I catch a cold.

And with umbrella out I tramp,
In mackintosh and coat,
Goloshes to keep out the damp,
And scarf around my throat.

But though the ducks wear none of these,
And never, never will,
I haven't heard them cough or sneeze
Because they've got a chill.

And when it's raining very hard,
I wish *I* had the luck
To go splish-splashing round the yard
And be a dripping duck !

Enid Blyton.

There was an Old Woman

THERE was an old woman, as I've heard tell,
 She went to market her eggs for to sell;
She went to market all on a market day;
And she fell asleep on the king's highway.

There came by a pedlar whose name was Stout,
He cut her petticoats all round about;
He cut her petticoats up to her knees,
Which made the old woman to shiver and freeze.

When this little woman first did wake,
She began to shiver and she began to shake.
She began to wonder and she began to cry,
 "Lauk-a-mercy on me, this is none of I:

"But if it be I, as I do hope it be,
I've a little dog at home, and he'll know me;
If it be I, he'll wag his little tail,
And if it be not I, he'll loudly bark and wail!"

Home went the little woman all in the dark,
Up got the little dog, and he began to bark;
He began to bark, so she began to cry,
"Lauk-a-mercy on me, this is none of I!"

Anon.

Drake's Drum

DRAKE he's in his hammock an' a thousand mile away,
(Capten, art tha sleepin' there below ?)
Slung atween the round shot in Nombre Dios Bay,
An' dreamin' arl the time o' Plymouth Hoe.
Yarnder lumes the Island, yarnder lie the ships,
Wi' sailor lads a dancin' heel-an'-toe,
An' the shore-lights flashin', an' the night-tide dashin',
He sees it arl so plainly as he saw et long ago.

Drake he was a Devon man, an' ruled the Devon seas,
(Capten, art tha sleepin' there below ?)
Rovin' tho' his death fell, he went wi' heart at ease,
An' dreamin' arl the time o' Plymouth Hoe.
" Take my drum to England, hang et by the shore,
Strike et when your powder's runnin' low ;
If the Dons sight Devon, I'll quit the port o' Heaven,
An' drum them up the Channel as we drummed them long ago."

Drake he's in his hammock till the great Armadas come,
(Capten, art tha sleepin' there below ?)
Slung atween the round shot, listenin' for the drum,
An' dreamin' arl the time o' Plymouth Hoe.
Call him on the deep sea, call him up the Sound,
Call him when ye sail to meet the foe ;
Where the old trade's plyin' an' the old flag flyin'
They shall find him ware and wakin', as they found him long ago !

Henry Newbolt

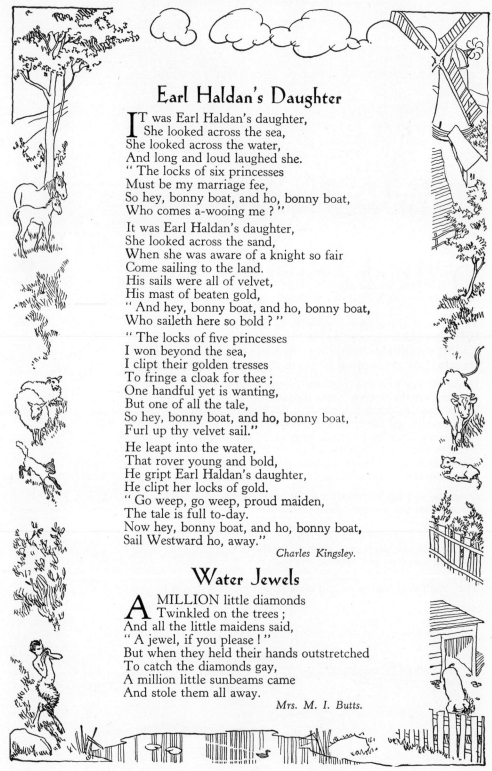

Earl Haldan's Daughter

IT was Earl Haldan's daughter,
She looked across the sea,
She looked across the water,
And long and loud laughed she.
" The locks of six princesses
Must be my marriage fee,
So hey, bonny boat, and ho, bonny boat,
Who comes a-wooing me ? "

It was Earl Haldan's daughter,
She looked across the sand,
When she was aware of a knight so fair
Come sailing to the land.
His sails were all of velvet,
His mast of beaten gold,
" And hey, bonny boat, and ho, bonny boat,
Who saileth here so bold ? "

" The locks of five princesses
I won beyond the sea,
I clipt their golden tresses
To fringe a cloak for thee ;
One handful yet is wanting,
But one of all the tale,
So hey, bonny boat, and ho, bonny boat,
Furl up thy velvet sail."

He leapt into the water,
That rover young and bold,
He gript Earl Haldan's daughter,
He clipt her locks of gold.
" Go weep, go weep, proud maiden,
The tale is full to-day.
Now hey, bonny boat, and ho, bonny boat,
Sail Westward ho, away."

Charles Kingsley.

Water Jewels

A MILLION little diamonds
Twinkled on the trees ;
And all the little maidens said,
" A jewel, if you please ! "
But when they held their hands outstretched
To catch the diamonds gay,
A million little sunbeams came
And stole them all away.

Mrs. M. I. Butts.

The Owl and The Pussy=Cat

THE Owl and the Pussy-Cat went to sea
In a beautiful pea-green boat :
They took some honey, and plenty of money
Wrapped up in a five-pound note.
The Owl looked up to the moon above,
And sang to a small guitar :
"O lovely Pussy ! O Pussy, my love !
What a beautiful Pussy you are—
        You are,
What a beautiful Pussy you are ! "

Pussy said to the Owl : "You elegant fowl !
How charmingly sweet you sing !
O let us be married—too long we have tarried—
But what shall we do for a ring ? "
They sailed away for a year and a day
To the land where the Bong-tree grows,
And there in a wood, a Piggy-wig stood
With a ring in the end of his nose—
        His nose,
With a ring in the end of his nose.

"Dear Pig, are you willing to sell for one shilling
Your ring ? " Said the Piggy, "I will."
So they took it away, and were married next day
By the turkey who lives on the hill.
They dined upon mince and slices of quince,
Which they ate with a runcible spoon,
And hand in hand on the edge of the sand
They danced by the light of the moon—
        The moon,
They danced by the light of the moon.

Edward Lear.

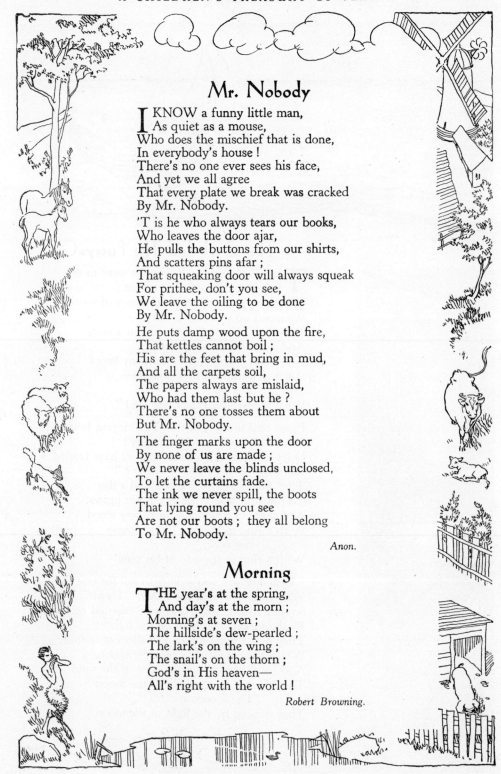

Mr. Nobody

I KNOW a funny little man,
As quiet as a mouse,
Who does the mischief that is done,
In everybody's house !
There's no one ever sees his face,
And yet we all agree
That every plate we break was cracked
By Mr. Nobody.

'T is he who always tears our books,
Who leaves the door ajar,
He pulls the buttons from our shirts,
And scatters pins afar ;
That squeaking door will always squeak
For prithee, don't you see,
We leave the oiling to be done
By Mr. Nobody.

He puts damp wood upon the fire,
That kettles cannot boil ;
His are the feet that bring in mud,
And all the carpets soil,
The papers always are mislaid,
Who had them last but he ?
There's no one tosses them about
But Mr. Nobody.

The finger marks upon the door
By none of us are made ;
We never leave the blinds unclosed,
To let the curtains fade.
The ink we never spill, the boots
That lying round you see
Are not our boots ; they all belong
To Mr. Nobody.

Anon.

Morning

THE year's at the spring,
And day's at the morn ;
Morning's at seven ;
The hillside's dew-pearled ;
The lark's on the wing ;
The snail's on the thorn ;
God's in His heaven—
All's right with the world !

Robert Browning.

Goblins' Lanterns

IT'S dark outside—but I can see
A big red glow beside the hill :
The man who makes the horses' shoes
Goes hammer, hammer, hammer still.

And sparks fly out up in the air,
And fall away into the night ;
But as they're falling, one by one,
They vanish, suddenly, from sight.

I think they're Goblins in the wood,
Who pass at night and catch each spark,
To put inside their lanterns when
They're hobblin' homewards in the dark.

Marion St. John Webb.

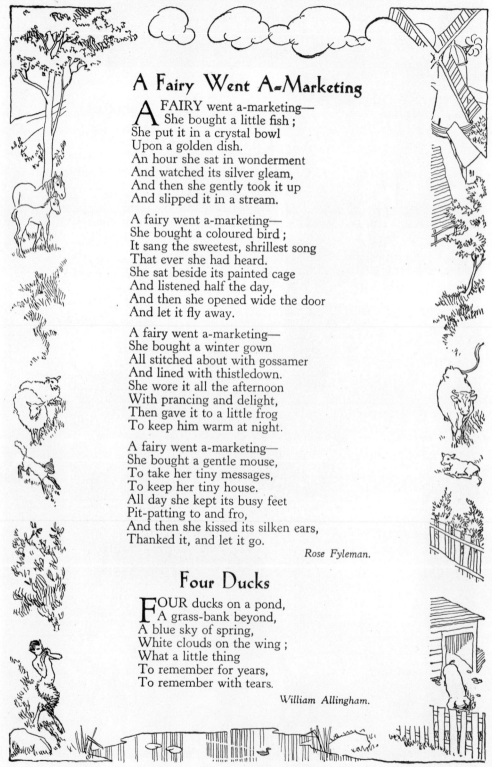

A Fairy Went A-Marketing

A FAIRY went a-marketing—
　　She bought a little fish;
She put it in a crystal bowl
Upon a golden dish.
An hour she sat in wonderment
And watched its silver gleam,
And then she gently took it up
And slipped it in a stream.

A fairy went a-marketing—
She bought a coloured bird;
It sang the sweetest, shrillest song
That ever she had heard.
She sat beside its painted cage
And listened half the day,
And then she opened wide the door
And let it fly away.

A fairy went a-marketing—
She bought a winter gown
All stitched about with gossamer
And lined with thistledown.
She wore it all the afternoon
With prancing and delight,
Then gave it to a little frog
To keep him warm at night.

A fairy went a-marketing—
She bought a gentle mouse,
To take her tiny messages,
To keep her tiny house.
All day she kept its busy feet
Pit-patting to and fro,
And then she kissed its silken ears,
Thanked it, and let it go.

Rose Fyleman.

Four Ducks

FOUR ducks on a pond,
　　A grass-bank beyond,
A blue sky of spring,
White clouds on the wing;
What a little thing
To remember for years,
To remember with tears.

William Allingham.

The First Wild Rose

OYEZ, oyez, there is news to-day !
Come, you folk of the woodland way,
Hasten, folk of the velvet toes,
And see the birth of the first wild rose.
Follow me soft between the trees,
Bunnies and butterflies, birds and bees.
Run, little dormouse, bring your mate,
And tell the squirrel I may not wait.
For the kiss of the sun will wake the rose,
So hasten, Wings and Velvety Toes.

Low on the hedge she lies asleep.
Come, you bunnies, and softly peep !
Fly, you butterflies hovering near
And kiss the sweetest rose of the year.
Palest pink will her petals be
When from the bud they are shaken free,
And sweet as honey her scent will come,
(Hush, little bees, too loud you hum),

. . . . . .

And hush now, folk of the velvet toes,
For the sun is waking the first wild rose !

Enid Blyton.

Old Shellover

"COME ! " said Old Shellover,
"What ? " says Creep.
" The horny old Gardener's fast asleep ;
The fat cock Thrush
To his nest has gone,
And the dew shines bright
In the rising Moon ;
Old Sallie Worm from her hole doth peep ;
Come ! " said Old Shellover.
"Ay ! " said Creep.

Walter De La Mare.

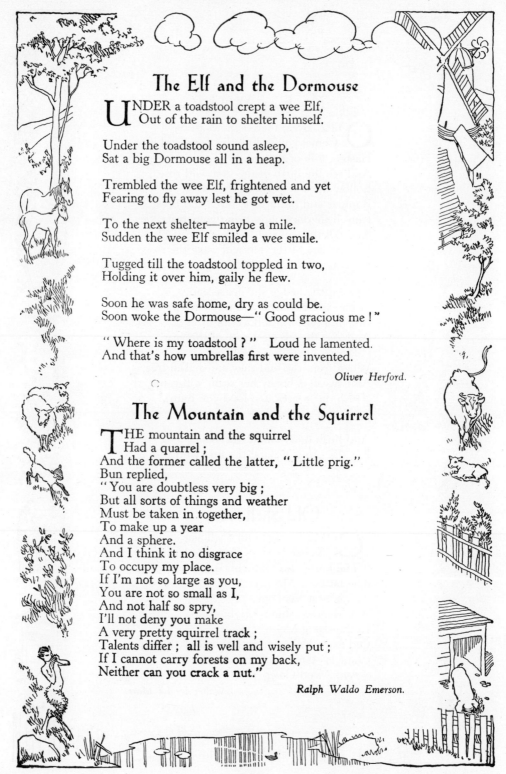

The Elf and the Dormouse

UNDER a toadstool crept a wee Elf,
  Out of the rain to shelter himself.

Under the toadstool sound asleep,
Sat a big Dormouse all in a heap.

Trembled the wee Elf, frightened and yet
Fearing to fly away lest he got wet.

To the next shelter—maybe a mile.
Sudden the wee Elf smiled a wee smile.

Tugged till the toadstool toppled in two,
Holding it over him, gaily he flew.

Soon he was safe home, dry as could be.
Soon woke the Dormouse—" Good gracious me ! "

" Where is my toadstool ? " Loud he lamented.
And that's how umbrellas first were invented.

Oliver Herford.

The Mountain and the Squirrel

THE mountain and the squirrel
  Had a quarrel ;
And the former called the latter, " Little prig."
Bun replied,
" You are doubtless very big ;
But all sorts of things and weather
Must be taken in together,
To make up a year
And a sphere.
And I think it no disgrace
To occupy my place.
If I'm not so large as you,
You are not so small as I,
And not half so spry,
I'll not deny you make
A very pretty squirrel track ;
Talents differ ; all is well and wisely put ;
If I cannot carry forests on my back,
Neither can you crack a nut."

Ralph Waldo Emerson.

Reading, Writing
and
Arithmetic

A Helping Hand
for
Tiny folk

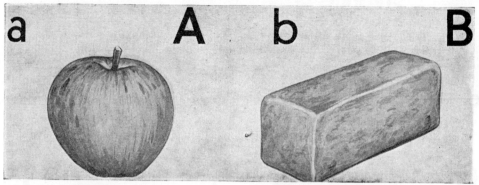

A is for apple
so round and so red.

B is for bread
which all children eat.

THE LETTERS OF THE ALPHABET (1)

There are twenty-six letters in our alphabet, and in this picture you are shown the first two of them, A and B. When we speak of an *alphabet* we mean the letters needed in building up the words used in our language. It is not a difficult word to understand, being formed by joining together the first two Greek letters which were called *alpha* and *beta*.

YOUR OWN SPECIAL CORNER

HERE is a very special corner prepared for you, the boys and girls who have loved to look at the pictures in this book, but who are as yet too small to read the printing by yourselves.

The pictures have shown you that the world is full of marvels, but you must not forget that some of the most wonderful things it contains have been made by men and women who were once no bigger than you are.

Great Chances Ahead

Some day, perhaps, many of you, when you are quite grown up, will go out into the world and help to do things better even than they are done to-day.

If you, to whom this is being read, are a little boy, you may one day design an aeroplane engine which will travel faster than anything has ever done before; you may build a great ship or a mighty bridge. Possibly, who knows? you may follow in the footsteps of the great inventors and help to make life easier and better for others than it is now.

Great chances lie ahead of you, boys and girls of to-day, but before you can grasp them you must learn to read that you may gain the knowledge that others have provided for you. You must learn to write and also to count. These in themselves are great things for little folk to do, and here in your own corner you can make a start to-day.

THE LETTERS OF THE ALPHABET—(2)

c C  d D

C is for cat
who can see in the dark.

D is for dog
with a very loud bark.

e E 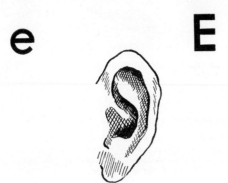 f F

E is for ears
with which we all hear.

F is for fire.
Take care when you're near.

g G  h H

G is for gate,
and for goat in the sun.

H is for hen.
How fast she can run!

LETTER C TO LETTER H

i I j J

I is for ink,
so black and so red.

J is for jam
that we spread on our bread.

k K l L

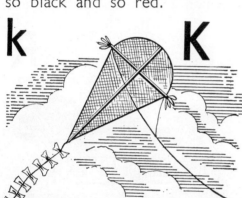

K is for kite,
please make one for me.

L is for little lamb,
frisky and wee.

m M n N

M is for mother.
We love her, we do.

N is for newspaper.
Read it all through.

LETTER I TO LETTER N

THE LETTERS OF THE ALPHABET—(4)

o O

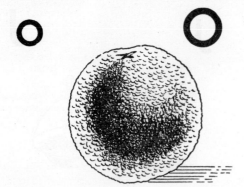

O is for orange,
golden and round.

P P

P is for potato
which grows in the ground.

q Q

Q is for queen
on a throne she is found.

r R

R is for rain
that falls from the sky.

s S

S is for sun
shining down from on high.

t T

T is for tree
and for top and for train.

LETTER **O** TO LETTER **T**

THE LETTERS OF THE ALPHABET—(5)

u **U**

V **V**

U is for umbrella
we take in the rain.

V is for van
and for vine with grapes blue.

W **W**

X **X**

W is for well
and the water it gives you.

X is for—let me see—
x is for Xmas.

y **Y**

z **Z**

Y is for yesterday,
yellow and yes.

Z is for zig-zag
and away we go and zig-zag
around the room just so.

LETTER U TO LETTER Z

Specially drawn for this work.

SIX MOST IMPORTANT FAIRIES

Here are some quaint little people. Although they are not very big they are well worth taking notice of. If you get to know them really well, they will teach you how to spell.

WE are six happy little fairies. We carry our names on our flags. We will teach you how to read. You will find one or more of us in every little word you meet. You must listen carefully to how we say our names in different words. Say our names carefully now: ā, ē, i, ō, u, y.

I am *Fairy " a."* You can hear my real name in bake, and cake; but I also say ă as in *apple*. You can see and hear me in cat, rat, bat, sat.

Can you think of some *Fairy " a "* words that rhyme with Jack? Be sure you can see and hear Fairy " a " in Jack.

Can you think of *Fairy " a "* words that rhyme with am, ash, an, crab, dad, and, camp, bag, tap?

The little fairies are very polite, and when there are two fairies in a word, the first fairy says her real name very clearly and the other one keeps silent.

Which fairy speaks in cake, day, rain?

Find Fairy "a" words that rhyme with (1) Jane, (2) ate, (3) came, (4) bake, (5) train, (6) play.

I am *Fairy "e."* You can hear my real name in *me*, but I also say e as in *egg*. You can see and hear me in Ted, fed, led, and the boys' name Ed.

Find *Fairy "e"* words that rhyme with (1) Ned, (2) bend, (3) bell, (4) den.

Fairy "e" speaks loud and clear in these words and *Fairy "a"* keeps silent: Beak, ear, eat, bead, cream, beach. Do you know why?

What rule are we helping the fairies to keep when we say these words?

Specially drawn for this work.

A FAIRY SONG

Happy fairies, six are we,
To all words we hold the key;
One or more is in each word
That you ever saw or heard.

Find *Fairy* " *e* " words that rhyme with:

(1) feast, (2) speak, (3) dream, (4) meat, (5) teach, (6) dear.

In these words *Fairy* " *e* " speaks very clearly indeed.

Find other words to rhyme with these:

(1) eel, (2) green, (3) deer, (4) bee,
    feel,   seen,   cheer,   see,
  (5) deep, (6) deed, (7) feet,
    keep,   feed,   meet.

I am *Fairy* " *i*." You can hear my real name in kite, but I often say i as in *it* and *ink*.

Find Fairy " i " words that rhyme with:

(1) ink,   (2) sit,   (3) ill,   (4) ring.

Remember when there are two fairies in a word the first one says its real name and the second one keeps silent. Fairy " i " says her real name in *ride* and *sprite*. Can you find Fairy " i " words to rhyme with these?

I am *Fairy* " *o*." You can hear my real name in no and toe, but I also say o as in orange, cot, got, trot.

Now find Fairy " o " words that rhyme with:

(1) cot, (2) clock, (3) nod, (4) hop, (5) dog.

In these words kind Fairy " e " is helping Fairy " o " to say her real name— doe, joke, note, bone, hope, pole, home.

I am *Fairy* " *u*." You can hear my real name in *use*, but I generally say ŭ as in *up* and *cup*.

Can you find words that rhyme with:

(1) gun, (2) rug, (3) bun, (4) dust, (5) sum, (6) blush, (7) cluck, (8) bump ?

I am *Fairy* " *y*," but I sound just like Fairy " i," for I am her twin sister. You will find me in these words: by, my, cry, dry, fly, fry, shy, sky, spy, try, why.

Here is a word in which you will find three fairies side by side, Fairy " y," Fairy " o " and Fairy " u," and it is the last fairy that speaks. What does she say ? Look at the word you.

You may have noticed what a kind little fairy is Fairy " e." She often helps the other fairies to say their real names very clearly and she keeps silent.

Here she helps Fairy " a "—bake.
Here she helps Fairy " i "—kite.
Here she helps Fairy " o "—poke.
Here she helps Fairy " u "—rule.
Here she helps Fairy " y "—eye.
And here she helps herself—deep.

Which fairy says her name in these words:

tea, sea, boat, coal, soap, rain, meat, play, grain, sail, you, sky ?

Look at any books you have to find the six little fairies.

When there is only one fairy and it is at the end of a very little word, it often says its real name.

Can you read these words:
go, my, me, he, be, she, lo, so ?

The Brownies

You have noticed that, though the little fairies can speak so nicely and say their names long and clear,

a, e, i, o, u,

and short and clear,

at, et, it, ot, ut,

they need many friends to help them to speak in words. You see how t helps them above.

Now here are some of their helpers:

The Puffing Brownies

The puffing brownies are p, b, t, d, c, k, g.

Look at the picture on page 133.

Brownie " *p* " smokes a pipe and says " p, p, p." Here he is helping the Fairies to make new words: pay, peep, pie, pop, pup, pig, pipe.

Brownie " *b* " shoots with his pop-gun. If you say his name with your lips you can hear his gun.

Here he is helping the Fairies " e," " a," " y," " u," " i ":
bee, bay, by, but, bit.

Brownie " *t* " likes playing trains and he makes the sound the engine makes when it goes along very gently before it gets up speed.

Here he is helping the fairies with the Brownies " p " and " b ":
top, tape, tea, tub, tap, beat, bat.

Brownie " *d* " makes the sound the

Brownie **p** smokes a pipe.

Brownie **b** shoots with his pop gun.

Brownie **t** plays with a train.

Brownie **d** hears the rain on the roof d d d.

Brownies **k** and **c** are twin brothers and go arm in arm.

Brownie **g** pours water from a bottle to hear it gurgling and copy the sound.

Specially drawn for this work.

THE PUFFING BROWNIES
Here are some of the little folk that work with the fairies. Take a good look at them, for you will meet them all again.

rain makes dripping or falling on the roof.

Here he is helping the fairies: dot, day, deep, deed, bed, add.

Brownie " c " speaks in his throat. He has a twin brother, Brownie " k." Although they have different names they nearly always make the same sound. You can hear the sound they make when they are helping the fairies: cat, cut, cup, kite, keep, kit.

Can you make the sound Brownie " c " or Brownie " k " makes? You can if you say the words, cat and kite, and listen to the sound at the beginning.

Brownie " g " also speaks in his throat. He makes a sound like water gurgling out of a bottle.

Here he is helping the fairies and the other brownies to make new words: goat, dog, gate, dig, get, tug, gay, go.

The Humming Brownies
Besides the puffing brownies, the fairies have the humming and buzzing brownies to help them.

The humming brownies are m, n, ng; and the buzzing brownie is z.

On page 135 is a picture of these brownies.

Brownie "*m*" makes a sound like bees humming, or a humming-top spinning, or a cow just going to say m-m-moo.

Here he is working with the other brownies and fairies and making words: am, me, make, mop, mud, my, mug, mum.

Brownie "*n*" makes a sound that you sometimes hear in the telegraph wires.

Here he is making words with the other brownies and the fairies; nut, no, nap, net, nip, neat, near.

Brownie "*ng*" makes the sound a bell makes when it is leaving off ringing.

Here he is making words: king, ring, swing, sing, wing.

You can hear him ringing very clearly if you say these words: ringing, bringing, swinging, singing, clinging, stinging.

Brownie "*z*" buzzes like a bumble-bee. You can hear him in the word buzz.

He does not help the fairies very

The Brownie **p** helping the Fairies to make a new word. Which fairy speaks and which is silent?

A Brownie and a Fairy. What do they say?

Specially drawn for this work.

THE BROWNIES AND THE FAIRIES AT WORK

Here the Brownies and the Fairies are working together. They are making words. You have met all these little folk before, and so you should know what they are trying to tell you.

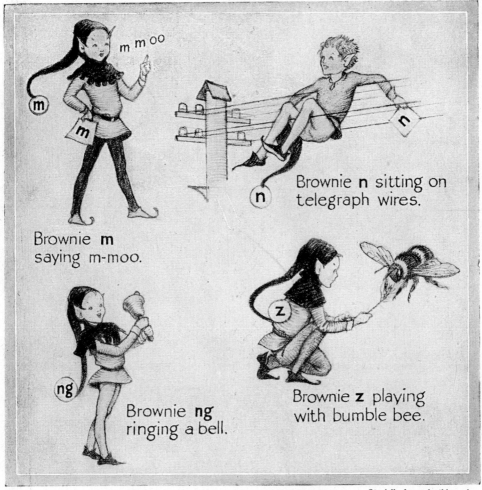

Brownie **m** saying m-moo.

Brownie **n** sitting on telegraph wires.

Brownie **ng** ringing a bell.

Brownie **z** playing with bumble bee.

Specially drawn for this work.

THE HUMMING BROWNIES

Now you see here Brownies " m," " n," " ng " and " z." Each one of them is showing what he can do. They are fine little chaps, so please don't forget them.

often, perhaps he is too noisy. Here he is helping to make words: zoo, zig-zag, zebra.

The Blowing Brownies

The Blowing Brownies make all sorts of funny sounds. They like the fairies to help them to speak.

Here are the names of the Blowing Brownies and pictures of them are on page 136: Brownies " w," " f," " v," " s," " j," " l," " h," " r."

Brownie " w " makes the wind sound and says " oo, oo."

Here he is making words with the fairies and other brownies: weep, wind, wave, well.

Brownie " f " makes the sound of bellows blowing or the puffing sound made by an engine.

Here he is making words: fan, fat.

Brownie " v " makes a sound like a cockchafer flying, or a clock being wound up, or an electric car. You can sometimes hear Brownie " v " in the wheels of a machine. Here he is help-ing the fairies and other brownies to speak. The fairies help him a great deal because he cannot say much with-out them: van, vain, vane, veer, vine.

Specially drawn for this work.

THE BLOWING BROWNIES

The Blowing Brownies are a large family and a busy one. They make many funny sounds, and are always ready to work for you.

Brownie " s " everyone knows well. He likes to make a hissing sound like a snake; you can sometimes hear him in the siphon as the liquid (lemonade, etc.) is being driven out.

Here he is helping to make words: so, sad, soap, say, see, sing, site.

Brownie " j " you can hear when a knife or scissors' blade is being ground on stone. He makes the sound the steel makes as it touches the grindstone.

He helps to make words that you know very well: Jack, jam, jar.

Brownie " l " makes a sound like a threshing machine.

Here he is helping to make words: low, lie, late, leave, lute.

Brownie " h " pants like a dog. Can you do this?

You can hear him panting in these words that he helps to make with fairies and other brownies: he, hay, hop, hip, hug, him, here.

Brownie **ch** has a cold and sneezes.

Brownie **ck** says the same as Brownie k.

Brownie **sh** hushes a baby to sleep.

Brownie **qu** tries to quack like a duck.

Brownie **th** tries to hiss like the gander.

Brownie **wh** Blows like the wind.

Specially drawn for this work.

THE SONG OF THE DOUBLE BROWNIES

Brownies all, in number six—
Troublesome and full of tricks,
Ever ready with some fun,
Never still till work is done.
ch, ck, sh, qu, th, wh.

Brownie " r " you will like because he purrs like a cat or growls like a dog. You can hear him when you say these words: run, rat, ripe, red, roll, ride, read, rain.

Can you tell the names of the fairies in these words?

The Double Brownies

These are strange little brownies.

Look at them carefully above and see what they are doing in the picture. Can you write their names? Their names are just two letters each. That is why they are called the double brownies. Most of the brownies, you remember, have only one letter on their caps. The double brownies have two—ch, ck, sh, qu, th, wh.

Brownie " ch " often has a cold and makes a sneezing sound.

You can hear him in church, chick, chew, chill, child, much, such, chip, chirp, chat, chap.

Brownie " ck " is a dull little brownie. He says the same as his brother " k." Here he is helping to make words with his brothers and the fairies: Dick, chick, lock, luck, duck, clock.

Brownie " sh " makes a hushing sound. He likes to hush babies to rest. You can hear him in hush.

Here are some other words he helps to make—bush, push, shut, shake, sash, she, shy, rush, shave, shall.

Brownie " qu " likes the quacking of the ducks. He helps to make only a few words, such as: quack, queen, quake, queer.

Brownie " th " sometimes tries to make a sound like the gander when he wants to drive you away.

He helps to make many useful words: this, that, thick, thin, thank.

Brownie " wh " makes a blowing sound. He is a little like the Blowing Brownies " w " and " h." Here are some words which he helps to make: what, where, whack, whither.

The Four Strange Goblins

Below are four strange little goblins who often help the brownies. You can hear what they say if you repeat their names carefully—Boy, Bow-wow, Scout, and Oily. They like Fairy " o " so much that they try to make her sound. But if you listen to what they say it is not a bit like the way Fairy " o " speaks. With the help of the brownies they make the following words. Can you read them ?

Goblin Boy. Toy, joy.

Goblin Bow-wow. Bow, cow, how, now, owl, fowl, howl.

Goblin Scout. Out, shout, stout, spout, trout, house.

Goblin Oily. Oil, toil, coil, boil, spoil.

Here is the song of the Goblins:

Gay and funny Goblins four,
Only four and not one more;
Bearing letters always two,
That we like to read to you.

Listen !

oy, ow, ou, oi.

" GAY AND FUNNY GOBLINS FOUR "   *Specially drawn for this work.*

THE BIG LETTERS
1. THE ROUND LETTERS

Round o, round o,
is like a ring
and we can
easily draw him.
Draw him little
or draw him big.

O

Big q is a queer letter,
you make him
you know
By adding a nice
little tail to an O.

Q

Big c
is quick to make,
if from your O
a piece you take.

C

Big u is not so hard.
Take away the top
of o, that is all
you have to do,
to make the
pretty letter U.

U

Big g needs some care.
Put a shelf
upon your C
and then it is
like big letter G.

G

2. CURVES AND STRAIGHT LINES

Big j is a letter
that we can draw fine
It is like a fish hook
at the end of a line.

J

To make big letter s,
draw a line that bends
and curves like a snake.
Wriggly, wriggly,
like a snake
Is the letter s you make.

S

To make big letter d,
draw a line and then
a curve.
Half an apple
you will also see
If you draw big letter D.

D

Big p is easy with straight
stroke and little curve.
Some say they think
the letter P
Is like a flag
that's flying free.

P

Specially drawn for this work.

LETTER BUILDING (1)

Big b is easy
when p you boldly try
A look at its picture
will tell you just why.

B

Big r is like big b
But you must
open the curve
at the bottom you see.

R

3. THE SOLDIER LETTERS
All Straight Lines

Big l is easy
if two lines you take
And put them together
this letter to make.

L

Big e is easy.
Draw a line,
give it three shelves,
one on the ground
and then the letter e
is found.

E

If you really
want big f,
then leave out
your bottom shelf.

F

Big t is like a table,
to make it every one
is able.
But draw it straight
or not at all
A table must not
have a fall.

T

Big i is like a soldier tall
It stands up straight
before us all,
Draw it straight
or not at all
A soldier must not
have a fall.

I

Two soldiers
and a stick between
Then big letter h
at once is seen
Draw them straight
or not at all
For soldiers must
not have a fall.

H

4. SLANTING LINES AND THE CROSS
LETTER AND THE ZIG-ZAG

Before you draw
big letter v
Open your first two
fingers and see
How much they are like
the letter called V.

V

Two V's together
make a w
This is a letter that
need never trouble
you.

W

Specially drawn for this work.

LETTER BUILDING (2)

Big y is easy
for you to make
If this advice
you'll quickly take
Put a letter v
at the top of a stem
And thus the letter y
is made with them.

Y

Big a is very easy.
First draw big v
upside down
Then "I see letter A,"
you'll cry
When the line I add
you spy.

A

Put a v on its side
close up to an I
And the big letter k
you will quickly spy.

K

Two straight lines
and a v between
That will make
big letter m
The finest ever
seen.

M

Here we have
Big letter n,
Straight up
and sloping down
and straight up again.

N

If you want big letter x
Cross two lines
and your work is done
And away you run
to have some fun
But when you cry
and fret and vex
Just think of your cross letter x.

X

Here we have
big letter z
To draw it you are able
Go straight along,
then sloping down
and straight along again.

Z

Some call z a zig-zag
if this is true,
find z's in the zig-zag line
that I have drawn for you.

You can make all the big letters that
are soldier letters and the slanting line
letters with match sticks. Look at the
letters carefully then get some sticks
and see how many you can copy....

Specially drawn for this work.

LETTER BUILDING (3)

WRITING LETTERS IN A ROW

MAKING THE LITTLE LETTERS
See what pretty patterns you get by writing letters in a row.

Here is the pattern that a makes —

a   aaaaaaaaaaaaaaaaaaaa

e   eeeeeeeeeeeeeeeeeeeeeeeeeeee

u   uuuuuuuuuuuuuuuuuuuuuuuuuu

o   ooooooooooooooooooooooooo

l   llllllllllllllllllllllllll

m   mmmmmmmmmmmmm

p   ppppppppppppppppppppppppp

f   ffffffffffffffffffffffffffff

Which row of letters do you think makes the best border?

Try a row of some of these — *ccc, sss, www,*
hhh, ggg, yyy, ddd, bbb, kkk.

Specially drawn for this work.

LETTER BUILDING (4)

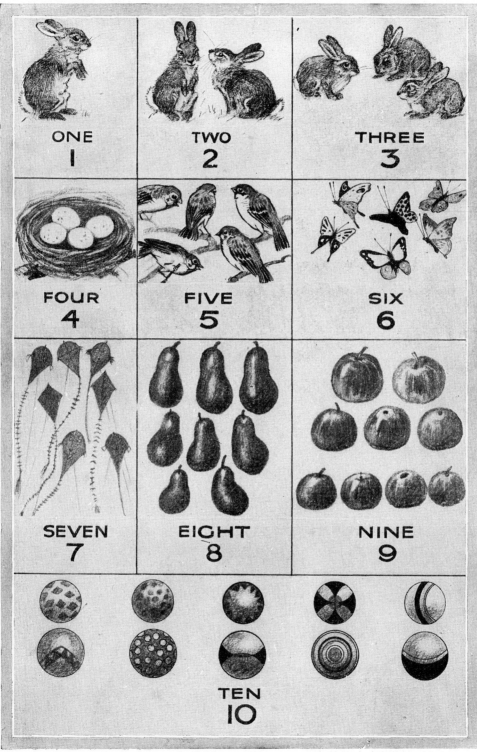

ONE
1

TWO
2

THREE
3

FOUR
4

FIVE
5

SIX
6

SEVEN
7

EIGHT
8

NINE
9

TEN
10

Specially drawn for this work.

COUNTING UP TO TEN

COUNTING AND BUILDING—(1)

1, 2, 3, 4, 5!
I caught a hare alive.

6, 7, 8, 9, 10!
I let her go again.

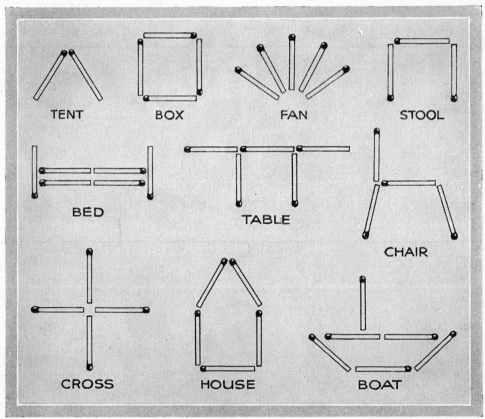

TENT   BOX   FAN   STOOL

BED   TABLE   CHAIR

CROSS   HOUSE   BOAT

Specially drawn for this work.

Count the number of sticks you will want to make each of the objects shown above. You can use match sticks. When you are sure that you have the exact number needed for each, arrange the sticks carefully in their places.

COUNTING AND BUILDING—(2)

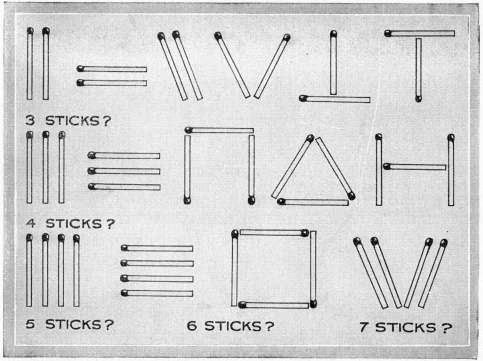

3 STICKS?

4 STICKS?

5 STICKS? 6 STICKS? 7 STICKS?

In how many different ways can you arrange 2 sticks? 3 sticks? 4 sticks?

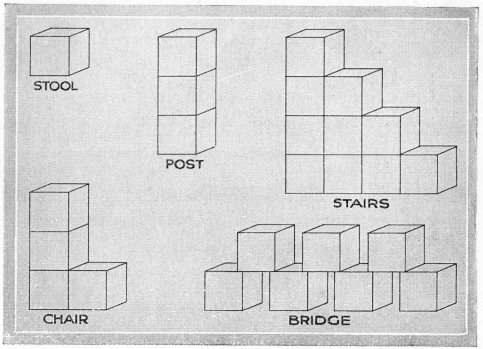

STOOL

POST

STAIRS

CHAIR BRIDGE

Specially drawn for this work.

How many blocks are needed to make each of these objects? If you have a box
of bricks count out the number you need for each and make it for yourself.

1 AND 1 ARE ———

2 AND 1 ARE ———   1 AND 2 ARE ———

3 AND 1 ARE ———   1 AND 3 ARE ———

4 AND 1 ARE ———   1 AND 4 ARE ———

5 AND 1 ARE ———   1 AND 5 ARE ———

6 AND 1 ARE ———   1 AND 6 ARE ———

Specially drawn for this work.

SIMPLE ADDITION

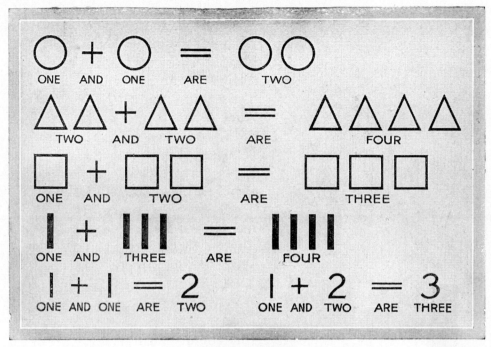

MAKING SUMS

Can you make sums like these? You must draw triangles, circles, squares or lines like those above. If you play at this game for a little every day it will soon become quite easy.

Specially drawn for this work.

A NUMBER STORY

Little Bo Peep lost her sheep. But presently one sheep came home, and then one more. That made —— sheep. Soon, another arrived. That made —— sheep. And just before tea, yet another. That made —— sheep.

Bo Peep locked her four sheep up and along came another, and that made —— sheep.

There was now only one more to come and soon he was in the fold too. That made — sheep.

THE STORY OF THE BOAT BOYS

Twice one is two,
Two boat boys dressed in blue;

Twice two is four,
Each wants a pinafore;
Twice three is six,
They fish with nets and sticks;
Twice four is eight,
They've caught a lot of skate;
Twice five is ten,
How well they help the men!
Twice six is twelve,
Look! in the sea they delve!
Twice seven is fourteen,
And the net they're caught in!
Twice eight is sixteen,
With the cold fish mixed in!
Twice nine is eighteen!
Do not keep them waiting;
Twice ten is twenty,
Rub and dry them plenty!
Twice eleven is twenty-two
Oh, dear! what will they do?
Twice twelve is twenty-four,
Here they are upon the shore!

Specially drawn for this work.

This is a very important little story. When you have read it through and can say it from
memory then you will know your first multiplication table.

THREE TIMES AND FOUR TIMES

SQUIRRELS AND PIGS
A tiny tale to tell the Three Times Table.

Three times one is three,
Three squirrels up a tree;
Three times two is six,
They play pretty tricks;
Three times three is nine,
Nine little pigs of mine,

DRYING THE PINAFORE

Four times one is four,
Where's your pinafore?
Four times two is eight,
I put it near the grate;
Four times three is twelve,
My name is Kitty Kelve.

Specially drawn for this work.

Now can you go on and complete the stories of the Squirrels and Pigs and the Pinafore?

THE LITTLE FISHES

Five times one is five,
Five little fishes all alive;

Five times two is ten,
Ten big, wet fishermen;

Specially drawn for this work.

Five times three is fifteen,
Fifteen fish lines swift in;
Five times four is twenty;
Twenty baits is plenty;
Five times five is twenty-five,
Twenty-five fishes caught alive!
But they've slipped from the grass with
    a sort of a shiver,
And they're back again now in their
    own flowing river.

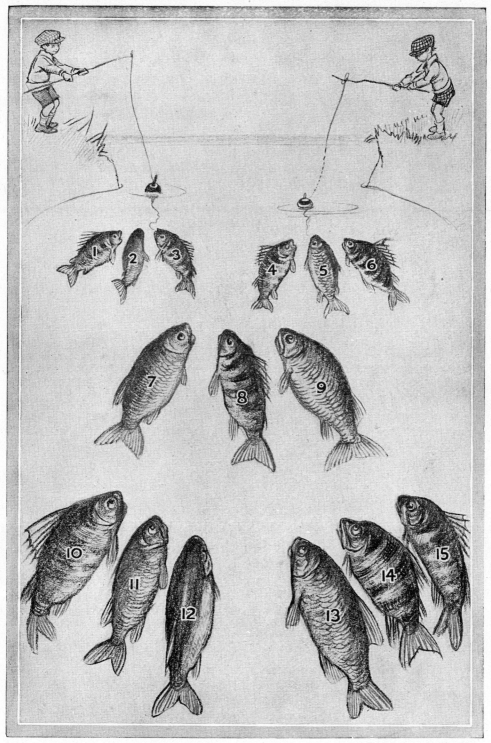

Specially drawn for this work.

Look at the fish in the river and see if you can catch any. You can catch them by naming the number of each.

THE PRETTY FLOWERS

CANDLESTICKS AND NIGHT LIGHTS

Six times one is six,
Six night lights with wicks.

Six times two is twelve,
Here is Kitty Kelve !
She bears a candle stick,
Let's hope it has a wick.

THE PRETTY FLOWERS

Seven times one
is seven,
Seven flowers
from Devon.

Seven times two is fourteen,
Pretty maids brought them in.

Specially drawn for this work.

You will soon find that there is nothing so very difficult about multiplication tables. A few
simple little rhymes with pictures will take you safely through them all.

Specially drawn for this work.

FINDING SUBJECTS TO DRAW

The children above are looking through their books to see what they can draw or paint. Many simple subjects can easily be drawn merely with straight lines, or with curves and circles, as clearly shown in the pages that follow. Now see what you can draw by copying the examples given.

EASY DRAWING

DRAWING with a pencil is great fun. Collect all your pencils and see that they have good points. Draw some lines with them. Do some of your pencils make blacker lines than others? If you look at them carefully perhaps you will find different letters on them. They may be marked B, or BB, or even BBB. The pencils with the B's on them make soft black lines. The more B's there are the softer and blacker your pencil is.

Drawing in Straight Lines

Pencils with H on them make fine hard lines. You cannot shade with them so well, or draw thick black lines. You will find these letters on hard pencils—HB, H, or HH, etc. Are any of these letters on your pencils?

If you cannot find any letters draw with your pencils and see what kind of lines they make. Then, perhaps, you can guess the letters that should be on them. When you have chosen the pencil or pencils you like best begin to make the drawings on the next page.

Notice that these drawings are made from straight lines in different positions. They look simple at first, but you may find your pencil does many things it should not do. It will soon begin to obey you, however. When you have finished one page, plan a new page of objects that can be pictured by straight lines, but do not cut or draw on the pages of this book.

FUN WITH LINES

Practise drawing some straight lines.　Then see what you can turn them into :—

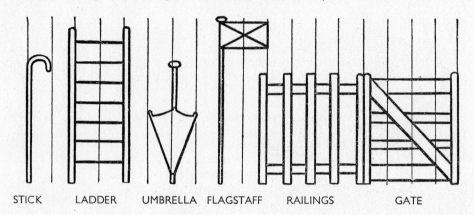

STICK　　　LADDER　　　UMBRELLA　FLAGSTAFF　　RAILINGS　　　　GATE

Now draw some slanting lines for rain.　See what a pretty pattern you can make with your lines.　Here is one :—

Who can make the neatest row of tents ?

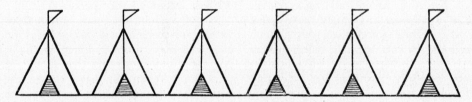

Give each tent a flag.

Draw a row of funny animals and shade them.

Draw a train to take you away for your holidays. Who can draw the neatest longest train for a large party ?

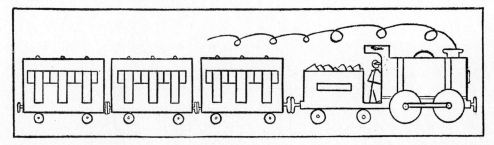

Draw the rows of houses the train passes.

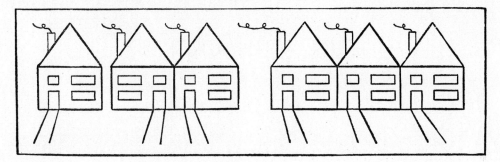

Draw some aeroplanes flying over the houses.

FUN WITH LINES AND CURVES

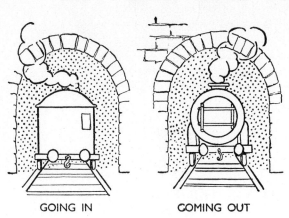

GOING IN   COMING OUT

Draw the tunnels the train went *under* ; two straight lines and a curve. Shade the tunnel with your pencil to make it dark. Perhaps you can draw a train going into the tunnel, and one coming out.

Draw the tall bridge, the viaduct, that the train passed over.

How many long straight lines do you need?

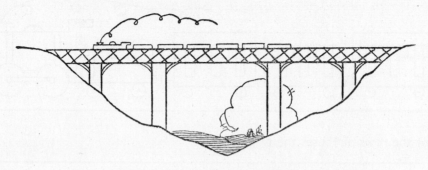

FUN WITH CIRCLES

Make circles by drawing round halfpennies and pennies. See what you can turn them into. Here are some pictures made from circles :—

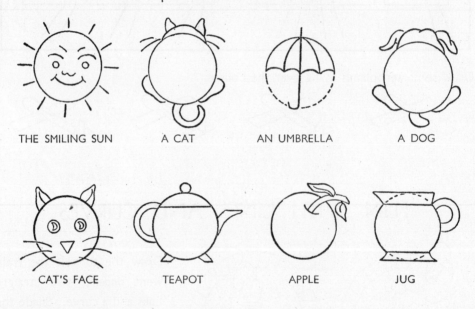

THE SMILING SUN   A CAT   AN UMBRELLA   A DOG

CAT'S FACE   TEAPOT   APPLE   JUG

What can you make from half-circles?

A CUP   PUDDING   CAP   DISH-COVER

MORE FUN WITH CIRCLES AND CURVES

Now practise drawing some circles and curves without using anything to draw around. Never mind if they are not perfectly round; you may be able to make some interesting pictures with them like these :—

RABBIT   CHICKEN   TULIP

A DRUM   A NEST OF EGGS   A CHAIN—DRAW OVERLAPPING OVALS
THEN FILL IN AS SHOWN

AN ELEPHANT   A FISH

A SNAKE   A ROUND TABLE

TREE   BOAT AND MOON   PRAM AND SUN

LINES, CURVES AND CIRCLES

Now see how many more things you can draw with the help of straight lines, slanting lines, curves and circles, such as telegraph posts and wires, railway signals, carts, boxes, toys, windows, fireplaces, pictures, etc. Perhaps you will want to do what a little boy once tried to do " draw everything in the world." Here is the little boy and some of the many things he drew :—

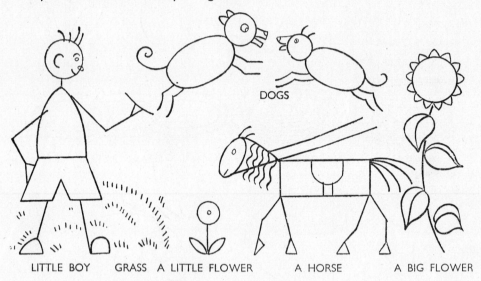

DOGS

LITTLE BOY   GRASS A LITTLE FLOWER   A HORSE   A BIG FLOWER

STICK FIGURES

Can you draw stick figures ? Try some of these :—

A FOOTBALL MATCH

Specially drawn for this work.

FOLLOWING OUT THE INSTRUCTIONS

Lots of girls and boys are very clever indeed at making things—once they know what to make and how to do it. In this section you will read of many useful and pleasing articles, none of them beyond your powers, though if at first you don't succeed it will be simple to try again.

PRETTY WORK FOR LITTLE FINGERS

WITH some odd pieces of paper, newspaper or old envelopes, we can make a number of interesting and pretty things. It is fun to make a newspaper tree (Fig. 1). Open a double sheet of newspaper and cut it in half lengthwise. You have now two strips. Roll up one of the strips, not too tightly. Paste the edge to keep the roll together. Then insert one point of your scissors and cut a slit half-way down as shown in the picture. Cut a slit the other side of this, and two more between these. Now hold the uncut end of the roll in the left hand. With the right grasp two or three of the inner strips you have cut. Pull them gently out and your tree will grow. You can make a forest for Red Riding Hood with your trees or a plume to decorate a paper cap. Ask your friends if they can grow a newspaper tree. You may need to practise a little before you make a really fine tree.

A Note-book (Fig. 2)

Little note-books can be made by opening all used envelopes of *one* size, tearing carefully or cutting off three of the triangular pieces, and using the fourth as a tying place, Fig. 2. Make a hole through this part and tie them together. A pencil can be attached to the tying string. Your mother may like a little note-book for shopping notes or for a telephone pad.

A Paper Cap (Figs. 3, 4 and 4a)

Fold a square of paper in half. Bend down the corners as in Fig. 3. Fold up

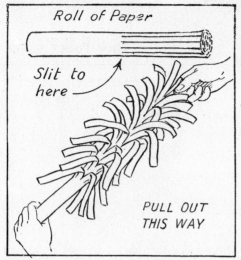

FIG. 1.   A Paper Tree.

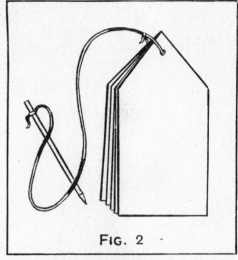

FIG. 2.   A Note-book.

the strips F, one on one side, and one on the other as in Fig. 4. You have now quite a nice paper hat to wear. You can alter the shape a little by folding back the corners A and B, and folding over them the corners C and D as in Fig. 4A. Paint your cap or decorate it with coloured paper. A feather stuck on one side looks gay. Newspaper caps are useful on a sunny day in the garden. Now notice that if you turn the cap, Fig. 4A, upside down you have a fine boat. It will float if you put something a little heavy in it, small stones for example.

A Pretty Bag (Figs. 5, 6, 7, 8, 9 and 10)

Begin with a square of paper. Any kind of paper will do, Fig. 5. Fold it in half along CD, and again in half along OA to get the smaller square shown in Fig. 6. Place your folded square so

that the open corner E is on top and to the right. Fold the square along OE to make the shape shown in Fig. 7. Make OF equal to OA, and join A to F by three pretty curves as in Fig. 7. This is to make a scalloped edge. Cut along AF so that AEF, the shaded part, is cut off. Open OAF and you get the pretty mat shown in Fig. 8. Put letters on your mat as shown in Fig. 8. Fold the mat in half along CD. Bend in OC and OD to meet each other as in Fig. 9. If you like you can put in a stitch to tie the bend OC, to OD, You now have a bag with two pockets. If your bag is made of brown paper or newspaper decorate it with coloured paper. If your bag is made of white paper, paint or crayon some pretty pattern on it as in Fig. 10. Make handles of string or raffia.

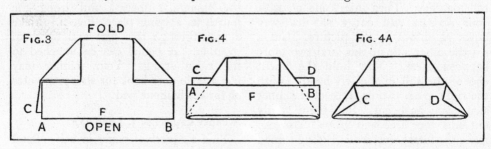

FIGS. 3, 4 and 4A.   A Paper Cap.

FUN WITH COLOURS

NOW clean your paint box and brushes and get your paints ready, or if you have no paints hunt up all your coloured pencils or crayons. Mix some red paint or choose a red crayon, and paint a large red ball. If you like, draw the outline first and fill it in with colour, or begin to colour the centre of your ball and work round and round until your ball is large enough and round enough. Draw a shelf and paint on it some red balls large and small. (Fig. 1.) Draw another shelf and fill it with balls of different colours.

A Pretty Garden

Draw and paint a pretty garden. Paint every flower a different colour. The green leaves, green stalks and brown earth will show up your flowers. You can paint it all with your brush alone if you like, without using a pencil. You can make pretty flowers, too, with your crayons. Look in gardens and parks for flower shapes to copy. (Fig. 2.)

A hollyhock garden is a pretty one to paint. Use your brush and yellow and green paint, or use red and green crayons. First crease your paper or draw a faint upright line to guide you in painting these tall flowers. Begin at the top and paint a round yellow flower, then one below, then two perhaps and so on down the stalk. Make the flowers a little larger as you go down. Now paint or crayon in the stalk and some green leaves. The flowers look pretty if you paint the edges of the petals a deeper colour than the centre. (Fig. 3.) Paint several tall hollyhocks in a row. Paint railings at the back, if you like.

A Fairy Tree is fun to paint because you can make it as pretty and gay as you like. With a brown crayon or brush and brown paint draw a graceful bending trunk and branches. Try to arrange your branches nicely *each* side of the tree. Now put on the green leaves. As it is a fairy tree the leaves may be arranged to make patterns.

Next choose your flowers—blue balls make a dainty tree. (Fig. 4.) Red and yellow balls make a more gaudy tree. See how many different fairy trees you can draw. Some can have straight branches, some curly branches and so on. Then there are flowers and fruits of all kinds to put on—star-like flowers and red apples and golden oranges. You will need to think to make a lovely fairy tree. Show your fairy trees to your mother, father and teacher, and ask them which they think is the best.

Ducks on a Pond

Paint a picture of a blue pond, some little yellow ducklings and some tall green rushes. It will help you to get the shape of a duck if you draw a figure 2 about the size you want your duck to be. (Fig. 5.)

Practise drawing some ducks with your paint brush or crayon before you begin your picture.

The Colours of the Rainbow

Do you know the colours of the rainbow ? Here they are : red, *orange*, yellow, *green*, blue, *violet*. Orange can be made by mixing red and yellow ; green by mixing yellow and blue, and violet or purple by mixing blue and red.

Paint or crayon six curved lines close together to show the colours of the rainbow. Look at your rainbow carefully and see if you can improve it. Try it again until you get a really good one. (Fig. 6.)

Paint a set of little pictures to show the colours of the rainbow. Choose simple pictures but try to paint lovely colours. (Fig. 7.)

You can choose many other pictures, red apples, oranges for orange, yellow butterflies, green grass, blue forget-me-nots, purple grapes.

A Picture of a Little House

Paint a picture of a little house with a red roof, pale yellow walls, brown door and windows, green or brown railings. Paint some flowers, trees and grass. If you can, paint a blue sky, leaving some white clouds. (Fig. 8.)

Drawing and Painting a Clown

Every child likes to draw and paint a funny clown. If you practise drawing and painting clowns, it will help you to draw real people one day. The picture shows an easy clown to draw and paint. Draw a ball for his head, add a smiling mouth, a little red nose and eyes. (Fig. 9.) Draw his pointed cap. Next draw his collar. It is easier to draw a collar than a neck. Drawing the collar will help to remind you that people have broad shoulders. Notice that his arms come from beneath his collar. Look carefully at the shape of his dress—coat and trousers all in one. Add his shoes. Now see how gay you can make him look by painting patterns on his clothes. First try a red and white clown, then try red and yellow, or orange and blue. Draw several clowns. Give them hats of different shapes, different collars, and put different patterns on their clothes.

Mr. Ballman

The clown is very gay in red and yellow. Paint by his side more sober Mr. Ballman. (Fig. 10.) Make him by drawing balls of different sizes. The largest ball for his body, the next largest for his head, then you can easily add small balls for his arms, legs and cap. Mr. Ballman is dressed quietly, so you must choose two colours that soften each other. These are the three pairs of colours that make each other less bright—blue and violet, green and blue, red and orange. Colour Mr. Ballman blue and violet. Give him black shoes and buttons. Draw two more Ballmen, colour one green and blue, and the other red and orange. These will help you to remember the colours that do not show each other up.

Some Little Studies in Colour

Humpty Dumpty—a picture in black, white, blue and red. Paint the sky blue, leave Humpty Dumpty white with black features, arms and legs. Paint the wall red. (Fig. 11.)

Coloured Alphabet Patterns.—Pretty patterns to colour may be made with letters of the alphabet. Look at the pattern made with V. Rule a piece of paper in squares (say half-inch squares). Draw a V with thick black lines in every other square. In this V draw another little V upside down. Colour your pattern black, white and green. Black and white show colours up. Paint or crayon the little diamond shapes black, and the vertical lines black. Choose the spaces you are going to colour green or leave white. (Fig. 12.)

Then try other letters. Good patterns may be made with A, Y, U, H and T. Colour each pattern with one of the six rainbow colours, adding black and leaving white spaces. If you compare your patterns, you can see which of the six rainbow colours are the brightest.

Red Riding Hood—in the Woods : a study in red and green. (Fig. 13.)

Paint Red Riding Hood's red cloak. If you cannot draw faces draw her back as she walks into the bushes. Paint green bushes and trees around her. Green and red are two colours that show each other up, so your picture ought to look very gay.

Colours that Show each Other up

Some colours never look so bright as when they are side by side. To remember the colours that show each other up, draw three squares, divide them by joining the corners, and then paint each square as shown—one square green and red, the second orange and blue, and the third yellow and violet. Now you have the three pairs of colours that brighten each other. (Fig. 14.)

Make some patterns with squares, lines, circles, letters or curves and colour them with these pairs of colours. Add black if you like. All kinds of interesting patterns can be made, as you will see in Figs. 15, 16, 17 and 18.

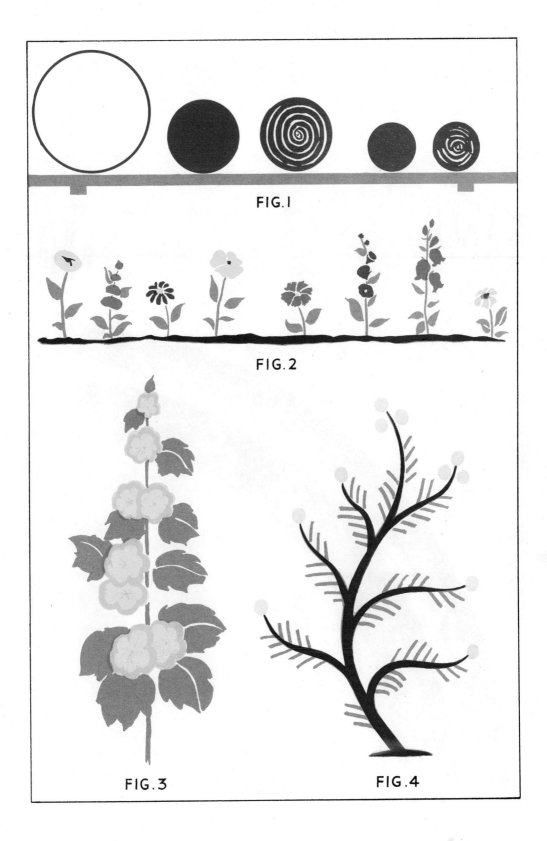

FIG.1

FIG.2

FIG.3

FIG.4

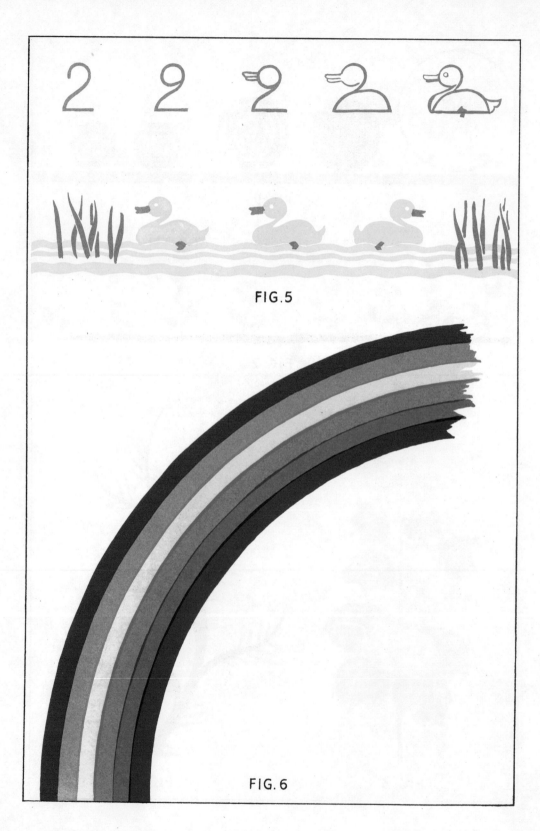

FIG. 5

FIG. 6

FIG.7

FIG.8

FIG.9

FIG.10

FIG. 11

FIG. 12

FIG.13

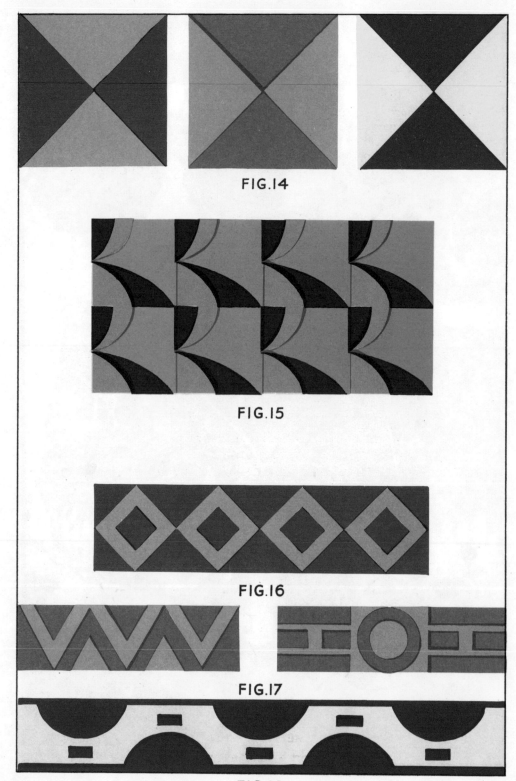

FIG.14

FIG.15

FIG.16

FIG.17

FIG.18

A Black Cat (Figs. 11, 12, 13, 14 and 15)

You will be very fond of this black pussy cat when you have made him. He can, of course, be a white cat if you like. It is best to colour him when he is finished. Take a piece of paper about 6 inches by 2½ inches and fold it in half. Any oblong piece of paper will really do. Narrow envelopes are useful. On your folded piece of paper draw the body of a cat as in Fig. 11. You can see how easy it is to draw. Cut away the shaded parts. Now make his head from a piece of round paper as in Fig. 12. Cut out two pointed ears and paste them on. Cut a furry neck for him as in Fig. 13 and a tail, Fig. 14. Paste all these parts together carefully as in Fig. 15. Notice the neck and tail are pasted *between* the folded body. If

the cat is made from black or dark brown paper, the eyes, etc., are painted or crayoned in white. If you tie a white bow around his neck and stand him on a match box your father will always be able to find the box. You can make some cats for your friends at Christmas time, cats of all colours, and write a greeting on them.

Making Paper Mats for the Table (Figs. 16, 17, 18 and 19)

Thin paper is best for these mats, but any kind of paper can be used. You can make square mats or round mats, so cut out some of both shapes. To make round mats draw around small boxes or plates. Fold a square of paper twice as you did for the bag, Figs. 5 and 6. Place the square in front of you

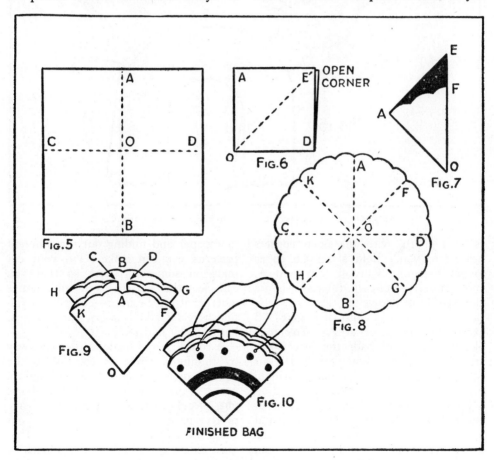

FIGS. 5, 6, 7, 8, 9 and 10. How to make a Pretty Bag.

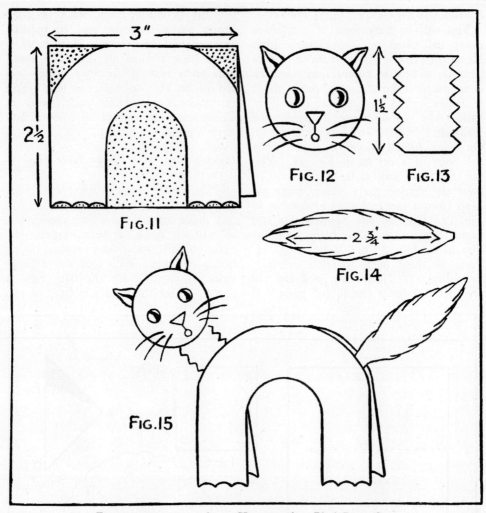

3"

2½

Fig. 11

Fig. 12

1½"

Fig. 13

2¾"

Fig. 14

Fig. 15

FIGS. 11, 12, 13, 14 and 15.   How to make a Black Pussy Cat.

as in Fig. 16, with the open corners nearest to you. Fold along AB so as to get Fig. 17. Cut off the point A, and cut out pieces of different shapes along AD as shown in Fig. 17. Be careful not to cut into the edge AB except for the piece at A. You may like to draw and shade the pieces you are going to cut out. Unfold your square and you have the mat shown in Fig. 18. The mat has been mounted on a piece of brown paper or a piece of paper of a contrasting colour so that it forms a border and shows through the holes that have been cut. You can spend a happy time cutting mats from newspaper and finding out the different patterns you can make. Put your cut mats on something dark so that you can see the pattern well and notice whether it can be improved. When you find a really good pattern cut it out of better paper and mount it.

A round mat is made in the same way by folding a circle as you folded the square so that it appears as in Fig. 19. Make a pretty scalloped edge and cut out pieces that you think will leave pretty spaces. You can cut pieces out along AB as well as AC, Fig. 19. It is quite exciting unfolding the square or circle to see the pattern made. Make some mats for your next birthday party.

A Pot of Flowers (Figs. 20, 22 and 23)

Draw a circle and draw another circle inside it so that you have what looks like a plate, Fig. 20. Make cuts in the rim as shown in Fig. 20. To get the cuts opposite to each other, fold your "plate" lightly in half twice. Bend up the tabs A, B, C, D, Fig. 21. This makes the stand for your pot. Cut a strip of paper the height you want your pot to be, roll it round to fit inside the tabs, paste or pin the overlapping edges of the roll together so that it will not unroll. Paste this roll to the tabs as in Fig. 22. Paint or crayon a pattern on your pot, or paste pieces of coloured paper of different shapes on it. Some patterns are best drawn on your pot when it is flat, that is before you fasten your roll up. Fill the pot with sand, sawdust or torn up pieces of brown paper to represent earth. Draw some flowers and leaves on stiff paper, colour them, cut them out, and stick them in your pot. Both sides of your flowers should be coloured. Tulips are easy flowers to draw, Fig. 23. You will enjoy cutting out flowers of different shapes. Try some from folded paper as well as

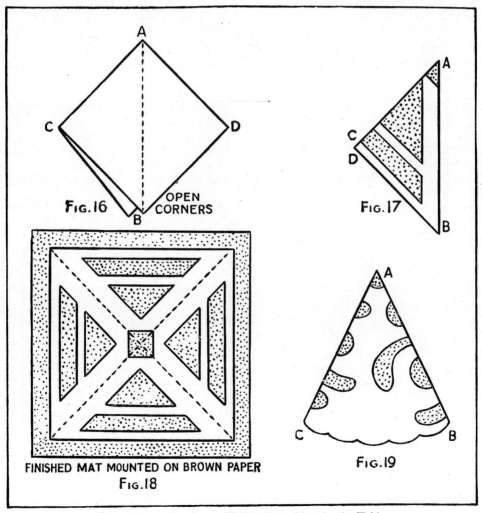

FIGS. 16, 17, 18 and 19.   Making Paper Mats for the Table.

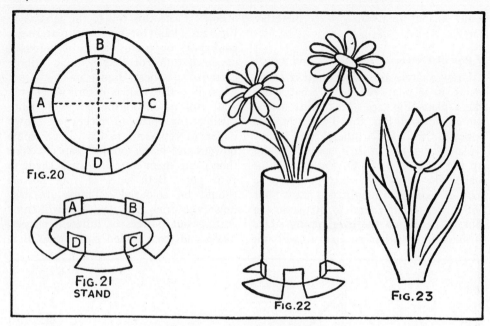

FIGS. 20, 21, 22 and 23.   A Pot of Flowers.

some little bushes for your pots like those in Fig. 24.

Flying Birds and Perching Birds (Figs. 25, 26, 27, 28 and 29)

Pretty little paper birds can be made

to decorate your room.   Use white paper and colour it, black for black-birds, yellow for canaries, blue for the blue bird of happiness, or the colours you have seen birds wear.   You can also use brown or any suitably coloured

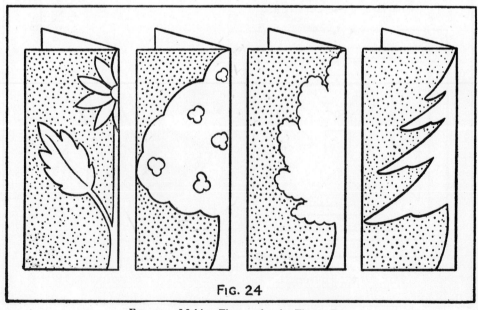

FIG. 24.   Making Flowers for the Flower Pot.

paper. Fold an oblong piece of paper in half as in Fig. 25 (3½ inches by 4½ inches will make a little bird). Keep the folded edge nearest to you. Find the middle point A of the top edge, Fig. 25. You can fold the paper lightly to get this point and then unfold. Draw a slanting line from A as AB in Fig. 25. Now bend up edge CB so that it lies along BA as in Fig. 26. Sketch in a bird's head and tail as shown in Fig. 26. Cut away the shaded parts. Draw feathers on the wings, and bend them out slightly, one on each side. A little daub of paste will help to keep the body together though it is not really necessary. Insert a piece of thread as in Fig. 27 for a flying bird.

To make the bird perch, fold a piece of paper (about 2 inches by ¾ inch) in half as in Fig. 29. Cut off the corners, the shaded parts in Fig. 29. Fold in half again to get the parts A and D. Now cut along B, C, the two pieces of paper thus obtained will form stands or " legs " for the birds. Paste one on each side of a bird by pasting the parts marked A as in Fig. 28. The parts marked D are bent out slightly so that the bird will stand as in Fig. 28.

A Cuckoo Clock (Figs. 30, 31 and 32)

You will like to play with this cuckoo clock when you have made it. Trace the clock, Fig. 30, on a piece of paper, and colour it. Cut out the opening above the clock face. This is for the cuckoo. Trace the cuckoos (colour them light brown), Fig. 31, also trace the hands of the clock, Fig. 32. If your paper is not very stiff, paste your three tracings on to thin cardboard and then cut them out. Push a pin through the centre of the hands and through the centre of the clock-face. Put the cuckoo strip of paper at the back of the clock face and pass the pin through this also. Push the pin into a small cork so that the hands and the cuckoo strip are kept in position and are not too loose. Bend back the sides of the clock along the dotted lines so that it will stand. By moving the cork the hands will turn and the cuckoo appear.

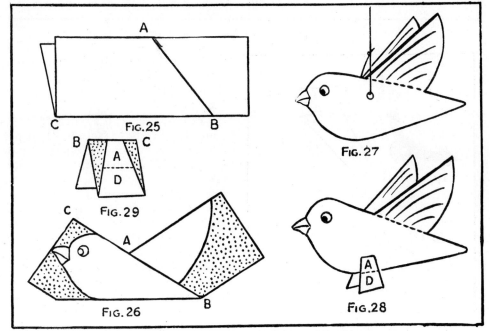

FIGS. 25, 26, 27, 28 and 29.   Flying Birds and Perching Birds.

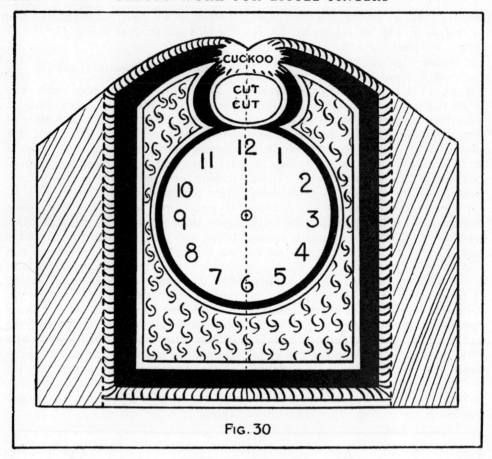

FIG. 30. A Cuckoo Clock.

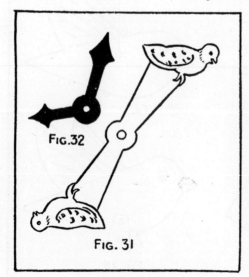

FIGS. 31 and 32. The Cuckoos and the Hands of the Clock.

A Toy to Make You Laugh—Willie Wrinkly (Figs. 33 and 34)

Make Willie's head from a circle of white paper about 6 inches in diameter. You can tear or cut a circle from a square by folding a square of paper twice to make a smaller square as in Fig. 34, and cutting off the corner. Make Willie's body from a strip of white paper or coloured paper about 6 inches by 12 inches. It must be a strip twice as long as it is broad. Now begin to fold the paper first one way and then another in small folds as though you were making a long screen. Try to keep the folds the same size, as they are narrow folds this will be fairly easy to do. If you have a page of an exercise book or a piece of foolscap, the blue lines will guide you. The arms are made from strips of paper 9 inches by 1¼ inches, and creased back and forth in the same way ; the legs are strips of paper 11 inches by 1½ inches. Paste or pin the legs, arms, and head to the body as in Fig. 33. Draw in the face and give Willie a hat cut from coloured paper. Paint his clothes what colours you like, for example, in stripes. On the whole it is better to paint the paper for the body, arms and legs, before folding it. Willie Wrinkly will dance, sit, and lie about in all sorts of amusing ways.

For Your Doll's House (Figs. 35, 36, 37, 38, 39, 40, 41 and 42)

It is fun to make paper furniture, and you can do it so easily by just folding paper squares and cutting them here and there.

Figs. 35, 36 and 37 show how to make a wash-bench, wash-tub and a pail from two squares. Fold each square into sixteen squares as in Fig. 35. For the wash-bench cut off one row of squares as in Fig. 35, and cut along the dark lines. Paste A over B, and C over both to make the bench shown in Fig. 37.

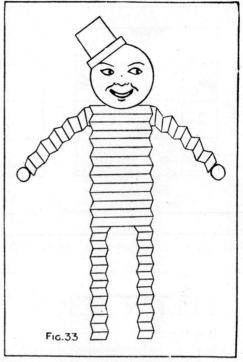

FIG. 33.

FIG. 33. Willie Wrinkly.

Cut one row of squares for the wash-tub. Make little cuts all the same length along the bottom as in Fig. 36. Bend the little cut pieces out to make a stand, and roll the strip around to make a tub, the little bent pieces that form part of the bottom or stand must be inside. Paste them to a square of paper to complete the bottom, cutting the paper round like the tub last of all. Fig. 37 shows the bench. A strip of paper folded back and forth will serve as a washboard. Three squares will make a pail in the same way as the tub. Odd pieces of paper will make the handle as in Fig. 37.

Chairs (Figs. 40, 41 and 42)

Fold and cut the square as in Fig. 40. The row of four squares cut off will make the arms of an armchair, Fig. 42. Bend back A, A, and fold B, B down over the A's to form the legs. Cut the back any shape you like, and the legs. You can make your chair an uphol-

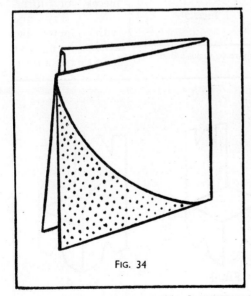

FIG. 34.

FIG. 34. How to make a Circle from a Square for Willie's Head.

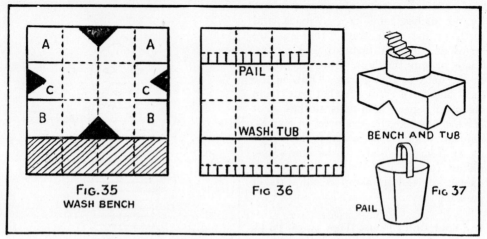

FIG. 35
WASH BENCH

FIG 36

BENCH AND TUB

FIG 37

PAIL

FIGS. 35, 36 and 37.   A Wash-bench, Wash-tub and Pail.

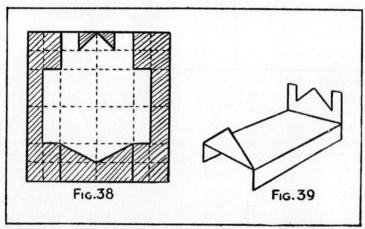

FIG. 38

FIG. 39

FIGS. 38 and 39.   How to cut and fold a square to make a bed.

stered chair by leaving the legs uncut and painting the chair some bright colour or colours. See what pretty chairs you can make. You can find out yourselves how to make tables, stools, and other pieces of furniture. Try first with newspaper and then use better paper.

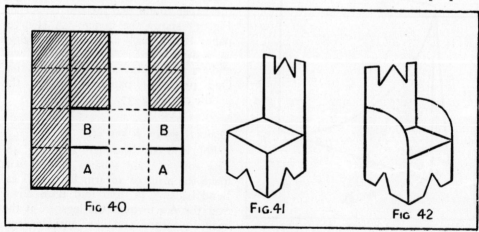

FIG 40

FIG. 41

FIG 42

FIGS. 40, 41 and 42.   How to make Chairs.

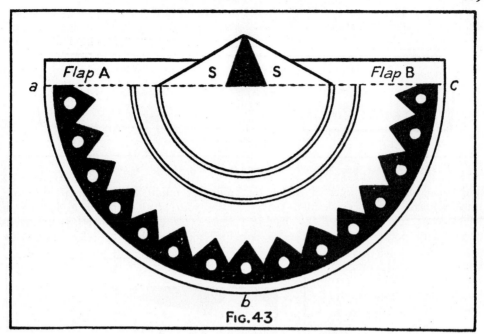

FIG. 43. Diagram for Hiawatha's Wigwam.

Begin by folding your square into sixteen squares.

Hiawatha's Wigwam (Figs. 43 and 44)

If you know the story of Hiawatha, as I am sure you do, it will be fun to make his wigwam. Fig. 43 shows how to plan it out. First make a semi-circle *abc*. Draw on *ac* the two flaps S, S, which are for opening the top of the tent to let out the smoke and direct it. They can be closed in bad weather. They are shown clearly in Fig. 44 with the poles attached to them for moving them. The flaps A and B, Fig. 43, also drawn on *ac*, are for joining the tent together. Before you join the wigwam together, draw and paint a pattern on it. Fig. 43 shows a Red Indian pattern, a row of brown triangles at the bottom with yellow discs on them and two red bands around the middle. Now fasten the tent together

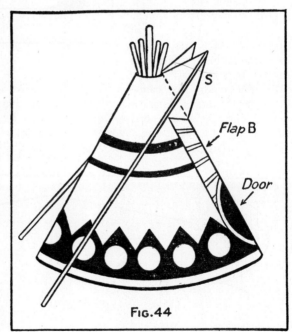

FIG. 44. Hiawatha's Wigwam—finished model.

by pinning or pasting Flap A under the edge of the tent, and Flap B over the edge. Paint the red bands over the flap. Bend out the smoke flaps S, S,

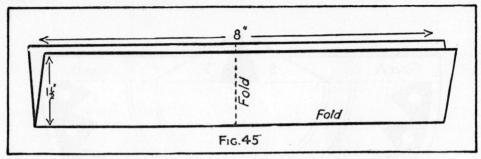

FIG. 45.   Hiawatha's Canoe.   Fold strip of paper as above.

and fasten them by pieces of cotton to bits of cane or very slender twigs. Make your tent more real by having several tent poles in the middle for it to rest on as in Fig. 44. Cut an oval opening for the door. Strips of cardboard can be used for tent poles.

Hiawatha's Canoe (Figs. 45, 46, 47 and 48)

Brown paper will make a strong canoe, very light brown or yellow paper will look something like the birch bark from which Hiawatha made his canoe. A piece of paper 8 inches long and 3 inches wide will make a fine canoe, but you can choose any size you like as long as you remember that the paper must be much longer than it is broad. Fold your strip of paper in half as in Fig. 45, and then in half again as in Fig. 46. See that the folded edges are

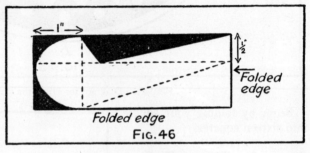

FIG. 46.   Showing folded edges.

to the right and at the bottom as in Fig. 46. Now draw on it half of the canoe as shown in Fig. 46. Notice the guide lines. Cut away the shaded parts and unfold, and

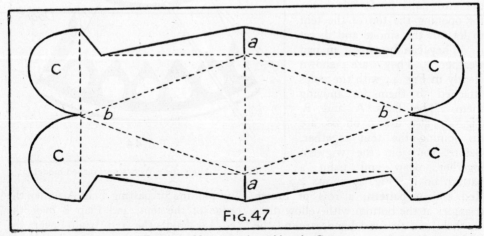

FIG. 47.   Next stage in making the Canoe.

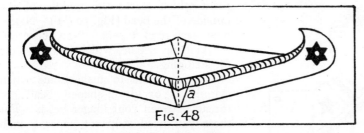

FIG. 48. Finished Canoe.

FIG. 49 (b). The Indian baby hanging up.

you have a canoe flattened out as is clearly illustrated in Fig. 47.

Canoes as Sweet Holders

Cut slits at *a, a*. Bend the sides up along *a b*. Paste the sides together at " *a* " as in Fig. 48. Paste the ends *c* together to make the finished canoe shown in Fig. 48. Do not apply the paste too heavily but see that it is evenly spread.

Paint a red star at each end and make a pattern round the edge. These little canoes can be made to hold sweets at your party.

Red Indian's Baby and Cradle

Make the cradle of a piece of brown paper 6 inches by $3\frac{1}{2}$ inches. Fold it into four parts each way so as to get sixteen divisions. Draw the cradle as shown and cut it out (Fig. 49). Bend up the bottom so that the baby will not fall out. Make holes along the flaps F F for lacing and bend them over. Draw the baby about $5\frac{1}{2}$ inches long as shown in Fig. 49 (*a*). Give it a gay blanket with stripes. Fold back the flaps and put a little cotton wool or some tissue paper at the back to make the baby more real. Lace the side pieces over this. Now put the baby in the cradle and lace it up with coloured wool or string as in the picture (Fig. 49 (*b*)). If you like you can paint a pattern on the cradle of stars or stripes. Hang the cradle up as shown in Fig. 49 (*b*).

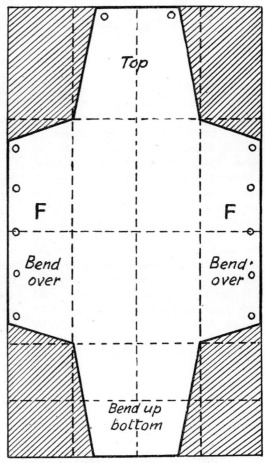

FIG. 49. A piece of brown paper 6 inches by $3\frac{1}{2}$ inches will make a Red Indian's cradle. First draw the cradle and then cut it out.

FIG. 49 (a).   The baby ready for lacing up.

Making Paper Beads

Making paper beads is a fine occupation for wet days. You need some paste, paper of different kinds, a knitting needle or small round stick of some kind, and a pair of scissors. Coloured paper makes pretty beads, but if you have some paints you can use paper of almost any kind, white paper, brown paper and so on. However, before you think of decorating the beads you must learn how to make them. Use newspaper for your first beads. Cut the newspaper into strips 2 inches wide and 9 inches long. Fold each strip of paper in half lengthwise, and cut to a point. Take one triangular strip and cover the surface with paste. Be sure to have it smooth. Place the knitting needle at the broad end as in Fig. 50 (a) and begin to roll tightly. Great care must be taken to roll the paper straight. Each layer becomes narrower and narrower, ending in a

point which marks the middle of the outside of the bead (Fig. 50 (b)). Notice how each end tapers. Now take out the knitting needle, which leaves a hole for stringing.

You may like to make some small cylindrical or drum-shaped beads to thread between your longer beads. For these you need strips of paper $\frac{1}{2}$ inch wide and 9 inches long. These strips must *not* be pointed. Paste and roll them as already described. When tightly rolled and before the paste is dry, press the layers gently to make sure the edges are straight. If they are made of white paper decorate them with bands or spots of bright colours as in Fig. 50 (c), which shows tapering beads and cylindrical beads strung together.

The pretty paper that lines envelopes can be used to decorate your tapering beads. Cut the lining paper into strips $\frac{1}{2}$ inch wide and 6 inches long. This time the strip must be pointed at each end. To do this fold it in half along the width, and then fold lengthwise and cut as before. Unfold the strip, paste it carefully, and roll it on the middle of the bead you wish to decorate. Perhaps your father will show you how to varnish your painted beads.

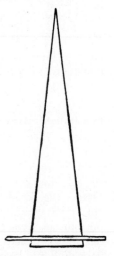

FIG. 50 (a).   Ready for rolling.

FIG. 50 (b).   How the rolling should finish.

FIG. 50 (c).   Here is a pretty necklace made of paper beads.

The First
Steps in
Geography

A Helping Hand
for
Tiny Folk

HOW THE SUN BEGINS HIS DAY

Specially drawn for this work.

June and Robin loved to watch the sun but it was only in the winter that they were up first and so could see him begin his journey across the sky. They soon found out that the sun rises every morning in the east and so started to learn **geography**.

JUNE AND ROBIN LEARN GEOGRAPHY

JUNE AND ROBIN LEARN FROM THE SUN

JUNE and Robin had a friend in the sun. They liked him because he made the days bright and warm for them. In the winter they loved to see him begin his journey across the sky. But in the summer the sun was always up before they were. One of the first things they learnt was that the sun begins his journey or rises *in the east* in the morning.

In the picture above you can see June and Robin learning geography from the sun.

In the winter evenings they watched him sink lower and lower in the sky. "He is going to bed," said June.

When the sun had gone he often left lovely colours in the sky. The children called them the sun's good-night gift. In the summer they knew he was shining while they slept, and they liked to see him peeping in at them through the curtains as he sank to his home *in the west*.

Mid-day or Noon

"The sun tells us where the east and west are," said June, "but how can he tell us where the south and north are?"

"Come into the garden at mid-day," said her father, "because at noon or mid-day the sun has done half of his daily journey and he is high up in the south."

At mid-day the children ran into the garden. The sun was shining at them from the south. His father told Robin to stand with his back to the sun. " Look at your shadow," he said. " It points to the north. The south is behind you."

" Your shadow is the sun's finger pointing to the north," cried June.

" Now hold out your arms," said his father. " Your right arm points to the east, your left arm points to the west."

The picture placed at the top of the next page shows how June and Robin found the north and south. Go into the garden one day at noon and let the sun point out the north to you by your shadow.

The picture at the bottom of the next page shows you June and Robin's house. You can see the back faces north and the front faces south. At noon the sun shines into their front rooms and makes them hot and sunny, but he never peeps into their north rooms. On which of the rooms does the sun shine in the morning ? From what windows can they see him in the evening ?

Draw a picture of your house. Show where E, S, W, N, are. You can watch the sun rise in the east and travel up the sky towards the south until it is due south. Then it begins to sink slowly towards the west.

Robin and June learnt how to draw the four chief points that show direction. Their father told them that these were the four chief points of the compass by which sailors steer, and he made a sketch like Picture A.

The children put the card on their table so that the black arrow pointed to the north. In their home it pointed to their back garden.

Said June, " On the east side the sun rises, on the opposite side, the west, it goes down. During the middle of the day it is always in the south. The north is the side where nothing happens."

The children learnt to say the points in clockwise or sunwise order round the

BED-TIME FOR THE SUN   *Specially drawn for this work.*

During winter evenings June and Robin would watch the sun sink lower and lower in the sky and say he was going to bed. They noticed how he left lovely colours in the sky and soon knew that he set in the west.

SEE WHERE THE SHADOW POINTS

Robin is standing in the garden at about twelve o'clock on a sunny day. This is when the sun is highest in the sky. He holds out his arms and knows that his right hand points east and his left hand west. The sun is behind him in the south so the shadow in front of him must point to the north.

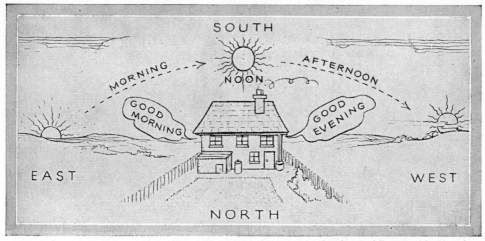

Drawings specially prepared for this work.

This is a picture of the house in which June and Robin live. It shows you that the back faces north and the front faces south. The sun makes the front rooms light and warm but he does not peep into the back rooms at all.

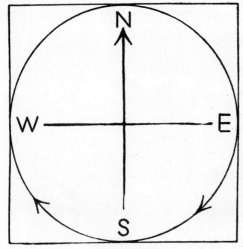

PICTURE A

This shows you the four chief points of the compass, E. S. W. and N. Sailors steer by these points.

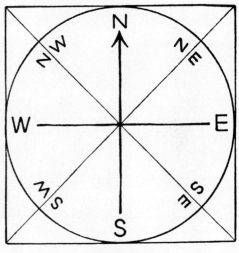

PICTURE B

You should make a card like this. It is different from Picture A, because it shows eight points of the compass.

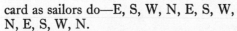

card as sailors do—E, S, W, N, E, S, W, N, E, S, W, N.

The children liked to see how far north they could walk without turning, and how far due east, south, and west.

They soon learnt to add four more points to their compass, thus making eight.

Eight Points of the Compass

Make a card like Picture B. Put it on the table in your room so that it points to the north and south. Tell what you can see in your room in each direction, thus: On the north side fireplace, on the east side a window, southeast a cupboard and so on.

Specially drawn for this work.

THE EAST WIND BLOWS TO THE WEST

In winter time particularly the east wind comes with its chilly breath to blow our hats and everything else towards the west. This wind reaches us from the point where the sun rises and brings with it air from cold countries.

THE WEST WIND BLOWS TO THE EAST

Specially drawn for this work.

June and Robin always liked the west wind because it was warm and gentle and brought rain for the garden flowers. It blows from the point where the sun sets and comes to us across the ocean.

JUNE AND ROBIN TALK TO THE WINDS

The winds often played with June and Robin. The East Wind was fond of blowing their hats off.

" Hold on your hat, here comes the East Wind," June cried when she heard him. " He is coming from the side of the sky where the sun rises. Listen to what he says."

The Winds and Their Names

" Woo-oo," puffed the East Wind, " I blow from the east. I am the East Wind—woo-oo-oo—I will blow your hats to the west; I will blow everything I can to the west. Woo-oo, I come from my home in the east."

The children liked the West Wind because he was often warm and gentle and brought rain for their garden.

" Woo-oo," sang the West Wind, " I bring fresh showers for your thirsty flowers."

Which Wind Is Blowing ?

The children found three things that told them which wind was blowing:—

(1) *Smoke from the Chimneys.*—If the smoke from a chimney points to the west, we know the east wind is blowing it to the west. A north wind blows the smoke to the south, and so on.

(2) *Flags.*—Flags, like smoke, point away from the wind that is blowing;

WATCH THE SMOKE

The smoke that comes pouring from a chimney tells from which point the wind is blowing.

FLAGS AND THE WIND

When a flag is flying from a pole it tells you at once which way the wind blows.

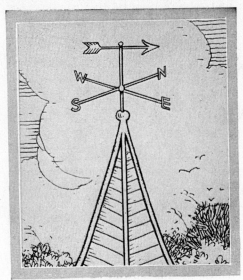

THE WEATHERVANE

There are weathervanes on many church steeples. Look at the arrow and it will say what wind is blowing.

with the wind. When the west wind blows it turns the arrow round so that its *point* points to the west. When an east wind blows round goes the arrow and points to the east. The " point " of the arrow always points to whatever wind is blowing. If you look at the arms you can tell in what direction the arrow points. If it points somewhere between the north arm and the west arm, a north-west wind is blowing. In the picture of the South Wind you can see the arrow pointing at him.

How Weathercocks Tell

Sometimes a weathervane has a cock on it instead of an arrow. It is then called a weathercock.

The beak of the cock always points to the wind that is blowing, and we can tell the name of the wind by looking at the arms. If the beak points in the same direction as the N-arm, a north wind is blowing.

" Woo-oo-oo," blusters the North Wind. " I bring the snow. My home is in the cold north. Woo-oo, I blow from the north."

The South Wind sighs gently in the summer and sings, " Woo-oo—I come from the south. I am the warm South Wind."

thus when a westerly wind is blowing the flag points east, being blown in that direction by the wind.

(3) *The Weathervane.*—A vane has four steady arms. Each arm bears a letter telling in which direction it points, E, S, W, or N. It is something like the compass June and Robin drew. These arms never move. Above the four arms is an arrow that turns about

Specially drawn for this work.

THE NORTH WIND BLOWS TO THE SOUTH

The north wind is always cold because it blows from the icy parts of the world. Often it brings snow with it for its real home is in the far, far north. We have to be well wrapped up when the north wind is about.

NORTH, SOUTH, EAST AND WEST

IN THE FAR NORTH

NORTH AMERICA

CHINA

IN THE HOT SOUTH

Great Britain is an island in the Temperate Zone, between the Far North of the Arctic regions and the warm South of the countries near the Equator. If we could fly to the Far North we should come to the lands of ice and snow where the Eskimos live. If we went South to the hot lands of Central Africa near the Equator we should find in the great forests the little people known as Pygmies, as well as other dark-skinned people. To the West across the wide seas the Red Indians still live in their homeland of North America, while far away to the East of Britain live the people of that big country called China.

Specially drawn for this work.

THE SOUTH WIND BLOWS TO THE NORTH

June and Robin have learned that the south wind sighs gently in summer. It is a warm, kindly wind because it comes to us from lands that are kissed by the sun. During the months of summer we often have breezes from the south.

JUNE AND ROBIN LEARN ABOUT THE LANDS FAR AWAY IN THE NORTH, EAST, SOUTH AND WEST

When the children walked along a road from their house that led due north, their father told them that if they kept on travelling northwards for a long time they would come at last to the land of snow and ice where the Eskimos live.

"Supposing we travelled on southwards for miles and miles and miles?" asked Robin.

Among the Pygmies

"We should come to the hot lands of the earth," said their father, "perhaps to the dry, hot deserts where the camels and the Arabs live, or the hot, wet forests where there are giant trees, creepers with strange flowers, and gaily-coloured birds. Here live little black people called the pygmies."

"Where should we get to if we travelled for miles and miles to the west?" asked June.

"To North America," said her father. "A land of great cities, forests and cornfields, once the home of Hiawatha and the Red Indians who lived in the forests and on the grasslands called the prairies. And if we travelled eastwards we should come to many strange lands, perhaps the land of China."

When they got home their father drew the four points of the compass on a large piece of paper and pasted pictures around of some of the peoples who lived in the far north, east, south, and west. You can see these pictures on the previous page.

In a House of Snow

The Eskimos' hut, built only of blocks of snow, tells you what a cold land it is. Notice the dogs that pull their sledge and their canoe made of skins. It is too cold for them to grow corn or vegetables so they have to live on fish, seals, polar bears, birds or any creatures they can catch.

The picture of the hot lands tells you it is hot by the huts made of leaves, and because the black people wear few or no clothes. Here grow all sorts of crops that we cannot raise in our own land.

On the east you see a picture of a Chinese boy eating rice with chopsticks, and on the west Hiawatha. He, as you know, was sent to bring peace and to be a teacher of the Red Indian tribes. There is a great poem written about him.

JUNE AND ROBIN DRAW PLANS AND MAPS

June and Robin loved drawing pictures of all the things in their home. Their father showed them how to draw a new kind of picture—a teapot *seen from above*. Looking down on a teapot one sees a big circle for the body of it, and a smaller circle for the lid, with the spout sticking out on one side and the handle on the other.

PICTURE OF TEAPOT

Here is a teapot as it appears when we look at it from the side.

PICTURE FROM ABOVE

This is the same teapot, but we are looking down on it from above.

CLOCK

PLAN OF CLOCK

DISH

PLAN OF DISH

SUGAR BOWL

PLAN OF SUGAR BOWL

These are very familiar objects and we see them here in two separate forms. In one form we have the object as it appears in front of us; and, in the other, how it seems when we look upon it from above. The second set of sketches are called plans.

This kind of picture is called a plan.

On this page are some pictures and plans the children drew.

Both June and Robin liked drawing plans of tables, especially dinner tables or breakfast-tables like the one seen below

What Does the Plan Tell ?

Notice in this plan, or map as their father called it, the chairs are just squares, the plates circles, the dishes oval, and the knives, forks and spoons straight lines. What does the finished map or plan tell you ?

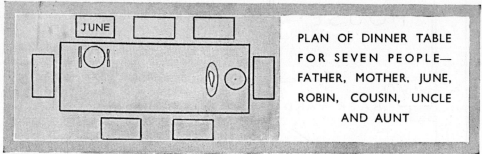

JUNE

PLAN OF DINNER TABLE FOR SEVEN PEOPLE— FATHER, MOTHER, JUNE, ROBIN, COUSIN, UNCLE AND AUNT

June and Robin are both fond of drawing plans of subjects they know very well such as a tea-table, dinner-table or breakfast-table. One such plan, which may be called a map, is reproduced above. What does the little drawing tell you? Copy it and complete it. Put names on the chairs.

Next the children drew maps of their rooms to show where the different things were placed. They began by drawing a square or oblong according to the shape of the room. They made thick lines for the four strong walls, leaving openings for the doors and windows.

They greatly enjoyed putting in chairs, tables and all the other things. They wrote names to show what their squares and oblongs were meant to represent. They put in the direction each wall faced, north, south, east or west.

Colours to Choose

Next they tried a map of their house and garden. They painted this map. The house was painted grey, the grass

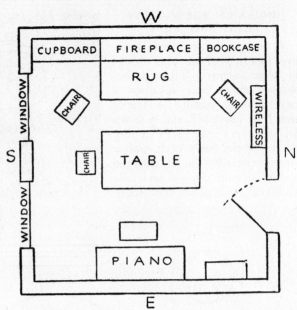

Above we see a map or plan of a living-room with all the contents in their proper places. Note the points of the compass.

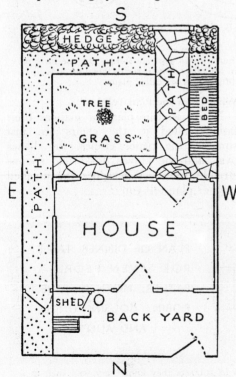

This is a map or plan which June and Robin drew and then painted. It shows the house where they live and its garden.

and hedge green, the tree a deeper green, the garden bed brown, the shed or outhouses light brown and the garden paths and backyard very pale brown or yellow. They thought this made a fine map. They were very proud to add the four chief points of the compass, S, W, N, E.

You will find the maps or plans of the living-room and those of the house and garden on this page, and perhaps before very long you will be able to make similar maps and plans yourself and colour them very neatly.

JUNE AND ROBIN VISIT A LAKE AND AN ISLAND

The first lake that June and Robin ever saw was in the Park. A path wound in and out close to the edge of the water, so the children were able to walk all round the lake.

"A lake has a path all round it," said June.

"I know what a lake is," cried Robin. "It is a piece of water with land all round it. This is a big lake because we cannot jump across it, but

I expect there are much bigger lakes in the world."

The Great Lakes

Their father told them that some lakes are so big that you can hardly see the opposite side. They are like inland seas, only their water is generally fresh water, not salt water like that of the sea. The most famous lakes in the world are the Great Lakes of North America.

"A big lake ought to have a different name from a little, little lake," said June.

Ponds and Pools

"A very little lake is called a pond," said their father.

"And I suppose a tiny, tiny lake is called a pool," suggested Robin.

When they got home they drew pictures of pools, ponds and lakes and you will find the sketches on the next page.

Their father took June and Robin into the country one day, where there was a large lake with hills all around it, and in the middle of the lake there was an island.

The children saw the island from the top of a hill.

Then they went down on the shore and looked across at the island.

"We cannot get to the island," said Robin. "There is water all round it."

The British Isles

Along came a boat with a man pulling hard at the oars. In jumped their father and the children. Very soon they were on the island, and exploring it.

"It is a very small island," said

Specially drawn for this work.

THE LAKE IN THE PARK

June and Robin knew of a lovely lake in a park with a pathway all round it and very soon they learned that a lake is a piece of water with land on every side. There are some lakes where you can hardly see the opposite side, but tiny lakes are called ponds, little ponds being pools.

A POOL   A POND   A LAKE

Specially drawn for this work.

AN ISLAND IN A LAKE

Sometimes a large lake has an island in the middle and you can always see the island best from a high hill. In this picture the children are looking down upon the lake and an island. The little drawings at the top show that they know the difference between a pool, a pond and a lake.

Robin, " but I should like to live on it. I suppose there are much bigger islands than this ? "

" Yes," answered his father. " There are little islands in lakes, but very large islands in oceans and seas. We live on an island called Great Britain, and west of it there is an island called Ireland, and around these two big islands are many little islands. All these islands are called the British Isles."

" I never knew we lived on an island," said June, " and I did not know there was an island called Great Britain."

" Well, you have learnt something," laughed her father.

" And I know what an island is," said Robin, " a piece of land surrounded by water."

The children made models of islands with clay and drew pictures and maps

GEOGRAPHICAL TERMS—Plate 1

1 ARCHIPELAGO

2 CONTINENT

3 EQUATOR

4 AVALANCHE

5 CATARACT

6 FJORD

7 ATOLL

8 VOLCANO

9 GLACIER

10 BAY

11 DESERT

12 DELTA

Specially painted for this work.

The need for maps and for names to describe the different features of a country, both inland and on the shores of the sea, was realised very early in the history of civilised man. Both the ancient Egyptians and the Greeks developed the science of map-making to a considerable degree. On this and the following pages are illustrated many of the terms used to describe the varying formations of land and sea.

GEOGRAPHICAL TERMS—Plate 2

13 KOPJE

14 TABLELAND

15 FRONTIER

16 PASS

17 RAPIDS

18 LITTORAL

19 REEF

20 ESCARPMENT

21 CAVE

22 STRAIT

23 PENINSULA

24 GEYSER

In the past men used to think that the world was flat, although wise men of ancient Greece knew that it was not. Much of the knowledge that the Greeks gained was largely lost during the centuries following their decline. Some of this knowledge was only re-discovered and accepted as truth when the explorers of the fourteenth and fifteenth centuries awakened a new interest in geography and in the science of making accurate maps in place of the imaginative and fanciful maps of the Middle Ages.

GEOGRAPHICAL TERMS—Plate 3

25 ICEBERG

26 DYKE

27 SUB-CONTINENT

UNION OF SOUTH AFRICA

28 CANYON

29 PRAIRIE

30 VALLEY

31 PROMONTORY

32 POLDER

Land reclaimed from the sea

33 KAROO

34 BROAD

35 HIGH SEAS

High Seas

3 Miles

Mainland

36 ZONE

North Frigid Zone

North Temperate Zone

Torrid Zone

South Temperate Zone

South Frigid Zone

The circumnavigation of the world led to the making of globes and to some understanding of how the newly-discovered lands of the West, now known as North and South America, were related to the fabled countries of the East. As soon as the map of the World was known in broad outline, sailors and explorers began to make more accurate maps of the coast-lines of new countries, and new names had to be found for the special and distinctive features of the newly-discovered lands.

The World according to Ptolemy, A.D. 150.

Plotting mountains with theodolite

Contour map of a small island

Surveying Sloop

The World as known in 1492 by Behaim

An Egyptian astronomer and geographer named Ptolemy (Claudius Ptolemæus) first introduced the complete network of lines for measurement purposes, but it was many centuries before Behaim and others made an attempt to show the world as a globe. To-day the coast-lines, mountains and valleys are surveyed from the sea and on the land by experts equipped with scientific instruments, and contour maps are produced showing the varying heights of the land above sea-level.

like those shown below and did not forget to colour them prettily, you may be sure. Pictures C and D and the larger drawings to the right of them show you exactly what to do to follow the example of June and Robin.

Making a Mountain Range and Plain

June and Robin knew that very high land is called a mountain. One day at the seaside their father showed them how to make a mountain range. June and Robin helped him to make heaps of sand. Some of the heaps had round tops and some were almost flat. They made them in a line, piling the sand up between them.

This line of high sand their father called a mountain range. At one side the sand was made rather low and flat. This low flat land, their father said, was called a *plain*. He then broke up an old match box into small pieces and stuck them in the sand to look like houses.

These houses were a village on the plain at the foot of the mountain range.

" Are mountains really made of sand ? " asked June.

" No," said her father, " the soil on them is hard, and there are great rocks there. I only wanted to show you with sand what a mountain range and plain are like."

Make a model of a mountain range and plain as June and Robin did. With blue wool make one or two little streams running down the mountain side.

Notice, too, that mountains have very high points, which are usually called *peaks*. Much lower heights on the sides of the range are often known as *foothills*. Only very short grass grows on mountain sides, but it is the sort of herbage sheep like best.

When June and Robin had made their mountain range, their father showed them these pictures and told them the following story.

PICTURE C

Here is the model the children made of an island in a lake.

A PICTURE OF THE ISLAND

This shows us some more of their work, a picture of the island. Note how easy it is to sketch in the water.

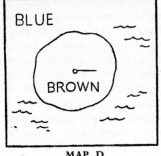

MAP D

Here we have a coloured map or plan of the clay model island above.

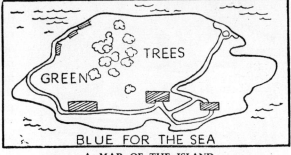

A MAP OF THE ISLAND

This shows you the map or plan of the island with the water all round. See how to sketch in houses and roads.

THE HILL-SIDE POOL
Water on mountain tops collects in small pools like this.

Travels of Water-drops

High up on a mountain side was a little pond, the home of many millions of water-drops. It was such a tiny pond that it was more like a pool. All the little drops in the pond wanted to travel and see the world. One stormy night when the wind blew, the rain brought a great number of water-drops to the pool. Some of them became very excited and they danced about singing, "Let us be off and see the world. There is no room for us here. Let us be off and see the world."

They rushed out of the pool and danced along until they tumbled into a *waterfall*. What a rushing and a roaring all the many water-drops seemed to make. They were carried by the waterfall down steep rocky sides, over great rocks and boulders to the foot of the mountain.

Here they ran along through the valley as a rippling singing *brook*, often winding round huge stones. Sometimes they were joined by other brooks or streams. Once they passed a lonely farm. Soon they ran into a great quiet *lake*, the meeting-place of other little brooks.

OVER THE FALL
From many mountain pools a stream is formed and this flows over a waterfall.

Boats and Steamers

But the lake was too quiet for the restless water-drops. They ran about it until they found an opening at the far end. Out they rushed in a stream soon to grow into a *river*. The river wound along through pleasant grassy land and past many farms. Sometimes the water-drops flowed under bridges, and they often saw boats and steamers. The river grew broader and broader and great towns were passed. The water-drops did not like the towns because near them the river became muddy and dirty, and they could not sparkle. Boats

A BROOK IN THE VALLEY
A brook is a small valley stream which has often to make its way among stone boulders.

FROM LAKE TO OCEAN

THE LAKE BELOW THE MOUNTAINS

Many brooks and countless tiny streams feed a lake, but when the basin is full its waters must run away, and this they do in the form of a river.

Specially drawn for this work.

A RIVER LEADING TO THE SEA

The river flows steadily from the lake to the sea. If it comes upon any high ground it sends its stream sideways and that is why most rivers wind. Where river and sea meet is the river's mouth.

Specially drawn for this work.

AT THE MOUTH OF THE RIVER

Here is the mouth of the river just where it joins with the sea. So we have followed water from the mountain-top to the pool, the brook, the lake and the river until we find it flowing into the ocean.

and steamers of all kinds stirred them up and sent them flying in the air or scurrying here and there. The water-drops really felt they were seeing the world.

The river now became very broad. To their surprise the water-drops found themselves being pressed back by other water-drops, salt water-drops hurrying towards them!

"Let us pass, let us pass," they cried.

"Presently, presently," sang the new water-drops. "We have come from our home in the sea; when we return we will take you back with us."

The water-drops had reached the *mouth* of the river where it ends and flows into the sea. As the tide was coming in they were checked in their journey for the time. They had to wait and mingle with the salt water-drops until the tide changed.

At last they heard a welcome cry.

"Off to sea, off to sea," shouted the salt water-drops. "We will take you to the great ocean."

"Off to sea," shouted the eager water-drops, and away they all floated out, out, out into the great *ocean*.

How different it was from the little pool on the mountain side.

There seemed no end to the vast ocean.

"Where is the ocean?" asked June. Her father told her that very deep and wide seas dividing land from land are called oceans, and there are five oceans. The children looked eagerly at their atlas to find the five oceans—the Atlantic Ocean, Pacific Ocean, Indian Ocean, Arctic Ocean and Antarctic Ocean. June thought the restless water-drops must have reached the Atlantic, but Robin thought the Pacific.

"And there," said his father, "we must leave them to rest."

Familiar Things
and How
They Are Made

Industries
That Serve
Our Everyday Needs

Topical Press.

THE FIRST ENGLISH TEAPOT

Tea was unknown in England until about 1657 and at first it was infused and kept in barrels, to be drawn and warmed as required. This teapot was made by the Dutch potter, Elers, who had settled in this country. Made about 1700 of red pottery, with raised moulding, and white enamel decoration, it is considered to be the first English teapot ever made.

THE POTTER'S ANCIENT CRAFT

THE making of pottery is one of the world's oldest industries. In Europe there is evidence that prehistoric man had learned how to make watertight vessels by firing clay, while in Britain pottery-making probably became a true industry as far back as the Early Iron Age. In modern times British pottery has become world famous and is exported to almost every country.

The Raw Materials

Clay is the chief raw material of pottery, the two most important types being china clay and ball clay, which are found in the counties of Cornwall, Devon and Dorset. But the pure white clay has to be mixed with several other materials before it is " china-slip." These include ground flint, which gives strength and increased whiteness; felspar, which helps to bind the other materials together; bone ash, from ground burnt animal bones; and Cornish stone or china stone.

The clay is mixed with water by the rotating blades of a machine called a " blunger." The other ingredients are

189

ground separately and kept in storage "arks" ready for blending. Only the correct amount of each ingredient must be used in the blending ark, where the liquid clay or "slip" is finally prepared.

This slip has to be passed through magnets to take out any iron that may be in the mixture, and is finally put through a filter press. The clay is now solid, but it has to be made more plastic before it can be handed over to the potter, and it is therefore churned and kneaded in the pug mill, rather like a huge mincing machine which disgorges the clay in a long, snake-like roll.

China clay of the best quality can only be worked by hand, for it is too "nesh" (brittle) to be handled by machinery. So if you go to the big workrooms at, say, the Royal Porcelain Works of Worcester, you will see the potter's wheel whirling and the "thrower" moulding his clay upon it in much the same fashion as the Egyptian potters of thousands of years ago. Only, whereas the ancient Egyptian worked his wheel with a foot treadle, the modern wheel is power-driven.

Modelled by Fingers

The wheel whirls and whirls and the thrower models the wet, soft clay in whatever fashion he wills. It is a fascinating sight to watch the shapeless mass grow into a beautiful form under the deft pressure of his fingers. These men are real artists, for they have not only a sure eye, but a true sense of proportion. Years of training and experience go into their work, which is often a family tradition, generation succeeding generation at the potter's wheel.

One of the difficulties of the craftsman who forms these beautifully-shaped cups and vases is that the clay shrinks so greatly when "fired"; that is, baked. He has to allow for this and, of course, it takes much practice to become perfect.

Much of to-day's ordinary "ware," but not fine china or individual pieces, is not made by the hand-throwing method just described. Machines called "jolleys" and "jiggers," and plaster

moulds and metal "profiles" are used. (You will have noticed already how many special terms are used in the pottery industry; each machine and process has its nick-name, as it were, and the products are not china, but "ware.")

The mould-maker usually deals in basins, bowls and similar articles. The moulds are made from plaster of paris, great care being taken to ensure that each part of the mould fits perfectly. But the *finishing* touches are put by the thrower. Handles, also made in moulds, are fixed deftly in position by the handler with a small dab of wet clay. It may seem strange, but it is perfectly safe for him to pick up a cup by its handle the moment he has put the handle in position.

The Cup Jolleyer

Cups are made on a "jolley." The clay is put in a plaster of paris mould, which shapes the outside of the cup. The mould is then put on the head of the "jolley." As this turns, the cupmaker draws up the clay inside the mould, then uses the metal "profile" to shape the inside of the cup correctly.

Plates are produced on the "jigger." Clay is flattened on a revolving disc, then shaped on one side by a mould and on the other by a profile.

Another craftsman we should see at work is the turner. On his lathe, dried "cheese-hard" cups and vases from the jolleyer or thrower are cleared of any surplus clay and burnished. Sometimes, he may also use a "runner"—a special tool for adding beading or filleting.

Firing the Work

Firing—that is, the baking of the clay pieces—takes place when they are "hard white." Some ware is fired only once, but fine china and earthenware will be fired at least three times and, if special colour effects are called for, there may be a number of additional firings.

When coal, gas or oil is used to heat the kilns or ovens, the ware must be protected from flames and fumes. Just as a cook puts his cake into a tin before

A CORNISH CHINA CLAY PIT

Central Press.

The foundation of English china ware is a pure white clay which is dug from pits, chiefly in Cornwall. Here you see one of the pits, with a background formed by the mighty heap of clay that has been excavated and the extremely steep narrow-gauge railway. This particular pit is situated near Fowey. Every year hundreds of thousands of tons of clay are produced in such Cornish pits as this.

THE HANDS OF THE THROWER

Fox Photos.

Though the potter's wheel is to-day power-driven, it remains much the same in principle as it has done through many centuries of pottery-making.

Central Press.

In this picture we have a close-up view of the clay-covered hands of the thrower as his fingers gently mould the wet clay into the perfect shape of the design.

Topical Press.

While the clay on the thrower's wheel before him swiftly revolves, it is fashioned into a classical shape by this skilled craftsman. In the Staffordshire Potteries there are some 300 factories, much of their production being sent to other countries.

Fox Photos.

HAND-DECORATED PORCELAIN

The more expensive china and porcelain is hand-painted by skilled artists, or decorated with ceramic colours by the enameller. The finest china is sometimes enriched by precious metals such as gold, silver and platinum. This picture shows a ceramic artist at work at Stoke-on-Trent, the heart of England's famous potteries.

it goes in the oven, so the potter puts his ware in saggars, or heavy fireclay containers. Saggars, however, are not needed when the oven is electrically fired.

" Biscuit Ware "

Let us assume that we are to see some fine bone china fired. The white-hard clay pieces, undecorated and unglazed at this stage, are carefully built up in tiers on the oven truck. The modern, electrically fired oven is very different from the one that mother uses. It is a tunnel more than 270 feet long and its maximum heat is more than 1,200° C.— more than enough to turn a joint of beef into dry ashes very quickly indeed! During the time that the truck passes through the oven, the clay pieces are transformed into hard, durable " biscuit ware."

Artists at Work

Now may be the time for the skilled artists and decorators to get to work.

The design may call for transfers to be applied, for ceramic colours to be delicately put on by the enameller, or for artistic painting by the hand-painter.

The addition of colours before the ware is glazed is known as " under-glaze decoration." But the number of colours that can be used is limited owing to the high temperature of the second, or " glost " firing. With the " on-glaze " method, however, there is no limit to the range that may be used. In this case, the biscuit ware is dipped in liquid glaze, dried and fired before the colours and enamels are applied. The ware is then fired a third time to fix the decoration.

Telling the Difference

We have been dealing with fine bone china and you may like to know how to distinguish between this and ordinary earthenware. If an earthenware and a china cup are both held up to the light, the latter will let a certain amount of

OLD WAYS AND NEW

Plates are made on a machine called a "jigger," the front being shaped by a plaster mould and the back by a metal "profile." Here we see the craftsman carefully shaping the rim.

This girl is a handler. With the help of a plaster mould, she is forming cup handles. A touch of moist clay and a little pressure will be sufficient to fix each handle firmly to its cup.

Photos: The Royal Worcester Porcelain Co. Ltd.

Here is a dipper coating a plate with liquid glaze. The plate will now be fired a second time ("glost" firing), then decorated with colours or enamels which will be fixed by another firing.

Using the old-fashioned kilns, firing took a week. Now it can be done in twenty minutes in this gas-fired continuous tunnel kiln. The man pushing the loaded truck into the oven is known as a "placer."

SPODE AND WORCESTER CHINA

A famous name among makers of pottery in England is Spode. It was in 1770 that Josiah Spode began to make felspar porcelain at Stoke-on-Trent and later introduced bone into the composition, thus giving a very transparent body. Spode china is usually highly decorated with flowers and gilding.

Photos: Central Press.

Worcester china is also famed among collectors. The factory was founded in 1751 by John Dale, who was both a scientific chemist and an artist. Soft paste porcelain, mixed with steatite, was employed, and early pieces include tea services and decorative pieces with embossed flowers and medallions.

Dorien Leigh.

The Duke of Portland, owner of the famous Barberini Vase, lent it to Josiah Wedgwood who made the first of the famous copies of what is now known as the Portland Vase.

Dorien Leigh.

Another example of Wedgwood's art is this piece from a dinner set of 952 pieces made to the order of Empress Catherine II of Russia. The paintings show famous English buildings.

Central Press.

The English porcelain industry was started at Chelsea in 1744, but afterwards transferred to Derby. In this photograph are seen several pieces of old Chelsea of the Red and Gold Anchor periods from the Lady Ludlow collection. Chelsea ware is noted for its rich groundwork of colour.

THE STORY OF WILLOW PATTERN

We have all seen Willow Pattern plates, for the design has been known and reproduced for a great many years. Of course, you will guess that the pattern came originally from China, but did you know there is a story or legend connected with it? The heroine of the romance was a beautiful Chinese girl whose father was a mandarin. Outside the girl's room was a willow tree (the one depicted by catkins) with a fruit tree not far away. The girl fell in love with her father's secretary, who was poor, and he sent her a letter floating in a nutshell across the lake (typified by the boat) asking her to fly with him. The girl assented, provided that her swain would fetch her from the little house where her father had made her live, and to this the sweetheart gladly agreed. We thus see three people crossing the bridge, first the girl carrying a bundle of flax on a staff for spinning; then the young man with her box; and, finally, her father bearing a whip. The lovers made their escape, were turned into doves and lived happily ever after.

light through; in other words, a china cup is translucent.

The colours used for decorating ware are made from metals such as iron, cobalt and copper. But very fine china is sometimes enriched by precious metals, such as gold, silver and platinum. These are fused to the ware in the last firing, but are dull when they come from the kiln and must be scoured with silver sand or burnished with an agate stone.

Some Famous Names

Among the many famous names in English pottery is that of Josiah Wedgwood, who started his own pottery in 1759, founding a world-famous firm which is still carried on by his direct descendants. Wedgwood did more to raise the quality of English ware than any other British pottery maker. In his designs he was inspired by the antique and produced beautiful shapes. He also improved the materials used in manufacture and carried out experiments to discover new mixtures. From 1744 till his death in 1795 he pursued his ideas and ideals and was the most versatile of potters. Among the artists he called on to help him was John Flaxman, but most of the famous artists of Wedgwood's day were enlisted to work on his designs. Another famous name is that of Spode. Josiah the elder began his factory at Stoke-upon-Trent about 1770 and the work was carried on by the younger Josiah who made the famous felspar porcelain.

Wedgwood, Spode, Royal Worcester, Royal Doulton, Minton, Royal Crown Derby, Coalport—these are some of the most famous British makes. If your mother has some china that she is very proud of, ask her if you may see the name on its base. Perhaps it will be one of those that we have just mentioned.

Doulton & Co. Ltd.

FIRING FINE EARTHENWARE

This is part of the continuous tunnel oven at the Burslem works of the Royal Doulton Potteries. The earthenware to be fired has been carefully placed on the tiers of fireclay bats on the oven trucks. These trucks move slowly through the oven, where the earthenware will be subjected to a heat of about 1,160° Centigrade. Royal Doulton is another of the famous names in the English pottery industry.

MAKING A DAILY NEWSPAPER

A CONFERENCE AT 10 DOWNING STREET

The Press photographer plays an important part in the production of the modern newspaper, and here we see a number of them at their work. Distinguished foreign statesmen have been to a conference at No. 10 Downing Street, and in the newspapers on the following morning, not only in this country but abroad, readers learn all that is known and see photographs of the visitors leaving the official residence of Britain's Prime Minister.

THE production of a daily news-paper brings us into contact with an industry remarkable for two outstanding features. The first is human skill; the second is the brilliance of the mechanical appliances involved.

Viewed casually, this statement might appear to be a little exaggerated, but a moment's analysis will, I think, prove to the most sceptical person that the two features I have named are indeed so remarkable that they are unsurpassed throughout the length and breadth of the mechanically controlled industries of the present day. Day by day, year in and year out, news must be gathered from all parts of the world, written into clear, concise English, laid out in an attractive and comprehensive form, set up in type, illustrated, printed in millions of copies, and dis-patched true to time to the many counties, cities, towns, and villages which make up Britain.

Now, although our main business in this section is to follow the activities of modern machinery, so dependent, in the present case, is machinery on human skill, and so closely are the two interwoven, that before we can fully appreciate the mechanical side of the newspaper industry, it is essential that we pay some attention to the human element.

We meet with it first in the men who sit at the apex of their profession; editors and heads of departments, keen brain-workers or engineering specialists, they control the movements of thousands of employees and all the magic of immense machinery. In them are vested policy and the *methods* of production; they see to it that the policy of the paper is properly followed, that the news they print is up-to-the-minute and as authentic as is possible, and that the lay-out of the paper conforms with the orders of the presiding genius—the Managing Editor.

Just as they are responsible to their powerful chief, so others are responsible to them. The editors control sub-editors, who " write-up," in swift, clear-cut journalese, all the hundreds of tersely-worded messages which come into the office by telephone, cable, tape-machine, and telegram; they control, too, the movements of the staff reporters, dramatic, literary, and film critics, special correspondents, photographers, and all the other members of the editorial staff.

The managing engineers, on the other hand, are responsible to the Managing Editor for the smooth running of actual production, the clarity of type and pictures, the evenness of printing, and the keenness of dispatch. The highest standard of organisation must be maintained, and failure in any of its many branches might well bring disaster.

Our Earliest Newspapers

The plant that these men employ is the direct result of more than three hundred years of constant experiment. The first newspaper printed, the *Avisa Relation oder Zeitung*, produced in Germany, bears the date 1609. Its compilation must have been a long and wearisome business, since the type, letter by letter, had to be carved by hand in small blocks of wood.

In England there were pamphlets published in the seventeenth century, and in the eighteenth century such brilliant writers as Swift, Addison and Steele began a type of journalism which still has its influence on our modern journals.

Printed newspapers and journals had become fairly well established by then, although they were read by only a small class. The earliest attempts to supply news were by means of the news-letters which were hand-written and copies made as the demand increased. In Elizabeth's reign the news-letter writers had become quite a flourishing body. It was not until the reign of James I that printed newspapers appeared. Probably the first real printed newspaper to be published in England was the *Weekly Newes from Italy, Germany and Hungaria*, which was issued by Nicholas Bourne and Thomas Archer in 1622.

A rival which was published by Nathaniel Butter came out soon afterwards, and as a result Butter and Bourne joined together and the first amalgamation of papers took place. In 1638, Charles I granted these two men a licence for the printing of foreign news. Oliver Cromwell was not very well disposed towards newspapers and suppressed several which had appeared during the Civil War. He had his own official newspaper, however, *Mercurius Politicus*, edited by Marchamont Nedham, while John Milton acted as censor of the Press.

Another licenser of the Press was Sir Roger L'Estrange, appointed by Charles II in 1663, and he became something of a monopolist by suppressing most of the newspapers and publishing his own. But while the Court was at Oxford during the Great Plague, Henry Muddiman was engaged to produce the *Oxford Gazette*. Its title was changed in 1666 to *The London Gazette*, and it has remained the official organ of the government ever since.

A Special Edition for a Great Victory

There were a good many handicaps with which early journalists had to contend. From about 1665 onwards there were Acts of Parliament controlling all printed matter, and the effect of these was to stop the ordinary kind of newspaper, while more or less secret news-letters were printed and sent to subscribers who lived away

HOW WE GET THE NEWS

Specially drawn for this work.

In stormy seas a ship runs aground. By the time a tug is able to put out the reporters and camera-men are there, ready to accompany the rescuers. (1) The shipwrecked crew are taken off and brought ashore, when (2) the pressmen make a quick return to their office. Photographs are developed and printed and the news editor (3) makes his selection, while the story is being written (4) and sent to the printer. Thousands of copies are presently on the night trains (5) and (6) at countless breakfast tables next morning the thrilling story is read.

NEWS FROM ABROAD

Apart from their reporting staff, the newspapers receive news from the Agencies such as the Press Association and Reuters. Here we see a Reuters man listening-in to a foreign news broadcast.

from London but were anxious to know the news from the capital.

Eventually these Acts were abolished, and in 1702 the *Daily Courant* was published. It was the first English daily newspaper, and it was also the first to publish a special evening edition. This came out in May, 1706, to give its readers the news of the great victory of Marlborough over the French at Ramillies.

Among the writers who contributed to the newspapers and reviews which began to be published about this time was Daniel Defoe, famous as the author of *Robinson Crusoe*. Eventually he brought out a journal of his own which became known as *The Review*. It was first published in 1704 and lasted till 1713. In this journal the " leading article " or " leader," which is still an important feature of every modern newspaper, was first introduced; so was the interview, which

still plays quite an important part in journalism to-day.

After Defoe, another hard fighter, John Wilkes, suffered, as Defoe had done, imprisonment for expressing his views too frankly and for criticising the government of the day. Wilkes founded the *North Briton* in 1762, and in No. 45 of that journal he violently attacked certain members of the government. For this he was committed to the Tower, but was eventually released to become a popular hero with the cry " Wilkes and Liberty! "

Later Wilkes was expelled from the House of Commons, sentenced to twenty-two months' imprisonment, and fined £1,000 for another article he published. However, in due course he became Lord Mayor of London and once again a member of Parliament. It was largely owing to the efforts of John Wilkes that the right of the Press

P.A.-Reuter.

DISTRIBUTING THE NEWS

Most of the news items broadcast by the B.B.C. come from the big news agencies, and in the photograph above a wireless operator at Reuters is seen at work sending out the news in Morse.

Associated Press.

CENTRE OF A FAR-FLUNG NEWS NETWORK

This photograph shows a section of the Fleet Street Office of the big American agency, Associated Press. Here a skilled team of editors, writers, wireless and cable operators, receive news from every corner of the globe. In this room the world's news is selected and written up for dispatch throughout the twenty-four hours by cable and radio to newspaper and other offices all over the world.

to enter Parliament and report the debates was recognised.

When "The Times" Began

The greatest handicaps under which newspapers suffered in the eighteenth and nineteenth centuries were the taxes put upon them. These stamp duties were not finally abolished until about 1850. Until that time there were no daily newspapers outside London though there were quite a number of weekly provincial newspapers. The total circulation of all the daily newspapers until the removal of the stamp duties was only about 75,000, and of this number *The Times* accounted for more than 50,000.

It was on January 1st, 1785, that John Walter brought out *The Daily Universal Register*, which was altered three years later to *The Times*. In due course it became the foremost newspaper in the world. For a century its rather ponderous and solid style was the model for all other journals. Then in the 'eighties of the last century, George Newnes, followed by Alfred Harmsworth and Arthur Pearson, began a new and brighter type of journalism which brought about a revolution in the world of print besides increasing the numbers of readers a hundredfold.

The Linotype Brings a Revolution

Where there were ten readers of the daily and weekly press in 1880 there are many thousands to-day. This rapid increase in print and readers demanded quicker printing, more paper, and more information about the world and all that happens in every sphere of human life. It led to the invention of wonderful machines and to the building up of a vast industry.

The old method of setting up by

hand all the different letters to make up the words to be printed has been replaced by machine-made type. Several kinds of machine are employed for type-setting, but the most widely used is that known as the *linotype*. To understand its working and the way in which a newspaper is printed, let us imagine that we are visiting the offices of a famous daily newspaper; the editors, sub-editors, reporters, critics, and photographers have prepared their " copy " and photographs for printing, and we are in the printing department watching machines bring typewritten and handwritten " copy " into newspaper life.

We are in an immense room housing dozens of curious-looking machines, all exactly alike, before each of which is sitting an operator. Every machine is about 7 feet high, 6 feet wide, and 5 feet deep. Viewed from the front it consists of a large keyboard, not unlike that of a typewriter, at which the operator is seated, a number of levers ready to his hand. To the left of the keyboard is a short, shining tray, above which is a narrow chute; while above the keyboard is a deep, inclining case connected at its top to mechanisms at the back of the machine.

A Machine and its Marvels

By stepping to the back of the machine we see that these mechanisms are a long, notched rod and a long revolving screw. At the far end of the rod, immediately above and slightly behind the shining tray beside the keyboard, is a steel arm, its " hand " touching the rod, its " shoulder " at the base of the machine. Beneath this arm, set in a complicated array of wheels and other apparatus, is a small furnace, heated by electricity and containing lead.

Now the operator starts work. He attaches a sheet of " copy " to a small easel, and begins to type out the words it contains. As he presses the keys (each of which is labelled with a letter) we hear the machine give short, sharp clicks; and, by looking over his shoulder, we see that little brass discs (known as *matrices* or moulds) are forming in an even row on a small carrier above the shining tray. These discs are being released, as the keys are pressed, from the sloping case at the top of the machine. If we could examine them, we should see that each is engraved with a letter.

Immediately the correct number of words to fill one line of type has been assembled, a bell rings, the operator presses another lever, and a mechanism known as a *delivery carriage* automatically collects the matrices and carries them, in a close row, to a spot immediately in front of the furnace. As soon as they are in correct position, molten lead flows from the furnace, enters the hollowed-out letters in the matrices, and waits for the next movement of the machine.

Sorting Every Letter

Now the arm at the back of the machine comes into play. The " hand " leaves the rod, drops to the matrices, grips them, and conveys them to the long revolving screw. The latter engages them and, carrying them along, drops them one at a time into channels leading to the case from which they were released but a moment ago! So cunningly does this " gadget " work that each letter is delivered into its correct channel—the a's together, the b's together, and so on.

But in the meantime the bar of lead bearing the line of type has been engaged in the hidden interior of the machine. Here it has been cooled, cut to exact size, and smoothly trimmed; and, as we watch, it is ejected through the narrow chute on to the shining tray, all ready for its future work of printing. Line after line of lettering is quickly assembled, for the machine is able to handle three processes simultaneously: assembling the matrices, casting assembled matrices, and dis-

AS THE NEWS FLOWS IN

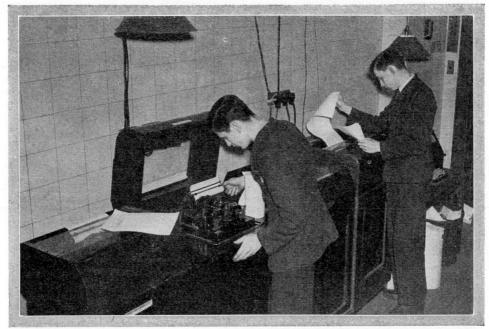

The Times.

From the big news agencies, with representatives all over the world, a continual stream of news is sent out to the newspapers. In this photograph we see the teleprinter machines in a newspaper office ; the typewritten sheets are taken out and handed to the news editor's staff.

Fox Photos.

Among the hardest-worked men on the staff of a daily newspaper are the sub-editors. Through their hands pass all the news stories of the day. Our photograph shows the sub-editors of the *Daily Telegraph* at their task.

tributing matrices already cast, at one and the same time. Expert operators, utilising all the immense capabilities of the machines, can produce as many as 20,000 *letters in one hour !*

From the linotype machine the bars of lead are laid out in a frame known as a *chase*, each chase being the size of a newspaper page. The illustrations (now in the form of metal *blocks*) are placed in position, and the columns of type and the blocks are securely locked. Actually, pages could be printed from the *forme*, as the completed frame is now called, while it is in this condition; but since newspapers must be printed in thousands, it is essential that many duplicates of the forme be made.

Work in the Foundry

This brings us to the foundry, where, by the aid of mechanical appliances, skilled workmen speedily transfer the printed matter from its bars of lead to curved " stereo " plates. Briefly, what happens is this. The forme is laid on a perfectly level steel table, a sheet of prepared material, called *flong*, is pressed upon it. When the flong is removed it bears an accurate impression of all the printed and photographic matter in the locked forme.

Our arrival in the foundry coincides with the fitting of this flong into a machine; the machine is closed, and a moment later ejects a curved metal plate, its outer surface engraved with all the type and illustrations, down to the finest detail. The machine is in fact a furnace containing molten metal which, at a moment, passes over the surface of the matrix (as the flong is now called); at the appropriate instant the apparatus stops the flow of metal, solidifies, and cools the plate, then cuts, trims, and ejects it in readiness for the important process of printing. This process is just as wonderful as those we have already seen.

It is here, in the

P.A.-Reuter.

THE STREET OF INK
The offices of practically all the national newspapers, as well as the London offices of many provincial papers and the big news agencies, are situated in or near Fleet Street. Throughout the twenty-four hours news from all parts of the world pours into the Street. Our photograph shows this famous thoroughfare looking eastwards towards Ludgate Hill and St. Paul's.

printing departments, that we meet with the gigantic machines that form the greatest engineering marvel of a newspaper works. The first thing that impresses itself on our minds is *noise*. There is a harsh, thunderous roar as machine after machine, each hundreds of feet long and between forty and fifty feet high, devours literally miles of virgin paper and ejects newspapers printed, counted, folded, and cut, ready for transport to every part of England. Blue-overalled men tend the machines; oil-can in hand, they scale steel ladders, adjusting a control here, checking a movement there. We marvel at their sure-footedness and seeming indifference to the immense energy of the machines beneath them.

But near at hand a machine is standing motionless, and men are preparing it for printing. Let us take the opportunity to examine it. It is composed almost entirely of brilliantly polished steel, surrounded halfway up by a platform, also of steel. Ladders run from the platform to ground-level, and here again the treads are of slender, strong steel. The workings of the machines are far too numerous and complicated to be taken in a short survey, but we see that they are mostly comprised of immense cylinders, some of which the workmen are covering with a type of smooth blanket.

Many Miles of Paper

Other men are clipping series of

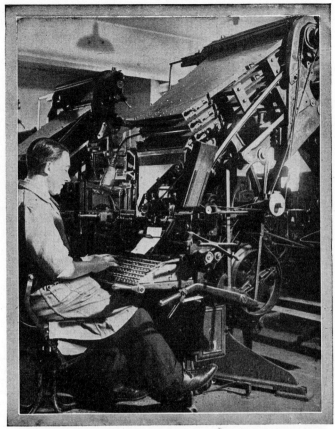

Daily Herald.

A LINOTYPE AND ITS OPERATOR

From Caxton's day until the invention of the linotype machine in 1886 all printed matter was set up by hand. The first linotype machine was made in the U.S.A., and it revolutionised the printing of newspapers. Our photograph shows a linotype machine with its operator setting up the " copy," which can be seen above the keyboard in front of him.

stereo plates to other cylinders, while a group is busily engaged in loading great reels of white paper on to one end of the machine. Here, however, light overhead cranes assist ; they lift the reels of paper with astonishing ease, and the men guide them to where steel jaws wait to grasp and hold them in position. These reels of paper (5 miles in each) are fitted to the machine, one above another; and their ends are taken and introduced into the mechanism.

Everything is now in readiness; a button is pressed, and slowly the great machine springs to life. There is a

The Times.

IN THE LINOTYPE ROOM

We have seen a close-up of a linotype machine and its operator, and this photograph gives a general view of linotype operators at work. The first flow of copy from the sub-editors' room has come down and has been divided into batches of convenient size for distribution to the men at the machines. The first stage of putting the world's news into the printed page has begun.

steady, swishing throb as the cylinders turn and the paper is drawn through the plant; another button is pressed and the throb changes to a thunderous din as the speed increases. A moment later the noise is lost in the general uproar of the immense building.

Cut, Folded and Counted

Now, as we walk down the length of the machine, we are able to observe some of its many marvellous components. We see that some cylinders, which bear stereos, are being automatically covered with an even coating of ink; as they turn, they press upon the paper threaded between them and other cylinders (covered with blanket) and print with an astonishing clearness every word and every picture-detail engraved upon the stereos. Farther on, the paper passes through an intricate arrangement of rollers that lead it down to more cylinders. These

print, in exactly the same way as the first, more reading and photographic matter on the *other side* of the paper.

Continuing our journey, we come to the far end of the plant, where hidden mechanisms work with an almost superhuman brilliance; and by listening carefully we are able to hear a steady and rapid *click! click! click!*

What is happening inside the machine is this: As each printed instalment of paper arrives at this section of the machine, it is cut and folded to form a complete newspaper; then, as the machine ejects it, a small device (which is responsible for the clicks that we hear) counts the papers into bundles or quires! With such magnificent precision does the machine work that it is able to print, cut, fold, and count no fewer than 80,000 *newspapers in one hour!*

From the machines the newspapers

are loaded into cars for distribution to every part of England and Wales, and often to Scotland and many places overseas as well, so that men, women, and children shall be kept informed of happenings in all parts of the world.

Occasionally it has been said, and by quite well-meaning people, that the use of machines in industry is directly responsible for the unemployment of many highly-skilled workers; but the newspaper business can justly claim that, were it not for its wonderful machines, news-matter, frequently of the most vital importance, would be seriously delayed in its distribution to the public. And in these days of international and political upheavals such delay could and would have the most damaging results.

So does the newspaper business employ the marvels of modern scientific machinery, and we, to whom our " daily paper " is a commonplace article, may well be grateful to the inventors and engineers who have made possible the superb mechanical methods of its production.

Many Millions of Readers

To-day there is practically no household in Great Britain where at least one newspaper is not taken regularly. London morning and evening newspapers have roughly a circulation of nearly twenty million copies. With the provincial and the Sunday newspapers added, a careful calculation shows the total to be nearly 60 millions. The Sunday newspapers alone account for more than 28 millions each week.

It is not only as distributors of news that our modern newspapers serve a highly important purpose. Other industries depend largely upon newspapers for the widest possible circulation of their advertisements in which they can tell the general public of the

News Chronicle.

MAKING THE STEREO

After the page has been set in type, the " forme " is taken to the stereotyping room, where skilled workmen make the papier mâché matrix from which the metal stereo is made. These half-cylindrical stereos are trimmed and bored to fit the cylinders of the printing machines in the deep basement of the newspaper office.

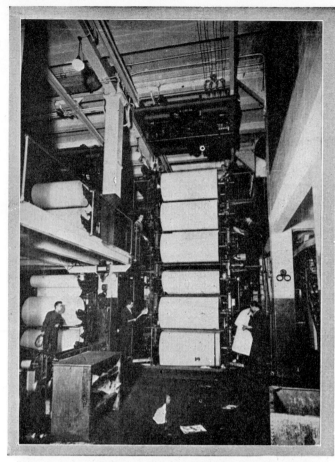

News Chronicle.

READY FOR THE RUN

Here we have an end view of one of the great printing presses which produce our newspapers each day. The reels of paper are in position and the crew of men who operate the monster machine are standing by in readiness for the signal which will set the machinery whirring, roaring and vibrating as the printing begins.

cheapest and surest way of acquainting the general public with important announcements which affect all of us. In various ways, too, the Press of any country can affect public opinion, but, generally speaking, where the Press is free and newspapers can express a variety of opinions, representing many different views, the public is well able to form its own opinions, based it may be on information given in different newspapers.

There has been much criticism of the newspapers right from the earliest days of their history, and this in itself is a safeguard. In America a Commission on the Freedom of the Press carried out extensive enquiries in quite recent years, while in our own country a Royal Commission was appointed in 1947 to enquire into the functions and control of the Press. This Commission made a number of useful recommendations.

goods they have to sell. Without the revenue derived from advertisements no modern newspaper could give its readers the service it now does in return for a very modest payment. Without the newspapers many manufacturers could not hope to inform the buying public to anything like the extent they can do through the Press of all the goods they have for sale. Increased sales mean reduced costs for the manufacturer.

Government and public bodies also find that newspaper advertising is the

Owing to the war the supply of newsprint was greatly reduced and in Britain newspapers were limited to about one-quarter their size in 1939. In some cases the reduction was even more drastic. Nor did the end of the war change the situation, and even in 1954 the newspapers of Britain were among the smallest in Europe, so far as the number of pages was concerned. The largest and most varied newspapers in the world are those of the U.S.A. Yet while America has more and bigger

FROM PRINTING PRESS TO PUBLIC

News Chronicle.

In this photograph we have a side view of one of the great printing presses. Each machine is several hundreds of feet long and from forty to fifty feet high, and is capable of printing, cutting, counting and folding up to 80,000 copies of the newspaper each hour.

The Times.

The newspapers have been printed and clerks and packers have seen the papers made up into bundles, addressed to the newsagents. Here we see them being loaded into the vans which will take them to the railway stations or distributing centres.

News Chronicle.

PRINTED AND FOLDED

In this photograph we see the concluding task performed by the modern printing-press shown in the preceding pages. Printed and cut, each separate newspaper is finally folded, counted and delivered all ready for handling by the packers.

evening papers are confined to a radius of about fifty miles of the city. The distribution of newspapers in this country is one of the many highly organised branches of a great industry.

Apart from their own staff of reporters and their local correspondents in the provinces, the London newspapers receive a more or less continuous supply of routine news from home and abroad through the news agencies. The chief of these are the Press Association, Reuters, Exchange Telegraph, Central News, and the two American agencies in this country, Associated Press and British United Press. The teleprinters in the newspaper offices are kept busy recording the news as it comes in from the agencies. Much of the news broadcast by the B.B.C. comes from these Press Agencies.

newspapers than this country the circulations of individual newspapers are not nearly so large, as a general rule.

This is due to the fact that there are no national newspapers in the U.S.A. owing to the great distances which would have to be covered if the whole country were served from New York. In Britain, London daily newspapers circulate throughout the whole country, though nowadays some of them are printed in the big provincial distributing centre of Manchester, and, in some cases, in Edinburgh. London

Fleet Street, which runs from Ludgate Circus to Temple Bar, has long been associated with the newspaper industry and the journalists and printers whose daily work it is to produce the newspapers. Many of the buildings in this famous street are wholly or in part newspaper offices, though some of these offices may be in the nature of branch offices while the newspaper itself is printed in one of the streets near at hand. Here, too, are the offices of the Provincial, Dominion and American journals as well as the London offices of European and South American journals.

OUR CLOCKS AND WATCHES

Fox Photos.

A COLLECTION OF AGED CLOCKS

Clock-making is an ancient craft that was practised by the blacksmith in medieval times. Some of the oldest clocks in Britain are seen in this picture ; their total age is 2,674 years and they are being inspected by a young pupil clockmaker.

HAVE YOU EVER paused to think what life would be like without clocks and watches ? It would be very difficult for us to plan our work and play, and well-nigh impossible for the life of the modern world to continue in its usual complicated pattern.

Early Water-clocks

Quite early in the history of the civilised world, man needed some more exact way of telling the time than the daily rising and setting of the sun. He had not progressed enough to make the intricate mechanisms that were later used; but he was sufficiently inventive to produce a primitive water-clock, and it is with timekeepers of this sort that the known history of clocks and watches begins.

In those far-off days of more than 3,000 years ago, man carved crude sundials in the stone and made rough stone vessels for use as water-clocks. The earliest " clock " that has survived is actually a water-bowl from Ancient Egypt. It has a scale marked inside and a small hole through which the water can leak away. As the water level falls, so its position in relation to the scale tells of the passing of time. This timekeeper dates from about 1400 B.C. and is made of alabaster. The original bowl is in a museum at Cairo, but you can see a copy in the Science Museum at South Kensington, London.

The sundials of ancient Egypt and of Greece and Rome were not of the kind that we have to-day to ornament our gardens. They were simple blocks of stone, so placed that the shadow of a part of one block fell across a scale of time marked upon the other block. In those times the day was divided (from sunrise to sunset) into twelve equal parts, and an " hour " therefore varied in length according to the season of the year. In summer, when the daylight period is long, the " hour " was long; in winter, the " hour " was shorter, because daylight then is also shorter. This rather unsatisfactory way of reckoning lasted until the fourteenth century when mechanical clocks and our present twenty-four hour day came into use.

Made by the Blacksmith

No one to-day would think of going to a blacksmith to buy a clock or of asking him to repair one that had broken. But in the fourteenth century the blacksmith was also the clockmaker —for the earliest mechanical clocks, such as those made in Italy, were constructed of iron. Similarly, the earliest watches were made of iron—and what cumbersome instruments they were! It is not surprising that they did not tell time accurately; in the case of the iron clocks, errors of as much as an hour a day were quite common.

Progress in the making of clocks and watches was dependent on the progress of general scientific knowledge and it was the swift scientific developments of the seventeenth century that made it possible to construct accurate timekeepers. Clocks were now given pendulums and watches balance-springs, the use of these being largely due to Huygens, a Dutch scientist and mathematician.

But by ten years or more after the middle of the seventeenth century, the lead in the clock and watchmakers' craft rested with England where such skilled men as Thomas Tompion, " the father of English clock-making," produced the grandfather and bracket clocks that proclaimed English preeminence. It has been estimated that during the seventeenth and eighteenth centuries, when the population of the country was less than ten millions, at least 70,000 people were employed in making clocks and watches. The industry is thus one of our oldest and one in which we led the world. We lost that leadership when other countries (Germany, France and Switzerland in particular) turned from the methods of the individual craftsman to mass production by machinery.

Cheap clocks and watches from these countries appeared in large quantities all over the world and the British industry fell rapidly behind. It is only in recent years that Britain has a revived clock and watchmaking industry which in part owes its recovery to a new form of clock, the synchronous electric, which draws its power from the electric mains and requires neither winding nor regulating. In the making of highly accurate timepieces Britain is to-day in the forefront.

Making the Works

If you have ever seen " the works " of a clock or watch, you will appreciate the high degree of accuracy and craftsmanship that is required to make so many small and exact parts and fit them together so that they tell time reliably. Your wrist-watch, for example, probably began its life on the draughtsman's board with drawings made on a scale fifty times greater than that of the watch itself. For to make the finished product and ensure its accuracy, measurements are used so minute in size that it is difficult for us to understand them. Our watchmaker will work in hundredths and thousandths of a millimetre, divisions no wider than— or not so wide as—a human hair.

He will work, too, in metals that have been carefully tested, making frames for the mechanism, cutting teeth in gear wheels, riveting the wheels themselves on to pivots, and cutting leaves in pinions. This work, involving perhaps 1,500 different operations, will produce what is called the " movement ": that is, the part of the watch which is worked by a mainspring to move the hands. Then comes the more complicated section of the watch, the escapement. This includes the balance wheel and hair spring and the regulator ; it is composed of nearly fifty different parts in the production of which nearly a hundred machines will have been used. But

ANTIQUE CLOCKS AND WATCHES

Sport & General.

This " Father Time Clock " with its quaint, mechanical figure was built in the year 1649, probably by Johannes Fromanteel.

Keystone.

This bracket clock was made by Tompion, " the father of English clock-making," during the reign of Charles II.

Keystone.

Kendall's First Marine Timekeeper (left) was taken to sea by Captain Cook on the second of his famous voyages. This was exhibited recently in London and is seen here in comparison with an up-to-date dress pocket watch.

A COLLEGE FOR CLOCKMAKERS

Clock- and watch-making is one of Britain's oldest crafts. This picture shows pupils at the National College of Horology at work on the assembly benches. Exacting tests have to be passed by the pupils before they are passed as qualified.

Photos: Topical Press.

Pupils at the College receive instruction in the automatic methods of clockmaking and also have to make watches to the highest standards. Here we see an instructor teaching the use of a precision tool room lathe.

PUTTING THEM TOGETHER

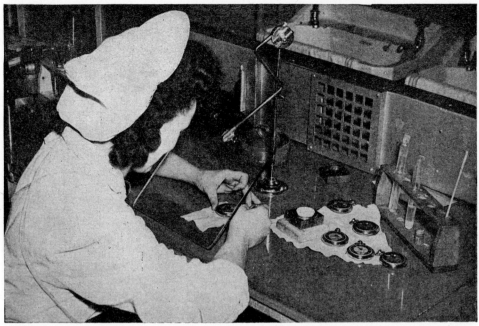

Clock- and watch-making requires great steadiness of hand and trueness of eye because the whole secret of its success lies in precision. Notice the care taken by this girl assembling watches in a British factory, aided by an adjustable glass.

This fifteen-year-old lad is working on a clock belonging to the South Kensington College of Science—and quite efficiently, too.

Here marine lever clocks for use by the Royal Navy are being assembled, the precision necessary demanding individual fitting.

though machinery is used to-day to bring our clocks and watches into being, their quality and reliability come from the skill and precision of the workers who have inherited their craft from the old clockmakers.

Look, for instance, at the famous astronomical clock at Hampton Court, made for Henry VIII in 1540. It not only tells the time of day, but is a calendar as well, and gives the moon's phases and the time of high water at London Bridge. Coming to more modern times, there is Big Ben, though the name rightly belongs only to its bell, famed throughout the world and now approaching its century. These, and many other famous clocks, have set the standard for our modern craftsmen.

And what a variety of timekeepers they have produced for us! Clocks with great dials and monstrous hands, watches no larger than a shilling, clocks which we can " plug in " to our electric circuit and others which tell us the time on the wireless and the telephone, wartime clock mechanisms that control fuses and detonators, and peacetime mechanisms that switch our street lights on and off. These are the wonderful means we now have instead of the sundial, the water-clock, and the clumsy devices of the medieval blacksmith. No longer do we depend for the time on the sand in an hour-glass or upon the sound of church bells; nor do we employ night watchmen to call the hours in the darkness. These are of the past. Modern time is told in modern ways.

International News Photos.

DENMARK'S " EIGHTH WONDER OF THE WORLD "

King Frederik of Denmark pressed the button that started this amazing clock at the end of 1955. It is claimed that this World Clock will lose only one second in 1,000 years, and it incorporates a calendar for 570,000 years as well as the eclipses of the sun and moon for 4,000 years. The dials on the left show how time is calculated locally and throughout the world. The clock was designed by Jens Holsen and stands in the Town Hall at Copenhagen.

A CAKE OF SOAP

ADDING PERFUME AND COLOUR

This picture shows one of the most skilled operations in soap manufacture—the adding of perfume and colour. With household soap this is done while the soap is still in liquid form. But with fine toilet soaps, perfume is added when the soap is in shredded form. Your toilet soap may contain no fewer than twenty-four delicate perfumes cleverly blended together.

A CAKE of soap is such an everyday thing that few of us pause to think of all the scientists, growers, seafarers and other workers, in lands near and far, whose skill and toil are necessary if we are to have soap to keep us clean and fresh.

The soap of long ago was very crude stuff and it was probably made from goat's fat and beech-ash. At one time, it was very heavily taxed; indeed, it was not until 1853 that the tax was abolished (in Mr. Gladstone's Budget of that year). Nowadays, of course, soap-making is a highly-skilled business, providing work for many thousands of people and using very different materials from the first crude tallow and wood-ash.

The Raw Materials

What raw materials are needed for making soap ? Firstly, oils or fats and, secondly, caustic soda or potash. The chief vegetable oil used by soap manufacturers is palm oil. Tallow (animal fat) and whale oil are also used, although some of our supplies of the latter are taken for foodstuffs.

By themselves, these fats would not make the sort of soap that you and I would like to use. They are therefore blended with soft oils, such as groundnut oil. Coconut oil and palm oil are commonly used to make good soap and are responsible for the ease with which it lathers.

You can understand, then, how much our soap-makers depend on raw materials from other countries. This explains why many of our most important soap-works are at large seaports or within easy reach of them. Now let us look at some of these raw materials from abroad and see how they are produced and what happens to them before they reach us in our cakes of soap.

The Valuable Oil Palm

Palm oil and palm kernel oil come to us from the oil palm, a tall, fronded tree that grows in the rain-forests of West Africa (especially Nigeria and Sierra Leone), Malaya, the Belgian Congo and Indonesia. Nigeria alone produces enough palm oil each year for some 150,000 tons of soap, and enough palm kernel oil for the same amount of margarine.

The tree starts to bear fruit when it is about five years old and will continue to bear fruit for a great many years. The fruit forms in " bunches " or " heads " at the top of the tree between the fronds which branch out from the trunk. Each " bunch " comprises anything from 1,000 to 3,000 fruits, or " drupes," packed tightly together on a tough fibre centre. The whole is about 2 feet long and weighs approximately 60 lb., perhaps more. One tree may produce a dozen such " bunches " during a season.

Each fruit has a pulpy outside, or pericarp, which yields palm oil, and a nut with a dark, oily kernel, which provides palm kernel oil.

When the fruit is ripe, it is harvested by agile cutters, who cut off the bunches, which fall to the ground where they are collected by the womenfolk to be stored under banana or plantain leaves until the fruits are soft enough to be picked off easily.

Extracting the Oil

The reddish oil is extracted from the pericarp either by pounding the fruits with long wooden poles or by heating them in one of the mills set up at convenient local centres. When the oil finally reaches the coast, it is purified and stored in large containers ready for the tankers which will carry it to Britain.

What about the nuts ? These are shelled by mechanical nut-crackers so that the kernels can be dried and bagged

Unilever Ltd.

SOAP PANS AS BIG AS ROOMS !

These are the large pans in which the mixture of oils is converted into soap. Each pan is 14 feet square, *i.e.*, about the size of an average room, and about 14 feet deep. Each can hold 60 tons of material. Note the feed pipes, which supply the oils, fats and caustic soda which will be boiled up in these huge receptacles.

ready for shipping. Large consignments go to Hull or Liverpool, where the oil is extracted by hydraulic and screw presses, or by the use of solvents, and then refined until it has neither colour nor smell.

Another palm also provides oil for the soap-maker. This is the coconut palm, which is widely cultivated in Malaya, Ceylon, Southern India, the West Indies, and throughout the Pacific (especially in Fiji and the Solomons). Like the oil palm, the coconut bears its fruit between the fronds at the top; from 30 to 150 coconuts may grow at a time on one tree. The nut itself, containing the white "meat," is sheathed in a thick, fibrous husk.

When the nuts have been split open, the halves are laid out in the sun for a few hours.

Unilever Ltd.

ON TO THE CHILLING ROLLER

The soap has been made, perfume and colour have been added, and the liquid soap is being drawn off from the mixer to the chilling roller. This cool steel roller causes rapid cooling, which gives the soap smoothness and improves its lathering qualities.

The white "meat" can then be separated from the shell quite easily. It is from the white flesh, dried in special kilns, that the oil is extracted. Sometimes this is done locally; at other times, the dried "meat," or copra, may be shipped and the oil extracted when it reaches its destination. Providing oil for the soap-maker is only one of many uses of the coconut palm.

One of the most valuable plants we have is the groundnut, whose "fruit" (the peanut or monkey-nut) is rich in vitamin and protein and goes to make margarine and cooking fats. Lower grades of groundnut oil are used in soap manufacture. The two chief Common-wealth producers of groundnuts are Nigeria and the Gambia, but the plant is also grown in East Africa and in other sub-tropical and tropical regions.

The groundnut is a small plant. Its flower is orange-yellow in colour and forms about a month after planting. When the flower has withered and fallen, the main stem or "peg" of the plant develops—not upwards, as you might expect, but downwards, forcing its way into the ground. It is here, from 2 to 7 inches below the surface, that the nuts grow and mature—hence, of course, the name "groundnut." When the leaves of the plant turn yellow, the farmer knows that the nuts are ripe.

Plants and nuts are pulled out of the ground and left in the hot sun to dry. Then the nuts are shelled and sold, bagged, and sent down to the coast ready for shipment.

The Evergreen Olive

If you visit any of the Mediterranean lands, you will be sure to see olive trees. Just as the coconut palm is the trade mark of the Pacific, so the olive is the trade mark of Italy, Spain and other Mediterranean countries. Olive oil has many uses; in some countries it is used instead of butter, and as a cooking oil. The finest oil comes from the first pressings, but this is too valuable to be handed over to the soap-maker. The oil he uses comes from the final pressing of the fruit.

Cottonseed also has a valuable oil content and may have helped in the making of our cake of soap. We import unrefined cottonseed oil from the Argentine and Brazil, and from other countries too; cottonseed for oil extrac-tion comes to us mostly from the Sudan and East Africa. The soya bean is another oil provider; it is cultivated in China, Japan and, to some extent, in Canada and the United States.

Whalers also serve the soap-maker, although whale oil is used not only for soap, but for margarine, glycerine and varnishes. From the great pine forests comes the resin which the soap manu-facturer needs to make his soaps more soluble. From many parts of the world come the perfumes that make soap more fragrant—lavender from our own fields, jasmine from the south of France, acacia from Australia, and citronella from Ceylon.

Chemical factories provide the soap-maker with caustic soda and potash, the former for making hard soaps and the latter for making soft soaps. These chemicals reach the soap works in block form and have to be broken up and dissolved in water to the strength required. It is important, of course, that the solution is not too strong—too

Unilever Ltd.

RIBBONS OF SOAP FROM THE COOLING MACHINE

A scraper removes the soap, in these thin ribbons, from the chilling roller to a moving belt. The shreds are then kneaded together and put into a refiner, which is rather like a large mincing machine and feeds short lengths of soap to another machine called a plodder.

Unilever Ltd.

CUTTING THE SOAP INTO BARS

In the plodder the soap is subjected to great pressure and finally comes out of a nozzle in the form of a long, continuous bar. As the picture shows, this bar feeds a cutting device which slices it up into convenient lengths ready for stamping and packing.

much of these alkalis might produce a soap that would burn the user. The more solid of the oils that have come to the works must be " melted out " and purified before they are ready for the soap-boiling pans.

At the Soap Works

Each of the large pans at a soap works can boil about 60 tons of soap. Round the edge of the pans run the pipes which feed in the properly mixed oils and fats and the caustic soda. At the bottom of the huge pans are the steam pipes which will bring the mixture to the boil.

The taps are turned on, the steam comes through, and before long the mixture begins to bubble like a witches' cauldron in a fairy story as alkali, oils and fats combine. Glycerine, as well as soap, is being formed and, since it is not required in the soap, something must be done to save this valuable by-product.

Salt is therefore added to the boiling mixture. This causes the soap, which is

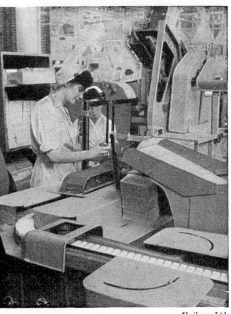

Unilever Ltd.

WRAPPING UP BARS OF TOILET SOAP

The long lengths from the plodder have been cut and stamped. The familiar tablets then pass to this wrapping machine which soon has them ready for packing and dispatch.

already beginning to thicken, to rise to the top of the pan while the liquid containing the glycerine collects at the bottom. When enough salt has been added, the steam is turned off and the curdled soap is allowed to settle. The glycerine water, or " spent lye " as it is called, is drawn off through pipes to another part of the works where the glycerine will be extracted.

When the boiling is over, the soap is left in the pan for three days. At this stage it looks like heavy syrup. Samples are taken to be tested in the laboratory, and if all is well, the soap is consigned to the mixing machine for its distinctive perfume to be added. If the tests reveal impurities or defects, however, the whole boiling is repeated.

After mixing, the soap (still in liquid form) is pumped from the mixer and allowed to flow over a chilling roller, from which it is scraped in thin shreds. These are kneaded together before being put through a refiner and plodder unit. Compressed in a vacuum in the plodder, the soap comes out in the form of a long, endless bar, which is cut up ready for stamping. Toilet soap is sliced into tablets at the amazing rate of about 10,000 an hour, ready for the packaging machine.

Fine Toilet Soaps

The finest toilet soaps contain special ingredients and require skilled mixing of perfume and colour. To begin with, the soap is made in the large boiling pan in the manner already described. But on leaving the pan it passes over water-cooled rollers and is shredded. The shreds are then dried, and colour and perfume are added, the mixing process being completed by heavy rollers, from which the soap emerges in long, pliable strips.

These strips are forced through a plodder, which converts them into long bars ready for cutting and stamping.

What an intricate and world-wide business is the making of soap! When you think of all the people involved, in lands near and far, and of all the complicated machines and processes used, it seems wonderful that a tablet of soap should cost so little.

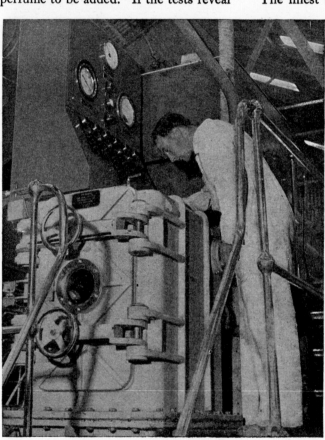

Unilever Ltd.

AT THE CONTROL PANEL

Many wonderful machines are to be seen in a modern soap factory. One of the most recent is a combined refiner and plodder unit, which has taken the place of the old cooling frames in the large scale production of soap. This picture shows the control panel of this remarkable invention.

Specially painted for this work by Dennis Adams.

AN ABORIGINAL CEREMONIAL DANCE

The Australian Aborigines have many strange festivals and ceremonies, most of which are connected with religion. The *kunapipi* rituals are widespread and originated, according to mythology, when Lumaluma, a troublesome man, left the land and became a whale. These Arnhem Land Aborigines dance round two huge *jelmalandji* emblems, constructed from wood, grass, paper-bark, clay and white bird's down, and on these are painted the symbolic snake design. The dancers are decorated with tufts of bird's down and totemic markings. The conical headdress, always worn by one of the older men, is made of paper-bark. The dances are performed to the singing of sacred chants, the beat of clapping sticks and the drone of the *didjeridoo*.

By courtesy of the Glass Manufacturers' Federation.

A WINE GLASS IN THE MAKING

Molten glass has been gathered from the fiery furnace in the background and is being fashioned by these craftsmen into a delicate wine glass. You can see the bowl and stem of the partly finished glass, which is shortly to receive its base, on the end of the rod held by the man on the right. He watches intently as his colleague shapes the foot of the glass. Only simple tools and methods are used to make mouth-blown glass in this way. The beauty and quality of the finished glass depends on the high skill of the craftsmen, not on the ingenious machines used in other sections of the British glass industry.

THE STORY OF LEATHER

Topical Press.

DRAWING SKINS FROM THE LIME PITS

These skins have been soaked in a series of lime solutions of increasing strength to loosen the hair and prepare the skins so that they will absorb the tanning liquid more readily. But before they go to the tanning pits, the skins will be cleaned of all remaining fleshy matter and washed in water or a weak acid solution.

OUR natural covering is our own skin, and the earliest people on the Earth had no other. But men soon learned to protect their bodies from heat and cold, using chiefly clothing from plants to keep out the heat, and clothing from animals to keep out the cold.

Cold they found worse than heat, especially when they learned how to make fires and found it necessary to wrap themselves up on going away from a fire on cold days. They wore the skins of animals to keep themselves warm or to protect their bodies from thorns and sharp rocks as well as from arrows and spears of enemies.

At first they simply dried the newly stripped skins and wore them with all the hair on. But such clothes grew stiff and uncomfortable and men therefore devised a way of making the skins pliable and tough—perhaps by accident, which even in our own days plays quite an important part in new discoveries.

Treating the Skins

They scraped off the hair, they hung the skins in the smoke of fires, they rubbed fat into them—and so made rough leather that was much better than untreated skins, which became stiff and smelly and were altogether uncomfortable.

The more men learned of the secrets of Nature, the better able they became to make themselves comfortable. But in doing so they became less able to stand heat and cold and rough ways of living, and they found it more than ever necessary to protect their bodies.

One good way of doing this was to protect their own skins by using parts of the skins of animals—especially by making leather for boots, shoes and leggings, and for gloves and gauntlets.

The great step forward was the discovery that the bark of oak and certain other trees could be used to convert raw hides into real leather. Men learned the art of tanning. They steeped their hides in a mixture of lime and water, finding this a good way of loosening the hair and making the skins easier to scrape. Then they placed the hides in a pit containing pieces of bark and filled it with water. The hides were allowed to soak for many months, perhaps even years, before they were taken from the pit, dried, stretched, and worked with oil and fat. This process remains the basis of modern methods, as we shall see presently.

Leather, in one form or another, is one of our oldest materials. In the British Museum, for example, can be seen a leather-seated stool made by the Egyptians some 3,500 years ago. In eighteenth-century England, jugs and bottles were often made of leather, and leather played its part in the great coaches used in those days. If you have ever seen the coach used by the Queen on State occasions, you may have noticed that it is hung on stout leather straps.

It is not until we begin to think about the matter that we realise how many different creatures provide us with hides and skins for the leather which plays such an important part in our daily lives.

Beneath our feet we wear the tough skin of cattle and horses, and above them (for the uppers of our boots and shoes) we wear calfskin—unless we are very young and wear shoe-leather made from sheepskin, lambskin or goatskin. Upon our hands we wear the soft velvety skin of kids, or lambs, or even dogs—unless we are wearing gloves of coarser leather for hard work, which may be made from goat, pony or even camel skin. Our suitcases may be of pigskin, like the fine saddles we put on the backs of horses when we go riding.

John W. Waterer.

WHERE HIDES BECOME LEATHER

These are the tanning pits. The hides are hung in a tanning liquid of exactly the right type and strength. Afterwards they will be scoured, rinsed and oiled, and then left partly dry until they are to be smoothed and stretched. There are various ways of tanning, the most important being vegetable tanning and chrome tannage.

W. Barratt & Co.

A CLICKING PRESS IN A BOOT AND SHOE FACTORY

This press, which gets its name from the noise it makes, is used with special knives to cut out many
pieces of leather of the same size and shape.   Some of the knives can be seen in the picture.   By
operating the lever, the clicker can apply pressure to the knives and so cut the leather.

Have you ever seen real parchment? Its manufacture is considered a part of the paper industry, but it is made from carefully worked sheepskins. You may have seen artificial flowers and other decorative things made of leather and it is also used at times for the buttons of sports jackets.

From Sea Creatures and Reptiles

The laces we use for our boots may be made from porpoise hide—for even sea creatures are caught to provide us with the leather we need. Perhaps you have seen bags or shoes made of sharkskin, and cigarette cases covered with shagreen, which is prepared from the skin of that strange fish, the sturgeon. Seals and walruses also provide skins for certain kinds of leather. Walrus-hide is especially tough.

Reptiles, too, are caught for the value of their strangely patterned skins. Most of us have seen fine shoes made of snake-skin, lizard-skin or crocodile-skin. Perhaps your mother has a crocodile-skin handbag. Small creatures such as rats and moles provide fine, soft leathers, and in Japan even frogskins have been made into delicate material for purses and other small things. The largest and heaviest of land animals—the elephant, the rhinoceros and the hippopotamus—have thick, tough skins which we might think unsuitable for leather. In fact, leather made from the hides of all three is in fairly common use—but not for clothing!

Where the Skins Come From

By far the most important animal-skins for leather are those of oxen, cows, sheep and goats. Almost everybody in civilised countries wears something made from them.

In Britain we rear cattle and sheep

15—2

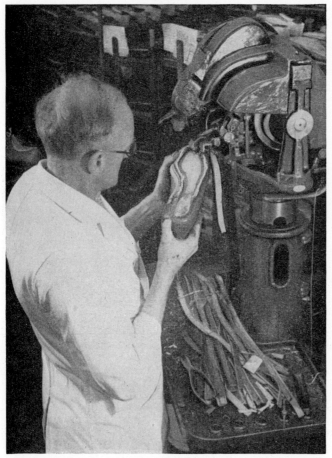

W. *Barratt & Co.*

WELT SEWING

In this picture we see the welt, or edging, of a shoe being stitched. The machine sews through the upper of the shoe and through a channel in the insole. When the job is done, the welt is levelled so that the sole can be sewn into it.

eat much veal in Britain, most of our calfskin also comes from abroad —from France and other European countries. Sheepskins come to us from Australia, New Zealand, South Africa and other countries where there are wide sheep lands. Most of our goatskins come from India, Nigeria, South Africa and other parts of the British Commonwealth.

Not all the hides and skins that we import are used in our country ; some are sold to other nations. But the British leather industry is one of the largest in the world. It employs more than 30,000 workers and exports goods to the value of more than £22 million.

From Raw Hide to Leather

Now let us see what happens to hides before they reach our shops as boots, shoes or other useful things. They

for our food supply, and it is from these animals that we get our home leather. But there are so many of us that all this leather is not nearly enough to make all the things we need, and we have to buy very large quantities of hides and skins from the great cattle and sheep lands of the world.

Most of our cattle hides come from the *pampas* of the Plate River lands— from the Argentine and Uruguay. Fair quantities are also supplied by New Zealand, Australia, East Africa, Nigeria, South Africa, the Irish Republic, Italy and other countries. Because we do not

come, let us say, from livestock in Nigeria, which exported some 9,000 tons of hides in 1952. Hides weighing 12½ pounds and more will probably be used to provide soles and heels for our boots and shoes; lighter hides and calfskins will be used to provide " box calf " and " willow calf " for the uppers. Goatskins will yield " suède kid " and other fancy leathers. Sheep and lambskins will be made into " grain " and " suède " for gloves.

A lot has to be done to hides, even before they are ready to leave Nigeria. When the hide has been removed from the animal, it has to be dried, washed, and then " cured," i.e., treated so that it will not decay during its journey to the tannery. The fleshy side of the hide is dressed with salt, after the hide has been immersed in brine. Sometimes a solution of arsenic is used, the hides being stretched on frames for drying after they have been treated.

When the hide is ready, it is put into its correct batch (according to type, size, condition and weight) and is then ready to be shipped to Britain.

There are many ways of converting raw hides and skins into leather—tawing, a way of tanning which uses solutions of alum ; chrome tanning, which uses solutions of chromium salts ; vegetable tanning, which uses tannin made from wattle bark, chestnut or quebracho wood, oak galls or acorn cups, and other vegetable materials ; and oil-tannage, which uses crude cod oil.

Chrome tanning is important because it produces leather which can resist heat and also keep out any amount of wet. It is sometimes combined with vegetable tanning in a process known as " semi-chrome." Oil-tannage is mainly used with sheepskin and gives us chamois, or " shammy " leather. But vegetable tanning, one of the oldest methods, is still one of the most important.

When the hides reach the tannery they are soaked in a chemical solution, which both cleans and softens them. The next task is to remove the hair. The hides are put into great open vats with lime to make the hair loose, and are then run through machines that scrape

W. Barratt & Co.

SEWING ON THE SOLE

This machine stitches into the welt of the shoe through a narrow channel in the sole, which is afterwards smoothed over by pressure. Sole and welt are thus united to make a firm base for the shoe. Some of the sewing machines used in a modern boot and shoe factory can make a thousand stitches in a minute.

off most of the hair, making it easier for men to finish the job by hand. It is unpleasant work, for the hides are slimy and give off an evil odour.

If leather thinner than the natural hide is required, the hide will next be split by machine into two or more layers, all of which can be used although the topmost layer is the best. Before this, any fleshy matter will have been removed from the underside of the skin, either by hand or by machine.

The hides are washed again, to remove any lime, and are then ready for the liquid that does the tanning. When they have been soaked in the tanyard pits, the hides are scoured, rinsed and oiled. Then they are " set out," i.e., smoothed and stretched, and undergo other processes before they are ready to be used by the manufacturer. Hides to be used as shoe-leather, for example, will be compressed by a rolling machine after they have been " set out." This compression makes them more waterproof and harder wearing.

If a coloured finish is required, the hides may be dyed or spray-painted. If a smooth surface is needed, the leather will be ''plated'' in a special machine; if the need is for a patterned or " grained " surface, it will be embossed. Suède leather will be given its distinctive nap by " buffing " with emery paper.

Tanneries in Britain

Our tanneries naturally grew up first in places where plenty of cattle-hides and sheepskins could easily be got, where there was good oak-bark to grind up for making tanning liquid, and where there was an abundant supply of clear, soft water. Think of the pastures of England, the oak forests there, and the many Midland rivers, and you will see at once the likeliest place for tanneries.

From early times to this very day there have been important tanning and leather businesses in the Midlands; the boot and shoe factories of Northampton and

W. Barratt & Co.

FIXING THE HEEL

At this machine the shoe receives its heel, which has already been built up to the proper height. The heel is attached by nails which penetrate to the insole and are clenched. More than a hundred mechanical operations may be carried out to complete a pair of boots or shoes.

neighbouring places are of great importance, and so are those of Leicester and Stafford. Another great shoe manufacturing centre, which, however, is not in the Midlands, is Norwich, the largest city in East Anglia, which is particularly famous for ladies' shoes.

Many of the big cities in Britain make some boots and shoes and other leather goods; but that is chiefly because there are so many ready customers.

Several of our great ports have their tanneries. Examples are Bristol, London, Liverpool, and Glasgow. Why is this? The answer is easy if we remember what vast quantities of hides and skins come to Britain from countries beyond the seas.

A Wonderful Industry

The greatest users of leather in Britain are probably our boot and shoe manufacturers. They need stout, hard-wearing leather for the soles and softer, more pliable leather for the uppers.

W. Barratt & Co

TRIMMING THE SOLE

Before the finished shoe can be waxed and polished, the edges of the sole must be trimmed. Scouring and glossing have still to be done, too.

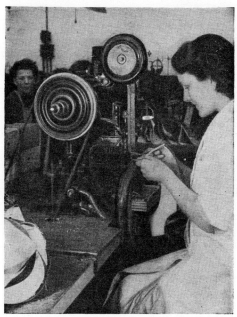

W. Barratt & Co.

FITTING EYELETS

Eyelets are inserted and clenched in position at quite an early stage in manufacture. The job is done neatly by this machine in a single operation.

At one time, all boots and shoes were made entirely by hand. Indeed, it was not until 1810 that any kind of machine was made available. Even to-day, you can still buy a pair of real " hand-made " shoes, carefully fashioned by a craftsman to suit the exact contours and measurements of your feet. They are more expensive, of course, than factory-made shoes, and you will have to wait for them to be made. But they will give you years of long and comfortable wear.

A boot and shoe factory is a wonderful place. More than a hundred, and sometimes as many as two hundred mechanical operations are carried out to complete a pair of boots or shoes. Many of the machines are not the property of the manufacturers, but are hired by them from the machine-makers. In such machines there is a disc on which is recorded the number of times each does its job, and the shoe manufacturer pays accordingly.

When boots and shoes are mass-produced, a large number of pieces of leather of the same shape and size are needed. This work is done by a clicking press, which gets its name from the noise it makes and is operated by a skilled workman called—can you guess? —a " clicker." Clickers must be able to get the most out of a piece of leather without much waste.

Other machines put the eyelets into the uppers and clench them in position. Linings are sewn in and the uppers trimmed by a machine called a post under-trimmer. One of the most marvellous of the machines is that which shapes the boot over a " last " or foot-shape, pulling over it the upper and tacking it to its sole.

From the cutting-out to the final polishing, the process of manufacture is by machines of many different kinds, working so fast under their skilled operators that the time taken for a single pair of shoes to be made is quite small. Even nailing is handled mechanically, while the special sewing machines may complete as many as a thousand stitches a minute. Where soles are not stitched to the uppers, but are stuck, the work of sticking is done mechanically at the rate of a thousand pairs of shoes an hour!

A Pair of Gloves

Machinery also plays its part in the making of leather gloves. The parts that go to make a pair of gloves are called " tranks " and they are cut from the soft, fine leather by a specially-shaped knife press. The tranks make up the back and the front of each glove. The small pieces which go between the fingers, called " forjets " or " fourchettes," are cut out separately.

The various pieces are stitched together by girls using electric sewing machines and the completed gloves are stretched over metal hands, or formers, containing steam. This gentle heat and the stretching give the gloves their proper shape. Elsewhere in the factory, buttons will be sewn on and the gloves packed ready for the shops.

Boots, shoes and gloves are certainly not the complete story of leather. You can probably think of many other useful things which come from our leather industry—leather wallets, suitcases, safety belts for telephone linesmen, saddlery, the straps on your school satchel, perhaps the whole satchel itself; and there are many others, too.

Fox Photos.

" LAYING OUT "

A newly-made glove has been drawn on to a metal former for "laying out " or ironing. The gentle heat and stretching ensure that the glove has its proper shape and a nice smooth finish.

THE WONDER OF GLASS

Fox Photos.

MAKING AN ENGRAVED GOBLET

Most of our ordinary glass is now made by machinery, but some of the finest glassware is still blown and fashioned by skilled craftsmen, who work with blowing irons and hand tools. In this picture we see such a craftsman carefully checking the engraved goblet he is making, to be sure that it is the correct size.

HAVE you ever thought of writing out a list of all the everyday things that are made of glass? What a long list it would be! It would range from window panes and ginger-beer bottles to spectacles, microscopes and other scientific instruments; from the heavy plate glass used for shop fronts to beautiful ornaments of fragile coloured glass and to spun glass so soft and pliable that you might mistake it for silk.

In Ancient Times

Who discovered glass? According to the Romans, the credit should go to some Phœnician merchants who stopped on a sandy shore in the eastern Mediterranean and used some blocks of natron (crude carbonate of soda) to support their cooking pots. When the meal was over and the fire had been put out, they discovered a strange, hard transparent substance. It was glass, formed from the fine beach sand and the natron, which had been melted together by the fire.

Although it is doubtful if the heat of their fire would have been strong enough to make crude glass in this way, something of this kind might possibly have happened. Even so, there is ample proof that glass was known long before the time of the Phœnicians.

It was in everyday use in Ancient Egypt as long ago as 1500 B.C., and glazed ornaments have been discovered

233

Crown Copyright.

MAKING GLASS TUBING

Slowly the two men walk away from each other, one using his blowing iron to keep the bore of the tube open. As the distance between them increases, so the syrupy molten glass stretches into a long, thin tube. Much glass tubing, of course, is also made by machine.

glass works there are many thousands of different formulæ for glass manufacture, and stocks have to be held of more than a hundred different substances ready for mixing with the sand, which is the basic material.

Obviously, the business of making glass has made great strides forward since the days when the Romans introduced glass-blowing to Britain. When they left Britain, the art of making glass vanished with them and it was probably not until the thirteenth century that England had glass-makers of her own.

How Glass was Made

For a long time, the making of even the most ordinary piece of glass was a slow and difficult affair. First the sand and other ingredients had to be mixed and then ground down into fine grains. Then the mixture had to be heated until a syrupy substance was obtained. This substance was taken from the furnace on the end of a hollow tube, or blowpipe, about 5 feet in length. Blowing down this pipe produced a large " bubble " of glass, which could be opened and spun so that the hot glass formed itself into a broad, flat disc. When the disc cooled, it was cut up into whatever sizes were required, the centre piece (where the glass had been attached to the blowpipe) having a characteristic bull's-eye pattern. You can often see this pattern in the window panes in old houses, where this " crown glass " has been used.

In time, it was discovered that the molten glass could be blown into a long cylindrical shape, split down the centre

in tombs of much earlier date. It may be, as Pliny the Elder says, that glass was first discovered in Syria, where there were rich deposits of fine sand and large forests to provide fuel for glass manufacture.

The main materials needed for making glass are sand, soda-ash and limestone. The sand is much purer and finer than ordinary beach sand, and in England it is obtained from quarries in north-west Lancashire, Surrey, Norfolk and other counties. Limestone for our glass industry comes from Derbyshire and north Wales.

Many other ingredients may be used as well, according to the type of glass to be made. We speak loosely of " glass," but there are, in fact, many types of glass. Indeed, it has been said that nowadays " there are more kinds of glass than there are of all the metals and alloys combined." At one modern

Pilkington Bros. Ltd.

A FURNACE IN A MODERN GLASS FACTORY

This picture shows the filling end of a glass melting tank furnace. Furnaces such as this may contain anything up to 1,200 tons of molten glass. The glass is drawn in a continuous ribbon from the tank, the edges of the sheet being gripped by two pairs of side rollers and pulled vertically upwards.

and then heated again so that it formed flat sheets. Then came the introduction of machinery, and glass-blowing was only needed for certain classes of work.

One of the difficulties that had to be overcome arose from the fact that molten glass does not solidify uniformly. The outside hardens before the inside. Strains are set up and unless something is done to counteract this natural process, the glass will break.

Annealing

The glass-makers therefore introduced the annealing process. What happens is this: the finished glass article is put into a heated chamber or tunnel called a lehr. The temperature in the lehr, which is higher at the entry end than at the exit, is carefully controlled so that the glass cools slowly and evenly as it travels through on a conveyor belt. This process makes the glass " stress proof."

Think of all the houses that are built every year. How slowly their windows would be fitted if the builders had to rely on supplies of old-fashioned crown glass! What a lot of glass-blowers would be needed! But nowadays, literally miles of sheet glass can be manufactured in a day.

The molten glass is drawn in a continuous ribbon from very large tank furnaces, which may contain anything up to 1,200 tons of molten glass. As the glass is drawn from the tank, the edges of the sheet are gripped by two pairs of side rollers and pulled vertically upwards.

After it has travelled a few feet, the glass has cooled sufficiently for it to be run between asbestos-covered rollers, which drive it upwards. The tower up which the ribbon of glass passes acts as an annealing lehr. On the top floor, which is 30 feet above the drawing point, the ribbon is automatically cut into sheets.

Plate Glass

Rollers of a different kind play an

important part in the making of plate glass. The raw materials are melted in a glass furnace similar in design to that used for making sheet glass. But the making of plate glass is a horizontal, not a vertical, process.

The molten glass passes from the tank between rollers and emerges in a continuous ribbon 100 inches wide. Without any break, it passes into the annealing lehr. Unlike sheet glass, plate glass has its surfaces marked by the rollers through which it passed. Both surfaces, therefore, must be ground and polished.

As the ribbon emerges from the lehr it comes into the open for a brief examination and then passes under a series of twin grinding heads. These grind top and bottom surfaces simultaneously. To complete the process, both surfaces of the glass are then polished by polishing heads, covered with felt, to produce the high-quality plate glass, with clear undistorted vision, so essential for shop windows, showcases, etc.

When the continuous ribbon of glass has been cut into sheets, it can be handled effortlessly by suckers operated and moved by electric cranes. These overhead cranes run on girders and transfer the sheets of glass to trolleys on which they can be moved to other parts of the works. Not only do the cranes save time ; they are also much safer. In the days when large sheets of plate glass had to be moved by hand, injuries were frequent.

Bending Flat Glass

Shop fronts sometimes need curved glass. This is produced with the help of a mould made of special metal. The mould is built in a furnace and the flat glass placed on top of it. Heated to an exact temperature, the glass will " bend " to the contour of the mould. Another method allows several sheets of glass to be bent at once.

What about bottles and electric light bulbs ? These are mass-produced by wonderful machines that take the molten glass and turn

Pilkington Bros. Ltd.

BOTH SIDES ARE GROUND AT ONCE

To remove the marks made by rollers during manufacture, plate glass must be ground and polished. After it has passed through the annealing lehr and been examined, the glass passes under a series of twin grinding heads, which grind both sides simultaneously. After this, polishing heads, covered with felt, complete the process.

Pilkington Bros. Ltd.

A SUCKER CRANE AT WORK

This large piece of plate glass is held in mid-air by suckers operated and moved by electric cranes.
These overhead cranes transfer the glass to trolleys on which it can be moved to other parts of the
works. The cranes save time and are also much safer than movement by hand, which often led to
injuries.

it into finished bottles or bulbs within twenty minutes. One of the newest machines can produce the glass envelopes of electric light bulbs at the rate of seven hundred a minute.

Bottle-making is one of the chief activities of the British glass industry; we manufacture nearly three million bottles every year. The machine used is a small glass factory in itself. As the machine revolves, its arms draw up molten glass, each arm taking enough for one bottle. Compressed air automatically blows the glass into a bubble, which is then shaped by a mould. Mechanical fingers lift the bottle from the mould and put it on a conveyor, which carries it through the annealing chamber at the right speed and temperatures. The finished bottle is made entirely by the machine; it is not blown by human breath or touched by human hands.

Perhaps your mother uses heat-resistant glass baking dishes. These have a hard, smooth surface that will last for a very long time without flaking or discolouring. Such dishes are made on an ingenious turntable press carrying about sixteen moulds. Molten glass is fed automatically into the moulds, stamped into shape, and then cooled by compressed air from tubes above the moulds.

Many a life has been saved because the glass-makers have discovered how to produce glass that is much stronger than the ordinary annealed type and that, if broken, cannot cause serious injury. Examples are found in armoured cars and aircraft.

The windscreen of your father's car could be made of either a laminated or a toughened glass. The laminated, or sandwich, glass prevents splintering. If the glass is broken, the pieces are held together by an interior layer of plastic instead of shattering into the car and injuring driver or passengers.

The toughened windscreen looks exactly like a piece of polished plate glass, but it has, in fact, undergone a special toughening process which makes it far more resistant to impact. Even if it is broken, this toughened glass disintegrates into very small particles which cannot cause serious injury.

Fine Glassware

Wine and other drinking glasses are now made by machine, but once they were entirely products of the glass-blower and he is still in demand for high-class work of this kind. Using his blowpipe, he first forms the bowl of the glass, which is then joined to its stem. Then the foot is added and carefully trimmed. The beautiful engraved glass that one sometimes sees is made with the help of copper cutters of various sizes, which are operated by a machine rather like a dentist's drill. This, too, is highly skilled work; an intricate pattern may take many hours to complete.

Some of the most wonderful glass in the world comes from Venice, which has been the home of beautiful decorative glass for many centuries. The Venetian craftsmen of old were so jealous of their skill that it was death for anyone to reveal the secrets of the craft to a foreigner. Murano is still the famous centre for Venetian glass, and there you can see skilled glass-makers turning out all kinds of elaborate designs.

The Venetians could "draw" glass in the form of very fine threads and used these to make elaborate patterns on other glass surfaces. To-day, glass threads and fibres are made by machine and used for many more ordinary purposes. Some are woven into cloth or tape; others go to make insulating material. The machine-made threads are so fine that fifteen of them may be needed to equal a human hair in diameter. Yet they are amazingly strong and flexible.

Colour is another quality in which Venetian glass has always excelled. It is colour, too, which gives such distinctive beauty to many of the stained windows in our churches and cathedrals. The oldest stained glass window in Britain may be seen in Canterbury Cathedral; it dates from the thirteenth century.

Glass was coloured by adding certain ingredients, e.g., cobalt, when blue glass was required. But the craftsmen responsible for the beautiful stained glass windows obtained their striking colours in another way. They mixed powdered glass with their paints and when the picture had been painted, heated the glass so that paint and glass became one.

Nowadays, stained-glass windows owe much of their beauty to the skill of the scientists and mixers at the glass works. One American company, for example, which specialises in the manufacture of stained glass can produce no fewer than 300 different shades and is ready to devise formulas for new hues should the artist require them.

This delicately coloured glass is blown in cylinders, which are afterwards cut, reheated and flattened into sheets. Working to the design prepared by the artist, the craftsman then cuts pieces of the right size and colour from the sheets and fits them together to make the complete window. The finished picture may tell some part of the Bible story, commemorate a saint or some event in Church history or serve as a memorial. Perhaps you have visited Westminster Abbey and seen the beautiful stained glass window dedicated as a memorial to the airmen who lost their lives during the Battle of Britain.

Lenses and Mirrors

You will sometimes hear people declare that "there is nothing new under the sun," and this certainly seems true when we come to consider the making

SPECIAL KINDS OF GLASS

John Topham.

Strangely-shaped glassware, like the bulbous tube which this glassblower is making, is often required by the medical profession. The small glass factory where this picture was taken specialises in work of this kind. Glassblowing is still a highly skilled art where all sorts of unusual shapes and sizes have to be made.

Central Press.

Another highly skilled craft is the making of stained glass for our churches and cathedrals. The picture in this window, which tells some part of the Bible story, is made from many pieces of beautifully coloured glass. The workman is soldering the joints, which will later be treated with a special mixture, to ensure that the finished window is waterproof.

of optical lenses and mirrors. For the peoples of old were not nearly so ignorant about such matters as you might suppose. It is said that a convex lens, or burning glass, was used in the fifth century B.C. for blanking out marks on the wax writing tablets of the time, and the emperor Nero is supposed to have used an emerald as an eyeglass. Spectacles were in use in the fourteenth century, and Dutch craftsmen were making telescopes in the early seventeenth century.

As you may imagine, making lensse for optical instruments such as telescopes and cameras is highly skilled work. The glass must be perfect—made without the tiniest bubble, shaped accurately, and carefully ground and polished. Special ingredients may well be needed in precise quantities and free from all impurities—lead, zinc, zirconium, antimony and barium are among the substances sometimes used. Some types of spectacle lenses undergo more than sixty different operations on twenty-six different machines during manufacture.

Glass mirrors were in use more than two thousand years ago, but it is only since 1840 that they have been silvered. To-day, mirrors find a place not only in our bathrooms and on our dressing tables, but in the very large telescopes of our chief observatories. The astronomer does not study the heavens by looking at them directly through lenses. He receives the picture with the help of two mirrors: one a large concave mirror at the base of the telescope, the other a smaller mirror fixed so that it can reflect the picture from the concave mirror to the eyepiece in the side of the telescope.

The reason for this arrangement is that while it is certainly difficult to make the large mirrors needed for these telescopes, it would be even more difficult to make accurate lenses of such a size.

Webb Corbett Ltd.

MAKING DECORATED GLASSWARE

This craftsman is cutting a detailed design into a water jug. It is slow and very skilled work, especially when a complicated pattern is required. The actual cutting is done by the small, power-driven wheel. Wheels of other sizes, from very small to quite large, can be fitted to suit the work in hand.

Reproduced by courtesy of Brooke Bond & Co. Ltd.

SOWING THE SEED ON A NEW TEA ESTATE

The forest has been beaten and the matted undergrowth and tangled vines have gone. Trees have been felled and uprooted, while shade trees have been planted. A new tea estate is born. In the nearby nursery seed is being sown and the beds will be shaded from the scorching sun by "tatties,"—thatches of grass and fern spread over bamboo frames. These will protect the young seedlings as they grow. When the seedlings are between six and eight weeks old most of them will be transplanted to the new plantation; others will go to old plantations to replace bushes past their prime. In approximately five years' time the bushes will be ready for plucking and will come to full bearing when they are six to eight years old.

Tivey & Hatton.

LUNCH-TIME WITH A GOLDFINCH FAMILY

Goldfinches feed their young in a rather remarkable way. The two parents go off to find and eat the seeds of thistles and other weeds. An hour or so later this food is regurgitated in pulpy form for the young. Young Goldfinches do not have the glorious colour pattern of their parents until their first winter-time and they are thus often called " grey pates." Two families a year are raised, occasionally three. The nest, in this picture in a clump of lilac trees, is a wonderful structure and is built almost entirely by the female. Although the male escorts her and is a proud spectator he will not deign to do any work himself.

Fox Photos.

MAKING LEAD CRYSTAL GLASS

Fine sand, lead and other materials are used to make high quality lead crystal glass. The tumblers seen in this picture still have the tubular tops by which they were attached to the blowing iron. With the help of simple machines, the girls are cracking off these unwanted tops.

The largest telescope in the world is at the Palomar observatory near Pasadena, California. This huge telescope has a mirror with a diameter of 200 inches. The mirror is 26 inches thick and weighs 20 tons.

A Giant Mirror

You can imagine what a difficult task it was for the glassmakers to produce so colossal a mirror. To lessen its weight, they cast it with a ribbed back. Special boro-silicate glass that would not be affected by changes in temperature had to be used and it was estimated that when the mirror had been cast, nearly a whole year would be required for the glass to cool.

Casting was successfully accomplished in December 1934. Just over a year later, grinding and polishing began. No fewer than 5¼ tons of glass were removed from the surface during this process! It was 1947 before the massive mirror could be taken to Palomar observatory, and nearly two more years passed before all was ready. Alas! at the eleventh hour an error of one twenty-millionth of an inch was discovered, and the glassmakers had to work for a further six months before their part in the building of the great telescope was done.

Have you ever been inside a lighthouse? If you have visited one of these signposts of the sea, you will know that its powerful, guiding beam depends not only on the men who tend the light and the power which keeps it alive, but on reflecting mirrors, lenses and prisms, which throw the beam out into the darkness.

Glass also plays a part in one of our most recent pleasures—our television set. The " screen " on which you see the televised picture is really the end of a glass cathode ray tube. The tube is bulbous in shape, and great precision is needed in its manufacture. The screen you watch at the cinema may also be made of glass.

GOOD THINGS FOR THE LARDER

MAKING OUR DAILY BREAD

Flour, water, salt and the proper amount of yeast have been mixed together mechanically in these large kneading pans or vats. The pans have been wheeled away from the mixers and are now being left for a short time to allow the dough to rise. This is a typical scene in a large modern bakery, where machines now do most of the work that was once done by hand.

WHAT lucky people we are to have enough food every day ! Yet only too often we take it for granted that mother will always be able to get good things for the larder and that there will always be something interesting to eat when the time comes for our next meal.

Have you ever wondered about the bread, butter, jam, tea, coffee, sugar, meat and all the other foodstuffs that mother buys ? People on farms and in factories, at home and across the seas, have worked hard so that we may have an unfailing supply. Yet we have become so used to finding good food on our tables at every meal that we hardly ever wonder where it all comes from, or what we should do if, for some reason, our supplies stopped suddenly.

" The Staff of Life "

One of the most ordinary foodstuffs, and one of the most important, is bread— called " The Staff of Life " because it is our main support. Because it is so important, we sometimes use the word " bread " in a much wider sense. We speak of " earning our daily bread," meaning " getting a living " and not merely earning enough actual bread to eat.

Bread of one kind or another is eaten by most of the world's people. In other lands bread may be made from barley, or oats, or rye, or maize, or millet, or rice. But here at home our bread is made chiefly from wheat. Some of that wheat is grown in the cornlands of eastern England and in the Scottish lowlands. But about four out of every five loaves of bread eaten in Britain are made from wheat grown in lands beyond the seas ; in Canada, Australia, the United States and other countries. In Vols. III and IV you can read more about the wheat that comes to us from abroad.

Bread is made from flour, which is made by grinding grains of wheat in mills. Once this work was done in old-fashioned mills driven by sails that whirled round in the wind or turned by the power of running water. Only a few mills of this kind are still in working order. Most of our flour is made in mills that are really " flour factories " in which ingenious machinery does nearly all the work, and where the few workers needed are engineers and engine-minders rather than millers.

At the Flour Mill

First the wheat must be cleaned. The outer husk is removed (unless the flour is needed for brown or wholemeal bread) and so is the inner skin. The grain is also passed over an electro-magnet in case any small pieces of iron—from harvest machinery, perhaps—have got into it. Stones and dust are taken out as the wheat, subjected to currents of air, passes through wire-mesh cylinders.

Next, the wheat has a bath in a large tank containing water that is churned continuously. At one end of the tank is a drying machine which removes all moisture from the golden grains before they are shot into storage bins. A further cleaning takes place, before the grain is ground, in a big rotating cylinder lined with emery. As the cylinder rotates at speed, the grains are rubbed clean and then given a final polish by revolving brushes which pass the grain through to the next lot of bins.

The actual grinding is done by a series of metal rollers that reduces the grains to the fine white flour that we know so well. From these rollers the flour passes down chutes and into sacks ready for the baker.

A. C. K. Ware.

A COOLING DRUM IN A MARGARINE FACTORY

When the oils, milk and vitamin concentrates that go to make margarine have been mixed and churned into creamy emulsion, this liquid mixture has to be converted into solid form. It is pumped into troughs, picked up by a small roller and transferred to this large cooling drum. Spread in a layer on the drum, the margarine solidifies during a single rotation of the drum and is scraped off in flakes by a blade.

Unilever Ltd.

PACKING MARGARINE MADE IN VOTATOR UNITS

At this Thames-side factory, all the processes needed to make margarine are carried out in one piece of plant called a Votator. The Votator units are totally enclosed and provide a continuous supply of margarine to the packing machines seen in this picture. These machines produce more than ninety packets a minute and automatically fill the 24 lb. and 48 lb. containers.

A Modern Bakery

The baker's first task is to mix the dough for his bread and nowadays this is done in a large kneading-pan. First the flour is put into the pan, and then the proper amounts of yeast, water and salt are added. The pan, which is on wheels, is moved under the electrically-driven mixing machine whose metal arms stir and knead the dough far more thoroughly than the baker himself could do it. During this process, the pan itself is kept revolving.

From the mixer, the dough goes down a chute to another machine which divides it into roughly-moulded pieces. These are taken by conveyor belt through a warm-air box. Already the dough has begun to " rise." The partly-finished loaves are then flattened and rolled, placed on well-greased trays, passed through another warm air chamber and, finally, through the electric or steam-heated oven.

Perhaps your mother buys wrapped loaves. The wrapping is done by another machine after the loaves have passed through cool air on leaving the oven. Such is the work of a modern bakery where machinery does most of the jobs.

Butter and Margarine

Bread by itself is a rather uninteresting food and most of us prefer to make it more palatable with butter or margarine and jam or marmalade, too. Butter makes us think at once of our dairy-farms, for it is made from the rich cream separated from the milk by machinery. Did you know that twenty pints of milk are needed to make one pound of butter ?

Unfortunately our dairy farms and creameries, good though they are, cannot produce anything like the quantity of butter that we need. So once again we have to buy abroad ; butter comes to us from New Zealand, Australia, Denmark, Holland and other countries.

FRUIT FOR JAMS AND JELLIES

Much of the fruit used at this jam factory comes from the large orchards and strawberry fields owned by the factory itself. Whether it is local fruit, reaching the factory in summer and autumn, or oranges from distant lands for marmalade making, it is all carefully inspected on arrival, as the picture shows.

Photos : Chivers & Sons Ltd.

The jam is made in these large silver-lined pans in the boiling rooms of the factory. Fruit and syruped sugar are brought to the correct temperature by steam-heat and presently the experts test the set of the jam with their long ladles. When the jam is ready, it is carried through silver troughs to the filling rooms.

Chivers & Sons Ltd.

FILLING THE JARS

In the filling rooms exactly the right weight of jam is put into the jars by automatic filling machines. Each of these machines can fill 180 jars per minute. The filled jars then pass through sterilisers and vacuum chambers where air is excluded and the lids are made fast.

In 1953 New Zealand provided more than forty per cent. of the butter we used.

If we visited the farms and creameries of New Zealand, we should find that the business of making butter—and cheese, too, for that matter—is wonderfully organised.

On most farms, the work of separating the cream from the milk is finished a few minutes after milking is complete. During the season, the cream is collected daily from the farms by lorries from the dairy companies. On reaching the creamery, the cream is carefully weighed, sampled and graded, and is then held overnight in large, cool vats lined with stainless steel. On the next day, the cream is piped to the large "end-delivery" churns, which may be capable of turning out anything from fifty to a hundred boxes of butter, each weighing 56 lb. The churns are called "end-delivery" machines simply because the butter is unloaded from the end of the churn.

Churning takes between half and three-quarters of an hour. The great mountain of rich butter which is taken from the churn has to be cut into conveniently sized blocks and this, too, is done by machine. New Zealanders are rightly proud of their dairy machinery, which is among the best in the world.

The work of making the butter is not yet finished. Before it leaves the creamery, it will be stored for at least a day in the cool room. Then off it goes to the grading stores and the refrigerating rooms at the docks, there to await shipment—some, perhaps, to Britain and your breakfast table.

"Butter" from Nuts and Whales

The next best thing to butter for our slice of bread is margarine. And people who know how it is made may tell you that it is, in fact, a sort of butter—a *vegetable* butter made from the oils of certain nuts.

One of the large factories where margarine is made stands on the banks of the Thames, not far from the mouth of that famous river. If we visited it, we should see drums and casks of these oils being unloaded at the big wharf. Many of these drums and casks would hold oil from nuts and seeds grown in hot lands, but others would contain whale-oil, for this is a most important raw material nowadays for the makers of margarine. Sufficient oil is produced, in a single season, by a typical whaling factory ship to provide a year's margarine for six million people!

The vegetable oils used in making margarine include coconut oil, palm kernel-oil, cottonseed oil and groundnut oil. If you have read the section in this volume dealing with Soap, you will know something about them.

If good margarine is to be made, the oils and fats must be free of fatty acids and impurities, and most manufacturers have their own refineries to produce the clear, purified oil they need. Lactic acid cultures (colonies of natural organisms occurring in milk) are used in the dairy industry to control the souring of milk when butter is being made, and milk used for margarine is similarly treated. Concentrates of vitamins A and D are also added to margarine; these vitamins are of especial importance to the proper growth and development of our bodies.

Margarine is made by what is known as the churn-drum process. Our tour of a typical factory would start in the milk room, where we should see pasteurised, fat-free milk—to which lactic acid cultures have been added—being slowly stirred in large containers. The stirring continues for about eighteen hours.

The next stage is to churn the ingredients (milk, oils, vitamin concentrates, all in exact proportions) until they form a creamy emulsion. This emulsion is pumped into troughs and then spread by a small roller on a large cooling drum. As this drum rotates, the layer of emulsion solidifies and is scraped off into containers below the drum.

Once the solid flakes have returned to normal temperature, they are passed through a series of kneading Multiplex rollers.

The partly-made margarine is rested for a time and then goes to be pommelled by the " S " shaped paddles of the blending machines, which give a further mixing to the proper texture and consistency. This completes the manufacturing process; the margarine is now ready for the remarkable machines which cut, wrap and package it.

There is now a single piece of plant, called the Votator, which carries out all the manufacturing processes (except packing). It is totally enclosed and operates continuously, feeding freshly-

Chivers & Sons Ltd.

PUTTING THE LABEL ON THE JAR

When the jars have been filled and sealed, they pass through cooling chambers and are then stored until needed for despatch. Then they are again inspected and the familiar label is put on by machine. All that remains is for the jars to be packed in their cartons ready to be sent to your grocer.

made margarine direct to the packing machines.

Do you know the origin of the word " margarine ?" It comes from an ancient Greek word meaning " pearl." A good name, don't you think, for the pearly-white substance first discovered by the French chemist Mège Mouriès in the eighteen-sixties, which so often takes the place of real butter ?

Jams and Marmalades

What could be better to put on our bread and butter than a rich strawberry jam, with whole strawberries in it, or marmalade made from the finest oranges ? One of the places where we can see fine jams and marmalades made is Histon, in Cambridgeshire. The factory there is only one of several owned by this particular manufacturer, who also has more than 10,000 acres of farmland where much of the fruit for his factories is grown. The oranges for the marmalade, of course, have to come from abroad, and during the winter they arrive by the train-load.

Whatever the fruit, it is carefully examined on arrival at the factory to ensure that it comes up to standard. Some will be used for jam-making, some will provide fruit juice for the jellies which are also made at the factory. Jam-making starts in the boiling rooms, where the fruit is put into large silver-lined pans, which also receive syruped sugar before steam-heat is applied. Experts check the set of the jam and when the latter is ready, it is carried by silver-lined troughs to the filling rooms.

Here are the wonderful automatic filling machines which can put exactly the correct weight of jam in no fewer than 180 jars a minute. These jars have been washed and checked for flaws before they reach the filler. When they have been filled, they pass through sterilisers and vacuum chambers for the air to be excluded and the lids firmly fixed down. Thoroughly cooled in the cooling chambers, the jam is now ready for storing. When the time comes for the jam to

leave the factory, it will be inspected again and then labelled.

Inspection is most important at a factory of this kind. You can imagine what serious losses there would be if the quality of its products was not maintained. That is why a large research laboratory is maintained to keep the purity and quality of the products under constant supervision.

Where the Fruit comes from

Large though they are, the farmlands surrounding this factory cannot produce all the fruit needed. Large tonnages of fruits of many kinds are used during the course of the year, and some inevitably has to come from other areas. Do you know where those areas are ?

Probably our most important orchard county is Kent, which has excellent soils for fruit-growing ; not too much rain, but enough ; plenty of sunshine and some winter frost ; and fruit-growers who are highly skilled at their business. Strawberries, cherries, plums, apples, pears and other fruits are produced in Kent, " the Garden of England."

Other good orchard lands are the Fen District, the county of Worcester with neighbouring orchards in Hereford and Gloucester, and Somerset, Devon and Cornwall, " where the cider apples grow." Moreover, fruit-growing has spread from Kent west into Surrey, Sussex and Hampshire, and north into Essex and Middlesex—perhaps because Greater London is so important a daily market for fruits of all kinds.

In Scotland, the most important fruit-growing lands are in the Carse of Gowrie between the Firth of Tay and the Sidlaw Hills which shelter the orchards from cold north winds. In Wales there are orchard lands in the northern coast plain and valleys.

Where does the factory get its oranges ? Probably from Spain, whose bitter Seville oranges are well suited for making marmalade. Originally, the orange— like other citrus fruits—was a native of Southern Asia. It is said to have reached

Cadbury Bros. Ltd., Bournville.

GRINDING COCOA " NIB " TO LIQUID PASTE

The roasted cocoa beans have been broken into small pieces and the shell extracted, leaving the pure cocoa, or " nib." The " nib " is then passed through the grinding mill seen in this picture. Since it is rich in cocoa butter, the heat and pressure of the rollers reduces the " nib " to a thick liquid paste, or " mass," from which the cocoa is made.

Spain by way of India and Arabia and to have been introduced by the Moors. Does your mother use candied orange-peel when she makes the Christmas puddings ? That, too, comes from Seville oranges.

The sweet, juicy oranges that are so refreshing on a hot summer's day come from several countries ; from South Africa, Cyprus, Israel (Jaffa oranges) and Brazil, to name the most important.

Tea and Coffee

If we wish to realise how much we depend on workers in other lands for some of the needs of our daily life, we have only to think of our common drinks—tea, coffee and cocoa—which are the products of hot lands beyond the seas.

The real home of tea is said to be Assam, in north-east India, on whose well-drained hillsides the kindly shrub is still grown in huge quantities. Our tea buyers look chiefly to India and Ceylon for their supplies of tea, although some comes from Pakistan and East Africa, and from Indonesia. You can read about the cultivation of tea elsewhere in this work.

Chinese and Japanese say that we *spoil* tea. They take it, always fresh and lightly brewed, without either sugar or milk, and in cups without handles. Well-brought-up girls are carefully taught the " tea-drinking ceremony " as part of their training as young ladies who know how to entertain guests with hospitality and dignity. Russians and many other Europeans (including many British) prefer to take tea without sugar and milk, but with a slice of fresh lemon in it. Have you ever taken tea this way ?

Is there a nicer smell than that of roasting coffee beans ? To the Americans and many Europeans, the aroma of the breakfast coffee is the best of morning welcomes. And although we cannot rival them as coffee drinkers, we do use a great deal of coffee.

The biggest coffee growers in the world are the Brazilians, who produce nearly half of the world's supply every year. Some of our coffee comes from Brazil, but recently even more has come from East Africa and from the Belgian Congo.

The coffee tree is an evergreen and in East Africa it is usually grown from seed, the seedlings being planted out when they are about a year old and a foot in height. The trees are allowed to grow to a height of about 5 feet and are then "topped" so that all fruit will be within easy reach of the pickers. The flowers are white, the berries dark red.

How quickly an expert picker can harvest the crop! His fingers and thumbs deftly twist the ripe berries off the trees and in the course of a day he may gather some 200 pounds of fruit. Pulping machines strip the berries of most of their outer pulp and water then carries them into the fermenting tanks. Fermentation makes easier the removal of sticky matter from the seeds, and this is done in washing channels— rather like large tanks—by Africans using long wooden paddles.

The seeds are then put out in the sun on trays, or drying floors, where they are turned with rakes every so often. Sometimes machines are used to dry the seeds. The coffee then goes to a curing works, where hulling machines remove the outer "parchment" and the "silver-skin," i.e., the layers protecting the seeds themselves. When this has been done, the seeds may be called "beans."

If roasting is to be properly done, only beans of about the same size should be roasted together. For this reason, they are graded by machine. As a conveyor belt carries the beans along, sharp-eyed workers remove any bad or discoloured beans. Finally, samples are carefully examined and coffee made from them is critically tasted. Then,

and only then, are the beans considered ready for marketing.

It is roasting that brings out the wonderful aroma and flavour of coffee. But once the beans are ground, this attractive fragrance will soon weaken unless the coffee is kept in an air-tight tin. Ideally, the beans should not be ground until just before the coffee is to be made.

"The Food of the Gods"

The cacao tree was classified by Linnaeus, the famous Swedish botanist as *Theobroma Cacao*, from the Greek words *theos* (god) and *broma* (food). The seeds of this tree are the raw materials of cocoa, that rich food-drink which most boys and girls like. The real home of the cacao is South America, but the tree is now grown in hot, wet lands in many parts of the world.

Columbus, they say, brought some cacao seeds back to Europe with him. The Spanish conqueror Cortes in 1519 found the Aztecs of Mexico drinking chocolate made from cacao beans as their national drink; their emperor Montezuma "took no other beverage than the *choco latl*, a potation of chocolate . . . served in golden goblets."

Most of our cocoa and chocolate to-day comes from African farmers in Ghana and Nigeria, but some comes from the British West Indies, Brazil and a little from Sierra Leone and French West Africa.

Let us have a look at the work of a typical Ghana cocoa farmer. His "farm" is ground cleared in the bush and shaded by a few trees which have been left standing for this very purpose. The beans are planted in a nursery patch; but when they have developed into seedlings, they are planted out about 10 to 15 feet apart. For several years the trees grow; then, at last, the small white, yellow or pink flowers appear on the main trunks and branches. After the flowers have dropped, the pods appear; they are green at first, but they soon change to yellow.

By harvest time (October-December) the pods are golden brown. They are cut from the tree with cutlasses and gathered into heaps, then split open so that the beans can be taken from their juicy bed of pulp. At the farmer's compound, the beans are laid out in the sun on drying platforms and are turned every day until they are dry enough to be put in sacks and sold. Then off to the port they go for their long sea voyage (more than 4,000 miles) to Britain. Bristol and Liverpool are the chief ports of entry.

At the Factory

On arrival at the factory, the sacks are stacked in a large warehouse. When the warehouse is full, it contains some 120,000 bags of cocoa beans. As they are required, the sacks are placed on a conveyor belt which takes them off to be examined, graded and blended. Blending depends on what is to be made; some mixtures are best for cocoa, some for chocolate, and others for special types of chocolate.

Once the beans have been cleaned and sieved (to remove loose shell and any small threads of sacking), they are ready for the roasting ovens, into which they are fed by chutes and hoppers. The ovens look like a row of large revolving drums and the room in which they stand is filled with the pleasant aroma of cocoa beans. The drums or ovens are heated by gas and each is capable of

Tate & Lyle Ltd.

CUTTING A SLAB OF SUGAR INTO CUBES

The sugar has been made and run into moulds, then cooled and spun to remove any surplus syrup. It is afterwards dried, in white slab form, until it is quite hard. As the slabs leave the drying ovens, they are passed through machines whose guillotine cutters divide the slabs into cubes. This picture shows us cubed slabs emerging from the cutter.

roasting 1,000 pounds of beans at a time. Roasting is skilled work, because only a man who has many years' experience can tell when the beans are done.

Roasting loosens the husk of the bean, which is not needed by the cocoa manufacturer. So after roasting, the beans are passed through heavy rollers, a process known as "kibbling." These rollers crack the shells and break them into small pieces, but do not crush the beans. " Winnowing "—the next process—separates shell and the pure cocoa, or " nib."

On goes the " nib " to the grinding mills, to be crushed by steel rollers or heavy revolving stones. But the result is not a powder ! Cocoa contains fat or butter, and when ground forms a dark sticky liquid, known to workers in cocoa factories as " mass." This " mass " is processed in the pressing room, where the surplus cocoa butter is squeezed from it by hydraulic rams. The resulting hard, dry cake is ground and sieved into our fine cocoa powder.

Cane Sugar and Beet Sugar

Sugar cane is a giant grass and it is grown in the hot, moist parts of the world. Most of our cane sugar comes from Cuba, Australia, Mauritius, British Guiana, the British West Indies, and the Dominican Republic.

Unlike the sugar-beet, sugar-cane, once planted, will go on throwing up new stalks for several years after the old stalks have been cut. On large plantations, the cut canes, trimmed and topped, are put on wagons and taken to the factory. Here, the cane is slashed into small pieces and fed into a large rolling machine which crushes the red-gold cane to squeeze out the juice.

The juice is then purified and concentrated for boiling in vacuum pans which convert it into " massecuite "— a mixture of sugar crystals and syrup. This massecuite is spun in swiftly-rotating containers which separate the crystals, or raw cane sugar, from the dark syrup, or molasses. The sticky brown crystals are now ready to be shipped to refineries in England.

Sugar-beet is now grown by about 50,000 farmers in the United Kingdom and provides some 750,000 tons of raw sugar. October and November are the harvesting months.

Trains, lorries and tractor trailers all take part in the work of getting the beet to the factory, where mountains of the roots soon pile up. When they have been washed and weighed, they are cut by machines into thin shreds and put into warm water which soon changes into a sugary liquid. This liquid is purified and then boiled until it changes to syrup, which is carefully heated in special containers until the small sugar crystals appear in its sticky mass. Then it is put into other containers, which whirl round at high speed and separate the crystals from the syrup. The crystals are brown and must be refined to make the white sugar we buy.

The pulp left after the first sugary juice was drawn off for sugar boiling is made into a valuable cattle food.

At the Refinery

Refining raw sugar is a long, expensive and very thorough process.

First, the sticky film of syrup has to be removed, by a process known as affination, so that only the hard crystals remain. The centrifugal machines used in the later stages of the process can be revolved at 720 revolutions per minute. The purer sugar which is produced, is dissolved and strained ready for the next process—carbonation and filtration. From this process, it emerges as a clear brown liquid.

This liquid is filtered through tanks containing charcoal, which absorbs impurities and leaves the liquid sugar ready for the vacuum pans. Boiling the sugar in these pans is a highly-skilled job which requires years of training.

More than one boiling takes place. After the first, the boiled sugar goes back to the centrifugal machines so that more syrup can be spun off. This syrup may be boiled to produce a further crop of sugar crystals.

After boiling, the small amount of water remaining in the now white sugar is removed in large rotating drums, or granulators through which warm, filtered air is drawn. Wire mesh drums, and vibrating sieves are then used to divide the sugar into the proper grades—coarse, medium and fine granulated sugar, and caster sugar.

HOW SCENT IS MADE

Central Press.

HARVESTING ENGLISH LAVENDER

English lavender water is world famous and Norfolk is the main growing area. This picture shows girls harvesting the lavender for the famous firm of Yardleys.

FROM the very early days of civilisation the making of sweet-smelling scents has been an art and an industry. There are several references in the Bible to the use of such scents as sweet cinnamon, sweet calamus and myrrh. Moses was commanded to take " sweet spices, stacte and onycha and galbanum ; these sweet spices with pure frankincense " and to make of them " a perfume, a confection after the art of the apothecary, tempered together, pure and holy."

When the wise men of the East set forth on their journey to seek the Child in Bethlehem they took with them valuable gifts. In addition to gold there were two scents, frankincense and myrrh. In Egypt, and throughout all the lands of Western Asia where the early civilisations first developed, the use of scent for ceremonial and domestic purposes was general.

Capturing the Flower's Fragrance

The apothecary, or chemist as we know him to-day, has continued as he did in those far-off times to blend together the oils from flowers and sweet herbs to make the perfumes which bring pleasure to one of our five senses, the sense of smell. A wider variety of flowers as well as scientific knowledge have added to the powers of the perfume-maker of to-day, but some of the principles of scent manufacture remain as they were in the days of old.

The earliest perfumes were made by dissolving odorous vegetable substances with sesame, or with almond or olive oil. To-day scent or perfume is obtained from the flowers, leaves, roots and the wood of plants by extracting the essential oils. This is but the first step and the method of extraction depends upon the nature of the substance. The separation of the sweet-smelling material, or the substance which causes the fragrant aroma, from the plant itself is not by any means a simple matter since one process that may be very useful in one case will in another destroy the very essence it is desired to obtain.

Of late years scents have been made from that most unlikely product of the gas-works, coal-tar. The expert perfume-maker is continually experiment-

WHERE PERFUMES ARE MADE

This picture shows one of the processes in the manufacture of lavender water. On the left is a condenser containing cold running water. Steam volatilised oil of lavender from the still enters a tin worm immersed in the cold water, and both oil and water emerge from the cock at the bottom, to be separated in the glass cylinder below.

Photos : Central Press.

This picture of a Perfume Compounder's laboratory shows just a few of the many essences needed to make fine perfumes of elusive fragrance. The Perfume Compounder is seen studying a horn of Abyssinian Civet and holding a flask of Bulgarian Attar of Roses.

ing to find the best way of preserving some new fragrant odour and it is often by a blending of the essence obtained from the flowers and some product of the laboratory, that is, a synthetic substance, that the best combination is found.

At one time it was thought that perfumes which made use of a coal-tar product were coarser and did not hold their fragrance so long as those in which no synthetic substances were used. That is scarcely true to-day, though it would be correct to say that nothing can take the place of the essential oils extracted from the flowers themselves. It is the skilful blending that makes the perfumes of to-day so fascinating and attractive. The tenacity of the scent is highly important and the longer its fragrance clings to the handkerchief or other garment the more highly is the scent regarded.

Brought From Many Lands

To the maker of perfumes to-day come the products of many countries. The South of France probably produces a wider range of the essential oils extracted from flowers than anywhere else. Bulgaria is famed for its attar of roses. In England the two main native perfumes produced are

lavender and mint. Orange-flower water is made in Sicily, while iris and bergamot are the special products of other Italian centres. Abyssinia supplies certain animal extracts which are essential. From Germany came the famous Eau-de-Cologne which is now largely made in England.

This particular perfume was invented by an Italian, Johann Maria Farina, who settled in Cologne in 1709. It is believed that Johann's original recipe

GRASSE, CAPITAL OF WORLD PERFUMERY

Nestling in France's Alpes-Maritimes, twelve miles from the Mediterranean coast and over 1,000 feet above sea-level, is the little town of Grasse, famous for the essential oils, distilled from the flowers of the sheltered hillsides, which are used by perfume-makers the world over.

WATER FOR THE FLOWERS OF GRASSE

Grasse, the famous French perfume town, has but a small rainfall at times when the flowers from which the essential oils are distilled need moisture. Water has, therefore, to be supplied from such large tanks as the one shown in this picture.

Bottling the Rose

It will be gathered that the first stage in the manufacture of scent is the production of the essential oils from the flowers. With these the chemist can experiment in his laboratory to produce a new and more wonderful scent. One of the most valuable of essential oils is attar (or otto) of roses and the export of this has for years been an important part of Bulgaria's trade. The scent manufacturers in other countries pay high prices for small flasks of Bulgaria's attar of roses.

This essential oil is not in itself very pleasant to smell. It is used sparingly with other scents and in combination helps to bring out the perfume the chemist wishes to create. All the time in the laboratories of the scent-manufacturers highly-skilled chemists are engaged on research to achieve that extra fragrance and subtle charm which will add to the pleasure, not of the beholder, but of the inhaler.

The capital of world perfumery is Grasse in the South of France. The town lies in a sheltered position in the Alpes-Maritimes, twelve miles inland from Cannes, and more than a thousand feet above the level of the blue waters of the Mediterranean. Here during

was lost after his death, but at one time there were many chemists in Cologne who used the name Farina and claimed to be the sole owner of the true recipe, though there is no longer much secret about the main ingredients. The usual recipe is twelve drops of each of the following essential oils : bergamot, citron, neroli, orange and rosemary, with one dram of Malabar cardamoms, all distilled with one gallon of rectified spirits.

the summer the hillsides are a blaze of colour. In June the carnations come to perfection and it is then that they are gathered in baskets and taken to the distilleries. Other flowers are gathered in their season and all in turn are deprived of their essential oils so that their fragrance may in due course be contained in a small bottle, to be discreetly and gently used by its owner and so waft its sweetness on the air in the home, or office, or in the dance hall.

Grasse has a population of some 20,000 people, the majority of whom are employed in one branch or another of the great industry for which it is famed. Broadly speaking, Grasse itself is not a great scent-making town, but it supplies a foundation for scent-makers all over the world in the flasks of essential oils, the distillation of the millions of flowers which cover its hill-sides.

Where Perfume Fills the Air

Another part of the world which has been endowed by Nature so that it is specially suitable for a certain flower is in Bulgaria. There are three places, Kasanlik, Kalofer and Karlovo, where the famous attar of roses is produced. In the valley as far as the eye can reach are rose gardens, miles and miles of wonderful blooms whose perfume fills the air. Generally

the roses are picked before sunrise, between 2 a.m. and 6 a.m., for at this time the perfume is considered to be at its best.

The whole population of the district works in the rose fields or distilleries, and even the children help when the time for gathering the flowers is at hand. Attar of roses is one of the most valuable of essential oils from the perfume-maker's point of view, and its manufacture means food and shelter to the peasants living in the valley in this out-of-the-way part of the world. The distilleries in the district deal with the rose harvest by modern methods and in due time the flasks of attar of roses,

HARVESTING CARNATIONS AT GRASSE
In June, carnations, roses, and jasmine blaze in all their glory on the hillsides around Grasse. Girls, dressed in typical peasant style, gather the flowers which then go to the factory for distillation.

DISTILLATION BY STEAM

This picture shows flowers being loaded into the distilling machine. Distillation by steam is the most effective method for many flowers, but where the essential oils might suffer from this process, another method called *enfleurage* is used.

soft fatty substance which is obtained from the civet cat found in North Africa. It is imported chiefly from Abyssinia and is stored in horns. In itself there is no pleasant fragrance about civet ; it is indeed distinctly disagreeable, but it is highly important in the laboratory of the scent expert. Ambergris is obtained from the whale, while castoreum comes from the beaver.

All these animal substances impart "life" and diffusiveness to the perfume to which they are added. They might be called *fixing* agents. A pure extract of flowers, though it might be skilfully compounded and possess a delightful sweetness for a time, would not last long. Hence the need for some other addition to act as a preservative of the delicate aroma produced by the chemist's skilful combination of flower essences. Other substances used as fixing agents include oils such as patchouli and sandalwood, and certain balsams and gums.

worth more than their weight in gold, are sent to other lands.

Fixing the Fragrance

Besides the essential oils obtained from flowers there are other important and valuable essences derived from animals which are valued by the scentmaker. Musk from the musk-deer comes from the Atlas and Himalayan mountains or from Tibet. It is costly but is among the essentials. Civet is a

Many mountain plants are also gathered for the sake of the sweet-smelling oils which can be extracted from them. Rosemary, thyme, mint and vermouth are valuable in this way. Not all are used for scent-making alone but are also employed to give subtle flavourings to medicines and to other liquids which can be rendered more pleasant by even a hint of some fragrant aroma.

Flowers picked for scent-making lose their perfume very quickly and it is necessary to deal with them as soon as they are gathered. Most of them, like the roses of Bulgaria, are gathered before the sun is up, but this is not an invariable rule as certain flowers are at their best when the sun is shining full on them. As soon as they reach the factory they are dealt with at once, but again the treatment varies with different flowers.

For many flowers a process of distillation by steam is the most effective method. When steam is used a separate boiler is erected close to the one in which the steam operates and this takes the mixture of distilled water and oil from the flowers. There is no risk of damaging the oil by burning with this method. In some cases some of the oil and water combine and then they are used in that form, as for instance in the case of rose-water or orange-flower water.

In other cases the oil rises to the top and the separation may be made by a system of high and low drainage taps, or dealt with in some other way. Each manufacturer adapts the method to suit the purpose he has in view. In

another method petrol is employed to extract the essential oil.

For certain flowers the steam method is unsuitable as the high temperature of steam would damage the flowers and destroy or seriously affect the essential oil. In this case the method used is known as *enfleurage*. The petals are spread upon specially-prepared sterilised fat which has the property of extracting the scent. This is done several times until one pound of fat holds the fragrance of about twelve pounds of flowers. A Grasse factory, for example, will have fifty to sixty thousand shallow glass frames on which

A GIRL WORKER IN A GRASSE PERFUME FACTORY
She is putting blooms upon specially-prepared sterilised fat which will extract the scent. This method is known as *enfleurage*.

the fragrant petals are placed and left for lengths of time varying from twelve to seventy-two hours.

The perfume-laden fat is then mixed with pure alchohol which absorbs all the scent from the fat. The alcohol is then treated to get rid of the last trace of the fat and thus leave a scent-laden spirit which is the essential oil desired by the scent manufacturer in Britain and other countries.

Maceration differs from *enfleurage*, as the flowers are immersed in hot fat or oils. Roses and a few other flowers are often treated in this way. Then there is the sponge process used for lemons and oranges in Sicily. The peel is removed and steeped in water, then the drained peel is pressed on sponges which absorb the oil. Later the sponges are very thoroughly squeezed and the oil runs into earthenware bowls.

Where Lavender Blooms

English lavender water is famous all over the world. At one time Mitcham in Surrey was a great lavender-growing district but nowadays Norfolk has become the main centre of lavender-growing and many acres are devoted to its cultivation. Here are the fields where the famous scent-makers, Yardleys, whose history goes back to the early days of George III's reign, grow vast quantities of lavender, the fragrant aroma of which is destined to be imprisoned in bottles which travel to every part of the world to sweeten the air, it may be, in some far-off camp, or add the fragrance of English fields to the heated air of a crowded tropical scene.

The horticultural expert watches over the crops and decides just when the right time has come for cutting. Then girls, armed with special knives, go into the fields and gather the lavender sprays which are transported as quickly as possible to the distillery. The steam method of distillation is used in the case of lavender and the essential oil is collected from the separate boiler into which the condensed water and oil is led.

In due course the oil of lavender goes to the chemist whose task it is to ensure that the aroma of the lavender will be brought out and preserved. But it is not merely lavender water in which the chemist is interested. There are other perfumes, each with its own special charm. To the cultivation of the flowers, the preparation of the blooms, and the art of distilling their sweetness from them, the chemist of to-day brings not only his scientific skill but also much ancient lore handed down from bygone generations of scent makers.

Soap and Toothpaste

Have you ever realised to what an extent the art of the perfume maker enters into many of the things we use in our daily life ? Scents and perfumes are not only used on a lady's handkerchief ; they add charm and attractiveness to many articles and preparations that are used in our daily routine.

Your bar of toilet soap, if it is neither carbolic nor coal-tar, has a pleasant smell that owes its existence to the cunning of the perfume maker. Toilet powders, toothpaste and notepaper are all materials on which the perfume maker may have worked, and some people even smoke scented cigarettes. Some floor polishes, too, have been specially treated so that when they are used they will make the room smell not merely clean, but fragrantly so. Commercial experts have often discovered that they can sell some commodity much more easily if an attractive aroma is bestowed upon it. Scent plays its part in our food, too, in the form of flavouring essences which give both a pleasant taste and odour.

As you go about, use your sense of smell and you will realise how important the age-old art of the perfume maker is to the comfort and pleasantness of daily life.

TOYS AND GAMES

Fox Photos.

WHERE WILL OUR HOME BE?

That is the question these delightful dogs seem to be asking. The love of all dumb animals is so natural an instinct in British children that practically every toyshop will have toys of this kind in its window. Their pleading expressions make you feel that you would like to buy every one of them.

FEW of us, whether we are young or old, can resist the temptation to stop to gaze at all the wonderful things to be seen in the window of a toyshop. There are teddy bears, dolls and dolls' houses, regiments of marching soldiers, farm animals, cuddly toys, rocking horses, racing cars, building sets—toys and games of every size and every description.

The toyshop is a wonderland where those of us who are grown up can escape back to the happy days of our youth, and where those of us who are still young can spend our pocket money or decide what we would really like Father Christmas to bring us when the time comes.

Toys of Ancient Egypt

Toys are almost as old as civilisation itself. If you go to the British Museum, you can see there a wooden doll which was once the plaything of a child of Ancient Egypt. Beside it are other dolls from this distant age, some of which have arms and legs that can be moved. There are also toy animals centuries old, some made of wood and others of porcelain. We know, too, that the little girls of ancient Greece and Rome had dolls' furniture and dolls, as well as balls, tops and rattles.

Many of our games have a very long history. Ball games and skipping were favourites among the children of thirteenth century England, who also played an early kind of blind man's buff, which they knew as " Hoodman Blind." A hundred years later, children were playing question games and forfeit games very similar to those we play at Christmas parties. Puppet shows are still with us to-day in the form of Punch and Judy, and puppetry itself seems to have come back to public favour. In his tale of Don Quixote, written in the sixteenth century, Cervantes gives an account of such a

Central Press.

TOY CAVALCADE

Arrayed on this table is a splendid cavalcade that is, in miniature, what you might see at a Victory parade or the Trooping of the Colour. Horsemen, bandsmen, and infantry are all painted by hand and are here seen receiving the finishing touches before they are finally inspected and packed.

performance in which a Spanish knight rescued a lady from the Moors.

Football is another game with a long history that might have come to a sudden end in the reign of James I, when it was decided to " debarre from this court all rough and violent exercise as the football, meeter (more suited) for laming than for making able the users thereof." But the game was too popular for a royal decree to bring it to an end. English men and boys continued to play football, and in the town of Chester the game was played in the city streets on every Shrove Tuesday.

How Toys Taught Great Men

Some toys not only amuse us, but have something to teach us, and many a great man has been helped by know-ledge he gained from his childhood playthings. In his young days George Stephenson, the inventor of the loco-motive, had the job of watching the sheep. He devoted the leisure time this work gave him to building model windmills and water wheels out of hemlock stalks. Nasmyth, the inventor of the steam hammer, obtained his start in life at a large engineering works by showing a model he had made when he was a schoolboy. Those of us who live by the seaside and long to go afloat know how much good seamanship is to be learnt from making and sailing model boats.

At one time there were no truly professional toymakers as there are to-day. Toys were made by ordinary craftsmen. The furniture maker, for example, could be prevailed upon to

DOLLS, CARS, AND HORSES THAT MOVE

Central Press.

Central Press.

British toys now enjoy world-wide popularity. In this picture we see girl workers in a doll factory painting the eyes on dolls' heads.

This picture of a South Wales toy factory shows us another type of doll. The girl worker is giving waves of beautiful hair to her tiny customers.

Fox Photos.

Fox Photos.

With the chassis before her, and the wheels in a box on her left, this girl is assembling dozens of model cars of the latest type.

Here we see work on a " Bronco," a toy horse that actually runs and gallops. They are produced at the rate of about 2,000 a week.

A CRICKET BAT IS MADE—

Here we see the bark being sheared from a felled willow log near Chelmsford. The roughly shaped "clefts" are stacked to dry and season before going to the manufacturers.

When spring comes, craftsmen work at high pressure to make bats for the season. This picture shows a worker at Manchester shaping a bat for the insertion of its handle.

Photos: Fox Photos.

Modern cricket bats have whalebone splices to increase their driving power and rubber in their handles to lessen the sting. Here we see a worker turning cricket bat handles on his lathe.

Shaping cricket bats is a skilled job for which a tool very like a spokeshave is used. Nearly all modern bats are made of willow, but early bats were made of oak.

—AND A CRICKET BALL

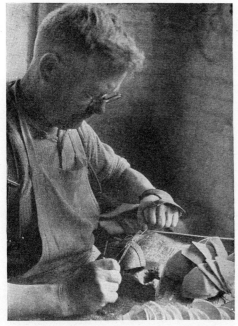

This shows the " closing " process in the making of a cricket ball, by which two " quarters " of leather from a hide are stitched together to form one half of the outer cover of the ball.

The next stage is " turning." Two cup-like half-covers are attached lightly together and blocked into perfect shape in a gunmetal mould. The edges are then trimmed.

Photos: Fox Photos.

This picture shows how the " quilt " or core of a cricket ball is hammered into shape. Holding a mould between his knees, the craftsman fits the core and works with his hammer.

The weight of a cricket ball is important, and official regulations say that its weight should be $5\frac{1}{2}$ ozs. This weight checker has been in his trade for half a century.

Balls for the royal and ancient game of golf will each contain about 192 yards of rubber thread, but the golf ball's centre core is filled with paste, and this process is done by means of the automatic filling machine seen in this picture.

Photos: Dunlop Rubber Co.

The rubber thread is wound under tension so that it is stretched, made into a core, and afterwards covered with gutta-percha. This picture shows us the tape being wound during the second stage of winding the core of the ball.

MAKING A FOOTBALL

Shaped pieces are cut out from a sheet of ox-hide. A regulation soccer ball consists of eight sections. A sheet like the one shown here provides two complete football covers.

The cut-out sections of specially stretched and tanned leather are sewn together, outside in. In the making of a first-rate ball all major operations are done by hand.

Photos: Keystone.

Before the cover is turned the right way round, the seams on the inside are carefully hammered and smoothed down. If this were not done, the seams might damage the inflated bladder.

The finished football, measuring 27–28 inches in circumference and weighing 14–16 ounces, is given a pressure test, the bladder being inflated to a pressure of 20 pounds per square inch.

make miniature chairs and tables for a doll's house. Even such famous designers as Sheraton and Chippendale made toy miniatures of their beautiful work for the children of the wealthy people of their day.

Nowadays the manufacture of toys is a great industry which, in Britain, not only fills our own toyshops, but makes toys and games for children in all parts of the world. The legions of soldiers and the beautiful jointed dolls which come from the moulds and paint-rooms of the modern British toy factory delight children in distant lands as well as those nearer home. Many of our finest toys to-day are exported for sale abroad to help to earn the foreign money which we need to buy the food and raw materials that keep us and our industries alive.

Making a Cricket Bat

Not all toys are mass produced. Look at the pictures of dolls and soldiers being made and you will see that individual craftsmanship of a very high skill is needed to make these as attractive as they are when we see them in the toyshop window.

This is also true of much of our games equipment, cricket bats in particular. Famous British firms make the bats for our great national sport, but their story begins in the country-side of East Anglia, where local craftsmen cut the " clefts," or rough blocks of willow, from the timber of special willow groves and sell them to manufacturers in London. These clefts are cut from the tree after it is felled, and each tree will probably provide sufficient clefts for from thirty to fifty

Central Press.

A " HOUSING ESTATE " FOR DOLLS

If you want a home for your doll the obvious place to find it is at this large factory where we see workers doing the interior decorating to row upon row of freshly-finished dolls' houses. Some of these will probably come to your toyshop, but many more will go abroad where there is a great demand for British toys.

FOR THE TENNIS COURT

Dunlop Rubber Co.

Lawn tennis balls are made from hollow india-rubber covered with felt known as melton. The first piece is stretched on the core by machine, but the second piece is carefully fitted by hand, as seen in this picture. Each ball is 2½ inches in diameter and must weigh just under, or exactly, 2 ounces.

bats. The greatest number to be cut from one tree is 1,179. These clefts were taken from a willow tree felled at Boreham, Essex, in 1888. The wood is not immediately ready to be worked on, but has to be stored for a year or more to mature, after which it passes into the hands of skilled craftsmen whose various work is illustrated in these pages. The manufacture of cricket bats is not, of course, confined to London; there are large firms in other parts of the country—in Manchester, for example.

Consider the skill and ingenuity that goes to the making of footballs, tennis balls and golf balls. Ox-hides are used for footballs, and an eight-sectioned ball for the Association game has to go through many processes before it is ready for the field. A golf ball contains about 192 yards of rubber thread, which has to be wound under tension so that it is stretched, made into a core, and afterwards covered with gutta-percha. Tennis balls are made from hollow india-rubber covered with a kind of felt; every ball has to be tested on sensitive scales to make sure that it is of the standard weight.

Making a New Toy

Many toys are moulded, and the most popular kind of moulded toy is the doll which, once made of wax, is now more frequently made from plastics or—in the case of the more expensive dolls—from china. Every toy factory has its timber department, and it is surprising to see how much work is needed for one toy.

When a new toy is invented the secrets of its construction must be very carefully kept. Different workmen may make the different parts, which are then put together in a room shut off from the rest. For a new toy, if it wins a way to popularity, may bring its inventor a considerable fortune.

Planet News.

EXAMINING COINS AT THE MINT

Our coins are made at the Royal Mint near the Tower of London. Before they are counted and packed, finished coins are carefully examined. Moving canvas belts carry them under the sharp eyes of the examiners who will extract any faulty coins and send them back to the furnace-room to be melted down and re-made.

WHAT exactly is money? This may seem a silly question, for we all know the coins and paper notes which we receive as pocket-money or for our work, enabling us to buy the things we want. In fact, money plays such an indispensable part in our daily life that we take its existence and use for granted. And yet, there have been advanced civilisations, such as that of Ancient Egypt, which flourished for centuries without money being used in everyday life.

At what stage in human history did people begin to give and accept money, and why? What gives money its value? What are the limits of its usefulness?

The Division of Labour

Imagine one of the small, self-contained communities that existed at the dawn of history, when each family built its own hut, found its own food,

and made its own clothes and simple tools. People did not buy anything then, and, therefore, needed no money. But when communities settled permanently on the land and grew larger, it was found that things could be produced better and faster by craftsmen who did only one particular kind of work. This "division of labour" brought with it a constant exchange of goods and services. A tool-maker would barter a spade for a pair of shoes made by the cobbler; a farmer would supply corn to the man who built his house; and so forth.

But this system of barter had obvious limitations. What if the tool-maker had all the shoes he wanted when the shoe-maker needed a tool? There was only one commodity which, as a rule, was equally useful to all at any time: cattle. And, indeed, cattle often went from one man to another in exchange for other things, just as money does nowadays. But cattle as a "medium of exchange" had its drawbacks, too, especially when distant communities started trading with each other; for cattle could not be easily transported from place to place; it might suddenly lose all or part of its value through death or disease; and it was useless for purchases worth less than at least one head of cattle.

Thus arose the need for money, that is to say, for something durable that could easily be distinguished, sub-divided and carried about, and which had a generally agreed value so that everybody would accept it in payment for his labour or goods.

Primitive Money

Coins (not to speak of paper money) make a comparatively late appearance on the historical scene; and it will help us to understand the nature of money if we consider some of the many odd things which have served as money in ancient days and, in remote parts of the world, sometimes until very recently.

Apart from the essential characteristics of money already mentioned, it stands to reason that people adopted as their money such things as they considered desirable possessions in themselves. During the early history of China, for example, knives, pieces of cloth and small tools, such as bill-hooks, chisels and spades, formed the local currency. Bricks of tea and bags of rice were another form of early Chinese money.

Salt bars were a medium of exchange in the interior of Africa, and in Tibet cakes of salt even bore a stamp of their value. Small mats were money in the New Hebrides and also on the west coast of Africa, where they were stamped by the Portuguese Government. Early settlers and traders in North America paid, first with beaver-skins, then with blankets. The millstones of the Caroline Islands and the squirrel skins of Siberia are other instances of primitive money in the form of useful commodities.

In tropical climates, where the necessities of life such as food, clothes and shelter, are easy to come by, it is things suitable for personal adornment that were in general demand. For that reason various types of shells became the most widespread of all primitive currency. Of these the cowrie shell is probably the best-known. It comes from a small mollusc found in the shallow spots of the Indian Ocean and off the east African shores. Cowrie shell money circulated in India, China, parts of the African Continent, and in many islands of the Pacific Ocean. As late as the last century, Indian natives still paid their taxes in cowries.

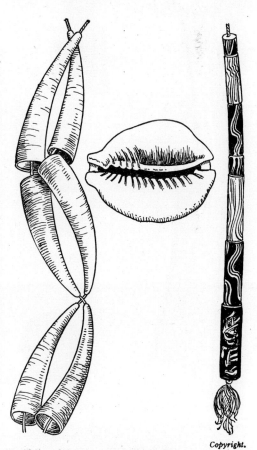

PRIMITIVE MONEY

Various kinds of shell money, such as strings of the dentalium shell (left), the cowrie (centre) and the wampum (right) have circulated in primitive communities until very recently.

The first colonists of New England found " wampum " in use among the natives as a medium of exchange, and adopted it as such for a period of time. Wampum consisted of beads made from the inner whorls of certain sea shells. In the Queen Charlotte Islands and in Washington Territory shells of the dentalium snail were gathered together on strings and thus used as money. The diwarra shells, in New Britain in the Bismarck group of islands,

British Museum.

" COINS " OF ODD SHAPE

Tokens of metal such as these served as an early form of coinage. The " knife " and " shirt " money of China and the ham-shaped coins of early Rome recall the objects originally used as a means of exchange.

were pierced and forced on to a stiff cane at an equal distance from one another. This made it possible to carry about a comparatively large amount of money, and to obtain smaller units by simply cutting a piece off the cane.

Of the many kinds of " adornment " money other than shells we will mention only the red feathers from the head of a tiny jungle bird in the Santa Cruz Islands; the porpoise teeth in the Solomons; boars' tusks in New Guinea; and the teeth of whales in Fiji.

It became apparent in the course of time that of all the materials that could be used for money, metal was by far the best, for it is extremely durable, and useful as well as beautiful things could always be made from it when it was no longer wanted as a medium of exchange. Precious metals, in particular, were found to be superior as they represented greater value in smaller bulk, and so were more convenient to carry. It is, therefore, not surprising that metal in the form of lumps, bars, rings and chains became a very widely used kind of primitive money. There was only one drawback: these pieces of metal had to be weighed every time they served in a bargain. You may remember the passage in the first book of the Bible where Abraham weighs out to Ephron " four hundred shekels of silver . . . current money with the merchant " for the purchase of a field. This inconvenience was overcome by cutting the metal into ingots of a fixed weight. Later, the ingots were reduced to a flat, handy shape, a stamp guaranteeing the weight and purity of the metal used was added— and there we have the first coins.

Coined Money

The history of coinage through the ages would fill a volume; here we can trace only a general outline. It is not certain where and when the first coins were struck, though probably it was in the Far East. But the oldest coin which has been preserved was made in Lydia, in Asia Minor, about 2,700 years ago. It was oval in shape, and the metal used was electrum, a mixture of gold and silver. It was also a Lydian king, the famous Crœsus, who issued the first coins made of pure gold.

Base metals were sometimes used for the coinage of a country; iron, for instance, in ancient Sparta, and bronze in early Rome. Most nations, however, adopted silver or gold, or sometimes both at the same time, as the standard metals of their money. True, even in countries with a silver or gold standard small change was often provided in the form of coins made from a baser metal; but these were then only "token" coins, a sufficient number of which could always be exchanged for a "true" coin of precious metal. The round shape of coins soon became common usage, though there were exceptions, such as the

ROMAN COINS

The earliest Roman coinage was of bronze only, but in the growing Roman Empire gold and silver became the basic metals. In our selection Figs. 6 and 9 depict gold coins, the rest silver coins. Fig. 7 is a denarius showing the head of the great Julius Caesar.

oblong eight-daler piece of seventeenth-century Sweden; and in China, *tao* coins in the form of a knife, and *pu* coins, roughly resembling a shirt, developed from the primitive money already described.

In the early days, merchants often issued their own private coinage, and occasionally this happened in comparatively recent times. Thus we read of an English inn-keeper in the seventeenth century who made his own money which was generally accepted in the local district. But the value of money being closely related to the value of the metal of which it is made, a dishonest person could easily cheat by giving a wrong weight or making a coin which looked

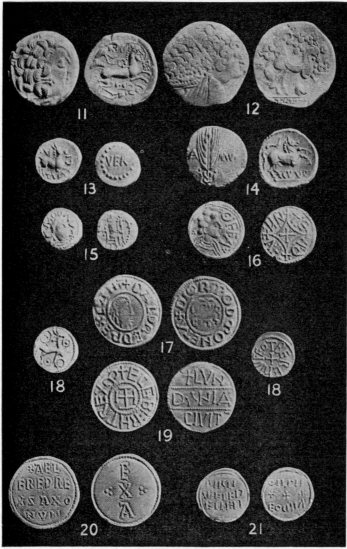

GAULISH AND EARLY BRITISH COINS

The illustration shows gold coins (Figs. 11, 12 and 14) and silver coins from Ancient Britain, Gaul and Saxon England. The earliest coins used in Britain were imitations of a Macedonian design. The Romans introduced their own coinage.

somebody might "debase" a coin by filing or clipping metal off its rim, and hence arose the custom of giving milled edges to the more valuable coins.

The forging of, or tampering with, the official coinage by private individuals has always been considered as a very grave crime. But it is sad to relate that kings and governments themselves were not always too scrupulous. We come here across an aspect of money which is a little complicated, but must be mentioned if we want to understand the nature of money at all. The point is this: a current coin has, as it were, two possible values—its metal value, and the face value which has been stamped upon it by the issuing authority. Thus a gold sovereign remained a sovereign even when it became worn and, therefore, less valuable as a piece of gold; but you could buy the same things with it, as long as it was "legal tender," which means that in accordance with the law it must be accepted on its face value in payment of debts. In a well-ordered economy the metal value and the face value of new coins should, of course, be the same; and worn coins should be withdrawn from circulation and replaced

like gold or silver, but was actually made from a less valuable alloy. For that reason the issuing of coins became, as a general rule, the sole right of the highest State authority; and as you know, most coins bear the portrait of the Sovereign or some national emblem of the country concerned. Even so

by new ones. But this has by no means always been the case. If you find the relationship between these two values puzzling, don't worry: the greatest economic experts also find it a bewildering problem. Here, however, we are only concerned with one, fairly simple, side of it.

Take an imaginary country where the standard coin is a gold ducat. The government has contracted a number of debts, but finds itself hard up for money. Now, all the government has to do is to coin a new issue of ducats containing only, say, half the amount of pure gold, and pay with this debased currency. In this simple way it has got rid of its whole debt by spending only half as much in gold.

It is hardly necessary to say that such measures bring only temporary relief, for people will soon ask a higher price for what they have to sell. Moreover, when there are both "good" and "bad" coins current at the same time, people tend to hoard the good and spend the bad. In the words of Sir Thomas Gresham, the financial minister to Queen Elizabeth I, "bad money drives out good"; once a State starts making coins of inferior metal value, it may find that the whole currency becomes debased to a much larger extent than originally intended. The last time the English coinage was severely debased in this manner was during the reign of Henry VIII.

How Coins are Made

A factory in which coins are made is called a Mint. In Britain there used to be several minting plants in different parts of the country, though all under royal supervision. Since the eighteenth century, however, all coins of the United Kingdom have been minted at the Royal Mint in London, which also produces coins for countries of the British Commonwealth of Nations, and some other countries. Not all the coinage of the Dominions, however, is minted in London. Australia, for instance, has branches of the Royal Mint at Melbourne and Perth, and some of her coins have been made in America and India. Let us take a look at one of these plants and watch the various stages in the birth of a " copper " penny.

The first thing to see is the furnace-room, for it is here that small but powerful furnaces melt the ore from which the coins are made, and which the government has bought in the ordinary markets.

" Coinage Blanks "

Copper ore takes about an hour and a half to melt under the fierce heat of

WORKS OF ART

These gold coins struck in the reigns of James I (Fig. 22) and Charles I (Fig. 23) are magnificent specimens from the great era of British coinage, which had begun under the Tudor monarchs and continued into the seventeenth century. Most of our present-day units of coinage derive from that period.

the furnace, and it is then put—in its molten state—into a crucible, from which it is carefully poured into steel moulds which have been wheeled into position beneath the crucible. After cooling, the metal (bronze) is removed from the moulds as a heavy, solid slab. The rough ends of the slab are then " guillotined " (cut) and filed, and the slabs then go to the rolling machines. Each of these is operated by a workman whose hands are protected by thick gloves made of leather. He passes a filed block of metal between the rollers of his machine, whose action increases the length of the block and diminishes its thickness.

This process is repeated several times, and on each occasion length increases and thickness decreases. The bar — for that is what it now becomes —also changes in colour and takes on the appearance of dull copper. The thickness of the bar must be the same throughout, and it is carefully tested before it passes on to the powerful steel punching - machines which actually cut the pennies in their crudest state. There may be as many as twenty of these punching - machines in one workroom, and the noise is almost deafening as they operate with rhythmical precision.

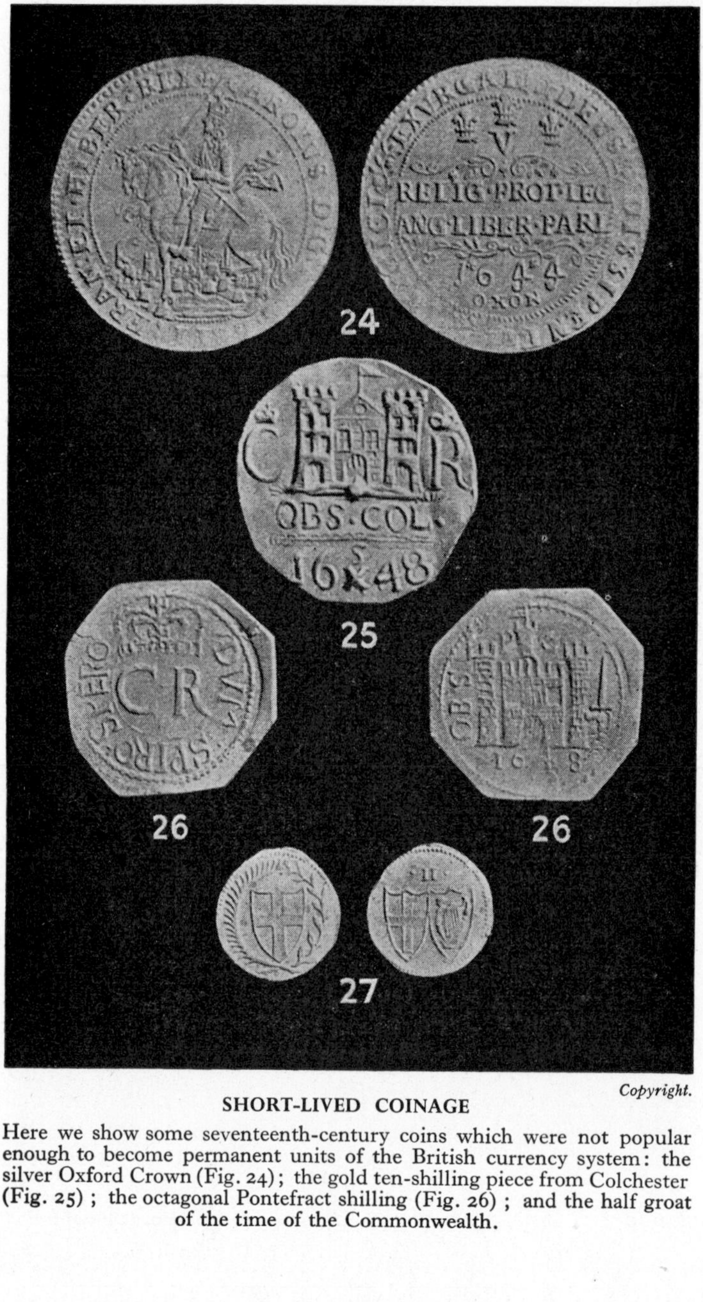

SHORT-LIVED COINAGE

Copyright.

Here we show some seventeenth-century coins which were not popular enough to become permanent units of the British currency system: the silver Oxford Crown (Fig. 24); the gold ten-shilling piece from Colchester (Fig. 25); the octagonal Pontefract shilling (Fig. 26); and the half groat of the time of the Commonwealth.

" Striking " Pennies

The penny-sized pieces, or " coinage blanks," as they are called, are collected and emptied into annealing vats. These are large brass barrels into which hot air is pumped. This has the effect of softening the metal, preparing it for washing and drying and so for the final process of stamping.

Washing is done in large revolving churns into which sulphuric acid, bichromate of soda, and water are run. As the churns swing round, the metal pieces crash against their sides with a loud swishing noise. Washed and dried the pieces are now shining metal discs ready for the press room.

The press room is where the coins are actually " struck " or pressed out. This is done by a machine containing dies of strong, tempered steel which will produce pennies from our metal discs at the rate of 120 every minute. As these machines work, the noise is considerable, for they strike the metal discs with a power of sixty tons.

The metal discs are now pennies, but before being packed ready for the banks, they are carefully examined. Faulty coins are extracted and sent back to the furnace-room to undergo the manufacturing process again.

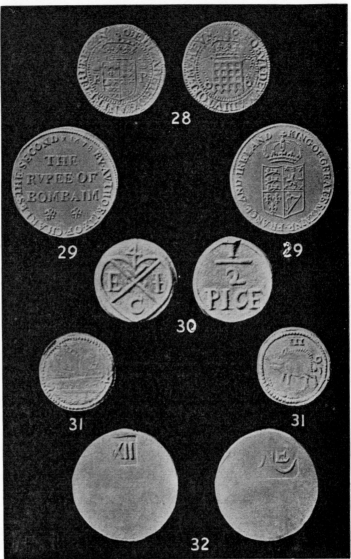

Copyright.

COLONIAL COINS

The history of the British Empire is reflected in colonial coinage. Fig. 28 shows a sixpence used in the American colonies in the time of Elizabeth I ; Fig. 29, an early Indian rupee ; Fig. 30, a coin of the East India Company ; Fig. 31, a threepenny piece from the Sommers Islands ; and Fig. 32, a New England shilling.

The Origin of Paper Money

In the London of the sixteenth and seventeenth centuries there was no police force in the modern sense; burglaries and street robberies were frequent happenings. For that reason, people in possession of a large amount of gold or silver coins often preferred to leave their money in the safe keeping of a goldsmith, who was better equipped to guard valuable property against thieves.

AUSTRALIAN COINS

When coins were scarce in Australia, the New South Wales Government had holes punched into Spanish silver dollars in order to prevent the coins from being smuggled abroad. Thus the "holey" dollar (top) and the "dump" (centre) came into existence. Private money (bottom) was another makeshift solution.

stead of giving one receipt for each deposit, they issued a series of receipts in round figures; and they undertook to pay the same amount in coins to anyone who would produce the receipt. These receipts were called bank-notes and could be passed from hand to hand exactly like coins.

The goldsmith-bankers of that time were mostly Italians from Lombardy, and a famous street in the financial heart of the City of London bears the name Lombard Street to this day. Their business prospered, and their bank-notes were accepted by the public with complete confidence. This encouraged the bankers to go a step further. When they were asked for a loan, as frequently happened, they again issued bank-notes instead of actual coins. This practice was the origin of modern banking.

Bank-notes proved to be a very popular form of currency, and it did not take long before all over the world hundreds of banks—which had ceased to be connected with the goldsmiths' trade—made their own paper money.

The Dangers of Paper Money

Bank-notes were thus a form of private money, just as coinage had often been in the beginning; and there were similar drawbacks. Bankers put into circulation considerably more money in the form of bank-notes than they held in coin. It was highly improbable that all the people would wish to cash their bank-notes at the same time, and as long as the bank's

The goldsmith would issue a receipt for any such deposit of money, and later return the money, when required, against the receipt.

Supposing now that a man who held such a receipt had to pay a debt to another person. It was then not necessary for him to handle any cash himself: he could simply instruct the goldsmith to pay the third person out of the deposit, altering the original receipt accordingly. But the third person might also wish to leave the money in safe keeping; and, in fact, the goldsmiths soon found that much of the money deposited with them passed from owner to owner, but never actually left their possession. This fact gave them the idea of simplifying the procedure. In-

INSIDE THE ROYAL MINT

From Roman times onwards there has been a Mint on Tower Hill. Within its walls is this furnace-room where we see molten metal being poured into moulds which have been wheeled into position. The Royal Mint makes coins for other countries besides Britain.

Photos : *Planet News.*

The raw metal has been moulded, rolled, and punched into pieces of the appropriate size. But before they can be stamped, the pieces must be washed and dried. Here are some of the " coinage blanks," as they are called, in the hot-air drying machine after washing.

reserves of gold were not too small, and the loans it had granted were safe and could be called in at short notice, those who did wish to exchange their notes for coin could always be satisfied. But when a bank issued paper money too rashly or fraudulently in excess of its resources, it was bound to fail sooner or later, and the people who had trustfully accepted its notes had to bear the loss. In the end, the State had to take control over the issuing of paper money, as it had in the case of coinage. Our present-day paper currency is, with few exceptions, State money. But again we must note that State control has not always proved to be a guarantee for the stability of a country's currency.

Since paper money has no material value, it cannot, of course, be debased in the same manner as coins, but there are other ways of lowering its value. We know that everything that is in plentiful supply is cheaper than something that is rare, and money is no exception. If, therefore, a government starts printing much more paper money than it had done before, the money will purchase less in goods and labour; that is to say, prices and wages will rise. This process is called " inflation," and within reasonable limits it may not be altogether harmful. When prices tend to rise, manufacturers are certain that the money they invest in production will bring them a good profit; and everybody will buy as many goods as he can afford before they become still more expensive.

A moderate inflation thus gives a boost to industry and trade. On the other hand, many elderly people are suddenly faced with the hard fact that their savings and pensions have lost a great deal of their real value, and young people are discouraged from making prudent savings.

If inflation is carried to an excess it may result in a complete breakdown of a country's currency system. A striking example was provided by Germany after the First World War. Germany had spent most of her gold reserves to buy war material from abroad, and after her defeat found herself saddled with

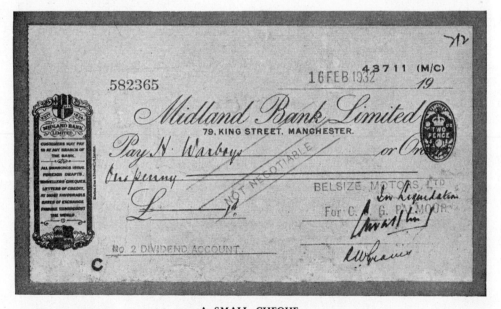

A SMALL CHEQUE

This cheque for one penny is, of course, an oddity, but in fact cheques are becoming increasingly popular as the most convenient method of making small as well as large payments. They are a safeguard against loss and theft, and make it much easier to keep a tidy record of one's expenditure. They are the most modern " means of exchange."

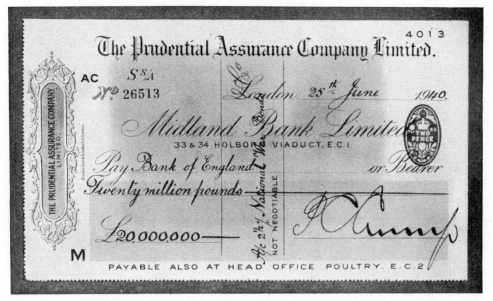

BIG MONEY

A few strokes of the pen on a small slip of paper is all that is needed to pay out twenty million pounds. Everybody uses money in its many forms, but few people realise its long and complex history since the early days when trading could be carried out only by means of barter. Without the invention and development of the money device, the growth of our civilisation would have been impossible.

a huge amount of debts. To provide the necessary money, more and more notes, in higher and higher figures, were issued. Prices first rose gradually, then soared with ever-increasing rapidity. At the height of the inflation, a workman would grab his weekly pay-packet and rush into the shops to spend the money at once; for if he waited only a day or two, his earnings of a week would buy him not more than a box of matches. In the end, a little article that had formerly cost but one or two *marks* was priced at many millions of *marks*; an entirely new currency had to be introduced, wiping out the savings which people had made during a lifetime of hard work.

In recent years, signs of milder inflation can be noticed from time to time almost everywhere; but governments have learnt from experience and by various methods prevent the situation from getting out of hand.

Measuring the Value of Money

From all that has been said it is quite clear that the real value of money cannot be taken from the figures to be found on the face of coins and bank-notes; for money is worth neither more nor less than the necessities of life which you can buy with it. How to measure the changing value of money is a vexing problem. Various methods have been evolved, none of them quite satisfactory. The most widely used is the Price Index Number, which works in this way: a certain year is chosen as the " basic " year, and the price of the most important commodities are recorded. It is then possible to measure the change of money value by comparing the prices in later years with those in the " basic " year. It is, however, only a rough-and-ready method, for you will find that the prices for different basic products do not always move upwards or downwards at the same rate; some prices may be influenced by circumstances which have nothing to do with the changing value of money.

The " Rate of Exchange "

We have explained how the value of money may change within individual countries; now we must briefly deal with the value of one country's currency as compared with that of another country—the " rate of exchange," as it is called, between the two currencies. This was an easy matter when most countries were " on the gold standard," which means that their currency consisted of gold coins or paper money which the country's Central Bank would redeem for gold on demand. In the beginning of this century, a French and a Belgian *franc* could be exchanged on equal terms because each contained exactly the same amount of gold. Again, a British sovereign (20 shillings) contained 113 grains of pure gold, and the American 10-dollar piece 232·2 grains (that is 23·22 per dollar): consequently, the rate of exchange between British and United States money was slightly under 5 dollars to the pound sterling.

After the First World War, however, very many countries went " off the gold standard ": gold coins went out of circulation, and paper money did not now represent a certain amount of gold. How was the rate of exchange to be determined then?

Money, as we have already said, is worth what it can buy. Now suppose that prices rose in France, but remained stable in Belgium, so that a certain amount of French *francs* might pay for 10 bushels of wheat in France, but the same amount of Belgian *francs* would buy, say, 12 bushels in Belgium. Obviously, nobody would then any longer exchange a Belgian for a French *franc*. We have also said that money is subject to the general laws of supply and demand. If the Belgians sold more goods to the French than they bought from them, French money would be plentiful in Belgium, and Belgian money scarce in France; and again the result would be that the exchange value of the French *franc* fell.

There were other and sometimes very complicated factors to be considered, but the main point is that rates of exchange altered or " fluctuated " all the time with the changing conditions of international trade. Foreign exchange was bought and sold like any other commodity, and the dealers in the Foreign Exchange Market fixed the rates of exchange by ordinary bargaining.

The system of freely fluctuating rates of exchange has an obvious drawback: lack of stability; and in order to maintain a fairly constant value of the currency, more and more governments have adopted the practice of keeping a more or less rigid control on the flow of money to and from foreign countries. Very few States nowadays allow their citizens to spend their money when and where they like.

Cheques

We have not yet mentioned a kind of bank money which in modern times has become the most important means of payment of all. When your father has to pay out a fairly large sum of money, or wants to make payment through the post, he will probably not use coins or notes, but pay by cheque. He has at one time paid money into his bank which is held to his credit—he has " a current account " with the bank. He has been given a small book with perforated cheque-forms, on which he can fill in the exact sum required each time. The cheque is simply an order on the banker to pay that sum out of the running account. The man who receives the cheque can go to your father's bank and obtain cash for it; or he can pay it into his own bank account; or he can write his name on the back of the cheque—" endorse " it—and pass it on to somebody else. Of course, a person may only draw cheques on his own bank, and only up to the amount of credit he has there; otherwise the cheque will be " dishonoured." A creditor is not obliged to accept cheques in payment: they are not " legal tender." But cheques given by a person of good repute are usually accepted without difficulty as the most convenient method of passing larger sums of money.

The British Currency System

After our brief survey of the general nature of money and the problems connected with it, let us take a particular case and consider the story of currency in this country. When the Romans invaded Britain, the only coins they found there in circulation were imitations of a Macedonian coin, issued by the successor of Alexander the Great. The Romans brought their own coinage; our own signs come from the Roman *librae, solidi, denarii*—£ *s. d.*—meaning pounds, shillings and pence. After the occupation no new coins were struck for some time. It was King Offa of Mercia who in the eighth century made the first truly English coins: the silver pound and silver penny. Silver continued to be the metal used for British coins in the centuries that followed until Edward III had the first gold noble struck in 1344.

The creative vigour of the Tudor age showed itself also in the field of coinage; it produced many coins which remained common units of British currency, such as the gold sovereign and half-sovereign, the silver shilling and the silver half-crown. The crown, on the other hand, also minted during that period, was found to be too large and heavy and did not survive. Gold and silver were now equally the standard metals. For the purpose of small change, copper half-pennies and farthings were introduced in 1672; the copper penny made its first appearance more than a hundred years later. For 150 years between 1663 and 1813 gold guineas, named after the gold-producing Guinea Coast of Africa, were in circulation, and the term " guinea " is still used for a sum of 21 shillings. Four-penny pieces, sometimes called " groats," were struck from time to time, but proved to be unpopular and were stopped. The Coinage Act of 1816, just after the

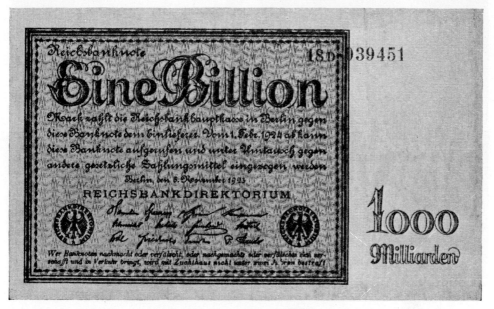

1,000,000,000,000 MARKS

As shown by this reproduction of a bank-note for a billion (i.e., a million times a million) *marks*, the process of inflation led to a complete breakdown of the currency system in Germany after the First World War. Eventually, the debased currency had to be replaced by a new one. The German inflation had far-reaching and disastrous effects.

victorious conclusion of the Napoleonic wars, established gold as the sole standard metal and the sovereign as the standard monetary unit. Only two pieces have been added to our coinage since: the florin, worth 2 shillings, in 1849, and the twelve-sided threepenny piece shortly before the last war.

In Victorian and Edwardian times, London was the centre of international finance, and the sovereign was the most highly esteemed coin in the world. The cost of the First World War, however, put a severe strain on Britain's economy, and like so many other countries she had to abandon the gold standard. At the present time, no gold coins are in circulation.

Bank-notes, as you will remember, were originally private bank money. The development of the British Empire and modern methods of finance offered many opportunities for profitable investments. But if banks were the first to gain by successful ventures, they were also the first to be hit when something went wrong.

Gradually the right of private banks to issue notes was restricted, and as a result of the Bank Charter Act of 1844, the Bank of England eventually became the sole bank of issue in England, though for a short period the British Treasury issued its own notes. Notes of the Scottish banks and those of Northern Ireland are still legal tender in these countries, but their issue is strictly limited by law. For a long time the Bank of England would pay gold for its notes on demand, and had ample gold reserves to do so. " Safe as the Bank of England " was a byword. But since the gold standard was abandoned, Bank of England notes are, of course, no longer " convertible." Only three denominations of bank-notes—ten shillings, one pound and five pounds—are in circulation at the present time.

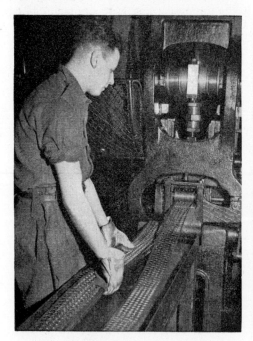

Photos : Topical Press.

" WASTE " BUT NOT WASTED

This strip of waste, called " Scissel," is seen leaving the power press after coinage blanks have been cut. It will be re-melted, re-rolled, and punched again.

BAGS OF MONEY

Once the coins are made and inspected, they are loaded by a special machine into bags which are labelled and sealed ready for issue to the banks.

Making
Pictures
for the
Screen

Behind the
Scenes
in the
Studios

Copyright.

FILMING ON LOCATION

The sunlight can often play its own tricks with the lighting of scenes taken on location at various intervals in the day's schedule. Here the outdoor lighting is being supplemented by gauzes to diffuse the light and reflectors to emphasize and concentrate it. This is just one aspect of the highly technical industry which makes films for our cinemas.

WHAT IS A FILM?

A CINEMATOGRAPH film, or movie, is quite simply a device for making a photograph appear to move. Actually, of course, it is not the photograph that moves at all. What we really see is a succession of hundreds of still photographs which are viewed one at a time, but at great speed.

Our eyes have a kind of memory—called persistence of vision—which makes us hold on to the picture or image of what we have just seen for a fraction of a second after it has been removed from our sight.

So when new types of cameras were invented towards the end of last century which could take sixteen pictures every second on a roll of celluloid film, and projectors were made of similar structure to throw the pictures onto a screen successively at the same speed at which they were photographed, one of mankind's oldest objectives seemed at last to have been realised—to give continuous life and movement to a picture he had created himself.

Yet the moving picture was, and still is, an optical illusion. As each separate still picture is shown for a fraction of a second, withdrawn and replaced by the

National Film Archives.

EARLY FILM SHOWS

Many early film programmes were given either as items in variety shows or as side-shows in fairs. Here is a typical travelling film show in the early years of the century. The programme was made up of a selection of short films playing only a few minutes each.

next, our eyes perceive no break. Through the persistence of our vision we combine the flow of pictures into one, and make of them a single continuous picture which moves with the natural speed of life.

The First Film Shows

Motion pictures were invented more or less simultaneously in a number of different countries where still photography had also been developed, more especially in Britain, America, France and Germany. The first film projection which the public paid to see took place at Christmas time in Paris, 1895. It is an odd coincidence that the family who became the first commercial producers and exhibitors of films should have had the name Lumière, the French word for light.

The invention of moving pictures was a source of tremendous excitement to their inventors as well as the public. Edison in America wanted to link them to his newly-developed phonograph (the ancestor of the gramophone) so that sound and picture could be reproduced. Friese-Greene, the British inventor, is said to have rushed blindly out into the London streets in the middle of the night and dragged a passing policeman in to see his triumphant achievement of a few seconds' movement on a little improvised screen. When he first saw a moving picture, Georges Méliès, the famous French conjurer and illusionist, offered the Lumière family all the money he could muster for the right to use their invention as part of his show.

The public flocked to see the early films in music-halls and fairgrounds as well as in specially adapted show-places. The age of the full-time cinema-theatre had not yet begun, but movie itself was successful from the start with the public as a part of other forms of entertainment.

The "Talkies"

For over thirty years films were silent—that is, the long reels of celluloid contained only pictures. These reels came eventually to be made up in standard lengths of a thousand feet each, and this is still the standard unit of measurement of a film today. A thousand feet in the silent days normally provided about a quarter of an hour of action on the screen—projected at sixteen pictures a second. When the sound film came at the end of the nineteen-twenties, the speed of photography and projection was increased by half-as-much again—twenty-four pictures a second instead of sixteen. The extra length of space gained on the sound track was found necessary in order to give a satisfactory quality to the photographically-recorded sound. This is still the standard rate of projection, and the reel now gives an average running time of about ten minutes.

The increase in projection rate, by the way, is the reason why the old silent films get quickened up when they are shown on a modern projector, unless it has a device for slowing back to silent film speed.

Until recently, all sound-on-film was what is called *optical*, that is it took the form of a narrow track with a *visible* pattern running alongside the picture-track, that could be turned back again into sound during projection in the cinema and amplified through the loud-speaker system in the theatre. The sound waves are converted into varying electric currents that modulate a sen-

National Film Archives.

AT THE BEGINNING OF THE CENTURY

This early British studio of the period 1902 consisted of a stage built in the open air, with a glazed roof to take advantage of the maximum amount of sunlight. The camera was mounted on a wheeled platform which could be positioned approximately for the scene.

sitively fluctuating light-beam which is turned into a photographic record, that is, the pattern of the sound track running down the length of the film. The process is reversed to enable the variable light to be transformed back in the form of variable current which is amplified and passed to the loudspeaker. More recently, with the introduction of magnetic tape recording, sound-on-film has become increasingly magnetic, and the optical sound-track has been replaced during production, and for more specialised forms of projection, by a magnetic stripe or series of stripes running down the side of the film. Theatres that have installed magnetic sound usually boast about it in their advertising — and rightly so, for its quality is superior in every way to optical sound reproduction.

Early Colour Films

Meanwhile, the moving picture itself had changed a great deal over the years. Films were first of all black-and-white only, not coloured. Then they began to be

National Film Archives.

AN EARLY FILM STUDIO

This was a film studio used in Brighton at the beginning of the century. The camera was mounted on a track for positioning, and the glass studio had sliding doors. Painted back-cloths were used as in the living theatre.

coloured by hand, a laborious process even when stencils were used to reduce the labour of colouring sixteen little pictures for each second of movement. Next, tinting the celluloid was introduced—the whole film becoming blue for night scenes, red for fire scenes, amber for romantic scenes or sunshine, and so on. This simple system of varying the black-and-white picture and giving it different kinds of dramatic colour for different times, moods or actions lasted almost throughout the silent period. But true colour began when a photographic process itself was used to reproduce a colour. Britain was the first country to develop a colour process. This was Kinemacolor (1908).

Soon the colour processes began to multiply and to gain range and accuracy, and familiar names put in their first appearances—in particular Technicolor (around 1928), Agfacolor (1936), Eastman Colour (around 1950).

With the arrival of television after the Second World War, the shape and size of the theatre screens was altered to make films more sensational and impressive. Cinema developed into two main directions—widescreen (such as Cinemascope) for normal theatres and giant screen (such as Cinerama) for specialised theatres.

Now there is a great difference between a moving picture on a screen which, however large in itself (like a Cinemascope picture) nevertheless fills only a fraction of your total field of vision, and a moving picture thrown on a screen which is designed to fill so large a part of your field of vision that you inevitably feel that you are physically involved in what is going on. You have been, as it were, passed through the vision barrier, and swept physically into the picture itself.

Let's be logical. There need be no limit theoretically to the development of these giant screens until a moving picture is produced that fills a complete sphere all round us while we sit on a transparent plastic seat fixed to a transparent plastic floor. Then we shall be able to fly magically over the Himalayas and, without any visible means of support, dip sickenly up and down on the air currents over the Grand Canyon. But there can be little question of the dynamic development of a film drama through a picture as large as this because it has done away with the vital principle of all art—the separation between the spectator and the work.

The man who is telling you a story through a film must have the freedom to use any device of which the art is capable to inspire your imagination—quicker or slower cutting, dynamic camera-set-ups, the sudden revealing of what matters to the total exclusion of what does not. The giant screen is simply not exclusive enough for any advanced form of film presentation. Most important of all, it does not exclude the spectator himself, so that when the film-maker wants to pull the stops out and use the wonderful artifice of the cinema to develop dramatic tension, he has most of the time to prevent himself doing so in order not to blow the nerves of the over-involved audience to pieces.

Types of Film

Bearing the new developments in mind, there are now several different widths and qualities of film used by professional and amateur film-makers. The main variations are :

8 mm. and 9.5 mm. film. Used almost entirely by amateurs who require only a silent film which will give a satisfactory result on a small screen at home at comparatively low cost.

16 mm. film. Used by amateurs and professionals alike, 16 mm. film (with or without sound) is highly adaptable. 16 mm. cameras and projectors are light and portable, and 16 mm. film is comparatively cheap. Many feature films are eventually distributed in 16 mm. for private projection, and this is the standard width used for all educational purposes, and often for television film projection (telecine). It is also widely used for

research and record purposes by science, industry and television.

35 *mm. film.* This is the so-called standard-width film used in cinema-theatres. With a special lens attachment for both camera and projector which *squeezes* a picture nearly two-and-a-half times as wide as it is high into the standard picture size, it is possible to use 35 mm. film for widescreen cinematography, such as Cinemascope. The camera lens squeezes the picture up and the projector lens readjusts the image back to its natural proportions on the screen.

Triple 35 *mm. and* 70 *mm. film.* The giant-screen systems (such as Cinerama, Cinemiracle and Todd-AO) use various methods to fill their specially large screens. Cinerama (first shown to the public in America in 1952) uses three separate projectors working together in synchronisation to make up a single enormous panoramic picture on a deeply curved screen. Later came Cinemiracle,

using a triple projector with three lenses to achieve a similar result. Both these systems (with their special triple-lensed cameras) use three reels of 35 mm. film simultaneously, each filling up a third of the screen. Todd-AO (Michael Todd and the American Optical Company) uses a single very wide-angled lens and a specially wide film (70 mm.) in order to get a photographic image of sufficient quality to show up well on the huge screen it has to fill.

All three of these systems use several separate magnetic sound tracks in order to fill the theatres where they are shown with sound coming from the same number of loud-speakers dispersed behind the screen and along the side-walls.

Three-dimensional Effects

Various systems have also been invented to produce moving pictures with solid, or three-dimensional illusion. The most effective of these so far makes use of polarised projection. Two images

TODD-AO

Among the giant-screen systems one of the most effective is Todd-AO (sponsored by Michael Todd and the American Optical Company). It uses a special 70 mm. film (shown here in comparison with a normal 35 mm. film). This wide film accommodates six separate magnetic sound tracks.

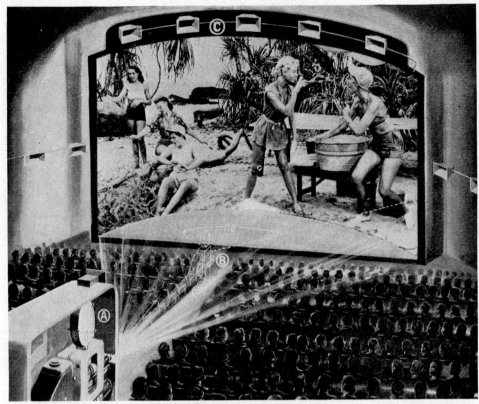

Todd-AO.

HOW TODD-AO WORKS

The Todd-AO camera uses a wide-angled lens of 128° field, as shown in the diagram at B. The projector (A) is specially designed to avoid viewing distortions when used in conjunction with the deeply curved giant screen. Note the placing of the loud-speakers above the screen and round the auditorium. These are served by six separate sound-channels corresponding to the six tracks on the 70 mm. film.

(either on two separate reels of film or combined together on one reel) are projected one on top of the other on the screen, but the images are polarised differently so that if each member of the audience wears similarly polarised glasses, the right eye sees only the right image and the left eye only the left image. This gives us the illusion of two-eyed vision such as we have in real life, giving space, depth, solidity and roundness to what we see.

Cover one of your eyes up with your hand for thirty seconds or so and look steadily at the furniture spaced over the room. Then remove your hand suddenly and see how at once the furniture takes on a new solidity in space. It is this illusion that the twin-images of the three-dimensional film reproduces, and as a result the picture seems no longer to be flat on the screen in the theatre, but to recede back to the horizon and even to project out into the auditorium.

But these three-dimensional films have not yet proved popular with the public. They are technically difficult both to produce and to project, and audiences dislike wearing the polarised glasses.

HOW FILMS ARE MADE AND WHO MAKES THEM

When a feature film is produced it has to go through three main stages. First come scripting and preparation; second, shooting in the studio or on location ; third,

A FULL VIEW INSIDE THE STUDIO

Sound City Film Studios.

This photograph gives a complete view of a scene inside a film studio. The upper half is what might be called the main lighting area, from which various effects can be produced. Below the temporary ceiling is the built-up scene of the hotel lounge, against which some of the action of the story takes place. A large group of workers, carpenters, plasterers, decorators, electricians and others have been employed to build up this setting.

final recording and editing. The chief people involved in this work are the producer, the writer, the director, the designer, the director of photography and his camera operator, the recordist and the editor. Let us have a look at what each of them does.

The producer either makes a film for himself or for a company. If he makes a film for himself he is called an independent producer, and this means he personally chooses each story that he wants to make into a film, buys the film rights for that story, and then gets together the money necessary to make the film. This is not likely to be less than £200,000 and may be considerably more.

If the producer makes the film for a company, then he will be assigned certain films to produce that the company is committed to make, and he will be responsible for seeing that the film does not cost more than the sum allotted for its production.

The independent producer assembles his own team of actors and technicians for the production and hires the studio he will need (together with its technical staff and its equipment) for the number of weeks he thinks it will take to shoot the film. The company producer, on the other hand, will use his company's stars, technicians and studios.

All producers must work out their schedule of productions very carefully in advance with the help and advice of their director and their senior technicians. By means of careful planning an independent producer can save himself many thousands of pounds in studio hire and fees for actors and technicians, and if he works for a company this saving is passed on to them. Directors vary considerably in the number of weeks they require to shoot a film, and films themselves vary considerably in the demands they make on time, due to the complication of their action. All this has to be planned in advance at what is called the script stage. So let us have a look at the script first.

Here is an example of a few scenes from a film-script. It is the opening to the British film *Great Expectations* from Charles Dickens' novel :

GREAT EXPECTATIONS
(A Cineguild Production, directed by David Lean)

After the film credits, a copy of the book *Great Expectations* appears on the screen, with Pip's voice as an adult reading the opening sentences which introduce him as a child. Then a gust of wind blows over the pages of the book, and the music that has accompanied the scene fades out. DISSOLVE to

Exterior Thames Estuary. Sunset

1. Very Long Shot of a small boy—Pip—running left to right along the bank of the Estuary. A wind is blowing and making a high-pitched and ghost-like whistling noise. The camera tracks and pans with Pip as he runs round a bend in the pathway and comes towards camera. A gibbet is built on the edge of the path camera-right, and Pip glances up at it as he passes—he continues running and moves out of picture camera-right.

Exterior Churchyard. Sunset

2. Medium Shot of Pip wearing long trousers, a short jacket and a woollen scarf tied round his neck. He is carrying a bunch of holly in his right hand. He climbs over a broken stone wall and the camera tracks left to right with him as he walks past the tombstones and old graves in the churchyard. Camera continues tracking as he makes his way towards one of the tombstones and kneels in front of it—he is now in Medium Long Shot.

3. Medium Shot of Pip kneeling at the foot of the grave. He pulls up an old rose bush which he throws aside, pats down the earth again and then places his bunch of holly at the head of the grave near the engraved tombstone. The wind is still howling.

4. Medium Close Shot. Pip kneeling near the tombstone; he looks round slowly and nervously as the wind gets louder.

5. Long Shot from Pip's eyeline of the leafless branches of a tree—the wind is blowing them, and to Pip they look like boney hands clutching at him. The branches creak.

Cineguild-J. Arthur Rank.

GREAT EXPECTATIONS

This is one of the most effective shots in the opening sequence of *Great Expectations*. Pip is seen standing beside his mother's grave. Everything, including the sinister tree, was reconstructed in the studio, and the church itself is a photographic background. The camera was mounted on a track running alongside the foreground of the graveyard.

6. Medium Close Shot. Pip looking round as in scene 4.

7. Medium Shot of the trunk of an old tree from Pip's eyeline—it looks very sinister and to him like a distorted human body. There is a creaking sound from the branches.

8. Medium Shot of Pip. He jumps up from the grave and runs away right to left towards the stone wall. The camera pans with him, and then becomes static as he runs towards the camera and into the arms of a large, dirty, uncouth and horrible-looking man. Pip screams loudly. From his clothes and shackles it is obvious that the man is an escaped convict.

9. Close Shot of Pip. His mouth is open as he screams, but a large and dirty hand is clapped over it, silencing him.

10. Close Shot of the convict. His face is dirty and scowling, his hair is closely cut. He leers down at Pip.

CONVICT (*to Pip*) : Keep still, you little devil, or I'll cut your throat!

The difference between this and a stage play is very obvious. In the theatre, once the curtain goes up a whole section of the story is acted continuously in front of the audience—perhaps even for a whole hour without stopping. But in a film a shot may last for only a second, and rarely lasts for more than a minute or two without interruption.

Like a Human Eye

The camera-lens is like a human eye that travels about spying into what is going on. The writer's job is to provide the director with the story told in a series of dramatic scenes (or sequences of shots) which will be exciting to watch. And in a good film a great deal of the excitement will be due to the telling details that single shots will bring to the story—details of people's faces, of

Cineguild-J. Arthur Rank.

FILMING IN THE STUDIO TANK

Large studios can usually provide directors with an extensive tank where shots involving water can be made. Here David Lean is directing the scene of the rescue of Magwich in *Great Expectations*, with a section of a paddle-steamer at work. Note the wall of the studio tank to the left at the base of the picture.

the things they are doing, of the places where they live and where they go, as well as the larger shots which show the whole of a room, the length of a street or some large, open space. The writer is thinking of these opportunities all the time he is preparing his script for the producer.

The Screen-writer

The screen-writer is normally a recognised professional of considerable experience. He may also be known as a novelist, a dramatist or a journalist, but his particular skill as a member of the film-making team lies in his ability to describe on paper how the camera can see the characters in action and the world in which they move. However wonderful he is as a descriptive writer, it is no good for him to describe some-

thing which would be either impossible or far too expensive to photograph effectively for the screen. And it is no good writing pages of wonderful dialogue or conversation which merely holds up the dramatic action of the story. Whether the screen writer is preparing an original story of his own for filming or adapting a novel or a play, he must be able to visualise in his mind's eye how what he writes will look on the screen.

As a first stage he prepares what is called a *treatment* for the producer. This is an outline of the story as he sees it in its rough screen shape. It may be only a few pages long, but it shows very clearly the sort of characters involved, what they do, and how the story should begin, develop and end. It also shows clearly where everything happens, because the producer must begin as a result of the treatment to plan where he will make the film, especially the locations he will require at home or abroad. A location is the term used for real-life settings in town or countryside, on hills, mountains or seas.

The producer must also decide how to cast the film, more especially the stars he wants for the main parts. If the producer or the company for which he works has any stars under contract, the story may well have been bought in the first place with their particular stars in mind for the main parts. From the screenwriter's treatment the producer can judge whether the parts are developing well for these star actors and actresses.

The treatment, too, is an easy form in which to adjust the story, strengthening a climax, eliminating an unnecessary scene with, perhaps, a difficult or expensive location. Characters may require changing, plots simplifying or made more exciting, and so on. The treatment goes backwards and forwards between the writer and the producer until both are satisfied that the screenplay itself can be started. This is the full scene-by-scene and even shot-by-shot presentation of the story on paper.

Director and Producer

By now the producer should have appointed his director. Some producers are even their own directors and will

make the film themselves, shot by shot, in the studio or on location. This is the case (or mostly the case) with highly individual film-makers such as Charles Chaplin, Alfred Hitchcock, Carol Reed or David Lean. But it is rare for a man to be able both to direct a film and at the same time watch over the complicated business of its day-by-day production costs and see that every detail of the advance arrangements for shooting are working out according to plan. It is usual for the producer to supervise these things and keep the director's task

Cineguild-J. Arthur Rank.

INSIDE THE STUDIO

Here is the British director David Lean (in the perch-chair fitted to the mobile crane carrying the camera) supervising a scene from *Brief Encounter* involving both a staircase and a lift. Note the positioning of the lighting, the simple white backings, and the way the camera is shooting through the iron-work of the lift-shaft to achieve a special effect on the screen.

as smooth as possible so that he can concentrate on the most effective rendering of the screenplay by the actors and film technicians.

Broadly speaking, the producer is the business manager as well as the promoter of the film for himself or his company, whereas the director is the creative talent responsible for turning the written screenplay into the photographed and recorded film. It is very much a matter of personal relationships how much the producer, director and writer contribute to the final film. If the team is a good one, they work it all out together at the planning stage.

When the shooting script, the shot-by-shot record of the film, is satisfactory in the view of the producer and his associates, other future colleagues will be brought into their consultations. Important members of the advance team are the designer (or art director) and the production manager. The designer's job is to produce advance sketches for all the sets and for the costumes and any important properties which are featured in the story ; it is the production manager's responsibility to examine the script in detail and begin to prepare the shooting schedules and, with the producer, estimates of the cost of the picture, which will depend very much on the length of time they reckon the film will take to make in the studio and on location (if any) and the cost of building the sets—of which there may well be thirty or more to construct —rooms, corridors, halls, sections of railway stations and shops, sides of streets and so on.

The larger companies will also assign a casting director to the production to help the producer make all the detailed arrangements for contracting the actors and actresses, the crowd artists and any specialist performers (from stand-ins to stunt-men) that the film requires. This is not an easy task. Most small parts need only two or three days' work, and the dates when the particular shots involving the smaller parts will be made have to be known in advance to ensure that the players will be available.

Careful Planning

It is impossible to over-emphasise the importance to film-making of these long days and weeks of preparation. Some directors, such as Alfred Hitchcock, plan every shot on paper with masses of little drawings inserted in the script like an endless strip-cartoon. Others, such as Sir Carol Reed, prefer to be more flexible and add details when they are actually at work on the film and have the actors around them. Sir Laurence Olivier is a meticulous planner of his Shakespearean films. The battle scenes in *Richard III* were planned in advance on location in Spain with numbered flags planted in every spot where the camera was to be set up. Even the film editor went along to ensure that the planning would include every shot that would be required when it came to cutting and assembling the lengths of celluloid into the final continuous action of the scenes.

Film production is team-work, and every team differs. But the best system is always to interest the senior technicians as early as possible in the film they are to make, and draw on their various skills to the utmost to make the film as rich a mixture as possible of their talents. The good producer and director, of course, have to keep all these talents under control. The job is to tell the story, not show off wonderful photography or beautiful sets for their own sake. A film is a dramatic campaign. The director is the commanding general and the top technicians his senior officers.

Once they enter the studio, every responsible technician must know as exactly as possible what they all want to achieve, because then they may well have hundreds of other technicians, craftsmen, electricians and actors working for them on the studio floor and in the workshops where the sets and properties are being made. It is vital to have reliable help from such people, for

THE ART DIRECTOR'S SKETCH

Cineguild-J. Arthur Rank

In many carefully designed productions the director and his designer work together, making perhaps hundreds of rough sketches. These sketches suggest the atmosphere and light of all the key shots, and what will be necessary in the way of set construction. For the British film *Brief Encounter*, the art director, John Bryan, drew many sketches like the one at the top of this page for the railway station sequence. The station at Carnforth in Lancashire was the model used; certain exterior scenes were shot at Carnforth itself at night when the station was out of service. Other sequences were shot in the studio, with sections of the station reconstructed.

SET DESIGN

Ealing Films Ltd.

The art director's sketch has to anticipate a practical set in which the director of photography can place his lights, the sound recordist operate his microphones and the director of the film move his actors. The best initial training for an art director is in architecture and interior decoration. The initial sketch has therefore to be turned into a carefully designed set which can be built in the studio workshops. Here is an art director's sketch and the luxurious bar realised from it by the set builders and decorators.

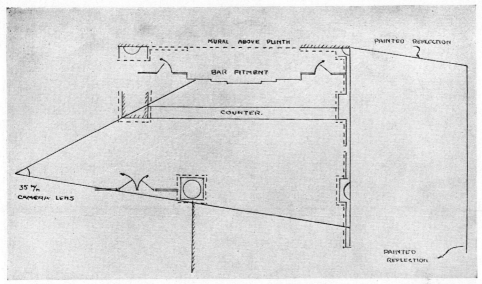

Ealing Films Ltd.

THE PLAN OF THE SET

Here is the plan of the set on the page opposite. The plan shows precisely the angle of vision of the camera, so that only that part of the set need be built which will, in fact, be included in the range of each set-up of the camera that the director contemplates using.

example, from the continuity girl and assistant director in order to ensure smooth operations, as well as from the experienced eye of the production manager watching over the practical details of the film campaign.

The Continuity Girl

The continuity girl's job is to watch every shot that is made and record every important detail ; she sits at a desk with a typewriter beside the set. She must notice that John, the hero, wore a blue tie in the living-room for shot 157, and see that he wears it again in shot 158 when he enters the kitchen set—for this shot is not planned to be made until the following Thursday week, and John will be wearing other clothes meantime and could easily forget about the blue tie.

Meanwhile the assistant director is out talking to the headmaster of the local school arranging for the party of lads required for shots 298–310 which are location scenes in a street near the school and are fixed to be done in three

weeks' time if the weather forecasts sound good.

In the Studios

The studios themselves—which our independent producer has hired (with the services of the technical staff) for, say, eight weeks at a cost of several thousand pounds a week—have many "stages" of various sizes, some looking as large as aircraft hangars, some smaller and more intimate like a village hall. These stages are specially insulated against outside sound. Round the upper walls are gangways hung with scores of lamps to give brilliant and highly adjustable illumination for every kind of photographic effect demanded by the director of photography—or lighting-cameraman, as he is sometimes called. He is responsible for the final quality of the photography ; he does not handle the camera himself ; that is done by the camera operator and his crew under the supervision of the lighting-cameraman, who spends literally hours setting the more difficult scenes and producing

A STRANGE WORLD

A remarkable picture of the strange world of the film studio. In the foreground the technicians adjust the lights, the wind machine and the fog-making apparatus for what is eventually to be a shot of an aircraft in flight that has lost its way in bad weather.

Ealing Films Ltd.

A fine example of the effective use of a model ship operated in a large tank within the studio. This shot from the war film *San Demetrio, London*, shows a blazing merchantman sinking after being torpedoed. The water in these tank shots is often filmed in slight slow motion in order to give the diminutive waves more scale and body.

Ealing Films.

PRODUCTION IN AUSTRALIA

The mail from England arrives in the British film *Eureka Stockade*, made on location in Australia by Harry Watt. This film, and especially its predecessor *The Overlanders*, were good examples of Commonwealth productions promoted by a British production company.

the right lighting effects. A cameraman once described this process to the writer as "painting the scene with light."

While the foreground sets before which the action takes place are as realistic as the same structures would be in real life, their surroundings are mostly highly artificial. The street-scene you see through the window is probably a huge, flat photographic backing, or (if movement is required) it may be an actual film of a street-scene projected on to a large screen. The floor, which looks like parquet, is actually only wall-paper pasted on the studio floor and varnished. All the scenes, in fact, are a contrivance to produce the right pictorial effect for the camera, using real things where these are best and artificial things for the rest.

One of the most enthralling jobs in a studio is to work in the plasterer's shop. Here everything is made at astonishing speed from sheets of brick wall or roof tiles to exquisite "carvings" for elaborate period settings—mantlepieces (for example) and statuary.

Building the Sets

Another department of the utmost importance in providing skilled work is the carpenters' workshop where the actual structures for the sets are put together. These are assembled on the empty stages of the studio while work is going on elsewhere. It is for this reason mainly that films are shot out of their proper order in the script. All the shots requiring a particular set are filmed together, and the sets themselves

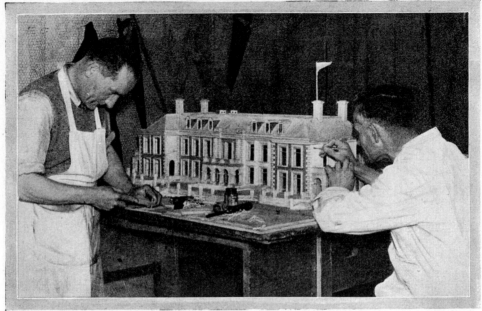

MODEL MAKERS AT WORK

Here is a mansion constructed in model form receiving its final touches. By expert use of the
camera or by super-imposing one picture on another, the house will appear in the finished film to
be life-size. Most people seeing the picture on the screen will not have the least suspicion that the
fine-looking building is not full size, but merely an example of the model-makers' art.

are built in the order of convenience
for the studio and the workshops according to the main schedule of work. It
may well be that two or more films are
being made at the same time, and the
producer has to take his turn in the use,
for example, of the largest stage.

Over all this work of set building the
art director presides, turning the original
sketches drawn for their atmosphere and
dramatic feeling into solid structures.
The art director has to combine a
designer's flair for atmosphere and colour
with an architect's knowledge of building
structure and materials.

As a kind of half-way stage between
staying in the artificial conditions of the
studio and filming on location in the
places and scenery of the real world,
sets are often built on the studio "lot",
a stretch of open ground which many
studios situated in the country-side have
as part of their property. Here streets
and other exterior sets can be built

with the added realism of being in the
open air.

Filming in the open air, however,
still requires the use of artificial lighting
aids to give the right degree of light and
shadow to make shots taken at different
times and (it may well be) different
places match together when the editor
starts his splicing. It is obviously no
good the light going up and down, or in
and out, shot by shot according to
whether the sun was in or out, high or
low at different times on different days.

Filming out of doors is always more
tricky than filming in the studio, where
everything is under the film-makers'
control. But locations and the sense
of being out-of-doors add greatly to the
feeling of reality in a film, and, since
the arrival of television, producers have
tended more and more to find exciting
locations for their films in every part
of the world in order to show off the
capacity of the big screen to bring the

A SPECIAL EXTERIOR SET

The erection of special exterior sets is a problem for experts, and here we see one of them looking through the camera view-finder to judge how the final result will appear. The foreground section of this set is constructed in model size for economy and will emerge in correct proportion with the full-size set in the background. The film studio buildings can be seen on the left.

Photos: Associated British.

Here is the finished result of the work as it finally appeared on the screen. The foreground buildings are really nothing more than models. Even the old tiled roofs are sheets turned out by the plasterers in sections about four feet long by three wide. In rough weather they would crumble away in a week or two.

farthest, most exotic places to the doorstep of your cinema. No device, however ingenious, can equal the effectiveness of the real thing.

Clever Technical Aids

There are many technical ingenuities, however, which are frequently used to save the expense of going on location in the more modestly budgeted films. Photography permits the use of many devices such as the combination in a single shot of model-size sections of an elaborate setting with full-size sections immediately surrounding the actors, and the famous device of the "matte," by means of which the film record of a moving background, such as a rough sea, can be combined with another separate film of actors taken in a boat inside the studio.

Cineguild—J. Arthur Rank.

THE COMPOSER

The director, director of music and the composer (on the right) discuss a point of detail in the score for a film. The director of music is responsible for conducting the music at the recording session, watching the film on a screen as he does so.

Many startling trick effects that you have seen in supernatural or science fiction films are achieved in this way.

There are many other departments that serve the film. The Property department ("Props") supplies from the studio store (or by hiring) everything used on the set from furniture to small articles, such as a pen. The Drapes department supplies soft furnishings — the curtains and cloths. The Wardrobe department looks after the clothes worn by both men and women ; the dresses of the women stars are often designed by famous fashion-designers. The Make-up department is responsible for the very special forms of make-up needed to survive the enormous magnification of the big close-up. An elaborate make-up, such as Laurence Olivier wore in *Richard III* or Alec Guinness in *Oliver*

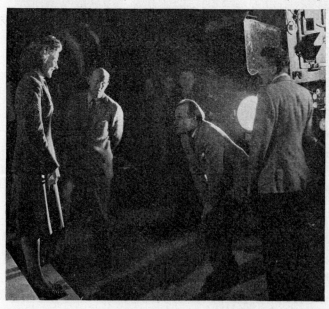

J. Arthur Rank Organisation Ltd.

THE DIRECTOR OF PHOTOGRAPHY

This picture shows Jack Cardiff, the famous British colour cinematographer, studying the lighting for a shot in Technicolor. The camera is seen in the background.

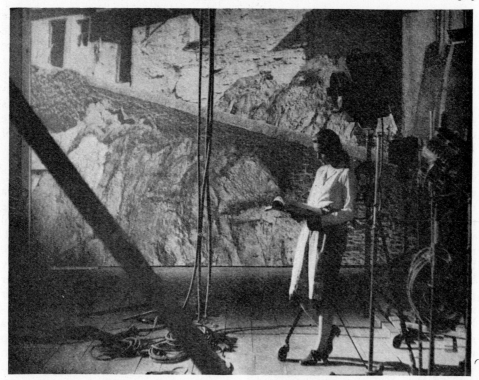

PHOTOGRAPHIC BACKING: THE MORE NORMAL TYPE

This is the more normal type of photographic backing used inside the studios. It shows a street in Mevagissey, Cornwall. Photographic backings save complicated location work and are the most economical form of static background. The backings can also be projected films giving movement, for example, to street backgrounds seen through windows or behind moving vehicles.

Twist, can take a matter of hours to apply, and has to be carefully charted so that it is made exactly the same in shape and colour at any time when it is needed, however long ago it was last put on. The Special Effects department deals with every unusual effect, photographic or otherwise, that the other departments cannot normally handle.

Camera and Sound

The Camera and Sound departments are obviously crucial to the film. The camera in the feature studio has its crew—its operator who carries out the instructions of the director of photography and keeps his eye on the view-finder throughout the shot to see that everything that should be included in the picture is seen properly in its place, the focus-puller who shifts the lens when the camera is moving to keep the focussing sharp, the man who pushes the dolly, or truck on rails on which the camera is mounted for moving during the shot, and the men responsible for loading and unloading the reels of film as they are used.

The camera may find itself mounted on the end of a mobile crane or set up on the roof of a special car for filming vehicles in motion, action on race-tracks, or, to take a famous example, the long tracking shot about a mile in length in which we keep alongside the charge of the French Knights in *Henry V*. Also, the aeroplane and the helicopter are old friends of the cameraman.

The camera itself can "pan" and tilt, twisting slowly to take in the panorama of a scene, to follow an actor's movement across a room, or to look up at the distant heights of a skyscraper or tower. The camera, like the human eye in the human head, moves to watch the thing that interests it. What you cannot see by turning your head, you run after ; so does the movie camera.

Other effects the camera can achieve are slow and quick motion by varying the speeds at which the film is shot. For dramatic purposes this can vastly increase the apparent speed of chasing cars, or make a raging sea even more titanic by filming it in slight slow-motion. The comic effects of quick motion are obvious, but very high and very low speeds are usually employed mostly for scientific and instructional films to show, for example, a shell bursting through armature, or a day's growth in a flower cut down to a few seconds. Photomicrography (the combination of the camera and the microscope) can show the movements of minute life and enlarge insects into gigantic monsters on the screen. The telephoto lens, like a telescope, can enable us to see details at a considerable distance away, such as the domestic habits of savage beasts. There is no end to the camera's resources in both black-and-white photography and colour. Its operation is a life-time's study, and the more famous cameramen earn some of the highest salaries in the industry.

The Clapper-boy

Before each scene is photographed, a clapper-boy stands in front of the camera holding in full vision a special number board, like a small black-board, with the name of the film at the top. At the bottom he chalks in very clearly the number of the shot and the number of the "take." He then calls the number of the shot and the take and (on instructions from the director) claps down a hinged section of the board ; this sharp noise is recorded by the sound men

J. Arthur Rank Organisation Ltd.

A STRIKING EXAMPLE OF SCREEN MAKE-UP

Character make-up for the film is much more elaborate and detailed than stage make-up because of the strong lighting used and the magnification of the face on the screen. Actors are often cast because of their natural facial suitability for the parts they are to perform. The British actor Alec Guinness has often appeared in films with a heavy make-up. He is seen here as Fagin in *Oliver Twist* and (in contrast) as he normally looks (except for the moustache, which he grew specially for the film *To Paris with Love*).

THE CHARGE OF THE KNIGHTS

The famous charge of the French knights in Sir Laurence Olivier's film version of Shakespeare's *Henry V* was shot from a camera which ran beside the line of galloping horsemen on the long track shown in this picture of technicians preparing for the scene.

This picture shows the use of a giant photographic backing of the Law Courts in London set up on the studio lot. (Note the local houses in the background on the extreme right.) The scene—from Alfred Hitchcock's early film *Sabotage*—shows a state coach together with a section of a crowd lining the street.

20—2

(you can see it plainly on an optical sound track) and enables the editor to synchronise exactly the sound and the action before the actors commence their work on a second instruction from the director that follows immediately— "Action!" All this is necessary because the editor will receive in the cutting-room the sound and the picture for each shot on separate lengths of celluloid, which he can project together for himself in a special viewing apparatus known as an editola (or movieola).

It is unlikely that the director will be satisfied with the first take or run-through of the shot—there is so much that can go wrong. An actor may forget his lines or make a clumsy movement in the confined space of a close-in shot. The camera may itself have to move during the shot, tracking along on a railway beside the moving actor, or gliding in towards him for a closer view while he remains still. Or there may be a complicated crane shot, with the camera hovering over the action perched at the end of a small mobile crane. Or a shadow may be cast by the long arm of the microphone boom, a crane almost like a large fishing-rod with the microphone hanging from it. This has to be swung over the heads of the speaking actors as they move about to catch their voices for the recording of the dialogue, and it is only too easy for its shadow to be cast over the set or the actor's faces when so many lights are shining down from overhead.

Editing the Film

The director normally repeats the shot (it may be only ten seconds of action, or thirty seconds, or perhaps, more rarely, a full minute) until he and his technicians and actors are fully satisfied they have done the best they can. Then the director orders the particular takes he favours to be printed. They will be viewed by the senior technicians and actors the following day when they have come back from the laboratory—an anxious moment. It is then that the best shots from the previous days' selected takes are chosen for the editor to cut and splice together as he builds up his "rough cut" of the film.

The rough cut is the editor's assembly of the film in line with the script. Directors often shoot alternative material for important scenes to give the editor plenty to work from—particularly close-ups, from which he can get his "reaction shots" (the expressions of the actors reacting to what is said or happening) or significant details of feeling

J. Arthur Rank Organisation Ltd.

EXTERIOR SHOTS

This looks like a real street, but it is in fact a street facade only, built on the studio lot. An astonishing realism of setting can be created by the art director and his craftsmen who build the sets he designs.

when actors are speaking. The editor can try out for the director different ways of presenting a scene, because the way a scene is cut is often the making of it dramatically.

For example, in the opening sequence of *Great Expectations* the convict is not seen until there is a sudden close-up of him gripping Pip by the throat in the eerie setting of the desolate grave-yard. An alternative way of presenting this scene was considered and rejected in which the audience would have seen the convict stealing up on Pip. But it seemed more dramatic to let the audience share Pip's own shock by this sudden, savage piece of cutting. In *Scott of the Antarctic*, to take another quite different example, the shots of the feet of Scott's men climbing the glacier and the more distant shots of them in the wastes of ice and snow are carefully cut to the rhythms of Vaughan Williams' magnificent music, which in this particular case was composed in advance of shooting and not, as is normal in all films other

National Film Archives.

THE CLAPPER-BOARD

The clapper-board marks the start of each shot, and the sharp sound of the wooden clap (visible on the sound track) synchronises the sound and the picture on their separate reels of film. The shots are numbered on the board, as are the takes and re-takes of them.

than musicals and cartoons, composed after the picture has reached the rough-cut stage.

Types of Shot

Films in practice are composed of different kinds of shot which are roughly indicated in the shooting script as *close-up* or close shot (which is a head-and-shoulders portrait), or a *big-close-up* (which is the face only) ; the *medium shot* (in which the camera is fairly close in on, perhaps, two or more people, their bodies dominating the screen rather than the setting in which they are grouped) ; and the *long shot* and distant shot which in varying degrees show off the full setting, ranging (for example) from a room to a railway station or several square miles of desert. One of the

Ealing Films Ltd.

FILM EDITING I

The various shots and sound tracks of films are assembled together by means of the editor's individual viewing-machine, known as an editola or movieola. The editor can hear the sound and see the picture and has an exact control over the movement of the film forwards or backwards.

most famous distant or panoramic shots in all films is the moving coach in John Ford's *Stagecoach* threading its minute way through the massive cathedral-like mesa rocks in the Arizona desert.

As the shots in the film are gradually completed, the editor pieces them together in his rough-cut like a jig-saw puzzle ; the blank sections are gradually filled in as the work is done. On the rough-cut he marks the film's punctuation for the laboratories to complete during processing, when this is not a direct cut from one shot straight to the next.

The main methods of punctuating a film are the fade-out, the fade-in and the dissolve (or mix). In the case of the fades the shots disappear and reappear slowly or fast according to the markings made by the editor ; when two successive shots are marked for a dissolve they will momentarily merge together on the screen, the first one disappearing at the same time as the second appears. Apart from these standard methods of change-over, there are many fancy devices for cutting that you

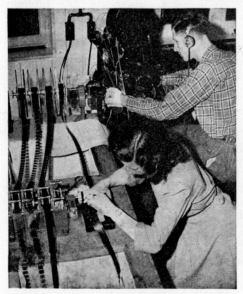

FILM EDITING II

When the editor has decided where he wants to make his cut, his assistants slice the film and then join it to the next shot on a film splicer.

will see take place in films. But the most effective are the fades and dissolves, with their strong time sense. Fades, in particular, bridge a lapse of time between one phase or sequence in the story and the next. But film technique to-day tends more and more to use sharp cutting even between sequences, using music to bridge the change-over in time or place.

The Sound Tracks

The Sound department looks after the many sound tracks needed in a film. First there is the actual soundtrack of the dialogue recorded during the action photographed in the studio ; if the quality of this proves not to be good enough to satisfy the high standards of modern film-making (especially when magnetic sound is being used), then the actors are brought back to make a post-synchronised record of what they said on the set under carefully controlled acoustic conditions. This means that they must follow the action with their eyes on the screen whilst short sequences of the film are projected for them and repeat what they said once more in perfect timing with the movements of their lips. This is not always easy to do with the right degree of feeling.

To the dialogue track are added other special tracks for individual sound effects —from the simplest footstep to the most elaborate effect, like the supernatural heart-beats when Hamlet meets his father's ghost in Laurence Olivier's film of Shakespeare's play. Finally, all these tracks are amalgamated together (that is, re-recorded or dubbed) in a single recording which accompanies the rough-cut of the film—everything is there except the music.

For this a composer is called in. Together with the director and other interested people in the production team he views the film, and a decision is reached about the various scenes and moments where music is felt to be needed. Good film music can be exciting, tense, eerie, dramatic—everything, in fact, that can heighten the effectiveness of the drama. Measured with a stop-watch, each music section is carefully timed and the composer is then responsible for creating the right music with the right timing for each section of the film. The music is recorded at a special music session, and is the last ingredient to be added to the sound track of the completed film.

For many film-makers the editing and re-recording of their films is the happiest period in production. Working quietly with a few highly-skilled technicians (the editor and the sound men), they can study the detailed effects which will give the right polish to their work. The final balance of pictures, dialogue, sound effects and music can be worked and reworked until they are all as nearly satisfied as possible. The noisy, anxious days in the studio are over, and the film is there in its maker's hands to shape.

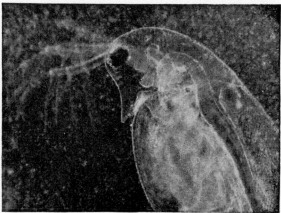

G.B. Instructional Ltd.

COMBINING MICROSCOPE AND CAMERA

The technical term used for combining the microscope and the film camera is photomicrography. This picture is from a photomicrographic film showing a water-flea, whose translucent body reveals the actual workings of its internal organs. Photomicrography is in constant use in scientific films.

DOCUMENTARY, SPECIALISED AND EXPERIMENTAL FILM-MAKING

The term *documentary* is still used to describe the ever-widening branch of film-making concerned with the facts of real life. These films are made for purposes that go beyond entertainment. They are made for instruction, information, propaganda, advertising. In time of war they may well become one of the most important links between Government and people, as was found during the Second World War.

The actual process of production for this very varied kind of film-making is the same as for a feature film, though the technicians who work in documentary are usually specialists. Films about science, medicine, engineering or agriculture require specialised knowledge of the subject in the film-maker himself, although he works with technical advisers and experts beside him. The application

of that wonderful instrument, the movie camera, to the needs of science and technology is growing every year, and many countries (especially Britain, and including Canada and Australia) have had long experience in this work.

These films are seldom intended for the cinema-theatres, though descriptive documentaries are, of course, highly entertaining if they are well made—such as *Back of Beyond*, the Australian film of life in the outback of southern Australia that has been widely shown to the public through every form of exhibition, including television, which has become a natural home for descriptive and factual films. For countries such as Australia, where feature-films with a world distribution are only now made occasionally, the first-class documentary is the best means of presenting an intimate portrait of some aspect of the national life and scene to the public of other countries as well as to the public at home.

On the borderline between professional and amateur film-making lie various kinds of specialised and experimental production. The professional may be called in to help record on film some scientific-research, or the research-worker with a ciné-camera may do this for himself. The traveller and explorer may find himself developing into a film-maker for the purpose of his work. Many professional film-makers have begun as amateurs, producing short films of life as they see it, sometimes highly experimental in their technique.

The amateur film movement itself is very widespread, with its own journals, societies and international associations. More recently it has begun to develop as a part of school activities. Making films yourself, on however modest a scale, is the best way of realising the powers and possibilities of motion pictures.

Animated Films

Another quite distinct branch of film-making is the completely artificial world of cartoon drawings, puppets and jointed cut-out figures. These films are called in general *animated films*, and the people who work in them are artists

Halas & Batchelor.

FILM ANIMATION—THE STORYBOARD

John Halas, the British cartoon film producer, is seen working on the storyboard sketches for *Animal Farm*. These sketches are like a detailed strip-cartoon of the future film.

with a special talent for being able to imagine how their sketches can most effectively come to life through the film.

Like almost all film-making, animation is a laborious and expensive process. For the British cartoon feature film *Animal Farm* a team of seventy artists of various grades worked nineteen months to make seventy-five minutes of dramatic action on the screen.

Once more you must remember that it takes twenty-four separate and slightly different pictures to make one second only of action on the screen. Lift your arm fairly quickly into the air; it takes a second to do this. Now imagine twenty-four drawings of your arm in successive moments between the two positions, at rest by your side and up in the air. To make these drawings correctly would be an example of the simplest form of animation. But in most cartoons several figures are moving with all their bodies and limbs in action. That is more complex animation. It takes a small team of artists perhaps three months or more to complete an eight minute animated cartoon. Even the simple little ninety-second cartoon commercials on television take quite a long time to make.

All cartoons begin with a story or an action sketched out in a series of drawings which is called a storyboard. The characters and the backgrounds are also worked out by means of innumerable trial sketches, which supplement the storyboard with details of facial expression and characteristic body movements. The final storyboard for *Animal Farm* was about 4,000 drawings showing every stage of the seventy-five minutes' drama, like a giant strip-cartoon. A large cartoon studio would include producers, directors, key animators, assistant animators, background artists, tracers, camera crew, editors and sound experts on its staff, and the composer is obviously an important additional member of the team. The composition and recording of the music often precedes the animation of the

COAT CAN
GROW A TRIFLE
LONGER FOR ANIMATION

PRODUCTION F I
SNOW WHITE
DOPEY MODELS
© 1936
W.D.P.

EARS CAN
REACT TO MOODS
LIKE (FIG ① + ②)

AND WILL
ALSO BE USED
IN ANIMATION
GAGS

Walt Disney Productions.

FILM ANIMATION—THE MODEL SHEET

The animators are artists and produce model sheets to show different expressions, gestures and positions for such characters as may be needed during the film. The animators will use them as a guide when they begin the detailed frame-by-frame drawings. Here we have a reproduction of an actual model sheet used for one of the popular characters in *Snow White and the Seven Dwarfs*.

figures, because their movements are normally very closely timed to the music and sound effects.

Again, preparation and careful planning means everything to a good cartoon, however short or long. Owing to the enormous labour involved, feature-length cartoons are very rare, and only Walt Disney has made a whole series of them; they represent two to three years' labour for a large studio. But the shorter cartoons are now used for every conceivable purpose—including particularly advertising and technical instruction, as well as entertainment. The output of cartoons has roughly-speaking trebled since the arrival of television, with its ceaseless demand for commercials.

Preparation consists, then, first of all in completing a satisfactory storyboard with the dialogue (of which there is usually comparatively little in a cartoon) typed underneath the pictures at the points where it occurs; secondly, in making a series of advance studies of the characters (humans and animals, chiefly) from every standard position; thirdly, in making more finished drawings of the main backgrounds against which the characters will perform; and, lastly, in working on the music score with the composer. Before the animators begin to move in on the job, a work-book is prepared analysing every movement in every shot; this is the master plan, an instruction chart on the timing and nature of the drawings.

Animation is graded. The most skilled

artists are the key animators, and they are responsible for drawing the characters in their chief positions for every movement—perhaps it might be phases 1, 5, 12, 14, 17, 21 and 24 in a particular second of action. The assistant animators complete the in-between movements, so building up the rest of the drawings into a smooth sequence.

If the scene has a number of important characters then these are divided among the key animators, each of whom specialises in working on one or more of the figures. Whilst the still sections of the backgrounds remain painted on paper, the moving parts of the drawing, which are chiefly the characters themselves, are outlined by the tracers on to transparent celluloid sheets and then painted over with paints and inks, which are opaque, and so cut out the background when they are placed over it. When it comes to the final stage of photographing, the layers of celluloid (one for each

Halas & Batchelor.

ANIMATION DRAWING AND TRACING

When the animators have made their finished drawings for each frame of the film, the tracers transfer them to the celluloid sheets which are to be placed over the backgrounds for photographing.

main character or object in motion) are fastened down very exactly over each other on top of the background painting. A new set of celluloids is required for each twenty-fourth part of a second in all fully-animated cartoon work.

To help the animator, his work is very carefully charted for him on work sheets taken from the work-book. These work-sheets, for example, analyse and time every beat of the music, for the ear alone is not keen enough to relate movement to sound to the exact degree of one twenty-fourth part of a second —and exactly synchronised animation will have to work as closely as this. The animator also checks his movements in outline only in what is called the line or pencil test stage ; these are roughly animated sketches which are photographed and projected to see if the work is progressing satisfactorily when seen in action on the screen itself.

The final film goes through the same processes of editing and recording as a feature film, simplified considerably because it is planned so precisely in advance.

Puppet Films

Puppet animation and cut-out jointed-figure animation (such as you find in silhouette films) go through the same processes, but with some variations. The jointed figures of a silhouette film are layed on a sheet of opaque but translucent glass, lit from underneath. The figures are adjusted by hand between each shot, a task which needs great skill and delicacy of touch. The movements again are carefully planned and rehearsed down to one twenty-fourth part of a second.

The puppet-film, on the other hand, deals with three-dimensional, not two-dimensional, settings and figures. These figures, until recently, also had to be adjusted by hand. Some kinds of modern puppet films, however, use dolls whose movements can be controlled electronically.

The Secret
of
Man's
Supremacy

About the
Mental Equipment
of the
Human Being

Copyright.

TRAINING YOUTH FOR MODERN INDUSTRY

Training for commerce and industry is essential, and in this photograph is seen the Drawing Office of the School of Motor Body Engineering at the Regent Street Polytechnic. Here youths are trained in the methods employed for the production of private cars, passenger-carrying, public service and other types of modern vehicles.

HOW THE BRAIN AND THE MIND WORK

THE human brain might be compared with the general headquarters of an army. The general headquarters receives information respecting the whole state of the army and what is happening in the various outposts. The brain is constantly receiving messages and kept informed of the state of the body, that is, of bodily movements, and changes within the body itself, as well as changes taking place outside.

Before, therefore, we consider the nature and work of the brain itself, it will be interesting to consider briefly the kinds of messages it receives.

The Brain Receives Messages

Diagram 1 illustrates these varying types of messages, or stimuli, as the scientists call them, which travel to the brain.

In the first place, there are those messages aroused by events happening in the outside world, giving us sensations of sound, sight, touch, both light and heavy, painful and non-painful, taste and smell. Secondly, there are messages informing us of the position of the body, both when it is at rest and when it is in motion. Some of these messages arise from nerve fibres in the muscles, ligaments, tendons and joints in the various parts of the body. Others are received by the brain from the internal organs of the ear.

You see, the ear is a very complicated organ which not only enables us to hear, but also to know of the equilibrium, or balance of the body. If this part of the ear, called the internal ear, is disturbed or damaged we are sometimes unable to maintain our balance. Thus, when you turn round rapidly many times, you disturb the smooth working of the internal ear and you become " giddy."

Thirdly, there are messages telling us of the changes taking place in the internal organs of the body, including the lungs for breathing, the heart for supply of blood to the body, the digestive system which deals with the food we eat and the eliminative system which gets rid of the waste products of the body.

The Human Telephone

The messages of which we have spoken travel along chains or relays of nerve fibres and nerve cells called neurons. These might be compared with the wires of the telephone system. Now, there are two-way messages, one series of messages from the body to the brain, Diagram 2a, and the other series from the brain to the body, Diagram 2b. In the body there are many millions of these nerve processes and Diagram 2 shows you what they look like. Let us suppose that an animal sees a dangerous object and runs away.

If we compare this sequence of events with the telephone system, then the voice of the caller, the sensory message, which for our animal is the sight of the dangerous object, travels along wires, the sensory nerves, to the exchange, the brain, where it is accepted and interpreted. Then the message is sent from the brain, along a series of wires, the motor nerves, to the receiver of the message, the muscles, which then carry out the appropriate movements of flight.

Just as in the telephone system we have the central exchange including local exchanges which can contact any area, and trunk exchanges which can contact any area over which the telephone wires run, so in the nervous system we have the central nervous system, consisting of the spinal cord and the brain, as well as the nerve processes lying outside the central nervous system. Most of our messages travel to the brain by way of the spinal cord. However, the nerves of the face are connected directly with the brain through small holes in the skull. These nerves carry messages relating to sensations of smell, taste, sight, and hearing and movements of the face and eyes. Moreover, there are certain messages which use only the local exchange, or the spinal cord.

Thus, when you unknowingly touch a hot plate, you immediately and automatically remove your hand. Such a non-willed automatic action is called a reflex action. We have spoken of a reflex action of the spinal cord, but parts of the brain also are responsible for such automatic bodily actions. The tasks which the lower parts of the brain perform are carried out without our consciously willing that they be performed. We will now consider the work of the brain, taking each part in turn.

THE HUMAN BRAIN

The Grey Matter

When we look at a brain, we see a mass of grey and white coloured matter. The grey matter consists of millions of tiny nerve cells, each of which has a fine nerve fibre. It is these fibres which give the brain its white appearance, and they serve either to link up various cells within the brain, or by passing to other parts of the body, to connect the brain with the rest of the body.

Parts of the Brain

The brain is a continuation of the spinal cord, and perhaps it will help us to understand the brain if we make a very rough comparison. Imagine a scout's pole, the top of which is divided into three by notches. The top division of our pole is placed between the cut halves of an orange, and another

TRAINING HAND AND EYE

In this picture we have a view of the School of Motor Body Building, where students are at work in the metal shop, shaping aluminium panels for car bodies. Finished work is hanging from the balcony and in the background are " wheeling machines," used to smooth off and polish the panels. Oxy-acetylene welding, painting, trimming, coach joinery and body assembly also are taught.

smaller orange, also cut in half, is placed against the third division as shown in Diagram 3. In the diagram, the main parts of the brain have been indicated and named.

However, this is a very crude comparison, and we must now consider the various parts of the brain as they really are. Diagrams 4, 5 and 6 are drawings of the brain as it actually appears. Diagram 4 shows how the human brain is situated inside the human skull, and Diagram 5 shows the parts in greater detail. In Diagram 5, the mid-brain and inter-brain are situated in between the two parts of the cerebrum and are not, therefore, seen in the diagram.

Brain Stem and Mid-Brain

The brain stem contains the pathway by means of which the spinal cord is joined to the rest of the brain, and along this pathway impulses or messages travel from the spinal cord to other parts of the brain, and from the brain to appropriate parts of the body. It contains nerve fibres which control our breathing, others which regulate the heart-beat, and therefore the control of blood throughout the body, and still other centres which control processes necessary to eating, swallowing, the secretion of saliva, as when our mouths water at the sight and smell of an appetising meal. The brain stem also controls the work of the digestive system during the assimilation of food.

Now, when you consciously move your eyes, your head automatically moves in the same direction. Similarly, if you consciously move your head, the eyes automatically move in the same direction. In short, they work together; you *will* the movement of the one, the movement of the other is automatic or reflex in character. Again, if you hear a noise, you tend to move the head in that direction, while some animals prick their ears also in response to sound.

These simultaneous movements of the eyes, ears, and head are protective devices which are especially useful to animals, enabling them to be able easily to inspect the events in the outside world so that they may then assess their danger value. The mid-brain contains the cells and fibres which enable the automatic or reflex actions of the eyes to follow a willed movement of the head, and the automatic or reflex action of the head to follow a willed movement of the eyes.

Concerning the Cerebellum

The cerebellum, or lower outgrowth of the brain, is sometimes called the hind-brain because it is situated just above the back of the neck, as you can see from Diagram 4. It is round in shape, but is divided into two hemispheres, which are connected by means of nerve fibres, while other nerve fibres connect the cerebellum with the rest of the brain and also with the joints and muscles of distant parts of the body. The outside of the cerebellum consists of a layer of grey matter which has deep folds, as, for example, has a handkerchief when it is lightly screwed up in the hand.

These folds have a special purpose in that they enable a large amount of grey matter to be tucked away within a very small space. The section of the brain called the pons, as marked in Diagram 5, consists of nerve fibres which connect the two hemispheres. The name " pons," meaning " the bridge," is most appropriate because this part of the brain is a kind of bridge which connects the brain stem with the upper parts of the brain as well as connecting the two hemispheres of the cerebellum. In appearance, you might compare the pons and the cerebellum with a signet ring on a finger, the pons being the ring and the cerebellum a very large signet.

Specially drawn for this work.

AN OPTICAL ILLUSION

Here are two squares of the same size. If you prepare similar squares for yourself and hold them a little apart, the one with the horizontal lines will seem higher than that with the vertical lines.

MESSAGES TO THE BRAIN

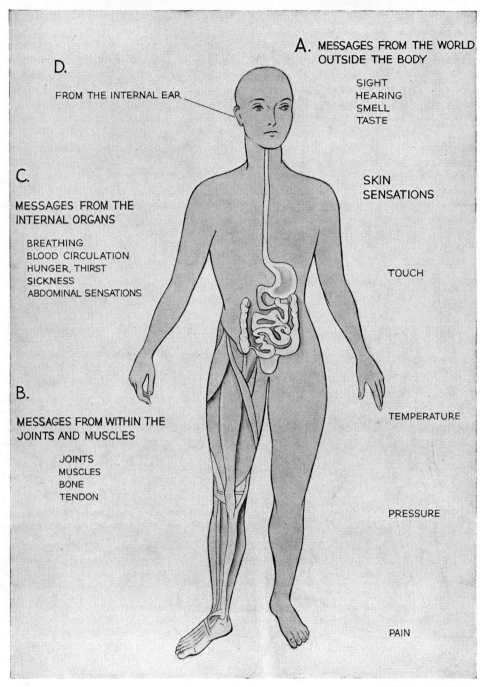

D.

FROM THE INTERNAL EAR

A. MESSAGES FROM THE WORLD
OUTSIDE THE BODY

SIGHT
HEARING
SMELL
TASTE

SKIN
SENSATIONS

C.

MESSAGES FROM THE
INTERNAL ORGANS

BREATHING
BLOOD CIRCULATION
HUNGER, THIRST
SICKNESS
ABDOMINAL SENSATIONS

TOUCH

B.

MESSAGES FROM WITHIN THE
JOINTS AND MUSCLES

JOINTS
MUSCLES
BONE
TENDON

TEMPERATURE

PRESSURE

PAIN

Specially drawn for this work.

Diagram 1. Here we can see the kind of messages received by the brain, and the sensations of which we are made aware. There are messages informing the brain of what is going on in the world outside the body (A), and other messages which tell the brain of what is happening inside the body (B, C, and D).

The Work of the Cerebellum

The chief work of the cerebellum is to co-ordinate the various movements of the body, so that the muscles work harmoniously together. For the tiny child, when he begins to learn, walking is a very difficult process. His movements tend to be jerky, one leg completing its movement before the other leg begins. The movements are carried out consciously, the higher parts of the brain taking part in these early attempts. Soon, however, the process of walking becomes a smooth, harmonious activity, carried out without conscious thought. By this time, the cerebellum has taken over this task, leaving the higher centres of the brain free for other work.

It has been discovered that an animal deprived of its cerebellum does not suffer from paralysis, or inability to move the muscles of the body, but its movements are shaky, jerky, and poorly controlled. In man, disease or injury to the cerebellum causes the same lack of muscular control, and he is unable to carry out the movement of his muscles smoothly and accurately. If, for example, he is asked to touch his nose with his finger, his arm moves jerkily and he fails to hit the mark.

The Inter-Brain

The inter-brain, as we shall call it, is a mass of grey matter lying just above the mid-brain and at the base of the cerebrum. It is the part of the brain which enables us to sense extreme sensations, extreme pain, extreme heat and extreme cold. There are nerve centres which enable the body to adapt itself to these extreme changes. Thus, for example, on a boiling hot day these centres enable the body to lose heat by controlling chemical changes in the body and by increasing the activity of the sweat glands. Further, these centres are concerned with violent reactions —emotions of hate, rage and fear. These violent reactions are usually controlled by the higher centres of the brain.

If, however, these higher centres are removed in an animal, there results a condition of uncontrolled emotional outbursts, such as anger, shown by snarling, clawing and lashing of the tail. Extreme fear is also seen. The heart beats fast, the blood travels at a very quick rate through the body, the pupils of the eyes enlarge and the hair on the body rises in much the same way as in a cat when it is chased by a dog. In man, alcohol tends to inhibit or prevent control being exercised by the higher centres of the brain. It sometimes

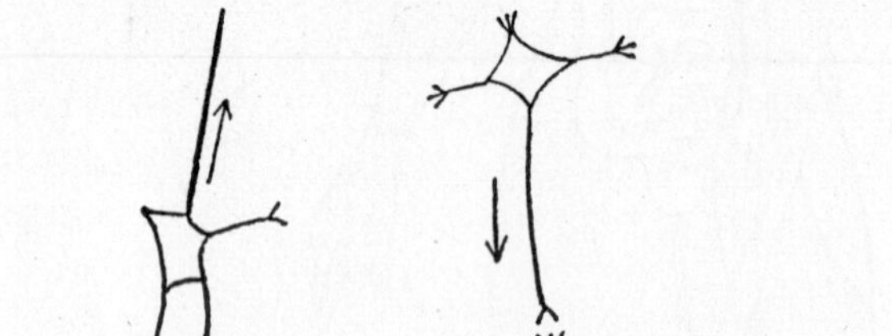

A.   B.   MESSAGES

MESSAGES ALONG THE NEURONS

Diagram 2. In A we see the beginning of the message, which a touch on the skin sends along the sensory neurons on the way to the spinal cord and the brain. In B is seen the final pathway of the message from the brain (or spinal cord) along the motor neurons to the muscle.

happens that a man who is intoxicated displays extreme emotions such as we have described in the animal deprived of the cerebrum.

The Cerebrum and Its Work

The cerebrum is the largest and most important part of the brain in man. In lower creatures, the cerebrum is smaller in proportion to the rest of the brain. As we ascend the evolutionary scale from the fish to man, the cerebrum becomes proportionately greater, until in the dog and monkey it is larger than all the other parts of the brain put together. In man it is so large that all the rest of the brain seems very insignificant.

In so far as it consists of a deeply folded, outer grey crust of nerve cells, and an inner layer of nerve fibres; in so far also as it has two hemispheres joined by nerve fibres, and has nerve fibres connecting it with the rest of the brain and with distant parts of the body, the cerebrum is not unlike the cerebellum in general structure. Diagram 6 shows the right half of the cerebrum. In the diagram, you can see the deep folds of which we have spoken. In appearance, the cerebrum is not unlike the kernel of a walnut which has been extracted from the shell. The cerebrum in human beings, however, is larger in bulk than the cerebellum, and fills most of the skull.

Moreover, the work it has to do is more varied. An interesting difference between the cerebellum and the cerebrum is that in the cerebellum, the right hemisphere controls the joints and muscles on the right side of the body, and the left hemisphere looks after the joints and the muscles on the left side of the body. In the cerebrum, however, this is not so, for here the left hemisphere controls and looks after the opposite or right side of the body; and the right hemisphere controls the left side. You see, the fibres leaving the cerebrum cross each other before they reach the spinal cord. Diagram 7

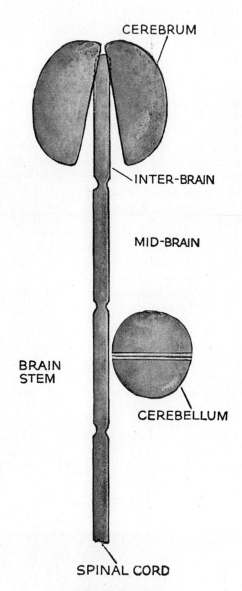

CEREBRUM

INTER-BRAIN

MID-BRAIN

BRAIN STEM

CEREBELLUM

SPINAL CORD

A SIMPLE COMPARISON

Diagram 3. In this drawing the brain is compared with a notched scout's pole, showing the inter-brain, the mid-brain, the brain stem and the spinal cord. The two cut oranges represent the two halves of the cerebrum and the cerebellum.

shows the pathway of nerve fibres from the cerebellum and cerebrum. You can see how the fibres from the cerebrum cross over to the other side of the body when they reach the brain stem.

The Cerebral Cortex

The cerebral cortex is the name given to the grey matter, or nerve cells, which cover the cerebrum. The cerebral cortex is the seat of conscious reactions. It contains centres by means of which we are made consciously aware of our surroundings ; it is the organ of volition or will, for when we will to move some muscle or to perform some task, the nerve cells in the cortex are first stimulated, and messages then sent to various parts of the body.

The cortex is also the centre for higher thought processes, reasoning, memory and speech. In short, this area of the brain firstly makes us conscious of bodily sensations, secondly enables us to use our will or volition, and thirdly, enables us to carry out thought processes.

The Map of the Cortex

Now, it has been found, as a result of experiments on animals, and from the observation of the effect of brain diseases and injuries suffered by man, that certain specific areas of the cortex perform, and are responsible for, certain specific tasks. Scientists have, as a result of their observations and experiments, been able to map out these various areas of the cortex, and Diagram 8 is a sketch of the left half of the cerebral cortex mapped out according to the tasks which the various parts perform. From a study of the diagram you can see that there is :—

1. A motor (or muscle movement) area from which summonses to action are dispatched to the muscles of the body. Each part of the body has its special small area within the motor cortex. When this part of the motor area of the right hemisphere is stimulated by a weak electric current in an animal under anæsthetic, it causes movement of the appropriate muscles on the left side of the body. Disease of, or removal of, the motor area in any one hemisphere produces paralysis of the opposite side of the body. If the motor areas of both the hemispheres are injured, the whole body becomes paralysed.

2. A sensory area which makes us conscious of sensations coming from the muscles and skin. Patients who have had to undergo brain operations using local anæsthetics only, have sometimes permitted the surgeon to stimulate these sensory areas. The patients reported definite sensations of numbness or tingling which they localised in specific parts of the body.

3. An auditory area, which is a special area for hearing, and

4. Another special area for visual per-

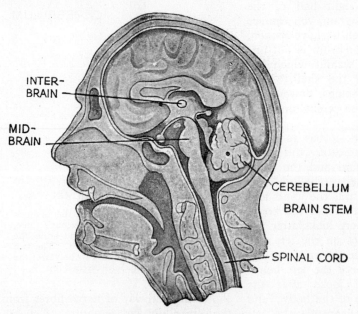

INTER-BRAIN

MID-BRAIN

CEREBELLUM

BRAIN STEM

SPINAL CORD

PROTECTOR OF THE BRAIN

Diagram 4. The skull acts as a protector of the brain. Between the brain and the skull are three layers of fine, supple skin, which protect the brain from the hardness of the inside surface of the skull.

ception, the visual area. In animals it is difficult to say when a sensation appears, but when the auditory area of an animal is stimulated there is a short delay, then a pricking up of the ears ; the stimulation of the visual area is followed by a turning of the head presumably in the direction from which the visual impulse is thought to come.

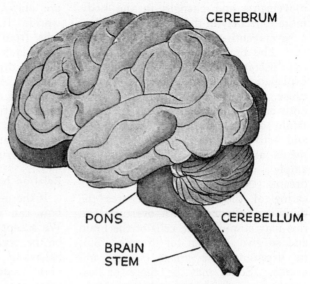

A SIDE VIEW OF THE BRAIN

Diagram 5. Here we see parts of the brain as they are seen on the left side. The mid-brain and the inter-brain are hidden from view.

The rest of the cerebral cortex is sometimes called the " Silent Area " as these parts do not carry out special functions, as do the specific areas considered above. They are also known as " Association areas." To associate means to link one, two or more ideas together. These areas are said to be concerned with learning and memory, thought and reasoning processes; in short, the mental processes which characterise man, and in the exercise of which he is distinguished from the animal.

HOW THE HUMAN MIND WORKS

So far we have been considering the brain, the scientific study of which is carried out by the physiologist. Now, we need to consider man's mind, the student of which is a psychologist. The work of the psychologist, like that of any other scientist, is to observe, to classify the facts which he observes, and then to make scientific laws concerning his observations.

A scientific law says, in effect, " Do so-and-so, and such-and-such will follow," or " If so-and-so happens, such-and-such will follow." Thus is man able to predict or foretell what will happen. It is this power of prediction which gives man control over the world in which he lives.

The psychologist is concerned with mental events or what happens in the mind. He is concerned, that is, with such facts as sensations, perceptions, emotions, feelings, memory, intelligence and character. Now, for Western man, this study of mental processes is comparatively new. Western man has, especially during the last four hundred years, expended most of his energies in examining objects and events in the world outside him. Thus, he has learned much about the laws which govern their movement and behaviour, and has built up a highly technical civilisation. But the study of the mind has been neglected, and often such a study is regarded by us as strange, if not a little mysterious, and one in which we do not feel quite as much at home as we do when we consider objects in the outside world.

What is Mind ?

Here we ask a question which philosophers have pondered throughout the ages.

Some consider the mind as something which is caused by and is the result of movements and changes in the body, more especially in the brain; as Hobbes, a seventeenth-century philosopher, put it, " The brain secretes thought as the liver secretes bile." However, such an explanation is hardly satisfactory because, as we shall see later, the mind is both active and creative, and it is certainly difficult to explain creativeness and activity in terms of bodily movements and changes. To take an example ; we eat a big supper, and we dream. Now, it may be true that the eating of the big supper causes the digestive system to work overtime and this may stimulate the cells of the brain and so give occasion for dreams. But, in dreaming, we create scenes and events. Some may be more or less repetitions of what we have experienced during our waking hours, others may be new and strange. We might even write a story, book or poem. Coleridge, the poet, created his poem " Kubla Khan " during sleep, and wrote it immediately on waking.

Thus, there is something creative and active, which is influenced by the brain and body but is nevertheless something other than either. The body, as a body, obeys the laws of chemistry and physics, the laws which are obeyed by objects in the outside world. If, for example, a human body falls from a height, it will obey the same laws as did the lead balls which Galileo dropped from the leaning tower of Pisa. A human body can be weighed and measured, but we can hardly measure the inspiration which enabled Beethoven to write his musical works. A brain and body, but not a thought, may be crushed with a hammer.

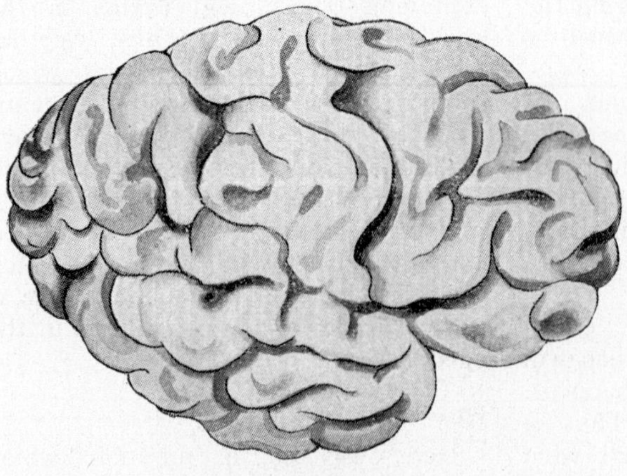

Relation between Body and Mind

If the mind and body are so different, how can they influence one another ? We accept the fact that one object can be the cause of movement or change of behaviour in another. They are both material objects, consisting of what the scientist calls " matter." But how can a thought cause changes in the body ? Yet, experience tells us that the mind does affect the body.

We decide to do something, that is, we make an act of will, which is a mental event, and the body obeys. Worry and anxiety, mental events again, have been found to cause bodily ills such as indigestion and stomach troubles, heart diseases and asthma, and in certain cases cures have been obtained by treating patients psychologically when the use of drugs has failed. Further, experience tells us that the state of our bodies can affect the state of our minds. We have indigestion and we feel gloomy and depressed. We take drugs and we have visions of ecstasy, or we lose our will power or become obstinate.

Philosophers have given many theories to account for these body-to-mind and mind-to-body influences, but it is perhaps true to say that our commonsense view is as satisfactory as any of the other theories of philosophers. The commonsense view is

THE FOLDS OF THE BRAIN

Diagram 6. Right side of brain, showing the deep folds which enable a large amount of grey matter to be tucked away in a very small space.

that the body and mind are two separate elements of man, and they obey separate laws. Nevertheless, one can affect the other. How they do this, we do not know, but by observing human behaviour, we must accept the fact that they do so influence each other.

Mental Behaviour is Purposive

The main feature of mental behaviour is that it is purposive. Objects obey mechanical laws and are moved to action by the force of other objects, or else are still. In mental activity, however, there is a goal or purpose and the mind works forward to accomplish its purpose, not blindly, but actively exploring all the time and changing its behaviour according to changing circumstances. Now, a rubber ball running downhill is impelled forward by the force of gravity. If, in its forward movement, it hits an obstacle, say a wall, there its " activity " ends.

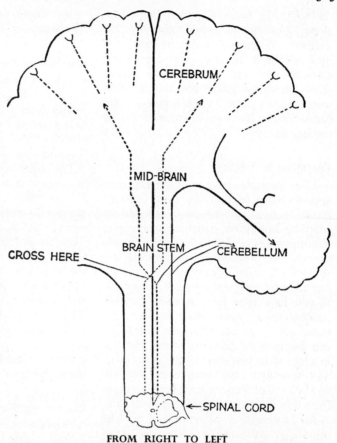

FROM RIGHT TO LEFT

Diagram 7. This shows the nerve fibres from the cerebellum and cerebrum to the spinal cord fibres. Notice how fibres from the cerebrum cross to the other side of the spinal cord. In the cerebrum the left hemisphere looks after the right side and the right after the left side of the body.

Compare the boy who wishes to obtain some apples on the trees on the other side of the wall. He runs down

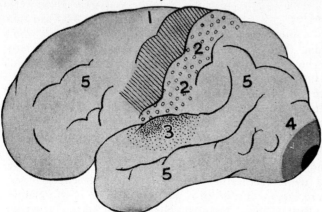

A MAP OF THE BRAIN

Diagram 8. This left view shows the special areas of the brain. 1. The motor area responsible for movements of the muscles. 2. The sensory area where sensations of touch, etc., are perceived. 3. The auditory or hearing area. 4. The visual area, responsible for understanding things seen by the eyes. 5. Association areas, responsible for learning, memory and thought processes.

the hill ; the force of gravity helps him along, but he is urged also by his desires. When he finds the wall too high to climb, he does not stop in his activities but will explore other means of obtaining his goal; nor will he stop, until either the circumstances are greater than he can overcome, or he reaches his goal.

The Mind is Active

The example of the boy and the apples shows us that the mind is constantly active, solving problems and so adapting bodily movements to changing circumstances. Even in the simple process of perceiving, our minds are active. A simple example of this is provided by Diagrams 9 (a, b, c and d). If you look separately at each diagram concentrating your attention all the time, you will see that each drawing can be seen in different ways, but not in more than one way at the same time. Try this little test with each diagram and you will experience these changes from one drawing to the other.

An interesting illustration of the mind's activity in perceiving is given when we look at those puzzle pictures which you find in children's books. For example, there is a forest scene and you are asked to find among the trees, the woodman, his wife and three children. At first you cannot see them, but by searching you find them.

Perceiving is a Form of Thinking

When you discover the woodman and his family, they stand out so obviously that you wonder how it was that you did not see them immediately. But in order to experience this, your mind had to be active. Then we make a judgment, to ourselves, if not in words to someone else, and we say, " There is the woodman." Perceiving is thus a form of thinking and is followed by a judgment of what to us is fact. But there are other processes of thinking which must be distinguished

from simple perception as we have so far considered it.

Discovering Relations

When two objects or ideas are given, we also discover that there is some relationship existing between them. When we say that we " see " that two objects are " similar," we do not see " similar " as we see " red " when we say " The pillar box is ' red '." The seeing of " red " is what the psychologist calls a " percept." The " seeing " of " similar " is a concept, that is, it is conceived by or produced by the mind. This mental process of discovering of relations is a very important ability of the mind, for it enables us to see how events and objects in the outside world are connected one with the other. Thus we speak of one event as being " the cause of," or " the result of," just as we speak of one thing being " more beautiful than " or " bigger than " another.

Discovering New Ideas

Suppose you were given the idea " black " and the relation " opposite." From these two you obtain the third and fresh idea " white." You obtain another idea from two ideas given.

Again, suppose you were given two terms, e.g., " coal " and " locomotive." You see there is a relationship between them, for coal enables the locomotive to run. Suppose you were given yet a third term " motor car." You can then find a term, namely " petrol," which stands to motor as coal stands to locomotive, that is, the fuel from which it obtains its energy to move.

We have shown here how the mind is active, first in seeing objects and the qualities they have; secondly, discovering relations between objects, and, thirdly, finding new ideas or objects. These are very simple examples, but the minds of great scientists work in this way to discover new relations between objects and new facts and

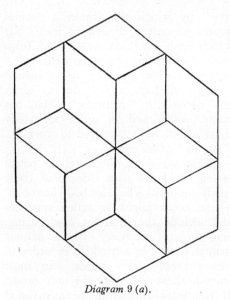

Diagram 9 (a).

laws which have not been discovered before.

Intelligence

Intelligence is the power to perform the types of mental activities we have described. Psychologists have made out special tests to find out how well you can perform these mental tasks. The relationships and new items can be made more and more difficult, and the more difficult the relations you can see, and the more difficult the new terms your mind can discover, the greater your intelligence score.

You must not confuse intelligence with knowledge. A man may gain a lot of knowledge, not only by reading and schooling, but also by travel and life experience. This increases the number of ideas he has in his mind, but not the power of seeing difficult relations and conceiving new ideas. We might compare intelligence with the maximum speed which a car can go; and compare the amount of knowledge a man has obtained, with the number of miles the car has travelled. Now, a car may have travelled 40,000 miles when its maximum speed is only 50 miles an hour. On the other hand, a car may have travelled only 10,000 miles, but have

a maximum speed of 95 miles per hour. In the same way, a man with a smaller intelligence may have greater knowledge than a man with a higher intelligence.

Aptitude

Psychologists call intelligence " general mental ability." In order to become a brilliant mathematician, philosopher and scientist, a great amount of " general mental ability " is needed. However, besides this general ability, we have also special abilities, for example, in music, drawing, painting, craftwork, and motor mechanics. To be good at these we need not necessarily have a high intelligence, or " general " ability, but we do need a " special " ability or special aptitude in the particular subject. Certain tests which psychologists have devised are attempts to predict what tasks you are best able to do. They are called Aptitude Tests.

Learning

There are two main ways of learning. We may learn without realising that we are learning. This we can call " unconscious " learning. A child learns more in the first five years of life than in any other five years of his life, though he may not go to school. Besides learning to walk and talk, he learns skill in handling objects, to know what they are used for. He learns also the kind of behaviour his parents

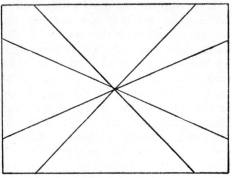

Diagram 9 (b).

expect from him. He learns to like some things, dislike others; he learns to like certain people and to hate and fear others.

In school, much learning is conscious learning. We " pay attention " to the teacher, and he explains facts to us.

In learning, we use our " memory." How we are able to " store up " so many memories, or what exactly " memory " is, is ultimately a mystery. All we can say is that we are able to remember, and that our minds can remember more easily, provided that we understand what we are learning, that is provided we see the relationships between the various items of what we are learning. We can learn merely by rote, or " by heart " (as we put it), without understanding. But this is a very poor way of learning, not only because it is more difficult, but also because things we learn merely " by heart " are easily forgotten. It is always a good rule, therefore, in all your learning to understand, and not merely learn " parrot fashion."

Secondly, learning depends on our feelings about the subject we are learning. Interest and desire to learn are the lubricating oil of the mind. They enable the mind to learn more easily and more quickly. That is why the good teacher is the one who arouses our interests and desires to learn by using pictures, diagrams and stories as aids to learning.

Mental Energy

If we compare the mind with a motorcar engine, we may say that so far we have described the engine of the mind, how the rods and pistons link up one with the other, and what work each does. But what is the source of energy of the mind ? What corresponds in the mind to the petrol of the car ? Here again, we are faced with an ultimate mystery. Some thinkers speak of " mental energy " which they call by various names including " libido," " élan vital " or " the will to

live " by which they mean a general source of energy unseen in itself, but which they conclude must exist from their observations of human behaviour.

Rather than speak of " mental energy " perhaps it is better to speak of " needs " or " instincts." Man has many needs, and in order to satisfy these needs, he is prepared to work the " engine " of his mind.

These needs are, therefore, the petrol which the mind uses. Some of these needs are needs which his body demands. These needs might be called appetites and include the need for food, drink, and physical exercise. Much of our mental energy is carried on in order to satisfy these bodily needs. In most animals these needs are the only needs. If you want an animal to learn, or if you wish to train an animal, the best way is to refuse him food till he is hungry, and then offer him food as a reward for carrying out the task you wish him to do.

Human beings acquire other needs, and these needs vary in strength from one person to another. We need to assert ourselves, and we gain much satisfaction from mastering a task.

We like also to please other people and win their affection and esteem so that they will say " What a good boy you are." We may also wish that other people will admire us, and we are urged to activity by this need to impress them so that they recognise how clever we are. Furthermore, we need to join with our fellows and to be able to do the many tasks they do. We would feel " out of it " if others in our little groups could do things which we could not do. It is pleasant to share the work, play and interests of others and to do so we must use our mental energy to learn the skills, the rules of the games which others play. When we are older, our needs may become less self-centred. We have a wife and children and we are urged on by the need to provide for them. Finally, we might feel that our efforts will

THROUGH THE MICROSCOPE

A. E. Smith

This is an artistically arranged group of insects' eggs, photographed through a microscope and magnified about 40 times. The large central egg is that of the Red Underwing Moth. It is surrounded by the fluted eggs of the Swallowtail Moth. The long white eggs on the outside of the group were laid by the common House Fly.

Here we see the flower of one of the Milkwort family as revealed under the microscope. Though only a small flower the design is charming, and an excellent model for the artist.

What might be a wonderful carving or ornate plaster cast for a ceiling is simply a magnification of the leaf rosette of one of the Saxifrages, the well-known rockery plants.

One need not look only to rare greenhouse or exotic plants for beauties hidden from our eyes except with the aid of the microscope. In this photograph we have the marvellous flowers and stalk of Comfrey, a herb of the stream-side. The photographs on this and the following two pages appear in a beautifully illustrated book "Art Forms in Nature," published by A. Zwemmer of 78 Charing Cross Road, London, England.

In disclosing to our vision the concealed beauties of nature, the microscope and camera have never been brought to bear upon a more interesting subject than this simple and well-known flower the Scabious. When enlarged, the blossom appears to be constructed of countless smaller blooms, massed and assembled in the most finished fashion, the spike-like leaves drooping after the manner of a beard, the whole covered with a veritable forest of hairs as fine as the most delicate tracery.

A CROZIER AND TOTEM POLES

There is a quite definite suggestion of the bishop's crozier in the design seen in this photograph. It shows the frond of an ordinary fern in the early stages when it is slowly unfolding.

These three extraordinary things, in appearance for all the world like the totem-poles of American Indians, are really young shoots taken from the Horse Chestnut tree.

This is a young shoot of Aconitum, often known as "Monkshood" from the hooded blooms, which bears gay blue flowers, though its root contains a deadly poison.

A queer weed of the ditch and marsh is the Teasel. Here the camera and microscope reveal the leaves dried on the stem in autumn, when the sap has left the plant to wither.

benefit not only ourselves and our families, but the whole of the human race, and this acts to further our mental efforts.

So, you see, when we are mentally and physically active, we are moved to

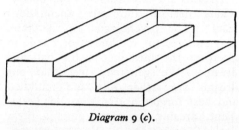

Diagram 9 (*c*).

action by motives or needs. Not all man's needs have been given here. Man has many needs which urge him to mental activity and these needs are sometimes called instincts. To understand why a person attempts to solve particular problems, it is necessary to explain not only how he thinks, but also why he thinks—that is, what real needs does he hope to satisfy by his activity.

The Unconscious Mind

So far we have spoken as if man is aware of all his mental processes. This however, is not generally so. Often we are not fully aware of our desires and needs. We often have feelings of anxiety though we know not why. It is because of these things that psychologists say we have an unconscious mind.

A boy has to take an examination. He has fears about it, but is not aware of them because he refuses to admit them. He " represses " his fears, as the psychologist puts it. So there arises a conflict in his mind. One part says, " I will take the exam.," the other says " You are afraid." Then he becomes ill, and so he does not take the exam., nor does he recognise his fears. In short, his unconscious mind discovered a way out of his fears.

In much the same way, a soldier who is about to perform some dangerous

manœuvre against the enemy may " repress " his fears, and develop paralysis of the arm.

Conquering Fears

In both these cases, the fears which they felt were natural, and most people would have similar fears in like situations. But their pride was so great that they were not prepared to admit fear, even to themselves, and because of this, they could not control their fears. The work of the psychologist would be to get them to admit their fears, and to see that such fears are natural to all men. Then they would understand why they had become ill. Having accepted their fears, they would not be overwhelmed by something of which they were unaware. If the treatment were successful, both the illness and the paralysis would disappear, and they would be prepared to carry out the difficult tasks.

Again, a person may " repress " a need for love and say, " I am tough, too tough to want sloppy love." Here

SEEN IN DIFFERENT WAYS

Diagrams 9 (*a*), (*b*), (*c*), (*d*). The mind is very active in perceiving. If you look carefully at each of the drawings on this page and on page 445, you will discover that each can be seen in two different ways.

there is a conflict in the mind between a vain need to be "tough" and a natural need for love and affection. Then suddenly, he begins to steal, and cannot stop himself, or tell why he must steal.

People often "repress" feelings and desires they think they ought not to have. As they repress them and are unaware of them, they experience fears and anxieties, and they cannot account for them. Their fears and anxieties arise because they are afraid these unconscious hatreds and desires will be unloosed. If, however, they can be shown these unconscious factors, they will then be able to control them, and do something about them. Thus, they may "work off" their hatred by "attacking" a mountain and making a tunnel through it, or becoming mountaineers and "overcoming" the mountain. Similarly, other energies may be deflected into socially useful channels by the care of, and service to, others. This the psychologist calls "sublimation," which means the turning of energy, which might but satisfy only an individual need, to work which is socially acceptable and maybe socially useful.

Understanding the Mind

Dreams are expressions of our unconscious desires and our unconscious fears. The psychologist is, therefore, very interested to know of, and to interpret the meaning of his patients' dreams. We generally feel that our dreams are rather silly and muddled and best forgotten. In the Old Testament, dreams are given quite a great deal of prominence. To the psychologist also, they are important and interesting, for they help him to understand the activity of the unconscious mind.

To-day the psychologist is playing an increasingly important part in our lives. The doctor of medicine deals with the ailments of the body; the psychologist is concerned with ailments of the mind and in learning how to test and develop our mental processes.

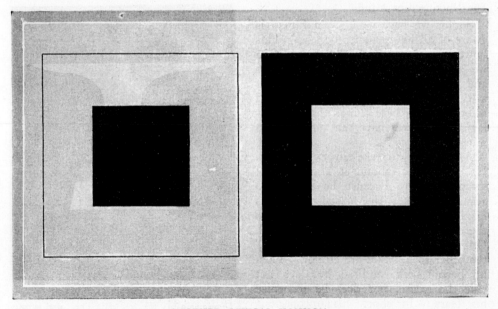

ANOTHER OPTICAL ILLUSION

Look carefully at the two squares in this picture. The white square has a black centre, and the black square has a white centre. The white central square seems larger than the black central square, although actually they are exactly the same size.

Questions
and
Answers

Who, What,
Why,
When and How?

Specially drawn for this work.

There are so many wonderful things in this world that most of us ask questions of other people who may be able to help us with their knowledge. It is only by asking questions that we can learn the things we want to know. In this section a great many questions which have been asked from time to time of the writers in these volumes are set forth and answered briefly under their different headings.

ON THINGS THAT INTEREST YOU AND ME

AIRCRAFT

Why does a Balloon rise?

Because it is lighter than the volume of air which it displaces. It is forced upwards by the difference between the upward and the downward pressure of the air on it.

When did a Man first ascend in a Balloon?

On November 21st, 1783, when two Frenchmen rose in a huge fire-balloon from Paris. The balloon attained a height of 300 feet, and came to earth about two miles from the starting-point. The first ascent in a gas balloon was made at Paris on December 1st, 1783, by Professor Charles, who used hydrogen gas. He rose after sunset to a height of 3,000 feet, and at that elevation was the first man to see the sun set a second time on the same day.

What is a Barrage-balloon?

A captive balloon used in time of war to impede the movements of enemy aircraft and restrict dive-bombing attacks. The balloon is attached to a cable and flies like a kite on a string, except that it requires no wind to keep it aloft.

Chambers at the rear, shaped like ears or wings, serve as fins when inflated, keeping the balloon head to wind and preventing it from swinging sideways. Barrage-balloons in war-time were stationed at convenient points in large cities, naval and military centres, and were also employed in the protection of ships at sea when sailing in convoy.

Why is an Aeroplane able to keep in the Air?

Because of the curved shape of the upper surface of its wings and the power of its engines to drive it forward. The air is deflected upwards by the fore-edge of the wings, leaving a partial vacuum over the greater part of the wing-surface, so that the aeroplane is drawn or " sucked " upwards. It is not maintained in the air by wind-pressure from below, as is a kite.

Who first crossed the Atlantic in an Aeroplane?

Commander A. C. Read, of the United States Navy, and three companions. They left Newfoundland in a flying-boat on May 15th, 1919; and, after calling at Horta and Ponta Delgada, in the Azores, reached Lisbon on May 27th. The first non-stop flight across the Atlantic was made by Captain John Alcock and Lieutenant Whitten Brown, in about sixteen hours, on June 14th and 15th, 1919. These two airmen were knighted in recognition of their feat.

Who made the first Aeroplane Flight from England to Australia ?

Captain Sir Ross Smith, accompanied by his brother, Sir Keith Smith, and Sergeants W. H. Shiers and J. M. Bennett. They left England, in a twin-engined Vickers biplane, on November 12th, 1919, and reached Port Darwin, in Australia, on December 10th, 1919, thereby winning the prize of £10,000 offered by the Australian Commonwealth Government to the first Australians making the journey in thirty days or under. The distance flown was 11,293 miles, and the actual flying time taken 124 hours.

Who made the first Circuit of the World by Air ?

Six men of the United States Army Air Service, flying in three machines. They left Seattle on April 6th, 1924, crossed the Pacific from Alaska to Kamchatka, flew southwards to Japan, China and Siam, traversed the Malay Peninsula, and followed the Burmese coast northwards to India. In Calcutta the floats of their machines were replaced by wheels, for the overland flight across Asia and Europe to England. At Hull the floats were resumed for the flight over the North Sea to Iceland and Greenland, and thence across the Atlantic to Labrador and down the American coast to Boston. At the last place a change back to wheels was made for the final lap across the continent to Seattle, which was reached on September 28th, 1924. The total distance of 26,345 miles was covered in 336 flying hours.

Has an Airship ever flown round the World ?

Yes! The German airship " Graf Zeppelin " left Friedrichshafen (on Lake Constance) on August 15th, 1929, and flew eastwards across Europe and Asia to Tokyo; then crossed the Pacific Ocean to California; and, after passing over the United States and the Atlantic Ocean, arrived back at its starting-point on September 4th, twenty days, four hours and thirteen minutes after the beginning of the voyage. During that time the airship had been in the air just over 300 hours and covered 21,000 miles.

Has an Aeroplane ever flown Non-Stop Round the World ?

A Boeing B-50 machine of the U.S.A. Air Force made the first non-stop flight round the world in Feb.-March, 1949. The machine, carrying a crew of fourteen, was refuelled from the air four times. The aeroplane travelled 23,108 miles in 94 hours 1 minute.

What is meant by Mach number ?

Mach number is used to relate the speed of an aircraft to the speed at which sound travels in air. If the Mach number of an aeroplane is 0·5 then it is travelling at half the speed of sound. At Mach 1·0 it is moving at the speed of sound, at Mach 2·0 it is moving at twice the speed of sound, and so forth. The expression comes from the work of Professor Ernst Mach who studied fluid flow in the 1870's.

Why is the Speed of Sound so important to Aircraft ?

Sound consists of small waves or pressure disturbances travelling through the air. The speed of sound is the natural speed at which such disturbances move, and it is always the same for any given temperature. When an aircraft moves through the air at less than the speed of sound, small pressure disturbances travel ahead of it. This means that the air some distance in front of the aircraft begins to move aside before the aircraft itself arrives. Thus the air resistance is lessened. When the aircraft reaches the speed of sound, or some figure near it, the " warning " time for the air ahead is reduced, and resistance is increased.

What is the " Sound Barrier ? "

As has already been explained, the resistance of the air to a moving body increases when the body reaches a speed near the speed of sound. The increase is rather sudden near the speed of sound and considerably more engine power is needed to overcome it. Hence the expression " sound barrier " came into use because there was a delay in reaching higher speeds until more powerful engines became available.

What is a Shock Wave ?

As aircraft approach the speed of sound the nature of the flow of air over the wings and other parts undergoes important changes. One of the most important effects is the formation of shock waves, which are thin bands where there is a marked change in the pressure and density of the air. These waves cannot normally be seen, but they can be photographed in the wind tunnel with the aid of special equipment. When shock waves begin to form, the flow over the wings and control surfaces tends to become turbulent, and buffeting, or shuddering, of the aircraft can follow. When the aircraft is flying faster than sound the flow steadies down again, and it is during the period of changing from sub-sonic to super-sonic speed that the greatest irregularities are found.

What is the Speed of Sound ?

At 0° C. (or 32° F.) the speed of sound in air is 742 miles an hour. The speed increases as the temperature rises. The increase is at the rate of about 12·5 miles an hour for each 10° C. rise in temperature, or about 7 miles an hour for each 10° F.

What is Jet Propulsion ?

The conventional way of propelling an aircraft is to accelerate a mass of air rearward. When a propeller, or airscrew, is used, the mass of air is unconfined. On the other hand, if the mass of air issues from a pipe or tube in which it is confined until the moment of release, then the term " jet propulsion " applies. The ordinary rocket motor is a form of jet propulsion, but the most common form is the turbojet engine. This takes in air at the front, compresses it, heats it by burning fuel, and ejects it at the rear. The compressor is driven by a turbine, which is a multi-bladed windmill, and the turbine is driven by the hot exhaust gases flowing over its blades. Another form of jet engine, the ram-jet, needs no turbine or compressor, because it is used in super-sonic aircraft where the speed of forward flight is sufficient to " ram " the air into the intake and compress it without further ado.

What is a Turboprop Engine ?

The gas turbine engine which drives a propeller is often wrongly called a jet engine. This is because it is very similar in its internal workings to a turbojet engine, and it does give some propulsive force from the jet of exhaust gases at the rear. But the greater part of the turboprop's energy goes into driving the propeller.

Why are Gas Turbines so valuable to Aviation ?

The gas turbine engine, which uses the energy of rushing exhaust gases to drive a multi-blade windmill, or turbine wheel, has two very great advantages. In the first place it is capable of giving greater powers than would ever be feasible with the internal combustion piston engine. Secondly, it is very light in relation to the power it can give. For a given horsepower a gas turbine may weigh one-fifth as much as the best piston engine. In addition to these two qualities, the gas turbine is easily able to produce a fast-moving gas jet of the kind needed for jet propulsion.

What is the difference between buried and podded Aero Engines ?

Some designers consider the thinnest possible wings necessary for efficient flying at high speed. In such wings there is not enough room for the engines, so that they have to be carried outside. A good way of doing this is to mount each engine, or pair of engines, in a streamlined casing and to attach this to the wings by a thin streamlined structure, in the form of a fin or web. Such engines are said to be podded. Buried engines are installed inside the wings, usually at the root ends where they are thickest.

What is the meaning of " g " ?

The term " g " is an abbreviation of the force, or more properly, the acceleration, due to gravity. When at rest any object or person is normally subjected to 1 g downwards : that is a downward force of its, or his, own weight. But when an aircraft makes a sharp turn or pulls up sharply to climb from the bottom of a dive, it is subjected to a centrifugal force resulting from its tendency to continue moving in its original course. The effect of this is to increase the effective weight of the aeroplane and all its occupants. If the centrifugal force is sufficient to double the effective weight, the manœuvre would, for example, be referred to as a " 2 g turn." Sometimes the forces generated by manœuvres act in the same direction as the earth's gravity, and sometimes in the opposite direction. Thus, if a very fast aircraft flies a " rainbow " course, arcing high up into the sky, an upward force of 1 g may be generated, exactly counter-balancing the earth's attraction and giving the feeling of weightlessness to the crew.

Why does an Airman carry a Parachute ?

So that he may jump out and land safely if his machine catches fire or gets out of control. The parachute opens of its own accord, or when a string is pulled by the person attached to it, and its great umbrella-like surface offers so much resistance to the air that the airman falls slowly and reaches the ground without severe shock.

For very fast-moving aeroplanes, particularly jet-propelled machines, the ordinary parachute cannot be used in the normal way since the force of the air current would make it difficult for the airman to leave the machine, or, if he did get out, he would in all probability be swept against the rear part of the machine with considerable violence. The Martin-Baker pilot-ejection seat has been evolved to avoid these risks, and the escaping airman, once clear of the slipstream from the machine, can then descend safely by means of the ordinary parachute.

ASTRONOMY

What is Astronomy ?

Astronomy is the science of the stars and other heavenly bodies. Having at one time considered the earth as the centre of all things, and later thought of the sun as the centre, man has found that the sun is just a star at the centre of one system of planets. Beyond this " Solar System " we know there exists an immeasurable universe with millions of stars and possibly many other systems of planets. The astronomers of ancient Egypt, Greece and China discovered a great deal, and the Middle Ages of Europe saw some of their old errors corrected. In the sixteenth century Copernicus showed that the planets move round the sun. This theory was not accepted at once, and Galileo was summoned to appear before the Inquisition in 1633 because he supported it. On this foundation, on Kepler's laws of the motions of the planets, and on Newton's theory of gravitation, the science of modern astronomy has built up a wonderful description of the universe. Many of its most important discoveries have been made by means of observatories equipped with telescopes and other instruments of tremendous power. More recently, Newton's theory has given place to Einstein's theory of relativity, which has enabled the age, size and shape of the universe to be estimated. The science of astronomy has also resulted in discoveries of great importance to mankind, especially in conjunction with the science of physics.

Was the Earth ever a Part of the Sun ?

In 1796 the great French mathematician, Laplace, put forward a theory that the sun and all the planets were formed out of a gigantic glowing mass of gas-like matter. As it cooled, this threw off whirling rings, each of which solidified into a planet. The central mass became the sun. A more recent theory pictured a near collision between the sun and another star, the gravitational attraction of the passing star drawing a long cigar-shaped mass of vaporised matter out of the sun. This was left revolving about the sun, and condensed into liquid drops which finally cooled and solidified to form the planets. However, since the sun consists chiefly of hydrogen, it is now doubted if the earth could have had such an origin, and it seems more likely that its materials were gathered out of space by the sun's passing through clouds of solid particles.

TO SAFETY BY PARACHUTE

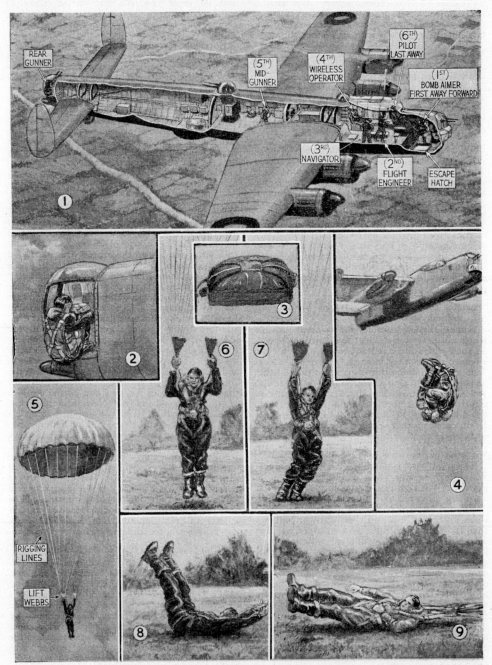

Specially drawn for this work.

The Lincoln bomber seen at the top is in difficulties, and orders have been given to leave the plane by *parachute* (see p. 333). 1. Shows the order in which the crew leave. 2. The rear gunner turns his turret, discards his headgear, opens escape door and falls out. 3. The parachute pack. 4. Another member of the crew escapes from front hatch, body doubled, making free fall until well clear. 5. Cord is pulled and parachute opens. 6. Nearing the earth airman pulls himself up, legs together. 7. On landing, body relaxed, knees and feet together. 8. Rolling over, body relaxed, chin tucked in. 9. On the back, a blow on the release button frees parachute and prevents airman being dragged.

ESCAPE FROM JET-PROPELLED AIRCRAFT

For jet-propelled aircraft, travelling at over 500 miles an hour, the ordinary escape method is unsafe. The pilot must be thrown clear of the aircraft, and the Martin-Baker pilot-ejection seat has been adopted by the R.A.F. after thorough tests. A piston-gun, operated by the pilot when he pulls down the face-blind to protect him from injury, ejects pilot and seat. A drogue, or small parachute, then comes into operation to prevent the seat from turning over. The gun operating the drogue is freed from the seat by the line attached to the aircraft.

Illustrated London News.

Well clear of the aeroplane, the pilot falls forward from the seat with his right hand on the release lever of his own parachute.

After a short fall the pilot pulls the rip-cord of his parachute and makes a safe descent, while the 80-lb. seat also falls steadily to earth.

Is the Earth's Shape changing?

Only to a negligible extent. The slight alterations that take place in its surface are so small in proportion to the earth as a whole that they need not be considered.

How fast does the Earth travel through Space?

The orbit of the earth round the sun measures 580,000,000 miles. The earth completes the orbit in 365 days (about). So it must be moving through space at an average speed of 66,250 miles an hour.

What is the Earth like at the Centre?

Probably the earth's core is composed largely of iron and nickel. Outside the core is a shell of nearly molten rocks many thousands of miles thick, and this is enclosed in a crust of cooler rocks about thirty miles thick.

How is it that, though the Earth is very hot inside, there is always Ice at the Poles?

Between the hot interior of the earth and the surface there is a cooled crust, through which enough heat does not penetrate to keep the surface above freezing point. The heat of the surface is derived almost entirely from the sun, and is not sufficient to melt the polar ice during the short polar summers.

Has the Earth ever been weighed?

Yes, by several scientists. Its weight was first found by experiment in 1797–98 by an Englishman, Henry Cavendish, who estimated by means of the gravitational attraction between two lead balls that our globe weighs about 12,500,000,000,000,000,000,000,000 pounds. His estimate agrees very closely with the calculations of later scientists.

Will the Earth ever become Cold like the Moon?

Undoubtedly it will, but not till millions of years have passed.

Why would it be impossible to make a hole right through the Earth?

Because the interior of the earth is intensely hot. In mines the temperature rises about 1° Fahrenheit with every 60 to 70 feet of depth, and to make things comfortable for miners in deep mines large quantities of cold air have to be circulated through the workings.

How large across is the Moon?

2,162 miles.

How far away from the Earth is the Moon?

The distance varies slightly at different points on the moon's course round the earth, but the average distance is 238,840 miles.

Was the Moon ever a part of the Earth?

At one time it was thought that the earth and the moon were one body, much softer than either is now—being much hotter—and spinning much faster. This theory held that the rate at which it spun made it fly into two parts; the smaller became the moon, and the larger the earth. In support of this attractive theory it was pointed out that the hollow which is now the Pacific Ocean would just about take the material of the moon. It now seems more likely that the moon, like the earth itself, consists of matter gathered out of space by the sun on its journeys through clouds of solid particles.

Could we live on the Moon?

No, because the moon has no atmosphere, is waterless, and is intensely hot by day and terribly cold at night.

Why is the Moon without an Atmosphere though the Earth has one?

Because, owing to its small size, the moon had not sufficient attractive power to retain the atmosphere which may once have enveloped it. The atoms of this would have gradually escaped into space. The earth, being much larger than the moon, and having a greater pull, has been able to prevent its atmosphere leaving it.

Why do we always see the same side of the Moon?

Because while the moon makes one complete revolution round the earth it revolves exactly once on its own axis in the same direction.

Does the Moon affect the Motions of the Earth?

The moon is very, very slowly checking the revolution of the earth round its own axis. For the moon is the main cause of the tides, which move from east to west while the earth turns from west to east. The friction between the water and the earth acts as a brake. But the slowing down is so extremely gradual that it lengthens our year at the rate of only a second in 100,000 years.

How does the Moon give us Light?

By reflecting to us light which falls on it from the sun. Being cold on the outside it cannot give out light of its own.

Does the Moon shine only at Night?

No, it shines whenever it is above the horizon. The fact that we can see it by day as a white object in the sky proves that it must be reflecting light and therefore shining.

What is " the Old Moon in the New Moon's Arms "?

When only a thin crescent of the moon is illuminated by the sun, the rest of the moon's face is sometimes faintly visible as a copper-coloured disc. This is because it is illuminated by earth-shine—just as the earth is sometimes illuminated by moon-shine.

Why are Coloured Circles sometimes seen round the Moon?

They appear when the sky is overspread with the very lofty clouds called cirrus clouds, composed of tiny particles of ice. These particles transmit earthwards rays which strike them at certain angles, forming a halo like a weakly-tinted rainbow.

What is known about the recently discovered Planet Pluto?

That it is farther from the sun than any other planet, and forty times farther than the earth is. Its year, that is, the time taken by it in making one complete revolution round the sun, is equal in length to 248 of our years. If there

Tivey and Hatton.

A MISTLE THRUSH AND ITS YOUNG

The Mistle Thrush likes to build its home about eight feet off the ground. This nest has been built in the fork of an ivy-covered alder tree. Outwardly it is rather untidy, but the inside is neatly lined with dry grasses on which the eggs, usually about four, are laid. Few birds guard their territory with greater zeal than the " Storm Cock," as country folk term the bird. Such wandering rogues as the Jay and Magpie are given short shrift. With an angry " churring " the Mistle Thrush will dash straight at any intruder that happens to come near the nest. Fledgling Mistle Thrushes are fed on insects and earth worms, but when adult they eat mainly fruit and berries.

Satour.

CONSULTING THE WITCH-DOCTOR

Wearing his elaborate ostrich-feather head-dress, the witch-doctor gravely listens to the troubles of an elderly Xhosa man. The braided blanket worn by the latter is typical Xhosa dress and is impregnated with red ochre. On the counter can be seen the symbols of the witch-doctor's craft. The photograph was taken at Umtata, about 150 miles by road from East London, in Cape Province, South Africa. Umtata is a cathedral city and the capital of the Transkeian Territories (lying between the river Kei and Natal). Not far from the city are the beautiful Umtata Falls, while the Tsitsa Waterfall (the highest in Cape Province) is only 40 miles distant.

is water on Pluto it must be frozen solid by the intense cold.

What is the Sun ?

It is a star, round which the earth and the other planets of the solar system revolve in space. We know very little about the core or central part of the sun beyond that it is intensely hot and the site of the violent release of atomic energy. Outside the core are three layers of glowing or flaming gases, through which the fierce white light of the sun finds its way. The sun is about 93,000,000 miles away from the earth, and almost 110 times as large across as the earth.

Is the Sun the hottest of the Heavenly Bodies ?

The sun's surface heat is estimated at about 10,000° Fahrenheit. Its heat at the centre is, owing to the enormous pressure of the sun's fluid mass, probably 40,000 times greater. Yet the sun is cool in comparison with some stars, which have a surface temperature of 70,000° and a correspondingly higher central heat.

What is a Sun-spot ?

A comparatively dark area on the surface of the sun. It consists of a vast uprush of gases from below the outer layers, and some sun-spots cover many thousands of square miles. Round the edges of a spot the telescope reveals great tongues of flame. The appearance of spots on the sun is often accompanied by what are called magnetic storms on the earth, which upset the working of electrical apparatus.

What causes an Eclipse of the Sun ?

The passage of the moon directly between the sun and the earth. The moon is just large and near enough to cover the sun completely for a few moments during a total eclipse.

What is a Nebula ?

A faint misty patch of light in the sky. Very few nebulæ are visible to the naked eye, but a large telescope reveals many thousands. There are two principal kinds, one consisting of a vast mass of luminous gas, and the other a complete system of stars so remote that the individual stars within it cannot be distinguished. This type is sometimes called an " island universe."

Why are Shadows shortest at Mid-day ?

Because the sun is then at its highest point in the heavens.

Why is it that we have the Different Seasons of the Year ?

Imagine the sun to be an electric lamp fixed by strings at the centre of a very large hoop, laid flatwise, but somewhat tilted. The hoop represents the path taken by the earth round the sun, and the earth is represented by a spherical spinning-top moving along a groove in the upper side of the hoop. Then picture the top making a circuit of the hoop once in a year. Twice during the year it will be level, or nearly level, with the lamp, and its upper and lower halves be lit equally. These periods are like our spring and autumn. When the top is at the highest point of the hoop, its lower half is lighted

more strongly than its upper half. This position corresponds to midsummer in the southern hemisphere of the earth; and to midwinter in the northern hemisphere. On the other hand, the northern hemisphere has reached midsummer, and the southern hemisphere midwinter, when the top has got to the lowest point of its path.

What is meant by a Light-year ?

The distance that light will travel in one year, that is, about 6,000,000,000,000 miles. Astronomers use it for expressing the vast distances between us and the stars.

Why do we see more Stars on some Nights than on others ?

Because the clearness of the atmosphere varies.

What is the Milky Way ?

A narrow band of faint light which reaches right across the sky. It is made up of the light from millions of stars which are too far away to be distinguished separately. It represents a vast, wheel-shaped system of stars known as the Galaxy, of which the sun is an unimportant member.

How does a Star differ from a Planet ?

Stars can be readily distinguished from planets, owing to the fact that stars twinkle while planets give a steady light. Planets move round the sun in their particular orbits and so their positions in respect to each other, and to the stars, are always changing.

The stars do not move round the sun. They are very much further away from the earth than the planets and may themselves be suns with planets revolving around them. Because of their great distances their own movements are imperceptible from the earth, and they appear to have fixed positions in the sky. For this reason they are often called " fixed stars."

How many Planets are there ?

Nine. In order from the sun they are Mercury, Venus, Earth, Mars, Jupiter, Saturn, Uranus, Neptune and Pluto.

Which is the Largest Star ?

It is impossible to say, as the sizes of but comparatively few stars have been measured. Betelgeuse, one of the two bright stars in Orion, is one of the largest stars of which we know the diameter. It is over 200 million miles across, so the orbit of the earth round the sun would fall entirely within the compass of this gigantic body. It is so immensely distant that through the telescope it has only the size of a bright halfpenny placed seventy miles away ! Such stars are known as " Red Giants " because their comparatively low temperature gives their light a red colour. These enormous stars are only bodies of gas, and not heavy relatively to their size. Betelgeuse weighs only forty times as much as the sun.

Which is the Brightest Star in the Sky ?

Sirius, also called the Dog Star, a star in the constellation of Canis Major (the Greater Dog)

It gives out twenty-six times as much light as the sun; but, being 500,000 times further from us than the sun is, it is much less bright. Another star, S. Doradus, has actually 10,000 times greater light-giving power than Sirius, though it seems dull by comparison, owing to its vastly greater distance from us.

What kind of a Star is called " White Dwarf " ?

A small star which gives out white light, owing to its intense heat. Stars of this kind are immensely heavy for their size. A certain one of them, though no larger than the earth, is believed to weigh 50,000 times as much as the earth. In such a star the terrific heat and pressure is thought to break down the nature of the atom, so that its parts, instead of reserving to themselves a space vastly greater than their own bulk, are crowded closely together. The heat at the centre of a " White Dwarf " may be anything up to fifty times that at the centre of the sun.

What is a Shooting-Star or Meteor ?

A small body, usually no larger than a sand-grain or small pebble, flying through space at a terrific speed. When it enters our atmosphere the friction between it and the air makes it white-hot and therefore visible. The term shooting-star describes its appearance as it streaks across the sky, but it has, of course, nothing to do with the stars.

What is an Asteroid ?

One of the two thousand or so tiny " minor planets " which revolve round the sun between the orbits of Mars and Jupiter. They are of all sizes, but average a few miles in diameter.

THE CALENDAR

How did the Days of the Week get their Names ?

The names are of Scandinavian origin. Sunday is the day of the sun; Monday the day of the moon; Tuesday is named after Tiw, the god of war; Wednesday after Woden, the Scandinavian Mercury; Thursday is the day of Thor, the god of thunder; Friday the day of Freya or Frigga, goddess of friendship; and Saturday is Saturn's day.

How did the Months get their Names ?

All the months have Roman names. January is the month of the god Janus; February the month of Februa, the goddess of purification; March the month sacred to Mars, the god of war; April is the " opening " month, from *aperire*, to open, as flowers and trees then blossom; May is named after Maia, the mother of Mercury, June after the goddess Juno. July after Julius Cæsar, and August after the Emperor Augustus; September, October, November and December were originally the seventh, eighth, ninth and tenth months of the old Roman year. When the year was made to begin with January instead of March the old names were retained, though some were no longer correct.

Which Days of the Year are called the Quarter Days in England ?

March 25th (Lady Day); June 24th (Midsummer Day); September 29th (Michaelmas Day); and December 25th (Christmas Day).

Why is the Day after Christmas Day named Boxing Day ?

Because on that day alms-boxes used to be set up in public places to receive alms to help poor people.

What is meant by Twelfth Night ?

The evening of the twelfth day after Christmas Day, January 6th, known better under the name of Epiphany—the day on which Christ was made known to the Gentiles. In olden time Twelfth Night was marked by much merrymaking and feasting, and looked upon as the finish-up of the Christmas festivities. It gives the title to one of Shakespeare's plays.

How did Shrove Tuesday get its Name ?

On the day before the first day in Lent (Ash Wednesday) people used to prepare for the fast by confessing their sins and being *shriven*, that is, given pardon by the priest. After being shriven people feasted, and this is the origin of our eating pancakes on Shrove Tuesday.

What does Good Friday mean ?

The words are a corruption of God's Friday.

What does the word Easter mean ?

Spring. The old pagan " feast of spring " has become the Christian Easter.

What does Whit Sunday mean ?

White Sunday, because on that day candidates for baptism wore white garments. This is the usual derivation. But Whit Sunday is also thought to mean the Sunday of *whit*, the Anglo-Saxon word for wisdom or understanding, because at the first Pentecost (another name for Whit Sunday) the Holy Spirit enabled people to understand what was spoken in a strange tongue.

What are Ember Days ?

Days set apart by the Church as special days of prayer and fasting for persons about to be ordained to the ministry. They are the Wednesday, Friday and Saturday following the first Sunday in Lent, Whit Sunday, September 14th, and December 13th.

Why does one have to alter one's Watch periodically when travelling East or West round the Globe ?

Because, as compared with Greenwich time, noon arrives 4 minutes sooner for every meridian crossed when travelling eastwards; and 4 minutes later for every meridian crossed westwards. In the first case one is travelling towards the sun; in the second, away from it. If one did not adjust one's watch periodically, it would get completely out of step with the time of the place in which one happened to be.

What is Standard Time ?

If every town and city in the world kept its local time, there would be endless confusion because, as we know, time varies from place to place. In Britain, every place takes its time from Greenwich, but in countries such as Australia and

Canada, which extend far in longitude, such a system would not be practicable. Most countries therefore use what is known as the *Standard Time* system. Meridians which can be divided by fifteen have been selected as the centre of certain time zones or belts, and it is from these central meridians that the zones take their time. Thus in Europe there are three Standard Times: *West European* (Greenwich Time), *Central European* (Greenwich Time plus one hour), and *East European* (Greenwich Time plus two hours). A further example is found in Australia where there are also three times—Western, Central, and Eastern. Division is made by fifteen because it is through fifteen degrees that the earth rotates in one hour.

What is the International Date Line?

Suppose you set off from London and travelled round the world without altering your time. When at last you reached London again, you would find that in your journey you had either lost a day (if you had travelled westwards), or gained a day (if you had travelled eastwards). So somewhere or other the date has to be changed, and the easiest place to do this is along the 180th meridian, most of which lies in the ocean. Thus, with one or two exceptions (made to provide for certain islands), the International Date Line follows this meridian. A ship approaching the Line from the west drops a day (going from Monday to Wednesday) if it crosses the Line; a ship crossing the Line from east to west repeats a day (going thus:—Monday, Monday, Tuesday).

What are the Equinoxes?

The two days of the year, March 21st and September 23rd, on which the night has the same length as the day. On them the sun is exactly over the Equator; in the first case, while the days are lengthening in spring, and in the second while shortening in autumn.

What is a " Geophysical Year "?

Geophysics is the science concerned with the earth and its atmosphere. It covers many subjects, including the weather, cosmic rays, glaciology (the study of the build-up and movement of large masses of ice), the oceans, and seismology (the study of earthquakes).

Some of these subjects cannot be studied properly unless information is collected simultaneously from observation points spread out right across the world. In other words, the co-operation of many nations is needed to make the work of the scientists effective.

More than thirty nations co-operated in studies of this kind in the International Geophysical Year which began on June 1st, 1957. During the period the Soviet Union launched their first artificial satellite, and upper atmosphere rockets were successfully launched from many parts of the world. More efforts were also made to gain information of the whole of the Antarctic Continent and about sixty observation stations were established during the period to record weather observations and changes in the Southern Lights and other polar phenomena.

The International Geophysical Year period proved to be the highest peak in the sun's eleven year cycle of activity since records were first taken over two hundred years ago.

Originally scheduled to end on December 31st, 1958, the Year was such an outstanding success that it was extended throughout 1959.

This was the third International Geophysical Year; the first was held in 1882–83, and the second in 1932–33. The normal practice is for a Year of this kind to take place once every twenty-five years.

How are Time-signals sent out from Greenwich Observatory?

By a clock, called the Mean Solar (sun) Time Clock. This is corrected frequently from another clock, which keeps sidereal (star) time, and is itself corrected by observations of the stars. The actual sending of the signals is done automatieally by special mechanism in the clock. Signals are sent hourly to the G.P.O. for telegraphing all over the country, and every quarter of an hour to the offices of the British Broadcasting Corporation; and at 10 a.m. and 6 p.m. to Rugby for broadcasting by wireless all over the world.

CHEMISTRY

What is a Chemical Element?

A substance which cannot be broken up into different substances. Or we may say, a substance that is made up of nothing else but itself. At present ninety-four elements are known; four of them, Neptunium, Plutonium, Americium and Berkelium were discovered as recently as 1944–5. Chemists give each a symbol (one or more letters of its name) by which it is known everywhere. Thus, Hydrogen is called H, Oxygen O, Silicon Si, Sulphur S, and so on. These symbols represent one atom of the element, but solitary atoms do not commonly exist at ordinary temperatures, the atoms of most elements assembling in pairs or other such groups called " molecules." The number of atoms in a molecule is represented by a small figure slightly below the element. Thus, O_2 is a molecule of oxygen, O_3 a molecule of ozone, N_2 a molecule of nitrogen, and so on. The atoms of the elements in chemical compounds are similarly represented. Thus, H_2O = Water; H_2SO_4 = Sulphuric Acid.

What is an Atom like?

The old idea was that atoms are very tiny hard balls incapable of being broken, but we now picture each atom as a little solar system, with a central body called the " nucleus " about which revolve numbers of electrons like the planets revolving about the sun. This is the general form of all the atoms, the various elements differing only in the weight of the nucleus and the number of electrons revolving about it.

Why do some Gases refuse to Burn?

Because they will not combine with oxygen alone.

Why is a Glass Chimney used on an Oil Lamp?

The air heated by the flame rises through the chimney and compels fresh air to enter at the bottom and pass close to the flame. Besides protecting the flame, the chimney keeps it supplied with sufficient air to make it burn the carbon in the oil completely without smoke, and give out a bright light.

Why does an Oil Lamp smoke if turned up too high?

Because the supply of air reaching the flame is not sufficient to allow all the carbon coming away from the wick to burn.

What is a Will-o'-the-Wisp?

A light seen in marshy places, due to the burning of marsh gas, which is produced by decaying vegetable matter. It is believed to be ignited by traces in it of another gas, phosphine, which catches fire spontaneously on contact with the air. To follow such a light in the belief that it comes from a lamp ends in disaster; hence the words have come to mean also any misleading guide. Other names for the phenomenon are Jack-o'-Lantern, corpse candle, and *ignis fatuus* (Latin).

Is it possible for a Flame to burn in Water?

Yes! if the flame be supplied with air or oxygen at a pressure which prevents the water actually touching it. Divers are now able to use blow-pipes under water to cut through ships' plates and other parts; and a steam boiler has been invented in which liquid fuel is burned as an open flame in the midst of the water.

What are the Causes of Explosions in Coal Mines?

In many mines a great deal of gas is enclosed in the coal seams, sometimes under great pressure. This escapes into the workings and is ordinarily carried away safely by the ventilating air. In a large colliery as much as 2,000,000 cubic feet of gas may be given off in a day. Should a sudden large outburst of gas occur, or gas collect in an imperfectly ventilated part of the mine, it forms an explosive mixture with the air in the mine, and a naked flame or spark may ignite it. Some mine explosions are due to the air in the workings becoming charged with coal dust, which may catch fire when blasting is done. A gas explosion may, by stirring up coal dust, be prolonged as a dust explosion with disastrous results. Dust explosions are less likely to occur if the workings are sprinkled with non-combustible stone ground into a fine powder.

Why do Coal-miners sometimes take Canaries into the Mines with them?

Canaries are very sensitive to dangerous gases, and their behaviour warns the miners if such gases are present in the workings.

Why do Iron and Steel rust?

The metal at the surface combines with oxygen of the air to form oxide of iron, commonly called rust. This combination takes place only in the presence of moisture. By adding certain other substances (such as chromium) to steel it can be rendered rustless or " stainless."

Why does an Apple turn brown after being peeled?

The removal of the peel exposes the pulp of the apple to the oxygen of the air, and chemical changes take place which discolour the surface.

Why have Explosives such enormous power?

An explosive of the gunpowder type is a mixture of some compound of oxygen with combustible materials. When the explosive is fired, the oxygen is set free and combines with the other substances in the mixture. Gases are formed and at the same time heated, and their tremendous effort to find room for themselves in which to swell gives the explosive its power. Explosives of the T.N.T. and dynamite types are unstable nitrogen compounds, ready to change suddenly from a small volume of solid into a large volume of hot gases when given a violent shock.

What is Helium?

A gas, and one of the elements. It is the lightest gas known after hydrogen. It weighs just twice as much as that gas, and only one-seventh as much as air. Helium is extracted from natural gas which is tapped from the ground in certain parts of the United States and Canada. As it cannot take fire it is ideal for inflating balloons; but, owing to the great expense of separating it, it has been used for this purpose only in a few airships. It is also an important product of many radio-active changes, and is the chief substance produced by the explosion of a hydrogen bomb.

What is Radium?

An element obtained in very small quantities from a mineral called pitchblende. It has the curious property of sending out rays or streams of helium atoms, electrons and gamma-rays without losing weight perceptibly. The rays are used in curing certain diseases. Radium was discovered in 1898 by the French scientist, the late Madame Curie and her husband.

Why does Water, though made up of Oxygen and Hydrogen, extinguish Flames?

Oxygen by itself makes substances burn, and hydrogen by itself burns with great heat. But in water each is fully combined with the other, and cannot combine quickly with anything else. When flung on a flame, water has the triple effect of smothering the flame by turning into steam and preventing air getting at it, of making things which it wets less ready to take fire, and of cooling down things which have become dangerously hot.

Why is Rain Water softer than ordinary Tap Water?

Because it has no dissolved minerals or " hardening " substances in it, being water evaporated by the sun and afterwards condensed by the cold of the upper air.

How does " Soft " Water differ from " Hard " Water?

Soft water lathers freely with soap; hard water does not, because it contains compounds of calcium or magnesium. Rain water caught off a clean roof is soft, being almost entirely free from chemical impurities. But it has in it some carbonic acid gas, which, though it does not make it hard, enables it to dissolve calcium and magnesium easily. This accounts for the hardness of water drawn from deep wells, which is rain water that has penetrated the ground, dissolving chemicals on the way. Hard water can be softened to a certain extent by boiling, which deposits some of the dissolved matter on

SAFETY IN THE COAL MINES

Glasgow Herald.

Glasgow Herald.

A canary is put into a "humane" cage at the start of a rescue exercise. Canaries are quickly affected by fire-damp and thus give timely warning. To revive the bird if overcome by gas a cylinder of oxygen is fitted to the cage.

While the rescue team is fighting a mock fire at one of the several British Rescue Test Stations, the senior instructor receives their minute-to-minute progress reports over the portable telephone. In return he transmits orders and criticism.

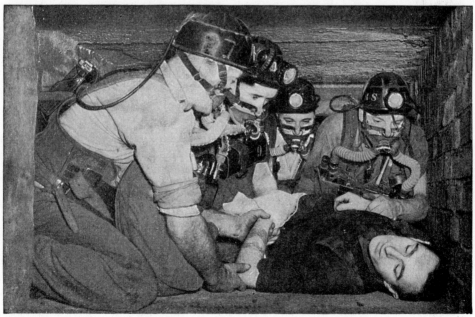

Yorkshire Post.

At the end of the exercise, rescuers give first-aid to a *coal-miner* (see p. 340) found in a low roadway after a supposed explosion. The men are wearing their heavy breathing apparatus which enables them to remain in a smoke-filled or gas-filled atmosphere for two hours. A permanent staff of 250, and 4,000 fully trained part-time rescue workers are at the disposal of the British Mines Rescue Service.

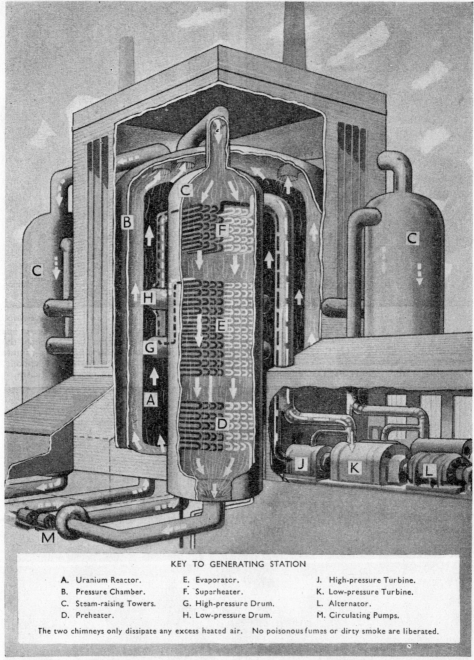

KEY TO GENERATING STATION

A. Uranium Reactor.	**E.** Evaporator.	**J.** High-pressure Turbine.
B. Pressure Chamber.	**F.** Superheater.	**K.** Low-pressure Turbine.
C. Steam-raising Towers.	**G.** High-pressure Drum.	**L.** Alternator.
D. Preheater.	**H.** Low-pressure Drum.	**M.** Circulating Pumps.

The two chimneys only dissipate any excess heated air. No poisonous fumes or dirty smoke are liberated.

Specially drawn for this work.

This generating station, embodying a graphite moderated uranium reactor, or *atomic pile* (see p. 343), is in the North of England. It contains a pressure chamber through which is circulated carbon dioxide gas under pressure at 100 lb. per sq. in. This absorbs heat from the reactor around 400° C. and, passing through the steam-raising towers, re-enters the circulating pumps and passes back to the pressure chamber. Passing through the towers the hot gas heats, evaporates and superheats water in two systems, one high pressure, one low. The steam from these two systems passes to a high-pressure turbine and a low-pressure turbine which are in turn coupled to an alternator, and from here the current is passed to the National grid.

the inside of the vessel as "fur"; and more thoroughly by being treated with chemicals.

Why do Kettles become encrusted with Lime inside?

Because the lime in water is deposited when the water boils; so that a kettle which has been in use some time gets lined with it.

How is Water from Rivers made safe for Drinking?

It is first exposed in large reservoirs to sunlight, which has great germ-killing power; and then filtered through gravel and sand or other materials, to be freed of all solid matter. In some cases it is also treated with chemicals, or has air or ozone blown through it, or is exposed to ultra-violet rays from electric lamps.

What is meant by the Elixir of Life and the Philosopher's Stone?

The first was the name given by the old alchemists to an imaginary fluid which, if discovered, would give very long life or immortality to anyone who drank it. The second was a supposed substance which would change base metals into gold or silver.

What are Molecules?

Molecules are the smallest possible particles of any substance which can exist as that substance. If you break up a molecule you separate it into the atoms of which it consists. Thus, you cannot have a smaller quantity of water than one molecule (H_2O), because further division would break it up into hydrogen and oxygen.

What is Atomic Energy?

When substances such as wood and coal are burnt we obtain energy in the form of heat. This is called molecular energy, because it is obtained from the splitting up or re-arrangement of the molecules of various substances. Now molecules are composed of atoms, and though you can separate molecules into their constituent atoms, it was thought until about fifty years ago that the atoms themselves could not be broken up into anything simpler.

In 1919 Lord Rutherford succeeded in breaking up an atom of nitrogen into two entirely different atoms, namely, oxygen and hydrogen. Since then many different atomic changes have been brought about, for example, a special kind of uranium called U235 splits up very readily and in doing so releases enormous amounts of energy. This is what is known as atomic energy.

What is an Atomic Pile?

An atomic pile, or "nuclear reactor," is a device for obtaining atomic energy under control. One kind is built of carbon blocks through which holes are drilled, and rods of pure uranium are inserted in the holes. Some tons of uranium are used, and its radio-activity produces heat which can be made to drive turbines and generate electricity. To protect workers from harmful radiations the pile is enclosed in a thick concrete shell.

What are Protons, Electrons and Neutrons?

These are the chief particles of which atoms are composed. The centre, or nucleus, of an atom consists of protons, which carry a positive electric charge, and neutrons, which have no electric charge. Electrons are minute charges of negative electricity which revolve about the nucleus of an atom like planets round the sun. Protons and neutrons are about 1,836 times as heavy as electrons.

EDUCATION

What is meant by "Education"?

In its broadest sense education covers all the knowledge we gain from books, travel, social contacts and from all our experiences in life. In its usual sense, however, the word is confined to the teaching and bringing up of children so that they can play a useful and intelligent part in the life of the community and of the world.

How did our Education System come into being?

In the earlier days of ancient Greek civilisation Greek youths of the citizen class received their education, as individual pupils, by visiting professional teachers of various subjects in their homes. At a later date, Plato (428–348 B.C.) was the first Greek to establish a school, called the Academy.

From its beginnings in Greece the school survived as an institution through Roman times, and was developed during medieval times by the Church. In England there were schools attached to the monasteries from the tenth century and, later, grammar schools attended by noblemen's sons as well as those of ordinary freemen.

Until the reign of Queen Victoria, education was not considered a matter for the government. Then, in 1832, State grants were made to "elementary schools" and this was followed by a system of inspection, and the seeds of the present Ministry of Education were sown.

When was our present system of Education founded?

It was under the great Education Act of 1870 that the foundations of a national system of education were laid.

The Elementary Education Act of 1870 was intended to "complete the voluntary system and fill the gaps." Under it School Boards were established and given the duty of providing new elementary schools at the public expense, and the existing voluntary schools received increased grants.

A few years later the Elementary Education Act of 1876 introduced compulsory attendance. The Local Government Act of 1888 brought the then new county councils into the field of higher education, giving them the power to aid "technical" instruction. The improved grant system made it possible after 1891 to abolish fees at many public elementary schools. The Education Act of 1892 ended the life of the School Boards and made the county councils and county boroughs the local authorities for both elementary and higher education. Under the same Act the local authorities were required to maintain at public expense the voluntary elementary schools provided and managed by the Church and other bodies.

The Education Act of 1921 raised the compulsory limit of age to fourteen, abolished part-time attendance and extended medical inspection. This Act was eventually superseded by the Act of 1944, which, among other provisions, laid it down that every child shall receive both elementary and secondary education, raising the school-leaving age to fifteen, with powers to raise it later to sixteen. It also set up a system of part-time education in county colleges and abolished fees at all schools maintained by the local education authorities and at the county colleges.

What is a University?

This place of learning may be defined as an institution designed for the instruction or examination or both of adult students in all or many of the more important branches of learning. It may consist of a single college or of a group of colleges, and it usually has a proportion of its students in residence. The different departments of a University are known as " faculties," as for instance the faculties of arts, medicine, science, theology, and degrees are conferred in each faculty, Bachelor of Arts (B.A.), Bachelor of Science (B.Sc.), and so on.

The Middle Ages saw the rise of many famous universities in Europe. One of the earliest and best-known was that at Paris, on which were modelled our own Oxford and Cambridge Universities, founded in the thirteenth century. During the next century or two were founded St. Andrews, Glasgow, Aberdeen and Edinburgh. The more modern foundations in Great Britain are Birmingham, Bristol, Durham, Manchester, Leeds, Liverpool, London, Reading, Sheffield and Wales. Some of these Universities relate a portion of their activities to the character of the local industries. Another University is in course of provision near Stoke-on-Trent. London University has a unique character. Its numerous " schools " are found in different parts of London, although it has a large central nucleus. It covers a wide range of studies and includes in its " schools " special institutions such as the School of Tropical Medicine, the School of Oriental and African Studies, and the Lister Institute.

The British Universities are independent institutions, but receive monetary aid from the State and from some of the local education authorities.

How many children and students attend our Schools and Universities?

Schools and universities in the United Kingdom are attended by about 8½ million children and students. More than 90 per cent. of the children attend schools provided by public authorities or assisted by grants from public funds.

What is a Public School?

Broadly, they are fee-charging secondary schools controlled by a body of governors, as distinct from privately-owned schools (such as many preparatory schools) and the State schools.

The public school system was developed in England and has made an important contribution to education in this country. It was in the public schools that the prefect and house systems were developed. They consider character-building particularly important. They are usually boarding schools and take pupils when they are about thirteen years of age.

Many of our public schools were founded in the sixteenth century, e.g., Harrow (1571), but some are much older, e.g., Winchester (1382) and Eton (1440).

What Youth Organisations are there in Britain?

There are at least twenty major organisations catering for the spare-time activities and interests of our young people. Among the best-known are the *Boy Scouts' Association* and *Girl Guides' Association,* which were founded by Lord Baden-Powell (in 1908 and 1910 respectively). In 1959, the active membership of the Boy Scouts' Association in the United Kingdom was 571,402; active membership of the Girl Guides at the end of 1958 was 545,998.

The *Boys' Brigade* (founded in 1883) is a youth organisation associated with the Protestant religion, while the *Church Lads' Brigade* is connected with the Anglican Church. Then there are the *National Association of Boys' Clubs,* the *National Association of Mixed Clubs and Girls' Clubs;* various organisations which train both boys and girls for entry into one of the Services (e.g., the *Army Cadet Force,* the *Girls' Nautical Training Corps*); the *Outward Bound Trust,* which maintains sea and mountain schools where character-building courses are run for boys; young people's branches of various adult organisations, such as the *British Red Cross Society* and the *St. John Ambulance Brigade;* and a number of other bodies, e.g., *National Federation of Young Farmers' Clubs,* the *Youth Hostels Association,* the *Central Council of Physical Recreation,* and the *National Playing Fields Association.*

In addition, the leading political parties have junior sections.

Which are our Oldest Schools?

The following are the best-known of the early foundations: King's School, Canterbury (founded A.D. 600); King's School, Rochester (founded A.D. 604); and St. Peter's, York (founded A.D. 627).

ELECTRICITY

Why should Electric Light Switches in Bathrooms have no bare metal on them?

Because while the skin is damp after a bath electricity can pass much more easily through the body, and any leakage at the switch might cause a very serious shock. It is now forbidden to fit the ordinary type of electric switch in a bathroom, which is why modern bathrooms often have the switch just outside the door.

Why does an Electric Lamp light up when one moves the Switch?

The switch lets current pass through the thin filament of the lamp, which becomes so intensely hot that it glows fiercely.

Why are Lightning Conductors put on Tall Chimneys, Church Spires, Buildings, etc.?

To allow electricity to leak away gradually between clouds and earth and prevent a dan-

MADE BY NATURE

Icebergs (see p. 348) are large masses of ice which have broken away from polar ice-fields or glaciers. Only one-ninth of the total bulk of the iceberg appears above the surface of the sea. Dwarfed by the iceberg in this picture is a ship of the International Ice Patrol, which is maintained to report on the location and movement of icebergs and give warning to ships on North Atlantic routes.

This carboniferous limestone *escarpment* (see p. 351 occurs near Llangollen, North Wales. The picture shows the Ty-nant ravine breaching the escarpment and the Berwyn Hills, beyond the Dee Valley, on the extreme right. Escarpments are found where uptilted layers of hard rock rest on layers of softer rock.

OVER THE CURVE OF THE WORLD

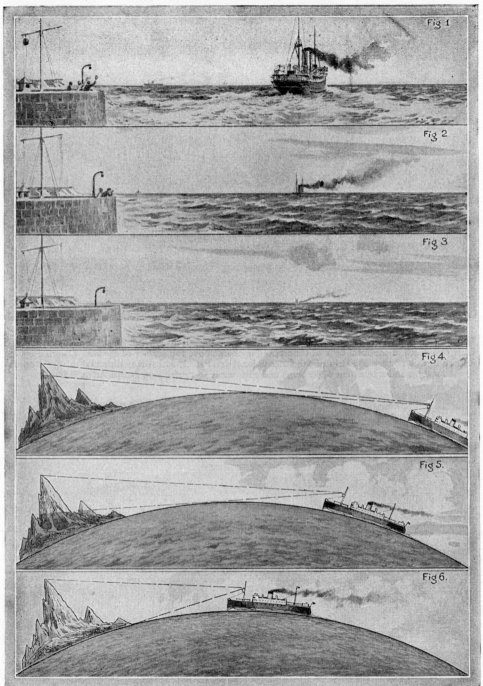

Specially drawn for this work.

One proof of the earth being a *sphere* (see p. 347) is the fact that a ship disappears over the *horizon* no matter in what direction it sails. In Fig. 1 a ship is leaving port. In Fig. 2 the ship is "hull-down," only its funnel and masts being visible, and in Fig. 3 even its masts have almost vanished. In Fig. 4 the lookout-man in a ship's "crow's nest" can just see the crest of a lofty and distant mountain. Closer approach reveals more of the mountain (**Fig. 5**); and in Fig. 6 the whole mountain and the island at its foot come into sight.

gerous piling-up of a charge. If a flash should occur, a conductor gives the current an easy path to the earth, and protects the building to which it is fixed.

Why are Fuses fitted on an Electrical Switchboard?

They prevent the current rising above a certain figure in the circuits of which they form part. A fuse will melt and break the circuit before the copper wire beyond it (which it protects) can become dangerously hot.

How is it that Men are able to handle the Electric Conductors of Tramways with their bare hands while the Current is still on?

The platforms on which the men stand are made entirely of wood, which is a very bad conductor of electricity. It is therefore impossible for the current to pass through the men's bodies.

How does Radar Work?

A wireless wave is sent out from a transmitter, and a receiver detects its reflection from distant objects. The time taken for a signal to be reflected enables the distance of the object to be calculated. By using a narrow beam and tracing out the outlines of objects their form can be made visible on a screen like that of a television set. Since wireless waves can travel easily through fog, radar enables ships to " see " rocks, icebergs and other ships when they would otherwise have to rely on sound signals for their safety.

Where are the chief Water-power Stations in Great Britain?

In the Highlands of Scotland, the Snowdon district of North Wales, and a few in Yorkshire.

How is an Article Electro-plated?

Suppose that a spoon is to be plated with silver. It is hung in a chemical solution of silver and connected with the negative pole of a battery or dynamo. The other pole of the battery, etc., is connected with a plate of pure silver, also suspended in the solution. The flow of current through the spoon, solution and plate causes silver to be deposited on the spoon from the solution, while an equal amount of silver is dissolved in the solution from the plate.

How does an Electricity Meter work?

In most meters a tiny motor is kept revolving by the current passing through the meter at a speed proportionate to the current multiplied by the pressure. The motor drives a train of wheels which indicate on dials, in Board of Trade units (kilowatt-hours), the amount of electricity used.

Why are Electric Bell Wires covered with Rubber and Cotton?

To prevent the current leaking from the wires, rubber and cotton being bad conductors of electricity.

Why isn't a Bird electrocuted when it perches on the Overhead Electric Cable?

Because, like the wire itself, it is insulated from the earth. But if anything which can conduct electricity were to touch both it and the ground, the circuit would be completed through its body and it would die instantly.

How does an Electric Bell work?

The hammer arm has on it a small mass of iron, which is attracted by an electro-magnet when the bell push is pressed in and the electric circuit completed. Before the hammer strikes the bell, a contact at the back of the arm leaves another contact and breaks the circuit. The hammer strikes the bell by its own momentum, and is then pulled away by the spring on which the arm is fixed. As soon as the two contacts come together again the magnet pulls the hammer forward once more. This cycle of operations is repeated rapidly as long as the circuit is kept closed by the bell-push.

Who invented the Electric Telegraph?

The first practical telegraphic apparatus was the needle instrument invented jointly by two Englishmen, Fothergill Cooke and Charles Wheatstone, in 1835. It is now used only on some railways. In the following year an American, Samuel Finley Breese Morse, produced another instrument which recorded messages as dots and dashes on a moving strip of paper and laid the foundation of modern overland telegraphy.

When was the first Telegraphic Message sent from the Old World to the New?

On August 16th, 1858, through the first Atlantic cable laid from Ireland to Newfoundland. It ran: " Europe and America are united by telegraph. Glory to God in the highest, on earth peace, goodwill toward men," and was followed by a greeting from Queen Victoria to Mr. James Buchanan, President of the United States.

What is a Telegraphic Code?

A system of words, or of groups of letters or figures, each of which means a sentence. It is used to reduce the cost of telegraphing, or to ensure secrecy. Several different codes, published in book form, are employed for general commercial purposes. Anyone may use a telegraph code of his own, if it conforms to certain rules laid down by the postal authorities.

GEOGRAPHY

How do we know that the Earth is a Sphere?

In several ways. (a) A ship in mid-ocean gradually disappears over the horizon, in whatever direction it moves. (b) Anyone travelling in the same direction continuously will return to his starting-point. (c) The earth always casts a circular shadow, or part of one, on to the moon. (d) The curvature of the earth can be seen in photographs taken automatically in rockets from a height of a 100 miles or more.

How much is the Earth flattened at the Poles?

The diameter of the earth at the Equator is 7,926 miles, and the distance between the poles is 7,899 miles. So the flattening is very small indeed. The earth is commonly compared to an orange in shape; but an orange of exactly the same form as the earth would appear to the eye to be perfectly spherical. Assuming the orange to be 3 inches in diameter at its " equator," its " polar " diameter would be only one-hundredth part of an inch less than 3 inches.

How did Men measure the Circumference of the Earth?

If one knows the length of a definite part of a circle, one can easily calculate the circumference of the circle. To measure the girth of the earth through the poles, astronomical observations were made at different points along north-and-south lines measured on the earth's surface. In this way the length of one degree, that is, one 360th part of the earth's circumference, was found to be 69½ miles. So the circumference must be 69½ × 360, or 25,020 miles (approx).

Why does the Sun appear to rise in the East and set in the West?

Because the earth turns towards the east.

Why are Summer Days longer than Winter Days?

Because the sun is higher above the horizon in the summer and describes a larger part of a circle between its rising and setting.

Why is Sunshine hotter in Summer than in Winter?

Because the sun's rays then strike the earth less slantingly, and, in consequence, a larger number fall on every square yard of it.

How do Days and Nights at the Equator differ from those in England?

At the Equator a day is of almost the same length as a night all the year round. In England the lengths vary greatly at different seasons. At the Equator a day begins and ends very suddenly with practically no dawn or twilight.

What causes the Tides?

The attraction of the moon and, to a much smaller extent, that of the sun. The water, being able to move, bulges out slightly at the points nearest to and farthest from these bodies.

Why do the Tides vary in Height?

Because the sun and moon are sometimes acting together and sometimes against one another. When the earth, moon and sun are all in one line, as at " new moon " and " full moon," the moon-waves and sun-waves come together and we get the highest, or " spring " tides. But when the moon is half full or half waned the moon-waves and sun-waves are in different places and the lowest, or " neap," tides occur. One should notice that spring tides have no connection with the season of spring.

Where do the Tides rise and fall most?

In the Bay of Fundy, between New Brunswick and Nova Scotia, Canada. At spring tides the difference between high and low water levels is from 45 to 50 feet.

Did the Tides ever have a larger Rise and Fall than they have To-day?

Yes, when the moon was much nearer to the earth, as it was millions of years ago, its attraction was very much greater and the tides were probably so high that they would have swamped much land that is now far above tide-level.

What are Ocean Currents and by what are they caused?

Ocean currents are movements of the waters of the ocean. Where there is an ocean current, the water flows strongly and surely in a definite stream. In the upper layers of ocean, currents are caused mainly by the wind; in lower layers, in some parts, changes of temperature and salinity at the surface may lead to movement of the waters.

The prevailing winds help to determine the direction in which ocean currents flow, but this is also affected by the shape of the coast-line and by the rotation of the Earth. Ocean currents in Trade Wind latitudes follow a general counter-clockwise direction in the Southern Hemisphere, and a general clockwise direction in the Northern Hemisphere.

For example, in the area of the Equator, the currents (North Equatorial Current) moves in a westerly direction. The piling up of waters by this North Equatorial Current in the Gulf of Mexico is the beginning of one of the best-known ocean currents—the Gulf Stream.

The Gulf Stream flows out north-eastwards. Its narrowest width is about fifty miles, it is some 350 fathoms deep, and it flows at a rate of about five miles per hour. As it moves across the Atlantic, it spreads out into the North Atlantic Drift, but another part of the Gulf Stream (the Canaries Current) moves southwards to rejoin the Equatorial Current.

The Gulf Stream, which is a warm-water current, flows in a north-westerly direction, i.e., towards the British Isles, by the prevailing south-westerly winds. From it these winds bring warmth and moisture to western Europe.

In the South Atlantic, the Brazil Current is turned southwards by the protruding shoulder of South America, and then meets the colder Westerly Drift and circles eastwards and north-wards to flow up the coast of West Africa (Benguela Current).

In the Pacific the same pattern can be seen. Here the North Equatorial Current flows in a westerly direction, part of it sweeping past Japan as the Kuro Siwo. In the South Pacific, the Equatorial Current flows in a counter-clockwise direction and turns north up the coast of South America as the cold Peru Current.

Why is the Sea salt?

Because rivers are constantly pouring into it water charged with salt dissolved out of the land. The water evaporated from the sea by the sun and winds leaves the salt behind it, so the sea is becoming more and more salt.

How much Salt is there in the Sea?

Sea water contains on the average about one part in forty of salt, or, say, 4 ounces in a gallon. Were all the salt in the oceans and seas piled together it would fill a space of nearly 5,000,000 cubic miles.

How are Icebergs formed?

They are in most cases masses broken off from polar ice-rivers (glaciers) at the points where they enter the sea. In the Antarctic regions many icebergs come from the Great Ice Barrier, a huge ice plateau in the Ross Sea, which probably is afloat.

What are the Doldrums?

A part of the ocean near the Equator where winds are very light, or absent altogether, for long spells. Sailing ships may be becalmed for weeks in the Doldrums. Being held up in this manner has a depressing effect; and the phrase, " To be in the doldrums," has thus come to mean being in low spirits.

What is the Sargasso Sea?

A large tract of the Atlantic Ocean lying between Florida and the Canary Islands, in which great masses of floating seaweed are found. The weed is carried into it by the Gulf Stream and North Equatorial Current, and stays there, as this part of the ocean is generally calm. Columbus ran through the Sargasso Sea during his famous voyage of discovery in 1492. The weed is thick enough in places to impede the movements of ships. It is notable as a breeding-place of eels. Similar collections of weed are found in the South Atlantic and South Pacific Oceans.

Why is the Mediterranean Sea so named?

The word " mediterranean " comes from the Latin *medius* = middle, and *terra* = earth, and means in the midst of the land, or surrounded by land. The description is almost a true one, for the only breaks in the coastline are at the fourteen-miles wide Straits of Gibraltar and the much narrower Dardanelles. The Mediterranean Sea is by far the largest land-locked sheet of water in the world. It has an area of nearly a million square miles. As more water is evaporated from it than comes from rivers emptying into it, there is always an inward current through the Straits of Gibraltar, and the water is salter than that of the Atlantic Ocean. Its deepest portions are in the eastern half, where depths of up to about 14,500 feet are found. The Mediterranean Sea is not tideless, but the tidal range in many parts is only a few inches.

Which are the World's most Important Straits?

The Straits of Dover, Gibraltar, Messina, Bab-el-Mandeb (entrance to the Red Sea), Ormuz (entrance to the Persian Gulf), Malacca (between the Malay Peninsula and Sumatra), Sunda (between Sumatra and Java), Torres (between Queensland and New Guinea), Cook (between North Island and South Island, New Zealand), Belle Isle (between Newfoundland and Labrador), Cabot (between Newfoundland and Nova Scotia), and Juan de Fuca (between Vancouver Island and the mainland). Also, the Dardanelles and Bosporus (between Europe and Asia Minor), the Sound (between Denmark and Sweden, at the entrance to the Baltic), and Windward Passage (between Cuba and Haiti).

What and where is the Dogger Bank?

A sandbank about 170 miles long and 60 miles broad, in the middle of the North Sea, covered by water only from 60 to 120 feet deep. It is a famous fishing-ground, over which much trawling is done by British and Dutch fishermen.

Where are the Goodwin Sands?

Above five miles off the east coast of Kent, from which they are separated by a channel called the Downs. At low tide parts of them appear above water. The sands are very dangerous to shipping, which is warned off them by four lightships. They serve a useful purpose, too, as a natural breakwater, behind which ships can shelter in the Downs from easterly gales. According to tradition they were once part of the property of the Saxon earl Godwin, father of King Harold, and were submerged by the sea in 1097.

What do the Terms " Far East " and " Near East " mean?

There is no definite rule governing these terms, but broadly it may be said that the Near East covers Turkey to Persia (25° to 60° E. long.); the Middle East includes Baluchistan to Burma (60° to 100° E. long.), while the Far East is from Siam to Japan (100° to 160° E. long.).

How many People are there in the World?

The number has been estimated at about 2,795,000,000. Exact figures cannot be given as in some countries there is no census, and the total is always growing. According to the United Nations' statistics for 1958, Africa contained about 225,000,000 people; the Americas, 381,000,000; Asia (excluding U.S.S.R.), 1,556,000,000; Europe (excluding U.S.S.R.), 414,000,000; U.S.S.R., 204,000,000; Oceania, 15,000,000.

How did we get the Words " County " and " Shire "?

England was built up out of small kingdoms, each under an earl or count. " Shire " comes from an Anglo-Saxon word meaning a division. One may say that county and shire now mean the same thing; but that in some cases (Kent and Cornwall, for example) the kingdom name has survived, while in others this has given way to the division name.

Which is the Largest County in England?

Yorkshire, which has an area of over 4,000,000 acres, equal to one-eighth of the whole area of England. It is more than twice as extensive as the next largest county, Lincolnshire. For administrative purposes Yorkshire is divided into three separate Ridings—East, North and West. (Riding is a shortened form of the Anglo-Saxon " thriding " or " trithing," meaning a third part.)

What are the Broads?

Shallow lakes in those low-lying districts of Norfolk and Suffolk through which flow the rivers Yare, Bure, Waveney and Ant. They are expansions of these rivers, or are connected with them by wide ditches or waterways. Their edges are fringed with reeds, which would invade the water space if they were not cut back. Some of the Broads are still large enough to give plenty of sailing room for small yachts. They are popular with holiday-makers.

Where are the English Fens?

They cover an area about seventy miles long from north to south, and thirty miles wide, in the counties of Lincoln, Norfolk, Suffolk, Northampton, Huntingdon and Cambridge. They are a low-lying region, much of the country being below high spring-tide level. The sea and rivers are prevented by banks, called dykes, from flooding the land. On occasion, notably in the early part of 1947, the heavy rainfall has caused the rivers to burst their banks and great damage has been caused, with farm lands and buildings flooded out. Early in 1953 there was also severe flooding as a result of abnormally high tides along the east coast. An important part of the area drained for cultivation is named the Bedford Level, after the Earl of Bedford, who played a leading part in reclaiming it during the seventeenth century.

How were the Fens formed?

By silt from the sea and soil brought down by rivers, intermingled with decaying vegetation. Eventually they were protected from the sea and rivers by embankments and drained, large areas of what formerly was useless swamp being converted into valuable pasture and agricultural land.

What is the Red Plain of England?

The Midland Plain, bounded on the south by the Cotswolds, on the west by the Welsh hills, on the north by the Pennines, and on the east by the Eastern Plain. It is named from the red colour of its soil.

Where is the Black Country?

The name is given to the southern part of Staffordshire, on account of the large number of coal mines, blast furnaces and factories in it. It contains many large towns, including Wolverhampton, Walsall, Dudley and West Bromwich, which produce iron and steel goods of all kinds.

What is the longest Land Journey that can be made in the British Isles?

From John o' Groat's House, in the very north of Scotland, to Land's End, in Cornwall. The distance by road between these two points is usually given as about 880 miles.

Where does the Thames rise?

In the Cotswold Hills. Thames Head, near Cirencester, the source of the Kemble Stream, and Seven Springs, near Cheltenham, the source of the River Churn, dispute the honour of being called the true source of our most important river. Seven Springs are farther from the sea; but the Kemble Stream contributes more water than the Churn. The two streams unite at Lechlade.

What are the Names of the chief British Lakes?

In England: Derwentwater (Cumberland), Ullswater and Windermere (Westmorland), Coniston Water (Lancashire).
In Scotland: Lochs Awe, Lochy, Lomond, Ness, Tay, Rannoch and Earn.
In Wales: Bala.
In Ireland: Loughs Neagh, Erne, Ree, Derg, Mask, Corrib and Leane (Killarney).

Which are the most Mountainous Counties of England?

Cumberland and Westmorland. They contain most of the Cumbrian group of mountains and the northern part of the Pennine range. In these are the highest English peaks—Scafell Pike (3,210 feet), Helvellyn (3,118 feet) and Skiddaw (3,054 feet).

Why is Cornwall warmer than Norfolk in Winter?

Cornwall is warmed by winds blowing in from the sea after having passed over a great expanse of ocean heated by the Gulf Stream drift. The sea breezes that reach Norfolk have come from a colder quarter, over the waters of the North Sea.

Where and what are the " Seven Sisters," the " Needles," the " Nore," the " Downs " and the " Longships "?

The Seven Sisters: a series of seven bold chalk cliffs between Seaford and Beachy Head, on the Sussex Coast. The Needles: detached chalk rocks standing out of the sea at the western end of the Isle of Wight. The Nore: a sandbank in the Thames estuary, midway between the Essex Coast and the Isle of Sheppey. The Downs: a roadstead between the Kentish Coast and the Goodwin Sands, measuring eight by six miles, and protected from all but southerly gales. The Longships: a lighthouse on Cara Bras, a rocky islet to the N.W. of Land's End, in Cornwall.

Where is Shakespeare's Cliff?

On the south coast, a little to the west of Dover. Rising to a height of over 350 feet, it is a prominent feature of the " White Walls of Old England."

What is Old Sarum?

The site of an old fortress and town, about two miles north of Salisbury, in Wiltshire. Under the Romans and Saxons it was of importance as a stronghold, and during the eleventh, twelfth and thirteenth centuries it was a bishop's see. Owing to lack of water the inhabitants were obliged to abandon the place, and move to New Sarum, or Salisbury, as we now call it. By the end of the fifteenth century, the site was quite deserted, and now only the remains of extensive earthworks and the ruins of fortifications tell of its former occupation.

What Town is called " The English Naples " ?

Torquay, on Tor Bay, on the south coast of Devonshire. It commands a beautiful view over the bay, and enjoys a climate which is cool in summer and mild in winter. Another claimant to this title is Weymouth.

Where is " The Garden of England " ?

The county of Kent, renowned for its orchards. The Isle of Wight is also sometimes given this name on account of its small cultivated fields and fuchsia hedges.

What is meant by the " Three Towns " Western England?

Plymouth, Devonport and Stonehouse, lying close together at the head of Plymouth Sound, on the tongue of land between the two branches of the Sound called the Hamoaze and Catwater. Plymouth is essentially a seaport. Devonport is famous for its naval dockyard, and Stonehouse, lying between the other two, contains a naval hospital and marine barracks.

What British Town is a County in itself?

Berwick-on-Tweed, including Tweedmouth and Spittal. Whether it belonged to England or Scotland was settled by an Act of Parliament passed in 1885, which included it in England. Inner London, with a population of over 3¼ millions, is now also an administrative county, which includes the City of London, and covers 117 square miles.

What is the Smallest City in England?

The City of London, which measures approximately 1 square mile.

Which are the Chief English Ports used by Travellers to the Continent?

Dover (Kent), for Calais (France), 22 miles; Folkestone (Kent), for Boulogne (France), 26 miles; Newhaven (Sussex), for Dieppe (France), 67 miles; Harwich (Essex), for Hook of Holland, 106 miles.

Was Glasgow always an Important Port?

No. At one time it was possible to ford the Clyde on foot twelve miles below Glasgow, so shallow was the water. In the eighteenth century sandbanks so obstructed the river that no vessel drawing more than 3½ feet of water could reach Glasgow even at high spring tides. Glasgow has been made, and is kept, accessible to large ocean-going ships by the constant dredging of vast quantities of sand from the channel.

What is an Escarpment?

A steep rock face appearing high above the surrounding countryside and usually sloping away more gradually on the opposite side to the escarpment.

Why are Rivers bent in their course so that they do not run straight?

Over a stretch of level country a river does run straight. It is when the level of the land varies that the course of the stream twists and turns because it must always run in a downward direction. If a river comes to a slight rise in the ground it cannot pass over the top and so it bends and curves to find a way round.

What is the Federation of Rhodesia and Nyasaland?

The Federation of Rhodesia and Nyasaland is a self-governing unit of the British Commonwealth of Nations. It is made up of the self-governing territory of Southern Rhodesia and the protectorates of Northern Rhodesia and Nyasaland, and was brought into being on August 1st, 1953. On this day the Queen signed the Order-in-Council which proclaimed the new Federal State. The capital of the Federation is Salisbury. The first elections for the Federal Assembly were held on December 15th, 1953.

What Countries make up British East Africa?

(1) Uganda, between the Anglo-Egyptian Sudan on the north and Lake Victoria Nyanza on the south; a protectorate including areas ruled by native kings. (2) Kenya Colony and protectorate (capital, Nairobi), extending eastwards from Uganda to the Indian Ocean. (3) Tanganyika Territory (formerly German East Africa), bounded on the north by Uganda, Kenya and Lake Victoria Nyanza, on the west by Lake Tanganyika, on the east by the Indian Ocean, and on the south by Portuguese East Africa.

Tanganyika is governed by Britain under United Nations' trusteeship which replaced the former League of Nations' mandate in 1946. (4) The islands of Zanzibar and Pemba, off the East African coast, under their own Sultan and the protection of Britain.

What City is called "the City of Gold"?

Johannesburg, in the Transvaal, South Africa. In 1886 its site was open veldt. To-day its population is reckoned in hundreds of thousands. The rapid rise and title of the city are explained by its being the centre of the gold-mining industry of the Rand, whence comes more than a half of the world's supply of gold.

Why was the New World called America?

After Amerigo Vespucci, a Florentine who sailed with Columbus on his third voyage, and did some exploring on his own account. He was the first European explorer to enter the Antarctic regions and to see the constellation called the Southern Cross.

Where are Colombia, the District of Columbia, and British Columbia?

Colombia is a republic in the north-west corner of South America. It covers about 500,000 square miles, and its capital is Bogotá. The *District of Columbia* is an area of the United States between Maryland and Virginia, in which stands Washington, the Federal capital of the United States. *British Columbia* is a province of Canada between the Pacific Ocean and Alberta, bounded on the south by the United States and on the north by the sixtieth parallel of north latitude. It includes Vancouver Island, and has an area of some 350,000 square miles.

Which is the World's Greatest River?

The Amazon (or Amazons), which drains about 2,700,000 square miles of South America, including most of Brazil, Bolivia and Ecuador, and parts of Peru and Colombia. Its length, 4,000 miles, is less than that of the Mississippi and Missouri combined (4,240 miles), but it discharges such a mass of water at its mouth, which is 200 miles wide, that the saltness of the Atlantic Ocean is much reduced even 150 miles from land. Ocean-going steamers are able to ascend the river to Manaus (also spelt "Manaos"), 1,000 miles from the mouth, and smaller vessels twice as far, to Iquitos, in Peru. Its main tributaries are the Rio Negro on the left bank, and the Madeira on the right bank.

Why are the Descendants of the Original Inhabitants of America called Indians?

Because when America was discovered it was believed to be part of India. For the same reason the name of West Indies was given to groups of islands off the American coast. The name Red Indians, and sometimes Redskins, has persisted ever since.

What is meant by the Spanish Main?

The lands in Central and South America, on the coasts of the Caribbean Sea, once held by Spain. The words mean "Spanish mainland," as opposed to Spanish islands in the West Indies, and not—as is often incorrectly supposed—the Caribbean Sea itself.

What is the " Forbidden Land "?

Tibet, in Central Asia, just north of India, has borne this name because the Tibetans were long hostile to any foreigners entering the country. Until 1904 only one Englishman, Thomas Manning (1811), and half a dozen or so other Europeans had succeeded in reaching Lhasa, the capital of the country. In 1950, Chinese troops entered Tibet and in 1951 a treaty was signed placing the foreign affairs and defence of the country under Chinese control. In 1959, after a revolt in Eastern Tibet against the Chinese, one of the religious leaders of the Tibetans, the Dalai Lama, left the country and sought asylum in India.

Where is the Great Barrier Reef?

Off the eastern coast of Queensland, Australia. It runs more or less parallel to the coast for more than a thousand miles, at a distance of from twenty to sixty miles from the mainland. The Reef is entirely the work of the coral "insect," and marks the original coastline, which has been sinking slowly for ages. There are gaps in the Reef at a few places opposite the mouths of rivers, where the water is too fresh to suit the coral-makers. At many points the Reef widens out into islands, many of them well covered with vegetation, and many swarming with bird life. The long strip of water between the Reef and the land is one of the busiest waterways in the Pacific.

Which are the most Northerly, Southerly and Westerly Points on the Mainland of Europe?

Cape Nordkyn, in Lapland (Lat. 71° N.) is the most northerly point. North Cape is about ten miles further north, but is on an island. Cape Marroqui (Lat. 36° N.), near Gibraltar, is the most southerly point; and Cape da Roca (Long. 9° 30' W.) in Portugal, the most westerly point.

What is the Holy Land?

The country to which we refer as the Holy Land is Palestine, but large parts of what is now called Syria were included in the Holy Land of ancient times. The Holy Land, where Christ walked and talked nearly 2,000 years ago, was a country actually no larger than Wales, and Palestine as we know it to-day is smaller still. Britain held Palestine under mandate from the League of Nations and then under trusteeship for UNO until 1948. In that year, British troops were withdrawn from Palestine where the Jewish National Council proclaimed the State of Israel.

Fighting broke out between the Arabs and their supporters, on the one hand, and the new state of Israel on the other. The armistice agreements signed in 1949 divided Palestine, giving much of the eastern area, including part of Jerusalem itself, to Jordan, and a small sector of the south-west to Egypt.

What was the Zuider Zee?

A great gulf formed in Holland during the twelfth to fifteenth centuries by the bursting in of the waters of the North Sea. The original outline of the coasts of Holland is shown plainly enough by a chain of islands—Texel, Vlieland, Terschelling, Ameland, Schiermonnikoog and Borkum. In all, about 2,000 square miles of fertile land were covered by the sea to a depth of from 10 to 18 feet. The Dutch Government was for many years engaged in building an embankment to separate the Zuider Zee from the outer ocean and this great dyke was actually completed on May 28th, 1932. The embankment, 400 feet wide at the bottom, tapers to 120 feet at the top and provision is made for both a road and railway line. The area within, which is still being reclaimed, is divided into four polders and also contains the Ijssel Lake.

What is the U.S.S.R.?

The Union of Socialist Soviet Republics. As a result of the War of 1914–18 and revolution in Russia the former Russian Empire in Europe and Asia broke up into a large number of republics; these form the U.S.S.R., which has its headquarters at Moscow.

Which is the Sunny Side of a House in New Zealand?

The north side, because New Zealand is south of the Equator. The warm winds there come from the north, the cold winds from the south.

Which of the World's Cities lie very high above Sea-level?

Cerro de Pasco, in Peru, is the loftiest town, lying at an elevation of 14,270 feet. La Paz, capital of Bolivia, is 12,000 feet; Lhasa, capital of Tibet, 11,800 feet; Cuzco, in Peru, 11,400 feet; Quito, capital of Ecuador, 9,350 feet; and Mexico City, capital of Mexico, 7,410 feet.

What Cities or Towns are on or very near to the Equator?

Quito, in Ecuador, South America; Stanleyville, in the Belgian Congo, Africa; Kisumu, Port Victoria and Entebbe, on Lake Victoria Nyanza; Padang, in Sumatra; and Pontianak, in Borneo.

Where is the Island of Tristan da Cunha?

About half-way between the Cape of Good Hope and South America, in the middle of the South Atlantic. It has been called the "Empire's loneliest island " as, except for two uninhabited islands close by, there is no land nearer than St. Helena, which is over 1,300 miles distant. The island is a volcanic rock about twenty-one miles round, projecting from the ocean. In one part is a plateau, measuring nine by one and a half miles. On this live about 160 people, descended from British soldiers who settled there in 1816. Ships very seldom call at the island, which has no harbour and lies off the ocean routes. During the Second World War, the island became H.M.S. *Atlantic Isle*, and it is now an important radio and weather station.

Where are the Islands known as New Guinea and the Solomon Islands, and to whom do they belong?

New Guinea is a large island to the north of Australia, the western part of the island being Dutch New Guinea, or West Irian, while the eastern part, which includes Papua, is under the government of Australia. The Solomon Islands lie to the east of New Guinea, and the southern

Paul Popper.

TWO MEMBERS OF THE ANTELOPE FAMILY

Danger from other fiercer wild animals often threatens these two inmates of the Wankie Game Reserve in Southern Rhodesia. Nature has given a form of protection to the Kudu Cow who stands alert by the waterside. It is easy to see how well its tan coat blends with the surroundings. Kudu Cows are a species of large antelope and grow up to 4½ feet at the shoulder. The Waterbuck is never seen far from water and is brown to roan in colour with a white band on the rump and white markings. It is found from Kenya to northern Transvaal. Antelopes are very abundant in Africa generally and some 90 species are to be found there.

A REMARKABLE EXAMPLE OF NATURAL CAMOUFLAGE

Animal camouflage and mimicry, which are Nature's strange devices to enable weaker creatures to survive in a world peopled with fierce and destructive beasts, birds, insects and reptiles, as well as that dangerous enemy man, make a very fascinating study. There are beetles which look like leaves, moths which cannot be seen when resting on a tree, and other creatures that have protective colouring which makes it almost impossible to observe them against a background of field, wood or moorland. The colour photograph seen here is a wonderful example of this protective colouring or mimicry in shape. It shows on the left an owl, and on the right a Caligo, or Owl Butterfly, whose markings make it an excellent example of the "lamb in wolf's clothing,"—a harmless insect which is able to mimic a fierce predatory one.

group have been a British Protectorate since 1893–99. The Northern Solomons, which include Bougainville, Buka and adjacent islands, have been governed by Australia since the end of the war of 1914–18. New Zealand also has certain islands in the Pacific, including Western Samoa and the Cook Islands.

Which are the World's most famous Volcanoes?

Vesuvius, near the Bay of Naples, in Italy; Etna, in Sicily; Stromboli, on one of the Lipari Islands; Hecla and Skaptar Jokul, in Iceland; Popocatepetl, in Mexico; Cotopaxi, in Ecuador; Mont Pelée, in Martinique, and La Soufrière, in St. Vincent, in the West Indies; Kilauea, in Hawaii; and Erebus, in the Antarctic. Vesuvius blotted out the towns of Pompeii and Herculaneum in A.D. 79, and has erupted many times since, though for over 1,100 years, between A.D. 512 and 1631, it gave few signs of life, and its top was covered with forests. Etna also has sent out destructive lava streams on many occasions. Mont Pelée destroyed the city of St. Pierre and 40,000 inhabitants in a few minutes in 1902. Cotopaxi, one of the loftiest volcanoes in the world, is now quiescent. Kilauea has a crater measuring eight to nine miles round and surrounded by vertical walls 800 feet high. In the centre of the bottom is a lake of boiling lava.

Which are the World's Greatest Waterfalls?

The Victoria Falls, on the River Zambezi (South Africa); Niagara Falls; the Kaieteur Falls, on the Potaro River (British Guiana); the Guaira Falls, on the River Paraná (Brazil); the Iguassu Falls, on the Iguassu river, a tributary of the Paraná; the Grand Falls of Labrador, on the Hamilton River; and the Gersoppa Falls, on the Sharavari River (India). Of waterfalls having a great fall, but comparatively small volume, the Yosemite Falls (United States), and the Sutherland Falls (New Zealand) are good examples.

Which is the Highest Mountain in the World?

Mount Everest, a giant peak in the Himalayas named in 1858 after Sir George Everest, the Surveyor-General of India. The mountain stands partly in Nepal and partly in Tibet. It rises to a height of 29,028 feet and it was first climbed by the British expedition of 1953 led by Col. (now Sir John) Hunt. The members of the expedition who reached the summit were Edmund (now Sir Edmund) Hillary and the Sherpa Tensing.

Who were the First Men to reach the North and South Poles?

An American, Commander Robert E. Peary, of the United States Navy, was the first man to reach the North Pole, on April 6th, 1909. A Norwegian explorer, Roald Amundsen, reached the South Pole on December 16th, 1911, beating the British expedition, led by Captain R. F. Scott, R.N., by just a month.

GEOLOGY

How were Mountains and Valleys formed?

The great groups and chains of mountains were raised by upheavals of the earth's crust, which was bent into folds by the forces beneath it. Almost all the individual mountains and valleys are due to the action of the weather and rivers, and bear no direct relation to the folds in the crust. The weather and rivers have loosened and washed away the softer rocks, carving out deep valleys, and the mountains consist of the harder rocks remaining.

How can we tell that some kinds of Rock are older than others?

Rocks may be (a) stratified: that is, occurring in layers deposited in ancient seas and prehistoric lakes, or (b) igneous: rocks which have cooled from a state of fusion, or (c) metamorphic: rocks which have undergone changes due to heat or pressure or both since their formation. The stratified rocks were formed by deposition of material from igneous and other rocks as a result of the action of running water, frost, snow and ice, wind and rain. In the stratified rocks there may be fossils (traces of former life), from which the age and type of the rock may be deduced. Obviously the stratified rocks are, generally speaking, younger than the igneous or metamorphic rocks from whose fragmentation many types of stratified rock have been formed. Igneous rocks which have been formed by cooling from a state of fusion bear no fossils for obvious reasons, but their age—and that of metamorphic rocks—can sometimes be determined by examination of the rock structure under the microscope. The ages of very old rocks can be estimated from the traces of radio-active minerals they contain.

Why do the Faces of Sea-cliffs keep breaking away in some places?

Because no cliffs are hard enough to withstand the battering of the waves, which undermines them at the foot until a fall takes place. As soon as the fallen matter has been cleared away by the waves and currents, the sea attacks the cliff again. Even the hardest of rocky cliffs have in the course of ages been eaten into by the sea, as the rocks on the shore near them testify.

What is Chalk?

A soft, white, earthy rock, almost pure carbonate of lime. It was once thought to consist chiefly of the tiny skeletons and shells of creatures which lived in an ancient sea. It is now believed that the chalk was originally an ooze deposited on the sea-floor by the chemical action of bacteria. It was later raised by movements of the earth's crust and now forms our chalk downs and wolds.

What is Clay?

Tiny particles of rock, usually held together loosely by moisture. The purest kind of clay, called china clay, is felspar, which was separated from granite by the action of the atmosphere. It is a compound of silica and alumina. But many clays are very impure, containing a large proportion of powdered rocks of other kinds.

What is Coal?

A rock made up chiefly of carbon. It is what remains of trees, plants, mosses and other vegetation which once grew on the earth's surface and were afterwards covered by layers of other rocks. Great pressure and chemical changes, lasting for hundreds of millions of years, gradually drove out the larger part of the gases, so that coal, as we now know it, is mostly carbon, squeezed into a hard, compact form.

What is Sandstone?

A mass of grains of granite and other rocks once carried down by rivers and laid on the sea-floor in beds. The grains are cemented together by mineral matter dissolved in the water and compacted by the pressure of layers of other rocks deposited on top of the sandstone.

Why does Slate split so easily?

Because the particles composing it have been arranged in sheets by great pressure, during movements of the earth's crust. Slate is a form of clay, much hardened by the squeezing it has undergone.

Why are many Hills steepest at the Top?

Because the earth, etc., washed from the top by rain in the course of ages has been spread over the lower slopes and made them less steep.

How can Geologists tell where Ancient Glaciers once flowed?

By deep scratches left on the rocks over which they moved. The marks were made by stones and boulders carried down with the ice. The surface of the rocks is in places worn smooth by the friction of the ice, sand, etc. In places, again, there may be moraines, which are piles of stones left by the ice when it melted. Valleys made by glaciers are U-shaped, and have steep sides and flat bottoms.

Why do Earthquakes occur?

They are due chiefly to the breaking of rocks inside the earth's crust, and to slips at places where large masses of rock are in a state of great strain. There are two great " earthquake belts " in which disturbances of the earth's crust most frequently occur. One runs from Spain through South Italy, the Caucasus and the Himalayas to China. The other includes the western coasts of North and South America, Japan and New Zealand.

What is a Volcano?

A conical mountain, with a central hole reaching down to a depth at which very great heat prevails. A volcano may begin as an opening in level ground. Eruptions of ashes, dust and lava build up the cone round the hole, which is kept open by pressure from below.

What is Pumice Stone?

A light, porous, molten rock thrown out of volcanoes. It is lava which was charged with steam at great pressure in the depths of the earth, and expanded by the steam on reaching the surface, in much the same way as dough is " raised " by the gas from baking powder. Lumps of pumice are useful for smoothing the skin of the hands. Ground into a fine powder, pumice is a very good polishing material.

What are Fossils?

The petrified remains of plants and animals which became covered with the sediments which afterwards formed rocks. Most fossils are sea-shells whose limy substance has been replaced by harder minerals deposited by water soaking through the rocks containing them.

What is a Quicksand?

A stretch of very fine sand, mixed with water and clay or chalk, which make the sand particles move over one another too easily to support the weight of men or animals. In some cases a so-called quicksand is really only wet clay with a thin layer of sand on top.

Where does the Sand on the Sea-shore come from?

It is fine particles of rocks ground up by the action of the waves or brought down into the sea by rivers and carried about by currents. In places a good deal of it comes from sandy cliffs eaten into by the sea.

Why are Pebbles on the Beach more or less rounded?

The waves are continually rolling them over one another, and making them knock off their corners against each other. The process goes on until they are more or less spherical, when they move with far less wear.

What is the Transparent Material used in the Doors of Stoves?

Mica, also miscalled talc (which is really quite another substance). It is a compound of silicates of aluminium, magnesium and iron, found in masses in the ground. Mica splits easily into thin sheets, which are quite transparent, very flexible, and able to endure great heat. At one time mica was used instead of glass in windows.

GOVERNMENT, INSTITUTIONS AND CUSTOMS

To Whom is the Title of Princess Royal given?

It is bestowed during his lifetime upon his eldest daughter by the British sovereign.

On Whom is the Title Prince of Wales conferred?

The eldest son of the reigning Sovereign of England. He takes the title of Duke of Cornwall by heritage, but the Sovereign can, if and when desired, create the Heir Apparent to the Throne Prince of Wales and Earl of Chester, by letters patent. The title is not a heritable one.

What are the Names of the Royal Palaces?

Buckingham Palace, the London residence of the sovereign since 1837; purchased by George the Third and remodelled by George the Fourth. *Kensington Palace*, in which Queen Victoria was born, at the western end of Kensington Gardens; purchased by William the Third. *St. James's Palace*, built by Henry the Eighth, the London residence of many monarchs until the nineteenth century. Little of the original building remains. *Kew Palace*, bought by George the Third. *Hampton Court Palace*, erected by Cardinal Wolsey, and presented to Henry the Eighth. It has not been used as a royal residence since George the Second's time. *Windsor Castle*, the chief royal palace and residence of the sovereign since the time of

Henry the First. *Holyrood Palace*, Edinburgh, begun about 1501, twice partly destroyed in 1544 and 1650, and rebuilt by Charles the Second.

What is Voting by Ballot?

Recording votes in a secret manner. A law was passed in 1872 making voting by ballot compulsory at all parliamentary and municipal elections. Every voter at an election is given a voting paper at the station in which he records his vote. The paper has printed on it the names of all the candidates, but nothing by which it can be identified. The voter takes his paper into a screened booth, makes a cross against the name of the person whom he supports, folds the paper up, and drops it into a sealed box. Before voting by ballot was introduced, a voter had to give his vote publicly by word of mouth, so that many voters dared not vote as they wished to vote.

What is meant by the term British Constitution?

Broadly speaking, the word Constitution means the whole body of laws and customs which bind a State together. In most countries there is a written Constitution setting forth the principles on which the country must be governed. The British Constitution is for the most part an unwritten one, *i.e.*, certain guiding principles and general rules have become accepted over a long period of years but have never been written out and passed by Parliament.

The chief principles of the British Constitution are that the country shall be governed by a Sovereign and two Houses of Parliament, with a Cabinet of ministers which is responsible to Parliament. There are, however, certain written parts of our Constitution such as the Bill of Rights and the Act of Settlement which lay down the law concerning the succession to the Throne. Then the Parliament Act of 1911 states the powers of the House of Commons and House of Lords in relation to each other. But in the main the British Constitution is based on well-established customs and principles which have been generally accepted by the people of the country.

Who preside over the House of Lords and the House of Commons?

The Lord Chancellor presides over the House of Lords, sitting on an ottoman stuffed with wool, known as the Woolsack. He must himself be a peer. The House of Commons is presided over by the Speaker, who must be an elected member of the House, and be chosen on the assembling of a new Parliament. All speeches made during a debate in the House of Commons are addressed to " Mr. Speaker," whereas in the House of Lords they are addressed to the House generally, as " My Lords " or " Your Lordships."

What is the House of Keys?

The Lower House of the Tynwald, which is the Parliament of the Isle of Man. It consists of twenty-four members, elected by the parliamentary voters of the island. The Isle of Man makes its own laws. When a Bill has been passed by the House of Keys, and by the

Governor and his Council (corresponding to our House of Lords), it is sent for the Royal Assent. Even after receiving this it does not become law till it has been read out publicly on the Tynwald Hill, near Peel, in the Manx and English languages. The House of Keys is said to be one of the most ancient law-making bodies in the world.

Where is Downing Street, and why is it important?

It is a street opening into Whitehall, London, on the west side. No. 10 Downing Street is the official residence of the Prime Minister; and No. 11 that of the Chancellor of the Exchequer. Flanking it, or near it, are the Foreign Office, the Dominions Office, the Colonial Office, and other Government offices.

Who takes first place among Commoners?

The Prime Minister is first among commoners. He takes precedence of everyone except the Royal Family, ambassadors, the two Archbishops, and the Lord High Chancellor.

What are the duties of the Chancellor of the Exchequer?

He has to manage all matters relating to the collecting and spending of public money; and to draw up every year an estimate of the cost of carrying on the public services during the next twelve months, as well as a statement of the manner in which he proposes to raise any extra money that may be needed. The estimate is called the Budget.

What is the Referendum?

A method of giving the whole body of voters in a country the final decision as to whether a law which has already been sanctioned by Parliament shall or shall not appear in the statute book. The voter must write either " Yes " or " No " on his voting paper. The referendum has never yet been used in Britain; but in 1898 the federation of the Australian colonies into the Australian Commonwealth was brought about by referendum in every colony, and in 1910 the referendum was used in Natal on the question of that country entering the Union of South Africa. In Switzerland the constitution demands that all bills of a certain kind must be submitted to a referendum.

How often is a Census of the Population taken?

Once every ten years, in Britain and most other countries. Our censuses come in the first year of each decade—1901, 1911, 1921, 1931 and 1951, but not in 1941 because of the World War.

When was a Census first taken in Britain?

In 1801, in England and Scotland; and in 1813, in Ireland.

How is a Census taken?

The whole country is divided for census purposes into about 1,800 areas, each under a local census officer. This official subdivides his area into districts, each containing about the same number of houses, and appoints an enumerator to each. Every enumerator visits every house in his district and leaves a schedule with every head of a family, to be filled up on

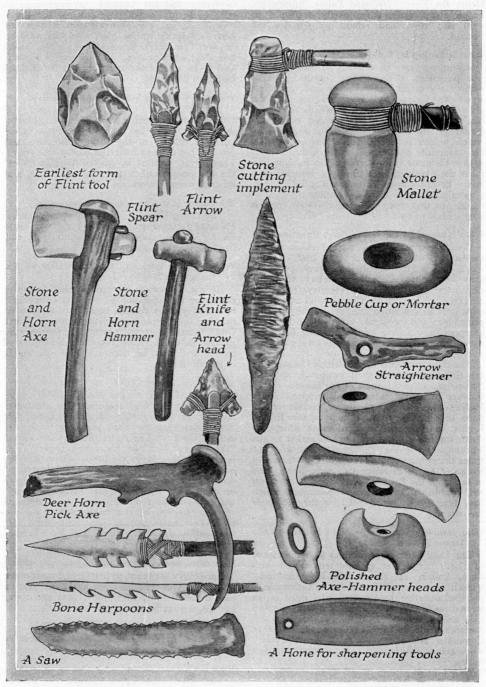

Earliest form
of Flint tool

Flint
Spear

Flint
Arrow

Stone
cutting
implement

Stone
Mallet

Stone
and
Horn
Axe

Stone
and
Horn
Hammer

Flint
Knife
and
Arrow
head

Pebble Cup or Mortar

Arrow
Straightener

Deer Horn
Pick Axe

Polished
Axe-Hammer heads

Bone Harpoons

A Saw

A Hone for sharpening tools

Specially drawn for this work.

These are representations of weapons and tools used by prehistoric men of the *Stone Age* (see p. 359) to whom the smelting and working of metals were unknown. The materials used were stone (especially flint) and bone. The improvement in workmanship that the lapse of time brought with it becomes evident when one compares the roughly-chipped objects at the top of the picture with the beautifully finished axe-hammer heads, the shaping of which by patient rubbing must have entailed an enormous amount of labour. Many of our museums contain collections of objects of this kind, which are constantly being unearthed.

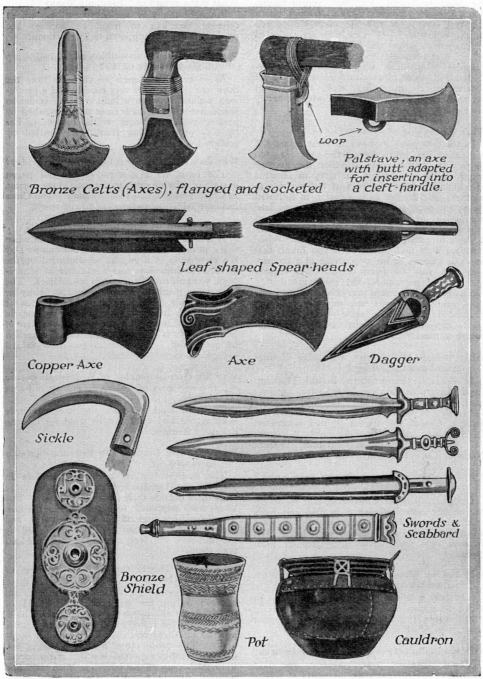

Bronze Celts (Axes), flanged and socketed

Palstave, an axe with butt adapted for inserting into a cleft handle.

LOOP

Leaf-shaped Spear-heads

Copper Axe   Axe   Dagger

Sickle

Swords & Scabbard

Bronze Shield

Pot   Cauldron

Specially drawn for this work.

The first metal to replace stone and bone was bronze. We speak of the period during which bronze was used for weapons and tools as the *Bronze Age* (see p. 359) of a country. Since metal could be beaten into any desired shape, design and workmanship became much more elaborate, as these specimens prove. The use of bronze probably spread westwards from Asia, and is believed by some authorities to have been introduced by a race of horsemen. The Britons of, and probably long before, Cæsar's time, far from being mere skin-clad savages, were skilled workers in this metal.

the day appointed for the census-taking. When the day arrives certain particulars about everyone staying in a house must be entered on the schedule. The schedules are collected by the enumerators and returned to the local officer, who prepares, from the figures received, statistics which are sent to the Registrar-General, in whose office all the facts and figures contributed by the many areas are brought together, and the results for the whole country are got out.

What is the value of a Census?

In the first place it shows to what extent the population has grown during the preceding ten years. It also reveals: whether the average length of life is increasing or not; movements of population from one part of the country to another; the density of population in different areas; the numbers of people engaged in various occupations or in none; and a whole host of other important facts which it would be very difficult to gather in any other manner. When censuses were first instituted it was found that previous guesses at the population of a country had been very far from correct. As regards the total of population, the great value of a census is that it is taken everywhere at the same time, and so prevents any one person being counted in more than once—which certainly would happen in very many cases if any other course were adopted.

What British Universities are there besides Oxford and Cambridge?

In England: Birmingham, Bristol, Durham, Leeds, Liverpool, London, Manchester, Nottingham, Reading, Sheffield. In Wales: The University of Wales (Colleges at Aberystwyth, Bangor, Cardiff and Swansea), and Lampeter. In Scotland: Aberdeen, Edinburgh, Glasgow, St. Andrews. In Ireland: Belfast, Dublin, National (Colleges at Cork, Dublin and Galway).

Why are there Buttons on the sleeves of a man's coat?

Originally they were fitted so that he might button his cuffs back when he did any work that might soil them. That was in the days when cuffs were ornamented with lace. The buttons now are merely decorative in most cases.

Why has the Ribbon on a man's hat got a Bow in it on the left side?

The bow is probably a relic of the plume or other decoration once worn on the left side of a hat, where it was out of the way of the right hand, with which the hat would be taken off.

Why has a tail-coat got two Buttons at the back?

The buttons are a survival from the days when a man buttoned back the skirts of a long coat to make riding or walking easier.

What is the purpose of the Sporran worn with Highland dress?

The sporran is an ornamental pocket or pouch. As there is no room in a kilt for a pocket, a separate one has to be provided.

What is the origin of " Touching Wood "?

Probably the very ancient pagan custom of offering sacrifices to trees, to appease the spirits which were supposed to live in them.

Why does a Gentleman walking with a Lady keep on the kerb side of her?

As an act of politeness which dates from the days when roads were very muddy and a gentleman walked between a lady and the traffic to shield her and her dress from being splashed by passing vehicles. Being on the outside of her he also protected her from being jostled by passers-by.

Why do we eat Hot Cross Buns on Good Friday?

The buns are a survival of the old pagan custom of offering cakes to the gods in the spring, in which season Good Friday comes. The Cross has been added as a symbol of Christianity.

What is meant by " Beating the Bounds "?

It is an old custom dating back to times when there were no parish maps. On Ascension Day the clergyman of a parish, accompanied by the clerk, churchwardens and a number of schoolboys, went all round the parish boundaries. The boys were made to strike them with withy or willow wands, and themselves were beaten at places which it was most important to keep in mind. In this way an accurate knowledge of boundaries was handed down from generation to generation. The custom has now ceased except in a very few places.

Why are circular patches of Whitewash put on the windows of houses in course of being built?

To warn workmen that the windows have been glazed and must not be used for passing materials through.

Why are Three Brass or Gilt Balls the sign of a pawnbroker?

The earliest bankers and moneylenders in England, the Lombards from Italy, hung three large discs outside their places of business. The discs were supposed to represent gold coins. The Lombards presently left the country, and the discs, changed into balls, were adopted by pawnbrokers, who lend money on goods pledged with them.

Why is the Thistle the National Emblem of Scotland?

If legend is to be trusted, the thistle was adopted during the reign of Malcolm II of Scotland, for the following reason: The Danes had invaded the country and designed to capture a castle in Aberdeenshire. They attacked it by night. The castle moat, instead of being full of water, as they expected, was dry and occupied by a thick crop of thistles. The men who first plunged into it uttered cries of pain which aroused the Scots, and the invaders were beaten off.

What is the Royal Standard?

The flag of the British Sovereign. It is divided into four quarters, in two of which three golden lions of England appear on a red ground; in one the red lion of Scotland on a yellow (gold) ground; and in one the yellow harp of Ireland on a blue ground. The flag is flown over the building or ship in which the Sovereign resides. No other person has the right to fly it even for decorative purposes.

Which is the British National Flag?

The Union Jack. It is made up of three flags placed one on top of the other. These three flags are the upright red cross of St. George (England) on a white ground; the cornerwise white cross of St. Andrew (Scotland) on a blue ground; and the cornerwise red cross of St. Patrick (Ireland) on a white ground.

What are the White Ensign, Blue Ensign and Red Ensign?

They are flags with a white, blue and red ground respectively, and a Union Jack in the upper quarter next the mast. The White Ensign, which has St. George's cross on it, is flown by the ships of the Royal Navy ; the Blue Ensign by vessels of the Royal Naval Reserve, Government vessels, and Royal yacht clubs; and the Red Ensign (also called the " Red Duster ") by the ships of the British merchant service.

Which is the National Flag of the United States?

The " Stars and Stripes," also called " Old Glory." The ground of the flag is seven red stripes alternating with six white stripes, running lengthwise. These represent the original thirteen States of the Union of 1777. In the top inner corner there are as many white stars on a blue ground as there are States in the Union to-day.

HISTORY AND INTERNATIONAL AFFAIRS

How long has Man lived on the Earth?

It is certain that he has inhabited the globe for half a million years at least, and that his half-ape ancestors lived long before man attained to true form and development. There have been discovered near Peking, in China, the skulls of half-ape, half-human beings which must have lived from 750,000 to 1,000,000 years ago. The teeth and front part of the skulls are those of a human being, though the jaw is ape-like. Many scientists believe that in this find they have discovered the " missing link "—the object of eighty years' search—connecting the ape with the intelligent human being of later ages.

What are Lake Dwellings?

Huts or houses built on platforms supported by piles driven in shallow water near the edge of a lake or river. Dwellings of this kind may still be seen in Borneo, New Guinea and Celebes. During the Stone and Bronze Ages many such dwellings were erected by prehistoric man in Switzerland, Italy and Britain. The Irish used them as late as the reign of James the First. They gave security against wild animals and other foes. In many cases they were connected with the shore by bridges. The remains of such dwellings have been found in the marshes round Glastonbury, in Somerset, which once contained large lakes.

What is meant by Stone Age and Bronze Age?

That period in the history of a race during which stone or bronze was used for making weapons, tools and utensils. The Bronze Age followed the Stone Age, and preceded the Iron Age. Some races were in their Bronze Age when others had not yet emerged from the Stone Age of weapons and tools made from flints; and when others, again, had already learned how to smelt and use iron.

What Race of People still Surviving are Regarded as belonging to the Stone Age?

The Australian Aborigines are probably thousands of years older than any other race in existence. Until comparatively modern times Australia was an unknown land and these native people had lived for many centuries untouched by conquest or by any other circumstances to change their mode of life. They never learned to work metals at all and their cutting instruments were of stone, roughly ground. They wandered in groups or tribes from place to place, hunting and fishing for sustenance. Despite the coming of civilisation when the white men discovered and began to settle in Australia, they still remain a primitive Stone Age people, a legacy from the world of thousands of years ago.

What are Dolmens and Cromlechs?

Both words mean very much the same thing and are given to the prehistoric stone structures which mark the burial mounds of people who lived and died in that far-off period of human history known as the Stone Age. There are numerous structures of this kind in many countries of Europe. In England one of the best-known dolmens is Kit's Coty House, near Aylesford in Kent, while others exist in Devonshire, Cornwall and Anglesey as well as in Scotland. There are over 700 in Ireland and very many in France.

Where was Troy, and when was it beseiged?

Excavations made in a mound at Hissarlik, in Asia Minor, a few miles south of the western entrance to the Dardanelles, have revealed the position of Troy, or Ilium, as it was also called by the ancients. Several cities and settlements were built at different periods on the same site, including a very old town of considerable size, dating back to 2500 B.C. This was destroyed and rebuilt more than once. A thousand years or so later another and much larger city, with huge walls and towers, was reared, and this was probably the Troy that underwent the siege that became the subject of Homer's " Iliad." It is impossible to fix the date of the siege, or to distinguish legends about it from historical facts, but that the Greeks actually did besiege and capture Troy can hardly be doubted.

Who were the Leaders of the Greeks against Troy, according to Homer's Account?

Agamemnon, Achilles, Ajax, Diomedes Patroclus and Ulysses.

Who led the Defence of Troy?

Hector, Æneas, Helenus, Sarpedon, Glaucus, Paris and Polydamas.

What is the History of Cleopatra's Needle?

The Needle was cut, as a single block of red granite weighing about 186 tons, and measuring 68½ feet in length, in a quarry in Upper Egypt, about 3,500 years ago. It was floated down the Nile and set up with a sister Needle at Heliopolis, where it remained till 23 B.C., when the Emperor Augustus had it removed to Alexandria. Fifteen hundred years later it fell prostrate without suffering any damage. It was presented to England by a famous Pasha of Egypt, Mehemet Ali, in 1819, but no attempt to remove it was made until 1877, when it was encased in wooden baulks, covered with iron plates to form a water-tight cylinder. Having been rolled into the sea, the cylinder was taken in tow for England. In the Bay of Biscay it had to be cast adrift in a storm, and it was believed to have sunk, but soon afterwards it was found floating and brought into Vigo Harbour. Thence it was towed safely to the Thames and opened, for the Needle to be hauled out and erected on the Victoria Embankment. The Needle was lowered into place on September 12th, 1878. Its name is misleading, as Queen Cleopatra had no connection with its history.

What are the most famous Roman Remains in Britain?

Hadrian's Wall, running from Wallsend-on-Tyne to Bowness on the Solway Firth; the famous baths at Bath, Somerset; and the old town of Silchester (Calleva), in Hampshire, seven miles north of Basingstoke. As regards the last, the walls are still standing in a more or less ruinous condition for a large part of the circuit, and the whole area inside them has been systematically explored and mapped.

What were the Seven Wonders of the Ancient World?

(1) The Pyramids of Egypt.
(2) The Temple of Diana at Ephesus, said to have been supported on 127 columns 60 feet high.
(3) The Colossus at Rhodes. This was a bronze statue of Apollo, 120 feet high, which stood on one side of the entrance to the harbour.
(4) The statue of Zeus (Jupiter) at Olympia, in Greece, sculptured by Pheidias, the most famous of ancient sculptors, in ivory and gold.
(5) The walls and hanging (terraced) gardens of Babylon, said to have been made for the Queen Semiramis.
(6) The Mausoleum at Helicarnassus, in Asia Minor. This was a magnificent tomb built for Mausolus, King of Caria, by his Queen Artemisia.
(7) The Pharos or lighthouse at Alexandria. It was of white marble and the flames of the fire kindled on the top were said to be visible 100 miles away.

How did we get the Stories about King Arthur?

In the eighth century a writer named Nennius produced a " History of the Britons," written in Latin. This contained many stories about Arthur and his doings, and on it was based the " Chronicles of the British Kings," written by Geoffrey of Gloucester about 1135. The " Chronicles " were translated from the original Latin into French by Wace in 1150, and back into English by the monk Layamon in 1205. At each step additions were made as fancy prompted. During the Middle Ages French romances on the Arthurian legends were popular. In Wales, stories about Arthur formed part of the " Mabinogion," a series of Welsh legends. The question as to whether King Arthur was or was not an historical personage arises. It is more likely than not that a British chief of that name really existed and fought against the Saxons. But all the stories about the Round Table and the Knights are evidently mere legend, as " knights " of the type of the Arthurian romance did not exist till centuries after the times of British Arthur himself.

What is the Origin of the White Horses found carved on the surface of some English chalk hills?

Probably that the horse was the national emblem of the Saxons, as the lion is now of England, and the eagle of the United States. Perhaps they were monuments of victories. It will be remembered that the leaders of the Saxon invasion of England were named Hengist and Horsa, both of which words mean horse. The most famous, and perhaps the oldest, is that on the Berkshire Downs, near the old British camp, Uffington Castle. It has been " scored," or cleaned, many times, to prevent its disappearance.

Why was King Alfred called Alfred the Great?

One cannot answer this question better than by reproducing the inscription on the pedestal supporting the statue of the great King which was set up in 1877 at Wantage, Berkshire, Alfred's birthplace:

Alfred found learning dead,
  And he restored it;
Education neglected,
  And he revived it;
The laws powerless,
  And he gave them force;
The Church debased,
  And he raised it;
The land ravaged by a fearful enemy,
  From which he delivered it.

One may add that Alfred found Britain without a navy, and he created one; and that historians agree in regarding him as the greatest king that ever ruled in England.

What was Danegeld?

Money raised by taxation during the reign of Ethelred the Unready (978–1016) to bribe the Danes not to attack England. The Danes took the money, but returned to get more as soon as it was spent.

What is meant by the Middle Ages?

The period of European history lasting from near the end of the fifth century to the end of the fifteenth century—rather more than 1,000 years in all. It opened with the invasion of Western Europe by hordes of barbarians and the break-up of Roman civilisation, and ended at the time of the discovery of the New World.

THE RED MEN OF AMERICA

Mondiale

When Christopher Columbus landed in America in 1492 he believed that he had reached India. The islands where he first set foot in the New World became known as the West Indies, while the native people on the mainland were regarded as Indians. Red Indians or Redskins became their popular name and attempts to give them more correct names have not been successful. Our photograph shows a typical North American Indian wearing the traditional feather headdress of his race.

AT HOME, AND ON AN OFFICIAL VISIT

E.N.A.

Today the Red Indians live in special areas or reservations, both in Canada and the United States. Here the descendants of the original people of North America sometimes live their own lives much as they did when Columbus first discovered them. Our photograph shows a group of Blackfeet Indians outside their tent in one of the Indian reservations in the Glacier National Park, Montana, U.S.A.

Red Indians have their homes in all parts of North America, keeping to their different tribes and always preserving the traditions and customs of their forefathers. The governments of North America have made no attempt to change these customs and representatives of the Indians often attend the white men's functions. Here we see various types of Indians in their national dress photographed during an official ceremony.

BIG CHIEFS AND THEIR PEOPLE

The chiefs of the different tribes have considerable powers, which are exercised wisely. In this photograph is seen an old chief of the well-known Blackfeet Indians of Wyoming, U.S.A.

Great hunters, whether in their canoes, on foot, or on horseback, the Redskins still preserve many of their old methods. Here we see an Apache Indian, on horseback, in the reservation in Arizona, U.S.A.

Photos: E.N.A.

In this photograph are seen two more Indian chiefs, dressed in full regalia for some important ceremonial occasion. They belong to the Yakima tribe, living in the reservation in Washington State, U.S.A.

This photograph was taken in one of the Indian reservations in Canada and shows a Cree Indian mother with her small child, borne in the customary fashion in a carrier round the mother's shoulders.

THE SQUAW AND THE TWO PAPOOSES

The great reservations in which the Red Indians now live are truly the wide open spaces, as this photograph shows. Here we see an Apache squaw (married woman) travelling through the reservation in Arizona.

In this photograph are seen two papooses of the Chippewa or Ojibway tribe. Papoose is the Indian name for baby, used especially when the child is fixed to a board so that it can be carried safely.

Photo: E.N.A.

Here we have another typical scene on an Indian reservation. On the right is seen the "hogan," or house, in which some of the members of the tribe make their home. There is not the same need today for hunting expeditions now that flocks of sheep can be kept. This photograph of a Navajo encampment was taken in the great Indian reservation in Arizona, U.S.A.

LEGACIES OF LONG AGO

Polar Photos.

The *Australian Aborigines* (see p. 359) probably first reached the southern continent many thousands of years ago and, untouched by the struggles in other continents, have remained in their primitive state through the centuries. They still belong to the Stone Age and are the "oldest inhabitants" of all other races in existence. The picture shows young Aborigines with their *gunyah*, or bark shelter.

The British Travel and Holidays Association.

This *Dolmen* (see p. 359) or Cromlech may be seen near Dromara in Northern Ireland. Like other similar structures, it belongs to the Stone Age and was probably part of the central chamber of a burial mound which, in the course of time, has been bared of its protecting earth. Dolmens can be found in many parts of the British Isles and there are also large numbers in Brittany.

Who was Sir John Mandeville?

The author of a famous book of travels originally written in French or Latin, and translated into English in or about 1364. In his preface the writer says that he is an Englishman, born at St. Albans in 1300. But it is more probable that he was a Frenchman. In any case, his " Adventures " was the first book of travels—at least of any note—to appear in our language. The book describes Sir John's experiences and the sights seen by him in Turkey, Palestine, Arabia, Egypt, India and the East Indies. There is good reason to think that the writer never visited many of the countries on his list; and it is certain that he never saw the dog-headed men, double-headed geese, white lions, and many other wonders with which he claims to have met. Much of the book was doubtless borrowed from earlier writings, by other hands. Nevertheless, the " Adventures " make very interesting reading.

What was the Black Death?

A terrible plague which ravaged Europe during the middle part of the fourteenth century. It reached England from France in 1348, during the reign of Edward the Third, and swept off from a third to a half of the population of the country. The total number of victims in Europe is estimated at between 20 million and 25 million. The Black Death got its name from the black spots which appeared on the skin of a person stricken by it. The bubonic plague which breaks out at intervals in various parts of Asia is probably the same disease under another name.

What are the Cinque Ports?

The towns of Hastings, Winchelsea and Rye on the Sussex coast, and those of Romney, Hythe, Dover and Sandwich on the coast of Kent. They were all at one time ports, but the retreat of the sea has left Winchelsea, Rye, Romney and Sandwich " high and dry." The title means " The Five Ports," and originally there were only five in the group, Winchelsea and Rye not having been added to the number until the thirteenth century. So far back as Anglo-Saxon times the Cinque Ports enjoyed certain privileges, such as freedom from taxation, and the right to levy tolls, try criminal cases within their own boundaries, and hold a local parliament. In return for these they had, until about the beginning of the sixteenth century, to furnish all the ships and sailors needed to protect the coast from invasion by sea. Some traces of the old privileges remain, and the once important office of Lord Warden of the Cinque Ports is still in existence.

Who were the Friars?

Mendicant or " begging " orders of clergy, founded in the Middle Ages. Though they had convents as headquarters, they differed from monks in not being cloistered or confined. They were sent out to preach, teach and heal the sick in streets and country lanes, and had to live on alms and food given them. The most famous of the orders are: the Dominicans or Black Friars, founded by St. Dominic in 1216; the Franciscans or Grey Friars, founded by St. Francis of Assisi in 1209; the Carmelites or White Friars, whose origin is somewhat doubtful, and the Augustinian or Austin Friars, added by Pope Alexander the Fourth in 1256. Before the Reformation they were all represented in London, where Blackfriars, Whitefriars Street, Carmelite Street and Austin Friars still recall the sites on which their convents stood.

What were the Stocks and the Pillory?

Instruments of punishment. At one time every town and village had its stocks, in which persons guilty of begging, vagrancy, and other small offences were confined. They consisted of two horizontal boards on edge, one above the other. The bottom one was fixed and the top one movable. Holes were cut where they touched, half in each, and large enough to take a man's ankles. A person condemned to the stocks sat on the ground or on a seat behind them, imprisoned by the feet as long as the two boards were locked together. While in this position he was liable to be pelted by the boys and loafers of the place. The stocks went out of use in the latter part of last century, but a good number still survive as curiosities. They are a very old invention, for mention is made of them four times in the Bible. The pillory was similar in principle to the stocks, but it was mounted on a post, and had three holes in it, a large central hole for the neck and a smaller hole on each side for the wrists. A person " in the pillory " had to stand; and, as his hands were held fast, he could not protect himself from missiles. It was used to punish dishonesty, sedition and perjury, and was not done away with in England till 1837.

Who was William Tell?

The national hero of Switzerland. What we know of him is legendary, and it must be confessed that the famous story of his shooting an apple off the head of his son has a strong family resemblance to stories told about other heroes in other countries. It is even very doubtful whether any person of this name existed at the time (1307) when the apple-shooting incident is supposed to have taken place.

Who was John Huss?

The great religious reformer of Bohemia, born about 1370. While the head of Prague University he studied the writings of the English reformer, John Wycliffe, and in his preaching uttered opinions which got him into trouble with the authorities of the Church. In 1414 he was ordered to attend a Church Council at Constance, and was promised protection by the Emperor. But on his arrival he was imprisoned and tried, and condemned to death as a heretic. He was burned at the stake on July 6th, 1415. After his death the Hussites, supporters of the movement which he had set on foot, fought fiercely against the German supporters of the Pope; and the Hussite Wars, as they were called, did not end till 1436, when the two parties came to terms.

What Effect did the adoption of Coal as Fuel have on the Population of England?

It caused a great movement of people northwards into Lancashire, Yorkshire, Derbyshire and Staffordshire, where large manufacturing towns sprang up near the coalfields. Before the eighteenth century the greater part of England's population lived to the east of a straight line drawn from Hull to Southampton, engaged in agriculture and industries, such as iron-smelting, which used wood as fuel. When the southern forests became exhausted and the northern coalfields were opened up, industry went northwards, taking hundreds of thousands of people with it.

Who was the Admirable Crichton?

A Scotsman, James Crichton, born in 1560. He lived only twenty-two years, but before his death he had made a great name for himself as a scholar, poet, swordsman and speaker of foreign languages. Nowadays if a person is spoken of as an Admirable Crichton it means that he excels in a number of bodily and mental accomplishments.

Where was King Charles the First Beheaded?

On a scaffold erected on the east side of White-hall, London, outside the Whitehall Banqueting Hall, which is now part of the Royal United Service Institution. A hole was cut in the wall of the hall—then part of a Royal Palace—through which Charles stepped to the scaffold.

Who besides Samuel Pepys kept a Famous Diary?

John Evelyn (1620–1706), a contemporary of Pepys. He began his diary when only eleven years old, and kept it up till his death. Like Pepys, he wrote it merely to please himself, and this makes it all the more valuable, since it contains many interesting statements which probably would not have got into it had its author written for publication. As an historical document, as well as for the light which it throws on the manners of the day, Evelyn's diary is a national treasure.

What were the Seven Weeks' War, the Seven Years' War, the Thirty Years' War and the Hundred Years' War?

The Seven Weeks' War was fought in 1866 between Prussia and Austria, and ended in the crushing defeat of Austria at Sadowa on July 3rd. The Seven Years' War was one between the same countries for the possession of Silesia. It lasted from 1756 to 1763, and resulted in favour of Germany. The Thirty Years' War broke out in Germany in 1618, between the Protestant and Catholic parties, and lasted till 1648. In 1630 the Swedes intervened, under Gustavus Adolphus, on the side of the Protestants; and after that king's death at Lutzen, in 1632, the French aided them in crushing the German Emperor. This made France the leading military power in Europe. The Hundred Years' War was really a series of wars between England and France during the period 1338 to 1453. The chief battles in it were Crécy (1346), Poitiers (1356) and Agincourt (1415). From 1428 onwards the English steadily lost ground, and when the war ended they held Calais only.

Which were the Great Wars of the last Hundred Years?

The Crimean War, 1854–1856 (*England,* France and Turkey v. Russia); the American Civil War, 1861–1865 (*Northern States v.* Southern States); the Franco-German War, 1870–1871 (France v. *Germany*); the Russo-Turkish War, 1877–1878 (*Russia v.* Turkey); the Boer War, 1899–1902 (*Britain v.* Transvaal and Orange Free State); the Russo-Japanese War, 1904–1905 (Russia v. *Japan*); the First Balkan War, 1912–1913 (*Serbia, Greece, Bulgaria and Montenegro v.* Turkey); the Great War (now generally referred to as " the First World War "), 1914–1918 (Germany, Austria, Bulgaria and Turkey v. *France, Russia, Belgium, British Empire, Italy, Serbia, Rumania, Greece, Portugal, the United States and Japan*). The winning side in each war is indicated by italics. The Second World War lasted from September, 1939, to August, 1945.

Who were the Moss-troopers?

Bands of freebooters or robbers who haunted the border land between England and Scotland in the seventeenth century, before the two countries were united. Those on either side crossed the border to ravage property on the other side. They got their name from the mosses, or bogs, among which they found refuge.

Why were Cromwell's Soldiers called Round-heads?

Because they had their hair cut close to the head, which made them very different in appearance from the Cavaliers, whose hair was worn very long.

Who was Andreas Hofer?

A Tyrolese innkeeper who, when the Tyrol was transferred from Austria to Bavaria by Napoleon in 1805, headed a revolt and drove the Bavarians out of the country; and afterwards defeated combined Bavarian and French forces, freeing his country completely. But in 1810 he was betrayed by some of his most trusted followers, captured by the French, and executed by Napoleon's order.

What was the South Sea Bubble?

In 1719 a company, called the South Sea Company, made an offer to the Government to take over a large part of the National Debt. In return it was given exclusive rights of trading on the coasts of South America and with the Pacific Islands. The shares of the company rose to ten times their original value, and this caused the public to be attacked by a mania of speculation. Companies were floated by the hundred, and money was subscribed to them blindly. The natural result was a terrible financial crash, which ruined thousands of people. The South Sea Bubble, as the original scheme and its many imitations were termed, had burst.

Who are the Quakers?

Members of the Society of Friends, founded in the seventeenth century by George Fox and his adherents. They held that baptism and the Lord's Supper were not necessary to salvation; that there need be no ordained ministry, as any man or woman whom the spirit moved to do so should be allowed to preach; and that worship in public should be silent for the most part. The Quakers are opposed to war and the taking of oaths; and they hold strongly that religious principles should guide the actions of everyday life. Though they are now but a small sect, numbering only about 20,000 in Great Britain and Ireland, their record is a very fine one. The most famous of their old meeting-houses is Jordans near Beaconsfield, in Buckinghamshire, in the graveyard of which lies William Penn, the founder of Pennsylvania.

Why did Britain become the leading Manufacturing Country in the Nineteenth Century?

In the first place, she was exceptionally rich in iron and coal, conveniently close together. Second, the steam engine was developed in England before other countries. Third, the Napoleonic wars left her much less exhausted than the Continental nations, and undisputed mistress of the seas, with large fleets of merchant ships able to trade with all parts of the world.

What was the Industrial Revolution?

Industrial Revolution is the name given to all the amazingly rapid changes that befell Britain from about 1760 onwards, giving her great factories, new towns, railways, canals and good roads. A number of circumstances combined to bring this about, and chief among these were: new inventions including cotton-spinning machinery and steam engines; the extended use of coal and iron which, in Britain, were found close together; the sudden growth of the population and the spread of the factory system with what were at that time terrible conditions of work and appallingly low wages. Hand in hand with the Industrial Revolution went the Agricultural Revolution, for the movement of the people to the industrial towns and the increase in population demanded new methods of farming if everyone was to be fed. The small yeoman farmers began to disappear as, more and more, large farms became the rule. New crops and methods were introduced by such men as " turnip Townshend " and Coke, while others such as Robert Bakewell improved English stock-breeding.

When and where was British Soil last invaded?

In February, 1797, at Fishguard, in Pembrokeshire. A French force, called the " Black Legion," landed in Fishguard Bay. The first Baron Cawdor collected a troop of yeomanry, 300 men of the local militia, and an ill-armed mob of miners and peasants, to oppose the enemy who, having been deserted by the ships which brought them, surrendered without a blow. It is said that their surrender was hastened by the appearance of a large number of Welsh women in their red cloaks, which were mistaken by the French for the tunics of soldiers.

Who were the Jacobins and the Jacobites?

The *Jacobins* were the members of a political party formed in France in 1791, during the French Revolution. Under Robespierre, Danton, Marat and other leaders they were responsible for the massacres which took place during the Reign of Terror. In 1794, after the death of Robespierre, their power ceased. The *Jacobites* were the supporters of James the Second after he had been driven from the throne

into exile, and of his son, James, the " Old Pretender," and of his grandson, " Bonnie Prince Charlie," the " Young Pretender." Many of them were executed or banished after the unsuccessful rebellions of 1715 and 1745. The word Jacobite is derived from Jacobus, the Latin form of James.

Who were the Chartists?

Supporters of a popular movement in favour of sweeping political reforms which lasted from 1832 to 1848. Their demands were set out in a document called the People's Charter. Petitions were presented to the House of Commons, but were refused consideration. Riots broke out, and in 1848 a large number of Chartists gathered near London to march to the Houses of Parliament with a monster petition, bearing, so they claimed, over six million signatures. Government buildings were fortified and nearly 200,000 special constables enrolled because violence from the Chartists was expected. But the procession never took place, and the movement soon afterwards died out.

When were Postage Stamps first used?

In 1840, the year in which the penny post was introduced in the United Kingdom. The first stamps were the penny black, printed in sheets which had to be cut up with scissors.

Who began the building of Windsor Castle?

William the Conqueror, who built a round tower on the central mound now crowned by the more modern Round Tower of Edward the Third. This mound was doubtless the site of a fortress of much earlier date, and legend connects it with King Arthur. Under William the First the castle was a stronghold and nothing more. Henry the First made it a palace; Henry the Third enlarged and strengthened the fortifications; and millions of pounds were spent on additions by his successors.

When were the present Houses of Parliament built?

The foundation stone was laid in 1840. The House of Lords came into use in 1847, and the House of Commons in 1852, but construction was not completed till 1857, by which time £3,000,000 had been spent on the work. The buildings cover an area of 8 acres, and their river face is 313 yards. The House of Commons was almost completely destroyed by air attack during the last war but has been rebuilt, the new House being opened by King George VI on October 26th, 1950.

What are the Livery Companies of London?

They are corporations which had their beginnings in the old trade guilds of London. They now have little to do with trade. The leading men of the Companies, called the liverymen, elect the Lord Mayor and Sheriffs of London. The income of the Companies is spent mostly on education and charitable objects. There are now about eighty companies, the twelve most important of which are the Mercers, Grocers, Drapers, Fishmongers, Goldsmiths, Skinners, Merchant Taylors, Haberdashers, Salters, Ironmongers, Vintners and Cloth-

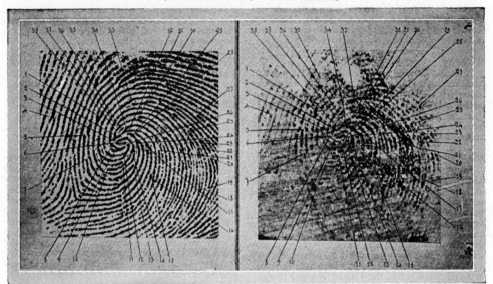

On the left is the finger-print of a criminal taken by the police and entered in their records. On the right is a photograph of a finger-mark found afterwards on a table. A comparison of this with the recorded print left no doubt as to the identity of the owner of the finger.

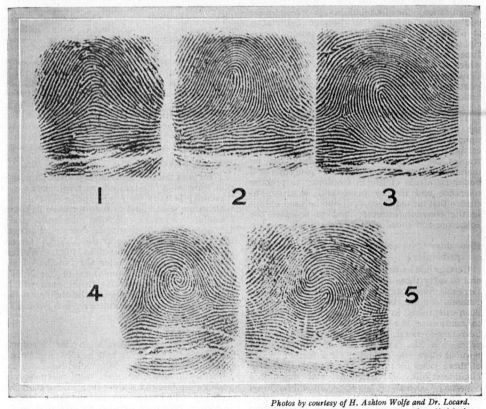

Photos by courtesy of H. Ashton Wolfe and Dr. Locard.

These are examples of the five groups into which all *finger-prints* (see p. 367) may be divided. In the first four there is a nucleus or centre round which the lines are grouped; most clearly in No. 4. In No. 5 there are two distinct centres. No one of these prints could possibly be mistaken for another.

workers. Among the lesser companies are the Bowyers, Fletchers (arrow-makers), Loriners (bridle and spurmakers), Cordwainers (shoemakers and Upholders (upholsterers).

Who was Father Damien?

A heroic Belgian priest who, in 1873, went to Molokai, one of the Hawaiian Islands, to devote himself to the service of the lepers there. For twelve years he escaped the terrible disease, and then he was attacked by it. Carrying on his labours to the last, he died in 1888, leaving behind him a name which will live for ever.

What was the League of Nations?

An alliance of most of the nations of the world which aimed at maintaining peace between nations and at reducing armaments. It was established under the Treaty of Versailles in 1919, which ended the War of 1914–18; and its first meeting was held in 1920. All nations that had signed the Covenant of the League bound themselves to submit any disputes among themselves to the Council of the League, which had its headquarters at Geneva. It ceased to exist in April, 1946, when the United Nations Organisation (UNO) took over its work.

What is UNO and when was it founded?

The initials stand for the United Nations Organisation, the foundations of which were laid at the Conference of Foreign Secretaries at Moscow in 1943. Later, the general principles were discussed at San Francisco in April–June, 1945, when a charter was drawn up to which the fifty Allied Nations present gave their signature. The Organisation came formally into existence on October 24th, 1945, when fifty-one nations became members. Others have been admitted to membership since then.

The Charter asserts its main purposes to be the prevention of the scourge of war and to uphold the fundamental human rights; to establish conditions under which justice and respect for obligations under treaties can be maintained; to promote social progress and better standards of life in freedom; to practise tolerance and live in peace and security; to ensure that armed force shall not be used except in the common interest; and to promote the economic and social advancement of all peoples.

How does UNO endeavour to carry out these principles?

Certain bodies have been set up to make plans and to carry them out under the main body, the General Assembly, of which all the United Nations are members. The headquarters have been established in New York with a Secretariat to administer the affairs of UNO. The first Secretary-General, who is appointed for five years, was Mr. Trygve Lie, of Norway. His term of office was extended for a further period of three years in 1950. Subsequently Mr. Dag Hammarskjöld, of Sweden, was appointed Secretary-General. A Security Council has been set up to maintain peace and security. The Economic and Social Council is investigating health, social, economic and educational problems, while the Trusteeship Council will safeguard the interests of territories which are not self-governing. There is also an International Court of Justice, which has its seat at the Hague, and this consists of fifteen judges elected by the Security Council and the General Assembly.

Other bodies acting under UNO include UNESCO (United Nations Educational, Scientific and Cultural Organisation); FAO (Food and Agriculture Organisation of the United Nations); IRO (International Refugee Organisation); WHO (World Health Organisation), and the International Labour Office which is now a United Nations agency.

What is the Council of Europe?

This important body met for the first time in August, 1949. It has been set up by the nations of Western Europe, who believe that there is need " of a closer unity between all like-minded countries of Europe," and affirm their devotion to the spiritual " and moral values which are the common heritage of their peoples and the true source of individual freedom, political liberty and the rule of law." The aim of the Council is to achieve a greater unity between its member nations and to facilitate their economic and social progress.

The Council of Europe consists of (a) a Committee formed by the Foreign Ministers of the countries concerned and (b) a Consultative Assembly formed by an agreed number of representatives from each State appointed as each Government shall decide. Questions of defence are ruled out from discussion. Other subjects for discussion by the Assembly must be approved by the Committee of Ministers.

The countries originally forming the Council were Belgium, Denmark, France, the Irish Republic, Italy, Luxemburg, the Netherlands, Norway, Sweden and the United Kingdom. Since 1949, the following countries and territories have joined the Council: Turkey, Greece, Iceland, the Saar (an associate member), and the German Federal Republic (West Germany). The Council has its headquarters at Strasbourg.

What is NATO?

NATO is the North Atlantic Treaty Organisation, formed by certain of the free nations as a " security league " in April, 1949. The nations which then subscribed to the pact were Belgium, Canada, Denmark, France, Iceland, Italy, Luxemburg, the Netherlands, Norway, Portugal, the United Kingdom, and the U.S.A. Greece and Turkey were admitted in 1952. Western Germany in 1955. Under the North Atlantic Pact, an armed attack on one of the NATO countries in Europe or North America will be considered as an attack against them all, requiring action by each of the countries. NATO has its headquarters in Paris.

What is OEEC?

OEEC is the Organisation for European Economic Co-operation and had its origins in a speech made by Mr. Marshall, the American Secretary of State, in June, 1947, when he suggested that America should help in the economic recovery of Europe (Marshall Aid). Many European countries decided to take part in the scheme and a permanent organisation was set up in 1948. OEEC now exists to develop cooperation between the countries of the organisation and to help the U.S.A. in assisting European recovery.

What is meant by a Mandated Territory?

A former possession of Germany or Turkey which, after the War of 1914–18, was handed over to one of the conquering Powers by a mandate of the Peace Treaty of Versailles. A Mandatory Power, that is, one to which a mandated territory has been entrusted, does not own it, but governs it in the interests of its inhabitants. Up till 1946 the Mandatory Power was responsible to the League of Nations whose authority in such matters is now exercised by UNO. To-day we speak of certain territories being " under United Nations Trusteeship." The territories thus entrusted to Great Britain and other parts of the Commonwealth were: Palestine, Iraq, Tanganyika, parts of Togoland and the Cameroons, South-West Africa, part of New Guinea, and Western Samoa. The Mandate over Iraq was relinquished by treaty in 1922, and that over Palestine came to an end in 1948.

What are the names of the Patron Saints of England, Wales, Scotland and Ireland?

St. George, Patron Saint of England, is believed to have been born in Cappodocia of Christian parents, in the latter half of the third century. He became a soldier under the Emperor Diocletian. According to the Golden Legend he slew the dragon, then put off his knightly attire, gave all he had to the poor, and went forth to preach Christianity. He was made a prisoner and put to death at Nicomedia on April 23rd, A.D. 303. This date was ordered to be kept in remembrance of him as a national festival in England in 1222, his fame having been brought to Western Europe by the Crusaders, but it was not until the reign of Edward III (1327–1357) that he was made the Patron Saint of England. In 1346 Edward III founded the Order of the Garter with St. George as the badge.

The Patron Saint of Wales, St. David, was the son of Prince Sandde of Cardiganshire and his wife, Non, who later became a Christian saint. An eloquent preacher, St. David became head of the Church in Wales and founded a monastery at Menevia, now known as St. David's. Canonised as a saint in the twelfth century, he became the Patron Saint of Wales, his festival being on March 1st. David died in 601.

Scotland's Patron Saint is St. Andrew. He was born at Bethsaida on the Lake of Galilee, and, with his brother, Simon Peter, was one of the first Apostles. He preached the Gospel in Asia Minor and in Scythia, along the shores of the Black Sea. At Patrae he suffered martyrdom about A.D. 70 on a cross shaped X. Part of this cross is said to be in one of the supporting pillars of the dome of St. Peter's in Rome. According to tradition his relics were first taken to Constantinople and from there to St. Andrews in Scotland, probably some time in the eighth century. Since that time he has been the Patron Saint of Scotland, his festival being held on November 30th.

St. Patrick was born in England about A.D. 389, and was carried off to Ireland as a slave when he was about sixteen. Later he escaped to France (Gaul), where eventually he became a Bishop, and returned to Ireland to preach Christianity. He died in 461, and later became the Patron Saint, his festival being held on March 17th.

Who were the " Seven Champions of Christendom "?

The name was given in medieval legend to the Patron Saints of seven countries whose deeds were recorded in various writings. The Seven Champions were St. George of England, St. Denis of France, St. Anthony of Italy, St. James of Spain, St. Andrew of Scotland, St. Patrick of Ireland and St. David of Wales.

Which European Monarch had the Longest Reign?

Louis the Fourteenth of France. He ascended the throne in 1643, at the age of five, and died seventy-two years later (1715). He did not, however, begin to *rule* till 1661. So as a ruling monarch he comes after the Emperor Francis Joseph of Austria, who both reigned and ruled from 1848 to 1918 (seventy years), and Queen Victoria, 1837 to 1901 (sixty-three-and-a-half years).

What are the Crown Jewels?

A collection of crowns, sceptres, precious stones and other articles kept in the Wakefield Tower of the Tower of London. They belong to the reigning sovereign. The most valuable items are perhaps two diamonds, parts of the Cullinan diamond—the world's largest diamond—which was presented to King Edward the Seventh by the Transvaal in 1908.

HUMAN BODY

Why has an Animal got a Skull?

The skull is a very strong protection to the brain, which must be carefully guarded, since on it depend the senses and the control of all parts of the body.

Why are Prints taken from a Criminal's Fingers?

Because it has been discovered that no two persons have exactly the same markings on their finger tips. A " print," made by pressing the fingers against an inked slab and then on a sheet of white paper, thus becomes a record by means of which a person can be unerringly identified on any future occasion.

Why do some Deaf People hear conversation most easily in very noisy surroundings?

People affected by what is called middle-ear deafness suffer from a thickening of the ear drums and from stiffness in the joints between the tiny bones which convey vibrations from the drum to the inner ear. The loud noises in, say, a railway train, keep the drums vibrating and in a condition which responds to spoken words. Amid quiet surroundings shouting is needed to make a deaf person's ear drums move with sufficient vigour. Victims of what is called nerve deafness hear worse in a noisy than in a quiet place.

Why does the Pupil of the Eye become smaller when one looks at a bright light?

Because the circular curtain of the eye, named

W. F. Mansell.

This slab of black basalt, famous under the name of the *Rosetta Stone* (see p. 373), gave scholars the key to the reading of ancient Egyptian hieroglyphic and demotic inscriptions. What made it so valuable was the Greek inscription in the lower half. This was easily read, and proved to be a decree of the priests of Memphis in honour of Ptolemy the Fifth of Egypt. By dint of long study and intelligent guessing, scholars managed to pair-off the hieroglyphics (at top) and the demotic script (middle) with their Greek equivalents. Through the knowledge thus gained it became possible to read Egyptian inscriptions generally, and learn many things about ancient Egyptian history.

the iris, contracts to regulate the amount of light entering the eye.

Why are some people Colour-blind?

Owing to their eyes being defective, in a way which is not yet understood, and insensitive to certain colours.

Why do falling Raindrops look like Streaks?

The retina of the eye, on to which images of things must fall for us to see them, is made up of a vast number of cells. An impression received by any one of them lasts for about one-tenth of a second. The image of a raindrop affects a whole vertical row of them so quickly that the drop is " seen " in a great number of different positions at what is in effect the same moment, and the drop appears to be a line.

What happens to our Eyes while they are becoming accustomed to darkness out of doors after we leave a well-lighted house?

At first we are practically blind, if it is a very dark night. But the pupils of the eyes quickly expand, allowing more of the faint light reflected from outdoor objects to enter them. It has been suggested that the retina contains a second set of nerves which are affected by light too weak to act on the ordinary sight nerves.

Why do the Telegraph Lines beside a Railway seem to go up and down when watched from a Train?

Because they sag slightly between the posts, so that the height of the part being watched is constantly changing.

Why does Laughter bring Tears to the Eyes?

On the outer side of each eye there is a gland which keeps exuding moisture between the eyeball and the upper eyelid. Ordinarily the fluid is carried away into the nose by a small passage. Hearty laughter, like its opposite emotion, great sorrow, makes the gland give out more liquid than the passage can deal with, and the surplus runs out of the eye down the face.

Why do Onions bring Tears to the Eyes of a person peeling them?

Because onions when cut give out a vapour which irritates the tear glands of the eyes and makes tears flow.

What makes an Eye Bloodshot?

Inflammation, which causes the tiny veins in the white part of the eyeball to become swollen with blood.

How do Spectacles assist the Sight?

Spectacles assist the lens of the eye to focus rays of light on to the focusing-screen of the eye, called the retina. In a short-sighted eye the rays meet, that is, come to a focus, *before* reaching the retina, and have spread out again by the time they arrive at it. If a lens thinner at the centre than at the edge is placed in front of the eye, the rays are bent outwards a little before they enter the eye lens, and then focus further back, on the retina itself. A long-sighted eye, on the other hand, focuses *beyond*

the retina, and needs a spectacle lens which is thickest at the centre to bend the rays inwards and make them come to a focus sooner.

Why does the Heart beat?

To pump blood into every part of the body through the arteries and veins.

Why is the Blood in the arteries bright red, and that in the veins dark red?

Arterial blood has been purified by the lungs, and has the normal colour of blood. Blood in the veins is on its way back to the lungs, and is discoloured by the loss of oxygen given up to the tissues, and by carbon dioxide which it has absorbed from them. When an artery is cut, blood comes from it in spurts, but the flow from a severed vein is steady.

Why does a Bruised part of the Body turn blue?

Because tiny blood-vessels just under the skin have been broken, allowing the blood to escape into the tissues and spread under the skin.

What is the cause of " Pins and Needles " in the Limbs?

A deficiency of the oxygen supply to the nerves, often due to a temporary checking of the circulation by pressing on an artery, as when one crosses one's legs. As soon as the pressure is removed and the blood flows again freely, the prickling sensation of " pins and needles " follows.

Why cannot we live under Water?

We need a constant supply of fresh air, which is drawn in and made use of by the lungs. The first breath taken under water would fill the lungs with water and render them useless. Fish get the air they need by extracting it from the water through their gills.

What becomes of the Foul Air which we breathe from our Lungs?

It becomes mixed with the air round us. The carbonic acid in it will probably be absorbed by trees and plants sooner or later.

Why should we keep Bedroom Windows open at Night?

To prevent the air in the room becoming foul with the carbonic acid gas breathed out from our lungs. The open windows ensure a constant supply of pure fresh air.

Why is it dangerous to descend into an unused well or pit?

Because foul air containing dangerous gases may have collected at the bottom. If a lighted candle be lowered and it burns brightly, the air may be considered fit for breathing.

Why do we Perspire?

To get rid of waste matter and to keep the heat of the body even by evaporation. During an attack of fever perspiration ceases and the patient's temperature then rises quickly. As soon as perspiration begins again the temperature falls and the patient's condition becomes less serious.

Why do we Perspire after running a Long Distance?

The work done by the muscles during violent exercise heats the body. The sweat glands of the skin then open, allowing water to exude and spread over the skin. The evaporation of the water cools the skin, and with it the body as a whole.

Why does one's Face tend to become dirty more easily when one is hot than when one is cool?

Getting hot makes the skin sticky with perspiration, and dust then adheres to it much more readily than when it is cool and dry.

Why do we eat Food?

In order (1) to build up the tissues of the body when growing; (2) to make good the waste of tissue that is always going on; (3) to produce heat; (4) to give us energy to do work.

Why do we eat Foods of many kinds?

Because different foods contain different substances needed by the body.

Why do we become Hungry?

The feeling called hunger is the warning given by the body that its supply of fuel (food) is running short.

Why should we chew solid food well before swallowing it?

So that it may be mixed thoroughly with saliva, which helps us to digest it.

Why do we not need Meals at night?

While we are in bed our muscles are at rest and doing no work, and while we are asleep the brain is inactive. Therefore much less food-fuel is needed, and the body is able to subsist on what was taken in during the previous day.

Why does one sometimes feel sleepy after a Heavy Meal?

The blood is drawn away from the brain to the stomach to take in the nourishment in the food, and the brain then becomes less active, causing drowsiness.

Where does our Hair come from?

Out of tiny pits in the skin, called follicles. A hair is composed of the same horny matter as our nails. An ordinary human hair is only three-thousandths of an inch thick, yet it is three or four times coarser than a hair from a rabbit's fur.

Why does Hair grow on our Heads?

To protect the brain and other organs of the head against heat and cold, and no doubt also to deaden blows which may fall on the skull.

Why does a Fright make a person's Hair stand on end?

Each hair has a tiny muscle at the root. When a person is frightened this contracts, causing the hair to become more erect. The erection is much more pronounced in the case of a frightened cat, or in that of a pugnacious dog, when it is doubtless intended to give the creature a more formidable appearance.

What causes Stammering?

Lack of proper control over the muscles of the mouth and tongue which are used in speech. Stammering is a nervous trouble.

Why does a Boy's Voice break, but not a Girl's?

When a boy reaches a certain age his larynx grows larger very quickly, and the vocal cords become longer and give out lower notes. During the " change-over " to his " man's voice " the boy is unable to adjust his vocal cords properly, and his voice is said to have " broken." A girl's larynx, on the other hand, grows much more slowly, and does not become as large as a man's, so there is only a slow and slight alteration in pitch.

Why do we Sneeze?

To expel irritating matter from the air passages of the nose.

Why do we Cough?

Because the air passages are irritated, and coughing tends to expel any irritating substance. Coughing is generally preceded by a deep breath. The opening between the windpipe and mouth is then closed, and the muscles which squeeze the lungs come into action. The pressure of the air in the lungs increases till the vocal cords in the larynx are suddenly driven apart and the air escapes noisily.

Why do we Blush?

Blushing is due to the tiny blood-vessels of the head and neck becoming distended. Why this should happen when we are overcome with shyness or shame is not fully understood.

Why do we Swing our Arms when we Walk?

Probably to help balance the body. As a leg moves forward, the arm on the same side swings backward.

What is the cause of Freckles?

Freckles are due to cells in the under part of the skin collecting pigment, which is seen through the outer layer of the skin. Some people are born with freckles, while others—especially fair-skinned people—develop them if exposed to strong sunlight. Sunburn is the same kind of thing, but evenly spread instead of appearing in patches.

Why should one give attention to even a small cut or graze?

The germs that cause blood-poisoning are very tiny, so that it is a safe rule to take precautions against them whenever the skin is broken. A cut or graze should always be well washed and treated with some germ-killing substance, such as boracic powder or iodine, and be covered over to prevent dirt getting into it.

What is Quinine?

An extremely bitter substance extracted from the bark of the cinchona, an evergreen forest tree native to Peru. It is very valuable for bringing down the temperature of a person suffering from fever, and for both preventing and curing malaria. In 1630—over 300 years ago—it was first given to a European—a Jesuit missionary in Peru. He was cured so quickly of malaria by it that he told all the Spanish settlers round about of its virtues, and presently it was brought to the notice of the Viceroy of the country. The Viceroy introduced it into Spain in 1639, and from that country its use spread over Europe. Most of the quinine now sold comes from trees grown in plantations in the East and West Indies, India, and Australia.

When was Chloroform discovered?

In 1831. It was first prepared by J. v. Liebig and E. Soubeiran, working independently of one another. It was first used as an anæsthetic at Edinburgh in 1848, by the Scottish surgeon, Sir James Young Simpson.

LANGUAGE

How did we get our Alphabet?

It came to us from the Romans, who adopted many letters in it from the Greeks, in the sixth century B.C. The Greeks got their alphabet in the main from the Phœnicians, who had adapted the Egyptian and other methods of writing. The letters are commonly supposed to be simplified pictures of objects, the names of which began with the sounds indicated by the various letters. But it is also held that the very early scribes, when trying to find symbols that would suggest sounds, took those in which the hand most closely followed the movements of the tongue and lips. To take one example: when one makes the sound "oh," the mouth naturally becomes more or less circular, and O is the symbol which suggests this.

How many Words are there in the English Language?

The most complete English dictionary ever compiled, the New English Dictionary, deals with 414,825 words. A considerable number of the words in this dictionary are, however, never or seldom used nowadays.

In what Proportions have Various Languages contributed to English?

On the average, out of every 100 words in our language 28 are of English origin, 54 are derived directly or indirectly from Latin, 5 from Greek and the remainder from French, Italian, Portuguese, Dutch, and other languages.

How did we get our truly Native Words?

Many of them are Celtic, and inherited from Britons of Cæsar's time. The rest are mainly of Scandinavian origin, imported by the invading Teutons or Germans of the north—Jutes, Saxons, Angles, and Danes.

Why does our Language contain so many Latin Words?

Some were left by the Romans during their 400-year occupation of Britain from A.D. 43 to 410. Augustine and his monks imported many more from Rome at the end of the sixth century, mostly words relating to religious matters. The conquest of England by the Normans under William the Conqueror brought with it the Norman-French language, which contained a vast number of words of Latin origin, picked up from the Romanised inhabitants of what is now France. These were intermingled thoroughly with the Anglo-Saxon speech, and most of them remained fixed in our language. Finally, the Revival of Learning, in the fifteenth century, increased greatly the study of Latin authors, and led to the adoption of many words which are used more in writing than in speech, and so had far less influence than the Norman-French invasion. It had, however, the effect of changing the spelling of many Norman-French words back into a more closely Latin form; for example, "aventure" and "dette" into our present "adventure" and "debt."

What is the Name of the oldest English Poem?

"Beowulf," an epic dating from the seventh century, though the MS. now in the Cottonian Library of the British Museum is ascribed to the tenth century. It is the oldest poem in any Teutonic language. Like all epics, it is a mixture of history and mythology, but its author is unknown. It tells the story of how Beowulf of Sweden went to Jutland to rid King Hrothgar of a monster which devoured his men, and how he succeeded in his enterprise. The "Beowulf" was a favourite after-dinner song among the old Vikings.

Who was the Author of the first English Poems written in England?

Caedmon, a herdsman of Whitby Abbey, in Yorkshire, who lived in the seventh century. The gift of song, so the story runs, came to him in a dream, when a celestial voice bade him sing of the beginning of created things. When he awoke he at once wrote down some lines composed during his sleep, and took them to Hilda, the Abbess of Whitby. She at once admitted him and made him a monk, and had him taught the Scriptures, parts of which he turned into English verse. Caedmon's songs existed in manuscript only for nearly 1,000 years, and then, in 1655, were printed.

Who wrote the first English Prose?

Baeda, a seventh-century monk of Jarrow-on-Tyne, generally called the Venerable Bede. Of his many works, the most important of which was an Ecclesiastical History, all but one were written in Latin. The one exception, a translation of St. John's Gospel, was written in English as he lay dying, and completed just before he drew his last breath. Unfortunately no copy of this translation—the first prose written in our language—has survived.

Which are the Romance Languages?

French, Italian, Spanish and Portuguese, all of which are derived from the language spoken by the old Romans—Latin. It follows that anyone who has a good knowledge of Latin will find it useful when learning one of these modern languages.

What is Esperanto?

An artificial "universal" language, invented by Dr. Louis Zamenhof, of Warsaw, and first

THE LONG ARM OF THE LAW

Specially drawn for this work.

This picture will give you a very good idea of what you would see in an English Court of Justice if present at a criminal trial. Facing the prisoner in the dock (1) is (2) the Judge, with a Sheriff (13) on his left, the Judge's Clerk (10) on his right, and the Clerk of the Court (14) below him. At (3) is the *jury* (see p. 373); at (4) a witness in the witness-box being cross-examined by (5) Counsel. At desk (6) are other Counsel engaged in the case. The solicitors (7) taking part have behind them ushers (11), reporters (8), and the police (9) in charge of the case. A warder (12) stands close to the prisoner.

published in 1887. It is based upon the roots of the principal European languages, and has so simple a grammar and forms of construction that it can be learned very quickly.

What is the Rosetta Stone?

A slab of basalt found near Rosetta, in the Nile Delta, by a French officer in 1799. It is now in the British Museum. The discovery of it was an important event, for the slab had on it three inscriptions: one in the symbols used by the old Egyptian priesthood on monuments and in manuscripts; one in the ordinary writing of the ancient Egyptian people; and one in Greek. The last inscription was easily read, and intelligent guesswork led to keys being found to the other two languages, which hitherto had been unreadable. The inscription, which is the same in all three languages, was made in or about 196 B.C.

What is Swahili?

A mixed Arabic and African language, containing a number of Indian and European words, which serves as a sort of universal language throughout Central East Africa. It is written in both Arabic and European characters.

LEGAL

What is a Justice of the Peace?

An unpaid magistrate appointed by the Lord Chancellor on behalf of the Crown. There are county justices and borough justices. They must be persons of some importance and of good character. Two or more justices sitting together in what are called petty sessions form a court which can try and pass sentence on persons charged with minor acts of lawbreaking; and in quarter sessions, held once every three months, they may deal with any but the most serious crimes, such as treason or murder. The letters "J.P." after a man's name show that he is a Justice of the Peace.

What are the Duties of the Lord Lieutenant and High Sheriff of a County?

The Lord Lieutenant is appointed by the King and is the head of the magistracy. He recommends the names of persons to be appointed magistrates of the county. The High Sheriff is the Crown's principal law officer in the county, acts as returning officer for County elections, attends the judge on circuit, and has the duty of keeping prisoners in safe custody.

What are the Duties of a Jury at a Trial?

To listen to the evidence given, and to the speeches made by counsel on both sides, and then to decide whether the charge brought against the person or persons on trial has been proved or not. Before a jury considers what its verdict or decision shall be, the judge sums up the whole case in the light of the evidence. In a criminal case the verdict must be unanimous; that is, all twelve jurors must agree either to "Guilty" or "Not Guilty." If an agreement is come to, the foreman of the jury tells the judge what the verdict is; and the judge sentences or discharges the prisoner in accordance with the verdict. Should the jurors be divided in opinion, so that no verdict can be given, the jury is discharged, and the trial is held over again with a new jury.

What is meant by Going Bail for a Person?

If a person is committed for trial at a future time, and the crime with which he is charged is not a very serious one, he may be allowed his freedom until the trial comes on if he can find persons who are willing to go bail for him. This means persons who will enter into a bond to produce the prisoner at the time appointed for the trial or, if they fail to do so, to forfeit a sum of money agreed upon with the magistrates. A person temporarily freed in this way is said to be released on bail.

What is meant by a Close Season?

A period of the year during which it is illegal to kill a certain species of game or fish, so that it may have a proper chance of breeding. In England the close season for partridges is from February 2nd to August 31st; for pheasants, from February 2nd to September 30th; for grouse, from December 11th to August 11th.

What is Treasure-Trove?

Money, gold or silver plate, or other valuables found hidden in the ground, and having no known owner. Valuables which have been merely abandoned or lost, and not purposely hidden, are not treasure-trove. As treasure-trove belongs by law to the Crown, it is a crime to conceal the discovery of it.

Are Burglary and Housebreaking the same thing?

A person who breaks into *any* building at *any* time of day or night, with intent to commit a crime, is guilty of housebreaking. If the building broken into be a dwelling-house, and the act be committed between 9 p.m. and 6 a.m., he is guilty of burglary, which is regarded as a more serious crime than ordinary housebreaking and is more severely punished.

What does the word Mayor mean?

The chief magistrate of a city or borough. He is elected on November 9th by the Aldermen and Councillors, and holds office for a year. His chief duty is to preside at meetings of the Council. The mayors of London, Belfast, Dublin, Birmingham, Bristol, Leeds, Bradford, Liverpool, Manchester, Newcastle-upon-Tyne, Hull, Sheffield, York and several other cities have the title of Lord Mayor.

What is meant by a Person becoming Naturalised?

That he goes through a legal form whereby he gives up his allegiance to the country to which he belongs by birth, and becomes a citizen of another country. An Englishman who takes out papers of naturalisation in the United States, for example, ceases to be a British citizen and becomes an American citizen. Before a foreigner can apply to become a naturalised Briton, he must have lived in this country for five years out of the past eight.

What and where is Scotland Yard?

A building on the Thames Embankment, London, which is the headquarters of the Metropolitan Police. It is called New Scotland Yard, to distinguish it from the original Scotland Yard in Whitehall. The change of headquarters was made in 1890. The former Scotland Yard, or Great Scotland Yard, was once occupied by a Palace built for the reception of the Kings of Scotland when they visited London, and the name has been retained.

LITERATURE AND ART

Who was Æsop, the Fable-writer?

A Greek of Phrygia, in Asia Minor, who is thought to have been born about 620 B.C.— more than 2,500 years ago. He left no writings; and, though he was famous among the Greeks as a relater of fables, the stories which go under his name were probably compiled by later writers. Some of them, including that of the Lion and the Mouse, are probably much older even than Æsop, exactly the same fables having been found in ancient Egyptian manuscripts.

What are the Sagas?

Stories and legends of old Norse families, kings, heroes and gods, generally in prose, but in some cases in verse. For generations they were handed down by word of mouth, but in the twelfth and thirteenth centuries many of them were collected and put into writing. The most famous Sagas are those of Icelandic origin. From the Sagas in general we gather a great deal of information about the mythology, customs and history of the Norsemen. Among the most interesting are those which describe the colonisation of Greenland by the Icelanders at the end of the ninth century, and of the discovery of Winland (America) by Leif, son of Eric the Red, in or about A.D. 1000.

Who wrote the "Arabian Nights Entertainments"?

It is not known. But probably several people had a hand in the tales, which may have been written at different periods, ranging from the eighth to the sixteenth centuries. Edward William Lane, a great Arabic scholar, who first translated the book into English from the Arabic, in 1838-40, believed the original work to have been of Persian origin, and to have been written not later than 1475.

In what branch of artistic culture has Britain excelled?

In literature. Shakespeare and his contemporaries of the Elizabethan Age created the modern drama and the modern theatre. In poetry no country has surpassed Britain. Chaucer, Spenser, Shakespeare, Milton, Byron, Shelley, Keats, Wordsworth, Browning and Tennyson are some only of her many great poets. A foreign writer of to-day describes our poetry as enjoying "an everlasting summer." The modern novel had its birth in Britain; but Britain's lead in this branch of literature is now increasingly challenged by the United States.

Who first translated the Bible into English?

John Wycliffe, in or about the year 1382. Parts of the Bible had been translated before, but Wycliffe made the first complete translation. This was in manuscript only. A complete printed translation did not appear till 1535— the Coverdale Bible.

How many Words are there in the Bible?

The Authorised Version contains rather more than 773,000 words.

What is the Apocrypha?

A group of fourteen books of the Bible, which are regarded as being of obscure origin and not of the same authority as what are called the canonical books. They were printed in all English Bibles till about the end of the seventeenth century, but now are seldom included. Some of the books are: the Book of Tobias, the Book of Judith, the Book of Wisdom, the Song of the Three Children, Bel and the Dragon, and the First and Second Books of Maccabees.

What is the Pentateuch?

The first five books of the Bible—Genesis, Exodus, Leviticus, Numbers and Deuteronomy— taken as a group. At one time they were thought to have been written entirely by Moses, but this view is held no longer. They tell the story of the Hebrew nation up to its invasion of Canaan, the Promised Land, and contain all the Laws of Moses, which the Jews were bound to observe.

What is meant by Blank Verse?

Poetry in which the lines do not rhyme. Greek and Latin poets and dramatists used blank verse only, and since Shakespeare's time practically all English poetical dramas have been written in such verse. Rhyming is replaced by equality in length of lines as regards metre. A complete line in one of Shakespeare's plays has ten syllables or five "feet." For example:—
" Sleep that/ knits up/ the rav/ell'd sleave/ of Care/,
The death/ of each/ day's life/, sore la/bour's bath."/

Why do so many People visit Stratford-on-Avon?

Because William Shakespeare, the greatest of our poets, was born and buried there. The house of his birth is still standing, and is held as a public trust for the nation. New Place, the house in which he lived during his last years, has disappeared, but the site is preserved as a public garden. On the banks of the Avon stands the Shakespeare Memorial, built in 1879, and including a theatre (since burned but re-built) in which the poet's plays are performed. A mile from the town is the village of Shottery, containing the cottage home of Anne Hathaway, who became Shakespeare's wife.

Who comes next in reputation to Shakespeare as a Writer of English Plays?

Ben Jonson (1573-1637), a contemporary and close friend of Shakespeare himself. He began life as a bricklayer, then turned soldier and fought against the Spanish on the Continent; and on his return to England settled down to writing plays, of which he produced a great number. The most famous of them are: " Every Man in his Humour," " Every Man out of his Humour," " Volpone," and " The Alchemist." In 1616 he was created Poet Laureate—the first poet to be appointed formally to the office under letters patent. His body was buried in Westminster Abbey, in, it is said, an upright position.

Who is believed by some People to have been the real author of Shakespeare's Plays?

Francis Bacon, Viscount St. Albans (1561–1626). In the middle of last century doubts began to be raised about the authorship of the Shakespearean plays, and since then many people have tried to prove, by means of hidden ciphers, which they claim to have discovered in the plays, and in other ways, that Lord Bacon wrote the plays, using Shakespeare's name to hide his own. But, in spite of the ingenuity of the champions of Bacon, the opinion of experts is heavily against them; and it is much easier to continue believing in Shakespeare as author than in the theories of Bacon's supporters.

Who was the earliest English Woman Writer?

Aphra Behn (1640–1689). When she was twenty-five years old she was sent by Charles the Second into Holland as a spy. On returning to England she devoted herself to writing plays and stories. The best known of her tales is " Orronoko, or the Royal Slave." Next after her came Sarah Fielding, sister of the much more famous Henry Fielding (1707–1754) and authoress of " David Simple "—a book which must not be confused with Marryat's " Peter Simple."

Who were Hans Andersen and the Brothers Grimm, the Fairy Tale Writers?

Hans Christian Andersen was the son of a poor Danish shoemaker. He was born at Odense, in Funen, in 1805. After suffering much hardship and poverty he produced, in 1835, his first series of fairy tales, which made him world-famous; and he continued to issue fresh volumes at intervals almost up to the time of his death in 1875. " Grimm's Fairy Tales " are the work of two German brothers, Jacob Ludwig Karl Grimm and Wilhelm Karl Grimm, both professors, who collected tales from people, old manuscripts and books, and published them as a single volume in 1815.

What was Excalibur?

The magic sword given to King Arthur by the Lady of the Lake. On one side of it was engraved " Take Me," and on the other " Cast me away." Just before his death King Arthur ordered his knight, Sir Bedivere, to throw the sword back into the lake. As it struck the surface an arm appeared, grasped it, and drew it down.

Who were the Fates?

Three goddesses of Greek mythology, named Clotho, Lachesis (pronounced Lak'-e-sis), and Atropos, who were supposed to govern human destinies. Clotho spun the thread of a man's life; Lachesis worked happiness and woe into it; and Atropos cut it with her shears at the time appointed for death.

Who wrote the first English Novels?

Daniel Defoe (1659–1731). His famous " Robinson Crusoe," produced in 1719, was not merely the first English novel, but the first novel in any language to deal with real life, as opposed to romance and stories about impossible happenings. Like " Robinson Crusoe," his " Plague Year " and " Memoirs of a Cavalier " are so realistic that for a long time they were supposed to be the autobiographies of persons who had been through the experiences described.

Who was Alexander Selkirk?

A Scotsman, born at Largo, in Fifeshire, in 1676. When nineteen years old he became a sailor and took part in a privateering expedition to the South Seas under Dampier. Having quarrelled with his captain, he asked to be put ashore, with provisions, on one of the islands of the Juan Fernandez group, about 400 miles west of Valparaiso, on the west coast of South America. He remained there for four years and four months, and was then taken off by Captain Woods Rogers, who made him mate and afterwards captain. Later on he became a lieutenant in the Royal Navy. Defoe is commonly supposed to have used Selkirk's adventures on the island as the basis for his famous " Robinson Crusoe." The poet Cowper wrote the well-known poem about Selkirk, beginning " I am monarch of all I survey."

How did we get our Christmas Cards?

They are the descendants of decorated sheets of paper on which schoolboys wrote compositions just before the Christmas holidays, to show how they had improved in composition and writing during the year. These " Christmas pieces," as they were called, were popular from 1800 to 1850. In 1845 some private people adopted the idea for Christmas greeting, to their friends, and soon afterwards printers began to prepare Christmas cards for sale to the public. Lewis Carroll, the author of " Alice in Wonderland," is said to have drawn the first Christmas card.

Who were the Old Masters?

The great painters of the thirteenth to the seventeenth centuries in all countries.

Who was Leonardo da Vinci?

An Italian genius who was born in 1452 and died in 1519. He was gifted by Nature with great physical beauty and strength, and with mental powers that made him perhaps the most distinguished " all round " man that the world has ever known. He was undoubtedly the greatest painter of his time, besides being an excellent sculptor, musician and architect. In addition, he interested himself in mechanics, botany, astronomy, geography, chemistry, geology and mathematics; and the writings which he left behind him suggest that, if he had specialised in any of these, he might easily have become as famous as a man of science as he became as an artist. The brain that put on to canvas the

" Last Supper " and " Mona Lisa " also invented the camera obscura, breech-loading cannon, a rope-making machine, and many other mechanisms; and in the field of physics put forward theories which show that he was far ahead of other thinkers of his time in such matters.

What is meant by Pre-Raphaelism in Painting?

A movement which the painters Ford Madox Brown, Holman Hunt, Millais and Dante Gabriel Rossetti set on foot in the middle of last century after studying the works of some of the predecessors of Raphael. In theory, it pursued truth in the representation of objects on canvas. But now it signifies an excessive attention to fine detail, such as characterises— and, some people will say, mars—some of the works by the artists named. Reaction from Pre-Raphaelism led the way to the very broad effects of modern Impressionism, which is concerned more with interpreting ideas than with the exact representation of things.

Which are the chief Picture Galleries of London?

The National Gallery and the National Portrait Gallery (Trafalgar Square) and the Tate Gallery (Millbank). Smaller collections are to be seen at the Soane Museum (Lincoln's Inn Fields); the Guildhall Art Gallery (in the City); the Wallace Collection (Manchester Square); and Hampton Court. Exhibitions are held yearly at the Royal Academy (Burlington House), the Whitechapel Art Gallery, the New Gallery (Regent Street), and elsewhere.

What is the Louvre?

A splendid pile of buildings in Paris, which now houses the finest collection of art treasures— pictures, statuary, gems and archæological remains—in the world. Until the French Revolution it was a royal palace, in an unfinished state. The Republicans made a museum of it, and Napoleon the First added to it. After 1848 it was completed and connected with the Tuileries, another palace. Most of the latter was burned down in 1817, but new galleries have been built on since.

When did the best known of the Great Musical Composers live?

Bach, 1685–1750; Handel, 1685–1759; Haydn, 1732–1809; Mozart, 1756–1791; Beethoven, 1770–1827; Schubert, 1797–1828; Mendelssohn, 1809–1847; Chopin, 1810–1849; Schumann, 1810–1856; Liszt, 1811–1886; Wagner, 1813–1883; Brahms, 1833–1897; Elgar, 1857–1934.

Which are the World's Largest Bells?

The famous Tsar Kolokol bell at Moscow, weighing about 198 tons, is easily the largest of bells, but it is imperfect and has never been used. Next comes the Krasnogvardersk bell, weighing 171 tons, and there are in Russia others weighing 121 and 110 tons. A bell in Burma weighs 80 tons. Pekin boasts a 57-ton bell. The largest English bell is Great Paul (16¾ tons) in St. Paul's Cathedral.

Why are First-rate Violins so expensive?

Because there are so few of them in existence. A violin is by no means the simple instrument it looks. It took centuries to ascertain the best materials, shape and proportions for it. A soft wood is used for the front or belly, and a hard wood (usually maple) for the back and sides. A very slight difference in the thickness of any part, or in the curves of the front or back, or in the depth of the body, or in the position of the little sound-post inside, connecting front with back, or in the shape of the f-holes in the front, or in the quality of the varnish used, may have a great influence on the tone. The violins made by Antonio Stradivari, of Cremona, during the first quarter of the eighteenth century, are still the best ever produced, and fetch huge sums. Some say that their remarkable quality is due to the special varnish prepared and used by Stradivari, but it may be partly due to the mellowing influence of time.

What is meant by Gothic Architecture?

The style of architecture which spread over many countries of Europe at the end of the twelfth century. It is distinguished by its pointed arches, as contrasted with the rounded arches of the Norman style which preceded it. Gothic architecture obtained a firm hold in England, and was adopted for most of our great medieval buildings, including many cathedrals and churches. English Gothic falls into three periods: the Early English, with slim columns and simple decoration; the Middle English, in which decoration is much more elaborate (Westminster Abbey is an example); and the Perpendicular, in which there is a return to a severer style, finely illustrated by the nave of Winchester Cathedral. The name is a misleading one, though generally adopted, as the Goths were destroyers rather than builders, and themselves had nothing to do with the introduction of the style.

How is a Marble Statue made?

The sculptor first prepares a small model in clay. If the statue is to be a large one, he then makes a full-sized clay model round an iron framework inside it. This model is coated with plaster of Paris to form a mould, which is removed in pieces and assembled again for a plaster cast to be made in it. The cast is an exact duplicate of the large clay model. The sculptor then places the cast near the block of marble out of which the statue will be cut. The model is marked all over at important points, and with the aid of an ingenious machine holes are sunk into the marble till their ends are in positions corresponding exactly to the various marks on the model. A workman hews away the marble all round to the depth of the holes, roughly shaping the statue; another, more skilled, man almost completes the cutting; and the sculptor himself gives the finishing touches.

How is a Bronze Statue made?

Since bronze is heavy and expensive, a bronze statue has to be hollow, and this means casting it in the space between an outside mould and an inside core. When the sculptor has prepared a full-sized model, the casting may be done by either of two methods. The first of these is called the sand-casting method. A sand mould, in separate parts, is made round the model, and, after being taken off and put together again, is filled with rammed sand. It is then removed, and the core is scraped down all over to a depth equal to the thickness of metal required. The sand mould having been assembled again round the core, molten bronze is poured into the space between the two. The second, named the *cire perdue* (lost wax), method, proceeds as follows: a plaster mould is taken from the model and lined with wax as thick as the bronze is to be. Workmen then fill the space inside the wax with a mixture of plaster and brickdust, and remove the plaster mould from outside the wax. A mould of the same materials as the core is formed round the wax, and the whole is then heated till the wax runs out, leaving a space which is afterwards filled with molten bronze.

What and where is the World's Largest Statue?

The statue of Liberty, standing on Bedloe's Island, at the entrance to New York Harbour. It represents Liberty holding a torch above her head. The statue, of beaten copper stiffened by an internal iron framework, is 151 feet high, not including the pedestal, which has about the same height. The designer was the eminent French sculptor, M. Auguste Bartholdi. The original model was a 7-foot figure, which was enlarged four times in a second model. This was cut up into pieces from which moulds for the shaping of the copper plates were made. After ten years of work the statue was completed, in France, in 1883, then taken to pieces, shipped across the Atlantic, re-erected, and finally presented by the French to the American nation on October 28th, 1886. In size it far exceeds the famous Colossus of Rhodes, one of the Seven Wonders of the ancient world, which is thought to have been 120 feet high. The Colossus was erected about the year 280 B.C. and was destroyed by earthquake in 225 B.C.

What are the Elgin Marbles?

Parts of the frieze and other external decorations of the Parthenon at Athens, the great temple dedicated to the goddess Athene in 438 B.C. The Marbles were purchased by the seventh Lord Elgin and brought to England in 1815. The following year they were sold to the British Museum—in which they can still be seen—for £36,000.

What is the Bayeux Tapestry?

The most famous piece of needlework in existence. It is a strip of linen, 231 feet long, and about 20 inches wide, on which are worked in coloured worsteds, seventy-two historical scenes connected with the invasion of England by William the Conqueror, and ending with one of the Battle of Hastings. The needlework is ascribed by tradition to William's wife, Matilda, and there is little doubt that this unique tapestry, which is housed in the museum of Bayeux, Normandy, dates from the time of the events which it records.

MECHANISMS

Who invented the Bicycle? And when?

A Dumfries blacksmith named Kirkpatrick Macmillan, in 1840 or thereabouts.

Why are there Ball Bearings in the Axles and Pedals of Bicycles?

To reduce friction to the lowest possible figure. If such bearings were not used it would need much more effort to propel a bicycle.

How does the Free-wheel of a Bicycle work?

The ring on which are the teeth for the chain is separate from the hub of the wheel, and between the ring and the hub are pawls, or catches, which enable the ring to drive the hub round, but go out of action if the ring is held fast or turned backwards.

Who invented the Pneumatic Tyre?

An engineer, R. W. Thompson, born at Stonehaven, Scotland, in 1822. In 1845 he patented a tyre which had an inner tube of canvas made airtight with rubber solution, and an outer cover of leather. A number of these tyres were fitted to road vehicles, but they went out of use because of the imperfections of the inner tube. The pneumatic tyre was re-invented in 1888 by John B. Dunlop, a veterinary surgeon of Belfast, in a much improved form, and soon came into universal use for bicycles, and, later on, for motor cars.

Why does the Rear Wheel of a Bicycle turn more often than the Pedals?

Because the chain-wheel turned by the pedals has more teeth on it than there are on the chain-wheel on the hub of the driving wheel. If the first has thirty teeth, and the second twelve teeth, every turn of the pedals will make the driving wheel revolve $\frac{30}{12} = 2\frac{1}{2}$ times. If the driving wheel is 28 inches across, the bicycle is said to be " geared " to $28 \times 2\frac{1}{2} = 70$ inches. This means that it advances as far for every turn of the pedals as it would do if the pedals were attached directly to a wheel 70 inches in diameter.

How does a Change-speed Gear help the Cyclist?

It enables him to alter his gear to suit different conditions. Downhill, or when a strong wind blows from behind, there is little resistance to be overcome, and he can use the high gear to get the greatest forward movement for every turn of the pedals. Uphill, or against a strong wind, he chooses the lowest gear, which gives him the greatest leverage at the expense of speed. The middle gear is useful for ordinary conditions.

How does a Petrol Engine work?

Each cylinder has two valves, one to admit an explosive mixture of gas and air, and the other to allow the burned gases to escape. The valves are opened at the proper moments by gearing driven off the crankshaft. During one outstroke the inlet valve opens, and the piston sucks the cylinder full of mixture. During the following instroke the valve is closed, and

THE WORLD'S MOST FAMOUS TAPESTRY

Made for Bishop Odo's Cathedral at Bayeux and 231 feet long and 20 inches wide, the *Bayeux Tapestry* (see p. 377) records the conquest of England by the Normans. Almost as old as the Conquest itself, the Tapestry has 72 scenes; here we see Harold being crowned King of England.

The linen from which the Bayeux Tapestry is made is now brown with age, but the eight different colours of the worsteds used to work the scenes remain clearly distinguishable. The scene shown here depicts the invasion fleet of William the Conqueror nearing Pevensey.

Picture Post Library.

To escape from captivity, and perhaps death, in Normandy, Harold had promised William the English throne: to enforce the fulfilment of this promise William crossed the Channel. The rival armies met at Hastings, and the Bayeux Tapestry vividly records the battle in scenes such as this.

Picture Post Library.

Almost at the end of its story, told in worsteds and linen, the Tapestry shows the death of King Harold. He is seen (left), plucking from his eye the fatal arrow. From noon till dusk the *huscarles*, Harold's picked troops, withstood the assault, but Harold's death ended their resistance.

the imprisoned mixture is squeezed by the piston. At the end of the stroke an electric spark is passed through the mixture, causing it to explode and drive the piston outwards again. When the second outstroke is almost completed, the second or exhaust valve opens, so that the burned gases may be driven out by the piston during its second instroke. The cycle of operations then begins again.

Why has a Motor Car got a Radiator?

To cool the water which circulates through the cylinder jackets, to prevent the cylinders becoming dangerously hot. The radiator is made up of a large number of tubes, through which water from the cylinders passes. The outsides of the tubes are gilled, *i.e.*, they have vanes fixed on them to provide a cooling surface. Cool air is passed through the vanes or gills, thus cooling the water in the tubes. The total surface of the tubes is so great that by the time the water has passed through the radiator it is cool enough to be used over again. The water is chilled so quickly by the radiator that quite a small amount of it is sufficient to cool a large engine.

What causes the Automatic Cancelling of Traffic Indicators on many Motor Cars?

"Cams" or protruding portions inside the head of the steering column. They automatically switch off the current as the wheel is turned to bring the car round a corner and this causes the indicator to fall.

Why do Pneumatic Tyres make a Vehicle travel more smoothly?

If an iron-tyred wheel strikes an obstacle, it has to rise over it and perhaps may jump some distance into the air. A pneumatic tyre laps round a small obstacle and flattens out on a large one, so the wheel is raised less. Even if it should be thrown up by a large obstacle, its elasticity makes it strike the ground more gently than a hard tyre does. The successful development of the motor-car was made possible by pneumatic tyres after their use on bicycles.

Why do the Rear Tyres of a Motor-Car wear more quickly than the Front Tyres?

Because they have to push the car forward, and in doing so slip more or less on the surface of the road, whereas the front tyres merely have to roll.

What are Machine Tools?

Machines used in engineering shops and shipyards for turning, drilling, planing, cutting, punching, pressing and riveting metals and other materials. The lathe in its various forms is the most widely used of them. These machines enable parts to be shaped and fitted together with great accuracy

How are Metal Plates and Bars bent into circular form?

By passing them between two rollers on one side and a single roller on the other. A plate will be curved in the direction of the single roller, and the closer this is set to the other two the smaller will be the circle to which the plate or bar is bent.

How does a Yale Lock work?

The part into which the key is pushed is a cylinder, able to revolve in a large cylinder outside it, which is fixed. The key cylinder has an arm on the inner end which moves the bolt of the lock when the key is turned. In the key cylinder is a row of upright holes, which are opposite an equal number of holes in the outside cylinder when the key slot is vertical. There are pins of various lengths in the holes, and springs above the upper ones to push each pair downwards. When a key is pushed into the lock it drives the pins upwards. If the correct key is used, the top of every lower pin and the bottom of every upper pin will be flush with the joint between the two cylinders, and the key cylinder is free to turn. A wrong key will drive one or more pins up too far, or not far enough, so that the two cylinders are locked together, and it is impossible to turn the key.

Why should the Hands of a Striking Clock not be put back?

Because if they are made to pass a striking-point the striking gear will be put out of step with the time-keeping mechanism.

How does an Escalator work?

Each step is mounted on a four-wheeled carriage, attached to an endless chain. The front wheels run on one pair of rails, and the rear wheels on another pair. The two sets of rails are so arranged that the carriage and its step are always level. At the bottom and top a number of steps form a platform. As they approach the incline they gradually separate vertically into a staircase, but become a platform again as they reach the top or bottom, as the case may be. The chain is driven at a steady speed by a powerful electric motor.

How does a Gas-meter work?

The ordinary household gas-meter is an air-tight casing divided into two gas chambers, which we will call A and B. The chambers each contain a bellows, respectively C and D, fixed at one end to a central division, and independent of one another. A slide valve, like that of a steam cylinder, and worked by the movements of the bellows, admits gas from the main to A and D, while allowing it to escape from B and C to the outlet pipe. As D fills it drives an equal amount of gas out of B, and at the same time the pressure of the gas in A squeezes the gas out of C. By the time that C is empty and D full, the valve has moved over, admitting gas into B and C. So the bellows keep opening and closing alternately, and at each stroke a definite amount of gas is delivered to the outlet pipe. The valve-shifting mechanism operates a train of wheels, which move pointers round dials to show how much gas has passed through the meter.

Why does the Cold Water Cistern of a House not overflow?

Because the entry of water from the main is regulated by a self-acting device called a ball-cock. The valve of the cock is opened and closed by a pivoted lever having a large copper float at its free end. When water is drawn off the float sinks, opening the valve. As the cistern

GOING UPSTAIRS WITHOUT WALKING

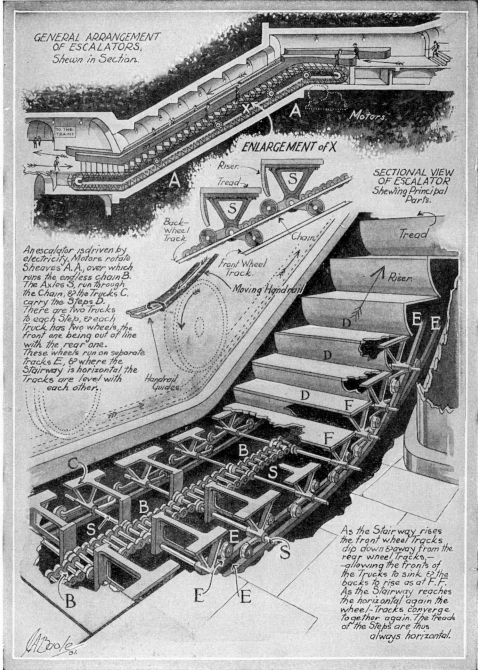

GENERAL ARRANGEMENT OF ESCALATORS, Shewn in Section.

ENLARGEMENT of X

SECTIONAL VIEW OF ESCALATOR Shewing Principal Parts.

Motors.

Riser

Tread

S

Back-Wheel Track

Front Wheel Track

Moving Handrail

Chain

Tread

Riser

Handrail Guides

An escalator is driven by electricity. Motors rotate Sheaves A.A., over which runs the endless chain B. The Axles S, run through the Chain, & the Trucks C. carry the Steps D. There are two Trucks to each Step, & each Truck has two wheels, the front one being out of line with the rear one. These wheels run on separate tracks E, & where the Stairway is horizontal the Tracks are level with each other.

As the Stairway rises the front wheel Tracks dip down & away from the rear wheel Tracks, allowing the fronts of the Trucks to sink & the backs to rise as at F.F. As the Stairway reaches the horizontal again the wheel-Tracks converge together again. The treads of the Steps are thus always horizontal.

Specially drawn for this work.

When travelling on the Underground Railways of London you have often made use of an *Escalator* (see p. 380) for getting up or down. These drawings will explain better than words only how it is that the moving steps of an escalator change from a flat platform at one end into a stairway during the ascent or descent and then back into a platform at the alighting end. The great advantages of an escalator are that it moves continuously, and allows one to add one's own speed of movement to that at which it runs. The escalators of London carry hundreds of thousands of people to and from the trains every day.

ALL ABOUT HURRICANES

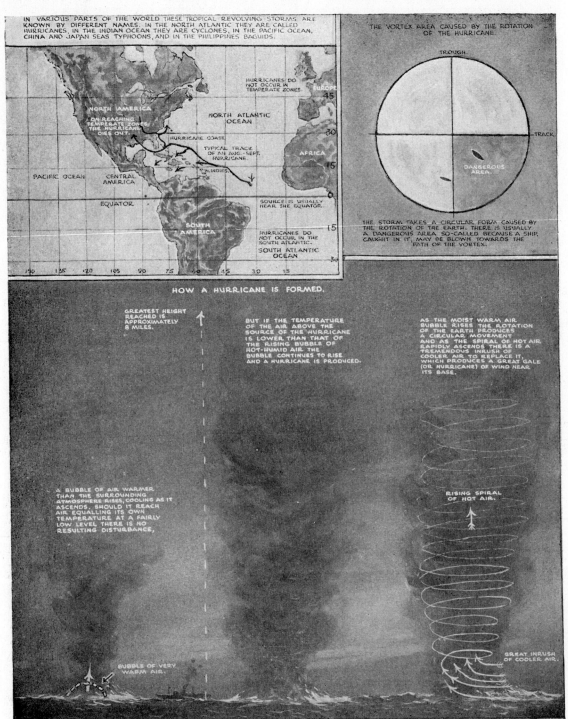

IN VARIOUS PARTS OF THE WORLD THESE TROPICAL REVOLVING STORMS ARE KNOWN BY DIFFERENT NAMES. IN THE NORTH ATLANTIC THEY ARE CALLED HURRICANES, IN THE INDIAN OCEAN THEY ARE CYCLONES, IN THE PACIFIC OCEAN, CHINA AND JAPAN SEAS TYPHOONS, AND IN THE PHILIPPINES BAGUIDS.

NORTH AMERICA

ON REACHING TEMPERATE ZONES THE HURRICANE DIES OUT.

HURRICANES DO NOT OCCUR IN TEMPERATE ZONES.

EUROPE

NORTH ATLANTIC OCEAN

HURRICANE COAST.

TYPICAL TRACK OF AN AUG.-SEPT. HURRICANE.

AFRICA

PACIFIC OCEAN

CENTRAL AMERICA

W. INDIES.

EQUATOR

SOURCE IS USUALLY NEAR THE EQUATOR.

SOUTH AMERICA

HURRICANES DO NOT OCCUR IN THE SOUTH ATLANTIC.

SOUTH ATLANTIC OCEAN

THE VORTEX AREA CAUSED BY THE ROTATION OF THE HURRICANE.

TROUGH.

TRACK

DANGEROUS AREA.

THE STORM TAKES A CIRCULAR FORM CAUSED BY THE ROTATION OF THE EARTH. THERE IS USUALLY A DANGEROUS AREA SO-CALLED BECAUSE A SHIP, CAUGHT IN IT, MAY BE BLOWN TOWARDS THE PATH OF THE VORTEX.

HOW A HURRICANE IS FORMED.

GREATEST HEIGHT REACHED IS APPROXIMATELY 8 MILES.

BUT IF THE TEMPERATURE OF THE AIR ABOVE THE SOURCE OF THE HURRICANE IS LOWER THAN THAT OF THE RISING BUBBLE OF HOT-HUMID AIR, THE BUBBLE CONTINUES TO RISE AND A HURRICANE IS PRODUCED.

AS THE MOIST WARM AIR BUBBLE RISES THE ROTATION OF THE EARTH PRODUCES A CIRCULAR MOVEMENT AND AS THE SPIRAL OF HOT AIR RAPIDLY ASCENDS THERE IS A TREMENDOUS INRUSH OF COOLER AIR TO REPLACE IT, WHICH PRODUCES A GREAT GALE (OR HURRICANE) OF WIND NEAR ITS BASE.

A BUBBLE OF AIR WARMER THAN THE SURROUNDING ATMOSPHERE RISES, COOLING AS IT ASCENDS. SHOULD IT REACH AIR EQUALLING ITS OWN TEMPERATURE AT A FAIRLY LOW LEVEL THERE IS NO RESULTING DISTURBANCE.

RISING SPIRAL OF HOT AIR.

BUBBLE OF VERY WARM AIR.

GREAT INRUSH OF COOLER AIR.

On these two pages is a pictorial explanation of hurricanes (*see* p. 386), showing how they are formed and the way in which their destructive forces strike in certain parts of the world. In 1955, there was a particularly bad series of these terrible revolving storms which caused untold death and destruction on the Eastern coast of the United States and, in some cases, in certain islands of the

THE DESTRUCTION THEY CAUSE

Illustrated London News.

West Indies.   Hurricanes are given girls' names as code names in alphabetical order.   On September 22nd, 1955, hurricane "Janet" hit the Windward Islands and caused immense destruction, especially in Grenada.   Barbados also suffered.   Numbers of people were killed, thousands were made homeless and crops were ruined during the comparatively short period in which the hurricane raged.

fills again, the float rises and cuts off the supply entirely before the water reaches the level of the overflow pipe.

How does a Refrigerator work?

The process of refrigeration involves three basic principles: *firstly*, that heat is absorbed when substances change their state from solid to liquid and from liquid to vapour. Latent heat, as it is called, is again given up by the substance when the reverse takes place. *Secondly*, that a liquid will boil—or vaporise—at a lower temperature, if the pressure of the atmosphere above the liquid is reduced. *Thirdly*, that the boiling-point of a liquid can be raised by increasing the pressure above the liquid. Thus some such liquid as ammonia, carbon dioxide, or sulphur dioxide, is caused to evaporate. As it evaporates, it draws its latent heat of vaporisation from its surroundings. The vapour is then compressed so that it is liquefied again, and the latent heat it gives out is removed by air- or water-cooling. Then the liquid is allowed to evaporate again, and so the process continues. The diagram on page 345, Vol. X, shows how this process occurs in a typical home refrigerator.

Does a Refrigerator help to Cool the Room?

No. A refrigerator is a form of heat-pump, and as it extracts the heat from the objects placed inside it, it gets rid of this heat by passing it to the air in the room. So a refrigerator actually *warms* the room!

METALS

Who discovered Aluminium?

A German chemist named Friedrich Wohler, who separated it in 1827. The alum minerals were actually known to the Egyptians, Greeks and Romans, but there was no way of separating the metal profitably until Wohler's successful experiments. To-day, the chief source of aluminium is bauxite, now found in various countries. In Jamaica the mining and processing of bauxite has become an important and rapidly-growing industry, the alumina obtained from the ore being sent to Canada, one of the greatest producers in the world to-day of aluminium and its many alloys.

What is Duralumin?

An alloy of aluminium containing small quantities of copper, magnesium, silicon, iron and manganese. It is only one-third as heavy as mild steel, bulk for bulk, but almost equally strong, and on this account is much used in the framework of aircraft.

What is Pewter?

An alloy of tin and lead (but it must not contain any free lead). In France the amount of lead is limited to 18 per cent.

What is Chromium?

A bluish-white metal related to nickel, cobalt and manganese. It is intensely hard and takes a very high polish. Another valuable property is that it is not affected at all by air, fresh or salt water, and many acids. Mixed with a much larger proportion of steel it gives us stainless steel, now used for a multitude of purposes. In the last few years the electro-plating of water taps and other household fittings, and the bright parts of motor cars, with chromium has made great strides. Dirty chromium plating merely needs wiping clean to become its bright self again.

Is Gold the most Precious Metal?

No! Cerium, palladium, osmium, platinum, rubidium, thorium and many other rare metals command much higher prices.

How can one tell whether an Article supposed to be Gold is really made of Gold?

The usual test is to apply nitric acid, which does not affect gold, but turns brass or copper green.

What is Cadmium?

A soft metal with a low melting point. It is used in some kinds of automatic fire-extinguishing apparatus as a plug to a water-supply. When fire breaks out the cadmium melts and releases water which sprays over the fire. Rods of cadmium are also used to control atomic piles, because the metal is able to absorb neutrons.

What is Galvanised Iron?

Iron covered with a thin coating of zinc, which protects it from the air and from rusting. The iron is galvanised by being dipped in a bath of molten zinc.

How is Steel made Stainless?

By mixing with it small quantities of nickel and chromium.

Why are Stoves and Fire-grates made of Cast Iron?

Because cast iron does not "burn," that is, flake away on the surface, like wrought iron or steel when it becomes red-hot. A wrought iron poker soon wastes if left in the fire, but firebars remain good for many years.

What is Mercury?

A very heavy metal which is liquid at ordinary temperatures. If spilt, it does not wet the surface it rests on, but runs about in little silver globules. This "activity" gives it its other name of "quicksilver." Mercury is used in thermometers, and was formerly used with tin for silvering mirrors.

What is a "Tin" Kettle made of?

Sheet steel or iron, coated on both sides with a thin layer of tin to prevent corrosion.

Why do Metals melt in a Furnace?

The heat of the furnace breaks down the cohesion between the molecules of a metal until it is not sufficient to overcome the pull of gravity. The metal then becomes liquid, its molecules moving over one another until it takes the shape of the vessel containing it.

METEOROLOGY AND GENERAL SCIENCE

What is Air?

A mixture of 78 parts of nitrogen gas, 21 parts of oxygen gas, 1 part of argon, and traces of carbonic acid gas and such rare gases as neon and helium.

What is the Weight of Air?

About 2 pounds 2 ounces per cubic yard at sea-level. Water is 800 times heavier than air; while hydrogen, the lightest gas known, is 14 times lighter.

Why cannot we see Air?

Because it is transparent, that is it allows light rays to pass straight through it. Being transparent, and having no surfaces like those of a sheet of glass, it cannot even reflect light.

Why does a Record-breaking Motor Car require an Engine of very great power?

Because at very high speeds the resistance of the air becomes tremendous, increasing much more quickly than the speed. At 240 miles an hour it is at least twenty-seven times what it is at eighty miles an hour. A car built specially for record-breaking is "stream-lined" as far as possible, that is, it is given a shape which enables it to pass through the air without causing violent eddies.

Why does the Column of Mercury in a Barometer rise and fall?

Because the pressure of the atmosphere on the mercury at the bottom of the column changes from time to time.

Why is a Barometer called a Weather-glass?

Because its movements help us to forecast the weather. When it rises, fine weather is likely; when it falls, rain is probable, because the fall shows that lighter, and therefore moister, air is overhead.

What is an Aneroid Barometer?

A barometer in which no liquid is used. It contains a flat, circular metal box from which air has been exhausted. The top and bottom of the box are corrugated, to stiffen them. The bottom is fixed at the centre to the base of the instrument. Changes in the pressure of the atmosphere make the top and bottom move in or out, and the movements are transmitted through levers to a pointer on a dial. A delicate aneroid will register the difference in pressure caused by raising the instrument 2 or 3 feet.

How does the Barometer help us to travel by Air?

A kind of aneroid barometer, called an altimeter, is carried in the cockpit of an aeroplane. The varying pressure of the air at different heights makes a pointer move on the dial of the instrument, which is graduated to show heights. When the ground is hidden by cloud or mist or darkness, the pilot is able to tell, by glancing at the altimeter, how high up he is.

Why should the Air be thinner the higher up one goes?

Because air is a very compressible fluid, and therefore is compressed by its own weight. The air nearest the ground has most air pressing on it, and so is densest. The water in the greatest depths of the ocean is only slightly denser than that at the surface; but then water, unlike air, is very incompressible.

Why would Tea brewed on the summit of Mt. Blanc be very weak?

Because at that height water would boil at 186° F., and be 26 degrees colder than boiling water at sea-level. So the tea would not "draw" properly.

Why does Snow lie permanently only on the peaks of High Mountains?

The higher up one goes the colder the air becomes. At a height where the air is never warmer than 32° F. at the hottest time of the year snow cannot melt. This height, called the snow-line, varies in different parts of the world. In the tropics it is about 18,000 feet above sea-level, in the Alps about 8,000 feet, and in the polar regions is practically at sea-level.

Why does a Garden Syringe fill with water when the handle is pulled out?

The handle draws the piston upwards, creating a vacuum in the space below it, and the pressure of the outside air forces water into this empty space.

Why does Ink become thick if left standing in an open inkpot?

Because the water in it is absorbed gradually by the air, while the other substances in it are not.

Why do Wet Clothes dry more quickly in a Wind than in still air?

Because the air touching them is constantly changing and carrying away moisture with it. In still air the change is much slower.

Why does the Draught from an Electric Fan cool the Skin?

Partly because it makes the moisture of the skin evaporate quickly, and partly because it carries away at once the air heated by the skin.

Why do Morning Mists disappear as the Day advances?

Because the moisture which forms the mist is absorbed by the sun's warmth and disappears as the air becomes warmer.

Why can one see one's Breath in frosty weather?

Because the warm breath is chilled by the much colder air and the moisture in it is condensed into visible particles of water.

Why does a Window Pane become damp if one breathes on it?

Because the cold glass condenses the moisture in the breath.

Why does Water sometimes run down Walls indoors?

This happens when the walls indoors are colder than the air coming in, as during a sudden thaw. Some of the moisture in the air is then condensed by the walls and trickles down them.

Why are many Mountainous Regions rainy?

Because the mountains drive the winds upwards into cold regions of the atmosphere, where the moisture carried by them is condensed into rain.

Why does the South-west Wind often bring Rain with it?

It reaches us after passing over the Atlantic Ocean, from which it picks up moisture. On reaching the colder air over the land this moisture is condensed into rain.

Why does Dew form on Grass?

Grass radiates heat quickly after sundown and becomes colder than the ground. Any vapour rising from the ground is condensed on the cold grass.

What is Hail?

Hailstones are not frozen raindrops, but crystals of ice which have grown larger and larger while being carried to great heights by strong upward currents of air. Many cases of hailstones as large as eggs have been recorded.

What is Snow?

When water vapour condenses in air which is below freezing-point it forms tiny, six-sided crystals of ice instead of liquid droplets. The ice-crystals get matted together to form snow-flakes, which then fall gently down to the ground.

What is a Cloud?

Water vapour condensed from the air into tiny drops or frozen into particles of ice. A fog is a cloud at ground level. In the upper air the cold sometimes causes the very small drops to run together into larger drops, which fall as drizzle or rain.

How high up are the Highest Clouds?

Clouds of the kind called cirrus, which is the Latin word for " curl," float higher than those of any other kind, their average height above sea-level being about 30,000 feet—more than that of the world's loftiest mountain. They are made up of tiny particles of ice, and are always white. They resemble feathers or ribbons, spreading out like the ribs of a fan, and are sometimes called mares'-tails. Cirrus clouds are usually regarded as a sign of coming wind.

What is the cause of a Thunderstorm?

A thunderstorm begins with a violent upward rush of air over a large area. When the speed of the air current exceeds twenty miles an hour or so, the drops of water carried up by the air are thought to be broken up into much smaller drops, which become charged with positive electricity in the process. The cloud of droplets presently gathers so much electricity that the air can no longer prevent a discharge in the form of a flash of lightning. The thunderstorm lasts until the upward current of air dies away.

What causes Thunder?

The sudden expansion of air by the heat of the lightning, followed by quick contraction. This produces violent movements in the air which reach us as a sound called a " thunder-clap." This may be prolonged owing to the fact that the sound from different parts of the lightning-flash (which may be a quarter of a mile long) reaches us at different times. The rumbling of the thunder is the series of echoes between the earth and the clouds of the thunder-clap.

What is the difference between Forked Lightning and Sheet Lightning?

Forked lightning is a very violent and sudden discharge of electricity, either between a cloud and the earth or between two clouds. It may be compared to the electric spark between the poles of a charged Leyden jar. Sheet lightning is a silent discharge over the surface of a cloud. Very little is as yet known about its nature. It should be pointed out that what is often referred to as sheet lightning is merely the lighting up of the sky by flashes occurring out of sight beyond the horizon.

What is a Thunderbolt?

Nothing more than an ordinary flash of lightning. In old times it was believed that something solid passed along the path of a flash. Now, small meteorites sometimes fall from the sky and bury themselves in the ground. They may have given rise to the idea of a solid thunderbolt, though they have no connection whatever with thunder and lightning. The objects exhibited in some country museums as " thunderbolts " are usually lumps of a mineral called iron pyrites, and the term " thunderbolt " is misleading.

What makes the Winds blow?

A wind is a current of cooler air rushing to take the place of warmer air rising in some other part of the world.

What is the Beaufort Scale?

The Beaufort Scale which is now used in weather forecasts for shipping and has long been used by the International Meteorological Committee as part of the code for communicating weather conditions, was invented in 1805 by Admiral Sir Francis Beaufort. It consists of a series of numbers from 0 to 12, each number indicating a certain strength or velocity of wind from calm to hurricane. These numbers, with wind velocity in brackets, are as follows: 0, calm (0 miles per hour); 1, light air (1–3 m.p.h.); 2, slight breeze (4–7 m.p.h.); 3, gentle breeze (8–12 m.p.h.); 4, moderate breeze (13–18 m.p.h.); 5, fresh breeze (19–24 m.p.h.); 6, strong breeze (25–31 m.p.h.); 7, high wind (32–38 m.p.h.); 8, gale (39–46 m.p.h.); 9, strong gale (47–54 m.p.h.); 10, whole gale (55–63 m.p.h.); 11, storm (64–75 m.p.h.); 12, hurricane (above 75 m.p.h.)

What are Hurricanes?

Hurricanes are violent, revolving tropical storms which occur in the Carribbean area and often cause great destruction. Similar storms occur in certain other parts of the world, e.g., the cyclones of the Bay of Bengal and the Arabian Sea, the typhoons of the China Sea and the " Willy-Willies " of Western Australia. In West Africa and parts of the United States (especially the Mississippi-Missouri Valley), small violent storms called *tornadoes* sometimes occur. In the United States these are frequently accompanied by thunder, lightning and heavy rain, and take the form of a swirling funnel of dark cloud, which moves across the country at a speed of about 40 m.p.h. Great damage is caused where the heart of the tornado strikes.

What is a Cyclone?

A wind which blows round in a circle, while the circle as a whole moves forward. A very violent cyclone in the tropics is called a typhoon, or, if its area is very small, a tornado. The damage done by a cyclone of this kind is very great, and sometimes accompanied by much loss of life.

Where do the Winds called Khamsin, Sirocco, Harmattan, Mistral and Chinook blow?

The *Khamsin* is a hot, dust-laden wind blowing northwards over Egypt in the spring. The *Sirocco* is another wind from the hot interior of Africa which blows from the south over the North African coast and over Sicily, Italy, Malta and Greece. The *Harmattan* blows westwards from the Sahara over countries on the west coast of Africa, and the Atlantic Ocean. Besides being very hot, it carries clouds of fine red dust, which have been met with several hundreds of miles out at sea. Its season is December, January and February. The *Mistral* is a cold, dry wind which blows southwards from the central highlands of France and from the Alps in winter and spring, and affects the north Mediterranean coast from Spain to the Gulf of Genoa. The *Chinook* is a warm dry wind blowing down the mountain-slopes in the Rockies of Canada. A similar wind in the Alps is called *Foehn*, and it clears away more snow in an hour or two than would many days of sunshine.

What are the Trade Winds?

Winds which blow with great constancy in two belts about 1,400 miles wide near and on each side of the equator. The northern " trades " blow from the north-east, and the southern trades from the south-east. Their name is due to the great help given by them to sailing ships bringing produce from distant lands.

What are the Monsoons?

Seasonal winds blowing over tropical Asia and Australia. In the northern summer Asia gets very hot and the winds blow in from all the bordering oceans. Over India these are called the south-west or wet monsoons, and they bring heavy summer rain. In the northern winter and southern summer the winds blow out of Asia and into Australia. They leave Asia as dry monsoons—India's north-east monsoons—but then gather moisture from the ocean and bring summer rain to northern Australia.

How is Rainfall measured?

By means of an apparatus called a rain-gauge. The usual form is a funnel measuring either 5 or 8 inches across the mouth. The rain falling into this is caught in a bottle and poured into a graduated measuring-glass, which shows to a tiny fraction of an inch what depth of rain-water has fallen on the gauge since it was last emptied. There are more expensive forms which register the rainfall mechanically on a dial or trace a record on a chart.

Why may Rain be expected when Swallows fly Low?

Because the chilling of the upper air which precedes rain drives down the insects on which swallows feed.

Why may Fine Weather be looked for when Spiders are busy spinning their webs?

Insects are very sensitive to changes in the weather. When fine weather approaches, the spiders spin to catch the flies which appear in large numbers during such conditions.

What is a Waterspout?

A column of wet cloud formed between the clouds and the sea by the action of a whirlwind. It begins as a funnel-shaped cloud, which descends slowly till it meets a conical body of water rising from the sea. After a time the waterspout bursts. Some authorities think that the water in the column is made up largely of rain gathered by the whirlwind into a small space. Waterspouts are most common in the tropics.

Why is there no Frost at Night in Summer?

Because the earth picks up sufficient heat during the day to keep it above freezing-point during the night.

Why do Fires sometimes fill a Room with Smoke when first lighted?

Because the air in the chimney is still cold and will not move, so preventing the escape of the smoke. For this reason it is wise, before the fire is laid, to burn a few newspapers in a grate that has not been used for some time, to create a current and get rid of this cold air.

How does a Chimney help to draw up a Fire?

The hot air and gases in it, being lighter than the air outside, rise and draw fresh air in, and part of this air passes through the fire.

Why are Factory Chimneys made so tall?

In order to carry smoke and fuel gases so high that they will be blown clear of the neighbourhood.

What causes a Rainbow?

The reflection of sunlight from falling drops of water. Rays of different colours are bent in different degrees while being reflected, so that the drops reflecting, say, red to the eye of the beholder must be in a different position from those reflecting blue. This accounts for the separate bands of colours.

Why does Water gurgle when poured out of a Bottle?

The gurgling is due to large bubbles of air entering the bottle. What happens is this: first some water flows out, reducing the air pressure inside the bottle till it is lower than that of the air outside. The water then flows with less force, and air enters through the neck, checking the flow for a moment. The balancing of the pressure inside the bottle allows more water to pour out and stop air entering till the air balance is again upset, when more air gains admission. And so on till the bottle is empty.

What attempts are being made to Harness the Energy of the Sun?

For many hundreds of years men have tried to harness the energy of the sun. In recent times solar ovens have been built for research, but have been too expensive to put to industrial uses.

One of the most powerful solar furnaces in the world has been built by French scientists at the old castle of Montlouis, in the Pyrenees. Large reflectors are used to trap the Sun's rays and reflect them to the oven, which can produce enough heat to melt 130 lb. of iron per hour.

Australian scientists hope that within the next fifty to a hundred years it will become possible to use energy from the Sun to take the salt out of seawater, which could then be used to irrigate the dry lands of Australia.

MONEY

Why is Money used?

As a medium of exchange; that is, as something which everyone is willing to accept or give in exchange for something else. It does away with the need for direct exchange or barter. A workman receives money in exchange for his labour, and gives it to other people in exchange for whatever he may want. This is a much more convenient system than the direct exchange of work for groceries, clothes, and so on. Civilised nations use as money, coins and pieces of paper, the value of which is guaranteed by a bank or government. Among savages, shells, salt, tobacco, or anything else that is scarce, and therefore highly valued, may serve the same purpose.

Why do we use £ s. d. as Symbols for Pounds, Shillings and Pence?

They are the first letters of the Roman words, *libræ* (pounds), *solidi* (shillings), and *denarii* (pence).

Why is the Symbol $ used to mean Dollars?

One explanation is that the Spaniards, who first colonised America, used a dollar called a " piece of eight," as it was worth 8 reals. The original symbol for this coin is said to have been /8/, the lines on each side of the figure serving to distinguish it from an ordinary arithmetical 8. Later on the two lines were drawn through the figure $ (one line only is sometimes used to-day). Another explanation traces the symbol back to the Pillars of Hercules, the arms of Cadiz, in Spain, adopted by Charles the Fifth of Spain, and stamped on " pillar pieces," which were exported to America. The two pillars of the design were joined by a scroll turned round them.

Have we got a Copper Coinage?

No. Our " coppers " are made of bronze, a mixture of copper, tin and zinc. Until 1860 pure copper was used for pence, halfpence and farthings, but in that year a Royal Proclamation substituted bronze, which is harder and wears better.

Why is the word "Pound" used as a Money Value?

In the time of William the Conquerer the money standard of value was a pound weight of almost pure silver, or pound sterling. This was divided into 240 pence. When, in 1816, the silver pound was abolished, and the gold sovereign became the standard of value, the name of pound was transferred to the sovereign.

How can Pennies, Halfpence and Farthings be made use of otherwise than as Coins?

A halfpenny is exactly an inch across, and thus is useful in making small measurements. Three pennies or five halfpence weigh exactly an ounce; two-halfpence and a farthing half an ounce.

Why is a Two-shilling Piece called a Florin?

The word is derived from the Italian *florino*, meaning " a little flower," and was first applied to a very beautiful Florentine coin of the twelfth century, stamped with the city's emblem, a lily. The name spread to coins of other countries, including England, where a gold florin was minted in the reign of Edward the Third. Our present florin was first issued in 1849.

Why are little Grooves formed in the edge of a Shilling?

The " milling " or fluting of the edges of gold and silver coins was adopted to prevent clipping or filing them away to get precious metal, for such treatment would be detected at once and render the coin " bad." The threepenny piece in use before the present twelve-sided coin was issued is not milled because originally it was, like the silver 4d., 2d. and 1d., a " Maundy " coin, not meant for general circulation. In 1845 it was issued for ordinary circulation, but its plain edge was retained.

What is meant by Interest on Money?

A lends £500 to B. This sum of £500 is called the " principal." As A has lost the use of his money for the time being, B agrees to pay A, say, " 5 per cent. per annum " on the principal. This means that B will make a payment, called interest, at the rate of £5 for every £100 borrowed, and will make it every year (per annum) until the principal is repaid. Interest is usually divided into two equal half-yearly payments. In this case, then, £12 10s. would be due to A every six months. Where the principal is repaid in stages, the amount to be paid as interest (but not the rate of interest) is, of course, reduced proportionately as the loan is paid off.

What is a Cheque?

A written order to a banker to pay a sum of money to the person or firm whose name appears on it. The banker will not, of course, pay unless the person who signs the cheque—called the " drawer " of it—has enough money in the bank to cover the sum mentioned on the cheque. Payment by cheque does away with the necessity for keeping and transferring large amounts of actual cash, and makes the transaction of business much easier.

SILVER PENNY. HENRY II   SILVER PENNY. STEPHEN   St EADMUND PENNY

WILLIAM I PENNY   AN EDWARD III NOBLE   A HENRY VI ANGEL

A HENRY VIII SHILLING   AN EDWARD VI SHILLING   A MARY GROAT

AN ELIZABETH SOVEREIGN   A JAMES I SIXPENCE   A NEWARK SIEGE SHILLING

A CHARLES I OXFORD CROWN   A COMMONWEALTH SHILLING   A CROMWELL SHILLING   A CHARLES II TWO GUINEA PIECE

SHILLING WILLIAM & MARY   SHILLING GEORGE II   SHILLING GEORGE IV   DOUBLE FLORIN VICTORIA

Specially drawn for this work.

On this page are represented some of the British coins minted during the last eight centuries. Perhaps the most interesting of these specimens of *money* (see p. 388) is the diamond-shaped shilling of Charles I., struck at Newark during the siege of that town in 1645 by the Parliamentarians—as the abbreviation OBS (= obsidium = siege) shows. The one instance of a head other than that of the reigning sovereign appearing on an English coin is the Cromwell Shilling.

Why is the Bank of England so named?

Because, when it was founded in 1694, it was the only bank allowed to do business in England. Until 1946 it was a private corporation but became nationalised in that year. It acts as the Government banker, managing the National Debt, paying interest on it, issuing loans, and other State business, including the issue of bank-notes. Ever since 1780, when there was a danger of the Bank being attacked during the Gordon Riots, it has been furnished every night with a military guard, supplied by the battalion of Foot Guards on duty.

What is a Stock Exchange?

A place where stocks and shares of public companies, and securities issued by governments or local authorities, are bought and sold. But for these markets of such things it would be difficult for private people to get into touch with other people wanting to sell or purchase securities. The only persons who have the right to do actual buying or selling on a stock exchange are the members of it, who are bound by strict rules. Any private person wishing to buy or sell has to employ a broker who is a member and charges a fee, called a commission, for doing the business. The chief stock exchange in Britain is that in Throgmorton Street, London, commonly called "The House." Most large cities have their own stock exchanges.

What are Consols?

The word is a shortened form of Consolidated Fund. In 1751 the public debt of the country was made up of a large number of loans dating from different periods. To save confusion and trouble, most of these loans were then put together, or consolidated, into one fund. Consols differ from other public loans in that the Government is not bound to pay them off at any definite time.

What is meant by the National Debt?

Money borrowed by the Government from time to time and not yet paid back. It consists mostly of debts incurred to carry on wars. The war against Napoleon added over £600,000,000 to it, swelling it to about £900,000,000. In spite of the South African War (1899–1902) the total had been reduced to £661,000,000 in 1914. But the cost of the First World War swelled the figure to £7,800,000,000, and it has since been enormously increased by the Second World War. On March 31st, 1958, the National Debt amounted to over £27,232 million.

Why do our Postage Stamps bear the words "Postage" and "Revenue"?

To show that they may legally be used either for paying postage on letters or parcels, or for revenue purposes, such as stamping a receipt or agreement. This provision does away with the need for issuing two separate series of stamps.

What is an Underwriter?

A person who, in return for a payment called a premium, undertakes certain responsibilities. A marine underwriter guarantees ships and their cargoes against loss and damage up to a certain amount. An underwriter of the shares of a company about to be floated agrees to take up and pay for a certain number of shares if the public does not subscribe for all the shares offered.

What does the word "Limited" after the name of a Company mean?

That the liability of a shareholder in the company is limited to the value of his shares. In other words, that no shareholder who has paid the company the full price at which his shares were issued can legally be called upon to make any further payments to help the company out of any difficulties into which it may get.

What are Rates?

Payments which the owner or occupier of buildings or land has to make half-yearly to the local authorities of the town, district, or county in which the property is situated. Every property is assessed, or valued, officially for rating purposes, and a rate of so much in the pound is levied on it. The money thus raised is used for education, drainage, roads, police, public assistance and for other local services. Rates may be called local taxes. They vary according to the needs of the district in which they are levied. Water companies have the right to levy a special rate, called a water rate, on houses which they supply with water.

What are Tithes?

Payments made by the owners of land in a parish to the rector of the parish. The rector may be a clergyman or a layman. In the second case the clergyman of the parish is called a vicar and is paid a fixed sum every year, while the lay rector receives what are called the great tithes. Originally tithes were a tenth part of the crops and livestock raised in a parish yearly. The rector had the right to take every tenth sheaf of corn from a field, and store it in his tithe barn. Some of the old tithe barns are still standing. This rather clumsy way of collecting tithe was done away with in 1836 by the Tithe Act, which enacted that a landlord, instead of paying in actual produce, should pay a sum called tithe rent-charge, varying from year to year with the price of corn. Tithes were instituted for the support of the clergy. At first they were voluntary, but later on they were made compulsory by law. Under recent legislation arrangements have been made for tithes to be eventually completely extinguished by the Exchequer taking over the rights of all present tithe-owners in exchange for Government stock.

What is a Tariff?

A list of duties placed on articles imported into a country. A tariff may be designed merely to provide revenue (as is mainly the case in Great Britain), or to protect home industries against injury by the importation of foreign-made goods.

What are Death Duties?

A tax payable out of property after the death of its owner is levied on the total value of an estate (which in this case means land, house property, investments, and any other kind of possession on which a value can be put), the rate increasing with total value. An estate that is less than £3,000 pays no tax at all. Above £3,000 the tax rises from £1 on every £100 to £80 out of every £100 when the value reaches a million pounds and over.

What is meant by the Gold Standard?

That a country's currency is by law linked with gold and made exchangeable for gold on a fixed basis. Thus, while we were on the gold standard pounds sterling could be exchanged for gold on the basis of £3 17s. 10½d. per ounce of gold. Going off the gold standard implies that the link is broken, and the pound sterling has whatever value other nations still on the gold standard choose to give it, which probably will be lower than its previous value. During the war of 1914–18 and for a period afterwards, we were off the standard, but in 1925 we went back to it at the old pre-war rate. In 1931, however, following a period of acute depression, we found it necessary once more to abandon the gold standard. The 1914–18 war drove France, Italy, Germany, and other nations off the gold standard, and when they returned to it the " stabilised " values of their currencies, relatively to our own, were very much lower than before. For example, whereas in 1913 about 25 francs would purchase a pound sterling, the franc was stabilised at rather more than 124 francs to the pound. In 1949, after the Second World War, over a thousand francs were needed to buy one pound. Our pound sterling has still a link with gold as it is linked to the U.S.A. dollar; and the dollar equals in value a fixed weight of gold. An ounce of gold in the U.S.A. is equal to $35.

NAMES AND PHRASES

How did Americans come to be called Yankees?

The explanation generally accepted is that, when the North American Indians met the first English settlers, and tried to say " English," the nearest they could get to the sound was " Yankee." Over here Americans in general are spoken of as Yankees, but in the United States the word is used particularly of the inhabitants of the New England States.

What is an Eurasian?

A person of mixed European and Asian ancestry.

How are the following Surnames and Title Names pronounced?

Abergavenny, Beauchamp, Beaulieu, Bethune, Cholmondeley, Colquhoun, Farquharson, Knollys, Marjoribanks, Mainwaring, McLeod, Tredegar and Wemyss.

Abergavenny	Aber gen' ny.
Beauchamp	Beech' am.
Beaulieu	Bew' ly.
Bethune	Bee' ton.
Cholmondeley	Chum' ly.
Colquhoun	Ko hoon'.
Farquharson	Fark' a son.
Knollys	Knowls.
Marjoribanks	Marsh' banks or March' banks.
Mainwaring	Man' ner ing.
McLeod	Ma Cloud.
Tredegar	Tre dee' gar.
Wemyss	Weems.

What are the Origins of " Sir," " Mr." and " Esq." used in addressing a man in talk or on paper?

" Sir " is a shortened form of " Sire," which itself is derived from the Latin word *senior* (elder). " Mr." is a contraction of " Mister " or " Master." " Esq." is the abbreviation of " Esquire," which is a title of dignity ranking below knight, and should strictly be given only to sons of barons, baronets and knights, J.P.'s and barristers, but is to-day used indiscriminately.

What are the Meanings of " Mrs." and " Madam "?

" Mrs." is a contraction of " mistress "; " Madam " is the English form of the French " Madame " (my lady).

What is meant by " The Old Lady of Threadneedle Street "?

The Bank of England.

How did the Streets in London called Cheapside, Fetter Lane, Gracechurch Street, Holborn, Threadneedle Street and the Strand come to be so named?

Cheapside is derived from the Anglo-Saxon *ceapan*, to buy. A market was once held in it. Fetter Lane is a corruption of Faitour Lane, the Lane of Ruffians. It was once a favourite haunt of footpads. Gracechurch Street was formerly Grass Church Street, being named after the herbs once sold there. Holborn is a shortened form of Hollow Bourne—the stream running through the hollow now crossed by Holborn Viaduct. Threadneedle Street means Three Needle Street. In it were displayed the three needles which formed the arms of the Needlemakers' Company. The Strand was so called because it was on the banks of the Thames; it was the main road from the City to Westminster.

Why is England sometimes called Albion?

The word comes from the Latin *albus* = white. Perhaps the Romans, when they first landed in Britain, were particularly struck by the whiteness of the cliffs near Dover.

How did the Isle of Man gets its Name, and to whom did it originally belong?

Probably in the first place from Manannan, a god of Gaelic mythology. Later it was sometimes known as Mona, though this name rightly belongs to Anglesey. In early times the island was inhabited by Celtic people. Before A.D. 700 it was conquered by Scandinavian " rovers " who were eventually expelled by Norwegians. Later it was handed over to Scotland, but the Manx appealed to England and Edward I took charge of the island.

In 1406, Henry IV gave the island to the Stanley family and the Earls of Derby were Lords of Man until 1736, when it passed to the Duke of Atholl. Certain rights were bought by the English crown from the Duke for £70,000 in 1765 owing to the fact that the island had become a great centre for smuggling. In 1828 the remaining rights were bought for over £400,000, but the Island still has its own Parliament.

STRANGE CREATURES OF THE SEA:

A bewildering variety of fish live in the sea and some of their strange ways are illustrated here. There are several fish which can fly, while the Gurnard can fly and walk ; both the mud-skipper and climbing Perch spend some of their time out of water. The Sargasso fish, like the Brill, protects itself by camouflage, the Puffer distends itself and presents a skin beset with spines, and the Lion fish has poison spines. Sawfish are

SAILFISH

SAWFISH

FOX
SHARK
AND
SUCKER FISH

SPOTTED
EAGLE RAY

LION FISH

ELECTRIC EEL

THE FIGHTING-FISH'S
NEST OF BUBBLES

LASIOGNATHUS
SACCOSTOMA

SARGASSO FISH

SEA HORSE

CHAMELEON OF
THE SEA BED
BRILL

GYMNARCHUS NILOTICUS

PREHENSILE TAIL

NEAVE
PARKER

I.L.N.

among the most savage of sea creatures ; the Electric Eel can give a severe shock.   With a form of radar in its tail the Nile fish (*Gymnarchus niloticus*) can avoid obstacles when swimming backwards.   Nest-builders include the three-spined Stickleback and the Fighting fish, and among anglers are the Angler fish, the *Lasiognathus saccostoma*, and the deep-sea Angler (*Linophryne arborifer*), while the Archer fish is an expert marksman.

Why is the Bishop of the Island known as the Bishop of Sodor and Man?

Originally the Isle of Man was included with the Hebrides and other Scottish islands in the Norwegian possessions known as the Sodorenses. When Norway lost these Islands changes took place and in 1344 the English bishopric was limited to the Isle of Man, but the name Sodor was still retained in the Bishop's title.

Why is the Dead Sea so named?

Because its waters are so salt that no fish can live in it.

What is meant by El Dorado?

A city or district in South America supposed by explorers of the sixteenth century to abound in wealth, especially gold. The words mean " the gilded man," and originally referred to the imaginary ruler of this equally imaginary country, who was reported to cover himself with gold dust. Sir Walter Raleigh's last expedition was made in search of El Dorado, which he naturally failed to discover. We now speak of any place very rich in minerals, or where fortunes can be made quickly, as an El Dorado.

What are Jetsam and Flotsam?

Jetsam is anything thrown deliberately overboard to lighten a ship when it is in danger of sinking. Flotsam includes anything left floating by a ship that has sunk.

Why is Foolscap Paper so named?

Because the first sheets of paper of this size (13½ by 8 inches) had a fool's cap on them as the watermark.

Why is Calico so named?

After Calicut, a seaport on the western coast of India, which for a long time was famous for weaving this kind of cotton cloth. Calico was first imported from there into Europe by the Portuguese in the fifteenth century.

Why is an Omnibus so named?

The word is Latin, meaning " for all," and was very fittingly chosen to describe a public vehicle in which anyone may ride on payment of a fare.

What is a Dower House?

A house built on a large estate to which the widow of the previous owner may retire when his heir occupies the chief residence.

Why is an Umbrella so called?

The name is an Italian word meaning " a little shade." The umbrella was invented many centuries ago in the East, where it was used as a sunshade. It was introduced into England as a protection against rain rather than sun. The first man brave enough to carry an umbrella in the streets of London was Jonas Hanway. After his death in 1786 a monument was erected in his memory in the North Transept of Westminster Abbey, where it may still be seen.

Why are Sailors called Jack Tars?

Jack is the name given half-affectionately to bluejackets as a class, as " Tommy " to soldiers.

The word " tar " is here probably a shortened form of tarpaulin, meaning a hat made of or covered with tarred cloth, once worn in the Navy.

What is meant by " Conscience Money "?

The conscience of some people who have defrauded the revenue by not paying all the taxes they should leads them to send to the Chancellor of the Exchequer all or part of what they have held back. Such money is called conscience money. It is usually—for a very good reason—sent without any name being given, and therefore has to be acknowledged by an announcement in the daily papers.

What is a Dutch Auction?

An auction at which the thing to be sold is first put up at a higher price than anyone is likely to bid. The price is then gradually lowered, and the first person to make a bid has the thing knocked down to him. This method of selling is the reverse of a real auction, in which the price is run up in stages, and the highest bidder secures the article.

Why is the Canter of a Horse so named?

In the Middle Ages pilgrims riding to the shrine of Thomas à Becket at Canterbury made their horses develop a pace which was called a Canterbury Gallop. The name has since been shortened to canter.

Why is the public system of distributing Letters called the Post?

Before there were any railways, relays of horses were kept at certain posts, or fixed places, along a road, to enable people to travel along it continuously at a good speed. The earliest post offices were thus the offices at which one applied for a fresh horse or horses. Making a journey as fast as possible was called travelling post. The riders of coaches carrying the mails travelled post; and presently the method of travelling was adopted as the name of the general system of distributing letters.

What is the Origin of the word " Mile "?

Mile is a slightly altered form of the Latin word " mille," meaning a thousand. The Roman measure used for reckoning large distances was " a thousand paces," a pace being the distance between two successive points at which the same heel came down—what we should call two paces. Taking the Roman pace as 5 feet the " thousand paces " was about 93 yards shorter than our mile

What distinctive names are given to groups of animals and birds when moving about together?

One speaks of a flock of sheep, a herd (or drove) of cattle, a pack of hounds or wolves, a pride of lions, a tribe of goats, a nest of rabbits, a down of hares, a herd of buffaloes, giraffes and deer, a kindle of kittens, a litter of pups or pigs, a troop of monkeys, a sculk of foxes, and a sounder of hogs. For birds: a bevy of quails, a brood of grouse, a cast of hawks, a covey of partridges, a fall of woodcocks, a gaggle of geese (ground), a skein of geese (flying), a flock of geese (driven), a muster of peacocks, a flight of doves

ALUMINIUM FROM JAMAICA

A rapidly-growing industry of Jamaica is the mining and processing of bauxite, the raw material of *aluminium* (see p. 384). At the Kirkvine plant (above) and other centres, the red ore is converted into alumina, which is shipped from Port Esquivel to the great new plant of the Aluminium Company of Canada at Kitimat, British Columbia, as well as to ports in Norway, Sweden and France.

Photos: Alumina Jamaica Ltd.

This is Port Esquivel, Jamaica, where ore-ships collect their cargoes of alumina for Kitimat in distant British Columbia. Alumina, the raw material of aluminium, is really processed bauxite and looks rather like salt. The picture shows the alumina storage silos and the conveyor belt which loads it into the holds of the ore vessels at the rate of about 12,000 tons in 24 hours.

or swallows, a nide of pheasants, a watch of nightingales, a herd of swans, cranes or curlews, a spring of teals, a covert of coots, a congregation of plovers, a walk (or wisp) of snipe, a murmuration of starlings, an enchantment (or exaltation) of larks, a host of sparrows, a charm of goldfinches, a brood of hens, and a chattering of choughs.

Why is the Paid Driver of a Private Motor Car called a Chauffeur?

The word is the French for stoker. Many of the earliest motor cars were driven by steam and needed the services of a stoker. When the petrol engine ousted steam the name was transferred, more or less in fun, to the driver.

What is a Round Robin?

A petition with the names of all the people who sign it arranged all round it like the spokes of a wheel, or end-to-end in a circle, so that no name shall draw special attention to itself. The words are a corruption of the French " rond ruban " (circular ribbon). Many years ago French Government officials wishing to make complaints wrote their names on a band of ribbon attached to the petition.

Who are the Beef-eaters?

Members of a corps called the Yeomen of the Guard, who act as a royal bodyguard on State occasions. They still wear the Tudor uniform assigned to them when the corps was founded in Henry the Seventh's reign to wait at the royal table. The word beef-eater is commonly thought to be a corruption of the French " buffetier "—one who waits at a buffet or sideboard, but there is good reason to believe that it is to be taken literally, as indicating a servant fed on the best of food. The Warders of the Tower of London wear a similar uniform and are allied to the Yeomen, but their duties are distinct.

Who was the Flying Dutchman?

A legendary Dutch sea-captain, named Van Straaten, who committed a dreadful crime and was doomed to try vainly for ever to sail round the Cape of Good Hope. Sailors believed that if the Flying Dutchman's ship were sighted a disaster would happen to them. In the English version of the legend his name is usually given as Vanderdecken. The great composer, Wagner, took the legend as the subject of one of his operas—" Der Fliegende Holländer."

Why is a Policeman nicknamed a " Bobby "?

After the founder of our present police force, Sir Robert Peel, whose name also appears in the less familiar " peeler."

Why is a general Holiday called a Bank Holiday?

Many years ago a law was passed which allowed all banks to be closed on Christmas Day and Good Friday (as well as, of course, on Sundays). In 1871 an Act of Parliament added Easter Monday, Whit Monday, the first Monday in August, and Boxing Day (the day after Christmas Day). The closing of banks on these days naturally led to the closing of other places of business, and " bank holiday " now means a day on which all except absolutely necessary work is suspended. In Scotland the bank holidays are New Year's Day, Good Friday, the first Mondays in May and August, and Christmas Day.

Why is the place in a Railway Station where tickets are sold called a Booking-office?

In the days of stage coaches a person wishing to engage a seat on a coach went to an office where his or her name was entered in a *book*. When railways first came in, a passenger's name was written on a page of a book of tickets together with the fare, and the torn-out page was handed to him. Presently tickets were printed and issued in the stations from offices to which the name of booking-office was transferred, since in them a passenger purchased his right to travel on a train.

What were Scylla and Charybdis?

Scylla was a six-headed monster, mentioned by Homer. This creature lived on a rock in the Straits of Messina, between Italy and Sicily; Charybdis was a dangerous whirlpool close by. Homer describes in his " Odyssey " how six of Odysseus' companions were seized by Scylla as his ship passed her lair, and how, later on, Odysseus himself was nearly engulfed by Charybdis. The proverb " to go between Scylla and Charybdis " means to be on a course which may lead you into one danger if you try to avoid another.

What is a Ricksha?

A light two-wheeled carriage for two passengers, drawn by a man running in front between shafts. The jinriksha, to give it its full name, is of Japanese origin. It is used in Japan, other countries of the East, and South Africa, where it does much of the work done by cabs here.

What is " Toc H "?

In 1915 the Rev. P. B. Clayton opened at Poperinghe, in Belgium, a rest and recreation house for soldiers, named Talbot House, the title of which was soon shortened into its initials (" Toc " stands for " T " in signalling). In 1917 a Little Talbot House was added at Ypres. To quote from *Punch*, " both brought a corner of heaven into the hell of men's and officers' lives." After the war, Toc H was developed into a big Christian club having as its object the handing on to the younger generation of the teaching and practice of Christianity, fellowship, service, and fair-mindedness, for which Toc H stood during hostilities. It was incorporated by Royal Charter in 1922 with the Prince of Wales (H.R.H. the Duke of Windsor) as patron, and now has a membership of many thousands; some hundreds of groups and branches in Britain, the Dominions, the U.S.A. and South America; and Toc H houses in many places.

What is meant by " Act of God "?

It is a legal phrase signifying some act of Nature, such as an earthquake or storm, which cannot be foreseen or resisted.

What is meant by giving Parole?

An officer captured in war is said to be released on parole if he has given his parole, or word of honour, that he will not go beyond certain limits and will not try to escape; or, if given complete freedom, that he will take no further part in the war. To break parole is regarded as a deep disgrace by friends and foes alike.

What is the meaning of " to Cross the Rubicon "?

To take a decisive step that commits one to a risky enterprise from which there is no retreat. For example, a man may be said to Cross the Rubicon when he stakes all the money he possesses on a horse. The origin of the phrase is as follows: in 49 B.C. Julius Cæsar, at the head of an army, was proconsul of Cisalpine Gaul, the name then given to the part of Italy north of the little River Rubicon. Cæsar quarrelled with the Government at Rome, and by Crossing the Rubicon into Italy proper on January 6th, at the head of his troops—which as proconsul he had no right to do—he practically made a declaration of war.

What is meant by a thing being " Taboo "?

That it is forbidden by custom or public opinion. Thus we say that it is taboo for a man to keep his hat on in a place of religious worship. The word has been imported from Polynesia, where certain persons or things are shunned as being accursed or sacred.

Why is a very Wealthy Man said to be as rich as Crœsus?

Crœsus was a King of Lydia, in Asia Minor, who lived in the sixth century before Christ and was considered to be the wealthiest monarch of his time. His name has ever since been proverbial for wealth.

Why is a very highly valued Honour, Post, or Pride, called a " Blue Ribbon "?

Because the ribbon of the highest order of knighthood—that of the Garter—is a blue one. The Derby is the blue ribbon of horse-racing, the Wimbledon Championship that of lawn tennis; and the Lord Chancellorship is the blue ribbon of the law.

What happens to a Person who is " Sent to Coventry "?

His companions take no notice of him, as a punishment for having offended them or transgressed some rule of behaviour. The expression dates from the time when soldiers quartered on the citizens of Coventry were cold-shouldered by all the people of the town as a silent protest.

What is meant by having Blue Blood in one's Veins?

Being of noble birth or very good family. The expression is thought to have originated in Spain, where centuries ago the families of pure Spanish descent were lighter skinned than those which had intermarried with the Moors, and showed the veins more clearly through their more transparent skin.

NATURAL HISTORY

MAMMALS

How do we get our Knowledge of what extinct Animals, Birds and Fish were like?

In some cases the complete creature has been found in a fossilised condition. In others, bones, teeth and other parts give clues as to species, size and form. And in a very few cases animals have been preserved by intense cold in their original condition.

How can we tell the Order in which Various Kinds of Extinct Creatures came into existence and disappeared?

By noting the rock strata in which their remains are found. Those occurring in the older rocks must have lived before those occurring in later rocks.

What kinds of Creatures were a Dinosaur, a Pterodactyl and a Mammoth?

A dinosaur was a giant reptile, which fed on vegetation or other animals; and the pterodactyl a winged reptile. The mammoth was a prehistoric elephant, covered with a thick coat of hair to protect it from intense cold. It lived at a much later date than the other two, and was hunted by our very early ancestors.

Could Prehistoric Animals live now?

Many of them no doubt could in those parts of the world where conditions are now much the same as those to which they were accustomed. But a great deal would depend upon whether food of the right kind were plentiful.

What is Animal Camouflage?

Camouflage is a method of hiding from view by trying to look like something else. The tiger, for example, has stripes which blend perfectly with the tall tropical grasses among which he lurks, while the lion is the same colour as the sand of his native desert. The patterns of giraffes, and the dappled skins of deer and antelopes, resemble the patterns cast by the sun as it shines through the leaves of the trees. Nevertheless, an animal's body is solid, and even if it lay down its lower parts would be in shadow and cause its form to stand out. To counteract this Nature has given light underparts to nearly all her creatures.

Some creatures, especially harmless insects, conceal themselves by having forms and colours like those of their more dangerous cousins. Their enemies mistake them for creatures they have learned to leave alone, and so they escape molestation. The hover-fly, for example, cannot bite or sting, but it looks so much like a wasp that no creature which has ever been stung by a wasp would risk attacking it.

Under the water it is not uncommon to find creatures dressing themselves up in heavy clothes so that they cannot be recognized. The caddis-worm covers his soft body with pebbles and little bits of stick, while some crabs deck themselves out in seaweed, or even cover their backs with other living creatures like sea-anemones !

What does the syllable " Brock " in the placenames Brockley, Brockenhurst, Brockhall and Brockhampton tell us?

That these places were once favourite haunts of the brock or badger.

Why does a Bat sleep during the Winter?

Because at that season the insects on which

WHERE BIRDS KEEP HOUSE

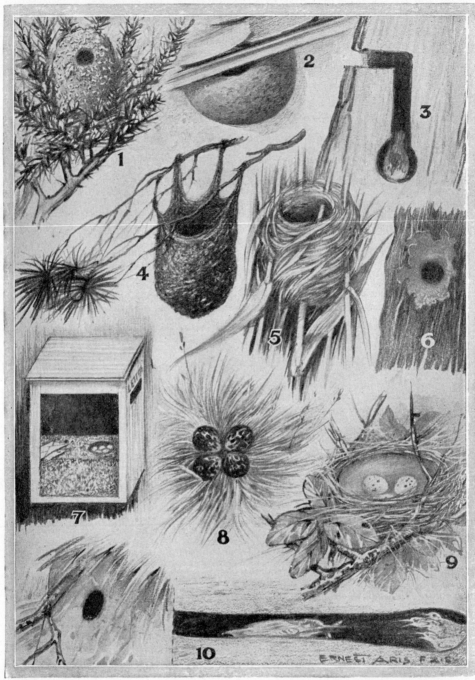

Specially drawn for this work.

The nests of birds vary much in character. The long-tailed tit (1) and the golden-crested wren (4) build lovely little nests among slender twigs ; the willow wren (5) weaves a nest among the stems of reeds ; and the thrush (9) lines its nest with mud. The house martin builds a nest (2) with pellets of clay under eaves. The woodpecker (3) bores a hole in a tree, while the nuthatch (6) makes use of an existing hole, the entrance to which it plasters round with mud. The kingfisher (10) excavates a hole in a river bank ; the peewit (8) adopts any convenient hollow in the ground ; and robins (7) often nest in strange places.

a bat feeds disappear. While asleep a bat needs very little nourishment to keep it alive, and exists on the reserve of fat with which it has clothed itself in the autumn. If it flew about, this reserve would soon be used up and the bat would die of starvation.

Why has a Cat got Whiskers?

A whisker is a very sensitive feeler and helps a cat to find its way in the dark and avoid obstacles. At the base of each whisker is a nerve which responds to the lightest touch.

Why has a Cat got padded feet?

So that it may tread quietly when stalking its prey.

Why is a Cat able to move about so easily in the dark?

Its eyes are sensitive to very weak light. It has been suggested that the eyes of cats, owls and other creatures which hunt by night may be able to use rays that do not affect our eyes.

Why does a Cat eat slowly and a Dog eat fast?

The ancestors of our domestic cat were solitary animals, hunting singly. When one made a kill, it could eat in peace. Our dogs are descended from animals which hunted in packs and all fell on a kill together, each eating fast to get the largest possible share.

Why does a Dog bury Bones?

Because its instinct tells it that, if it were to leave them about, other dogs might get them. It has doubtless inherited the habit from its wild ancestors.

How do a Cat's Eyes differ from a Dog's?

The pupil of a cat's eye is, when closed, a narrow vertical slit. When it opens, the iris moves to the sides, as if two tiny curtains were being drawn apart. The pupil of a dog's eye is round, as in the human eye, and expands equally in all directions.

From what Animals are Dogs descended?

From the wolf and the jackal. In the course of thousands of years six great groups have been developed from these: wolf-like dogs, greyhounds, spaniels, hounds, mastiffs and terriers.

Why have Dogs, Cats and Tigers got long pointed Teeth called Fangs?

To enable them to hold their prey fast when they seize it. They serve the same purpose as the talons of a bird of prey.

Why are Dogs more Sociable Animals than Cats?

In its wild state the dog is a member of a pack and used to company, whereas the cat is a solitary animal. The habits resulting from different modes of life have descended to the domesticated animals.

What is a Flying Fox?

A species of very large bat, found in Australia, India and the Pacific Islands. It lives on fruit.

What is the Difference between a Camel and a Dromedary?

The word dromedary is commonly used as meaning the one-humped Arabian camel, as opposed to the two-humped Bactrian camel. But its more correct meaning is an Arabian camel trained for riding and accustomed to trot, as distinguished from a baggage-camel.

How does the Indian Elephant differ from the African Elephant?

The Indian elephant has smaller ears than its African cousin, and smaller tusks. The African female elephant has tusks, but the Indian female is tuskless. The African elephant is the larger animal, and is said to be too wild for domestication.

Does an Elephant drink through its Trunk?

No. It draws water into its trunk, and then squirts the water from its trunk into its open mouth.

Whereabouts on a horse are the following parts: Withers, Forearm, Hock, Cannon, Fetlock and Pastern?

The *withers* are a ridge on the back at the base of the neck, just in front of where a riding saddle reaches to. A *forearm* is the upper part of a front leg. A *hock* is the joint half-way up a back leg, which looks like a knee turned the wrong way round. A *cannon* is the straight portion of the lower part of any leg. At the bottom end of a cannon is a bulge and joint called a *fetlock*. Between fetlock and hoof is the bone named *pastern*.

Why does a mother Kangaroo carry its young in a Pouch?

Because when the little kangaroos are born they are very weak and helpless, and could not possibly keep up with their mother, who moves in great leaps. So they are carried in the pouch until large and strong enough to look after themselves.

Do any other Animals carry their young in the same way as the Kangaroo?

Yes. The wombat, the dasyure, the bandicoot, the phalanger, the opossum, wallaby, koala, and a species of mole. All but the opossum, which is an American animal, belong to Australasia. They are grouped in a class called marsupials, a name derived from the Latin word "marsupium," meaning a pouch.

In what Countries are Lions found?

In Africa, India and Iran. The so-called mountain lion, or puma, of the New World is not a lion, but closely related to the leopard and jaguar.

Why is a Mole's Fur very short and glossy?

So that it may offer little resistance when the mole is forcing its way through the earth and may keep clean. The fur turns forwards as easily as backwards, making it easy for the mole to move in either direction.

What is a Molehill like inside?

The little mounds, commonly called molehills, seen scattered about a field in which moles have been active are merely the earth thrown up by moles from runs made in search of food. A mole's "fortress" or home is a much larger affair. It encloses a large central cavity in which he makes a snug globular nest of dead leaves or dry grass. Tunnels enter it from various directions, and it generally has a special " bolt " run for use if the mole should be surprised while in his nest. This slopes downwards from the bottom of the nest, and turns upwards again some distance from the " fortress."

What is the difference between a Monkey and an Ape?

Both " monkey " and " ape " are applied loosely to any animal of the monkey family. But the word " ape " is used more particularly of the gorilla, orang-utan, chimpanzee and gibbon, which have very long fore limbs, are tailless, and most closely resemble man in size and structure.

What Animal has most plagued the Country into which it was introduced from outside?

The rabbit. About a century ago a pair of rabbits were taken from England to Australia and let loose. The soil and climate suited them admirably. As there were no animals there to prey on them, rabbits multiplied so fast that they soon became the scourge of the Australian farmer. Trapping, shooting and poisoning on a huge scale made no noticeable difference in their numbers, which ran into many hundreds of millions. In recent years a method of infecting rabbits with a virus disease, myxomatosis, has been tried with excellent results. It is estimated that this campaign has resulted in an increase in wool and crops amounting to more than £50,000,000 within a few years. Research work is being carried out by the Australian National University in Canberra.

In what respects does the Indian Rhinoceros differ from the African?

The common Indian rhinoceros has deep folds in its skin and only one horn. The common African rhinoceros is two-horned, and its skin is not folded.

How many Kinds of Animals of the Weasel Family are found in Great Britain?

The true weasel, the stoat, the polecat and the pine marten. The ferret is probably only a hybrid descendant of a domesticated polecat.

How does a Stoat differ from a Weasel?

The stoat is larger than a weasel and has a much longer tail, which is tipped with black. The weasel is rather redder than the stoat, and the fur on its throat and belly is pure white, whereas that on the same parts of a stoat has a yellowish tinge.

Which is the largest of Living Creatures?

The blue rorqual, or fin-whale, which attains a length of 85 feet. Its nearest rival is probably the cachalot, or sperm whale, which, though not exceeding 60 feet in length, has a more massive head and body.

Is a Whale a Fish?

No, it is a mammal, that is, an animal which suckles its young. It differs also from a fish in having no scales on its body and in being warm-blooded. Moreover, it is an air-breather as much as a dog or horse, and has to come to the surface at intervals for air. In order that it may do this easily its tail is set across its body, and not up and down like that of a fish.

Why has a Whale got a thick coating of Blubber?

The blubber takes the place of a quadruped's hair or fur, or a bird's feathers, for keeping its body warm. It also helps to make the whale more buoyant.

What is Ambergris?

A grey substance from the intestines of a sperm whale. It has the peculiar property of strengthening the odour of scents, though it is itself practically odourless. Scent-distillers pay very high prices for it—more than its weight in gold—so that the man who finds a large lump of it floating about in the sea is lucky indeed.

What is Spermaceti?

A waxy substance which collects on the surface of oil taken from the head of the sperm whale. It is used for making candles and ointments.

What is the difference between a Hair Seal and a Fur Seal?

A hair seal has only one coat, of rather coarse and long hairs. A fur seal has a dense coat of short, fine and very soft hair, from which longer coarse hairs project. When a fur-seal skin is dressed the long hairs have their roots cut away very carefully on the inside of the skin and are all pulled out, leaving the valuable fur in place.

What Mammals lay Eggs?

Many people have heard of the curious creature found in Australia and Tasmania which goes by the various names of ornithorhynchus, duck-billed platypus and duck-mole. It has a beak like a duck and fur like that of a mole; it lives in the water, and it lays eggs. A full-grown specimen is about 20 inches long. The limbs are short, and the feet webbed, the front feet having powerful claws used in burrowing into river banks. The peculiarity of laying eggs, from which the young are hatched, is shared by two other much less well-known mammals, the common echidna and the three-toed echidna. Both of these are ant-eaters, whose bodies are covered with spines and stiff hairs. The first belongs to Australia, Tasmania and New Guinea; the second is found in New Guinea only. These three animals make up a class of mammals called Prototheria, which means primitive animals, belonging to a stage of development just above that of the reptiles.

Why do Grass-eating Animals spend so much time grazing?

Because their food contains very little nourishment and they must therefore eat a great deal of it. A flesh-eating animal, on the other hand, consumes enough food in a few minutes to satisfy its appetite for a long time, meat being highly nutritious.

Do Animals dream?

Dogs and cats certainly do so. Dogs sometimes bark and growl in their sleep, and, like

THE

DOG ROSE

The rose is one of the most typical flowers of the British countryside. A number of different species are to be found wild including the Sweetbriar, the Dog Rose, the Field Rose, the Downy Rose and the Scots (Burnet) Rose.

The Dog Rose (*Rosa Canina*) is the commonest of these wild roses, occurring throughout Europe. Abundant in Britain in hedgerows and thickets, it forms bushes about six feet high.

The stems (1) are of several years' duration and branch extensively. Each stem carries out the usual functions of supporting the leaves and flowers, of transporting water containing dissolved mineral salts and oxygen up to the leaves by means of the xylem or wood (5), and of conducting manufactured foods down the plant in the phloem or bast (3). The xylem and phloem are divided by a thin layer, cambium (4). The centre of the stem consists of pith (6). Suckers, which are branch stems arising underground, are frequently produced by the plant as a means of vegetative spread.

The leaves are borne at the nodes of the stem. Each leaf consists of a leaf base bearing very distinct stipules (15), a petiole or leaf stalk (16), and a lamina. The lamina is compound pinnate (14), made up usually of five oval, toothed leaflets (13). These leaflets are bounded by epidermal cells overlaid by a thin cuticle forming the upper and lower surfaces of the leaflet (7). Beneath the upper epidermis (9) is the photosynthetic tissue (10), containing chlorophyll in abundance. Carbohydrates are manufactured in these photosynthetic cells by the combination of carbon dioxide and water in the presence of chlorophyll and light. Above the lower epidermis (12) is the spongy tissue (11), with many air-spaces among the cells. It is here that a most gaseous exchange, necessary for the plant's life processes, takes place. Conduction is mainly carried out by the midrib of the leaflet (8). Curved prickles (2) occur on the stems and on the undersides of the leaves. These prickles are outgrowths from outer tissues only: they contain no xylem or phloem.

The inflorescence is a terminal corymb of three or four flowers which open rather early in the summer, *i.e.* May and June. The structure of each flower is that typical of the *Rosaceae*. On the receptacle (27), at the top of the pedicel (28), the floral parts are borne in whorls. The calyx consists of five green sepals, which protect the inner flower parts in the bud and which persist after fertilisation. Two of these sepals are smooth-edged (17), while the other three have lobed edges (18). The corolla is regular, and is made up of five, notched petals (19), varying in colour from deep to very pale pink. Bees and other insects are attracted to the flower by the coloured petals and the sweet scent, and bring about pollination.

(continued on page 4)

1

Insects visit the flowers mainly to collect pollen from the stamens (22). These stamens are numerous, and each consists of a filament (21) supporting an anther (20), which sheds its pollen towards the flower centre.

Within the flask-shaped receptacle (27), is an indefinite number of carpels (25). These are not joined together; each separate carpel surrounds one ovule (26). The styles (24), borne on the carpels, are distinct from each other, but form a hairy mass which scarcely projects through the opening of the receptacle. At the tip of each style is the stigma (23), for the reception of pollen. As the result of fertilisation each carpel becomes the wall of a fruit called an achene. The one-seeded achenes are the true fruits of the plant. But they are enclosed by the receptacle (27), which becomes orange-red, swollen and juicy. Thus is formed the false fruit of the Dog Rose — the scarlet hip, rich in Vitamin C — so familiar to all.

cats, twitch their noses and paws. Evidently they are dreaming of a chase or fight. So one may conclude that other animals dream as well.

Why have Lambs, Calves, and Foals disproportionately long legs?

In their wild state sheep, cattle and horses are hunted by wolves and other animals, and their young need long legs to enable them to escape.

BIRDS

Why does not Gravity pull a Bird down when it is Flying?

Because the bird's wings, beating on the air, give an upward thrust which counteracts the downward pull of the earth.

What Species of Birds cannot fly?

The ostrich; its relatives the emu, rhea and cassowary: the apteryx of New Zealand; and the penguin.

Why do Birds fluff their Feathers out in cold weather?

To keep themselves warm. The ruffled feathers imprison air, which is a bad conductor of heat and hinders heat from leaving the body. The long fur of many animals and the thick woollen clothes which we wear in winter act in the same way.

Why do Wild Geese fly in ∧-shaped lines?

This formation enables them to keep their leader in sight with less fatigue than if they flew abreast in straight lines.

Why do some Blackbirds have White Plumage?

Because their feathers have never received the usual dark pigment. Such plumage is a freak of Nature, like the hair of a white mouse or white rabbit.

Why do a Duck's Feathers throw off Water?

They are coated by a thin film of oil, procured by the duck from a gland near its tail, and applied with the bill during the process of preening the feathers.

Why are the back claws on Partridges' Feet undeveloped?

Because partridges live on the ground and do not perch on trees. A perching bird must have back claws in order that it may grip branches.

Why have Ducks and many other kinds of Water Birds got webbed feet?

To propel them easily through the water. A duck's foot closes as it draws it forwards, and opens during the backstroke, offering a large surface to the water.

Why do most Long-legged Birds have short Tails?

Such birds are usually wading birds, and the shortness of their tails prevents them getting wet. When flying, these birds trail their legs behind them and use them in place of a tail for steering and balancing.

Why have Ostriches got long Legs?

To enable them to escape from their enemies by running, as their wings are useless for flight.

Which is the smallest British Bird?

The golden-crested wren. It is only 3½ inches long, and weighs less than one-fifth of an ounce.

What Birds build the Largest Nests?

The Australian megapode, or mound-bird, which is of about the size of a turkey. It piles up a mound of sand, earth, pebbles and shells, and lays its eggs in it to be hatched by the heat of the sun. The mound may measure anything up to 150 feet round at the base, and contain many tons of material.

Why do Gulls fly Inland in Stormy and Cold Weather?

Because they are unable to find food in the sea at such times, and are driven to feed on worms and insects found on land.

How can one tell a Crow from a Rook?

Crows usually are seen singly or in pairs; rooks go about in flocks. A rook has a white or greyish membrane round the base of its beak, but a crow has not.

Why does a Hen cackle after laying an Egg?

Probably because having got rid of the egg makes her feel more comfortable and happy, and cackling is her way of expressing pleasure.

What was the Dodo?

A bird of the pigeon family which was found in the island of Mauritius until about the end of the seventeenth century, when it became extinct. It had a huge bill, hooked at the end, a body larger than a turkey's, and very small wings, which were useless for flight. We use the phrase " Extinct as the Dodo " of things that have gone entirely out of fashion.

FISH

Why cannot a Fish live out of Water?

A fish breathes through its gills, which extract from water the air dissolved in it. When a fish is taken out of water its gills become dry and useless, and it dies of suffocation.

Why are Fishes without Eyelids?

As their eyeballs are always in contact with water they have no need of eyelids to wipe and moisten them.

Why is a Flatfish dark above and white below?

Its dark upper side makes it difficult to see against the sand over which it moves. Its white under side makes it less visible when looked at from below. A flatfish always swims on its side, and this accounts for both its eyes being on the same side of its head.

Does a Flying-fish really Fly?

Many naturalists have held that its large fins merely enable it to glide through the air for a distance, under the impetus given by a blow of its tail as it leaves the water. But it is now more or less established that the fish does really fly. In his "Idylls of the Sea" Mr. Frank Bullen, a very competent observer, wrote: "A flying-fish of mature size can fly a thousand yards. It does not flap its fins, but they vibrate like the wings of an insect, with a distinct hum. The only thing which terminates its flight involuntarily is the drying of its fin membranes and their consequent stiffening."

What kind of Fish can swallow another Fish as large as itself?

The Angler fish or fishing-frog. It has a huge mouth, armed with long, inward-curving teeth, and a very large and elastic stomach. It has been known to gulp down a fish three times as long as itself.

Why do Fish lie with their heads pointing upstream?

So that they may maintain their positions by using their tails to counteract the current, and may keep a lookout for any food floating downstream towards them. Moreover, while in this position they cannot have their gills forced open by the current.

How are Herrings caught?

By means of drift nets, each 12 to 24 feet deep and 40 to 120 yards long. A net is held upright in the water by corks and buoys attached to its upper edge and a heavy rope running along the bottom edge. Its meshes are just large enough for a herring to get its head, but not its body, through. A fish that does this is trapped, for its gills act like the barbs of an arrow and prevent the head being withdrawn. A number of nets are usually fastened together end to end, forming a "fleet," one end of which is attached to the boat. As the boat drifts to leeward it keeps the fleet of nets extended like a long wall in the water.

How are Fish living on or near the Bottom of the Sea caught?

Most of them with a large bag-net, called a trawl net, tapering from its open mouth towards the rear. The mouth is kept open by a long beam or by two large boards arranged slantwise, so that they pull in opposite directions. The trawl is dragged along the sea-bottom, scooping up any flatfish, haddock, whiting, turbot, brill and other fish which may get in its way. After the trawl has been hauled aboard it is emptied by untying its small end, in which the fish have collected.

What Names are given to Young Salmon at different stages of growth?

During the first two years or so of its life a young salmon is called a *parr*, *samlet*, or *pink*. At this stage it is brown, with dark bars and orange spots. Its scales then become silvery, and it is known as a *smolt*. The smolt makes its first visit to the sea while still weighing but a few ounces, and returns some months later to its native river weighing anything up to 10 pounds. It is now a *grilse* or *salmon peel*. After its second visit to the sea the fish is a salmon proper.

What is a Sponge?

The ordinary bath sponge is the skeleton of a curious animal which lives on the sea-bottom. It is made of fine and very flexible horny fibres. Sponges are raised by divers in the western parts of the Mediterranean Sea, in the Red Sea, round the coasts of Australia and round the Bahamas. After being landed, the sponges are exposed to the air till they begin to decay, and are then pounded and trampled in running water till they have been rid of all once living matter. They are then dried and sent to wholesale purchasers, who give them a further thorough cleansing before putting them on the market.

What Living creatures Can give Electric Shocks?

Three species of fish: the electric eel, or gymnotus; the electric ray; and the electric cat-fish. The first of these gives shocks powerful enough to injure seriously, and even kill, any animal to which they are administered.

What makes the Sea phosphorescent?

Swarms of tiny creatures moving on or near the surface. These give out light like a glow-worm.

What is Bêche-de-mer?

A large sea-slug, growing up to 2 feet in length, which is found on coral reefs off the coasts of Australia and the East Indies. It has the appearance of a prickly cucumber. After being boiled, split open and dried in the sun or wood smoke, bêche-de-mer is shipped to China where it is considered a great dainty. Another name for the creature is *trepang*.

What are Sea-shells made of?

Mostly of lime. On the outside a shell is coated with a substance called conchiolin, and inside is usually lined with mother-of-pearl.

What Creature is able to bore holes in Rock?

The pholas, or piddock, a two-shelled shellfish somewhat like a long, thin mussel. It can sink holes in limestone, chalk, shale and other rocks. Whether it uses the edges of its shells or its large foot for doing the actual boring is uncertain, but probably the foot is the tool employed, aided by a secretion which softens or dissolves the rock.

REPTILES

How does an Alligator differ from a Crocodile?

Alligators have broader and shorter heads than crocodiles, and the toes of their hind feet are less completely webbed. Alligators belong chiefly to the New World, crocodiles to the Old World.

What is the difference between a Frog and a Toad?

A frog is usually of a yellowish-brown colour and has a moist, shiny skin; a toad's skin is a dull dark brown, covered with little warts. The frog is a good jumper and swimmer, and fond of water; the toad usually crawls, as its limbs are not adapted for jumping, and lives almost entirely on land, in damp places.

HOW WHALES AND FISH BREATHE

Specially drawn for this work.

The whale, a warm-blooded mammal, breathes atmospheric air just as we do. Its " nose " is on the top of its head. In the upper right-hand corner we have a view of its two nostrils (seen from above) when closed under water, and open for " blowing." Below, the expanded nostrils are seen from behind. Fish take in water through their mouths and expel it between the plates of the gills (see the two lower illustrations). The gills extract air dissolved in the water.

26—2

What does a Toad do with its Old Skin after shedding it?

It rolls it into a ball and swallows it.

Is a Slow-worm a Snake?

No. Nor is it a worm; but a legless lizard. It is also called a " blind-worm," but this is a misnomer because it has very good eyes.

What is a Rattlesnake's Rattle, and where is it on the Snake?

The rattle is a number of horny rings on the end of the tail, each attached loosely to the one in front of it. When the snake shakes its tail these rings clash together, making a noise which can be heard several yards away.

Is there such a thing as a Sea-serpent?

Nothing that could rightly be called a sea-serpent has ever been caught or washed ashore. But from time to time persons whose truthfulness can hardly be called in question have described marine monsters, having the shape of a huge serpent, seen by them. The correctness of their observations can, of course, only be proved beyond doubt by the capture of something which agrees with the description given.

How does the Chameleon change Colour?

By means of differently coloured cells in the inner skin, which it can contract or expand, making one colour or another more visible, or causing two colours to blend together into a third. The chameleon has several rivals, and is beaten as a " quick-change artist " by the Æsop prawn.

INSECTS

What is the Difference between a Butterfly and a Moth?

Butterflies have thin bodies, moths usually have thick ones. The antennæ or " feelers " of all butterflies end in a knob or " club." Those of moths are never clubbed, but pointed, and they may also be feathered. A butterfly when at rest brings its wings together in an upright position over its back; a moth has its wings folded level with its body. The upper and lower wings of most moths are fastened together by a kind of hook-and-eye arrangement, which is absent in butterflies. Most butterflies fly by day only ; most moths by night only.

Why do Flies and Mosquitoes bite, and Wasps and Bees sting?

Insects which bite do so to suck blood from the body bitten. Bees and wasps use their stings, which are their weapons, in self-defence.

A bee's sting is barbed, and cannot be withdrawn from the wound, but a wasp's sting is merely pointed and can stab repeatedly.

Why is a Spider's Web so sticky?

When a spider is spinning its web it first fixes the threads running spokewise from the centre to the edges. These threads are quite smooth. When they are in place the spider circles round and round over the spokes, attaching to them a spiral thread on which globules of gummy matter are deposited at tiny intervals. These globules act like birdlime, and make the web so sticky that any fly which strikes it is held fast.

A spider is not correctly described as an insect, but is a member of the class known as Arachnida.

What Creature uses a Diving-bell?

A species of water-spider. It spins an underwater bell, open at the bottom only, against the stem of a water plant, and drives the water out of it by carrying down bubbles of air and releasing them in the bell, which serves as its home during the winter.

How is a House-fly dangerous to Health?

It carries on to food the germs of disease picked up from any garbage on which it may have settled.

Why are Flies able to walk on the Ceiling?

A fly's foot bears two small flat pads which behave as suckers.

Where do Flies go in the Winter?

Many of them die of old age or are killed by the cold; others hibernate in window-frames, under floors, or in cracks. Flies' eggs laid in the later part of the year do not hatch out till spring comes.

What insect " keeps Cows "?

The ant. Its " cows " are the aphides which swarm on the tender shoots of roses and other plants; and the milk is honeydew, a sweet liquid which an aphis distils. The " cows " may be left on their pastures and milked there, or carried off and kept in tiny stables.

What is the Death-watch?

A ticking or rapping sound which at one time was thought to foretell the death of a human being. It is now known to be made by a beetle, the death-watch beetle, which has a habit of striking its head against wood. The eggs laid by this beetle develop into grubs which bore into wood and make it " worm-eaten." They are particularly destructive to old oak, and many fine oak-timbered roofs have been destroyed by them.

How did the Earwig get its Name?

From the fact that its wings, when unfolded, are shaped somewhat like an ear.

What does an Earwig use its " Pincers " for?

They are not weapons, and cannot do you any harm, though they are sometimes flourished to frighten enemies. Their real use is to fold up the wings, which are packed away in a very small space when not in use.

Why do Bees make the cells in their Combs six-sided?

Because six-sided cells fill up all the space, fitting in with one another and leaving no empty gaps. Square cells, or cells with three equal sides, would do the same thing, but they would not be so strong.

How is it that Locusts are so destructive?

Because of their vast numbers and their great appetite for vegetable food. When a swarm of locusts alights in a district the insects may, however, not do much damage before moving on. But they leave behind them millions of eggs, laid in the ground. These soon hatch out, and the ground becomes alive with tiny locust larvæ, ⅛ inch long. By the end of three or four weeks they have grown sufficiently to be able to hop—at this stage they have no wings—and then begin to march steadily forward, like a vast army, in one direction. It is these hungry " hoppers " which do the worst damage. They eat every vegetable thing, even the bark of trees, that comes in their way, leaving devastation behind them. Fortunately, their inability to fly makes it possible to collect and destroy huge numbers by poisoning or burning them.

PLANTS

How do Flowers attract Insects?

By providing them with food in the form of nectar. Their scents, and perhaps their colour also, help to draw insects to them.

Do Flowers really contain Honey?

What the bees extract from flowers is a nectar, containing a large proportion of cane-sugar. When placed in a bee's honey-bag it undergoes a chemical change into the sugary substance which we call honey.

How are Flowers Scented?

By oily liquids distributed through their petals. Many plants carry sweet-smelling oils in their seeds, buds and leaves. Thyme, mint and sweetbriar are common examples of scented-leaf plants.

Are all Garden Flowers descended from Wild Flowers?

Yes! Directly or indirectly.

What does a Gardener mean by " Annuals," " Biennials " and " Perennials "?

Annuals are plants which flower in the year in which their seed is sown, and then die. Among well-known annuals are nasturtiums, sweet peas and marigolds. A biennial is a plant which is sown and puts out foliage in one summer, flowers the next, and dies, or at least is not worth keeping any longer. Examples: Canterbury bells, foxgloves, honesty, wallflowers. Perennials are plants such as hollyhocks, primroses, violas and pæonies, which continue to bloom year after year.

What Wild Flower is called the Poor Man's Weather-glass?

The scarlet pimpernel, which keeps its flowers open only in fine weather, and closes them when rain threatens. The flowers are doubtless affected by the increase of moisture in the air which precedes rain. Other flowers which behave in a similar manner are the dandelion, wild geranium and mock strawberry.

What are the popular English names of the Flowers called in seed catalogues Antirrhinum, Aquilegia, Cheiranthus, Delphinium, Galanthus, Helianthus, Myosotis, Œnothera, Sedum and Tritoma?

Antirrhinum is snapdragon; aquilegia, columbine; cheiranthus, Siberian wallflower; delphinium, larkspur; galanthus, snowdrop; helianthus, sunflower; myosotis, forget-me-not; œnothera, evening primrose; sedum, stonecrop; tritoma, red-hot poker.

Why is the Daisy so named?

The name is a shortened form of " day's eye," and was bestowed on the plant because of its habit of opening its flowers in daylight.

Which is the Largest Flower known?

That of the *Rafflesia Arnoldii*, found in Sumatra. It measures more than a yard across. The plant, which is practically all flower, grows out of the roots of fig and other trees.

Why are Tulip Bulbs not moved after Flowering until the Leaves have withered?

Because during the withering process the bulbs absorb nourishment from the dying leaves and from the soil, and swell till ready for the next season's growth, which will exhaust their substance. Also, during the withering period the small side bulbs are formed on the parent bulbs, and these, if separated, will in time become large bulbs.

Of what use is its Fruit to a Plant?

The fruit protects the seeds and attracts birds and animals which, by eating the fruit, scatter the seeds.

How do Gorse and Broom scatter their Seeds?

When a seed-pod is ripe it suddenly splits, and each half curls itself into a spiral. The effect is to fling the seeds outwards, and give them a spin like that given to a rifle bullet, which makes them fly further and straighter.

What is a Jumping Bean?

A small Mexican bean containing a grub which at times makes violent movements, causing the bean to jump about.

How do its Leaves help a Plant?

They absorb carbonic acid gas from the atmosphere and supply the plant with carbon. They also evaporate surplus water, and bring oxygen to the sap.

Why do Leaves change their Colour in Autumn?

The yellowness of dying leaves is due to the breaking up of the green colouring matter called chlorophyll. Red, brown and other tints are given by pigments which collect in the leaves during the summer.

Why do Leaves Fall in Autumn?

Because they have done their work and their hold on the plant or tree is loosened by the formation of new leaf-buds.

Which Plant has the Largest Leaves?

Probably the giant tropical water-lily, *Victoria Regia*, the leaves of which are 6 feet or more across. The edges of a leaf are turned up, converting it into a raft which will support a child or large dog.

What are the curious Mossy Growths, called "Robins' Pincushions." sometimes seen on Rose Bushes?

They are galls caused by a small insect which lays its eggs in leafstalks. Instead of developing in the usual way, a leaf affected takes the form of a globular lump, covered with soft reddish hairs.

How does a Nettle sting?

By means of tiny hair-like prickles covering its leaves. These are hollow and filled with a very powerful irritant, which is squeezed out when they enter the skin.

Why are Different Crops grown on a Field in successive Seasons?

Because different crops have different effects on the soil. Wheat, for example, consumes nitrogen, whereas clover, peas and beans transfer nitrogen from the air to the soil. So a clover crop following a wheat crop helps to restore to the soil what the wheat took out of it.

When and where was the Potato first planted in England?

In 1585, near London.

What kind of Crop is grown in a "Paddy" Field?

Rice. The word paddy is the English form of the Malay *padi*, meaning rice.

Why is it that a Bare Patch of Land so soon becomes covered with Weeds?

Because the seeds of many kinds of plants are distributed by winds, rain, birds and animals. Some seeds are so small that the slightest current of air keeps them aloft until rain brings them down. Others, like those of the dandelion and thistle, are provided with plumes which enable them to travel hundreds of miles. Then, again, the seeds of many plants are swallowed by birds, carried about, and dropped while still in a condition to grow. And others are transported by the feet of animals, or even by the mud on people's boots.

What Plants have proved a great nuisance when taken abroad from their Native Countries?

The English blackberry, gorse and watercress and the Scotch thistle and broom, introduced into New Zealand; the South African prickly pear, planted in Australia; the South American water hyacinth, taken to Florida; and the Canadian water thyme, brought to England.

How do Plants benefit our Health?

The carbonic acid gas which we breathe out from our lungs is injurious to us, but useful to plants, which absorb it and make use of it. By removing large quantities of this gas from the air they help to keep the atmosphere sweet and healthy.

Why do Plants droop in Hot Weather?

Because their cells then contain little water and lose their stiffness. Each cell becomes like a balloon which has lost some of its gas.

How does a Virginia Creeper cling to a House Wall?

It throws out many little tentacles from the stem and branches, and these, when they touch the wall, exude a sticky substance from their tips. As this hardens it anchors the tentacles firmly to the wall.

Why does Grass that has been covered up for some time become bleached?

Because lack of sunlight deprives it of the green colouring matter called chlorophyll.

How does Mistletoe get on to the Branches of Trees?

The seeds are carried by birds that eat the berries. In cleaning its beak on a branch a bird may force a seed into a crevice in the bark, where it takes root.

What are the so-called Fairy Rings seen in Meadows?

They are the work of an underground fungus, which spreads outwards from a centre. The fungus attacks the roots of the grass just outside the circle, causing the grass to wither. The remains of the spent fungus act as a manure which makes new grass grow luxuriantly and form a ring of dark green. So a moving ring of dying grass and vigorous fungus is constantly being followed up by a ring of dead fungus and vigorous grass. The fungus fruits as a ring of toadstools.

Why is it unwise to Water Plants sparingly during a Drought?

The surface only being damped, the roots grow upwards towards it in search of moisture. They are then more easily injured when the top soil dries again. If watering be done at all, it should be done thoroughly.

What Plants win Land from Water?

Reeds and mangroves. They first choke up shallow lakes, such as the Sea of Aral and Lake Chad, and their decaying leaves gradually form soil. The shores of West and East Africa, Polynesia, India and many other parts of Asia, Central and South America and Australia are in many places fringed with great mangrove forests, the roots of which collect soil, sand and vegetable matter until at last new land is formed. The seaward fringe of a mangrove forest is continually advancing into deeper water, while its landward edge retreats and gives place to forest trees.

How do Plants get on to Islands very far from a Mainland?

The seeds of some are washed ashore by the waves, those of others are transported by birds or by the winds.

What is a Lichen?

A very curious combination of a lowly alga (a plant related to seaweed) and a fungus. It is found on trees, walls, roofs and rocks. The alga part extracts carbonic acid from the air, and the fungus part supplies water and other nutriment. Between them they perform all the

BADGES OF RANK

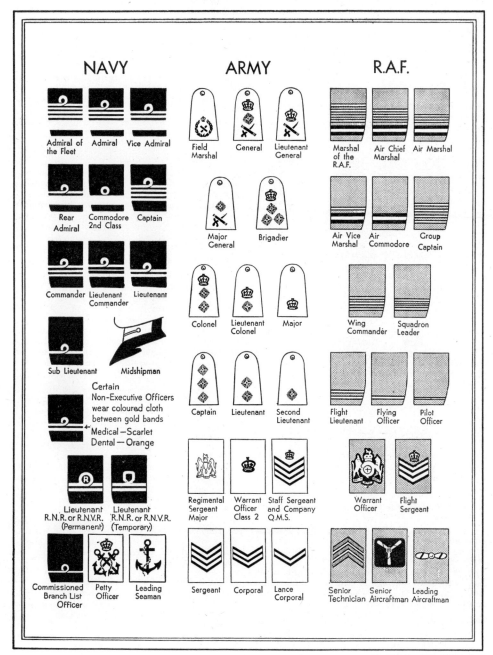

Specially drawn for this work.

In all three branches of our Fighting Forces, the rank of every man above the lowest is shown by special badges, usually worn on the sleeves or shoulder-straps. In the Navy, commissioned officers' badges are of gold braid; in the Army they are in metal or embroidery, while Air Force officers use lighter-coloured braid on the cuffs. The badges of the R.N.V.R. (the "wavy Navy") and those of the R.N.R. were replaced in 1951 by straight rings similar to those worn by R.N. officers, but with slight variations in the "curl." In the R.A.F., N.C.O. badges in the normal command ranks are similar to Army badges, but a new Technician class has its own distinctive badges for N.C.O. ranks.

functions of an ordinary plant. Some lichens yield useful dyes.

What Plant grown in Conservatories should be handled with care?

The *primula obconica*, which has its leaves fringed with sharp little hairs that cause great irritation if they enter the skin. Some people are much more affected than others.

Name some British Trees and Plants the fruit of which is poisonous?

The yew, spindle and wayfaring trees; the guelder rose and buckthorn; mistletoe, henbane, cuckoo-pint (lords and ladies), honeysuckle, bittersweet and deadly nightshade.

What was the Origin of Kew Gardens?

The Royal Botanic Gardens, at the northern end, were begun in 1759. Soon afterwards, George the Third purchased what became Kew Palace, close by. In 1840 Queen Victoria handed over the Gardens to the public, and the grounds have been greatly enlarged since then, now covering 288 acres, or nearly half a square mile. The Temperate House, completed at the end of last century, is probably the largest plant house in the world.

Are Kew Gardens merely Pleasure Grounds?

No! Important botanical research is carried on in them, and botanists from all parts of the world go to Kew to study plants and trees, of both of which there is a splendid collection. At Kew were grown, from seed, the rubber trees which became the ancestors of the great rubber plantations in Malaya.

TREES

In what ways do Trees benefit Mankind?

In addition to supplying us with fruit, timber and the many substances extracted from wood, they purify the air, attract rain, protect the ground from being washed away, and enrich the soil with their fallen leaves.

How much of the Earth's Surface is covered with Trees?

About one-sixth, equal to about 9,000,000 square miles.

How can one tell the Age of a Tree?

It is possible to do so only when the trunk has been sawn through. One can then count the number of rings in the trunk. Each ring represents a year's growth.

Why is it dangerous to camp under Elm Trees?

Because elm trees, especially old ones, are liable to shed a branch without any warning. Elm trees are subject to a form of decay of which there are no outward signs.

Why are some kinds of Pines and Fir Trees shaped like a Cone?

These trees have a straight stem with a leading shoot at the top. This grows vertically, throwing off branch shoots at intervals. The length of a branch developed from a side shoot depends on the age of the branch, so naturally the branches nearest the ground are the largest and the tree tapers towards the top.

Why is a Horse-chestnut so named?

Two wrong explanations are often given : (1) because there is a mark like the print of the nails in a horseshoe on the underside of a twig where it joins a branch; (2) because at one time the nuts were given to horses as medicine. The true explanation is that by common usage the word " horse " can be applied to a number of things to qualify them as crude or coarse. Thus we get horse-radish, horse-vetch, etc.

What is Teak?

The timber of a large forest tree (*Tectona grandis*) that grows in Burma. It is stronger and stiffer than oak, which it resembles in appearance, and has the valuable qualities of resisting the attack of insects, withstanding damp, and not rusting nails or screws driven into it. Teak is imported as logs from 10 to 30 inches square and from 20 to 50 feet long. It is used chiefly for shipbuilding and heavy engineering work.

Why are Yew Trees often found in Churchyards?

Some people think that in olden days they were planted there to furnish staves for bows. Being on consecrated ground they were protected. Another view is that they were used as being evergreen and the best substitute for the cypress, which has for many centuries been grown in cemeteries. As they live to an enormous age they may have been adopted as a symbol of immortality.

What Trees have benefited us greatly during the last fifty years by being introduced from their Native Countries into other parts of the World?

The rubber tree and the cocoa tree. Rubber seeds brought from Brazil to Kew Gardens in 1876 laid the foundations of rubber-planting in Malaya and the East Indies, which now employs hundreds of millions of pounds of capital, and yields annually hundreds of thousands of tons of rubber—is, in short, the great source of the world's rubber supply. The cocoa tree was introduced into the Gold Coast of West Africa in 1887 from the West Indies, and flourished there so exceedingly that now about £70,000,000 worth of cocoa is exported yearly from that country (the modern Ghana).

Which is the most useful of Trees?

The coconut palm is usually considered to be. The kernel of its nut supplies millions of people with food, besides yielding a valuable oil. The fibres of the nut-husk are made into ropes, mats, and other articles. The leaves of the tree are a useful thatch; the wood is valued for many purposes, and the root yields a drug.

Which are the World's greatest Trees?

The Californian sequoia or redwood tree and the Australian eucalyptus. Specimens of both kinds can claim a height of over 430 feet. There is an instance of a sequoia trunk measuring over 35 feet through near the ground, and of a eucalyptus reaching a height of 380 feet before throwing out a branch.

BRITISH UNIFORMS: THE DEFENCE FORCES—Plate 1

Specially drawn for this work.

The wearing of uniform by the armed forces dates in Britain from 1645 when the New Model Army was raised by Parliament to fight against the King, Charles I. In the plate above are seen uniforms of the land and sea forces during the century 1645–1745. 1. Soldier, 1645; 2. Soldier, 1650; 3. Soldier, 1660; 4. Seaman, 1660; 5. Soldier, 1680; 6. Soldier, 1690; 7. Admiral, 1705; 8. Seaman, 1705; 9. Soldier, 1715; 10. Soldier, 1740; 11. Soldier, 1745; 12. Seaman, 1745.

BRITISH UNIFORMS: THE DEFENCE FORCES—Plate 2

Naval uniform for officers was a matter of personal taste until the middle of the eighteenth century, while regular uniform for the men was not officially ordered until 1875, though the ships' captains did much to ensure uniformity among their sailors long before then. Above are shown: 13. Soldier, 1770; 14. Naval Lieutenant, 1775; 15. Seaman, 1780; 16. Admiral, 1805; 17. Seaman, 1805; 18. Soldier, 1810; 19. Cavalry Officer, 1810; 20. Highlander, 1815; 21. Cavalry Officer, 1815; 22. Soldier, 1815; 23. Flag Officer, 1833; 24. Boatswain, 1833.

BRITISH UNIFORMS: THE DEFENCE FORCES—Plate 3

Changes in Army uniform have been much more frequent than in the Navy, but until nearing the end of the nineteenth century the red coat was the general basic principle for all military uniform. Khaki was first adopted on Indian service around 1850 and gradually became adopted for service use generally. In this plate are seen: 25. Soldier, 1833; 26. Marine, 1855; 27. Petty Officer, 1855; 28. Soldier, 1865; 29. Seaman, 1890; 30. Highlander, 1895; 31. Soldier, 1900; 32. Soldier, 1918; 33. Flag Captain, 1939; 34. Seaman, 1939; 35. Marine, 1939; 36. Guardsman, 1939.

BRITISH UNIFORMS: COMMONWEALTH FORCES—Plate 4

The countries which form the British Commonwealth of Nations now have their own separate Defence Forces, and the uniforms of some of these are shown in this plate : CANADA : 1. Leading Aircraftman, R.C.A.F. ; 2. Private (full dress) Highlanders of Ottawa ; 3. Army corporal, battle dress ; 4. Seaman, Royal Canadian Navy. AUSTRALIA : 5. Royal Australian Air Force (walking-out uniform) ; 6. Lieutenant, Navy (tropical rig) ; 7. Private, Army ; 8. Seaman, Royal Australian Navy. NEW ZEALAND : 9. Lieutenant, Royal New Zealand Navy ; 10. Private, Army ; 11. Observer, R.N.Z. Air Force ; 12. Sergeant, Air Force.

What is Cork?

The outer part of the bark of an evergreen oak which grows chiefly in Spain and Portugal. It is stripped from the trees every eight to ten years. The cork obtained when a tree is stripped for the first time is called " virgin " cork, and, being very rough, it is of little use except for ornamental purposes, such as covering window boxes.

What is Amber?

Gum or resin which, long ages ago, exuded from an extinct pine tree, was buried in the ground, and became fossilised. Pieces of it are washed by the sea out of layers of clay or sand in which it was deposited, and thrown ashore, especially on to the coasts of Germany and Denmark. It usually has a pretty yellow colour, and is more or less transparent. White, red and green varieties are also found, and some specimens contain the embalmed bodies of flies and other insects.

Why is it that Insects are sometimes found embedded in Amber?

They settled on the resin while it was oozing from the tree, and stuck to it. Then more resin covered them over.

What is Kauri Gum?

The hardened resin of the Kauri pine, a large tree which grows only in New Zealand. The gum is found by probing the sites of ancient Kauri forests with iron rods.

What is Plywood?

It is the name given to boards made of plies or thin veneers of wood. A log is revolved in a special machine which cuts a continuous " peel " from the surface of the log. This peeling is then cut to the required size, and, when thoroughly dry, two or more plies are cemented together under pressure. In this way any thickness may be made and exceptional widths are possible.

The advantages of plywood are that it is extremely light, has great strength, does not warp or split easily, and can be used in the manufacture of a wide variety of goods, from aeroplanes and panelling to packing-cases. It is said to have been used by the Egyptians in making mummy cases.

What is Turpentine?

A colourless liquid obtained by distilling the resinous sap of certain pines. Heating drives off the volatile turpentine (usually called oil or spirit of turpentine), leaving solid resin behind. Turpentine is a very valuable liquid, as it dissolves the oils and resins used in paints and varnishes.

Which is the Hardest Wood known?

Probably Indian ironwood. It is too hard to work, as it quickly breaks the edge of the best tool. Lignum vitæ is another very hard wood.

Which is the Heaviest and which the Lightest Wood?

Cocus wood is perhaps the heaviest, but black ironwood runs it close, both being half as heavy again as water. The lightest of woods is undoubtedly balsa, which is lighter than cork. It comes principally from Ecuador but also from Brazil and Peru.

NAVAL AND MILITARY

Why do Naval Officers wear Epaulettes?

Originally epaulettes were made of metal and worn to protect the shoulders from sword-cuts, and they formed part of the uniform of both sailors and soldiers. They now serve merely as ornaments.

What is the difference between a Warship and a Battleship?

Any ship built for war purposes is a warship. A battleship is a warship of the largest size, protected by thick armour and carrying very heavy guns.

What is an Aircraft Carrier?

A large warship which acts as aerodrome and mother-ship to naval aeroplanes. It has a very spacious upper deck, extending the full length and width of the vessel, and clear of all obstructions. The funnels are placed on one side of the ship, or dispersed with altogether. Below this flight deck are hangars for aircraft, repair workshops and stores. Such a ship is only lightly armed and armoured, but she has a very high speed, to assist aeroplanes at starting or landing by steaming fast upwind. The British Navy is well to the fore with aircraft carriers, some of these vessels exceeding 30,000 tons.

When were Submarines first used in the Royal Navy?

In 1901–2 when five British submarines of the type designed by John P. Holland, an Irishman who had emigrated to the U.S.A., were built by Vickers. Apart from certain under-water craft used in the American Civil War, submarines were first used in naval warfare in 1914–18.

What are the Royal Marines?

Soldiers whose main purpose is service aboard ships of the Royal Navy and the provision of landing parties. Their history goes back to 1664, but they were officially established in 1755. They are nicknamed the " Jollies."

How long has Britain had a Standing Army?

For just over three hundred years. The soldiers who fought the early wars in our history were usually milita or levies. Not until the Great Rebellion was a standing, or permanent, force raised. The date usually given as the birthday of our standing army is February 15th, 1645, when Cromwell's " New Model " Army was concentrated at Windsor. The wearing of uniform also dates from this time.

The army was disbanded in 1660, when King Charles II was restored to the throne, except for General Monk's regiment of foot (now the Coldstream Guards). But a further regiment of foot (now the Grenadier Guards) was formed, and so were the troops of the Household Cavalry. The latter are now two famous regiments—the Royal Horse Guards (" the Blues ") and the Life Guards.

Other regiments were formed later as need arose.

What Regiments form the Brigade of Guards ?

There are five regiments in the Brigade of Guards—the Coldstream Guards, the Grenadier Guards, the Scots Guards, the Irish Guards and the Welsh Guards. When they are wearing their familiar scarlet tunics and bearskins (not busbies), they can most easily be distinguished by the colour of the plumes in their bearskins : red (Coldstream), white (Grenadier), blue (Irish), white and blue (Welsh). The Scots Guards have no plume.

What is the Territorial Army ?

The Territorial Army is really a part-time army. Its officers and men are citizens who carry out military training in their spare time. The backbone of the Territorial Army is the volunteer, but since 1950 National Service men have been required to give 3½ years' part-time service in the Territorials after completing their period of National Service with the Regular Army.

In the event of war, the Territorial Army would provide most of our anti-aircraft and coast defences as well as units to serve in the field with the Regular Army.

When was the last occasion on which a British Sovereign personally commanded his Army on a Field of Battle ?

June 16th, 1743. King George II commanded the British, Hanoverian and Austrian troops at the Battle of Dettingen and won a decisive victory over the opposing French.

Why are Soldiers dressed in Khaki-coloured Uniforms ?

Because uniforms of that colour blend with natural surroundings and are not easily seen at a distance. Khaki uniforms were worn first in India, and adopted for the British Army generally after the South African War of 1899–1902.

What are Non-commissioned Officers ?

Junior officers of the Army who do not hold commissions, that is, appointments direct from the sovereign. They rank below the commissioned officers (ranging from general down to second lieutenant) and below warrant officers but above privates. The various grades from top to bottom in the infantry are: sergeant, lance-sergeant, corporal and lance-corporal.

Who are the Sappers ?

Soldiers of the corps of Royal Engineers. Strictly, a sapper is a private, but the word is often applied to officers of the Royal Engineers as well.

How did the Moving Forts called " Tanks " get their name ?

It was given to them purposely by the British Army authorities to hide the real purpose for which they were being made. Rumours got about that the tanks were intended for carrying water for troops across the deserts of Egypt and Mesopotamia; and, of course, they were not contradicted.

What is the Foreign Legion ?

A regiment of the French Army, formed in 1831 for service in Africa and French colonial possessions and recruited from men of all nations, but the officers are French. The training and discipline are severe, and a legionary is called on to do many kinds of work in addition to his military duties. No regiment has been so much written about, and none has done more fighting. The French name for it is La Légion Étrangère.

PHOTOGRAPHY

Who invented Photography ?

The first photographic prints were made by Thomas Wedgwood, fourth son of the famous potter, in 1802, but he was unable to " fix " them. A Frenchman, Joseph Nicéphore Niepce, began experiments in 1814, and obtained his first " sun picture " with a camera about 1822. Another Frenchman, J. L. M. Daguerre, who invented another process in 1839, became Niepce's partner, and " Daguerrotypes " became very popular. In England, four years before Daguerre announced his invention, W. H. Fox Talbot invented the calotype process, though he did not make this known until after Daguerre's demonstration. Sir John Herschel made further improvements, and was also responsible for coining the word " photography " and using the terms " negative " and " positive." In 1851 Scott Archer invented the " wet plate " process, and eventually J. W. Swan devised the " dry plate " which was first put on the market in 1877. Improvements have followed steadily since then.

How is the Image of an Object impressed on a Photographic Plate ?

The plate is coated with a film containing a salt of silver. Wherever light strikes the film in the camera, the silver tends to separate from the salt into particles of pure silver, which are black. The process of separation is completed by " developing " the film with chemicals.

What are Orthochromatic and Panchromatic Photographic Plates ?

Orthochromatic plates are those coated with a film which is sensitive to rays of all colours except orange and red. They must be developed in a dim red light only. Panchromatic plates are affected by all colours, and therefore must be developed in total darkness. Both kinds are used to obtain a truer reproduction of tones when subjects containing many colours are photographed.

Who invented the Roll Film now so largely used in cameras ?

George Eastman, an American inventor, who began the manufacture of dry plates for photography in 1880 and in 1884–85 succeeded in making the first roll film for photography. In 1888 he perfected his first Kodak camera and in 1890 patented the first machine for making rolls of transparent film.

Can a Photograph be taken with a Camera that has no Lens ?

Yes, if light be admitted through a tiny hole

A LONG-RANGE CAMERA

Associated Press.

This camera is known as the " Peeping Tom " in the United States Army Signal Corps, by whom it has been developed. Fitted with a telephoto lens having a focal length of 100 inches, the camera can record scenes up to thirty miles away. It is designed to work with infra-red plates so that a clear day is not essential for good *photography* (see p. 410). With a lens of this type it is hoped in due course to take moving pictures and also make it suitable for use with a television camera.

situated where the centre of a lens would be. The smallness of the hole allows only a very few rays from any point of the object to reach the plate, so the image is fairly " sharp," or distinct, in its small details. The smaller the hole the sharper the image is, and the longer the exposure must be. The " pinhole " is of little practical use, because it means very long exposures, usually the same number of minutes that a lens requires seconds.

How long have Cinemas been in existence?

The basis of the cinematograph or moving-picture camera was the patent taken out in England by William Friese-Green of Bristol who took the first pictures with his machine in Hyde Park in 1889. In America Edison invented his kinetoscope which he patented in 1893. The adoption of the roller film, invented by George Eastman of America around 1884–5, increased the possibilities of the moving-picture camera enormously.

In February 1895 a moving picture was shown on the screen at the Finsbury Technical College. The camera was made by R. W. Paul of Hatton Garden, London. Others followed, including Charles Urban, with his bioscope, which marked another advance in cinematography. The first public exhibition on the lines of the modern cinema was given in London in 1896 by Messrs. Lumière.

Picture-making developed rapidly under the ideal conditions for photography in California, and by 1926 the " film industry " had become an extensive business. It has developed very considerably in the past quarter of a century and there are to-day few countries in the world where the cinema is not a popular form of entertainment.

PHYSICS (GENERAL)

If our Eyes enabled us to see Atoms, what would Solid Bodies look like?

They would be seen to be mostly empty spaces, in which are scattered about the protons, or positive cores, of atoms, each accompanied by one or more negative electrons revolving round it. If the proton of an atom were represented in size by a golf ball, the space occupied by an atom, that is, not intruded on by any other atom, would measure about half a mile across in all directions.

What is Dust?

The dust which gives trouble indoors consists of particles of matter of many kinds, small enough to be easily carried about by currents of air. A puff of smoke from a tobacco pipe sends thousands of millions of dust particles into the air. It has been proved that water vapour in the atmosphere cannot condense without having dust particles to condense round. So if there were no dust in the air we should have no mists, clouds or rain.

How does a Soap Bubble hold together?

A soap bubble holds together because the molecules (or particles) comprising it attract each other. In every liquid this force of attraction (or cohesion, as it is called) enables the liquid to form thin films or drops, and liquids seem to be especially elastic on their surfaces. Of course, this cohesion is much stronger with some liquids than with others; for example, soapy water compared with tap water. When a bubble is blown up, the pressure of the air inside increases. Under this pressure the molecules are stretched and the bubble grows larger; but when the stretching force due to the pressure becomes greater than the attractive force between each molecule, the molecules suddenly separate from each other and the bubble " bursts." When a bubble has been successfully released, it often bursts before reaching the ground because the force of gravity, which is stronger than the molecular attraction, tends to pull off drops of liquid from the bubble, weakening its film or skin.

Why do Things fall if dropped?

In obedience to the law of gravitation, under which every particle of matter in the universe attracts every other. The weight of a thing is really only the force with which the earth is pulling it towards its centre.

Why does fine Sand sink more slowly than Pebbles when dropped into Water?

Because each grain of sand has much more surface, relatively to its weight, than a pebble, and therefore has greater difficulty in making its way down through the water.

What is meant by Horse-power?

The early steam-engines were used to replace horses for pumping, winding and similar work. So an engine was said to be equal to so many horses, or have so many horse-power. The question arose: " What is a horse's power? " About 150 years ago the great engineer, James Watt, carried out experiments with powerful dray horses, making them lift a heavy weight attached to the end of a rope running over a pulley. He calculated from the results that on the average a horse-power was equivalent to raising 33,000 pounds 1 foot in a minute, and this has ever since been the unit in which mechanical power is expressed. We should note that an electrical power unit or kilowatt is about one-third greater than a mechanical horse-power.

Does it take as much Power to stop a Train as to make it get up Speed?

It takes much less power, because the brake gear has great leverage and stopping is helped by the friction at axle-boxes and other rubbing points. Most of the energy of the train is dissipated as heat by the friction between the brake-blocks and the wheels. This takes some time, and the brakes may have to be applied to a fast train a mile before the station is reached.

Why does Beating a Carpet rid it of Dust?

When the carpet is beaten from the back, the dust is set in motion by a blow of the stick and continues to move by its own inertia after the carpet has stopped moving. If the carpet be laid on the ground, face upwards, the stick compresses the carpet, which in its rebound flings the dust up to the surface.

Why are Pendulums used in Clocks?

Because the time which a pendulum takes to make a swing is the same for all pendulums of the same length, no matter what their weight. The pendulum is therefore perfectly fitted for controlling the rate at which a clock works.

Why do Engines have Fly-wheels?

A flywheel stores up the energy of the engine, and makes the engine run more steadily. Its weight prevents both sudden increases and decreases of speed. A piston engine turns its cranks with more force at some points of a revolution than at others, and but for the flywheel its action would be jerky. A locomotive does not need a flywheel, as its own weight, added to that of the train behind it, has the same effect.

Why does Ice float in Water?

Because water expands as it turns into ice, and a pound of ice must therefore take up more room than a pound of water and is consequently lighter. Only about one-ninth of an iceberg floating in the sea is above water, which shows that though ice is lighter than water it is only slightly so.

Does a Pound of Ice make a Pound of Water when melted?

Certainly it does. For the water is merely the ice with heat added to it, and heat weighs nothing.

Why does a Soap-bubble rise when first blown up?

Because the air from the lungs blown into it is warmer and lighter than the air outside it.

What is meant by Centrifugal Force?

If you tie a weight to the end of a string and whirl it round and round in a circle, the weight tries to fly away in a direction at right angles to the string. The string compels it to follow a circular path, so the string is pulled on by the weight; or, to look at the matter the other way round, the string pulls on the weight—with a force which is called centrifugal force. The force increases much more quickly than the number of revolutions per minute. Every particle of a revolving wheel is subjected to centrifugal force, tending to pull the wheel to bits. Anything intended to revolve at very high speeds must be carefully designed to resist this force. Terrible damage has been done on several occasions by large flywheels bursting. A blade, weighing only a third of an ounce, of a turbine wheel 6 inches in diameter will exert a pull of over 12 hundredweight at 30,000 revolutions a minute.

Is Centrifugal Force of any use to us?

Yes; it is turned to account in many ways. The speed of many engines is controlled by a centrifugal governor, with whirling balls which fly further apart as the speed increases and move levers that reduce the supply of steam or gas. Cream is separated from milk, water from wet clothes, molasses from sugar, by centrifugal apparatus. Pipes are cast centrifugally by pouring molten metal into rapidly revolving moulds. Centrifugal force keeps a circular saw stiff, is applied to the pumping of water, and is depended on to release the safety-bolt in a shell fuse as the shell leaves the gun. Resisting it provides the fun of a " joy-wheel."

Why are we not thrown off the Earth by Centrifugal Force?

A person at the equator is being carried round the earth's axis at the rate of about $17\frac{1}{2}$ miles a minute. But the earth is so large that he is travelling in an almost straight line; and the earth turns round its axis only once in twenty-four hours. So the centrifugal outward pull on his body is only about $\frac{1}{150}$th of the opposing pull of the earth, which we call his weight. The tendency to fly off is greatest at the equator, and decreases steadily towards the poles, at which it disappears.

Has the secret of Perpetual Motion been discovered?

No; and, so far as we can see, never will be; for the very idea of perpetual motion conflicts with our knowledge of the physical laws controlling all kinds of matter.

Why does Blotting-paper suck up Ink so readily?

Because its fibres are loosely compacted and the spaces between them act as tiny tubes into which the ink runs by what is called capillary attraction.

Why does a Wick draw up Oil?

Because the oil forces its way into the very small channels between the fibres of the wick by capillary attraction. If you dip the end of a very fine glass tube into water you will see that the water rises higher inside than it is outside. Capillary attraction is at work here, too.

Can Water be compressed?

Yes, but only if very great pressure be used. It loses about one-tenth of its bulk under a pressure of 20 tons to the square inch.

Why is it that, if you lay a needle very gently on the surface of water, it will float?

Because water has a " skin," which is reluctant to be broken and can withstand the weight of a needle. Water may be poured into a sieve of fine wire gauze that has been smoked in a candle flame, without running through. Here, again, the resistance of the skin supplies the explanation.

Why does not all the Ink on a Pen run off at once?

Because most liquids stick to anything dipped into them. When you write with a pen the force of gravity tends to make the ink run off, and this is helped by the ink at the tip clinging to the paper and pulling on the ink left on the pen.

Why does not the Ink run quickly out of a Fountain Pen?

Because the ink itself prevents air entering the ink reservoir and releasing the ink. The pressure of the air acts against the ink's weight. Ink can nevertheless be drawn slowly from the reservoir by the action of writing, as the paper exerts a pull on it.

Why does a Garden Hose tend to straighten out when the Water is turned on?

Because wherever there is a curve in it the tube is a bit flattened. The water expands the hose into a circular form, to make more room for itself, and in doing so it compels the hose to straighten itself. Just the same thing happens with the toy paper tubes which naturally coil up flat, but straighten out suddenly when one blows air into them.

Why does a Garden Hose squirt Water further if its end is pinched?

Because the size of the opening is reduced and the pressure inside the pipe rises, giving the water a stronger push as it leaves the hose. At the same time, of course, the rate of flow is reduced.

If you jump off a moving Vehicle, you should face the Direction in which it is travelling. Why?

Your body tries to keep up with the vehicle after your feet touch the ground, and unless you are in the proper attitude for taking some quick steps while slowing down you will topple over.

If one jumps upwards in a Train moving at sixty miles an hour one comes down on the spot from which one jumped. Why is this?

Because, while you are in the air, you are travelling in the same direction and at the same speed as the train, and consequently you are over the jumping-off spot all the time.

Why is a Fly able to flit about easily in a railway carriage travelling much faster than it can fly?

Because the air in the carriage is travelling at the same rate as the train, and for practical purposes the fly is moving in still air.

Why does Sugar dissolve more quickly in Tea or Coffee if stirred?

Because all parts of the granules are constantly being introduced to water which saturates them.

Why is Grease put in the axle-boxes of Railway Wagons?

To form a film between the axles and the brass bearings in which they turn, and so prevent them rubbing together and becoming hot.

How does a Kite fly?

The wind strikes it slantingly from below and forces it upwards until its weight is just balanced by the upward pressure.

Photographs show that Air-bubbles become larger as they rise through water. Why should this be the case?

Because the pressure of the water on them decreases. While a bubble rises from, say, 12 inches to 6 inches from the surface the pressure is halved, and the bubble's volume is therefore able to double

Who discovered X-rays?

Professor Wilhelm Konrad Röntgen, a German. He made his great discovery in 1895. The rays are also called Röntgen rays, after their discoverer.

What are Cosmic Rays?

Atomic particles such as protons, travelling through space at enormous speeds, enter the earth's atmosphere, where they smash up some of the atoms of the atmospheric gases. The result is a shower of mixed rays and particles, many of the kind known as "mesons." Nobody knows the origin of the cosmic rays, though some of them have sufficient energy to penetrate several feet of lead, and they are found even at the bottom of mines. About twenty atoms in every cubic inch of the atmosphere are smashed by cosmic rays every second.

HEAT

What is meant by degrees Fahrenheit and degrees Centigrade?

Degrees of heat as measured by the scales applied to thermometers by Gabriel Daniel Fahrenheit, a German, in 1714, and by Anders Celsius, a Swedish astronomer, in or about 1725. The Fahrenheit scale, which is that more commonly used in the British Empire and America, is divided into 180 degrees or equal parts between the freezing- and boiling-points of water; and its zero or starting-point is 32 degrees below freezing-point. By this scale therefore the boiling-point of water is 212 degrees (written 212° F.) above zero. The Centigrade scale of Celsius takes the freezing-point of water as its zero, and its boiling-point is 100 degrees (written 100° C.) above zero. The Centigrade scale is used by scientific men of all nations, and for general purposes in most European countries. Since a degree Centigrade is almost equal to two degrees Fahrenheit, one should be careful to note which scale is used when temperatures are referred to.

Why is coloured Alcohol used in some thermometers instead of Mercury?

Usually because it is cheaper. But it *must* be employed in thermometers required to measure very low temperatures, as mercury freezes at 38·87° below zero Centigrade, whereas alcohol remains liquid down to 130° below zero Centigrade (= 202° below zero Fahrenheit).

What is meant by Latent Heat?

The heat which a solid body takes in while melting, or a liquid while boiling, without becoming any hotter. If you put a kettle of ice-cold water on the fire, it will take in a certain amount of heat before it begins to boil. To make all the water boil away will require about five-and-a-half times as much heat again. Yet the water's temperature never rises above boiling-point. What has become of all this extra heat? It has become latent, or hidden, in the steam. Suppose all the steam to have been caught in a condenser surrounded by water. The steam will turn back into boiling-hot water, and the latent heat will appear again as heat in the water outside the condenser.

Why does Heat make substances expand?

Heat is a form of energy or motion. As a substance is warmed up, its molecules become more vigorous and agitated, and repel each other

THATCHERS AT WORK

Topical Press.

In some ways thatch is better than slates or tiles (see p. 418). The reeds used by thatchers are cut when the foliage has withered. Reed cutters at Abbotsbury Swannery, Dorset, cut as many as ten thousand bundles in a good season.

Fox Photos.

Central Press.

It is fascinating to watch thatchers and see how methodically and skilfully they work. Very often, the craft is handed down from father to son.

The reeds are carefully tucked in before being pegged down. Thatch of unthreshed straw will last about 25 years, thatch of reeds 40 years.

with greater force. The distance between them increases slightly, and the substance expands.

Has the swelling of Water when it freezes any important effects?

If water followed the general law, and kept shrinking as it gets colder, life would be impossible on a large part of the earth's surface. Ice would sink instead of floating, and during the winter many rivers, and some oceans and seas would be frozen solid from the bottom upwards. The heat of summer would thaw them only slightly, winds would be chilled by blowing over them, and the climate of the temperate zones would be very much colder. As things are, the ice on the surface protects the water below from intense cold. Other important effects of the swelling of freezing water are the breaking up of the soil, and the splitting of rocks into the crevices of which water has found its way.

Why do Water-pipes burst when frozen?

Because the water inside them expands as it freezes.

Why does a Pendulum Clock tend to lose time in Hot Weather?

Because heat lengthens the pendulum rod and makes the pendulum swing more slowly. The pendulums of good clocks carry devices which neutralise the alterations in length.

Why does Paint blister in hot sunshine?

Because heat softens the paint in places and makes it expand. To make room for itself the paint curves outwards.

Why should one not fill a Kettle brim-full with Cold Water before putting it on to boil?

Because heat expands water considerably, and some of the water would overflow.

Why should Bicycle Tyres not be pumped up very hard in Hot Weather?

Because heat makes the air inside them try to expand, and if the tyres are blown up hard to begin with they may be unable to stand the extra pressure caused by heating.

Is it right to fill Jampots right to the top with Hot Jam from the Preserving Pan?

Yes! because jam shrinks a good deal as it cools.

How can one cool Water in Hot Weather without using Ice?

By encasing the vessel containing it in a wet cloth and hanging it up in a draught out of the sun. The rapid evaporation of the moisture in the cloth extracts heat from the vessel and the water. In hot climates porous vessels are commonly used for the purpose. The water oozing through the earthenware keeps the outside damp, so that evaporation is continuous. Air is cooled in a similar way in India by hanging grass curtains in doorways and sprinkling them frequently with water.

Why do Damp Stockings chill the Legs?

Because the evaporation of the moisture in them takes heat from the skin.

Why does not the Water from the River Jordan keep on raising the level of the Dead Sea?

Because the intense heat of the sun in that region evaporates the water fast enough to prevent the level rising. Similarly, the Caspian Sea, which receives the water of the Volga, the largest river in Europe, and of five other rivers, does not increase its depth, but is actually becoming shallower, owing to evaporation.

Why do Blankets feel warmer than Sheets when we first get into them?

Because blankets absorb heat less readily than sheets.

Why does Linoleum feel colder to the Feet than does a Carpet?

Because it absorbs heat more quickly from the feet, being a better conductor and touching them at more points, owing to its smoothness.

Why is a Kettle-holder made of Cloth?

Because cloth is a bad conductor of heat.

How does Snow protect plants against injury by Frost?

Snow is a very bad emitter of heat, and therefore prevents the heat of the earth below it escaping. Also, it prevents intense night cold reaching the plants.

Why does Water bubble when it boils?

Because the steam rising from the bottom of the vessel keeps forcing up the surface of the water.

Why cannot Water in a Kettle become any Hotter after it has come to the boil?

Because all the heat taken in is then used up in changing water into steam. But in a steam boiler the boiling-point and the heat of the water rise with the pressure, and if the boiler is strong enough to stand the pressure the heat may rise to over 700 degrees Fahrenheit.

Why does Water in a Saucepan boil more quickly if the Lid is kept on?

Because the air between the water and the lid becomes heated by the water and lessens the escape of heat. If the lid be left off, heat is constantly carried away by air circulating close to the water.

Why should one prick a Chestnut before roasting it?

The heat of the fire generates steam in the moist interior of the nut, and if this cannot escape freely it may blow the nut to pieces.

Why is there a Hole in the Lid of a Kettle?

The hole acts as a vent for the steam, and allows air to enter the kettle when water is poured out from it.

What makes a Kettle sing?

Just before a kettle comes to the boil, small bubbles of steam begin to rise from the hottest parts of it. These are condensed before they reach the surface, and set up vibrations which cause the " singing " noise.

When one begins to toast a Slice of Bread it becomes damp at the back. Why is this?

The surface next the fire is hardened by the heat. Steam from the moisture in the bread therefore escapes more freely through the back surface, on which a good deal of it is condensed.

Why does Milk boil over so quickly?

Probably because it " lathers " readily. Steam, instead of escaping from it easily, as it does from water, blows the milk into bubbles which suddenly fill the saucepan and pour over the top.

What becomes of the Steam from a Locomotive when it disappears?

The steam inside the boiler is an invisible vapour or gas, and what we see coming from a locomotive's chimney is not steam but the particles of water into which the steam has been condensed. These are quickly scattered and are absorbed again into the air as invisible water vapour. In cold weather absorption is slow, and the so-called steam " hangs about " longer than on a hot day.

Why do Liquids keep hot so long in a Vacuum Flask?

Because the container is surrounded by a hollow double jacket of glass from which air has been removed. This airless space prevents heat being conducted from the inside to the outside of the flask, while silvering on the glass checks the radiation of heat.

Why do people wear White Clothes in Hot Climates?

Because they reflect heat better than coloured clothes.

Why are Dark-coloured Clothes hotter in Summer than Light-coloured Clothes?

Because dark colours absorb a larger part of the radiation from the sun which falls on them. White repels radiation, and for this reason we wear white flannels for summer games, and whitewash roofs in hot weather.

Why should Metal Vessels for holding Hot Liquids be kept brightly polished?

Because a brightly polished metal surface radiates heat more slowly than a dull one.

Does a Silver Teapot keep the Tea hot longer than a China one?

No, for china is a poor conductor of heat and allows less to escape. A metal pot feels hotter because the heat is coming out through it all the time, but this can be checked by using a tea-cosy.

Why does a glowing Coal blacken very quickly if broken up?

Because its heat then has a much larger surface through which to escape.

How does a Fire dry a Room?

By warming the air in it until the air can take in more moisture from everything in the room that is damp.

Why does an Electric Radiator begin to warm one almost immediately after it has been switched on?

The current quickly makes certain parts of the radiator glow and send out rays of radiant heat, which warm anything on which they fall. Even if the air of a room be icy cold, the temperature will rise rapidly.

Why does a Hot-water Radiator take so long to make a Room comfortably warm?

A radiator of this kind heats in the same way as a closed stove, by what is called convection. The air immediately touching it becomes hot and rises, and is replaced by colder air, which is warmed in turn. Until all the air in the room has repeatedly picked up heat in this manner the atmosphere in the room will not be warm throughout, and this process naturally takes a considerable time.

Why do Grapes ripen better against a Wall than in the open?

Because the wall stores up sun-heat and radiates it by night as well as by day.

Why does blowing with Bellows make a dull fire burn up?

Because the rate at which air reaches the burning fuel is increased.

Why are dirty Plates and Dishes washed in Hot Water?

Because hot water softens grease and allows it to be removed easily. Also, it dissolves sugary substances more quickly than cold water.

Why do Haystacks sometimes catch fire of their own accord?

If the hay is gathered in a damp condition it may ferment in the stack. The chemical processes of fermentation generate heat which, if unable to escape, may become great enough to set the stack alight.

Why does Friction produce Heat?

When two bodies rub together, the force called friction resists their moving over one another. The overcoming of this force means that work is done, and the doing of work is always accompanied by heat.

Why do things near the Ground seem to quiver on a Hot Day?

The air is then rising from the ground in hot waves, and its density is constantly changing at any one level. As its density varies, so are light rays bent in different degrees while passing from an object to the eye of a beholder. Consequently the object itself seems to move about or quiver.

Why does a Burning-glass set paper alight?

Because the glass bends the heat rays in such a manner that they all fall on the same small spot, where the heat becomes intense.

Why is Spring Water cool in the Hottest Weather?

Because it comes from a depth to which summer heat does not penetrate.

What becomes of the Heat leaving a cooling Flat-iron?

It is transferred to the surrounding air. Though it is lost so far as human use is concerned, it has not ceased to be.

Why do Stones on thawing Ice melt pits in it?

In the first place, the stones absorb heat from the air. In the second, the pressure due to their weight generates a little heat. If a bar of ice be supported at the ends and a weight be hung on a wire encircling it, the weight will draw the wire through the ice, which will freeze again behind it if the temperature is low enough.

In what respect is Thatch preferable to Tiles and Slates for covering Roofs?

It conducts heat much less readily, since it contains a large number of air-spaces, and therefore keeps a house cooler in summer and warmer in winter.

LIGHT

How is the Speed of Light measured?

In several different ways, all of which give almost the same results. The method most easily explained is that used by a French scientist, Fizeau, in 1849. He had a wheel made with 720 teeth round the edge, separated by spaces of the same width as the teeth. This was mounted in a way that enabled it to be turned steadily at any speed. A beam of light from a lamp was reflected from a mirror through the spaces between the wheel's teeth to another mirror set up about $5\frac{1}{3}$ miles away. The mirror near the wheel had a hole at the centre so that an observer looking through it might watch the reflections of light from the distant mirror. Fizeau found that when the wheel was run up to a certain speed no reflection of light could be seen. This meant that each flash passing through a gap was obstructed by the next tooth after travelling the $10\frac{2}{3}$ miles to the far mirror and back. So, to find the speed of light, it was only necessary to multiply $10\frac{2}{3}$ miles by the number of times per second (about 17,437) that a gap was replaced by a tooth. The result, as you will find, if you care to work it out, is about 186,000 miles a second.

Does Green Light travel faster than Red Light?

No! Light rays all travel at the same speed (about 186,000 miles a second), whatever their colour may be.

Can we have Heat without Light, or Light without Heat?

If water be poured on to unslaked lime, great heat is generated without any light accompanying it. One may heat things by merely rubbing them together. Here, again, there is no light. But we are at present unable to produce light without producing heat as well. Whether the light from glow-worms, fire-flies, and phosphorescent substances is heatless or not is uncertain, but it must be very nearly so.

Why does a Grease-stain on a piece of paper look more transparent than the surrounding paper if held up to the Light, but darker than the paper if this is laid on the floor?

The effect of grease is to make paper pass light more freely. This accounts for a grease-stain looking more transparent against the light. In the second case, as more light gets through the grease-spot than through the rest of the paper, the greasy part reflects less light and looks darker.

Place a Coin in an empty basin and step back till the coin is just hidden by the rim. If water be poured into the basin, the coin comes into sight again. Why is this?

Light rays are bent when they pass from air into water, or from water into air. Rays reflected from the coin are bent downwards at the surface of the water; and it is those reaching the part of the surface visible above the basin's rim which enter your eye.

Why does a Stick appear bent if part of it is immersed in Water?

Because rays from the under-water part are bent downward towards the observer, so that this part appears nearer the surface than it really is.

Does Water of which you can see the bottom appear deeper or shallower than it actually is?

Shallower, by about a quarter of its real depth. A pool 8 feet deep would appear to be 6 feet deep.

How does a Triangular Glass prism split white light into various Colours?

When a ray of light passes through a surface of a prism, it is turned towards that side of its original path on which the thicker part of the prism lies. On leaving the prism it is again bent in the same direction. Rays of different colours are bent in different degrees, red rays being bent least, and violet rays most. Therefore a beam of white light, which contains rays of all the colours of the solar spectrum, has the colours separated by passage through the prism.

Why are White Flowers the last to be visible when Darkness falls?

Because they reflect rays of all colours, whereas coloured flowers reflect some colours only.

Why does a Soap-bubble exhibit so many different Colours?

Because its film is thinner at some places than at others, and different thicknesses reflect different colours. The black parts are the thinnest, and reflect no light at all. They have been found to be only one three-millionth part of an inch thick.

Why is it difficult to match Ribbons and Coloured Fabrics by artificial light?

Because artificial light does not contain all the colours of the solar spectrum, or at least not all the colours in the same proportions as in daylight. Consequently, objects tend to take on the colours which predominate in the light used.

THE WONDERS OF SPEED

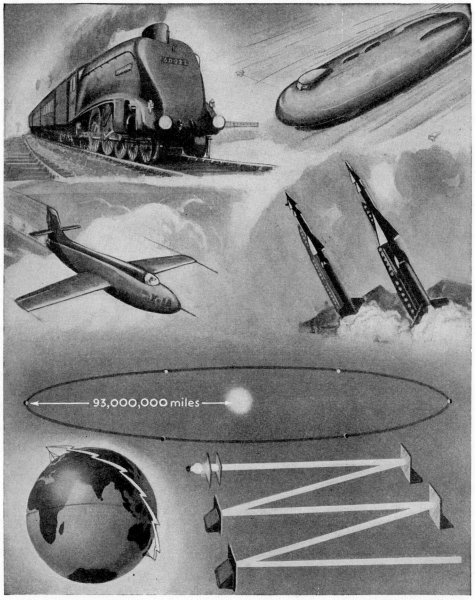

Specially drawn for this work.

Here we have some pictorial examples of speed: a Pacific Mallard locomotive attained 126 miles per hour on British Railways (Eastern Region). The fastest racing car made the record for the flying mile at 394 miles per hour, while the Bell X-IA aircraft reached 1,600 m.p.h. The rockets shown here travel at mach 2 and over, that is at over 1,500 m.p.h. All these speeds, however, are slow compared with the speed of the Earth round the Sun, which is about 66,000 m.p.h., while the speed of light as well as electrical and wireless impulses are all in the region of 186,000 miles per second. Thus *light* (see p. 418) from the Sun to the Earth takes about 8 minutes and a wireless message would travel round the Earth in one-seventh of a second.

Why does the sea look Blue on a Sunny Day and Grey on a Dull One?

Its colour is that of what it reflects—a blue sky in the first case, and grey clouds in the second.

Why does the Image of the Moon appear as a long streak on ruffled water?

Because the light is reflected from the tops and sides of many ripples at different distances from the eye.

Why do many inexpensive Looking-glasses give distorted Reflections?

Because the cheap glass which is used in them is not perfectly flat.

Why do Objects seen through a Window sometimes appear out of shape?

Because the two surfaces of the glass are not perfectly parallel to one another, so that the thickness of the glass varies in different parts.

Why does one see a Number of Reflections of a Candle-flame held near a thick mirror and viewed from one side?

The image nearest the flame is reflected from the front surface of the glass. The one next to it, which is by far the brightest, comes from the silvered back surface. Part of the light from the last is reflected to and fro inside the glass, and some of it escapes into the air after each reflection, causing the other faint images.

How is it that a Cloud, though made up of Water, which is a transparent substance, can hide the Sun?

The water in a cloud is composed of a vast number of isolated particles, which scatter the sun's light in all directions, and absorb a great deal of it. The rays being thus dispersed, we cannot see the sun, unless the cloud be thin, though some of its light penetrates the cloud. The water particles act in just the same way as the roughnesses on the surface of a piece of ground glass.

Why are Sunsets often Red?

Because when the sun is setting its rays have to travel through a great thickness of the atmosphere, and the water and dust particles in the air are able to scatter all the blue rays. The red rays, which are not scattered to the same extent, come through without difficulty.

Why does Total Darkness reign in the Depths of the Ocean?

Because even the clearest of water absorbs light. Tests made by lowering photographic plates seem to show that sunlight fails to reach a greater depth than about 3,600 feet anywhere in the oceans; and that blue rays penetrate water furthest and red rays least. In 1930 Dr. Beebe, an American naturalist, descended to a depth of 1,426 feet in a steel ball. At that depth the water appeared blue-black.

Why does an Incandescent Electric Lamp need a Glass Bulb?

In the first place, the glass protects the very delicate filament. In the second, it prevents the oxygen of the air reaching the filament and causing it to burn away. All air is exhausted from the bulb during manufacture, but this is usually replaced by an inert gas at low pressure to prevent the filament evaporating and blackening the glass.

Why is the Outline of a Shadow cast by a Candle on to a Wall somewhat blurred?

Because light rays come from many different points of the flame. Some are stopped entirely by the edge of the object and others are not. The further the object is from the shadow-catching surface, the greater is the dispersion of the rays, and the more indistinct the outline. For this reason it is not very easy to tell where the shadow of, say, a church steeple ends.

Why do some Motor Cars carry Yellow Headlights?

Because yellow light penetrates fog and mist better than white light. Red light is more penetrating still. At some aerodromes pilots are guided by powerful electric lamps filled with neon gas, which emits a red light having remarkable fog-piercing qualities.

Why should the Wallpapers used in Rooms facing north be of a Light Colour?

Because such rooms get no direct sunlight, and the paper should therefore be able to reflect a good part of such light as enters the windows.

Why, when Pictures are taken down, does the wall-paper behind them seem to be darker than it is elsewhere?

Because the paper behind the pictures has been screened from light and has faded less than the rest of the paper.

Why is it difficult to see through a Window at night from a Lighted Room?

Because the glass reflects images of things in the room. If the light be switched off, reflection ceases, and one can see outside objects much more clearly.

SOUND

How fast does Sound travel?

Through air, 1,120 feet per second; through water, 4,700 feet per second; through metals, from 4,000 feet (lead) to 16,800 feet (iron) per second; through wood, from 11,000 to 16,700 feet per second.

Why does a Violin String change its note as a finger is moved up or down it?

Because the length and tension of the part of the string that emits sound is being altered, and the number of its vibrations per second varies with them.

Why does a Violin String give out a higher note when tightened up?

Because it then vibrates faster, and the waves set up by it in the air strike the ear in quicker succession.

Why are Wooden Houses noisier than Brick Houses?

Because boards vibrate more easily than bricks and wooden walls act as sounding-boards.

Why are Noises heard more plainly in an Empty than in a Furnished House?

Because an empty house contains no carpets and other floor-coverings to muffle footsteps, and no curtains, other hangings, or furniture to deaden echoes.

Why do Empty Vessels give out Louder Sounds than full ones?

Because they are able to vibrate more freely.

Why is a Bell's Sound stopped by touching the Rim?

Touching the rim stops the bell vibrating, so it can no longer give rise to sound-waves in the air.

Why is it often difficult to make out the Words of a Person preaching or speaking in a lofty building?

Because echoes from the roof and walls of words that have already been uttered are mixed up with words being spoken.

Why are flat Sounding Boards hung over some Pulpits?

To turn the sounds of the preacher's words downwards towards the congregation, and to prevent echo from the roof.

Who invented the first " Talking Machine "?

The Phonograph, as the first talking machine was named, was invented by Thomas Alva Edison in the U.S.A. in 1876–7. Later, in 1887, A. Berliner of Washington devised an improved type of talking machine which was named the Gramophone. The principles of the original Phonograph are retained in the modern Dictation machines, largely used in business offices to-day for correspondence, reports, etc.

Why is the Hum of Telegraph Wires heard much more plainly when one places an ear against a Telegraph Post?

Because the wood of the post is a much better conductor of sound than air. The vibrations of the wires are sent through it from the insulators. The vibrations themselves are caused by the wind blowing through the wires.

Why do Hunters move Up-wind when Stalking Game?

Because any sounds they may make and the scent of their bodies are then carried by the wind away from their quarry.

Why does the Sound of a Passing Locomotive's Whistle change its pitch?

While the locomotive approaches, the sound-vibrations reach the air more frequently than they would if the engine were standing still. The pitch therefore rises above the natural pitch of the whistle. As the engine recedes, the vibrations are spaced out more, as each has further to travel than that before it, and the pitch falls.

Why do Soldiers marching to a band seem to be out of step with the music when watched from a distance?

Because sight is quicker than sound. We see the movements of the soldiers' legs practically at the actual moments when they are made, but the corresponding beats of the music do not reach our ears till a little later.

Why is there sometimes a loud Knocking Noise when one turns on a water tap?

The valve of the tap is out of order and jumps up and down on its seating. Every time it touches the seating the flow is suddenly checked, causing a rise of pressure which produces a knock in the pipe.

PRINTING

Who invented Printing?

It is impossible to say. Printing from blocks and type was practised by the Chinese many centuries before it became known in Europe. The earliest European examples of printing done with movable metal type are ascribed to Johann Gutenberg, of Mainz, in Germany, and belong to the year 1454.

How does Photography help the Printer?

It has quickened and cheapened the illustration of books, magazines and newspapers very greatly. Almost every illustration which one sees nowadays has been made from a block in the preparation of which photography played an important part. Most photographic printing blocks are divided into two classes: " line " or " black and white " blocks, and " half-tone " blocks. Line blocks are used for reproducing diagrams and pen-and-ink drawings as plain black lines or patches on a white ground. Half-tone blocks (almost all the blocks used in " Pictorial Knowledge " belong to this class) are employed in reproducing direct from photographs, pictures, etc., in which there are several different tones intermediate between black and white.

How are " Line " Printing Blocks made?

Suppose that a block has to be made of an ornamental black A on a white ground. First, a photograph of the A is taken on a glass plate, which shows a transparent A on a black background. This " negative " plate is placed in a printing frame touching a zinc plate coated with a sensitive film, and is exposed to light for a certain time. The light passing through the A, the only transparent part of the negative, renders all the film which it reaches insoluble in water. The zinc " positive " is held under a tap and all the film that the light could not get at dissolves and disappears, leaving the A on the surface of the zinc. After further treatment, which includes varnishing the back, the plate is placed in a dish and flooded with acid, which bites into the metal everywhere except where the A protects it. The " etching," as this process is called, is continued until the A stands up far enough above the rest of the plate to be printed from.

How are Half-tone Printing Blocks made?

If you examine with a magnifying glass a printed illustration made from a photograph, you will see that the black parts are speckled with small white dots; that the dark grey parts are larger white dots surrounded by black; that the light grey parts are small black dots surrounded by white, and that the white parts are white sprinkled over with tiny black dots. You will further notice that the dots are in parallel straight lines crossing one another at right angles. Let us suppose that a half-tone block has to be made from a photographic portrait of a person wearing a black coat, a grey waistcoat, and a white collar. First of all, a negative of the photograph is taken with a camera. Just in front of the plate is fixed a glass screen, consisting of two glass plates ruled with parallel black lines a tiny fraction of an inch apart. The screen plates are placed face to face, with the lines on one crossing those of the other, and forming a black network enclosing tiny squares of clear glass. Each square acts as a minute lens, and throws a dot of light on to the photographic plates. The size of the dot depends on the intensity of the light. The collar will cast dots so large that they overlap each other almost entirely, enclosing tiny spots of darkness wherever two lines of the screen cross. The waistcoat dots are smaller, and do not cross the shadow meshwork of the screen, while the coat dots are very small indeed. In the developed negative the blacks and whites are, of course, reversed. A print is taken from the negative on to a sensitised copper plate, coated with a film which becomes insoluble in water wherever light reaches it. When this metal " positive " is washed, areas of film are left wherever the negative was not blackened. The positive is etched with acid, which eats away the unprotected parts of the plate, and the result is a half-tone block, having small points of metal standing up over the collar area, a projecting meshwork over the waistcoat area, and a flat surface pitted with tiny depressions over the coat area. Wherever the metal has been left at its original level it will pick up ink from a roller passed over it. At reading distance the individual dots cannot be distinguished. They blend together, giving a tone which depends on the predominance of black over white, or of white over black, as the case may be.

Are the Pictures in the Photo-tone Supplements in these Volumes produced by the Half-Tone Process?

No; the Photo-tone Supplements in " Pictorial Knowledge " are printed by the Photogravure Process. In this process the original is photographed, a positive made from the negative and then this is printed on what is known as Carbon Tissue which carries a very fine cross-line screen. It is then printed down on to the copper plate or cylinder and etched. The effect of this screen is to divide the illustrations into numerous cells of equal area, but varying depth, and gives this process the advantage of being able to apply a lot of ink to the darker portions thus giving a wide range of tone. The whole plate is covered with ink and then wiped with a steel blade which leaves each of these small cells filled to capacity. When brought into contact with the paper under pressure the ink leaves the plate and lies on the paper, and provided the paper is of reasonable quality it is possible to give a printed result very close in quality to the original from which it has been reproduced.

What is meant by Stereotyping?

Making casts from set-up type for printing from. A soft pad of tissue paper and blotting-paper mixed with size is laid over the type and beaten or squeezed hard against it till the underside contains an exact impression of the type. The pad is then dried, lifted from the type and placed in a casting-box, for its back to be flooded with molten lead which, when it has hardened, is a plate with an exact duplicate of the original type standing up on one face of it.

What is Lithography?

A process of printing from flat stones. The design or picture to be printed is drawn on the stone in a special ink. A wet roller is then passed over the stone, damping it wherever there is no ink. Next, an inked roller is applied, and this leaves ink on the non-wetted parts only, that is, on the design. When a piece of paper is pressed hard against the stone it picks up the ink, taking a print of the original. Any number of prints can be taken, but the stone must be wetted and inked for each print. Lithography is now used chiefly for large coloured prints, such as posters.

What are the meanings of " 4to," " 8vo," " 12mo," and " 16mo," printed in Book Catalogues after the names of Books?

They are abbreviations of " quarto," " octavo," " duodecimo," and " sexto-decimo," indicating that the size of a page of the book is respectively a quarter, an eighth, a twelfth, or a sixteenth of a standard-sized sheet of printing paper. The size of the sheet itself is usually indicated by the word " royal," " crown," " imperial," etc.

What is the Purpose of a letter of the Alphabet printed at the bottom of some pages of a book?

This letter, called the " sheet mark," is printed for the guidance of the bookbinder, to ensure the correct sequence of pages. It appears on the first page of each sheet in alphabetical order, but sometimes numbers are used for this purpose instead of letters. A printed sheet is called a " signature," and usually consists of 16 pages, although it is sometimes necessary to vary this.

RAILWAYS

Which was the First Railway opened for Public Use?

The Grand Surrey Iron Railway, running from Wandsworth, London, to Croydon. It was opened in 1804, and had a gauge of 4 feet. The trains, which carried coals and other minerals, were hauled by horses.

On which Public Railway were Steam Locomotives first used?

On the Stockton and Darlington Railway, opened in 1825. Horses were used as well as locomotives during the early years of the railway.

When and where did the first Railway Accident take place?

On September 15th, 1830, at Parkside, on

THE DICTATION MACHINE IN BUSINESS

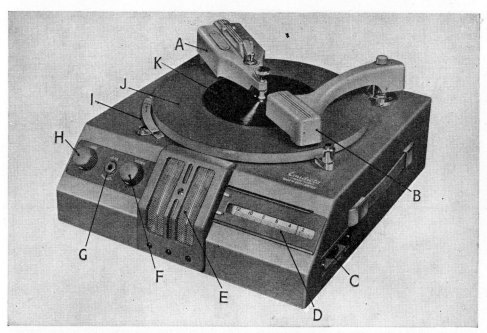

A modern dictation machine, the Emidicta, is shown here, with key to the parts indicated by letters: A. The erase head, which enables the recording disc to be used again and again. B. The record/replay head. C. Telephone recording switch. D. Cueing scale, which shows how much recording time is left on the disc. E. The loudspeaker. F. Volume control. G. Socket for typist's " stethophone." H. Tone control. I. On/off switch. J. The plastic recording disc. K. The tracking disc.

E.M.I. Sales and Service Ltd.

Here is an office scene with typists listening through their stethophones to the letters, reports, etc., which have been recorded, and typing as they listen. The on/off switch (I) enables them to slow down the speed of the dictation if it is too fast. Records can be filed for reference or erased by the erase head (A) and the disc used again. Records can be replayed through the loudspeaker, the master microphone, or the typists' lightweight stethophones.

HOW DOTS MAKE PICTURES

This is a "*half-tone*" (see p. 421) reproduction of a photographic print of the head of a dog. It has been printed from a block made through a "55" screen, which is suitable for newspaper work.

For this a "100" screen, that is, one having 100 rows of openings per inch each way, or 10,000 in a square inch, has been used. The "grain" of the illustration is sufficiently fine for ordinary periodicals.

F. W. Simons.

Here we have an example of the use of a "150" screen, which yields very fine blocks, suitable for printing only on paper having a highly finished surface. The "grain" is almost invisible.

In this instance a portion of the first illustration has been enlarged to show how the size and nature of the dots give different tones. At reading distance the dots in a half-tone reproduction cannot be seen.

the Liverpool and Manchester Railway, which was opened to the public on that day. The ceremonies included the running of special trains from Liverpool to Manchester. The trains stopped at Parkside to take in water. During the halt Mr. William Huskisson, M.P. for Liverpool and President of the Board of Trade, got out on the line to speak to the Duke of Wellington, who was travelling in a special coach. While he was talking with the Duke a train approached on the other track. In trying to get back hastily into his carriage, Huskisson fell in front of the train and had one of his legs crushed so badly that he died a few hours later.

What Far-reaching Change in the Control of Britain's Railways took place in 1948?

From January 1st, 1948, all the railways in Great Britain were nationalised; they became the property of the State, and the companies which had owned them ceased to exist. The four chief companies were the London, Midland and Scottish Railway; the London and North Eastern Railway; the Great Western Railway and the Southern Railway, but altogether some sixty companies were transferred to public ownership. All these are now known as British Railways.

What is meant by the "Permanent Way" of a Railway?

All that portion of the track which lies between the levelled surface of the ground and the upper surface of the rails. It includes the ballast, sleepers, chairs, keys, rails and fishplates.

Why are new Railway Sleepers black or very dark in colour?

Because they have been soaked in creosote, a black liquid obtained from tar, to preserve them against the effects of damp. The creosote is forced in under great pressure and fills the spaces in the wood, so preventing the entry of water. It also kills tiny fungi and bacteria which cause the decay of wood.

Why is the outer rail of a Railway Track running in a curve raised higher than the inner rail?

To give a train an inward tilt to counteract centrifugal force tending to make the train upset towards the outside of the curve. For the same reason motor racing tracks are "banked" or sloped inwards, on the curves, the steepness of the slope increasing towards the outside edge to make it suitable for different speeds.

Why are Men who look after Railway Tracks called Platelayers?

Because the earliest metal tracks for wagons to run on were made of iron *plates*. The plates had a raised rim to prevent the wheels running off them. Presently rails were used instead, the rims being replaced by flanges on the wheels; but the old word "platelayer" was still applied to the men who laid them.

What is the Purpose of Short Posts with two projecting arms which one sees beside a Railway Track?

They are placed at points where a change of gradient occurs, to inform drivers of locomotives.

An arm marked "Level" points in the direction where there is a level stretch of track. One pointing upwards or downwards indicates that the track rises or falls in that direction. The steepness of a slope is shown by figures. Thus, "1 in 165" means that the track rises or falls 1 foot in every 165 feet.

Why are Grass, Lucerne, Bushes and Small Trees planted on Railway Embankments?

So that their roots may bind the earth together and prevent it slipping.

What is the Purpose of a curved iron bar suspended from a kind of gallows over a Railway Siding?

It is a loading gauge. If the load on an open truck is able to pass under the gauge, there is no danger of it striking a bridge or the roof of a tunnel.

What is meant by the Gauge of a Railway?

The distance between the two rails of a track. The standard gauges used in various countries are as follows:

5 ft. 6 in. (1·676 m.): India, Ceylon, Spain, Portugal, Argentina and Chile.

5 ft. 3 in. (1·600 m.): Ireland, S. Australia, Victoria and Brazil.

5 ft. 0 in. (1·524 m.): U.S.S.R.

4 ft. 8½ in. (1·435 m.): Standard Gauge for Great Britain, Canada, U.S.A., Mexico, European Continent (except Spain, Portugal and U.S.S.R.), Egypt, Turkey, Australian Commonwealth, New South Wales and China.

3 ft. 6 in. (1·067 m.): Queensland, S. Australia, W. Australia, Tasmania, New Zealand, South and East Africa, Gold Coast, Nigeria, Sudan, Japan, East Indies, Sweden and Norway.

3 ft. 5¼ in. (1·05 m.): Asia Minor (part) and Algeria.

3 ft. 3⅜ in. (1 m.): India, South America, East and West Africa, Burma, Malaya, Siam, Indo-China.

3 ft. 0 in. (0·914 m.): Ireland.

2 ft. 11 in. (0·891 m.): Sweden.

2 ft. 5½ in. (0·750 m.): India and Ceylon.

1 ft. 11½ in. (0·600 m.): Wales, India and South America.

It will be noted that certain countries or Continents have two or three different gauges. Australian States, for example, have three different gauges. Some of the smaller gauges are, of course, used only on special railways in the countries mentioned.

Why do Railway Station Platforms slope down at the end?

So that people working on the line may easily mount them, and to enable luggage to be wheeled across the track from one platform to another.

Why are the edges of Railway Platforms painted white?

To warn people, especially at night, of their exact position.

Why are very Long Buffers fixed at the end of a Track in a Railway Terminus?

To bring a moving engine or train to a standstill without damaging it. The plunger of a

Since the motor-car first came on to the *roads* (see p. 428) the problem of making highways which will carry the ever-increasing traffic has become an urgent one. In this picture is a model of the new type of road, showing a fly-over roundabout junction, with an all-purpose road passing over a motor-way.

Photos : Central Press.

Here is the model for another roadway which has been planned. In this case the motorway passes over an all-purpose road which has a roundabout. Special arrangements have also been made in both these models for pedestrians and cyclists.

buffer is attached to a piston sliding in a cylinder. When the plunger is driven in, oil inside the cylinder is forced from one side of the piston to the other through an opening which becomes smaller as the piston moves. The friction of the oil passing through this opening causes a steady resistance which soon checks motion.

What is the Purpose of the Large Clocks seen at the ends of " Tube " Railway Platforms?

To inform the driver of a train how many minutes have elapsed since the train next ahead passed out of the station. The face of a clock is divided into minutes only. When a train leaves the station, the hand of the clock goes back automatically to o (the twelve-o'clock position) and begins to advance again at once. Railwaymen call these clocks " headway " clocks.

What is meant by the " Block " System of working a Railway?

The system of dividing a track up into a number of sections or lengths, and never allowing two trains to be in the same section at the same time. Each section is protected at the entry end by signals, worked from a signal box which is connected electrically with the boxes of the sections next to it in both directions. Before a signalman may lower his signals to let a train pass he must receive permission from the signalman in the box next ahead.

How is a Signalman partly guarded against making mistakes?

By very ingenious apparatus called interlocking gear, which makes it impossible to work signals in the wrong order, and to set signals so that they conflict with each other. To take an example: Two trains are approaching junction C on converging tracks A and B. The interlocking gear prevents the signals being set at " All Clear " on A and B simultaneously. The danger of a collision is thus avoided, since right of way cannot be given to both trains at the same time.

How can a Signalman tell at night what kind of a Train is approaching his Box?

By observing the headlights on the front of the engine. They are arranged according to a code, and the signalman knows from their positions what class of train is behind the locomotive.

What is meant by Automatic Signalling?

The use of signals which are worked by the trains themselves. The track is divided up into sections, and each wheel rail of a section is bonded together at the joints to form a continuous conductor. When the first pair of wheels of a train enters a section, current is able to pass from one rail to the other through the wheels and axle, and through a motor which sets a signal at danger behind the train. The circuit is not broken until the last pair of wheels of the train has passed out of the section at the other end. The signals then return to the " All Clear " position. The London " tube " railways are among those which have automatic signalling.

Was George Stephenson the inventor of the Railway Locomotive?

No. The title belongs by right to Richard Trevithick, a Cornishman, who built the first locomotive that ever ran on rails in 1804. Between him and Stephenson came Blenkinsop, Blackett and Hedley, all of whom introduced improvements. Stephenson's claim to fame is that he went much further than his predecessors, and, by making use of many-tubed boilers, high-pressure steam, easily-worked reversing gear, coupling rods, and the exhaust-steam blast in the chimney, produced the locomotives from which all modern locomotives may be said to be descended.

Why does a Railway Engine puff ?

At the end of every stroke of a piston the steam is released suddenly from the cylinder and escapes violently into the air. When a locomotive starts a train, the puffing is loudest, since the steam is then emitted at a higher pressure than it is after speed has been got up and the reversing gear has been " notched up " to make the steam expand more fully in the cylinders before it is released.

Why are the large wheels of a Railway Locomotive joined together by rods?

So that the cylinders may drive all the wheels thus coupled. The pull which an engine can exert is limited by the weight on its driving wheels, that is, by the friction between them and the rails. By using a number of coupled wheels a large part of the engine's weight can be used for pulling without throwing enough weight on to any one pair of wheels to cause damage to the track.

Why do Express Passenger Locomotives have much larger driving wheels than Goods Engines?

The first are built specially for speed, the second for pulling power. At each turn a big driving wheel moves forward further than a small one; but a small one has greater leverage, since its rim is nearer to the crank-pin.

What is a Tank Engine?

A locomotive which has its water-tanks and coal bunker on its own frames, and not in a separate tender. The absence of a tender enables it to run equally well either end first, so that it does not need turning round, and the tanks help to conserve heat by acting as a jacket to the boiler and fire-box. Tank engines are used mainly for hauling suburban and other passenger trains which stop frequently, but large and powerful engines of this class are also employed for working express trains and heavy goods trains.

Why does a Locomotive whistle before entering a Tunnel?

To warn any men who may be working in the tunnel.

How does the Vacuum Railway Brake act?

Under each carriage there is a cylinder containing a piston, which is connected with the brake gear of the carriage. The cylinder is joined by a short pipe to a main air-pipe (called the train pipe) running along the train to the locomotive. When the driver starts an air-ejector working, air is sucked from the train pipe and from the cylinders, both above and below their pistons. The latter then fall to the bottom of the cylinders, and the brakes are " off." To apply the brakes, air is admitted into the train pipe. It reaches the under side only of each piston, being prevented by a valve from reaching the space above it. The pressure on the under side of a piston now being greater than that on the upper side, the piston is forced upwards, and the brakes are pressed against the wheels.

How does the Westinghouse Air Brake work?

Each carriage has underneath it a brake cylinder and an air reservoir, both of which are connected, through a " triple-valve," with an air-pipe running along the train. When air is pumped into the pipe, the valve directs it into the reservoirs, which become filled with air under high pressure. If the pressure in the pipe be suddenly reduced, by the driver or guard opening a valve, or by the train breaking in half, the trip-valve of each vehicle shifts, admitting air from the reservoir to the brake cylinder of every vehicle. The brakes are then applied. To release the brakes, air has to be pumped into the air-pipe till its pressure exceeds that in the reservoirs. The valves then shift back, putting the reservoirs again in connection with the pipe, while allowing air to escape from the cylinders into the atmosphere.

How can one tell the Speed of a Train in which one is travelling?

On one side of the track distance-posts are set up a quarter of a mile apart. Using the second hand of your watch, note the time occupied in passing from one post to the next. If you divide 900 by the number of seconds taken, you have the speed of the train in miles per hour.

Why do men tap the Wheels of a Train with hammers at some stations?

To find out whether the tyres are in good condition. If a tyre has a crack in it, it gives out a dull instead of a clear ringing sound.

Why are Railway Goods Wagons coupled loosely together?

Partly because coupling and uncoupling are thereby made quicker; and partly in order that the locomotive may set a heavy train in motion more easily by starting up one truck after another.

Why do Bright Flashes come from a moving Electric Train?

Because the shoes which pick up current from the conductor-rail jump away from it now and then, especially at points and crossings. As a shoe leaves the conductor-rail an electric arc is formed between the two for a moment, and this gives out an intense light.

What is a Train Ferry?

A ship built specially for transporting railway trains across stretches of water. It has rails along the deck, on to or off which trains are run over bridges hinged at one end to the quay. A train ferry on the Harwich-Zeebrugge (Belgium) service can accommodate fifty-four 12-ton wagons. The use of train-ferries does away with the need for moving goods and passengers from train to ship, and back from ship to train.

Where in Britain is there a Mountain Railway?

Between Llanberis, in North Wales, and the summit of Mount Snowdon. In a course of about five miles it rises to an elevation of 3,560 feet. Trains are moved and controlled by cog-wheels engaging with a rack laid between the rails. The railway was opened in 1895.

Which Two Ports in England are connected by both Rail and Road Tunnels?

Liverpool, in Lancashire, and Birkenhead, in Cheshire, both at the mouth of the River Mersey, are connected by a railway running through the Mersey Railway Tunnel and by the Queensway Traffic Tunnel for motor vehicles, now more generally known as the Mersey Tunnel. The railway tunnel was opened in 1886 by the Prince of Wales (later King Edward VII) and the famous road tunnel was opened by King George V in 1934.

ROADS

Why does a Road slope from the middle towards the sides?

To throw off rain into the gutters, which are provided with drains to carry the water away. If the road were made flat, water would stand on it and work in, causing damage to the surface. The degree to which the top of a road is rounded is called its camber.

Why are Kerbstones often made of Granite?

Because granite is extremely hard and tough, and therefore able to withstand the impact of wheels against it.

Why are Stone or Metal Posts placed on the kerb at some street corners?

To prevent vehicles running on to the kerb and injuring foot passengers.

Why are White (or Yellow) Lines made along the centre of a Road at corners?

To warn motorists to keep to their side of the road. If a collision occurs, the line shows which driver was at fault.

Why do old British Roads twist about so much?

Probably because they have been developed out of bridle-paths and rough tracks which ran along the boundaries of properties or took routes where the going was easiest.

SHIPS

Why do Steel Ships float?

Because they are hollow and able to displace a weight of water equal to their own weight. If the water round a steel ship could suddenly be frozen solid and the ship be lifted out, the " mould " left in the ice would hold a weight of water exactly equal to the weight of the ship.

Which is the Port and which the Starboard side of a Ship?

The port side is the left side looking forwards towards the bows, and the starboard the right side. Port was originally called larboard, but the word was altered to avoid confusion in sound. Starboard means steer-board, or steering side, for the great oar used for steering ancient ships was on the right side of the stern. At night a ship shows a red light on her port side and a green light on her starboard side. Both of these lights can be seen at the same time only when the ship is coming straight at the observer.

What are a Ship's Scuppers?

Holes through which water runs overboard off the decks.

What are a Ship's Davits?

The swinging arms supporting the tackle by which boats are lowered into the water over the ship's side.

What are the Quarters and Poop of a Ship?

The quarters are the parts of a ship's sides nearest the stern. A poop is a raised deck at the stern.

What is a Ship's Binnacle?

A stand which supports and protects the compass. The top part or hood, covering the compass bowl, has glass windows in it, and a lamp on each side to illuminate the compass card at night.

How does its Rudder make a Ship change direction?

By pushing the stern to port or starboard. The ship swings about a point somewhere near the bows—not at its centre, as might be supposed.

What is meant by " Electric Drive " on a Ship?

That power is transmitted electrically from the ship's engines to the propellers. The engines, which may be steam engines or oil engines, or steam turbines, drive generators, the current from which is led to motors coupled to the propeller shafts. By means of switches one generator can be coupled with two or more propellers, for slow speeds, or each generator be made to drive a separate propeller.

Why is Oil Fuel used so much now on Steamships?

Because it can be put aboard easily and cleanly, takes up less room and can be stowed away in odd corners, enables fewer men to be employed in the boiler rooms, and is more efficient than coal, weight for weight.

What Type of Compass is now increasingly used on Ships?

It is named the gyroscopic compass or " gyrocompass." It is a kind of top, kept revolving by an electric motor, and so mounted that it is free to swing round and tilt. It is first set so that the compass gives a true reading, and then, so long as the top is kept spinning its axis will not vary in its direction, no matter how the ship moves. The gyroscopic compass, being purely mechanical, is more reliable than the old magnetic compass, which was influenced both by the steel of the ship itself and by magnetic rocks ashore.

What does a Man do when he " Boxes the Compass "?

He names the thirty-two points of the compass in their proper order, starting at north and working through east, south, and west back to north.

What are a Ship's Articles?

The agreement between the ship's owner and the crew, regarding an intended voyage, the food and wages to be given, and other details. It is signed by the captain and all members of the crew before the voyage begins.

When is a Ship on her Beam Ends?

When she is lying so far over on her side that she is out of control.

What are the " Dog " Watches?

The hours of the evening on board ship from 4 p.m. to 6 p.m. and from 6 p.m. to 8 p.m. A ship's day of twenty-four hours is divided into watches or spells of duty, all of four hours except the dog watches. The two working parties into which a crew is divided take them alternately, and the purpose of the dog watches is to prevent the same men being on duty at the same hours two nights running.

What is meant by " Heaving the Log "?

The old-fashioned way of finding a ship's speed is to throw overboard a triangular board, called a log-ship, attached at each corner to a line 720 feet long. The line has equally spaced knots in it, about 47 feet apart. At the moment of heaving the log a sand-glass which " runs " for twenty-eight seconds is turned over. The log-ship is weighted, so as to stand upright in the water and drag the line off a reel. When the sand has all run through, the line is suddenly checked. The number of knots on the line that have run out gives the ship's speed in knots, that is, sea-miles per hour.

How can one tell to what Line a big Steamship belongs?

By the painting of the funnels, or by the " house " flag, that is, the special flag of the line, flown. In some cases rings of different colours on the funnels indicate the line clearly enough, but in others the painting may be of the same colour throughout and the same for several lines, so the house flag is needed to give complete identification. Half a dozen important lines, for example, have all-black funnels, and as many all-buff funnels, but no two house flags are sufficiently alike to be mistaken for one another, when " read " along with the funnels.

How do Sailing Ships move against the Wind?

By sailing to-and-fro across the wind in directions which make an angle less than a right angle with that of the wind. Thus, if the wind be blowing from the north, and the ship is making for a port to northwards of her, she will sail first in a N.E. direction, and then come about and sail N.W. By repeating these movements again and again she works her way up-wind. This method of sailing is called " tacking."

AIR FOR THE MERSEY TUNNEL

Herbert J. Rowse.

Opened by King George V in 1934, the Mersey Tunnel (see p. 428) links Liverpool and Birkenhead, running for nearly three miles beneath the river. This picture shows us one of the six ventilating stations, each of which contains blower and exhaust fans to force fresh air into the tunnel at the rate of two and a half million cubic feet per minute and withdraw a similar amount of stale air at the same time.

How are Sailing Ships distinguished from each other by their rigs?

A *schooner* has two, three or four masts, and carries fore-and-aft sails only. A *topsail schooner* has two masts, but she carries square topsails on the foremast. A *brig* is an entirely square-rigged two-master. A *barquentine* is a three-master, with the foremast square-rigged and the other two fore-and-aft rigged. A *barque* has three or more masts, all square-rigged except the mizzen (aft) mast. A *full-rigged ship* has three or more masts, all square-rigged.

How does a Submarine keep below the Surface?

A submarine sinks if her water-ballast tanks are filled till the total weight of the boat exceeds that of the water she displaces. The ballasting can be so adjusted that the boat only just sinks, and in this condition she can be steered up and down, as she moves forward, by horizontal rudders.

What is a Floating Dock?

A great hollow floating structure which can be sunk to allow a ship to come above it, and then be raised with the ship by pumping water out of large chambers in it. It lifts the ship clear of the water, and in a different manner serves the same purpose as a dry dock. The largest floating dock yet built is at Southampton. It is 960 feet long and can raise ships weighing anything up to 60,000 tons.

What is a Dry Dock?

A chamber like a lock, but with an opening at one end, into which ships are brought for repairs or cleaning externally. The sides of a dry dock are sloped in steps. After a ship has been floated in, the entrance is closed and the water is pumped out. When the ship touches bottom, stout timbers are wedged between her sides and the steps on the dock to keep her upright.

What is a Sea-anchor?

Usually a large canvas cone attached to a rope at its big end, which is open. When flung into the sea it acts as a drag (hence its other name of " drogue ") and keeps a ship or boat that is not under control head-on to the waves and wind.

How are Lighthouses made to show their light at regular intervals?

In some cases the light is obscured periodically by a cover which descends and envelops the lamp; in others the lamp has a screen revolving round it, so that the light is seen from one direction only at any moment. The most powerful lighthouses employ revolving lenses or reflectors which concentrate the light into one or more beams, which sweep the horizon all round.

What is the latest method of sending Signals from Lighthouses during Fogs?

By means of a wireless transmitting set the lighthouse sends out its name at regular intervals. Simultaneously with every " call " it emits an ordinary sound signal through the air. The wireless signal is received as soon as sent, while the sound signal, travelling far less quickly, lags behind it. The navigator on a ship receiving the signals can tell, by multiplying the lag of the sound signal, in seconds, by 1,120 feet, exactly how far he is from the lighthouse. Thus, if the name of the lighthouse is heard every time six seconds before the sound signal, the distance between ship and lighthouse must be 6,720 feet.

Which are the most famous British Lighthouses?

The Eddystone, fourteen miles S. of Plymouth; the Bishop Rock, at the S.W. end of the Scilly Islands group; the Fastnet Rock, five miles from Cape Clear, at the S.W. corner of Eire; the Skerryvore, twelve miles S. of Tiree, in the Inner Hebrides; the Dhu Heartach, twenty miles S.E. of the Skerryvore; the Bell Rock (Inchcape Rock), twelve miles E. of the mouth of the Firth of Tay. The present Eddystone Lighthouse is the fourth built on the site; the present Bishop Rock the second, or perhaps it might be called the third, being the second greatly enlarged. All these lighthouses have their foundations almost at sea-level, and are exposed to the full violence of the waves of the open coast. The oldest of them is the Bell Rock, built during the years 1808–11.

What is the Blue Peter?

A blue flag with a white square in the centre, used for signalling the letter " P " in the alphabetical code. It is hoisted when a ship is about to put to sea, as a signal to passengers and absent members of the crew to come aboard. It also warns anyone who has accounts to settle with anyone aboard to do so at once.

SPORT

What is our oldest Outdoor Game or Sport?

Cricket is probably the oldest of our games, the history of its early forms being lost in antiquity. The earliest cricket score we possess, however, is that of a match played on the parade ground of the Honourable Artillery Company, City Road, London, in 1744: and this match probably marks the beginning of scientific cricket. Football is another ancient game, and its earlier forms were so brutal that more than once it suffered the disapproval of England's monarchs. It survived all attempts to suppress it, however, and when the nineteenth century brought an era of " muscular Christianity," football and other outdoor games and sports became well-organised with strict rules of play. Rugby football was developed from a game played at Rugby School, in which the ball might be carried by a player. Association football, commonly called " soccer," is a development of the older " foot " ball game.

What is the M.C.C.?

The initials of the Marylebone Cricket Club, first established in Thomas Lord's ground in 1787; in 1814 it moved to St. John's Wood and became owner of what is still known as Lord's. The Club is recognised as the controlling body for cricket, and all alterations in the rules of the game must be accepted by a two-thirds majority of the members.

What is the F.A.?

The Football Association is the governing body

of English amateur and professional Association football. It was founded in 1863 to establish a definite set of rules to govern both Rugby and Association games, but the Rugby clubs objected to certain proposals and in 1871 the Rugby Union was formed. The F.A. is responsible for the rules governing Association football; it promoted, in 1871, a cup competition open to all clubs: the final for this F.A. Cup, which is now held annually at Wembley, has become the most important event in English football.

What is the Difference between Rugby Union football and the Rugby League game?

The main difference is that Rugby Union football is played only by amateurs and professional players are strictly barred; the Rugby League, founded in 1895 and known as the Northern Union at first, organised Rugby football as a professional game. While the game of both Union and League is similar, the Union rules retain the rule of fifteen players a side, while Rugby League teams are only thirteen on each side. There are certain minor differences in the rules governing the two games.

How and when did the Game of Lawn Tennis originate?

The game of tennis, or real tennis as it is often called, is a very ancient game, but requires a fairly elaborate building, costly to erect even in the nineteenth century. A portable court for a similar game, named Sphairsticke, was devised by Major Wingfield about 1874, and from this came the game we now know as lawn tennis. The All-England Croquet Club took it up and drew up a set of rules for the first championship played at Wimbledon in 1877.

As the game became more popular a Lawn Tennis Association was formed in 1888 and has since been the governing body of the game.

When did Hockey become a Popular Game in this Country?

Hockey has been played under various names in many countries for centuries. In Ireland it was known as hurley, in Scotland as shinty, in Wales as bandy. It became a recognised game in England in 1883 when a standard set of rules was framed by the Wimbledon Club. In the same year the game was adopted by Cambridge University and later by Oxford. The Hockey Association was founded in 1886 and the All-England Women's Hockey Association in 1895.

What is the Meaning of the term " l.b.w. " in Cricket?

Leg before wicket. Law 39 says that if with any part of his person except his hand, which is in a straight line between wicket and wicket, even though the point of impact be above the level of the bails, the batsman intercepts a ball which has not first touched his bat or hand, and which, in the opinion of the Umpire, shall have, or would have, pitched on a straight line from the Bowler's wicket to the Striker's wicket, or shall have pitched on the offside of the Striker's wicket, provided always that the ball would have hit the wicket the batsman (striker) is out l.b.w.

What are the regulation weights and sizes of a Cricket Ball, a Golf Ball and a Lawn Tennis Ball?

A cricket ball must weigh not less than $5\frac{1}{2}$ ounces and not more than $5\frac{3}{4}$ ounces, and measure round not less than $8\frac{13}{16}$ inches and not more than 9 inches. A golf ball must not weigh more than 1·62 ounces, and its diameter must not be less than 1·62 inches. A lawn tennis ball must not be less than $2\frac{1}{2}$ inches nor more than $2\frac{5}{8}$ inches in diameter; and its weight must not be less than 2 ounces and not more than $2\frac{1}{16}$ ounces.

What is the Weight of the " Hammer " thrown at Athletic Meetings?

Sixteen pounds.

What is the Height of the Hurdles used for a Hurdle Race?

For the 120-yards race, 3 feet 6 inches. For the 440-yards (low hurdle) race, 3 feet.

What is meant by " Tossing the Caber "?

A sport popular at Scottish athletic gatherings. The caber is a heavy pole tapering towards one end. A competitor raises it vertically in his hands, small end down, and throws it from him, at the same time giving it a heave so that its larger end shall strike the ground first. The longest throw wins.

What was the Origin of the Olympic Games?

The original Olympic Games were an ancient Greek festival, held at the end of every fourth year at Olympia, in Southern Greece. They had a semi-religious character, and were open to members of all branches of the Greek race. During the festival no fighting was allowed anywhere in Greece. The winner of the Games received only a wreath of wild olive, but the prize was valued above anything else that a Greek could obtain. The winning of it conferred permanent glory on the country as well as the family of the victor. The first Games of which there is a record were held in 776 B.C., from which year Greek dates were reckoned, each games year being called an Olympiad. Thus, 772 B.C. was the second Olympiad, 768 B.C. the third Olympiad, and so on. The fact that the Olympiads were made the basis of Greek chronology shows the great importance attached to these contests. The Games continued to be observed for over 1,100 years, and were not finally abolished till A.D. 394. The *modern* Olympic Games date from 1896, when an athletic meeting open to the whole world was held at Athens. They preserve a link with the Games of Ancient Greece in the Olympic Flame which is kindled in the ruins of the Temple of Zeus in Greece and borne by runners to the place where the Games are being held.

What is the Origin of the Marathon Race?

After the great defeat of the Persians by the Greeks in 490 B.C. at Marathon, a runner, named Pheidippides, ran at full speed to Athens, carrying the good news. So exhausted was he by his effort that on his arrival he fell dead. The distance from Marathon to Athens by road (calculated at 26 miles 385 yards) was taken as that for the race introduced into the modern Olympic

TO GUIDE THE SHIPS AT NIGHT

J. Dixon-Scott.

One of the Seven Wonders of the World was the Alexandria lighthouse built about 260 B.C. In this country Trinity House has been responsible for lighthouses and other marks of the sea round our coasts since 1514. This photograph is of the Godrevy Lighthouse at Gwithian in Cornwall.

Fox Photos.

There have been four Eddystone *Lighthouses* (see p. 431). The first was destroyed by a hurricane in 1703; the second was burned down in 1755. Smeaton's granite building, erected in 1759, became unsafe; the fourth, built in 1882, stands on Eddystone Rocks, 14 miles south-west of Plymouth.

Games when they were instituted in 1896. Many so-called Marathon races have been run on other occasions than at the Games. At present the best time for the distance is 2 hours 23 minutes, 3·2 seconds, this record being set up by E. Zatopek of Czechoslovakia at Helsinki in 1952.

What is the America's Cup?

The cup offered by the New York Yacht Club as the trophy of an international yachting competition. The Cup was originally called the Queen's Cup, and offered by the Royal Yacht Squadron, Cowes, as prize in a yacht race open to all comers. In 1851 the United States' *America* easily won the cup, and the owner afterwards gave the cup to the New York Yacht Club, which changed its name to the America's Cup. British yacht owners have tried fifteen times, and Canadian owners twice, to recover the Cup, but without success. An original condition of the race was that any challenger must sail to the scene of the race in American waters, but this condition was recently nullified and British yachts can now cross the Atlantic Ocean aboard ship.

What is the Weight of the Javelin thrown in Athletic Sports?

A little under 2 pounds.

What is the Length of the Oxford and Cambridge Boat Race Course?

Four and a quarter miles. The shortest time in which the course has been rowed is seventeen minutes fifty seconds in 1948, by Cambridge.

What is the Difference between Rowing and Sculling?

In rowing a person uses a single oar, pulled on with both hands; in sculling, a pair of light oars, called sculls, one in each hand.

What is the Schneider Trophy?

A statuette presented by the late M. Jacques Schneider to be competed for by seaplanes of all nations over a distance of not less than 150 sea-miles. The winners of the contests were: 1913, France; 1914, Great Britain; 1920 and 1921, Italy; 1922, Great Britain; 1923 and 1925, United States; 1926, Italy; 1927, 1929 and 1931, Great Britain, which, by winning three successive victories, became the owner of the Trophy. The average speed in 1931 was 340·08 miles an hour.

STEAM

What was the earliest form of Steam Engine?

The turbine of Hero of Alexandria, who lived in the second century before Christ. It was a hollow metal sphere, pivoted between two points on opposite sides, and having bent tubes projecting from it. When the water in the sphere was boiled by a fire underneath, the steam spurted from the pipes and made the sphere revolve.

Why has a Steam Boiler got so many small tubes in it?

These conduct the flames and hot gases from the furnace through the water so that the greatest possible amount of heat goes into it. The smaller a tube is, the larger is its surface proportionately to the room which it takes up. A single tube 6 inches across occupies as much space as nine tubes each 2 inches across and of equal length; but it has only one-third as much surface as the nine smaller tubes taken together. A large number of small tubes provides a great total surface of thin metal, with water on one side and the hot furnace gases on the other, through which heat passes to the water.

How does a Steam Pressure-gauge work?

The form most commonly used has in it a curved and flattened tube of thin metal. One end of this is closed and free to move, the other is fixed and open to steam from the boiler. The pressure of the steam inside the tube makes it swell slightly, and in doing so it has to straighten. The free end is connected with a toothed rack engaging with a toothed wheel on the spindle of a pointer. As the tube straightens out, the pointer moves round a dial, which shows the pressure in the boiler.

What is the Greatest Pressure yet attained in a Steam Boiler?

About 3,200 pounds (nearly 1½ tons) to the square inch. At this pressure the water in the boiler has a temperature of 706° Fahrenheit and changes into steam without expanding. This extraordinary pressure was obtained with a boiler invented by Mr. Mark Benson. It consists of coils of steel tubes, having a bore of ¾ inch and a thickness of ¼ inch.

What is a "Compound" Steam Engine?

An engine which expands steam in two stages. The steam, after being partly expanded in a high-pressure cylinder, passes into another cylinder of larger bore, called the low-pressure cylinder. In this it is expanded further. In triple-expansion and quadruple-expansion engines the expansion is done in three and four stages respectively. At each stage the cylinder is of larger bore than that of the preceding stage, or two cylinders of the same size as that from which they receive the steam may be used.

MISCELLANEOUS

What are Aerated Waters?

Water, which may be flavoured, containing carbonic acid gas forced in under pressure. When the pressure is released, as in uncorking a bottle, the gas escapes in a "fizz" of bubbles.

What is the purpose of the S-shaped Flat Bars or Round Plates of Iron sometimes seen on the walls of buildings?

They are used at the ends of tie-rods running through the building to hold its walls together.

Which are the best-known Forms of Cross?

The Latin cross, which has the part above the arms shorter than the upright below them; the St. Andrew's cross, shaped like an X; the Greek cross, which is upright and has four parts of equal length; and the St. Anthony's cross, shaped like a T.

How can one count quickly a number of Small Objects of the same kind and weight, such as Nails, Screws, or Bullets?

First find out how many of them it takes to weigh an ounce or other fraction of a pound. Then weigh the whole lot and multiply by the number of times that the quantity weighed goes into the total weight. Thus, if an ounce contains 55, there will be $55 \times 32 = 1,760$ in 2 pounds.

Why are Feathers fitted to the back ends of Darts and Arrows?

To make them travel point first. They act like rudders, and prevent the dart or arrow turning sideways.

Who founded Eton College?

Henry VI, in 1440, who endowed it with the revenues of certain priories which had been suppressed by Henry V. At first the members included a schoolmaster; 25 scholars, sons of poor parents; and as many poor men. In 1443, the number of scholars was increased to 70, and that of the men halved.

Why does a Horse wear Blinkers?

To prevent it seeing and being startled by things which it is passing.

How far away is the Horizon at Sea?

The distance depends upon the height of the observer's eye above the water. To a person standing in a row-boat it is three miles; to a sailor 150 feet above the sea on a mast it would be thirteen miles. In perfectly clear weather an airman 10,000 feet up would be able to see 120 miles in all directions if his glasses were powerful enough.

Why is writing done in Ink more permanent than writing done in Pencil?

Because ink soaks some distance into the paper, whereas the marks left by a pencil are merely surface films of plumbago. One can rub out pencil marks easily enough, but ink requires the use of an eraser, which grinds away the surface of the paper.

What is Jade?

A hard, green stone, composed of magnesia, lime and silica. It is found in many parts of Asia, and is very widely valued in China as an ornamental stone for vases, jewellery, etc. Its name is derived from the Spanish word for flank or side, as it was once believed to cure pains in that part of the body.

How is Knighthood conferred on a Man?

The person to be knighted kneels before the sovereign, who lays a drawn sword flatways on his shoulder and says, " Arise, Sir John " (or whatever his Christian name may be).

What do the letters O.S. or A.B. after a sailor's name signify?

An O.S. is an Ordinary Seaman. After serving aboard ship for three years an O.S. is promoted to the rating of A.B. that is Able-Bodied or fully qualified seaman.

What is Lime?

A compound of calcium and oxygen. To obtain it a carbonate of calcium—chalk or limestone—is heated in a kiln. The heat drives off the carbonic acid gas in the carbonate, leaving quicklime behind. When wetted, quicklime combines with the water, setting up great heat, and crumbles into powder as " slaked " lime.

What and where is London Stone?

A stone in the wall of St. Swithin's Church, Cannon Street, London. It is one of the most famous relics of ancient London, and is supposed by some authorities to have been the stone from which the Romans measured distances along their great highroads radiating from London.

Where are London's great Meat, Fruit, Fish, Wheat and Tea Markets?

Meat: Smithfield, a third of a mile north of St. Paul's Cathedral. Fruit: Covent Garden, north of the Strand; and, on a smaller scale, the Borough Market, at the south end of London Bridge, and Leadenhall Market, in Leadenhall Street. Fish: Billingsgate, on the north bank of the Thames, just below London Bridge. Wheat: the Corn Exchanges, in Mark Lane, and the Baltic Exchange, in St. Mary Axe. Tea: Mincing Lane.

What is a Lych-gate?

A gate at the entrance to a churchyard, covered by a roof. The word lych means corpse. Formerly, the first part of a burial service was read while the coffin stood in the lych-gate, instead of in the church, as now. A lych-gate now serves as a waiting-place at which the clergyman meets the funeral procession.

Why does Cream collect on the top of Milk?

Because cream contains almost all the butterfat, which is the lightest part of milk. The fat is in the form of millions of tiny globules, which when the milk is churned, stick together as butter.

How did we get our Inch, Foot and Yard?

Originally a foot was a measure supposed to be equal to the average length of a man's foot; the inch was a twelfth part of this (the word inch is derived from a Latin word meaning a twelfth); and the yard was a measuring stick 3 feet long. To do away with confusion and inexactitude, an Act of Parliament was passed in 1824, making the Imperial Standard Yard the legal standard of measurement, and the foot and inch exact sub-divisions of it. The standard now used for deciding the exact length of the Imperial Standard Yard is the distance, at 62° Fahrenheit, between the centres of two gold studs let into a bronze bar 38 inches long and 1 inch square. This bar, which was made in 1845, is preserved very carefully in London.

How are Lengths measured to a tiny fraction of an Inch?

In workshops, what are called micrometer gauges are used. The thing to be measured is placed between a fixed part of the gauge and a sliding part which is moved forward or backward

MEASUREMENTS OF OUR PLAYING FIELDS

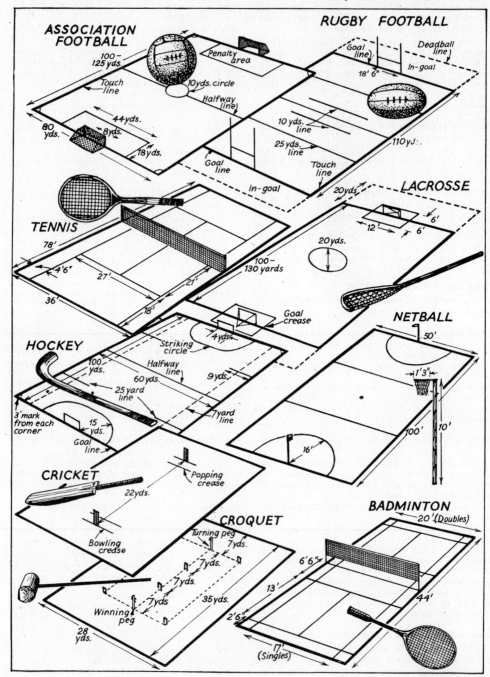

Specially drawn for this work.

Outdoor *games and sports* (see p. 431) have been a feature of British social life for centuries, though it was not until about the middle of the nineteenth century, the era of "muscular Christianity," that field games became well organised with strict rules of play. Cricket is probably the oldest of our games, its history being lost in antiquity. Badminton came from India about 1873 and is to-day played indoors as well as on lawns outside. The drawing above gives the measurements of the fields of play, though small variations may be permitted.

by turning a very carefully made screw. The screw usually has forty threads to the inch, and the thimble which turns it has twenty-five equally spaced marks round its edge, any one of which can be brought opposite a fixed mark on the gauge. A twenty-fifth turn of the screw therefore moves the sliding part 1-1,000th inch. Gauges of this kind may be graduated to read to 1-10,000th inch. Still greater accuracy is given by large measuring machines, working on the same principle. That made by Sir Joseph Whitworth is capable of measuring to one-millionth of an inch.

What is the Metric System?

A system of weights and measures based upon the standard of length called the metre, which is equal to about 39½ inches. The hundredth part of a metre is called a centimetre, and a thousandth part a millimetre. Geographical distances are measured in kilometres, a kilometre being 1,000 metres (about 5 furlongs). The unit of *area* is the square metre. For measuring land the hectare (10,000 square metres) is used. The metric standard of *weight* is the gram, which is the weight of a cube of water measuring a centimetre every way at 3° Centigrade. For weighing ordinary goods the kilogram (1,000 grams) is used. The metric unit of *volume* or capacity is the litre, the space that a kilogram of water occupies at 3° Centigrade. A litre of water would exactly fill a hollow cube measuring one-tenth of a metre (a decimetre) every way. Thus length, area, weight and volume are tied together. The metric system was instituted by the French Government in 1801, and has been adopted by many countries. It is used throughout the world for scientific purposes. In Britain, however, the Metric System is not generally employed.

What are the Nobel Prizes?

Five prizes, worth about £13,500 each, awarded each year to the persons who, in the preceding year, have made the greatest discoveries in (1) physics, (2) chemistry, (3) physiology or medicine, or (4) produced the most remarkable literary work, or (5) done the greatest work in the cause of peace between nations. They are awarded by Swedish and Norwegian committees to persons of any race and either sex. The money is provided by the income from a large fortune left by Alfred Bernhard Nobel, a Swedish chemist. To gain one of these prizes is regarded as a great honour.

Why should one not pour Water over burning Oil or Petrol?

Because the burning liquid is lighter than water and floats on the top of it, so spreading the flame. The proper thing to use is earth or sand, which smothers the flame. A mixture of sand is used in the treatment of " oil slick " (water oil) which may cover the waters of a harbour and be easily set alight by some chance spark.

How does the scattering of Sand or Earth on blazing Petrol help to extinguish the Flame?

The sand or earth, which is itself unable to burn, smothers the flame, that is, prevents air reaching it. So the flame dies from lack of oxygen.

What is a Diamond?

Pure carbon, which probably has been changed into a transparent and intensely hard stone by great heat and enormous pressure.

Which is the Hardest Substance known?

Diamond. Circular saws having diamonds as teeth are used for cutting hard stone; and tubular drills, armed at the end with diamonds, for boring holes through rock.

Which is the most costly Precious Stone?

The deep red ruby of what is called " pigeon's blood " colour. A large ruby of this kind is much more costly than a diamond of equal weight, and the difference in value grows rapidly with size. At the present time fine emeralds come next to rubies in value.

Why is Woodwork in New Houses painted Pink?

The pink paint is the " priming " coat, containing red lead, given to new woodwork to prepare it for the following coats by filling up the pores of the wood and making it less absorbent.

What happens to Paint when it Dries?

The turpentine in it evaporates, and the linseed oil or varnish combines with oxygen from the air, forming a tough, elastic and waterproof envelope to the particles of pigment and to the object that has been painted. It would be more correct to speak of the hardening of paint than of its drying.

What is Luminous Paint made of?

There are several kinds of luminous paint. Some contain compounds of strontium, calcium, sodium, bismuth and potassium. The light emitted is purple, green or yellow, according to what substances are used in making the paint, but they will only shine for a certain time after first being exposed to light. The luminous paint used on watches and clocks contains a trace of radioactive material, often a salt of radium, mixed with a substance which glows when bombarded with atomic particles. A watch may thus contain about three pennyworth of radium, an amount which would be quite invisible by itself. Such paints will shine continuously in the dark without being previously exposed to the light.

Which is the Largest Park in London proper?

Hyde Park and Kensington Gardens, which adjoin and were one park until Queen Caroline, wife of George II, appropriated about 300 acres out of Hyde Park to make pleasure grounds for Kensington Palace. Taken together, they have an area of 636 acres.

What is meant by Patenting an Invention?

Obtaining a grant from the Crown which gives the inventor the sole right to make, sell, or use a thing invented by him. Before he can get the grant he must prove that his invention is a really new one and is of some practical use. If he succeeds in doing so, he is granted a document called letters patent, which allows him to retain his rights if he pays a fee to the Crown every year after the fourth from the date of the patent. The fee increases year by year till the end of the fourteenth year, when the patent lapses, unless it be extended for special reasons.

Why does a Straight Road seem to become narrower in the Distance?

Because the farther off an object is the smaller it appears to be. If you focus the road on the screen of a camera you will find by measuring that the road at a point 200 yards away appears to have half the width it has at 100 yards.

Why is an Eiderdown Quilt stitched through into Squares or Diamonds?

To prevent the fine down moving about inside the cover and collecting into lumps.

Why does a Boat travel upstream most easily near the Bank of a river, and most easily downstream in Mid-channel?

The water is deeper in the middle of a river than at the sides, and less affected by friction against the bottom. So the current runs most strongly in mid-stream.

What makes a Rocket shoot Upwards?

The recoil from the stream of hot gases forced out of its rear end. The rocket is kept pointing upwards by the long stick fastened to it, which acts like a tail. Very large rockets are used for carrying cords from shore to stranded ships; and they have been applied to the propulsion of vehicles. Larger rockets still, driven by the burning of alcohol in liquid oxygen or by other violent fuel-mixtures, have been sent to great heights in the stratosphere, where they automatically record the state of the air and sometimes photograph the earth far below. Heights of about 200 miles have been attained.

If you have to walk along a Road without Footpaths at night, to which side of it should you keep?

To the right-hand side. You will then be much less likely to be run down by anything coming up behind you; while you will be able to see in good time anything coming towards you.

Why has a pair of Scissors got one Pointed and one Round-Ended Blade?

The pointed end is used for pushing through material; and the rounded end is kept underneath when cutting a length of material, as it does not tend to catch in the fabric or table on which the material is supported.

What is the Purpose of the large round Plates often seen in the Middle of a Street?

They are the covers of manholes giving access to sewers.

What is the Purpose of the square-cornered, pillar-like Iron Boxes seen on Pavements near the Kerb?

They are disconnecting boxes, containing switches, by means of which sections of the electric mains of the towns may be cut out of circuit when work has to be done on them. Some of them contain transformers for stepping down the high voltage of the mains supply to the 250 volts required for houses. Others control the automatic traffic-lights.

What is Tortoiseshell?

The outer layers of the carapace or shell of the hawksbill turtle. The most valuable shell comes from the large plates on the turtle's back.

Who are the Trinity Brethren?

A corporation having their headquarters at Trinity House, near the Tower of London. They control the lighthouses round the British coasts, are responsible for buoying channels, and issue licences to pilots. The corporation was given its charter by Henry VIII in 1514. It consists of a Master, Deputy-Master, twenty-four Elder Brethren and a number of Younger Brethren. The money needed for the lighthouse service is raised by levying dues, called light dues, on all ships using British ports.

What are Vitamins?

Certain substances in foods of different kinds which have important effects on our bodily health. The word vitamin comes from the Latin word for life. Many distinct varieties of vitamins are known, and to distinguish them they are given letters such as A, B, C, D, E and F. It is now recognised that a deficiency of vitamins A and B makes people more liable to catch infectious diseases; that lack of vitamin C causes scurvy; and that a want of vitamin D produces the ailment called rickets, from which some children suffer.

Where is Whipsnade, and what is it now famous for?

Near the southern border of Bedfordshire, and about three miles south of Dunstable. A park, 500 acres in extent, has here been converted by the Zoological Society into a second " Zoo," wherein zebras, wombats, wallabies, bison, bears, wolves, deer, ostriches, flamingoes and many other animals and birds are able to roam about in large enclosures, enjoying much more spacious quarters than it is possible to give them in Regent's Park.

Why does Wood crackle as it burns?

Because the air imprisoned in the cells of the wood expands, and the moisture in the wood turns into steam, causing it to split in one place after another.

Why does Wood that has been a very long time in the water lose its Buoyancy?

A piece of dry wood contains a vast number of tiny hollows, or cells, filled with air. The solid matter in it is actually heavier than water, but the air-spaces more than counteract this fact (except in the case of very heavy woods). During long immersion water gradually finds its way into the cells, displacing the air, and the wood finally becomes too heavy to float. If a piece of wood be weighted, sunk into the depths of the ocean, and raised again, it will be found to have lost its buoyancy, owing to great pressure having forced water into all its internal cells.

Why are some Bricks Yellow and others Red?

The colour of a brick depends largely on the composition of the clay out of which it is made. Clay containing magnesia and a little oxide of iron makes yellow bricks, while clay richer in oxide yields light red or dark red bricks, according to the quantity of oxide present. The permanent colour is given to a brick during the firing, or burning, which changes the character of the material, making it hard, tough and lasting.

Why does Mortar hold Bricks together?

The lime in the hardening mortar combines with the surfaces of the bricks and becomes, as it were, welded to them.

What is the Damp-proof Course of a House?

A course of slates set in cement, or asphalt, sheet lead, bituminised felt, or other waterproof material, laid in the walls of a house between ground level and the lowest floor, to prevent damp passing up from the ground through the bricks.

What is the Purpose of a Projecting Window-ledge?

To throw rain clear of the wall below it.

What is a Dormer Window?

A window projecting from the steep slope of roof and covered by a little roof of its own.

Why is a Small fillet of Wood sometimes nailed on the Floor round the skirting of a room?

To prevent the backs of chairs touching and marking the walls when the chairs are pushed back.

Why are the Roofs of Buildings sometimes painted white?

To make them reflect some of the sun's heat that falls on them, and keep the buildings below cooler.

Why do long Flights of Stairs have flat landings in them at intervals?

To give people a chance of resting, and to prevent long falls down the stairs.

How was the Great Pyramid raised?

Since some of the blocks used weigh over 40 tons apiece, and the uppermost blocks had to be raised nearly 500 feet from the ground, there has been a good deal of doubt as to how the Egyptian engineers did their work. One theory is that a huge incline of earth or sand was raised, running from the banks of the Nile

to the site, up which to drag the stones, and that it was raised as the work proceeded. But the construction and removal of such an incline would have been an even more gigantic task than erecting the Pyramid itself. It is more likely that the explanation given by Herodotus is the correct one; namely, that the stones were lifted from course to course by levers and man-power.

Where are the largest Hewn Building Stones in the World?

At Baalbek, in Syria, which was the Roman colony of Heliopolis. The temples at Baalbek were built from the first to the third centuries A.D. The ruins of the Temple of the Sun there include stones over 63 feet long, 13 feet high, and of unknown thickness, forming part of a wall. In a quarry close by lies a hewn stone measuring 69 by 14 by 17 feet, and estimated to weigh 1,500 tons.

How did the Ancients transport Huge Stones?

By harnessing a great number of men to them and using rollers, which were repeatedly picked up from behind and relaid in front. Assyrian and Egyptian sculptures and paintings illustrate this method, which was employed in modern times for moving a single block of stone weighing 1,200 tons into St. Petersburg (Leningrad) to form the pedestal for a statue of Peter the Great. A drummer seated on the stone signalled with his drum the moments for hauling.

Which is the World's Tallest Structure?

The Empire State Building, in New York. It contains 102 storeys above street level, and is 1,250 feet high. To this may be added the television tower, which was erected on top of the building in 1950, making its height 1,472 feet.

What is a Transporter Bridge?

A long girder supported at the ends on tall towers and spanning the water to be crossed. The girder acts as runway for trolleys moved by electrical power, from which cars for vehicles and passengers are suspended at shore level by cables. The largest bridge of the kind is between Runcorn and Widnes, over the Manchester Ship Canal and the Mersey River. It has a span of 1,000 feet. Other bridges of the same type are found at Newport (Monmouthshire); Marseilles, Nantes and Rouen (France); Portugalete (Spain); Duluth (U.S.A.); and elsewhere. Transporter bridges provide transport without hindering navigation, their girders being raised high enough to clear ships' masts.

What are the chief Ship Canals in Britain?

(1) The Manchester Ship Canal, from the Mersey Estuary to Manchester, thirty-five and a half miles long. (2) The Caledonian Canal, connecting Loch Linnhe with the Moray Firth, sixty miles long. (3) The Crinan Canal, in Argyllshire, connecting Loch Fyne with the Sound of Jura, nine miles long. The first is 26 feet, the second 17 feet, and the last only 10 feet deep. The traffic on the Caledonian and Crinan Canals is small.

What is the New River?

An artificial channel which brings drinking water from wells and the River Lea near Hertford into the heart of London at Clerkenwell. It was constructed through the enterprise of Hugh Myddleton, a London jeweller, who persuaded James the First to undertake half the expense of making it in return for half the profits. The New River was completed in 1613; and for a century was the chief source of London's water supply. At one time the shares of the New River Company had a value of under £5 each, but eventually they became more valuable than the shares of any other commercial undertaking. Towards the end of last century a single share was sold for £125,000! In July, 1904, the New River was sold to the Metropolitan Water Board for over £6,000,000 worth of stock bearing 3 per cent. interest.

What is the Greatest Depth to which a Hole has been sunk into the earth?

The deepest holes yet made are oil wells. Two in California have a depth of 10,000 feet (nearly two miles). Trial holes have been bored to 15,000 feet.

Why are Windmills used so little nowadays?

First, because they are larger and more expensive than steam or oil engines of the same power; and second, because they are useless during periods of windless weather. However, light windmills have now been designed for erection on mountains where the air is seldom still, and it is hoped that these may be used to generate electricity and add a constant supply to the grid system.

Why does a Modern Candle not require snuffing?

Because the wick is woven in such a way that it bends to one side, and the tip is continually being burned away in the very hot outer part of the flame.

What is Celluloid?

A mixture of camphor and gun-cotton, worked up with alcohol into a dough, kneaded and pressed. When heated, celluloid softens and can be squeezed into any desired shape. Much imitation ivory and tortoise-shell is celluloid. Common celluloid is very inflammable, and is being largely replaced by fire-proof celluloids and other new plastics.

What is Portland Cement?

A mixture of chalk or limestone with clay ground up dry or with water. The mixture is passed through a revolving kiln, which burns it into hard clinker. The clinker is ground up into a very fine powder, and this is called Portland cement because, when mixed with water and allowed to harden, it resembles the building stone quarried in the Isle of Portland. Portland cement was invented by Joseph Aspdin, a Leeds bricklayer, in 1824, and was first used in large quantities in the construction of the Thames Tunnel in 1828. Mixed with sand and broken stone it forms concrete, now so widely used in making roads, and building bridges, houses, factories and other structures.

How is Charcoal made?

The best charcoal is made by placing wood in chambers which are heated from outside until all moisture and gas has been driven out of the wood. Charcoal used for fuel is commonly produced by partly burning wood in heaps, covered with earth. Some of the wood burns, giving out enough heat to char the rest.

What is the difference between Butter and Cheese?

Butter is made up almost entirely of the fat in milk. Churning causes the globules of fat to separate from the rest of the milk and cling together as butter. Cheese contains both the butter-fat and the casein, which in butter-making remains in the butter-milk. To make cheese, milk is curdled by adding rennet to it, and the curds are separated from the watery whey. After being allowed to " ripen " till partly sour, the curds are salted, placed in cloths in moulds, and squeezed by a press into cheese. Soft and " cream " cheeses are not pressed.

How is Cider made?

Apples of special varieties most suitable for the purpose are passed through mills, which cut the apples up into small pieces. The " pomace," as the chopped apple is called, is wrapped in cotton cloths and put into hydraulic presses which squeeze about 140 gallons of juice from a ton of fruit. The juice is allowed to ferment for a week, and then strained off into maturing vats, whence it is transferred, when ready, into casks or bottles.

What is Coffee?

The ground-up seeds of a small shrub which is cultivated on a large scale in Brazil, the East and West Indies, Ceylon, India, Kenya and Uganda. Each coffee berry or fruit contains two seeds, called beans. When the fruit is ripe the beans are knocked out and allowed to ferment for a time. They are next dried in the sun and passed through a machine which removes a hard parchment-like skin enclosing each bean. The beans are then ready for market.

What is Copra?

The dried kernels of coconuts. Huge quantities of it are used in the manufacture of coconut oil, soap, candles, and margarine. Most copra comes from Ceylon, Malaya, New Guinea, and the islands of the South Pacific.

What is Glass made of?

Flint glass, used for making tumblers and moulded glassware, contains silica (in the form of quartz), red lead and carbonate of potassium. Window or *crown* glass consists of sand, carbonate of soda and lime; and *bottle* glass of sand, gas-lime and salt.

How is the Gold Leaf used in gilding made?

Gold is first rolled out into thin strips, 1½ inches wide, which are cut up into squares. The squares of gold are arranged, alternately with larger squares of very tough paper, in a pile, which is beaten with hammers till the gold has spread

Photo : W. G. Davis.

" Big Ben " is the name of the bell of the great clock in the Clock Tower of the Houses of Parliament, but the name is often used to include the clock itself. The bell was originally hung in 1856, but it was not till 1859 that the clock was actually started. *Big Ben* (see p. 442) weighs 13½ tons, and the Clock Tower is 320 feet high. The minute hand of the clock is 14 feet long, while the hour hand measures 11 feet. The clock has been described as the " grandfather of all clocks," and it is still, as when first erected, one of the most accurate as well as one of the largest in the world.

to the size of the paper. Each square is then cut into four parts, and the piling and beating are repeated. The process is carried through again and again, gold-beater's skin being used in the later stages instead of paper, till the gold is only about 1/300,000th of an inch thick.

What is Ink made of ?

The old-fashioned black writing ink is composed of water, extract of galls, sulphate of iron and gum. Modern inks are made of coloured dyes. Printing ink is a pigment ground up with boiled linseed oil or varnish.

What is Linoleum?

A mixture of cork dust, colouring matter and linseed oil—hardened by the action of the oxygen of the air—spread on a backing of canvas. Some linoleums have designs printed on the top in colours. Wherever wear is great, such designs naturally disappear. More expensive linoleums, with the pattern going right through, so that wear has no effect on it, are made with the aid of wonderfully ingenious machines which cut pieces out of linoleums of different colours and assemble them in exactly the right places, like parts of a jigsaw puzzle, to form the desired design.

Why is it difficult to ignite a " Safety " Match if it is not rubbed on the box?

The " strike anywhere " match is tipped with two substances, mixed together, which combine when heated by friction. In the case of the safety match one substance is put into the head, the other into the special rubbing surface on the box. When the head is rubbed on this surface the two substances set up enough heat to ignite the head.

Why has a Pen Nib got a hole in it?

The hole acts as a kind of reservoir, the ink forming a film across it. It also makes the nib more flexible.

Why is a Pen Nib slit down the middle?

To make it flexible and to assist the ink to flow off the tip. When the nib is pressed against the paper the points separate slightly and the crack between them acts somewhat like a tube.

What is the Marking Material used in a " Lead " Pencil?

Graphite, also called plumbago and black lead. It is a very pure form of carbon which is found in a natural state in the ground and can be made artificially from coke. After being ground into a very fine powder, the graphite is mixed with clay. The larger the proportion of clay, the " softer " the " lead " will be. The mixture is placed in a cylinder and forced out of it through a hole as a square or round thread. This is allowed to dry, and is then cut up into lengths, which are hardened by being baked in a furnace. They are then ready for encasing in wood.

Why is the Clock Tower of the Houses of Parliament popularly known as Big Ben?

Strictly speaking, " Big Ben " is the name given to the bell which hangs in the tower, the chimes of which are regularly broadcast by the B.B.C. Popularly, the name is often used to include the clock itself, of which the bell is a part. The name of Big Ben was taken from Sir Benjamin Hall, a big genial man who was First Commissioner of Works during the years when the great clock and bell were installed. The clock was successfully started on May 31st, 1859, after the weight of the bell had been reduced from 15 to 13½ tons. The clapper was also reduced to 4 cwt. It is without doubt the best-known clock in the world and there are few countries in which the chimes and strike of Big Ben have not been heard by radio.

What is Plaster of Paris?

Gypsum (sulphate of calcium) burned in a kiln and ground into a fine powder. When mixed with water into a paste it hardens very quickly. It is used for making casts in moulds, for cementing things together and in farming for soil conditioning.

What is the difference between China and Earthenware?

China allows some light to pass through it; earthenware is quite opaque to light. Porcelain—another name for china—owes its semitransparency to the purity of the kaolin (a kind of clay), feldspar and quartz of which it is made.

What are Ropes and String made of ?

Hemp, jute, coir (the fibre from coconut husks) and cotton. Metal ropes are made of wire.

How were the Rubber Plantations in Malaya started?

In 1876, Mr. Henry Wickham, while in Brazil, chartered a steamer of the Inman Line which had brought a cargo to the Amazon and was about to return empty. He then entered the forests with a band of natives and quickly collected 70,000 rubber seeds, packed them carefully, and met the steamer at a prearranged point. Special arrangements prevented difficulties with the Portuguese Custom authorities, and the seeds reached Kew safely. The young rubber plants grown from them were sent to Ceylon, Singapore, and other places in the East, and became the parents of most of the great plantations.

From what substances are Sago and Tapioca prepared?

Sago is obtained from the starchy pith of certain varieties of palm-trees. The pith is washed and pressed through a strainer, which separates the starch from the useless woody fibres. The starch is made into a paste and forced through sieves containing holes which give it the size of " grain " desired. Tapioca comes from the large roots of the cassava or manioc shrub, a tropical plant. The roots are pulped and well washed to extract the starch which, when dried, is ready for use.

How do we get Salt?

English salt is obtained from underground deposits of rock salt, into which water is forced to dissolve the salt. The liquid brine is pumped up and boiled in large pans to drive off the water. In some other countries a great deal of salt is got by evaporating sea water, which contains an inexhaustible supply of the substance. It has been calculated that the oceans and seas of the world have dissolved in them nearly five million cubic miles of salt, which would be sufficient to cover the whole area of the United States with a layer over one and a half miles thick. At Stassfurt, in Germany, Wieliczka, in Poland, and elsewhere, huge underground deposits of rock salt are mined by the same methods as coal. Vast surface deposits of salt occur in many parts of the world on the sites of dried-up lakes. Salt has always been a very important article of commerce, as being necessary for the flavouring and preserving of food. The ancient Roman allowed every soldier a ration of salt, or money—*argentum salarium*—with which to buy it. The second word (derived from sal, salt) is the origin of our word salary, meaning the stipend or pay of an official.

What system of numerals do we use to-day and what are Roman numerals?

The system in general use to-day is known as the " Arabic " system of numerals (1, 2, 3, 4, 5, etc.). The origin of this form of figures is not very certain and the name Arabic is not really justified. The system is believed to have originated in India and was carried to Bagdad during the eighth century A.D. From there it eventually reached Europe, probably about the tenth century.

Roman, or Etruscan, numerals were in use some centuries before the Arabic system. The origin of these is still obscure, apart from the numbers I to IIII, which are represented by simple strokes (I, II, III, IIII). The symbol C (100) probably came originally from a Greek letter which the Romans did not use, but it bore some resemblance eventually to their initial letter for Centum (meaning 100). In the same way M (for Mille) became 1,000 and so on. The following list gives the numerals most frequently used and from which other numbers can be made up:

Arabic	Roman	Arabic	Roman	Arabic	Roman
1.	I	15.	XV	70.	LXX
2.	II	16.	XVI	80.	LXXX
3.	III	17.	XVII	90.	XC
4.	IIII or IV	18.	XVIII	100.	C
5.	V	19.	XIX	200.	CC
6.	VI	20.	XX	400.	CD
7.	VII	25.	XXV	500.	D
8.	VIII	30.	XXX	600.	DC
9.	IX	40.	XL	900.	CM
10.	X	45.	XLV	1,000.	M
11.	XI	50.	L	1,500.	MD
12.	XII	55.	LV	1,900.	MCM
13.	XIII	60.	LX	2,000.	MM
14.	XIV				

A line over any letter increases it a thousand-fold, thus: $\overline{V}$—5,000, $\overline{D}$—500,000, $\overline{M}$—1,000,000.

What is Nylon?

An artificial substance prepared from coal-tar, petroleum and ammonia. Its actual constituents are all found in air and ammonia, but its molecules are extremely complex in structure, and are of the same kind as those of natural silk. Nylon is both stronger and more water-resisting than silk, for which reasons it is used for making parachutes.

How is Sugar Obtained from Beet?

The beetroots, after being thoroughly washed in running water, are cut into slices by machinery. The slices are soaked in warm water, which extracts the sugar, forming a syrup. The exhausted pulp is then strained off from the juice, which is treated with lime and carbonic acid gas to remove impurities. After further straining the juice goes to evaporating pans, wherein much of the water is removed from it, and a large part of the sugar present crystallises. The sugar crystals are separated from the syrup by centrifugal machines. The raw sugar thus obtained then undergoes refining, which includes dissolving in water, treatment with charcoal, boiling, and a second wringing in centrifugal machines.

Where does Sulphur come from?

From the volcanic regions of Italy, Sicily and Japan, and from districts in the United States bordering the Gulf of Mexico. The last are now the chief source of the world's sulphur supply. Sulphur occurs there as vast underground deposits saturating a stratum of limestone. In 1890 a Mr. H. Frasch, an engineer, conceived the idea of melting the sulphur out of the limestone and pumping it to the surface while fluid. He sank pipes into the deposits and forced down water heated far above ordinary boiling-point. His experiment proved quite successful, and vast quantities of sulphur are now " mined " yearly in this manner.

How is Vinegar obtained?

By fermenting either a kind of beer, which yields " malt " vinegar; or wine or cider, from which " wine " vinegar is derived. The sharp taste of vinegar is due to acetic acid, of which there may be present six or seven parts in every hundred parts of the liquid. Fermentation is caused by a tiny bacterium, called " mother of vinegar."

What are Hall Marks?

Marks stamped upon gold and silver articles to show the purity of the metal in them, as found by tests. If a spoon has a lion mark on it, one knows that it contains silver in the proportion of 11 ounces 2 dwt. per 12 ounces. A gold watch-case impressed with a crown and the figure 18 is of 18-carat gold; that is, it contains eighteen parts of pure gold out of twenty-four. The offices, or " halls," in which the marks are stamped are in London, Birmingham, Sheffield, Chester, Edinburgh, Glasgow and Dublin.

What is a Trade Mark?

A mark stamped or engraved on goods to show that they are made or sold by some particular person or firm. It may be a design, or an invented word or words, or a signature, or a name represented in some special manner. If a trade mark be registered through the Patent Office, the trader or manufacturer obtains the sole right to use it, provided that he pays a yearly fee to the Crown.

STENCILLING AS A HOMECRAFT

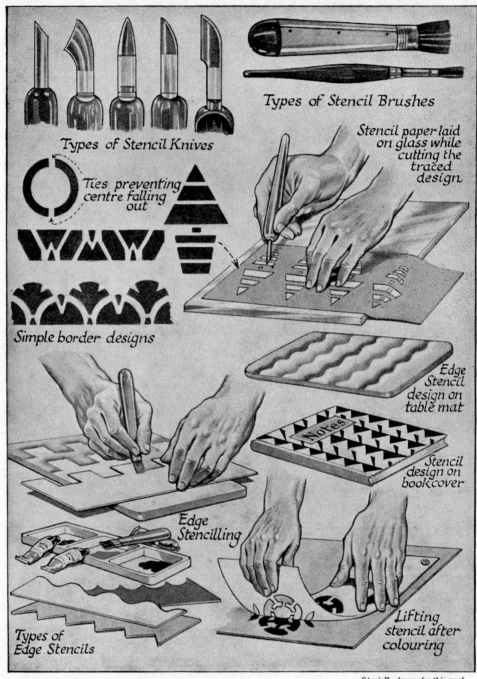

Types of Stencil Knives

Types of Stencil Brushes

Ties preventing centre falling out

Stencil paper laid on glass while cutting the traced design

Simple border designs

Edge Stencil design on table mat

Stencil design on bookcover

Notes

Edge Stencilling

Types of Edge Stencils

Lifting stencil after colouring

Specially drawn for this work.

Stencilling (see p. 445) is the filling-in with paint of the holes cut in a thin plate so that a pattern is formed. In the drawing above five different knives are shown for cutting out the stencil plate, but one or two will be sufficient at first. These should be kept sharp and the knife held nearly upright when cutting. Strong cartridge paper, smooth brown paper, or thin card can be used for the stencil plate. It can be made waterproof by coating each side with French polish or " knotting." Flat-ended hog-hair brushes should be used when painting in the design.

What is meant by Mean Sea Level and how is this decided?

Mean Sea Level (m.s.l.) or, more simply, " sea level," can broadly be defined as half-way between the levels of high and low water. In Britain the sea level at Newlyn, Cornwall, is taken from the average (or mean) hourly readings of the tide gauge between May 1st, 1915, and April 30th, 1921.

Before 1921 the levels were taken from those in Victoria Dock, Liverpool, but this " mean sea level " was considered to have been based on far too short a period (March 7th to 16th, 1844), and it has been replaced by the Newlyn sea level, taken over a period of six years. Each country uses its own M.S.L. (Mean Sea Level): Ostend for Belgium (recorded in 1878–85); Amsterdam for Holland (1922–36 records), and so in different countries.

On charts for shipping, however, the sea level, which is generally referred to as " reduction level," is the mean, or average, of low water spring tides, since this gives the minimum depth of water available for ships; corrections can be made for the state of the tide, of course, by the navigating officer. But for land-surveying the simple answer is that " sea level " is the average level of the water between high and low tides, based on official records taken as described.

What is meant by an Artesian Basin?

Imagine a bowl to be lined with a layer of sponge, reaching to the rim, and the sponge to be covered—except round the edges—with a layer of clay. On a very small scale this represents the conditions of an artesian basin in nature, where the bowl and clay are replaced by watertight strata, and the sponge by gravel or other material in which water can lodge. At the edges of the basin, which may be hundreds or thousands of square miles in extent, the gravel, etc., comes to the surface in high ground. Any water falling on its edges travels down towards the lowest points; and, as the stratum fills, the pressure at those points increases. If a pipe be sunk through the upper stratum into the gravel in the lower parts of the basin, water will rise to the surface by its own pressure, and what is called an artesian well will have been made. Artesian basins of enormous size exist in the eastern half of Australia and in Dakota (U.S.A.).

In what Country are Artesian Wells most used?

Australia, where thousands of artesian bores have been sunk in Queensland, New South Wales, and South Australia. Many of them are extraordinarily productive, yielding up to 5,000,000 gallons of water a day, and some of them nearly a mile deep. They supply among them sufficient water for hundreds of thousands of sheep and cattle.

What is Stencilling?

A stencil is a thin card or plate, through which a pattern has been cut. The pattern can be transferred to the desired surface by painting in the holes cut in the card or plate. As many as five knives may be used to cut the stencil, but for beginners one or two will be sufficient. An oilstone will be needed, because the knives must be kept very sharp. In use, the knife must be held nearly upright so that the cuts are cleanly made. Cartridge paper on thin card, or brown paper, form suitable materials for a stencil plate; and whichever is used should be spread on a sheet of glass for cutting. The stencil plate, too, must be made waterproof, and this can be done by coating its two sides with French polish or " knotting." For painting, flat-ended hog-hair brushes are best, and it is wisest to use a separate brush for each colour. Water-colours are quite suitable for work which will not have to be washed or exposed to the weather; but oils are best for fabrics, used with a little varnish or drying medium. The paint is put on with a dabbing motion.

How did the present system of putting the Clock forward by one hour during the Summer Months come about, and who first advocated the idea?

Daylight Saving, or Summer Time, was first mooted in America by Benjamin Franklin (1706–90), but nothing came of it. In England the credit for advocating such a scheme goes to William Willett (1856–1915), head of a well-known firm of London builders. The first Day-light Saving Bill was introduced in 1908 and in 1909 the Bill passed the second reading, but was rejected in committee by a majority of one. The war of 1914–18 emphasised the advantages that might be obtained by daylight saving, and the Summer Time Act came into operation at 2 a.m. on May 21st, 1916.

There was much propaganda for and against its continuance, but it was carried on by a series of Acts of Parliament until 1925 when the Summer Time Act made it a permanent measure. During the 1939–45 war the duration of Summer Time was extended from that provided in the Acts, which lay down that the clocks shall be put forward one hour from 2 a.m. on the day next following the third Saturday in April, or, if that day is Easter Day, the day next following the second Saturday in April, and that this " summer time " shall end at 2 a.m. on the day following the first Saturday in October. In some years during the 1939–45 war Double Summer Time was in force (1943–45 and again in 1947).

Summer Time has been adopted by many other countries, though the number of minutes that clocks are moved forward varies in a few cases. In America some of the States favour Summer Time, while others refuse to entertain it.

What was the Origin of St. Swithin's Day?

Swithin, or Swithun, was an English saint and bishop. He was bishop of Winchester A.D. 852–862 and was famed as a builder of churches. He died in 862 and the cathedral was dedicated to him. It was not until 971 that his body was removed from its first resting place for reburial in the cathedral. The day chosen, July 15th, 971, was so wet that it was impossible to carry out the task, and owing to the heavy rains the delay lasted for forty days. From this originated the popular superstition that if it rains on July 15th, now known as St. Swithin's day, it will be rainy for the following forty days.

A.A., Automobile Association; anti-aircraft.
A.A.A., Amateur Athletic Association.
A.B., able-bodied seaman.
A.B.A., Amateur Boxing Association.
A.C., Alpine Club; alternating current.
a/c, account; in account with.
A.C.G.B., Arts Council of Great Britain.
A.C.I.S., Associate of the Chartered Institute of Secretaries.
A.C.P., Associate of the College of Preceptors.
A.D., *anno Domini* = in the year of our Lord.
A.D.C., Aide-de-camp.
Adjt.-Gen., Adjutant-General.
ad. lib., *ad libitum* = at anyone's discretion or pleasure.
Adm., Admiral.
A.E.C., Allied Expeditionary Corps.
A.F., Admiral of the Fleet.
A.F.A., Amateur Football Association.
A.F.C., Air Force Cross.
Ala., Alabama (U.S.A.).
alt., altitude.
a.m., *ante meridiem* = before noon.
A.M.I.C.E., Associate Member of the Institution of Civil Engineers.
A.M.I.E.E., Associate Member of the Institution of Electrical Engineers.
amp., ampère.
anon., anonymous.
A.O.C.-in-C., Air Officer Commanding-in-Chief.
A.O.F., Ancient Order of Foresters.
A.P., Associated Press.
Apoc., Apocalypse; Apocrypha.
approx., approximately.
ar., arr., arrives; arrival.
A.R.A., Associate of the Royal Academy.
A.R.A.M., Associate of the Royal Academy of Music.
A.R.C.M., Associate of the Royal College of Music.
A.R.C.O., Associate of the Royal College of Organists.
A.R.C.S., Associate of the Royal College of Science.
A.R.I.B.A., Associate of the Royal Institute of British Architects.
A.R.I.C., Associate of the Royal Institute of Chemistry.
Ariz., Arizona (U.S.A.).
Ark., Arkansas (U.S.A.).
A.R.P., Air Raid Precautions.
A.R.S.A., Associate of the Royal Scottish Academy; Associate of the Royal Society of Arts.
A.S.A., Amateur Swimming Association.
A.T.C., Air Training Corps.
A.T.S., Auxiliary Territorial Service (now W.R.A.C.).
A.V., Authorised Version.
av. or ave., avenue.

B., Baron.
b., born.
B.A., Bachelor of Arts.
B.A.O.R., British Army of the Rhine.
Bart., Bt., Baronet.
B.B.C., British Broadcasting Corporation.
B.C., Before Christ; British Columbia.
B.D., Bachelor of Divinity.
B.E., Board of Education.
B.E.A., British European Airways; British East Africa.

B.E.F., British Expeditionary Force.
B.E.M., British Empire Medal.
B.I.F., British Industries Fair.
B.M., British Museum.
B.M.A., British Medical Association.
B.Mus., Bachelor of Music.
B.O.A.C., British Overseas Airways Corporation.
B. of T., Board of Trade.
B.R., British Railways.
Brig.-Gen., Brigadier-General.
B.S.A., British South Africa.
B.Sc., Bachelor of Science.
B.S.T., British Summer Time.
B.U.P., British United Press.
B.W.I., British West Indies.

c., cent; centime.
C.A., Chartered Accountant.
Cal., California (U.S.A.).
Cam., Cambridge.
Cantab., *Cantabrigiensis* = of Cambridge.
caps., capital.
Capt., Captain.
Card., Cardinal.
C.B., Companion (of the Order) of the Bath.
C.B.E., Commander (of the Order) of the British Empire.
C.C., County Council.
c.c., cubic centimetre(s).
C.F., Chaplain to the Forces.
cf., *confer* = compare.
C.H., Companion of Honour.
ch. or chap., chapter.
Ch.B., *Chirurgiæ Baccalaureus,* Bachelor of Surgery.
C.I.D., Criminal Investigation Department.
c.i.f., cost, insurance, freight.
C.I.G.S., Chief of the Imperial General Staff.
C.-in-C., Commander-in-Chief.
cm., centimetre(s).
C.M.G., Companion (of the Order) of St. Michael and St. George.
C.O., Commanding Officer; Colonial Office; conscientious objector.
Co., Company; County.
c/o, care of.
c.o.d., cash on delivery.
C. of E., Church of England.
Col., Colonel; Colorado (U.S.A.).
contd., continued.
Co-op., Co-operative Society.
c.p., candle-power.
Cpl., Corporal.
C.P.R., Canadian Pacific Railways.
C.S.I., Companion of the Star of India.
ct., carat.
Ct., Connecticut (U.S.A.).
C.V.O., Commander of the Royal Victorian Order.
cwt., hundredweight(s).

d., penny; pence; died.
Dak., Dakota (U.S.A.).
D.B.E., Dame Commander (of the Order) of the British Empire.
D.C., direct current; District of Columbia (U.S.A.).
D.C.M., Distinguished Conduct Medal.
D.D., Doctor of Divinity.
D.D.S., Doctor of Dental Surgery.
D.D.T., dichlorodiphenyltrichloroethane (an insecticide).
deg., degree(s).
Del., Delaware (U.S.A.).
dep., departs; departure.

Dept., Department.
Deut., Deuteronomy.
D.F., Defender of the Faith.
D.F.C., Distinguished Flying Cross.
D.F.M., Distinguished Flying Medal.
D.Lit., Doctor of Literature.
D.N.B., Dictionary of National Biography.
D.O.R.A., Defence of the Realm Act.
doz., dozen.
D.P., Displaced Person.
Dr., Doctor.
D.Sc., Doctor of Science.
D.S.C., Distinguished Service Cross.
D.S.M., Distinguished Service Medal.
D.S.O., Distinguished Service Order.
D.V., *Deo volente* = God willing.
dwt., pennyweight.

E., East.
Eccl., Ecclesiastes.
Ed., Editor.
ed., edition.
e.g., *exempli gratia* = for example.
E.I., East Indies.
E.N.E., East-north-east.
E.N.S.A., Entertainments National Services Association.
E.R.P., European Recovery Plan.
E.S.E., East-south-east.
Esq., Esquire.
et. al., *et alibi* = and elsewhere; *et alii* = and others.
etc., *et cetera* = and the rest.
Ex., Exodus.
E. & O.E., Errors and Omissions Excepted.

f., following; feminine; forte.
Fa., Florida (U.S.A.).
F.A., Football Association.
F.B.I., Federation of British Industries; Federal Bureau of Investigation (U.S.A.).
F.C.I.S., Fellow of the Chartered Institute of Secretaries.
F.C.P., Fellow of the College of Preceptors.
ff., following (plural); fortissimo.
F.I.D.O., Fog Investigation Dispersal Organisation.
fig., figure; figuratively.
fm., fathom.
F.M., Field-Marshal.
F.O., Foreign Office.
f.o.b., free on board.
fol., folio.
f.o.r., free on rail.
fr., franc.
F.R.A.M., Fellow of the Royal Academy of Music.
F.R.C.O., Fellow of the Royal College of Organists.
F.R.C.P., Fellow of the Royal College of Physicians.
F.R.C.S., Fellow of the Royal College of Surgeons.
F.R.I.B.A., Fellow of the Royal Institute of British Architects.
F.R.I.C., Fellow of the Royal Institute of Chemistry.
F.R.S.A., Fellow of the Royal Society of Arts.
ft., foot.

g., gram(s).
Ga., Georgia (U.S.A.).
gal. or gall., gallon(s).
G.B., Great Britain.

G.B.E., Grand Cross of the British Empire.
G.C., George Cross.
G.C.B., Grand Cross of the Bath.
G.C.M.G., Grand Cross of St. Michael and St. George.
Gen., Genesis; General.
G.H.Q., General Headquarters.
G.I., general issue, hence: common soldier (in the U.S. Army).
G.M., George Medal.
G.M.T., Greenwich Mean Time.
G.O.C., General Officer Commanding.
G.P., general practitioner.
G.P.O., General Post Office.
gr., grain(s).
gs., guineas.

H.A.C., Honourable Artillery Company.
h. and c., hot and cold (water).
H.E., His Excellency; His Eminence; high explosive.
H.G., His (or Her) Grace.
H.M., His (or Her) Majesty.
H.M.A.S., His (or Her) Majesty's Australian Ship.
H.M.C.S., His (or Her) Majesty's Canadian Ship.
H.M.S., His (or Her) Majesty's Ship.
Hon., Honourable; Honorary.
h.p., horse-power.
H.Q., headquarters.
H.R.H., His (or Her) Royal Highness.

Ia., Iowa (U.S.A.).
ib., *ibidem* = in the same place.
I.C.I., Imperial Chemical Industries.
i.e., *id est* = that is.
Ill., Illinois (U.S.A.).
I.L.O., International Labour Office.
in., inch(es).
Ind., Indiana (U.S.A.).
I.N.R.I., *Jesus Nazarenus Rex Judæorum* = Jesus of Nazareth, King of the Jews.
inst., instant = the present month.
I.O.U., I owe you.
I.Q., intelligence quotient.
I.R.A., Irish Republican Army.
I.T.A., Independent Television Authority.
ital., italics.

J.P., Justice of the Peace.
Jr. or **Jun.**, Junior.

Kan., Kansas (U.S.A.).
K.B., Knight Bachelor; King's Bench.
K.B.E., Knight Commander of the British Empire.
K.C., King's Counsel.
K.C.B., Knight Commander of the Bath.
K.C.M.G., Knight Commander of St. Michael and St. George.
kg., kilogram(s).
K.G., Knight of the Garter.
km., kilometre(s).
k.o., knock-out.
Kt., Knight.
kw., kilowatt.
Ky., Kentucky (U.S.A.).

La., Louisiana (U.S.A.).
lab., laboratory.
lat., latitude.
lb., *libra* = pound.
L.C.B., Lord Chief Baron.
L.C.C., London County Council.
L.C.J., Lord Chief Justice.

l.c.m., lowest common multiple.
Ld., Lord.
L.D.S., Licentiate in Dental Surgery.
Lev., Leviticus.
L.I., Long Island (U.S.A.).
LL.B., Bachelor of Laws.
LL.D., Doctor of Laws.
LL.M., Master of Laws.
loc. cit., *loco citato* = in the place quoted.
long., longitude.
L.R.C.P., Licentiate of the Royal College of Physicians.
L.R.C.S., Licentiate of the Royal College of Surgeons.
L.S.D., *libræ, solidi, denarii* = pounds, shillings, pence.
Lt., Lieutenant.
Lt.-Col., Lieutenant-Colonel.
Lt.-Gen., Lieutenant-General.
Ltd., Limited.

M., *Monsieur*.
m., masculine; married; mile(s).
M.A., Master of Arts.
Maj., Major.
Mass., Massachusetts (U.S.A.).
maths., mathematics.
max., maximum.
M.B., Bachelor of Medicine.
M.B.E., Member of the Order of the British Empire.
M.C., Military Cross; Master of Ceremonies.
M.C.C., Marylebone Cricket Club.
Md., Maryland (U.S.A.).
M.D., Doctor of Medicine.
Me., Maine (U.S.A.).
memo., memorandum.
Messrs., Sirs; Gentlemen.
mfd., manufactured.
M.F.H., Master of Foxhounds.
M.G., Machine Gun.
Mgr., *Monseigneur*.
Mi., Mississippi (U.S.A.).
Mich., Michigan (U.S.A.).
M.I.E.E., Member of the Institute of Electrical Engineers.
M.I.Mech.E., Member of the Institution of Mechanical Engineers.
M.Inst.C.E., Member of the Institution of Civil Engineers.
min., minimum.
Minn., Minnesota (U.S.A.).
Mlle., *Mademoiselle*.
M.M., Military Medal.
mm., millimetre(s).
Mme., *Madame*.
Mo., Missouri (U.S.A.).
M.O., Medical Officer.
Mont., Montana (U.S.A.).
mos., months.
M.O.W.B., Ministry of Works and Buildings.
M.P., Member of Parliament; Military Police; Metropolitan Police.
m.p.h., miles per hour.
M.P.S., Member of the Pharmaceutical Society; Member of the Philological Society.
M.R., Master of the Rolls.
Mr., Mister or Master.
M.R.A.S., Member of the Royal Academy of Sciences; Member of the Royal Asiatic Society.
M.R.C.C., Member of the Royal College of Chemistry.
M.R.C.P., Member of the Royal College of Physicians.
M.R.C.S., Member of the Royal College of Surgeons.

M.R.C.V.S., Member of the Royal College of Veterinary Surgeons.
M.R.G.S., Member of the Royal Geographical Society.
M.R.I., Member of the Royal Institution.
Mrs., Mistress.
MS., manuscript.
M.S., Master of Surgery.
m.s.l., mean sea-level.
MSS., manuscripts.
Mt., Mount.
M.T., Mechanical Transport.
MTB., motor torpedo-boat.
Mus.B., Bachelor of Music.
Mus.D., Doctor of Music.
Mus.M., Master of Music.
m.v., merchant vessel; motor vessel; muzzle velocity.
M.V.O., Member of the (Royal) Victorian Order.
M & B., May and Baker (a therapeutic drug).

N., North.
n., neuter.
N.A.A.F.I., Navy, Army and Air Force Institute.
Nat., National.
N.A.T.O., North Atlantic Treaty Organisation.
n.b., *nota bene* = note well.
N.C., North Carolina (U.S.A.).
N.C.B., National Coal Board.
N.C.O., non-commissioned officer.
N.D., North Dakota (U.S.A.).
n.d., not dated.
N.E., North-east.
Neb., Nebraska (U.S.A.).
neg., negative.
nem. con., *nemine contradicente* = no one contradicting.
nem. diss., *nemine dissentiente* = no one dissenting.
Nev., Nevada (U.S.A.).
N.F.S., National Fire Service.
N.F.U., National Farmers' Union.
N.H.I., National Health Insurance.
N.J., New Jersey (U.S.A.).
n.l., *non licet* = it is not permitted.
N.M., New Mexico (U.S.A.).
N.N.E., North-north-east.
N.N.W., North-north-west.
No., *numero* = (in) number.
n.o., not out.
Nos., numbers.
N.P., Notary Public.
N.R., Northern Rhodesia.
N.R.A., National Rifle Association.
N.S., Nova Scotia.
N.S.A., National Skating Association.
N.S.P.C.C., National Society for Prevention of Cruelty to Children.
N.S.W., New South Wales.
N.T., New Testament.
N.U.J., National Union of Journalists.
Num., Numbers.
N.U.R., National Union of Railwaymen.
N.U.T., National Union of Teachers.
N.W., North-west.
N.Y., New York (U.S.A.).
N.Z., New Zealand.
N. & Q., Notes and queries.

O., Ohio (U.S.A.).
o/a, on account of.
ob., *obiit* = died.
O.B.E., Officer of the Order of the British Empire.
O.C., Officer Commanding.

O.C.T.U., Officer Cadet Training Unit.
O.E.D., Oxford English Dictionary.
O.E.E.C., Organisation for European Economic Co-operation.
off., official.
O.H.M.S., On His (or Her) Majesty's Service.
Okla., Oklahoma (U.S.A.).
O.M., Order of Merit.
Ont., Ontario (U.S.A.).
op., *opus* = work.
o.p., out of print.
op. cit., *opere citato* = in the work quoted.
Or. or Ore., Oregon (U.S.A.).
O.T., Old Testament.
O.T.C., Officers' Training Corps.
Oxon., *Oxonia* = Oxford; *Oxoniensis* = of Oxford.
oz., ounce(s).

p., page; piano.
Pa., Pennsylvania.
p.a., *per annum* = by the year.
P.A., Press Association.
P.A.A., Pan American Airways.
par., paragraph.
P.A.Y.E., Pay as you earn (Income Tax).
P.C., Privy Councillor; Police Constable; post-card.
pd., paid.
P.E.N., Poets, Playwrights, Editors, Essayists, Novelists.
P.E.P., Political and Economic Planning.
per cent., *per centum* = by the hundred.
per pro., *per procurationem* = by the agency of.
Ph.D., Doctor of Philosophy.
P.L.A., Port of London Authority.
P.M., Prime Minister; Provost Marshal.
p.m., *post meridiem* = after noon.
P.M.G., Postmaster-General.
P.O.W., prisoner of war.
pp., pages; pianissimo.
P.P.S., additional postscript.
P.R.A., President of the Royal Academy.
P.S., postscript.
pt., pint(s).
P.T., physical training.
P.T.O., Please turn over.
P.W.D., Public Works Department.
P. & O., Peninsular and Oriental Company.

Q., Qy., query; question.
QANTAS, Queensland and Northern Territories Air Services.
Q.A.R.A.N.C., Queen Alexandra's Royal Army Nursing Corps.
Q.B., Queen's Bench.
Q.C., Queen's Counsel.
q.e., *quod est* = which is.
q.e.d., *quod erat demonstrandum* = which was to be demonstrated.
q.e.f., *quod erat faciendum* = which was to be done.
Q.M., Quartermaster.
Q.M.G., Quartermaster-General.
Q.M.S., Quartermaster-Sergeant.
qt., quart(s).
q.v., *quod vide* = which see.

R., *rex* = King; *regina* = Queen.
R.A., Royal Academy or Academician.
R.A.A.F., Royal Australian Air Force.
R.A.C., Royal Automobile Club.
R.A.D.C., Royal Army Dental Corps.

R.A.E.C., Royal Army Educational Corps.
R.A.F., Royal Air Force.
R.A.M., Royal Academy of Music.
R.A.M.C., Royal Army Medical Corps.
R.A.N., Royal Australian Navy.
R.A.O.C., Royal Army Ordnance Corps.
R.A.P.C., Royal Army Pay Corps.
R.A.S., Royal Asiatic Society.
R.A.S.C., Royal Army Service Corps.
R.B., Rifle Brigade.
R.B.A., Royal Society of British Artists.
R.C., Roman Catholic.
R.C.A., Royal Canadian Academy.
R.C.A.F., Royal Canadian Air Force.
R.C.N., Royal Canadian Navy.
R.C.P., Royal College of Physicians.
R.C.S., Royal College of Surgeons.
Rd., road.
R.E., Royal Engineers; Royal Exchange.
recd., received.
R.E.M.E., Royal Electrical and Mechanical Engineers.
retd., retired; returned.
Rev., Reverend.
R.G.S., Royal Geographical Society.
Rgt., Regiment.
R.H.S., Royal Humane Society; Royal Horticultural Society; Royal Historical Society.
R.I., Rhode Island (U.S.A.); Royal Institute of Painters in Water Colours.
R.I.B.A., Royal Institute of British Architects.
R.I.C., Royal Institute of Chemistry.
R.I.C.S., Royal Institute of Chartered Surveyors.
R.I.P., *requiescat in pace* = may he (or she) rest in peace.
R.M., Royal Mail; Royal Marines.
R.M.A., Royal Military Academy.
R.N., Royal Navy.
R.N.A.S., Royal Naval Air Service.
R.N.R., Royal Naval Reserve.
R.N.V.R., Royal Naval Volunteer Reserve.
R.N.Z.A.F., Royal New Zealand Air Force.
R.N.Z.N., Royal New Zealand Navy.
R.O.C., Royal Observer Corps.
R.S., Royal Society.
R.S.A., Royal Scottish Academy; Royal Society of Arts.
R.S.A.A.F., Royal South African Air Force.
R.S.M., Regimental Sergeant-Major.
R.S.P.C.A., Royal Society for the Prevention of Cruelty to Animals.
R.S.V.P., *répondez, s'il vous plait* = kindly reply.
R.T., radio-telegraphy.
Rt. Hon., Right Honourable.
R.T.O., Railway Transport Officer.
Rt. Rev., Right Reverend.
R.V., Revised Version.
R.W.S., Royal Society of Painters in Water Colours.
R.Y.S., Royal Yacht Squadron.

S., South.
s., shilling(s); second(s).
S.A., South Africa; South America; South Australia.
S.C., South Carolina (U.S.A.).
S.D., South Dakota (U.S.A.).
S.E., South-east.
S.E.A.C., South-east Asia Command.

S.E.A.T.O., South-east Asia Treaty Organisation.
s.g., specific gravity.
S.H.A.P.E., Supreme Headquarters Allied Powers in Europe.
sig., signature.
Sol.-Gen., Solicitor-General.
S.P.C.K., Society for Promoting Christian Knowledge.
S.P.G., Society for the Propagation of the Gospel.
Sq., Square.
Sr., Señor.
S.R.N., State Registered Nurse.
s.s., steamship.
S.S.E., South-south-east.
S.S.W., South-south-west.
St., Saint; Street.
Supt., Superintendent.
S.W., South-west.

T.A., Territorial Army.
T.B., tuberculosis.
T.D., Territorial Decoration.
Ten., Tennessee (U.S.A.).
Ter., Territory.
Tex., Texas (U.S.A.).
T.N.T., trinitrotoluene (an explosive).
T.T., Tourist Trophy; teetotaller.
T U.C., Trade Union Congress.
TV, television.
T.V.A., Tennessee Valley Authority.

U.D.C., Urban District Council.
U.K., United Kingdom.
ult., *ultimo* = last (month).
UNESCO, United Nations Educational Scientific and Cultural Organisation.
U.N.O., United Nations Organisation.
UNRRA, United Nations Relief and Rehabilitation Administration.
U.P., United Press.
U.S.A., United States of America.
U.S.S.R., Union of Soviet Socialist Republics.
Ut., Utah (U.S.A.).

v., *versus* = against.
Va., Virginia (U.S.A.).
V.C., Victoria Cross.
V.E., Victory in Europe.
verb. sap., *verbum sapienti* = a word to the wise.
V.I.P., Very Important Person.
viz., *videlicet* = namely.
V.J., Victory over Japan.
vol(s)., volume(s).
Vt., Vermont (U.S.A.).

W.A., West Africa; West Australia.
W.A.F.S., Women's Auxiliary Fire Service.
Wash., Washington (U.S.A.).
W.D., War Department.
W.E.A., Workers' Educational Association.
W.L.A., Women's Land Army.
W.O., War Office.
W.R.A.C., Women's Royal Army Corps.
W.R.A.F., Women's Royal Air Force.
W.R.N.S., Women's Royal Naval Service.
Wy., Wyoming (U.S.A.).

Y.H.A., Youth Hostels Association.
Y.M.C.A., Young Men's Christian Association.
Y.W.C.A., Young Women's Christian Association.